Family, Jonathan Glick, 1978. Private collection.

MARITAL

AND

FAMILY

THERAPY

Fourth Edition

Peruvian Wedding, Filemen Leon, 1983. Private collection.

MARITAL AND FAMILY THERAPY

Fourth Edition

Ira D. Glick, M.D.

Ellen M. Berman, M.D.

John F. Clarkin, Ph.D.

Douglas S. Rait, Ph.D.

With forewords by
Herta A. Guttman, M.D., and
Peter Steinglass, M.D.

Washington, DC
London, England

Copyright © 2000 Ira D. Glick, M.D., Ellen M. Berman, M.D., John F. Clarkin, Ph.D., and Douglas S. Rait, Ph.D.
ALL RIGHTS RESERVED
Manufactured in the United States of America on acid-free paper
Fourth Edition

03   02   01   00   4   3   2   1

American Psychiatric Press, Inc.
1400 K Street, N.W.
Washington, DC 20005
www.appi.org

Jacket photograph is the sculpture *Spirit of Life*, by Robert I. Russin, 1970. Photograph courtesy of the artist and the Palm Springs Desert Museum, Palm Springs, California. Used with permission of the artist.

Library of Congress Cataloging-in-Publication Data
Marital and family therapy / Ira D. Glick ... [et al.]; with forewords by Herta A. Guttman
and Peter Steinglass.—4th ed.
     p. ; cm.
     Includes bibliographical references and index.
     ISBN 0-88048-548-5 (alk. paper)
     1. Family psychotherapy. 2. Marital psychotherapy. I. Glick, Ira D., 1935-
     [DNLM: 1. Family Therapy. 2. Marital Therapy. WM 430.5.F2 M341 2000]
   RC488.5 .G54 2000
   616.89'156—dc21

                                                                        99-047724

To our families—
past and present,
personal and
professional

Contents

SECTION I

Family Therapy in Context

CHAPTER 1

The Field of Marital and Family Therapy: Development and Definition

CHAPTER 2

SECTION 2

Functional and Dysfunctional Families

CHAPTER 3

CHAPTER 4

Understanding the Functional Family: Alternative Family Forms

CHAPTER 5

Problems and Dysfunction From a Family Systems Perspective

SECTION 3

Family Evaluation

CHAPTER 6

The Process of Evaluation 139

CHAPTER 7

The Content of Evaluation 151

CHAPTER 8

Formulating an Understanding of the Family Problem Areas 167

CHAPTER 9

SECTION 4

Family Treatment

CHAPTER 10

CHAPTER 11

CHAPTER 12

CHAPTER 13

SECTION 5

Couples Therapy

CHAPTER 19

Dysfunctional Couples and Couples Therapy   **377**

CHAPTER 20

Sex, Marriage, and Marital and Sex Therapy   **397**

CHAPTER 21

Separation and Divorce 417

With Richard M. Patel, M.D.

CHAPTER 22

The Couple and Reproductive Issues 439

CHAPTER 23

SECTION 6

Family Treatment When One Member Has a Psychiatric Disorder or Other Special Problem

CHAPTER 24

SECTION 7

Results of and Guidelines for
Recommending Family Therapy

CHAPTER 27

Indications for and the Sequence of
Family Therapy Evaluation and Treatment   **597**

CHAPTER 28

Controversies, Relative Contraindications, and the
Use and Misuse of Marital and Family Therapy

CHAPTER 29

SECTION 8

Family Systems Medicine and Ethical, Professional, and Training Issues

CHAPTER 30

Treating the Medically Ill Patient: A Family Systems Medicine Perspective

CHAPTER 31

Ethical and Professional Issues in Family Therapy

List of Tables

List of Figures

Contributors

Ellen M. Berman, M.D.
Clinical Professor of Psychiatry, Department of Psychiatry, University of Pennsylvania School of Medicine; Senior Consultant, PENN Council for Relationships

Amy Bronstone, Ph.D.
Postdoctoral Fellow, Alcohol and Substance Abuse Service, Department of Psychiatry and Behavioral Sciences, Stanford University School of Medicine

Audrey J. Clarkin, Ph.D.
Clinical Assistant Professor of Psychology in Psychiatry, Weill Medical College of Cornell University; Director of Psychology, Scarsdale School District, Scarsdale

John F. Clarkin, Ph.D.
Professor of Clinical Psychology in Psychiatry, Weill Medical College of Cornell University; Director of Psychology, Westchester Division, The New York Presbyterian Hospital

Lisa Dixon, M.D., M.P.H.
Associate Professor, Department of Psychiatry; Director of Education and Residency Training Director, Center for Mental Health Services Research, University of Maryland School of Medicine, Baltimore

Diana M. Doumas, Ph.D.
Family Project and Assessment Coordinator, Department of Psychiatry and Behavioral Sciences, Alcohol and Drug Treatment Center, Stanford University School of Medicine

Ira D. Glick, M.D.
Professor of Psychiatry and Behavioral Sciences, Stanford University School of Medicine; Chief, Schizophrenia Clinic, and Director of Inpatient Services, Stanford University School of Medicine and Stanford University Hospital

Herta A. Guttman, M.D.
Professor of Psychiatry, Faculty of Medicine, McGill University, Montreal

Gretchen L. Haas, Ph.D.
Associate Professor of Psychiatry; Director of the Family and Psychosocial Studies Program, Western Psychiatric Institute and Clinic, University of Pittsburgh Medical Center

Harvey S. Kaplan, M.D.
Chief of Pediatrics, San Mateo County General Hospital

James Lock, M.D., Ph.D.
Assistant Professor, Department of Psychiatry and Behavioral Sciences, Stanford University School of Medicine

Laura Markowitz, B.A.
Senior Editor, *The Family Therapy Networker;* Editor, *In the Family* magazine

Robert A. Matano, Ph.D.
Assistant Professor of Psychiatry and Behavioral Sciences; Director, Alcohol and Drug Treatment Center, Department of Psychiatry, Stanford University School of Medicine

John T. Patten, M.D.[†]
Clinical Assistant Professor of Psychiatry, Cornell University Medical College, New York, New York

Richard M. Patel, M.D.
Assistant Clinical Professor, Department of Psychiatry, University of California at San Francisco

---

[†]Deceased.

Douglas S. Rait, Ph.D.
Clinical Associate Professor of Psychiatry and Behavioral Sciences, Stanford University School of Medicine; Chief, Couples and Family Therapy Clinic, Stanford University Medical Center; Director, Family Therapy Program, VA Palo Alto Health Care System

Vernon Sharp, M.D.[†]
Associate Clinical Professor of Psychiatry; Director, Vanderbilt Family Treatment and Training Program, Vanderbilt University School of Medicine

Peter Steinglass, M.D.
Executive Director, Ackerman Institute for the Family and Clinical Professor of Psychiatry, Cornell University Medical College

John A. Talbott, M.D.
Professor and Chair, Department of Psychiatry, University of Maryland School of Medicine

Emily B. Visher, Ph.D.
Adjunct Faculty Member, California School of Professional Psychology

John S. Visher, M.D.
Lecturer in Psychiatry, Emeritus, Stanford University School of Medicine

Marlene F. Watson, Ph.D.
Assistant Professor, Department of Mental Health Science; Director, Masters of Family Therapy Program, Medical College of Pennsylvania and Hahnemann University

Sanford R. Weimer, M.D., M.P.H.
Clinical Professor of Psychiatry, School of Medicine, University of Southern California; CEO, World Wide Employee Assistance Programs

---

[†]Deceased.

Foreword

Since the early 1970s, family therapy has developed exponentially, both as a philosophy and as a treatment modality. To teach its theory and practice involves combining concepts and facts that come from anthropology, epistemology, sociology, history, ethics, psychology, the philosophy of science, communication theory, medicine and psychiatry, and the traditions of psychotherapy. In other words, such teaching—especially in a comprehensive textbook form—requires breadth of knowledge, the ability to communicate, and a great deal of courage. The authors of this book have met all of these requirements.

The authors of this book cover all the major themes that are important in family therapy today—systems theory; the historical evolution of the family; the family life cycle; social and ethical issues related to ethnicity, race, gender, and class; and the effect of illness on the family system. Particularly noteworthy is the consistent emphasis on issues raised by feminist family therapists concerning subjects such as gender equity in marriage, gender-related problems in family relationships, and the general question of taking moral responsibility for one's sexism and sexist actions within a male-dominated society. Moreover, as they introduce the reader to these subjects, the authors are always conscious of the nature of the audience that they wish to address. This is an introductory book, written for future professionals. Although it addresses all the current issues in the family therapy field, the book does not burden the reader with voluminous references and the arcane language that characterizes some of the current writing in the field of family therapy. It is meant, primarily, for people who are preparing themselves to help others. It contains case examples that illustrate and enliven the relevant theoretical and practical principles that are being demonstrated. Another important aspect of this book is that it contains a whole section on couples and couple therapy, thereby making it clear that, whereas some issues are relevant to couples alone, the couple is also an integral part of the family, its interaction governed by many of the same principles; that couples come in many configurations, inside and outside traditional heterosexual marriage;

and that the principles of couples therapy are both the same and different from the principles of family therapy.

The authors are mindful of the need to integrate research findings into clinical practice, and they devote special care to introducing the beginning therapist to this idea and its relevance to intervention. Last, but not least, the language in which the book is written is lively and down-to-earth, demonstrating that one can be professional without being stuffy.

I recommend this book to everybody who is interested in learning and teaching about marital and family therapy. I commend the authors for their thoughtful revision of one of the basic textbooks in the field.

Herta A. Guttman, M.D.

Foreword

A Psychiatrist's View of the Field of Marital and Family Therapy

Often the process of revising a basic textbook in a field is primarily a task of insertion of new material and minor changes in interpretation of historical trends and conclusions about research findings. New clinical techniques are described, greater emphasis is placed on research that has stood the test of time, and new data about treatment outcome are added to ensure the most complete picture of the current status of a field.

But the fourth edition of *Marital and Family Therapy* is not simply an updating of a textbook to fill in some new material about the field of family therapy, its new treatment innovations, and the latest research findings about its effectiveness. Although these topics are obviously included as part of the task of updating us regarding family therapy practice and research, this edition is also an opportunity to reflect on some quite extraordinary events in the family therapy field during the 1990s. In this sense, it represents an opportunity to document something quite different—a major reconceptualization of a field.

As you will be reading in the authors' account of the history of this field, family therapy's roots were in social psychiatry, the then very new approach to mental illness diagnosis and treatment. In the 1950s, when family therapy first came on the scene, the dominant perspective in psychiatry was psychoanalysis, a perspective that focused almost exclusively on the individual and conceptualized psychiatric disorders as the products of intrapsychic conflicts emanating from experiences in childhood. What was important was what was going on in a person's head, especially in his or her fantasy life. Families were important only insofar as family members were characters in this internal fantasy life. Thus it was not necessary for a therapist to meet with family members; the family was already known to the therapist through discussions with the individual patient.

The founders of family therapy contended that a person's behavior was not determined solely by internal thoughts. Rather, a person's social context was powerfully important in shaping individual behavior, a radical proposal at the time. The social context both placed constraints on what types of behaviors were possible and was the source of ideas about the world and strategies for problem solving. Although social contexts might include friendship networks, extended family, and community, the most influential context was assumed to be one's immediate family. Thus the simple but dramatic contribution of the founders of the family therapy field was twofold: first, the concept that individual psychopathology cannot be adequately understood without a detailed appreciation of the psychosocial environmental context (family) within which the person is living; and second, the proposal that changing a person's family context would be a potentially powerful way of changing dysfunctional behavior.

You will also be reading that this notion about the relationship between individual behavior and family context was influenced by the emergence in the 1950s of two very new sets of ideas—general systems theory and communication theory. What evolved was a model that has been called family systems theory, a key part of which was the focus on communication patterns as critical determinants of functionality within family systems.

Both of these sets of ideas were at the time being applied in other areas of medicine as well, especially in helping us understand the way the major regulatory systems of the body work, for example, hormonal and autonomic regulatory functioning. So one might think that the emergence of family therapy as a new approach to psychiatric problems would also have extended rapidly to other branches of medicine. But such was not the case. Even within psychiatry, family therapy and family therapists tended to become isolated from the larger field rather than becoming incorporated as a core psychotherapeutic approach. Ironically, even though many of the pioneers of this new field were themselves psychiatrists, as the field grew into an established discipline in the 1970s and 1980s, it became more removed from rather than more integrated with traditional psychiatry and medicine.

Two outcomes resulted from this schism. First, family therapy came to have less and less influence within traditional psychiatry and medicine. Second, family therapists became less and less familiar with new advances in psychiatry. The first outcome meant that the potential contributions family therapists might have been making to psychiatric and medical diagnosis and treatment were instead missed opportunities. The second outcome meant that family therapists were often being poorly trained in recognizing psychiatric disorders of individual family members, for example, serious depression or substance abuse, and were uncomfortable with integrating biological therapies into their treatment plans.

In the 1990s a growing number of family therapists have become aware of the opportunities missed by the relative isolation of their field from other mental health disciplines and medical specialties. At the same time, a larger trend has been afoot, urging cross-disciplinary collaboration as a more effective way to organize treatment approaches for serious medical and psychiatric illness, especially chronic illnesses such as schizophrenia, mood disorders, HIV disease, diabetes, and cancer. It has turned out, perhaps not surprisingly, that many of the more difficult problems associated with the treatment of these conditions have strong family-based components or are helped vastly by the inclusion of the family as an active partner in the design and implementation of long-term treatment planning.

For example, adherence to medication, a major problem often undermining, say, the effectiveness of psychopharmacology regimens, or the control of diet as a component of effective diabetes management, improves significantly if treatment planning is carried out with the entire family present rather than with the patient alone. But to do so, a clinician needs to be well trained in how to negotiate treatment plans with a family, rather than attempting to impose a standard treatment protocol on a family irrespective of its values or ideas about illness. Thus as we have moved ahead in the 1990s, the need for family interviewing skills on the part of all clinicians has become increasingly apparent. In this sense, the potential role of the family therapist (who is expert in these very skills) has potentially significantly expanded.

Hence one of the ways in which the family therapy field is being reconceptualized is to see it as a discipline with broad-based applicability rather than as a subspecialty of psychotherapy. This edition of *Marital and Family Therapy* reflects this new view. The authors use every opportunity to point out ways in which family interviewing skills, the ability to assess the family's psychosocial environment and emotional climate as part of understanding the context within which psychiatric or medical illness is unfolding, and the ability to work with families in developing and implementing treatment plans will be invaluable to the clinician.

A second major change that has been occurring in the marital and family therapy field during the 1990s is the gradual switch from an almost exclusive emphasis on those aspects of family life that exert negative influences on its members (i.e., an emphasis on family pathology) to a much more balanced view that sees the family sometimes as an exacerbating force in people's lives but more often as a potential resource, capable of creating a positive emotional climate that helps family members regulate affect, improve their

MARITAL AND FAMILY THERAPY

problem-solving capacities, and perhaps even improve their autonomic and immune functioning. This new perspective has also helped introduce a greater emphasis on prevention (i.e., factors that reduce risk to develop psychiatric or medical disorders).

The implications of this second major change in the field is that family therapists have significantly expanded the scope of their activities and broadened their ways of conceptualizing their roles. Whereas previously the focus was on therapy aimed exclusively at altering dysfunctional family interaction patterns, family therapists of today have multiple roles: 1) as in the past, developing an understanding of how the interactional dynamics of a particular family relates to existing individual pathology of family members; 2) mobilizing the family's inherent strengths and functional resources; 3) restructuring maladaptive family behavioral styles; and (importantly) 4) strengthening the family's natural problem-solving capabilities.

One cannot underscore too strongly how important a shift this has been in the way current family therapists see themselves (and families). Whereas previously the emphasis was on what was not working in family life and how to get rid of it, the emphasis now in on what is working well and how to strengthen these aspects of family life and bring them to bear on the presenting problems in a clinical situation. This increased respect for family strengths on the part of clinicians helps families to feel understood, appreciated, and listened to. Within this atmosphere, they are far more likely to develop positive, collaborative relationships with health care professionals. You will find examples of this new perspective appearing throughout this edition of the book, reflecting the changes in the way marital and family therapy is now being practiced.

Finally, but perhaps most important, is the emphasis now being placed by family therapists on the need to appreciate the astounding diversity and heterogeneity of family life. Whereas the family therapist of the 1960s and 1970s was working within a model that defined the standards for healthy family functioning (see, for example, the description of the systemic-strategic family therapy model in Chapter 10), the family therapist of the 1990s would be loath to identify any particular family structure, interactional behavior pattern, or value orientation as being invariably healthy. Instead, we are much more likely to stand in awe of how inventive families can be in devising solutions to very tough problems and to survive in the face of extraordinary stresses.

This is not to say that we are not also distressed and at times even angered by the abuses that can occur in intimate relationships—interpersonal violence, sexual abuse, emotional abuse, and the like (see Chapter 25). But until proven otherwise, we no longer are inclined to view the family as the source of a patient's problems. Even more important, we do not hold out a single family form as the gold standard toward which family and therapist should aspire.

Reflecting this third major change in the family therapy field, this edition is replete with chapters and references to the heterogeneity of family life in the current day. Although the authors still sketch out some of basic ideas about functionality and dysfunctionality in families (Section 2), this same section includes a description of alternative family forms (Chapter 4). In like fashion, the section of the book devoted to a discussion of the basics of family treatment (Section 4) includes a thorough discussion of how these principles look when one incorporates issues of ethnicity, race, gender, and class (Chapters 17 and 18).

As family therapists have opened themselves up to these new perspectives on families, an inevitable corollary process has been an opening up to a broader range of professional perspectives. After many years of relative isolation from other mental health and medical disciplines, family therapists are now actively forging linkages with these disciplines. Although frankly still at an early stage of development, these newly forming alliances are among the most exciting aspects of the family therapy field as it now exists. In addition to updating the reader about how family therapy is being applied these days to the assessment and treatment of psychiatric disorders and marital and family behavioral problems, in order to presage how marital and family therapy is likely to be defined in the next decade, we must also include a discussion of the family perspective as it applies in other branches of medicine, in the other mental health disciplines, and in related fields such as the law (Section 8).

It is for all these reasons that I feel justified in characterizing the fourth edition of *Marital and Family Therapy* as reflective of a field undergoing a major reconceptualization. As a psychiatrist, family researcher, and family therapist with a particular interest in understanding how chronic psychiatric and medical illnesses affect family life and are influenced by the family's response to illness, it is a reconceptualization I enthusiastically endorse.

Peter Steinglass, M.D.

Preface

The four editions of this textbook of family therapy reflect the history and development of the family field, which has evolved rapidly since the 1960s. The first edition was an outline about a field that was just beginning to grow and gain momentum. The second edition was a statement that the family field, which began in the minds of creative individuals in diverse settings (and often unknown to one another), was blossoming with great enthusiasm. The field had arrived with full gusto, and many clinicians were doing family work and clamoring for theoretical clarity and more training in this form of intervention. The third edition heralded a field that had come of age. It had expanded in scope and was being commonly used in clinical practice.

This, the fourth edition, makes a statement, like its predecessors, about the current state of the art of family intervention. As we see it, the field has gone beyond its heyday of enthusiasm and advocacy of family intervention for every clinical condition, to a more sophisticated time of differentiation. This differentiation is taking place on many levels. Examples include differentiating when family therapy is indicated, when the symptoms are under systems control, and when they are more strongly determined by other factors such as biological ones; how one evaluates in order to make both individual diagnoses and a family diagnosis; when the whole family is the patient and when the family is best seen as part of the treatment team and not sick or bad, to help the individual with symptoms; and when behavioral or educational strategies of family intervention are particularly helpful. New developments in theory and technique, and a widened lens in terms of specific problem areas, have enriched the field.

The most critical changes in family theory are the incorporation of new attitudes and information about ethnicity, race, gender, and class into our theory building. The rules that govern all aspects of family life, and the experience of persons in families, may be vastly different for men and women. Families may operate by systems principles, but men and women bring to the system different ways of thinking and different types of influence. Norms of closeness and distance, emotional expression, basic aspects of viewing and disciplining children also vary greatly across ethnic group, class, and age cohort. The integration of this knowledge into the broad principles of family therapy, enabling therapists to work with a wide variety of families, is one of our key goals. Theory building in this area is still in a period of rapid growth and will probably be altered again by the next edition.

More integrative ways of working have replaced narrowly based schools, and brief therapy models such as solution-focused and narrative therapy have been added to our armamentarium. New information about previously ignored or inadequately researched issues—such as gay and lesbian families, the sequelae of abuse, the complexities of AIDS, and family response to reproductive events—have enriched our understanding of family life. Family systems medicine has become a new subspecialty in recent years. We hope that this edition adequately reflects this growing sophistication of the field.

Since the publication of the first edition of this book, we have consistently been gratified by the response of both readers and many reviewers, as well as by its adoption by some teachers as the standard introductory text. Since the publication of the second edition, it has been translated into Japanese, and parts into Chinese; it has been adopted widely in Italy, England, and other European countries. Because of the growth and changes in the field, as well as suggestions received, we have decided that this is an opportune time to expand and rewrite the text. Most important, we are convinced that the field has matured. Presently there are many established schools of thought that continue to evolve. At the same time, just as in the adjacent field of individual psychotherapy, there is growing interest in adopting a more integrative (rather than parochial) perspective that highlights some of the factors shared by these different models. In this book, we offer our version of an integration, that is, a framework for trainees and practitioners in the family therapy field and those persons in various fields that need an introduction to family therapy.

Although the newer body of knowledge has required extensive rewriting, the basic organization of the book is largely unchanged. The history of the field precedes general concepts, which are followed by evaluation, treatment, indications, and finally, results.

For this edition, we have thoroughly updated our chapter on family life in its historical and sociological context, and throughout we have paid special attention to the new family forms such as single-parent and remarried families. Our sections on function and dysfunction have been expanded and rewritten to present the latest information on how families are coping with the rapid changes in our society. Given the publication of DSM-IV, we have made a thorough review of understanding and treatment of dysfunctional families both for Axis I conditions and for other problems of living together. In our treatment section we have added a special section on treating Axis I disorders by combining medication with family therapy. We have thoroughly rewritten the chapter on treatment as modified by ethnic, racial, gender, and class considerations and included a chapter on treatment of African American families.

Our section on marital/couples disorders has been revised thoroughly, including a focus on the work of J. S. Visher and E. B. Visher with stepfamilies. In addition we have rewritten our chapter on lesbian and gay families. We have added a section on couples and reproductive health. We have expanded in a major way the section on relational disorders including both Axis I disorders and other problems. The chapter on incest, violence, suicide, and the family responses to these problems is also revised markedly.

Based on new data, we have updated the section on guidelines and results (i.e., efficacy). Throughout the text we have made suggestions (where possible) to practitioners regarding how to practice the art of family therapy based on implications of research studies.

The section on family systems medicine has been rewritten thoroughly, adding a general overview of the field from the point of view of the physician (taking care of the medical problems of the patients) as well as from the family systems perspective. We close the book with guidelines and an overview of ethical, financial, and professional issues facing the field, including issues involved with training.

Past readers have been very helpful and generous with their comments for revisions. Partly because of their suggestions we have been able to add new chapters, revise chapters from the previous edition, and update the book. For this edition, we have been fortunate to add two new authors, both nationally known clinicians and teachers in the field (Ellen M. Berman, M.D., and Douglas S. Rait, Ph.D.). We have also included on our team Richard M. Patel, M.D., a former psychiatric resident in our program, who not only helped edit the book but also provided a unique prospective as a trainee to make the text user-friendly for students. Alan Manovitz, M.D., our colleague at the Payne Whitney Clinic, reviewed an earlier version of the manuscript and made helpful suggestions. David Kessler, M.D., was a coauthor of the first, second, and third editions, and much of his wisdom still can be found in this revision.

In the third edition, we invited readers to write with their suggestions. The response was not only astounding but also helpful in improving the text. We offer the same invitation now, so that we can continue to make this book as helpful and practical as possible.

Ira D. Glick, M.D., Ellen M. Berman, M.D.,
John F. Clarkin, Ph.D., and Douglas S. Rait, Ph.D.

Acknowledgments

We wish to thank the many individuals and families who have helped to make this book possible.

First, our own families of origin, Bernard and Gertrude Glick, Estelle and Harry Moskowitz, John and Helen Clarkin, and Joseph and Barbara Rait, who in addition to steadfastly attempting to socialize us, provided us with our first major models of family structure and function. Second, our teachers, who by their concern and enthusiasm first helped to stir our interest in family study and treatment and provided us with a family model of understanding human functioning. Third, our colleagues in family therapy, who by their stimulating and provocative comments tried their best to keep us honest. Fourth, our trainees, with whom we have been privileged to work on the teaching-learning process in family therapy. They have had the courage to ask the critical questions about the field, and it was for them that much of the didactic material in this book was formulated and used in courses we have taught.

Finally, to our spouses who supported us as we spent long hours preparing the book—Juannie Eng, Perry Berman, Audrey Clarkin, and Karlana Carpen; and to our children as well.

For the preparation of this edition, we wish to thank Edelen Stevens for a superlative secretarial job; the members of our departments at Cornell and Stanford Universities for extending help and cooperation; and the readers and reviewers of the three previous editions for their suggestions. We are especially grateful to Richard M. Patel, M.D., for his help in editing several drafts.

Most of all, we are indebted to the families whom we have treated. They shared our journey, lived with our successes (and errors), and have taught us at least as much as we have taught them.

A Guide for Using the Text

Because this book is intended to serve as a basic but comprehensive textbook for individuals at different training levels and orientations, complex clinical situations and their sequential management regimens have been simplified and compressed. We realize this may be a disadvantage for the more advanced therapist and so have included up-to-date references. The book probably will be most helpful when used with ongoing supervision or with an ongoing course, because most of the case examples and interventions are written in bare-bones detail in order to make one or two teaching points at a time. For the sake of clarity, some chapters reiterate concepts presented earlier in a different context. For example, goals are mentioned in the discussions of evaluation, the process of setting goals before starting treatment, and the course of treatment.

Likewise, a number of sections and short chapters are (in our view) much too brief to be of value to the experienced family clinician. Here, too, we opted to take the route of maximum breadth, providing appropriate references to flesh out the materials. References have been updated, but we retained classics and those that refer to a particular research project mentioned in the text. We have also accumulated a list of suggested readings to encourage the student to read more and to guide the instructor of family therapy for his or her choice of assigned readings, depending on class objectives. We believe that the alternative path (i.e., to be less inclusive and provide greater depth) would make this introductory text too narrow and less useful given the many situations in which the family model is now being used.

We recommend that the beginner read the text sequentially, although obviously the more experienced clinician initially may prefer to read particular sections or chapters only. The book is written for reading, not as a reference to sit on a shelf. Some chapters may be read out of order, like the chapters on results (Chapter 29) or the family in historical context (Chapter 2), because they are more specialized and should be read as needed, as appropriate, or as the reader's interest dictates.

In part, how this book is used depends on one's training goals. Accordingly, a reader may want to refer to the training section, where we discuss context, formats, and goals. That is, the material can guide the reader's priorities. The reason, of course, is that the learning needs of someone trying to master the family model at a family institute are quite different from a psychiatric resident who is learning family therapy as one model among other competing models.

A note on the teaching objectives—there are two reasons for their inclusion. First, many fields in medicine, psychiatry, and psychology are attempting to define the core knowledge and skill competencies required for a practitioner in that field. We do so in that spirit. However, a second and in many ways more essential reason is that the ground we cover is so broad and can be so confusing to the beginner that by using the enabling objectives for each chapter as a road map, the reader can use them to understand the logic, direction, and end point for each topic. Our terminal objectives include but are not limited to

- A general understanding of the underlying theoretical principles and hypotheses behind the family model
- An acquaintance with techniques, including an understanding of the advantages and limitations of such techniques and an ability to draw from the basic principles (underlying any and all of them) techniques to put them into practice in the process of treatment
- Development of an appreciation, through experience, of one's abilities and difficulties in using such techniques
- An understanding of how ethnicity, race, gender, and class affect the therapist and family as they work
- An appreciation of the ethical issues involved in all areas of the practice of family intervention

SECTION 1

Family Therapy in Context

For family therapists, context is everything. Family therapy is both a set of therapeutic techniques for treating family distress and a specific way of thinking about human behavior. It is a critical context for understanding normal behavior and psychopathology. In Chapter 1 we speak to the following three issues: 1) How did family therapy develop? 2) How is it defined? and 3) What are the core concepts that every family therapist must know? Finally, we examine the elements that distinguish family therapy from other psychotherapies. In this edition of the book, we pay particular attention to recent studies of how gender, ethnicity, race, and class affect family therapy and to how DSM-IV and managed care affect this treatment approach.

We placed Chapter 2, which puts the family and family life in historical and sociological perspective, early in the book to make the point that there is no way to understand and treat families without being aware of the changing social landscape within which the family is embedded.

To avoid unnecessary duplication we often use the word *family* (as in family therapy, family system, and family unit) instead of the more cumbersome term *marital and family*. When we refer to marital issues specifically we use only the word *marital*. We use the term *couples* to refer to both married and unmarried couples. Similarly, the terms *family therapy* and *family treatment* are synonymous. Throughout the text we use a broad definition of family to include both blood and nonblood relatives who may not be under the same roof, including those who have been referred to as *significant others* or who are considered family members by the family itself.

Portrait of a Man and His Wife, artist unknown, late Fifth Dynasty, circa 2500 B.C., Egypt. Courtesy of Honolulu Academy of Arts, Honolulu, Hawaii. Used with permission.

CHAPTER 1

The Field of Marital and Family Therapy: Development and Definition

Objectives for the Reader

⚬ To understand the historical development of family therapy as it influences theory and practice

⚬ To define family therapy and to begin to differentiate it from individual and group formats and strategies

⚬ To recognize and be able to use basic family system concepts in evaluation and treatment

Introduction

Although the field of marital and family therapy is relatively young, family life has always been the main building block of human connections. Families as basic human systems are different in several essential ways from other types of human groups and relationships. Love of and bonding or attachment to family members are to some extent biologically built into the nervous system as survival devices, and our most intense emotions, both positive and negative, are reserved for family members. In addition, marriages and families perform vital socialization tasks for children and for society at large.

It has been a commonsense view that we are all shaped by what we experience in our *families of origin* (i.e., comprising our parents, siblings, and extended family). For most people what occurs in their current marital or family system is a significant element in their general sense of well-being and functioning. Furthermore, as we discuss in subsequent chapters, the family has important effects on the quality of life and on the course of psychiatric illness (e.g., depression) and medical illness.

In the past three decades mental health professionals have moved past a singular focus on individual dynamics to examine the enigmatic processes that lead to family distress. They have developed a set of theories grouped loosely under the name *systems theory*, which examines how people or aspects of a system affect one another. Using this theory, they have devised both a paradigm for explaining human behavior, one that looks past the individual, and a set of techniques for reducing distress and improving family functioning. As we discuss in this book, the mental health field is gradually incorporating these changes so that a truly biopsychosocial model of behavior is becoming a reality.

Development of the Family Therapy Field

Although exciting and often efficacious, family therapy can be confusing for the beginner. Just as psychoanalysis has spawned a range of perspectives that include drive theory, ego psychology, object relations theory, and self psychology, the family therapy field is differentiated by approaches that include structural, strategic, psychodynamic, experiential, cognitive-behavioral, narrative, and systemic. For some it may be difficult to distinguish the thinking that lies behind the personal styles of charismatic family therapists. For others it may seem difficult to synthesize a coherent family theory from the variety of existing orientations. Yet, as in any field of academic study or clinical practice, family therapy's present state can be understood partly by looking at its own evolution. How did this state of affairs come about, and how is it changing today?

In a broad sense, the significance attributed to the family's role in relation to the psychic and social distress of any of its members has waxed and waned over the centuries. The important role of the family in the development of individual problems was mentioned by Confucius in his writings and by the Greeks in their myths. The early Hawaiians would meet as a kin network (i.e., family) to discuss solutions to an individual's problem. For a long time in Western culture, however, what we now call mental illness and other forms of interpersonal distress were ascribed to magical, religious, physical, or exclusively individual factors.

It was not until the early 1900s that individual psychodynamics was delineated as a major determinant of human behavior. Although Freud stressed the major role of the family in normal and abnormal development, he believed that the most effective technique for dealing with such individual psychopathology was treatment on a one-to-one basis (Sander 1978).

At about this same time, others working with the mentally ill began to suggest that families with a sick member should be seen together and not "as individuals removed from family relationships" (Smith 1890). In particular, psychiatric social workers in child guidance clinics began to recognize the importance of dealing with the entire family unit around child-focused issues. However, the psychiatric community in general was dominated by Freudian thinking until the late 1960s.

In the psychiatric literature, psychoanalysts reported experiences in treating a marital pair as early as the 1930s (Mittelman 1948; Oberndorf 1934). They began to see a series of marital partners in simultaneous, but separate, psychoanalyses in the following decade. This approach was quite unusual because psychoanalysts generally believed that this method of treatment would hinder the therapist in helping the patient, on the assumption that neither spouse would trust the same therapist and consequently would withhold important material. As a result, the other marital partner was usually referred to a colleague. The two earliest marriage counseling centers in the United States began to treat couples in the early 1930s.

The early 1950s, which might be considered the heyday of American social psychiatry, witnessed the first consistent use of family therapy in modern psychotherapeutic practice. In New York, Ackerman began to use family interviews consistently in his analytic work with children and adolescents (Ackerman 1958). In these postwar years, American psychiatric researchers also turned to the most pressing psychiatric problem of the time—schizophrenia. Funding for new clinical programs and clinical research—available through the newly created National Institute of Mental Health—offered workers in a number of different centers the opportunity to study schizophrenia and family interactions (Bowen 1960; R. Lidz and Lidz 1949; T. Lidz et al. 1958) and family communication (Bateson et al. 1956; Wynne et al. 1958). Throughout the 1950s clinical advances and research findings were followed by a small but increasingly committed group of mental health professionals.

Not until the early 1960s did the modern field of family therapy begin to take shape (Ackerman 1966; Satir 1964). A backlash against psychoanalytic orthodoxy coupled with the social activism of the era propelled a handful of early theorists into leading roles in a social revolution within the fields of psychiatry, psychology, and social work. This group assumed that family, group, and community were the keys to effective intervention. Group therapy, family therapy, and milieu therapy in inpatient settings flourished during this period, as did community mental health. Various schools of theory and practice emerged, and leading journals (e.g., *Family Process*) were established. At the same time, teaching practices were marked by innovation, as the use of one-way mirrors and videotaped interviews moved the practice of therapy out into the open for study and discussion. As a result, many mental health professionals were drawn to learning about and practicing family therapy.

During the 1970s the scope of family therapy was expanded to apply to a broad range of psychiatric problems with families differing widely in socio-economic background. In particular, Minuchin's contributions to the development of briefer, crisis-oriented methods began to address the needs of families with multiple problems (Minuchin 1974). This was a decade of ferment as well, as traditionalists proposing more psychodynamic or biological models battled with family clinicians over territory, training funds, and the right to the "best" explanation for how psychopathology occurs, is maintained, and is remedied. During this period, researchers also began to look at process variables that contributed to treatment efficacy (Gurman and Kniskern 1978; Wells and Dezen 1978). Finally, the number of available clinical models of marital and family therapy expanded exponentially. During meetings of the American Psychiatric Association considerable prominence was given to family therapy topics. Interdisciplinary organizations such as the American Orthopsychiatric Association became a home for family therapy presentations. Except for relatively infrequent, small conferences, family therapists presented their major findings at meetings of these other professional organizations and were published frequently in other professional journals until the early 1970s. Later that decade, various clinical techniques in family therapy became more distinctively identified as schools, and family therapy began to become a distinct entity. As the American Family Therapy Association and the American Association of Marital and Family Therapists grew, training conferences nationwide evolved. For many mental health professionals, family therapy seemed to be the right treatment at the right time.

During the 1980s the early polemics faded and clinicians and researchers continued to establish innovative practices and particular treatment packages for specific individual, marital, and family problems. For example, data had made clear the existence of an important biological component in the etiology of schizophrenia and other Axis I disorders, and psychopharmacological treatment became an accepted practice. Although most family therapists no longer viewed family therapy as the primary treatment for schizophrenia, they considered family psychoeducation—a particular form of family treatment—to be one important component of a multimodal intervention. In 1988 marriage and family therapy was added to the list of four core mental health professions eligible for mental health traineeships under the Public Health Service Act, Title III, Section 303(d). In addition, issues of gender and culture became more prominent in the field, and the differences and similarities in family function among ethnic groups were addressed clearly for the first time.

Throughout the 1990s some family therapists expended much effort to establish marital and family therapy as a differentiated, autonomous profession. The marital and family therapy degree is now widely established, and marital and family therapy has become a separate and licensed profession. However, the downside of this is that family psychology, master's and doctorate degrees in family therapy, and family psychiatry seem to be moving further apart.

Psychology, social work, and counseling psychology are developing active subspecialties in family therapy. At the same time the rapidly developing interest in the biological treatment of psychiatric problems is to a degree overshadowing the development of new effective psychotherapeutic therapies. To some extent the various fields involved in developing theoretical models of human function have continued an old tradition of not collaborating with one another.

The aim of this book is to continue the tradition of integrating the best of theory and data from all disciplines into a coherent model of family theory applicable to trainees and practitioners in all of the mental health professions.

The health of the family therapy field has always resided in its diversity and its unwillingness to simply accept narrow, linear explanations for psychopathology or narrow, linear treatments. As members of a field originally composed of mavericks and rebels, family therapists were initially unwilling to accept the dominant psychodynamic and biological ideas of American psychiatry. However, during the 1990s, the independence of family therapists has receded somewhat as mental health professionals of every discipline and theoretical commitment are gradually recognizing that no one perspective owns the truth and that multimodal treatments are frequently necessary, even desirable. There is also a movement toward specificity of treatments, in the development of diagnostic classification systems for families (see Chapter 8) and in the development of selection criteria for the application, focus, duration, and intensity of family and marital interventions.

Although treatment techniques have become more differentiated, so that one can speak of major orientations, such techniques must be integrated into a treatment package that is flexible and that meets the needs of individuals and families alike. The family therapy field is generating a body of treatment outcome research, primarily the fruits of systematic research by more behaviorally oriented marital researchers (Pinsof and Wynne 1995), studies of psychoeducational interventions with psychiatric patients (Glick et al. 1994), and research on childhood behavior problems (Szapocznik et al. 1990). These research efforts are growing in number and are becoming more sophisticated in design and execution. The findings that family therapy has demonstrated positive results with certain family problems, ranging from schizophrenia to childhood problems, are indeed encouraging (see Chapters 24 and 29 for a full discussion of these issues).

In the 1990s the major financial issue facing family therapists was the effect of managed care. We discuss this issue in Chapter 31, but here let us emphasize that it has forced the outpatient family therapist to plan therapy so that it is focused and feasible within the limits set by the managed care provider. Likewise, managed care has had major effects on inpatient family therapy by decreasing the allowed length of stay (and accordingly the number of family sessions). It has also decreased the possibility of family outreach and long-term family support in publicly funded settings.

Definition of Marital and Family Therapy

Family therapy is distinguished from other psychotherapies by its conceptual focus on the family system as a whole. In this view, major emphasis is placed on understanding how the system as a whole remains functional and on understanding individual behavior patterns as arising from and inevitably feeding back into the complex interactions within the family system. In other words, a person's thoughts, feelings, and behaviors are seen as multidetermined and partly a product of significant interpersonal relationships. From the family systems perspective, alterations in the larger marital and family unit may have positive consequences for the individual members and for the larger systems. The family system under consideration may be either two- or three-generational, depending on the problem and the model used. A major emphasis is generally placed on understanding and intervening in the family system's current patterns of interaction, with in some cases only a secondary interest in the origins and development of those patterns (depending on the model).

Marital and family treatment can be defined as a systematic effort to produce beneficial changes in a marital or family unit by introducing changes into the patterns of family interactions. Its aim is the establishment of more satisfying ways of living for the entire family and for individual family members.

In many families, a member or members may be singled out as the *identified patient*. Occasionally a marital or family unit presents itself as being in trouble without singling out any one member. For example, a couple may realize that their marriage is in trouble and that the cause of their problems stems from interaction with each other and not from either partner individually.

Family therapy might broadly be thought of as any type of psychosocial intervention using a conceptual framework that gives primary emphasis to the family system and that, in its therapeutic strategies, aims to affect the entire family structure. Thus any psychotherapeutic approach that attempts to understand or to intervene in a family system might fittingly be called family therapy. This is a very broad definition and allows many differing points of view, in theory and in therapy, to be placed under one heading.

Family therapy might be thought of as any type of psychosocial intervention using a conceptual framework that gives primary emphasis to the family system and aims to affect the entire family structure.

A continuum exists between the individual's intrapsychic processes, the interactional or family system, and the larger social/cultural system. Different conceptual frameworks are used when dealing with these different levels. A therapist may choose to emphasize any of the points on this continuum, but the family therapist is especially sensitive to and trained in those aspects relating specifically to the family system—to both its individual characteristics and the larger social matrix.

Although many clinicians agree that problematic interactions may occur in families in which one family member has a gross disturbance, it is not always clear whether the faulty interactions are the cause or the effect of the behavior of the disturbed individual. Some practitioners continue to perceive and treat the disequilibrium in the individual's psyche as the central issue, viewing the family and larger social system as context, which adds an important dimension to the conceptualization and treatment. Others see and treat as the central issue the disequilibrium in the family, viewing the individual symptoms as the result of, or the attempted solution to, a family problem (Committee on the Family 1970; Minuchin 1974).

There is reason to believe that both views are important. Pending further research and experience in this area, it seems prudent for the clinician to evaluate each clinical situation carefully, attempting to understand the phenomena and select intervention strategies designed to achieve the desired ends.

Core Concepts

General Systems Theory

Like other developing fields of knowledge, the family therapy field has needed to generate its own terminology. Although individual behavior and individual psychodynamics have had a long history and wealth of sophisticated terminology attached to them, the language available to describe specific interactions among people is already substantial. Family therapy is based on a set of theories that combine a general systems view of interactions, a cybernetic epistemology, traces of interpersonal psychiatry, and the most recent contributions of social constructivism. Thus there is a need to begin by delineating the basic concepts underlying the developments in understanding family process and family intervention. These concepts are not numerous, but their paucity belies the profound shift in focus that occurs when progressing from concepts about the individual to describing a system and its functioning.

The biologist Von Bertalanffy is credited as the first to introduce the principles of *general systems theory*, which provide an organismic approach to understanding biological beings (Von Bertalanffy 1968). Von Bertalanffy felt that the reductionistic, mechanistic tradition in science was insufficient to explain the behavior of living organisms, because this approach depended on a linear series of stepwise cause-and-effect equations. He developed general principles to explain biological processes that include considerable complexity and levels of organization. General systems theory was described as a "new approach to the unity of science problem which sees organization rather than reduction as the unifying principle, and which therefore searches for general structural isomorphisms in systems" (Gray et al. 1969, p. 7). Thus a systems approach places an emphasis on the relationship between the parts of a complex whole, and the context in which these events occur, rather than on an isolation of events from their context (Anonymous 1972). A system is a group of interacting parts. In nature, each system is nested within a larger one (see Figure 1–1). In the most general terms, a living system is organized, exerts control over and adapts to its environment, and possesses and uses energy. Let's see how these notions apply to families.

Organization. The first key concept relevant to living systems is that such systems have a high degree of organization; that is, there is a consistent relationship between the elements or parts of the organism. The systems view implies that the organism or entity is greater than the sum of the separate parts. No single element in the system can be thought of as acting completely independently. One might think of this as the difference between physiology and anatomy. According to Engel (1980),

> Each hierarchy represents an organized dynamic whole, a system of sufficient persistence and identification to justify being named. Its name reflects its distinctive properties and characteristics. Each system implies qualities and relationships distinctive for that level of organization and each requires criteria for study and explanation unique for that level.

In order to regulate its exchange with systems outside itself, the living system must have boundaries (Figures 1–1 and 1–2). The membrane around a cell defines the boundary or outer limit of that functional unit. While creating a boundary between the cell and the outside, the cell membrane also provides through its permeability an interactional relationship between the inside and outside of the cell, by selectively allowing transfer of chemicals across itself. Analogously, the organized family system has a membrane, or boundary, between itself and the surrounding neighborhood and community. This boundary is the set of implicit and explicit rules by which the family keeps information and activities to itself or allows outside information and

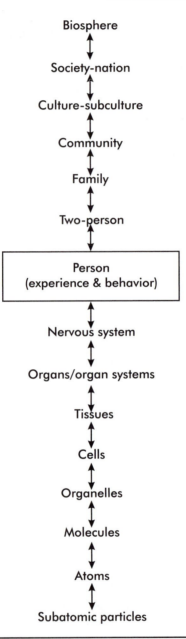

FIGURE 1–1. Hierarchy of natural systems, showing levels of organization. *Source.* Engel G: "The Clinical Application of the Biopsychosocial Model." *American Journal of Psychiatry* 137:535–544, 1980. Copyright 1980, American Psychiatric Association. Reprinted with permission.

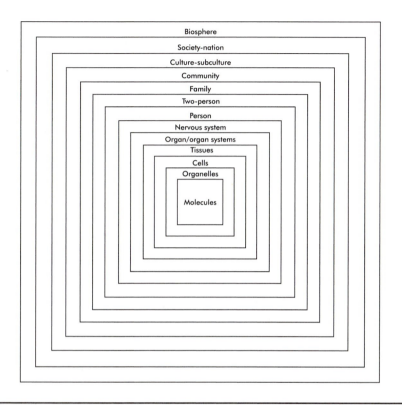

FIGURE 1–2.   Continuum of natural systems.
Source.   Engel G: "The Clinical Application of the Biopsychosocial Model." *American Journal of Psychiatry* 137:535–544, 1980. Copyright 1980, American Psychiatric Association. Reprinted with permission.

contact with people in the neighborhood and the community. A family must have clear boundaries to be functional. The same is true for subsystems within the family. For example, in order for the marital subsystem to function, it must have a boundary that separates it from other subsystems such as the sibling subsystem.

A family's boundary comprises the set of rules by which the family keeps information and activities to itself or allows outside information and contact with people in the neighborhood and the community.

Minuchin (1974) described families as being on a continuum from disengaged (i.e., having inappropriately rigid boundaries) to enmeshed (i.e., having overly permeable, diffuse boundaries). Families in the middle of this continuum (i.e., having clear boundaries) are considered to be the most functional (see Figure 1–3). Although no one-to-one correlation exists between extremes of boundary functioning and symptomatology, extremes are seen as more likely to lead to pathological behavior in one or more members of the family system. Because normative boundaries may vary considerably from one ethnic group to another and still allow development and growth of the child, families need to be considered using the norms of their cultural group as a reference point. For example, it is normal for some groups, such as upper-class English families, to send their children to boarding school by age 9 or 10 years, whereas in other groups children live at home until they are in their 20s or are married.

Recognition of the existence of subsystems within the family system relates to the notion of a hierarchical organization. The system itself is organized on one or many hierarchical levels entailing systems or subsystems (see Figures 1–1 and 1–2).

Control over and adaptation to the environment. A second key concept relevant to living systems is that a functional living system must have some means of controlled adaptation to its environment. In 1948, Wiener introduced the notion of *cybernetics* as a branch of science dealing with control mechanisms and the transmission of information. He pointed out the similari-

| Disengaged | Clear boundaries | Enmeshed |
| (inappropriately rigid boundaries) | (normal range) | (diffuse boundaries) |

FIGURE 1–3. Minuchin's description of the boundaries of the family system.
Source. Minuchin S: *Families and Family Therapy.* Copyright 1974 by the President and Fellows of Harvard College. Reprinted by permission of Harvard University Press.

ties between the mechanisms of internal control and communication in an animal and in machines. A key concept in cybernetics is that of *feedback* and the feedback loop. In such a circular sequence of events, element A influences element B, which influences element C, which in turn influences element A. For example, if the temperature in a room becomes too low, the thermostat initiates a mechanism, which turns on the furnace, which raises the temperature in the room, which registers on the thermostat, which then signals the furnace to shut off. Such mechanisms serve to control the state of the organism or environment (Wiener 1948). Control concepts such as homeostasis and feedback have been used by family theorists to understand and change family systems (Jackson 1957; Minuchin et al. 1975).

Corrective feedback (or negative feedback in the language of cybernetic theory) results in a sequence of events that returns a person to a previous, more balanced state (Strauss et al. 1985). Consider the following case example:

> Mr. A, a young father who had schizoaffective disorder, noted that as he became more hyperactive at home, his wife would become anxious. She would then say things like, "Why don't you slow down? I'll help you with the chores." This intervention appeared to help Mr. A to regain control of his activity level and his wife to become more comfortable.

A system always has feedback, but the result of a particular behavior is determined partly by each person's internal processing. Consider this case example:

> Mr. B, another patient with schizoaffective disorder, responded to his wife's request to slow down by becoming angry because he believed she was chastising him. She became more insistent, and he became more angry and upset. She finally started crying, and he calmed down. After a while, whenever he became upset she began crying, which kept her calm, but then she became depressed. In this instance, an attempted solution became a problem.

Energy.   A third and final key concept relevant to living systems is that of energy and information. Living systems are open systems in which energy can be transported in and out of the system. Instead of a tendency toward entropy and degradation of energy, which happens in nonliving systems, living systems have a tendency toward increased patterning, complexity, and organization. In human open systems such as the family, information (meaning knowledge from outside of the family) acts as a type of energy that informs the system and can lead to more complex interaction. For example, in families open to it, the women's movement brought many changes in how the spouses reacted to each other. In some families, however, these changes led to confusion and distress, whereas in others they led to improvement in function.

To summarize, a theoretical framework commonly used by family therapists is the family systems approach. The understanding of families is ecological, in that the capabilities of the family are viewed as greater than an arithmetic sum of its parts. Each person is viewed in interactive relations with the other family members, all functioning to maintain the family system coherently but also striving for their own unique goals. The family system is maintained by its members so as to preserve its essential traditions, myths, patterns, identities, and values.

A key concept here is that although to an outside observer some of a family's behavior may appear crazy or self-defeating, the behavior is assumed to be the family's best solution to its problems. For example, in Mr. B's family (see the case example mentioned earlier in this chapter), the wife's depression seemed to decrease her husband's symptoms.

The boundaries of the system are determined by the family and sometimes by the therapist. Most family therapists think of a family system as comprising at least three generations; however, a particular subsystem of couple or parents and children can also be seen as a system. In remarried families the system boundaries are more complex and permeable, and the total number of people involved tends to be much larger. Family organization shifts over time.

Often the family returns to an apparent steady state, but it must always deal with the inevitable changes that time and biological development bring. Sometimes it responds to stress with creative solutions but at other times with stagnation. The notion of the evolution of families as life events occur (e.g., when a child goes away to college) differentiates this view of coherence from that of a fixed homeostasis.

Family Systems Theory and Homeostasis Over Time

It can be said that the critical issue for families is which homeostasis to evolve toward, that is, what to preserve of the past (in order to manage the present competently) and what to look forward to in the future. Hoffman (1983) has developed a useful diagram (Figure 1–4), which she calls a time capsule, to illustrate the concepts of 1) how the family (and treating team) interface with the community and with its internal dynamics and 2) how each family has a long history (so-called mythic time) and is evolving constantly.

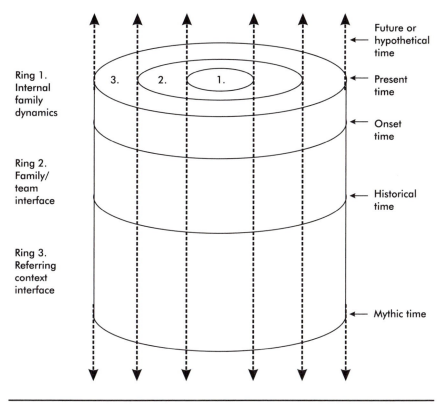

FIGURE 1–4.   Hoffman's time capsule.

Source.   Hoffman L: "A Co-evolutionary Framework for Systemic Family Therapy," in *Diagnosis and Assessment in Family Therapy, The Family Therapy Collections.* Edited by Hansen JC, Keeney BP. Rockville, MD, Aspen Publications, 1983, p. 42. Reprinted with permission.

Hoffman (1983, p. 42) describes the time capsule as follows:

> The figure presents a diagram of this construct, sometimes still referred to by me as my Cosmic Sausage, because so much depends on where you cut it. In this case, we will assume that the capsule's outer skin ends at the boundary of that imaginary entity called the family. The cuts in the cross-section correspond to different dimensions of time: present time, onset time, historical time, mythic time, and future or hypothetical time. At each position depicted by the Time Capsule, "difference" questions work to clarify family alignments in relation to the problem, by revealing five aspects:

1. Family alignments as they relate to the problem in the present
2. Family alignments as they relate to onset of the problem
3. Family alignments as they furnish a historical matrix for the problem
4. The effect on family alignments if the problem were to change
5. Family alignments related to paradigmatic values that the problem metaphorically represents

Information thus gathered can be used both to build a hypothesis and to suggest a positive connotation of the problem in whatever temporal context seems most relevant.

The capsule also contains subcylinders: Rings 1, 2, and 3, indicated within the cross-section, in the present. The idea of the rings is to show that there are several systems interfaces one might have to consider in targeting an intervention, and there seemed to be an order of priority, too. Interface dynamics within the family took second place to team/family system and professionals from the referring context. As I said before, the interface that seems most important in any interview can be called the "presenting edge."

To summarize, classical family therapy examines interpersonal relationships—rather than biological, intrapsychic, or societal processes—when attempting to understand human distress. That is not to say that family therapy ignores the intrapsychic or the biological, but its primary vision and interventions are focused on interpersonal relationships. For example, both chemistry and physics use versions of relativity theory and quantum theory. They are not separate disciplines because they embrace unique scientific approaches; rather, they are distinct because each uses its overlapping theories to concentrate on different natural phenomena.

An Integrative Interpersonal Model

An integrative model connects the systems concepts above with Lewis's work on interpersonal relationships and individual outcome. Our model is based on the notion that there is an ongoing and consistent interplay between psychopathology (related to biological and developmental factors) and the individual relationships with significant others. As Lewis (1998) noted,

At its center this perspective holds that relational structures—the more or less enduring patterns of interaction—either facilitate or impede the continued maturation of the participants. It is important to note that the relationship between an individual and his or her relational system is not linear; rather, individual characteristics influence system properties, and these properties shape individual characteristics.

We discuss Lewis's ideas about relationships in later chapters (see Chapters 15 and 19).

Differentiation of Family Therapy From Other Psychotherapies

Family therapy as a format of treatment can be distinguished from other psychotherapies by its fundamental paradigm shift, which assumes that people are best understood as operating in systems and that treatment must include, either in person or in theoretical understanding, conceptualization of all relevant parts of the system. From this assumption comes different goals, foci, participants, and so on (Table 1–1). The term *family therapy* connotes a format of intervention that attempts to include the relevant system members—this means at least the nuclear family but most often the three-generation family and perhaps significant others such as lovers, friends, or important adoptive kin (persons without ties of blood or marriage whom the family has designated as members of itself). The presence of family members is considered crucial to addressing the goal of family treatment, which is the improved functioning of the family as an interlocking system and network of individuals. This context allows a focus on the family system as a whole in order to understand current individual behavior as rising from, and inevitably feeding back into, the complicated matrix of the general family system.

The goal of family treatment is the improved functioning of the family as an interlocking system and network of individuals.

The final and the intermediate goals of the family format are different from those in the individual and group formats. The final goal of the family model is improved family functioning and improved individual functioning of its members. This goal is reached, for example, by intermediate goals of improving family communication and decreasing family conflict. Thus the focus of the family model is on the current family interactions with the various coalitions, boundary difficulties, and other features of systemic dysfunction. This model assumes that because a large part of a person's problem is connected to malfunction in the family system, mobilizing and reorganizing the

TABLE 1–1. Family therapy format compared with other psychosocial therapy formats

Therapy format	Intermediate goals	Final goals	Focus	Participants	Length or frequency of sessions	Mean overall duration of treatment
Family	Improve family communication; decrease family conflict	Improved family functioning	Family intervention: family coalitions and roles	Nuclear family unit; extended family; 1–2 therapists	Most 1–2 hours per week	2 months–2 years
Individual	Insight into intrapsychic conflicts; insight into interaction (transference)	Individual personality/symptom change	Unconscious conflicts: individual's thoughts, wishes, and behaviors	1 patient; 1 therapist	1 hour, 1–5 times per week	2 months–5 years
Group	Sharing with group; improved relating skills in group	Improved individual social functioning	Group participants and feedback	6–8 patients; 1–2 therapists	1½ hours, 1 time per week	6 months–2 years

system may be an effective way to solve the problem. In contrast, the final goal of the individual model is personality, symptom, or behavior change in one particular individual. In order to reach such a final goal, the focus of the individual format is often on the individual's behaviors, unconscious conflicts, or cognitive schema. With this final goal and focus, the intermediate goals of individual intervention (depending on the particular therapeutic strategies) include insight into intrapsychic conflicts or interpersonal interactions with others, or knowledge of one's individual cognitions/behaviors, and a progressive change therein. The group format has as its final goal improved individual social functioning. The focus (somewhat similar to family treatment) is on current group interaction and intermediate goals but would include the individual sharing with the group and manifesting an improved relating skill with other group members. The following case example illustrates how three different approaches could be applied to the same situation:

> Ms. C, a young depressed woman, is living at home and not dating. An individual therapist might determine that Ms. C's intrapsychic conflicts around dependence and autonomy and her early interactions with her father led her to be afraid of men. The therapist might choose an individual format to increase understanding or a group format to increase interpersonal interaction. A family therapist might see that Ms. C's grandmother just died, that her mother is grieving and hostile to her father, that she is the youngest child and last one home, and that she is staying at home because her mother desperately needs her as a companion. The family therapist would see the girl with her parents. A biological therapist would see the phenomenology of classic depression and prescribe medication.

The strategies and techniques of family therapy (see Chapter 12)—whether structural, strategic, behavioral, psychoeducational, experiential, supportive, or psychodynamic—overlap with these same techniques as they are used in individual and group formats, but they may take on added dimensions in a family session. For example, in individual insight-oriented psychotherapy, the therapist may interpret an individual's interaction with his wife as it relates to his earlier developmental interaction with his mother. A family therapist, with both spouses in the room, might also make a related interpretation about the wife's reaction to her husband's behavior and how it related to her behavior with him and perhaps to her earlier interactions with her father. The individual patient, hearing the therapist's interpretation alone, may integrate it in such a way that his behavior toward his wife changes. The couple hearing the family therapist's interpretation together can use it to jointly understand and shift their interaction. A therapist using a family-of-origin approach might ask the husband and wife to bring in their parents for a family-of-origin session, so that they could deal with unresolved conflict directly with their families rather than playing it out with each other. In that way, the larger family system is used as a resource instead of a source of aggravation.

The model of psychopathology underlying family treatment is quite different from other forms of intervention. The family model is based on the assumption that personality development, symptom formation, and therapeutic change result, at least in part, from the family's function as an interdependent transactional unit. The individual psychopathology model is based on the view that these factors are determined largely by the dynamic, intrapsychic function of the individual. If one takes a psychodynamic point of view (or a biological point of view), the individual has been the major focus of attention. In contrast, Schatzman (1975) states in his critique of the individual model that although this model is helpful, it is ultimately inadequate for understanding how people affect one another:

> Psychoanalytic theory cannot render intelligible someone's disturbed experience or behavior in terms of disturbing behavior by someone else on that person. In order to comprehend a relationship between two individuals—husband and wife, mother and child, or father and son—we must take into account that each individual experiences the world and originates behavior. Of course, psychoanalysts know that other persons' experiences act upon their patients and that certain persons who dealt with their patients as children influenced them greatly by their behavior. But insofar as psychoanalysts speak of object relations, their theory does not adequately account for this influence.

Schaztman's formulation (although somewhat dated) can be related to other therapeutic models. Modern biopsychiatry is concerned with the biological correlates of emotional disorders, whereas personality psychology and the psychotherapies are concerned with individual psychodynamics and their relation to mental disorders. Family therapy is concerned primarily with the relationships among persons and how these family relationships and disruptions are linked both to physical and mental disorders of individuals and to larger contexts in the community.

We return to the discussion of family therapy as compared with other psychotherapies in Chapter 15. For now, let us go to the context of marriage and family.

Suggested Readings

Guttman H: Systems theory, cybernetics and epistemology, in Handbook of Family Therapy, Vol 11. Edited by Gurman A, Kniskern D. New York, Brunner/Mazel, 1991, pp 41–64
This chapter summarizes key concepts in the development of systems theory.

Hoffman L: Foundations of Family Therapy. New York, Basic Books, 1981
This book provides a historical and conceptual overview of the field's early years and development. Of specific value are the chapters describing the elaboration and applications of the cybernetic and systems paradigms in family therapy.

Shields CG, McDaniel SH, Wynne LC, et al: The marginalization of family therapy: a historical and continuing problem. J Marital Fam Ther 20:117–138, 1994
This article offers an excellent view of development of the field through the early 1990s.

References

Ackerman NW: Psychodynamics of Family Life. New York, Basic Books, 1958

Ackerman NW: Treating the Troubled Family. New York, Basic Books, 1966

Anonymous: Towards the differentiation of a self in one's own family, in Family Interaction: A Dialogue Between Family Researchers and Family Therapists. Edited by Framo JL. New York, Springer, 1972, pp 111–166

Bateson G, Jackson DD, Haley J, et al: Towards a theory of schizophrenia. Behavioral Science 1:251–264, 1956

Bowen M: A family concept of schizophrenia, in The Etiology of Schizophrenia. Edited by Jackson DD. New York, Basic Books, 1960, pp 346–372

Committee on the Family: Field of Family Therapy, Report No. 78. New York, Group for the Advancement of Psychiatry, 1970, p 534

Engel G: The clinical application of the biopsychosocial model. Am J Psychiatry 137:535–544, 1980

Glick ID, Burti L, Okonogi K, et al: Effectiveness in psychiatric care; III. psychoeducation and outcome for patients with major affective disorders and their families. Br J Psychiatry 164:104–106, 1994

Gray W, Duhl FJ, Rizzo ND: General Systems Theory and Psychiatry. Boston, MA, Little, Brown, 1969, p 7

Gurman AS, Kniskern DP: Research on marital and family therapy: progress, perspective and prospect, in Handbook of Psychotherapy and Behavior Change: An Empirical Analysis, 2nd Edition. Edited by Garfield SL, Bergin AE. New York, Wiley, 1978

Hoffman L: A co-evolutionary framework for systemic family therapy, in Diagnosis and Assessment in Family Therapy, The Family Therapy Collections. Edited by Hansen JC, Keeney BP. Rockville, MD, Aspen, 1983, p 42

Jackson DD: The question of family homeostasis. Psychiatr Q Suppl 31:79–90, 1957

Lewis JM: For better or worse: interpersonal relationships and individual outcome. Am J Psychiatry 155:582–589, 1998

Lidz R, Lidz T: The family environment of schizophrenic patients. Am J Psychiatry 106:322–345, 1949

Lidz T, Cornelison A, Terry D, et al: Intrafamilial environment of the schizophrenic patient; VI. the transmission of irrationality. Arch Neurol Psychiatry 79:305–316, 1958

Minuchin S: Families and Family Therapy. Cambridge, MA, Harvard University Press, 1974

Minuchin S, Baker L, Rosman B, et al: A conceptual model of psychosomatic illness in children. Arch Gen Psychiatry 32:1031–1038, 1975

Mittelman B: The concurrent analysis of married couples. Psychoanal Q 17:182–197, 1948

Oberndorf CP: Folie à deux. Int J Psychoanal 15:14–24, 1934

Pinsof WM, Wynne LC: The efficacy of marital and family therapy: an empirical review, conclusions and recommendations. J Marital Fam Ther 21:585–613, 1995

Sander FM: Marriage and the family in Freud's writing. J Am Acad Psychoanal 6:157–174, 1978

Satir VM: Conjoint Family Therapy: A Guide to Theory and Technique. Palo Alto, CA, Science and Behavior Books, 1964

Schatzman M: The Schreber case. Fam Process 14:594–598, 1975

Shields CG, McDaniel SH, Wynne LC, et al: The marginalization of family therapy: a historical and continuing problem. J Marital Fam Ther 20:117–138, 1994

Smith ZE: Discussion on charity organizations. Proceedings of the National Conference on Charities and Correction, 1890, p 377

Strauss JS, Hafez H, Lieberman P, et al: The course of psychiatric disorder, III: longitudinal principles. Am J Psychiatry 142:289–296, 1985

Szapocznik J, Durtines W, Satisteban DA, et al: Interplay of advances between theory, research, and applications in treatment interventions aimed at behavior problems in children and adolescents. J Consult Clin Psychol 58:696–703, 1990

Von Bertalanffy L: General Systems Theory. New York, George Braziller, 1968

Wells RA, Dezen AE: The results of family therapy revisited: the nonbehavioral methods. Fam Process 17:251–274, 1978

Wiener N: Cybernetics, or Control and Communication in the Animal and the Machine. Cambridge, MA, MIT Press, 1948

Wynne L, Ryckoff I, Day J, et al: Pseudo-mutuality in the family relations of schizophrenics. Psychiatry 21:205–220, 1958

Family in Tenement, Lewis Hine, New York City, 1910. Courtesy of the International Museum of Photography, George Eastman House, Rochester, New York. Used with permission.

CHAPTER 2

Family Life in Historical and Sociological Perspective

With Richard M. Patel, M.D.

Objectives for the Reader

- ꙮ To be able to place in historical context the development of present-day family structure and function
- ꙮ To understand recent changes in the family and in marriage
- ꙮ To understand clinical implications of the current social context of the family

Introduction

Now that we have some notion of the genesis and meaning of the term *family therapy*, this information should be placed in the larger context of a historical, cultural, and sociological perspective. Our bias is that it is crucial for all mental health professionals (not just family therapists) to have a thorough understanding of current and evolving norms, patterns, and trends in family life. Knowing the historical development of family norms can guide treatment by placing specific cases in a conceptual framework, distinguishing what is dysfunctional from cultural extremes.

Admittedly most of this book is based on studies of Western society and families sprouting from the American cultural landscape. An understanding of how family form shifts with ethnicity and culture is just beginning. It is all too easy to assume that the family forms we grew up with are the normal, or correct, family forms, when instead they are products of a specific place and time. For example, in the time since our parents were married, families have changed in such dramatic ways that the differences in beliefs and family forms between generations is staggering. These differences have major implications for our ability to treat families, particularly those from a different generation than our own.

In this chapter we offer an overview and synthesis of contemporary, American familial trends in a historical context and also discuss the clinical implications of these trends. We discuss issues specific to other ethnic and cultural groups in Chapter 17.

Historical and Current Trends in Structure and Function of the American Family

The Past

Throughout history the structure of the family has altered in relation to the economic and social structures of the times. The particular roles and tasks of individual family members have also varied from one time period to another. For example, during colonial days the family was a self-sufficient economic unit that produced more of its daily sustenance than did the family in later periods. During that time period there was a greater emphasis on the economic basis of marriage than on romance. Traditional roles for husbands and wives were fixed and accepted with little possibility of role and task rearrangement. However, husbands and wives worked together on the land at home; and fathers were intimately involved with the day-to-day lives of their children and were responsible for their moral upbringing.

Before 1900 little recognition was given to the separate needs of children and adolescents. In rural and working class areas, family members as young as 7 years were treated as junior-sized adults and were expected to work; however, children were valued for their work and knew that they had important work to do. The prolonged adolescence of modern America, in which a 10-year period exists between puberty and acceptable adult role-taking, was absent—children reached puberty later and married earlier. Many current adolescent problems may be partly a result of there being a group of young people with adult bodies who do not yet have work in the adult world.

Before 1900, large families were common because there was no effective birth control, and childbirth was a major cause of early death in women. Life expectancy was shorter, so the couple had little time together without children before one or both partners died.

Throughout most of history, children (and women) were seen as subordinate, producing income or salable merchandise and existing mostly to help fulfill a parental (or family) need. Only in the last 100 years or so have most families been concerned with providing for the creative and developing needs of their children and for the development and equality of women. As we shall see, this has been a very difficult shift at both the cultural and the family levels.

Industrialization in the mid- and late nineteenth century saw the rise of the middle class and the so-called cult of domesticity. As men left the farms and homes to work in the city, work became separated from home, and women's and men's work diverged sharply, with women as the "angel of the house" and "haven in a heartless world" (Lasch 1977). In wealthier classes women eventually became primarily ornaments, to acquire and display their husband's wealth, but more women worked very hard at home. Poor women and children always worked in the developing factories and as domestics, but the ideal of the wife's domain as inside the house became very powerful. The ideal of the woman solely as homemaker dates from this time period, but many people believe it to be a panhistorical or even biological truth. The concept of romantic love as the raison d'être of marriage came to be widely accepted only in the late 1880s, at a time when in some ways men's and women's worlds were furthest apart.

During the twentieth century a number of powerful forces were at work:

1. Birth control and the possibility of spacing families. As soon as birth control became possible, the size of families began to drop. When women went to work it dropped further, so that in the latter half of the century the average American family had two or three children.
2. Increased medical and public health measures, and better nutrition, leading to a longer life span. Children were more apt to live to adulthood, married couples had a long postchildrearing phase in which both were alive and healthy, and families and society had a bigger job caring for a large number of elderly people.
3. The long struggle of women to find equality both at home and in public life. Because women still do more of the work of the home, and 60% also are in the workforce (including more than 60% of married women with young children [DeVanzo and Rahman 1993]), family life looks very dif-

ferent than it did 30 years ago. However, men's lives have not altered in order to take over half of the work of the home and children; therefore, the home is still in transition. Women have not yet found equality of pay or position in most work situations.

4. Geographical mobility, enabling nuclear families to move away from extended family and community, leading to less family and community support. Geographic stability is a key concept in the myth of the golden era of family life. Our society developed the image of a three-generation family living in a little house with a white picket fence (although this was seldom the reality). Geographic mobility has been and continues to be a way of life with Americans. The movement from rural to urban areas has been an important migration of the twentieth century, and migration patterns continue today, primarily to the west and the south.

These four events led to smaller family size, with longer time for a couple to be together both before and after childrearing. They also created an increased demand for more emotional connections and less tolerance for purely functional marriages. Children became more valued for themselves but changed from being an economic advantage to an economic burden. Increasing equality for women has changed many of the old rules and roles, leading to increasing freedom from sex-role constraints. Both men and women are in a process of negotiation as to what constitutes masculinity and femininity. The increased divorce rate, the lower remarriage rate for older women, and women's longer life expectancy have led to a larger number of single women, particularly in the older age groups. Because these changes developed slowly over time, couples of different ages seen in therapy may have vastly differing attitudes about intimacy, gender equality, and divorce, and the therapist must ascertain clearly the set of attitudes and beliefs with which he or she is dealing.

Couples of different ages seen in therapy may have very differing attitudes about intimacy, gender equality, and divorce, and the therapist must ascertain clearly the set of attitudes and beliefs with which he or she is dealing.

The Changing Model of the Family

The current state of the family is well described in the following UNICEF editorial concerning the changing family, written in 1976 but still true today:

> The family is the basic unit in all societies regardless of cultural diversities. Families everywhere consist of men, women, and children united by ties of kinship and mutual obligations. Within its capacity the family is expected to meet its members' basic needs for food, shelter, and clothing, and to provide the intangible needs for affection and a sense of belonging. It helps to transmit from one generation to the next the traditions and the cultural, moral, and spiritual values unique to each society. Inevitably, in each era there are changes, large or small, gradual or abrupt, that may alter or transform family patterns. Foremost among the forces influencing family life today is the rapid pace and nature of social change. First, the effect of national development is to change the economic, social, and physical environment, possibly to open up new horizons and opportunities, certainly to pose challenges for the family, if not to impose additional burdens on it. Second, development almost invariably involves adjustment within the family itself, in the roles and responsibilities of family members, and in relationships among the generations. Because of their complete dependence on adults, children are the first to suffer or benefit from changes affecting the family. Throughout the developing world, the past few decades have witnessed dramatic changes. The gradual awakening of women to their rights and dignities, the rapid rate of urbanization, population pressures, increasing education, and technology are factors that are affecting the family in countless ways. Change is a continuing and inescapable reality in today's world ("Coping with change" 1976).

Heated discussion continues concerning the extent to which the family is changing and whether the family is dying altogether. The "traditional" model of the average family—one made up of husband/breadwinner, wife/homemaker, and two children—represented less than 10% of the American population by 1991. Clearly there are other models of living together in an intimate relationship, in which adults are involved in family functions. Unmarried couples, single-parent and remarried families, and committed gay or lesbian couples are common viable family forms. In addition, it is helpful to think in terms of a much broader definition of the system, which Pattison and associates (1975) called the kinship model. By kinship they meant the individuals, extended families, community, and neighborhood that are seen as the family.

Because there are many possible and workable types of family organization, family therapists need to be careful not to project, knowingly or unknowingly, their own personal ideals of family structure and function when they are treating their patients. From the initial contact with a family, the therapist should pay special attention to the structure of that family: its goals, resources, motivation, and potentialities. Only after understanding the specifics of a particular family can the therapist begin to think about treatment.

Family therapists need to be careful not to project, knowingly or unknowingly, their own personal ideals of family structure and function when they are treating their patients.

Divorce and Remarriage

Many contemporary observers refer to the happy, extended multigenerational families of bygone times as the ideal to which we should aspire and lament the current so-called dismal state of family life, as though we have somehow fallen from grace. Although some writers attribute this fall to moral decay, others blame governmental intrusion into private and family matters (D. Davis 1979). Both sides agree, however, that things were seemingly better in the past and that family life today is deteriorating. We agree with others who note there is little evidence that different means worse.

The largest proportional increase of any marital status category in the last 30 years has occurred among divorced persons. The number of currently divorced persons more than tripled from 4.3 million in 1970 to 15.8 million in 1991, representing 9% of all adults age 18 years and older in 1991 (U.S. Bureau of the Census 1992).

High divorce rates create, among other things, a large pool of individuals eligible for remarriage. Remarriage in the United States has become a relatively common life course event. Currently more than 4 out of 10 marriages in the United States involve a second or higher-order marriage for the bride, groom, or both (Norton and Miller 1992).

Several variables seem to be causally linked with the likelihood of divorce or remarriage. Earlier studies documented an association between age at remarriage and divorce; educational attainment and divorce; premarital pregnancy and divorce; and age at divorce and likelihood of remarriage (Norton and Moorman 1987). Those who enter marriage before age 20 are more likely to divorce than those who are older. Overall, the data show no unidimensional association between education and divorce. The data appear to support the so-called Glick effect, which suggests that people with an incomplete education—those who apparently stopped short of a diploma or degree—are more likely to divorce than are people who do not have an incomplete education (Norton and Miller 1992). That is, people with lower levels of education are more likely to divorce than those with higher levels.

The increasing divorce rate is frequently taken as a single measure of family disintegration and is portrayed as a sign that marriage is no longer important to Americans. We believe that the issue men and women face is that of having more choices. Our position is that both the old and the new models have problems. There is no evidence that one set of problems is worse than the other. People's willingness to remarry quickly is, we believe, an indication of how strongly people believe in marriage.

In that context, one of the most significant marital constants has been the percentage of women who choose to marry and who become mothers. Women born between 1936 and 1940 married and had children with approximately the same frequency as did women born 100 years earlier. A hundred years ago, men would die or desert the family—now couples often agree to divorce. Up to very recently (1999; see the paragraph below), regardless of enormous cultural changes, most women continued to enter marriage and bear children, thus demonstrating the viability of marriage as an institution.

However, Americans are less inclined to get married now than at any previous time in history, leading to debate among social scientists over social and public policy consequences. A report from the National Marriage Project at Rutgers University in New Jersey found "a substantial weakening of the institution of marriage." The researchers said that the marriage rate had never been lower, births to unmarried women had skyrocketed, the divorce rate remained high, and marriages were less happy than in the past (International Herald Tribune 1999).

The report, citing census data, said that the marriage rate had plummeted by one-third since 1960, from 73 marriages per 1,000 women age 15 or older to 49 marriages per 1,000 in 1996, the last year for which figures were available. The report cited several factors: American are postponing marriage, sometimes until it is too late. There has been a huge jump in cohabiting partnerships and an explosion of sex outside marriage, and the movement of women into the labor market has made many less reliant on husbands (International Herald Tribune 1999).

The family therapist should appreciate that, from the proportion of individuals having children and the great extent of divorce activity, many children today are very likely to experience a divorce. There is a concomitant substantial increase in the number and proportion of single-parent families and remarried or stepfamilies. It has been estimated that stepfamilies make up 10%–15% of all households in the United States.

Nevertheless, the marriage rate continues to decline. U.S. Bureau of the Census data stated that one in four Americans age 18 years and older (i.e., about 41 million people) had never married (U.S. Bureau of the Census 1992). In 1970 that figure was about one in six adults. The proportion of Americans getting married in 1991 was lower than any year since 1965, a year when the oldest members of the post–World War II baby boom were just coming into prime marrying age. Although divorce rates peaked in the 1980s and have been leveling off since then, the drop in marriage rates was accompanied by continued increases in the number of single-parent families. Between 1970 and 1991 the proportion of children living in two-parent living arrangements declined from 85% to 72%, whereas the proportion living with a single parent more than doubled from 12% to 26%. There were sharp differences in the statistics for whites and blacks. More than half of the nation's black children (58%) were living with one parent in 1991, compared with 20% of white children.

More people, especially men, are postponing marriage until later ages. In the early 1990s, 17.6% of men in the age group 35–39 years had never married. This figure was up from 7.8% in 1980. For women the increase was almost as sharp; never-married women, who were 6.2% of females in the age group 35–39 years in 1980, accounted for 11.7% (of the same group) 10 years later.

A 1996 report by the Population Reference Bureau (De Vita 1996, p. C4) suggests that "after two decades of social pressures that caused many to fear that it might dissolve, the traditional American family is making a comeback in the 1990s. Increases in the number of two-parent households with children, decreases in the divorce rate and other changes suggest that the American family is stabilizing. The number of two-parent households with children increased by 700,000 from 1990 to 1995, reversing a 20-year decline. The divorce rate slowed to 20.5 divorces per 1,000 married women in 1994 from 23 divorces per 1,000 in 1980; the increase in the number of births to unmarried women slowed to a 2% annual average increase in the early 1990s, down from a 6% annual rise in the 1980s [Figure 2–1]. These changes can be attributed to the Baby Boom generation, which makes up a third of the country's population, has entered middle age and settled into the task of raising families."

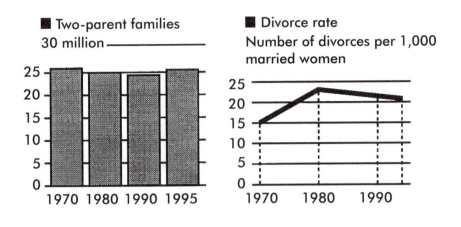

FIGURE 2-1.   Family portrait.
Source.   De Vita CJ: A Report Suggesting That the Traditional American Family Is Stabilizing. Washington, DC, Population Reference Bureau, 1996. Reprinted with permission.

Other Changes in the Late 1900s

Increased Status of Women

One of the most significant historical trends has been the gradual increase in the status of women, evidenced by at least two clearly measurable phenomena: employment and education. At the end of the nineteenth century and early in the twentieth, most employed women were single. In general, a single woman who had a job would quit when she married and usually would not re-enter the labor force. By the end of World War II, a reversal had taken place so that the majority of working women were married. This suggests that although single women continued to work, their married compatriots rejoined the labor force later on. Today, almost all women work during the early years of marriage, and the vast majority continue to work during the childrearing years. Over 50% of women with preschool children, and 75% of those with school-aged children, are now in the labor force. This shift has produced many changes in family life, which we detail later in this chapter, including busier, if often happier, mothers and a demand for husbands to take over a share of the housework as women take on more of a share of the financial burden. Conflicts in this area are at the heart of many arguments within couples.

The educational status of women has been improving dramatically. In the

1950s approximately 25% of women obtained degrees beyond high school. Today, over 50% of college and graduate students are women. The major implication of the increased educational and employment status of women is that they are able to support themselves and thus are increasingly independent.

Modifications in the Family Life Cycle

The majority of women continue to become mothers, although increasingly larger numbers delay childbearing and prefer to have fewer children. In 1900, women bore six children, on average, whereas today they usually have one or two. From 1970 through the 1990s, the number of families containing three or more children younger than 18 years has dwindled from 17% to just 7%.

One of the most profound changes in the evolution of marriage in the United States is the substantial modification of the life cycle of women. The average age at marriage remained the same from the mid-1800s to the mid-1900s, but by the end of the 1900s the age had risen. Because more children were born per family in the mid-1800s, the average time span between the birth of a woman's first child and her last was 12.5 years. In contrast, women now experience a corresponding period of only 2.5 years. The brevity of time from birth of first to last child, coupled with the fact that modern mothers also experience greater longevity, defines a rather extensive postchildrearing period.

Today it seems reasonable to think of essentially two phases of a marriage. The first might be referred to as a family-oriented phase, in which children are present, and the second a postchildrearing phase, after the children have left home. The adaptations and skills necessary for a successful family-oriented marriage cannot be assumed to apply necessarily in the postchildrearing phase, with its greater intimacy and couple orientation.

Today it may be reasonable to add a prechildbearing phase for those couples who decide to delay childbearing for various reasons. Couples may choose different sequences for their lives together—marriage first, then babies, then career (at least for one of the spouses); career first, then marriage and babies; or marriage first, then career and babies. The last combination leads to very busy and tired two-career parents (see next section).

Working Mothers and Fathers

The related phenomena of working women and two-career families are subjects of much contemporary marital and family research. The question of who is to be home with children during illness, during vacations, or after school is still a struggle in most households. Child care still falls mostly to women—mothers, grandmothers, or paid help who may be leaving their own children alone or with relatives. Although 35 years of research found no ill effects for children raised in well-functioning day care programs, there have been problems when day care programs are substandard or when both parents work such long hours that neither parent or no consistent caregiver is at home with the children, even when the children are older. Social change also lagged behind family changes, and only recently have companies begun to experiment with on-site child care, maternity and paternity leave, and enough flexibility to make family life manageable. Waite (1981) found that time management was one of the most critical matters faced by both men and women. It is for this reason that in most couples one of the partners, usually the woman, drops out of the labor force or decreases his or her hours when children are born. Whatever the couple's decision, it will be restructured several times over the course of the childrearing years, often with a great deal of conflict. Women in particular come to therapy feeling guilty that they are not working, guilty that they are working too much, or angry that they are not getting more help. However, for women who choose to be at home, or who find a good balance between home and work, these can be very satisfying years. Men are increasingly sharing the housework when their wives are sharing the financial burden but are often reluctant partners in the restructuring of household tasks.

Patterns of Sexual Behavior

With the sexual revolution in the United States during the 1960s and 1970s, attitudes and behaviors once considered radical have gradually come to be incorporated into everyday life. For example, premarital intercourse is commonplace today (although AIDS has made the character of sexual exploration far more complex), as is cohabitation. Surveys of adolescents indicate that most have premarital intercourse (Kaplan 1995). Because people are more sexually experienced when they enter marriage, they have higher expectations of sexual satisfaction from their marital partners. Sexual gratification alone is no longer a reason for getting married, as it once was.

Cohabitation has become increasingly common in the United States. In some states over half the couples who marry will live together first. Early research suggested that the divorce rate is higher among previously cohabiting married couples than among those who did not live together before marriage; more recent work, however, suggests a reversal of this trend.

Contemporary Living Arrangements

There is no one dominant family form of marital and family living arrangements in the United States today. Single-breadwinner, nuclear families, the usually idealized concept of the family, comprise only 13% of the population. The most prevalent form of household composition today is one in which people live in a child-free or postchildbearing marriage (23%); followed by single, widowed, separated, or divorced persons (21%); single-parent families (28%); and dual-breadwinner nuclear families (16%). Figure 2–2 illustrates another way of looking at household composition.

Anyone engaging in family or couples therapy must be cautioned against thinking of families in any single way. It is worthwhile to remember that for couples born before 1960 the ideal of husband/breadwinner and wife/homemaker may still be deeply present.

Aging of the Population

Another important change in American society is the aging of the population. Not only is the elderly population increasing in size relative to other age cohorts, but it is an older population. Life expectancy in the United States has increased substantially: In 1900 the average life expectancy from birth was 49.2 years, but by 1983 it had climbed to 74.6 years. As death rates fall, there is usually a secondary decline in birth rates due to changes in the perceived value of having many children and the wish to maintain the high quality of life that is often threatened by large families.

As life expectancy improves, larger cohorts of individuals remain alive into their later years. By the year 2050 more than 20% of the population will be older than 65 years, and approximately 30% of the population will be younger than 25 years. The over-85 age group is the fastest-growing segment of the population (Figure 2–3). One of the major effects of an improved life expectancy on family life is the changed composition of families, so that today we expect more multigenerational families than existed in the past. However, the current trend among couples to delay childbearing may offset this effect. Men and women age 50–60 years may be expected to spend time taking care of their elderly parents. Although women are the predominant care-

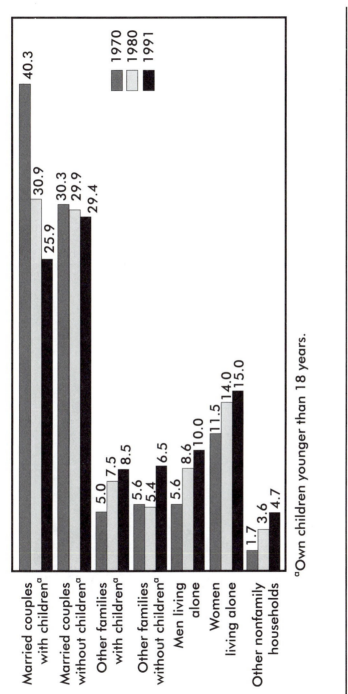

ᵃOwn children younger than 18 years.

FIGURE 2–2.   Household composition in the United States, 1970–1991, percent of total households.   *Note.*   Percentages may not add to 100% because of rounding.   *Source.*   U.S. Bureau of the Census (1992a).

takers of aging parents at present, this trend may change in the future. Childhood dependency will not only give way to adult autonomy and independence but in the future will also continue on to a caretaking role for the elderly.

Likewise, Schone and Pezzin (1999) recently reported that divorce reduces both caregiving and economic ties between elderly parents (especially fathers) and their adult children. Contrary to popular opinion, the elderly are using less medical services than expected, and they are resisting dependency. They are also becoming more assertive and demanding in their communities, expressing their expectations that their medical and social needs be met. Family therapists need to be aware of these changes as they manage elderly patients (see section on dementia in Chapter 24).

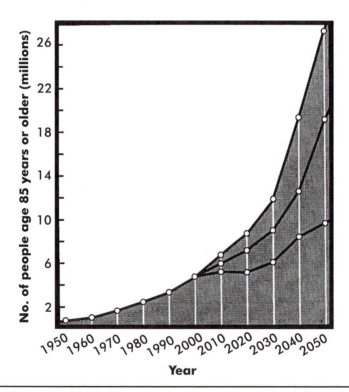

FIGURE 2–3.   The size of the U.S. population age 85 years or older, 1950–2050. The values are actual from 1950 to 1990 and three sets of estimates—low, intermediate, and high—from 1991 to 2050.

Source. U.S. Bureau of the Census (1993).

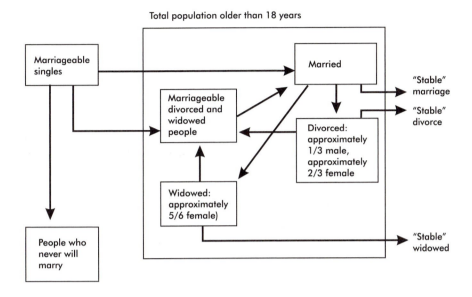

FIGURE 2–4.   A historical and sociological perspective of the marital cycle drawn schematically.

Source.   Adapted from Bjorksten OJW, Stewart TJ: "Contemporary Trends in American Marriage," in *Marriage and Divorce: A Contemporary Perspective.* Edited by Nadelson CC, Polonsky DC. New York, Guilford, 1984. Adapted with permission.

The Cycle of Marital Activity

Categories of marital status such as single, married, divorced, widowed, and so on are frequently conceived of as stable states. This view is no longer accurate. A much more dynamic picture of marital activity in the United States, in which a larger number of people shift between various marital statuses, is more accurate. We illustrate this with a schematic diagram showing the flow of marital activity (Stewart et al. 1985) (Figure 2–4). Although most Americans still marry before age 30 years, demographers and marital researchers have noted a general delay in marriage, with more marriages occurring in people age 25–44 years.

The extent of divorce activity in the United States is frequently referred to as an indicator of a general decline in the importance of marriage and family in the United States. The divorce rate increased markedly in the United

States during the twentieth century, although the rate stabilized, albeit at a higher level, over the last 15 years of the century. Perhaps the most useful type of divorce data is not the divorce rate but cohort studies that essentially track the marital and divorce history of selected subpopulations. For both first marriages and remarriages, by the time the 50th anniversary occurs for a couple, only slightly more than one half of the couples will still be married. Of interest is that remarried people seem to divorce sooner but with about the same frequency as people in first marriages. Thus a remarriage has about the same probability of success as first marriages. For both parents and children, divorce is still traumatic, regardless of how well-managed it is.

As expected from the proportion of individuals having children and the great extent of divorce activity, many children today are likely to experience a divorce. There is a concomitant substantial increase in the number and proportion of single-parent families and remarriage, stepfamilies, or blended families. Nearly 30% of nonmarital births occur within cohabiting unions (Bumpass et al. 1991). It has been estimated that stepfamilies make up 10%–15% of all households in the United States, and that percentage is increasing (Espinoza and Newman 1979). Stepfamily relationships are complex—we discuss them in Chapters 4 and 21.

In the mid-1980s it was estimated that after a first divorce, almost 80% of the partners would remarry. After a second divorce, almost 90% of the partners will remarry, although this is less likely for women older than 40 years. Currently more than 40% of marriages in the United States involve a second or higher-order marriage. The median duration of a first marriage before divorce is about 6.3 years for women ages 20–54 years. The median duration before remarriage for all women whose first marriage ended in divorce is 2.5 years. About 25% of those who remarry do so in the first year after the divorce; 75% repeat marriage within 5 years.

To understand the effect that current demographic trends have on the family therapist and mental health practitioners in general, we must consider how the current social context influences marital adjustment, pathology, and the overall treatment situation.

The Change From a Traditional to a Companionate Marriage

Traditional Marriage

Over the past several generations, major changes in marital style have occurred, moving from a traditional to a companionate pattern. Traditional marriages can be viewed from a structural perspective in which marital roles and duties were prescribed, nonnegotiable, and well defined. Marriage was functional, and each partner was expected to fulfill role obligations. James Thurber described love within the traditional marriage as "Love is what you've been through with somebody." Marital failure was synonymous with role failure, which was easy to determine because there was good cultural agreement about what husbands and wives should do. These marital functions were closely associated with gender: men were reluctant to perform women's duties and vice versa. These gendered sex roles connected marital-role behavior with individual identity and thus with related marital and individual pathology. These relationships served as one rationale for applying an individually oriented psychotherapy approach to the treatment of marital problems.

Before 1900 the key concepts in traditional marriage were *duty* and *responsibility*. Duty implied a known set of role functions that one accepted upon marriage; if a person did not want to perform these functions, then he or she would not marry. Thus in this sense traditional marriage was considered binary. Once married, each partner was responsible for his or her role functions (i.e., he or she was expected to perform them). If love occurred in a traditional marriage, it grew after marriage and was frequently not the essential requirement in the decision to marry; rather, one appraised a potential partner in terms of his or her ability to perform role functions (e.g., Will he be a good provider? or Will she be a good mother?).

Companionate Marriage

The traditional marital style began to shift with the onset of industrialization in the latter part of the nineteenth century, shifting slowly through the early part of the twentieth century. The companionate style of marriage can be viewed from a process perspective (i.e., how the marriage works) because it has an emotional focus in which roles evolve through negotiation and are often variable and vague. Communication and negotiation skills are vital in this style of marriage, and it is important that each partner has the maturity to know what he or she wants from the marriage. In contrast with the traditional style, roles in the companionate marriage are created by the partners so that role competency is difficult to evaluate, and marital failure is synonymous with a poor relationship rather than role incompetency. Partners in traditional marriages must tolerate the stresses of adaptation to marital roles, whereas in the companionate form they must tolerate role ambiguity.

Within the companionate model, however, wide discrepancies in power and influence can occur. The early companionate marriages still left the husband as principal breadwinner and wife as principal homemaker, whatever else she did. True equality, in which the wife has a job or career that is equally as valued as the husband's and the husband truly takes much responsibility for household day-to-day care, is still unusual. Time studies or careful interviewing show that in many couples who attempt such relationships, the wife is simply working harder, doing both work and the so-called second shift (housework and child care) (Hochschild 1989). In addition, the old idea that the man is head of the house dies hard.

The key concepts in companionate marriage are *love* and *choice*. The raison d'être for these marriages is that people want to be together because they love each other and expect to obtain fulfillment from their relationship with their partner. The actualization of this romantic ideal is an historically new phenomenon that implies a level of prosperity sufficient to release people from a survival orientation, and a degree of equality between partners hitherto unknown because of inadequate birth control, short life expectancy, and lack of economic opportunities and education for women.

Marital choice implies not only choice within the marriage but also of the marriage. The freedom of both partners to choose to marry each other is a recent historical phenomenon and now appears to be an ongoing matter after marriage because divorce is relatively easy to obtain. We take for granted that women can leave a marriage as easily as men, but this has become possible only in recent years, now that women have joined the workforce and have achieved the economic freedom that makes this option possible. (In reality, women cannot leave as easily because they will probably carry a disproportionate share of responsibility for the children.)

The partners in companionate marriages have high expectations of their partners and of the relationship. They expect to remain in love and be happy. These expectations often lead to disappointment when romance settles into routine and the relationship is no longer exciting. This has led to the development of (among other things) marital enrichment workshops designed to help partners achieve more fulfilling marriages.

The concept of the increasing status and freedom of women is not meant as a vague or philosophical term but rather as a description of demographic trends, supported by increasing employment rates and educational achievement of women, fewer children per woman, delayed childbearing, and curtailed childbearing years. With this increased status has come increased freedom of choice regarding intimate relationships. Although this freedom has permitted more love marriages and better psychological functioning for men and women, it has probably contributed to the higher divorce rate. In addition, increased status and genuine equality are not synonymous. Physical abuse of wives and children and spousal rape are still prevalent in this society. Traditionally the marital agenda focused on the development of a family with children and the acquisition of property (i.e., a home). This agenda usually implied a high degree of stability so that roots could be established. Thus psychiatric appraisal of marriage used children and property as one set of criteria to judge if a marriage was working. Today, mental health professionals are faced with a much more challenging dilemma in evaluating companionate marriages. Because the focus is on love and the relationship itself, rather than on children and property, the evaluation of marital success is based much more on the subjective appraisal by the partners than on external objective criteria. Couples may view their marriage as very successful, even though they have no children and move frequently. What are the criteria for evaluating such a marriage? For the couple, one answer is, "If it works." The following history of four generations of a middle-class family demonstrates this shift:

Ms. A's great-grandparents came from rural Pennsylvania. Each came from a family of seven children. They met at a dance in a nearby town in 1905. They had six children together. Ms. A's great-grandmother took care of the house, the children, and the garden, and she helped with the farmwork. Her friends and confidants were the women of the surrounding farms. Ms. A's great-grandfather farmed, and the boys helped as they grew older. On Saturdays he sometimes went hunting with local men. Both great-grandparents worked very hard. Their roles were distinct, and the great-grandfather made the decisions.

Ms. A's grandparents met in the same town in 1930, but they were both restless and moved to Philadelphia after high school. Her grandfather worked in a factory, and her grandmother worked at home. They had five children, one of whom died of pneumonia. Ms. A's grandmother enjoyed nice things and as time went on found ways to earn extra money by sewing at home or raising chickens in the small coop in the backyard. Although Ms. A's grandfather was clearly the head of the house, he listened carefully to his wife's opinions, although not in public.

Ms. A's mother was born in 1934. She was raised to be a lady and marry well. She was the first woman on her side of the family to start college, but the man she was engaged to was graduating, and she dropped out to get married after her freshman year. Ms. A's father became a doctor, and her mother was a doctor's wife all her life. Her mother enjoyed raising her three children, caring for the house, and preparing elaborate meals for her family. She and her husband considered themselves romantic partners and good friends.

Ms. A was born in 1960. She went to college, finished graduate school in business, and in 1988 married a man from her business school class. She and her husband both work long hours and earn about the same amount of money. They had put off having children until 1995 and are still trying to work out adequate child care because Ms. A had to be back to work 6 weeks after their baby was born. Her husband is uneasy about taking paternity leave, and both grandmothers have been working full time since their husbands died. Ms. A and her husband see themselves as equal partners but are still arguing about who will do the dishes.

Special Issues in the Marriages of Immigrants

One of the major historical trends in the United States has been massive immigration. About 9% of the current population was born in a foreign country. During the past 150 years an unprecedented number of immigrants from all over the world have settled in the United States. Married immigrant couples face very specific issues because they have to both mourn an old culture and adapt to a new one. Often they have come to the United States to escape grinding poverty or as political refugees. When they come from poor and nonwesternized cultures, they must also adapt to very different patterns of marriage and attitudes toward women and children. The struggle between traditional and companionate marriages then becomes an issue of differential Americanization. If the husband works while the wife remains at home, the wife may become the spokesperson for the culture left behind and for old traditions, whereas her husband, who is working, or the children who are at school become the spokespeople for the new. Alternatively, if the wife goes out into the wider community, she may chafe at old restrictions when her husband insists on the respect he received in the country of origin. The children must negotiate living in the new culture at school and the old one at home, with various family stresses that result. It usually takes three generations for the family to deal completely with issues of immigration. Immigrants who marry in the United States often marry people of different backgrounds or degrees of enculturation, and most struggle with issues of family and ethnic loyalty.

Issues Unique to the Historical Development of African American Families

The ancestors of African American families were brought to the United States as slaves, and efforts were made by slave owners to stamp out all aspects of native African culture and to decrease ties of marriage, family, and community. There was no guarantee that families could stay together, nor could men protect in any way the women or children they loved. Women were obviously expected to work very hard. Despite these hardships, couple bonding was still very strong, and after the Civil War (and in the north before then), African American families developed strong family and community bonds in the face of continued segregation and discrimination. In general African American women have been seen as very strong and have not had to contend to the same degree with the Caucasian ideal of the sweet, feminine, helpless woman, although they certainly are seen as nurturing. African American men have had to contend with a society that allows them few options for advancement or self-esteem outside their own community. African American families have tended to keep extended family together, to use family resources as support, and to adopt into the family nonblood members who become vital parts of family life. We explore these issues in greater detail in Chapter 18.

Summary and Relevance for the Family Therapist

The family has maintained itself as an institution throughout history and in all recognized cultures. In various subtle and major ways, it has also changed with respect to specific ways of carrying out its functions. The family therapist needs to examine a particular family to see to what degree it has carried out its functions within its cohort group and culture and to what extent extended family people and institutions are available to help the family continue to do so.

In this chapter we have discussed the past and present and alluded to the future of the family. In Chapter 3 we look at how families function.

Suggested Readings

McGoldrick M, Heiman M, Carter B: The changing family life cycle: a perspective on normalcy, in Normal Family Processes, 2nd Edition. Edited by Walsh F. New York, Guilford, 1993, pp 405–444
This is an excellent review of how historical and sociological changes in the past 30 years have affected all phases of the family life cycle.

Segraves RT: Marital status and psychiatric morbidity, in New Clinical Concepts in Marital Therapy. Edited by Bjorksten OJW. Washington, DC, American Psychiatric Press, 1985
This book offers an excellent review of the existing data relating marital status to psychopathology.

Shorter E: The Making of the Modern Family. New York, Basic Books, 1977
The book examines the history of courtship, the mother-child relationship, and the boundary between the family and the community, as influenced by the industrial and sexual revolutions.

References

Bumpass L, Sweet J, Cherlin A: The role of cohabiting in declining rates of marriage. Journal of Marriage and the Family 53:913–927, 1991

Coping with change. UNICEF News 89:3, 1976

Davis D: The American family and boundaries in historical perspective, in The American Family: Dying or Developing. Edited by Reiss D, Hoffman HA. New York, Plenum, 1979, pp 13–33

Davis K: The American family in relation to demographic change, in Demographic and Social Aspects of Population Growth, Vol 1. Edited by Westoff CF, Parke R. Washington, DC, U.S. Government Printing Office, 1972, p 256

DeVanzo J, Rahman O: American families: trends and correlates. Population Index 50:350–386, 1993

De Vita CJ: Population Reference Bureau. Quoted in San Francisco Chronicle, March 7, 1996, p C4

Espinoza R, Newman Y: Step-parenting (DHEW Publ No ADM-78-579). Washington, DC: U.S. Government Printing Office, 1979

Hochschild A: The Second Shift. New York, Avon, 1989

International Herald Tribune, September 30, 1999, p 6

Kaplan HS: The Sexual Desire Disorders: Dysfunctional Regulation of Sexual Motivation. New York, Brunner/Mazel, 1995, Chapter 18

Lasch C: Haven in a Heartless World. New York, Basic Books, 1977

Norton AJ, Miller LF: Marriage, divorce and remarriage in the 1990s. U.S. Bureau of the Census, Current Population Reports, Series P-23, No 180. Washington, DC, U.S. Government Printing Office, 1992

Norton AJ, Moorman JE: Current trends in marriage and divorce among American women. Journal of Marriage and the Family 49:3–14, 1987

Pattison EM, DeFrancisco D, Wood P, et al: A psychosocial kinship model for family therapy. Am J Psychiatry 132:1246–1251, 1975

Schone BS, Pezzin LE: Parental marital disruption and intergenerational transfers: an analysis of lone elderly parents and their children. Demography 36:287–297, 1999

Stewart TJ, Bjorksten OJW, Glick ID: Sociodemographic aspects of contemporary American marriage, in New Clinical Concepts in Marital Therapy. Edited by Bjorksten OJW. Washington, DC, American Psychiatric Press, 1985

U.S. Bureau of the Census: Marital status and living arrangements: March 1991. (Current Population Reports, Series P-20, No 461.) Washington, DC, U.S. Government Printing Office, 1992

U.S. Bureau of the Census: Special studies: Sixty five plus in America. (Current Population Reports, Series P-23, No 178 RU.) Washington, DC, U.S. Government Printing Office, 1993

Waite L: Women at work. Population Reference Bureau 36:1–44, 1981

SECTION 2

Functional and Dysfunctional Families

In the opening sentence of the book *Anna Karenina*, Tolstoy (1960) declares, "Happy families are all alike; every unhappy family is unhappy in its own way." Although one hesitates to disagree with Tolstoy, this and the next two chapters describe the ways in which functional families are alike, yet diverse, as well as the ways in which dysfunctional families are alike and yet unique.

Our bias is that to treat families, the family therapist must understand not only how families function but also how dysfunction develops. In Chapters 3 and 4 we consider the family as an organized system, its life cycle, and the family's tasks and functional characteristics as they relate to traditional and to newer, alternative family forms. In Chapter 5 we describe how dysfunctional families, which often have symptomatic members or members with problem areas, operate in these three dimensions.

Multiple models are available for understanding how families operate, but much remains to be learned. In this section we provide information on what is known, so that readers can formulate a working model for use in clinical situations. In Section 3 we discuss the assessment of families.

Sea & Mountains, Akihara Fijii, 1987. Private collection. (Literal translation of calligraphy: A father's love is as high as a mountain, and a mother's love is as deep as the sea.)

CHAPTER 3

Understanding the Functional Family

Objectives for the Reader

- To understand the concept of the family as a functional system
- To be able to characterize the phases of the family life cycle
- To be able to describe family structure
- To understand basic family tasks
- To understand characteristics of the functional family

Introduction

There is probably little need to stress the general importance of marriage and the family. These social institutions have existed throughout recorded history, and despite the talk in some quarters about the death of the family, marriage and the family are clearly very much with us. It is also true, however, that expectations regarding marriage and the family have changed, especially when we compare the traditional American family of the 1950s with multiple current alternatives. The variety of accepted patterns (including cohabitation, stepfamilies, and single-parent and two- and three-generation families) for marriage and the family is for many people a cause for uncertainty, instability, and distress. Nevertheless, this diversity offers richness of solutions that a more rigid, unchanging pattern could not offer. As we have learned over time, some dimensions of functional families are stable regardless of family form. All families, for example, need some form of organization, stable and clear ways of communicating, and protection for young children. The specifics, however, can vary considerably. In this chapter we try to locate the universals of family life as well as its diversity.

The frame of reference we provide for understanding the family is intended as a model for understanding what a family therapist sees. This model will be supplemented by individual and sociological frames of reference. Exclusion is not meant to imply that other models are unimportant, only that they are not in keeping with the general tenor of this book—that of presenting ideas of particular interest or use to the family therapist. Undoubtedly our model will not completely describe or explain the richness, complexity, and variety of marriages and families, nor will all of the categories used in our model fit precisely into every specific family system. It is hoped, however, that this material will offer a useful structure for thinking about all families, including those members in distress, who present themselves to professionals for help.

In this chapter we examine the concept of the family as a functional system by exploring the phases of the individual, marital, and family life cycles, from courtship and early marriage to older adulthood when children have moved on and started families of their own. We also discuss the basic family tasks, including providing for basic needs and socializing children, and the evolution of characteristic beliefs and patterns of behavior among family members.

Since this is both a long chapter and a key one, we provide here an outline to guide the reader:

The Family as a System
The Marital and Family Life Cycle
    The Individual Life Cycle
        Early adulthood
        Mid-adulthood
        Older adulthood
    The Marital Life Cycle
        Phase of Relationship and Tasks
            Courtship and early marriage
            Marriage in mid-adulthood
            Marriage in older adulthood
        Marital Coalition
        Sex, Intimacy, and Companionship
    The Family Life Cycle
        Children and shifts in function
        Family structure as it relates to the life cycle

Family Tasks
   Provision of Basic Needs
   Rearing and Socialization of Children
      Use of age-appropriate childrearing techniques
      Maintenance of the parental coalition and generational boundaries
      Sexuality, masculinity, and femininity
      Support of a sibling coalition
      Enculturation of offspring
   Family Belief Systems
   Summary

The Family as a System

Families and married couples differ from other human groups in many ways, including duration, intensity, and function of relationships. For most people, the family constitutes their most important group in relation to individual psychological development, emotional interaction, and maintenance of self-esteem. The family is a group in which they experience their strongest loves and strongest hates, enjoy their deepest satisfaction, and experience their most painful disappointments. The characteristics of the family (or couple) as a unit are different from the mere sum of its components. Knowing the attributes of all the individuals in the family is not the same as understanding the family system as an entity. The family has a history and function of its own, the specifics of which differ from those of its individual members.

As we discussed in Chapter 1, marriages and families need to be thought of as interactive contexts in which transactions between component parts are continually taking place. From this perspective, the action of one member will affect the entire family (and vice versa). A ripple set off anywhere, internally or externally, that impinges on the family will reverberate throughout the family system.

At the same time there is a basic, underlying stability in every family that maintains each member's position within the family. The family is a system in dynamic equilibrium, oscillating between periods of relative balance and periods of disequilibrium. Family members are usually bound together by social roles, mutual support and needs, expectations, and intense and long-lasting ties of experiences. Factors are at work constantly, more or less successfully, to keep the family system in equilibrium and to keep it from undergoing a too severe or rapid change.

As we pointed out in Chapter 1, *family homeostasis* refers most generally to the concept that the family is a system designed to maintain a relatively stable state so that when the whole system or any part of it is subjected to a disequilibrating force, feedback will restore the preexisting equilibrium. However, it is often necessary for the family to move to a new equilibrium. This happens at transition points in the family's life cycle, after a major life change (e.g., if the mother goes back to work), or after a major trauma (e.g., if a family member is injured in an auto accident and cannot continue his or her usual roles).

If one thinks of characteristic patterns of achieving equilibrium for the family, then families can be thought of as having personalities or styles analogous to those of individuals. These styles consist of patterns of problem solving and preferred patterns of thinking, feeling, and interacting (e.g., fun-loving and somewhat chaotic; organized and cheerful; angry and confusing). Studies have characterized families by their cognitive and problem-solving styles, by types of pathology, and by boundary patterns and organizational structure. No model has taken into account all variables. The key to defining a functional family is in whether the characteristic patterns allow for flexibility and movement in response to stress (Walsh 1993).

For the family system to be functional, it must have certain characteristics. Walsh (1993) identified 10 processes that characterize functional families (Table 3–1).

Another model is based on only three dimensions—problem solving, organization, and emotional climate. These dimensions are considered central for a rapid overview evaluation. They represent the core of the Global Assessment of Relational Functioning Scale now used in many clinical settings (Guttman et al. 1995). We discuss this scale in detail in Chapter 8.

All families have conflicts, and family members' feelings toward one another may be mixed, or their love may not always be constant. Furthermore, the completely well-functioning, growing, long-term marriage is a rarity (estimated by clinicians to represent about 5% of all marriages). Different cultures place differing emphasis on certain of the processes listed in Table 3–1. For example, some cultures place far more importance on the child's role as a family member than on fostering autonomy; patriarchal cultures are more interested in maintaining a clear hierarchy than in equitable sharing of power. Most of these processes are necessary for family function, regardless of form.

Focusing on the couple (as a system), Lewis (1998) suggested that the most important decision (and process) each partner in a couple makes is selecting the person he or she is going to spend his or her life with, jointly constructing a relationship. That decision does not occur in a vacuum and is aimed not just at autonomy but, more important, at connecting intimately with others. Marriage is commonly the most important relationship for individual growth of each spouse.

> The most important decision (and process) each partner in a couple makes is selecting the person he or she is going to spend his or her life with, jointly constructing a relationship.

The Marital and Family Life Cycle

Because a central family function is to raise children to adulthood, the system needs to ensure that various psychosocial tasks are mastered at each phase of

TABLE 3–1.   Processes that characterize functional families

1. Connectedness and commitment of members as a caring, mutually supportive relationship unit
2. Respect for individual differences, autonomy, and separate needs, fostering the development and well-being of members of each generation, from youngest to eldest
3. For couples, a relationship characterized by mutual respect, support, and equitable sharing of power and responsibilities
4. For nurturance, protection, and socialization of children and caretaking of other vulnerable family members, effective parental or executive leadership and authority
5. Organizational stability, characterized by clarity, consistency, and predictability in patterns of interaction
6. Adaptability: flexibility to meet internal or external demands for change, to cope effectively with stress and problems that arise, and to master normative and nonnormative challenges and transitions across the life cycle
7. Open communication characterized by clarity of rules and expectations, pleasurable interaction, and a range of emotional expression and empathic responsiveness
8. Effective problem-solving and conflict-resolution processes
9. A shared belief system that enables mutual trust, problem mastery, connectedness with past and future generations, ethical values, and concern for the larger human community
10. Adequate resources for basic economic security and psychosocial support in extended kin and friendship networks and from community and larger social systems

the family life cycle. The extent to which this mastery is accomplished will depend on the individual adaptation of family members and on the flexibility and functionality of the family as a whole. Stressors during any of these phases may interfere with the accomplishment of normal developmental tasks. Although the family's ability to pass successfully from one specific developmental phase to another may depend on how prior phases have been negotiated, families sometimes find themselves better suited to meet the challenges of one phase than another. For example, a couple may be at odds in the childrearing phase of a marriage but function quite well during the postchildrearing phase.

A couple's ability to communicate clearly, to solve problems, and to have a relationship reasonably free of projection and incompatible agendas is based on the intrapsychic needs of the individuals, the reflexive behaviors they bring from their families of origin, the evolving marital dynamics, and the state of marital development. In our version of these life cycles (Tables 3–2 and 3–3), certain normative patterns of stress are determined by the individual and family life cycles described in the next sections.

> A central issue in marriage is the meshing of individual needs with relationship needs. The behaviors and beliefs of dysfunctional couples tend to be more rigid than those of well-adapted couples.

The Individual Life Cycle

Issues of marital and family life are affected strongly by the age of the adult participants. One's attitudes, prospects, and emotional availability for intimacy and family life vary to some extent with age. In addition, the age at which one has children has become widely variable since 1980. Many young women have children in their teens, indeed their early teens—producing a family consisting of the teen, her child, and her parent(s)—and then marry later in life. At the other end of the spectrum, many men and now women are taking much longer to explore job opportunities and are marrying much later, so that a substantial number of couples do not begin their families until their 30s or 40s. Second marriages between 30- to 40-year-old women and 50- to 70-year-old men have produced a phenomenon of many men in their later years who are both grandfathers and new parents.

TABLE 3–2. The family life cycle and adult development

Early adulthood (age 20–40 years)	Mid-adulthood (age 40–60 years)	Older adulthood (age 60+ years)
Age 20–30 years	**Age 40–50 years**	**Age 60+ years**
1. Establish an independent life structure—home, friends, etc.	1. Deal with complexities of being command generation: may be responsible for children and/or aging parents	1. Conduct a life review
2. Renegotiate relationships with parents		2. Give up being command generation
3. Make first set of decisions around occupational choice	2. Midlife transition: reevaluate life goals, work, and relationships	3. Find function and direction in a world that values youth
4. Explore intimacy/sexuality	3. Forgive self for sins of omission and commission	4. Deal with physical changes of aging
5. Possibly deal with parenthood		**Age 75+ years**
Age 30 transition	**Age 50–60 years**	Focus on functioning despite physical aging
Sometimes rethink early choices—"course correction"	1. Settle into life one chose in 40s	
Age 30–40 years	2. Accept who one has become	
1. Settle into chosen life structure	3. Deal with grandparenthood	
2. Deepen commitment to work and intimate relationships	4. Deal with issues of aging and mortality	
3. Experience self as fully adult		

TABLE 3–3. The child-focused years of the family life cycle[a]

Childbearing family	Family with preschool children	Family with school-aged children	Family with teenagers	Family with launching center
Adjust from dyad to triad and beyond	Maintain couple connection	Maintain couple connection	Support children's autonomy while maintaining connection	Renegotiate marital dyad
Apportion household tasks	Find ways to balance home and work that support child's development	Realize increasing complexity of children		Develop adult-adult relationship with children
Renegotiate position in extended family	If additional children are born, restructure to make room for all			Include children's spouses and children in system

[a]This period, lasting perhaps 20–25 years, most commonly occurs when individuals are age 25–55 years.

Adult developmental phases can be divided roughly into early adulthood (age 20–40 years), mid-adulthood (age 40–60 years), and older adulthood (age 60 years and older).

Early adulthood.   Developmental issues in early adulthood include launching from one's family of origin and developing a sense of identity and life structure, a job or career track, and an intimate and committed relationship. The 20s tend to be a time of maximum energy and minimum life experience. By the 30s most people experience themselves as older and more settled. Particularly in the 20s, with a need to attend to all developmental tasks at once, both marital choice and couple development can be altered profoundly by one's relationship with parents and work. Early love relationships, in particular, can be in response to perceived parental demands, to wishes to prove oneself adult, or to a need for closure as a result of insecurity. In their 20s, men in particular, but many women also, may channel much time and emotional energy into work rather than relationships. However, the need to establish the security of emotional ties is high, and most people, no matter how hard they work, begin intense long-term relationships by their late 20s and want to establish a family soon after. For people who are pleased with their choices, their 30s can be a particularly stable and settled time.

Mid-adulthood.   Midlife issues are complex. The early 40s are not always a crisis period but are usually characterized by a sense of transition and a need to reevaluate one's life structure after 20 years of functioning adulthood. The sense of mortality and potential aging prompts many people to conduct a life review and to redirect some portion of their lives. In addition, people in midlife have often exchanged some measure of their enthusiasm for more patience and wisdom, which makes them less demanding and more accepting of themselves and others. Some people may be depressed and bitter. As spouses, people in midlife may be more willing to let go of an obsession with work and become more intimate or to let go of a focus on the family and become more world oriented. Some people become very dissatisfied with their marriages as part of their life review and seek affairs, separation, or divorce. Later midlife can be a source of satisfaction, in which people come to terms with who they are and are not. If a couple's marriage is good, it can be a particular source of comfort and strength at this time. Many divorced persons begin new marriages at midlife, starting new families with young children.

Older adulthood.   The tasks of older adulthood focus on developing a sense of purpose for the rest of life and conducting a life review. Because many older adults now can expect to live into their 80s or 90s, the task of finding purpose and function in a society that values youth and denigrates age is a difficult one. Key questions include how much to rely on adult children and how to construct a meaningful life. In the next decade we expect that many new alternatives to traditinoal retirement will be explored. For widows and widowers the question of whether to date is an important one. Because women live on average 7 years longer than men and tend to marry men older than themselves, the oldest population consists primarily of widowed and divorced women, who are subject to sexism, ageism, and poverty.

The Marital Life Cycle

The marital life cycle for most people in first marriages begins in their 20s, with both partners in the process of building a life structure. Generations of researchers have studied mate selection, with complex and confusing results. Some of the factors involved are propinquity, cultural similarity, and some complex matching of psychological needs. In addition, many researchers speculate that biological preference factors such as odor are involved.

Phase of Relationship and Tasks

In this section we first discuss tasks involved in the beginning family and then examine those tasks concerning the adult life cycle as they relate to the family form.

Courtship and early marriage. For many people, the most important decision made in the course of a lifetime is who to marry. Couple formation is best done when both individuals have completed tasks of restructuring their relationships with their parents, learned enough about themselves to become aware of their characteristic problems, and had enough freedom and adventure that the demands of an intense relationship feel comforting rather than constricting. The new couple, if they are preparing for marriage, must establish an identity as a couple, develop effective ways of communicating and solving problems, and begin to establish a mutual pattern of relating to parents, friends, and work. Decisions regarding sexuality and some pattern of sexual relating commonly occur before marriage. Planning for the wedding and the early months of marriage are early tasks that will test these skills.

It is important in this early stage for couples to understand what marriage is about. It is not simply about establishing a family, finding the right person, or being chosen by the right person. It is also about providing a setting for personal growth.

If the couple did not live together before marriage, they will deal with sexuality and mutuality in the early months of the marriage. Because ways of communicating and dividing tasks set up in the first months are often difficult to alter later on, it is critical to address these issues directly and early.

Marriage between people younger than 21 years often represents a search for a substitute parent, a way of getting out of a troubled home or getting revenge on a parent, or a search for security. Some early marriages function well and allow the partners to grow in them, but many interfere with further individuation, especially if children are born soon after.

Marriages undertaken during the usual time frame (i.e., from age 21 years to the early 30s) are embedded in the set of multiple, complex tasks of early adulthood. Competency at intimate life, work life, and parenting may need to be developed simultaneously. Because most women now move into the labor force before marriage and remain in it after marriage, the partners are apt to begin with an egalitarian model for connection that was impossible when women stayed at home until marriage and saw work as only a stopgap until they married. Spouses born before 1950, however, usually began marriage with the woman having little sense of herself as a person in the world and seeing her identity as tied completely to her marriage.

In general, marital satisfaction is greatest in the first year and begins to decline, reaching a low point with adolescent children. However, divorces are also highest in the first year as poorly matched couples dissolve. Common stress points in early adult marriages are childbearing, attempting an egalitarian marriage in a nonegalitarian culture, and enduring an age 30 transition if one or both of the partners go through a major reevaluation period. Couples married in their 20s or 30s often find a stable and well-functioning style in their 30s.

Marriage in mid-adulthood.   Marriages between people in midlife differ depending on whether they are long-term first marriages or new marriages. Long-term marriages are often threatened by the stirrings of midlife transition, the launching of children, and the beginning of illness. They may be stronger and deeper or may be structural shells. New marriages are usually second marriages and may profit from the mistakes of the past. Both partners may be more mellow about themselves and their work and more available for family life. As a result, the children of second marriages may be easier to raise; however, stepfamily issues may greatly complicate second marriages.

Marriage in older adulthood.   Marriages between older people may be relationships of habit and convenience, or they may involve a deep connection. Spouses have usually stopped trying to change each other and may be more accepting; however, the divorce rate has risen even in this age group in recent years. The husband's retirement (if he retires first) may put stress on the marriage, but health and illness are the biggest determinants of the couple's functioning in later years.

Marital Coalition

The core of the family is the *marital coalition* (i.e., the spouses working together). This term implies that the spouses have been able to loosen their ties appropriately from their families of origin and develop a sense of their own individuality and self-worth in addition to a joint identity as a couple. Marriage is not merely a joining together of two individuals; it is also a distillation of their families of origin, each with its own experiences, history, life style, and attitudes. One marries not only an individual but also the individual's family of origin. For example, if the parents are alive, they may be involved very clearly and specifically in the daily operations of the new couple. They may take sides, comment on childrearing practices, or live next door. Even when the extended family is not physically present, the patterns experienced by the spouses in their original families inevitably influence their current marital and family interactions.

The process of working out a satisfactory marital relationship involves tacit, shared agreements between the two people involved. These agreements may consist of explicit rules, implicit rules (rules that the couple adhere to without discussing), and rules that an observer would note but that the couple themselves probably would deny. Seen this way, conflicts in marriage arise when there are disagreements about the rules of living together, about who is to set those rules, and about who is to enforce those rules that are mutually incompatible. For example, there may be disagreements as to whether the husband or wife should wash the dishes, but there may be further disagreements as to who should make this decision. More complex still is the situation in which one spouse forces the other to agree "voluntarily" to wash the dishes.

The basic issues of interpersonal relationships are found in the following five dimensions, which determine the quality of a relationship (Lewis 1998):

1. *Power.* Who is in charge? This is a complex area because there are many kinds of power, ranging from expertise to physical coercion to custom. Although no one is completely without power in a relationship, and power may be shared in many ways, there is general agreement in most couples about who is in charge if a joint decision is impossible, and whose needs come first in the family. How a couple resolves conflict makes this factor most important of all.

2. *Closeness-distance (emotional intensity) and amount of shared activities and values.* Partners negotiate what type of emotional distance feels close and intimate and what feels too distant. Also, because different kinds of behaviors may connote intimacy to one partner and not the other, there usually are agreed-on behaviors that represent a bid for closeness.

3. *Inclusion and exclusion.* Who else is considered to be part of the marital system? This question of boundaries applies not only to relatives and other persons but also to time allocated for career and recreational interests.

4. *Marital commitment.* Both partners need to feel that they and their spouse are committed to the relationship and are primary in each other's lives.

5. *Intimacy (i.e., the reciprocal sharing of vulnerabilities).* Partners often vary in their need for verbal sharing, but for most couples, this is an important or essential part of bonding.

In married couples the spouses do not start with equal access to power or with similar ways of looking at issues of closeness and inclusion. Gender differences, both intrapsychic and sociocultural, affect the ways in which these issues play out. Traditionally men have been seen as family leaders and wives as the support system (i.e., the helpmate). Women were supposed to use indirect methods of influence rather than direct requests or, worse yet, demands. Although this tendency is changing, it has certainly not vanished. In addition, men's typically superior physical strength makes physically coercive behaviors by them more threatening, and their commonly superior earning power gives them other sources of power in the home, so that structural equality is difficult even when desired. In addition, men in general have been taught to have more ambivalent feelings about intimacy than women because intimacy is seen as unmanly or as linked to being controlled. Intimacy is also more difficult in situations of grossly disparate power.

Couples matched for variables of socioeconomic class; religious, ethnic, and racial backgrounds; political and social attitudes; and values tend to be more successful. However, dissimilarity or complementarity of personality styles may enhance a partnership, as might other subsidiary interests. The determining factor seems to be a match of roles to goals—that is, to achieve a specific goal, do you need to pick a partner the same as or different from yourself? Temperament and personality factors are other key determinants. Two studies (Markman, as quoted by Talan 1988; V. Thomas and Olson 1993) suggest that the best predictors of what can be thought of as a "good" (i.e., functional) marriage include "communication, the ability to resolve conflict, personality compatibility, realistic expectations, and agreement on religious values. What is common in both studies is the ability for couples to resolve differences and communicate differing needs."

In our experience, marriages that seem most stable over time are those in which the husband is willing to be influenced by his wife and to share power. Predictors of divorce include overt anger, criticism, and contempt toward one's spouse; defensiveness; and an unwillingness to discuss issues.

Sex, Intimacy, and Companionship

Marriage presents an opportunity for the spouses to deal with their sexual needs. It may offer, in part, a relationship more like a friendship, in which there is mutual sharing of feelings, interests, activities, availability, and emotional support. Marriage offers a practical and acceptable way to conceive and raise children. It offers a sense of stability, continuity, and meaningful direction into the future. For some people, marriage is a response to a variety of social pressures that sanction and reinforce it as an institution. For any two individuals, marriage may afford the opportunity for the meshing of particular psychological traits and needs.

The Family Life Cycle

Although stability and homeostasis are important elements of marital and family systems, inevitably other forces also are continually changing the family, pushing it in the direction of development and differentiation. Some of these forces constitute the growth pattern known as the *family life cycle*. The life cycle can be thought of as the expected life events that most families go through in a fairly predictable but varying sequence. Other stresses can be thought of as unexpected in that they are extraordinary. They are not necessarily experienced by most families, or they occur outside of the usual sequence of the life cycle. Thus each family finds its own balance between those forces that tend to keep it stable and those that encourage change.

The longitudinal view (what we refer to as the traditional view) of the family's development is analogous to the individual's life cycle (Duvall 1967). Figure 3–1 offers one model of the family life cycle. Lidz (1963) proposed a model that integrates both individual and family life cycle issues. Various authors have studied the specific tasks for each phase in an individ-

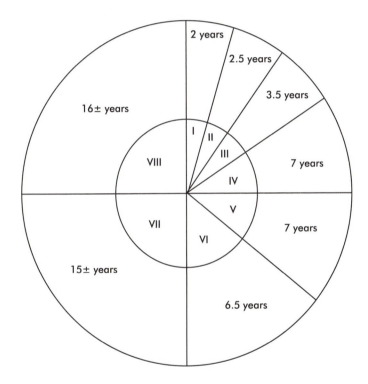

Phase	Family phase	Family description
I	Beginning family	Married couple without children
II	Childbearing family	Oldest child up to age 30 months
III	Family of preschool children	Oldest child age 30 months to 6 years
IV	Family of schoolchildren	Oldest child age 6–13 years
V	Family with teenagers	Oldest child age 13–20 years
VI	Family as launching center	First child gone to last child leaving home
VII	Family in the middle years	Empty nest to retirement
VIII	Aging family	Retirement to death of both spouses

FIGURE 3–1.   The family life cycle.

ual's and in a family's life. As in individual development, the family evolves through expected phases. The traditional phases include 1) couple formation (love, cohabitation or engagement, marriage); 2) the childbearing family (birth of the first child, oldest child younger than 5 years); 3) the family with school-aged children; 4) the family with teenagers; 5) the family as a launching center (the offspring begin their own adult life structure, usually but not always moving away from home); 6) the family in its middle years (which may include one or both spouses retiring and often includes grandparenthood); and 7) the couple as part of a three-generation family (and eventual death of a spouse). When one or both partners come to the marriage with a child, the couple may face the complex situation of having to deal with couple formation and child-related issues at the same time. In addition, families with many children, or with children spaced widely apart, may be dealing with issues of several phases at once.

Children and shifts in function. Family structure and organization change with each major developmental phase. For example, the marital couple's organization alters dramatically with the birth of the first child, the structure of this threesome will necessarily shift with the birth of a second child, and so on. Over time, it is to be hoped, the couple's ability to cope flexibly emerges. In assessing the life cycle stage of the family, the therapist can anticipate the tasks and challenges that family members of different generations usually face (Rapoport 1963).

The family with young children is characterized by closeness, bonding, and intense inward focus on the children. The family can also expect that boundaries formed during the formation of the couple will be relaxed as relatives and friends move into and out of the expanded family, although in some families boundaries tend to be tightened around the nuclear family members. In acquiring their role as parents, the married couple faces new responsibilities. Both parents cannot return to work full time without providing for the needs of the child, and parents must develop and revise strategies for meeting their own as well as their child's emerging requirements (Feldstein and Rait 1990). The couple must learn to operate in a triangular situation, to handle rapid decision making around the child's needs, and to negotiate around what are often very different ideas and styles of childrearing. Most often the mother is the one who does most of the child care and cuts back on her work, leaving the couple to find a way to negotiate roles in a system that pushes them back toward a traditional model.

It is important for the therapist to understand that children have a very different inner world than do adults. As Lively (1989, p. 43) suggests,

Children are not like us. They are a being apart: impenetrable, unapproachable. They inhabit not our world but a world we have lost and can never recover. We do not remember childhood—we imagine it. We search for it, in vain, through layers of obscuring dust, and recover some bedraggled shreds of what we think it was. And all the while the inhabitants of this world are among us, like aborigines, like Minoans, people from elsewhere safe in their own time capsule.

Although adults may not think like children, children can be very observant and even insightful to what is going on among adults. The family with school-aged children is opened up to the larger world of the school, families of the children's friends, and new peers. As children interact with others outside the family, so too are parents freed up to pursue their own interests. This is also a time when children and parents can become good companions and is often a warm and easy time for the family. Even grandparents contribute to the opening up of the family system by introducing their grandchildren to experiences in different contexts. Issues of discipline, values, and amount of freedom for growing children may become major areas of argument. Religious or cultural differences between the parents must be negotiated around the children because this issue directly affects the family's rituals and functioning.

As the children become adolescents, they press for greater autonomy. At the same time, parents also begin to struggle with contradictory desires for family closeness and safety on the one hand and freedom on the other. The years of adolescence are often difficult ones for many families. For the first time the teenager appears to be half in and half out of the family. He or she is neither part of the parental subsystem nor comfortably identified with the child subsystem. To manage these developmental tasks, the family must be strong, flexible, and able to support growth. However, for the majority of families, adolescence is not a time of chaos and rebellion. Parents and children still connect and learn from one another in powerful ways. At the same time, parents also may contend with changes in their own parents' health, leaving many spouses feeling sandwiched between the needs of their children and their parents. Sometimes, parents face midlife issues of mourning lost youth or wishing to change themselves or their situation, all of which complicate matters.

The situation changes again with young adult children. The primary task of the family is to continue the letting-go process that began when the children were in adolescence, which involves restructuring the relationship while continuing to be related. American folk wisdom has placed autonomy as the only goal of this stage, whereas most people remain connected in different ways.

Young adults particularly are still in the process of launching and are deeply connected to their parents. For parents, the process of watching and participating in the life course as their children marry, have children, and become middle aged is a continuous process of relationship shift. Some families experience this later stage as a time of fruition and completion, whereas for others this stage prompts reevaluation of life and marital goals. Parents eventually encounter illness and loss as their own relatives and friends become ill or die. As their own health status changes, children again reenter the family to provide support and assistance.

Family structure as it relates to the life cycle. In healthy families the basic roles and functions necessary for family adaptation are carried out by their subsystems (e.g., marital, spousal, sibling). These subsystems can be categorized according to the division of labor, or psychosocial tasks, within the family. For example, spouses generally offer each other social and emotional companionship and sexual intimacy, whereas parents provide nurturance, support, and guidance for children. In the sibling subsystem, children learn to share, trust, negotiate for resources, and develop social skills. Children provide parents with loyalty and a sense of purpose (or problems). The family's subsystems are arranged not only functionally but also hierarchically, with parents typically occupying positions of authority in relation to their offspring.

From a developmental perspective, we would expect the family's structure to change over time. For example, the arrival of children signals the need for the marital partners to broaden their roles to include those of being parents. The task is to form an appropriate parental coalition with respect to childrearing practices. It is beneficial to have parental agreement and consistency in these areas, with a sharing of responsibility and mutual support. Children may become confused if they do not know what is expected of them, or if they receive continually conflicting messages from each parent. Clearly parents cannot agree on everything, and there may be danger in attempting to present a facade of agreement. On basic, important matters, such as discipline, money, and central family values, however, it is preferable for parents to follow some sort of mutual, consistent childrearing guidelines.

The maintenance of generational boundaries tends to lessen role conflicts that follow the blurring of roles and the ambiguity this fosters. A totally democratic family in which all members, regardless of age, responsibility, and experience, have an equal voice in all decisions seems wholly unrealistic. Far from being something to be decried, a generation gap between parents and children is a necessity, if we mean by the term a difference in responsibilities, roles, and maturity. Such a gap, however, should not consist of a deficiency in communication. Different relationships need to exist between parents and between parent and child. At the same time, the parents must give the child emotional room to learn, interact with peer groups, develop an identity, and begin to acquire responsibility and maturity themselves.

There must also be a reliable way for family members to relate to the larger society in which they live. The overall style of family involvement in relation to outsiders is also dictated by beliefs and behaviors (i.e., boundaries) that protect the family unit. In some families, the boundary is permeable, permitting free movement in and out of the system. In other families, the boundary is more rigid. A family with rigid boundaries may be isolated from social input, whereas a family with boundaries that are too diffuse may be unable to protect itself from external stresses. In either case, the family's structure or organization must be flexible enough for a variety of family aims and tasks.

These issues are complicated by the rapid shift since the 1970s from a traditional gender-differentiated marriage to a more egalitarian one. The traditional model specified separate domains of responsibility for men and women and set the man at the head of the hierarchy. It also specified fairly rigid emotional roles for men and women, with men being valued for strength and aggressiveness and women for intuition and emotionality (although intuition and emotionality tend to be undervalued in American society). In the new model, roles are flexible, and both partners earn money, make decisions, have emotional sensitivity, and care for the children. Most couples are the most traditional behaviorally, if not emotionally, when their children are young. In couples with widely differing expectations of male-female behavior, communication and problem solving become more complex and difficult.

Family Tasks

Families can be viewed as laboratories for the social, psychological, and biological development and maintenance of family members. In providing this function, couples and families must accomplish vital tasks, including the provision of basic physical and material needs (e.g., food, shelter, clothing), the development of a marital coalition (see section "Marital Coalition" earlier in this chapter), and the socialization of children. Therefore, not only do families have a given structure that expresses the family's underlying belief system, but families also serve to fulfill essential functions.

Provision of Basic Needs

Some of the essential life-maintaining tasks of the family group may be over-looked by therapists treating middle-class families. Therapists working with poor families recognize immediately the fundamental requirement of addressing the family's basic needs. Depending on the extent to which these needs are not adequately met, the family's more complex functions will be affected in one way or another and become distorted or deficient. A therapist must pay attention to the family's safety, shelter, and nutrition, and, when indicated, the major or at least the initial effort may have to be to help the family deal more adequately with its basic needs. A family system already overwhelmed by gross deficiencies in basic needs will not usually be motivated to deal with more sophisticated or symbolic considerations.

Rearing and Socialization of Children

It is our bias that what we call *personality* is each person's adaptation to the biological equipment inherited at birth interacting with the demands of the family and the external world. Although much of a child's essential temperament is inborn, the child's ultimate stance in relation to the world, his or her knowledge of cultural norms, and his or her attitudes toward men and women are developed within the family and the neighborhood and through the media (especially television). Early neglect or trauma or a chaotic upbringing can produce permanent damage in a child's brain structure and function.

Children learn from who their parents are and from what they do, so that some aspects of learning cannot be controlled by education. An anxious parent will communicate some anxiety to the child regardless of his or her direct support. However, certain basic parenting skills are necessary for optimal child development.

Use of age-appropriate childrearing techniques.   Parents need to understand or intuit their children's capacities at different ages in order to parent adequately. For example, expecting a 1-year-old to demonstrate patience and self-control, or trying to reason with a 3-year-old who is having a temper tantrum, will result in rage and confusion for both child and parent. In addition, some parents may have difficulty when their children are at a particular age because of what they experienced in their own family of origin. For example, a parent who was sexually promiscuous as an adolescent may become frightened when his or her child reaches the same age and may be untrusting and overly controlling as a result.

Maintenance of the parental coalition and generational boundaries. It is beneficial to both the parents and the children for the parents to be clear that they are functioning as a team to parent the children, and that grownup roles are different from child roles. Although parents cannot agree on everything, they should follow some sort of mutual, consistent childrearing guidelines. Even when parents disagree, their children should know that their parents will find a way to deal with the disagreement rather than leave the children in limbo. Problems arise when the parents are in so much conflict that one or both turn to the children for support, leaving the children either with a loyalty conflict (e.g., "If I side with Dad, Mom will not love me") or in a parentified, caretaking role.

Are two parents necessary? It is a strain on any one adult to raise a child or children, and the lack of adult support plus the greater likelihood of living in poverty make it more difficult for single-parent families with multiple children. However, many single-parent families do extremely well by any standard of functioning. Although theory suggests that the parent of the same sex serves as a role model for identification whereas the parent of the opposite sex serves as the basic love object, children are very creative in finding love objects and role models in the caregiving parent and in the other people in their environment. What seems to be the most destructive for the children's development is fierce conflict between two parents (whether married or divorced) who are using their children as a weapon, or highly inconsistent, primarily neglectful behavior on the part of one parent, divorced or not (Hetherington et al. 1993).

Sexuality, masculinity, and femininity. It is becoming increasingly clear that in most cases sexual orientation is not a function of parental dynamics. The facts that no consistent patterns of parental behavior can be found in the parents of homosexuals and that children raised in homosexual homes do not show an increase in homosexuality, in addition to increasing evidence from molecular biology, suggest strongly that this is mostly a biologically based phenomenon. However, parents do powerfully influence children's attitudes toward sexuality, their sense of whether it is good to be a boy or a girl, how one exhibits masculine and feminine behavior, and whether one can trust members of one's own or the opposite sex. Because much of this behavior is nonverbal (e.g., a man who is happy with his masculinity will appear masculine whether he is cooking or playing football), it is learned mostly outside awareness. Parents today have the problem of teaching their sons to be warm and empathic and their daughters to be strong and self-confident in a culture that still defines masculine primarily in terms of aggression and control and that devalues women.

Support of a sibling coalition. The history of developmental theory has largely neglected the role of siblings in families. There has been greater emphasis on dysfunctional than functional relationships. For example, disproportionate attention has been paid to sibling rivalry.

A key issue is *microenvironments* for siblings (here meaning the world of the siblings as opposed to that of their parents). Research has found that siblings have a small degree of similarity in personality, but the commonalities in personality appear to result mostly from shared genes rather than from shared experience. Obviously other factors influence how siblings turn out differently, for example, the so-called nonshared environment such as life events, each child's perceptions about the parents, different attitudes of the parents to each sibling, and the friends that each child develops (Reiss et al. 1991). The differences in family and environment are more obvious to the children themselves than to the parents. This research overlaps with A. Thomas and Chess's (1985) work (discussed in Chapter 5), which has focused on the child-parent fit—the point being that some parents may make the same demands on two different children and get two different results (presumably because of the differences in the personality of each sibling).

Family theory has stressed the important role that siblings play in normal family functioning. Each sibling has a crucial role in the maintenance of homeostasis for that particular family system. Siblings often work together when their parents are continually at odds, when their parents have divorced, or when one or both parents have severe mental illness. That sibling bond is often the link that keeps a family functional when one or both parents cannot carry out parental roles.

Siblings can be both a source of stress and an enormous support to one another. Whether siblings support or befriend one another in childhood is to some extent a matter of temperament and age, but it is also a reflection of the parents' encouragement of kind behavior and their ability to keep the children out of parental conflict. In dysfunctional families, siblings often play stereotyped roles—the good kid, the bad kid, the clown, or the charmer—leaving little room for them to work out their own issues. How siblings connect in childhood does not always say much about how they will behave toward one another as adults.

Family therapists feel that issues of sibling loyalty, attachment, and bonding are important and useful in changing dysfunctional patterns. Dysfunctional families often exhibit dysfunctional sibling relationships. For example, siblings may mimic the parental relationship by always bickering in the same way the parents bicker or by one being dominant. The bottom line for the family therapist is that each sibling should be seen as a separate individual.

Family therapy should not presume that all siblings share the same experience and should be treated the same.

The bottom line for the family therapist (and often forgotten) is that each sibling should be seen as a separate individual.

Interventions focused on siblings may be included in family treatment models. Treatment can use older siblings as change agents or can focus on sibling conflict. When one parent has died, siblings are important in maintaining the family system while coping with the parental loss. When one sibling has a mental disorder, other siblings can be active supports. In addition, if one sibling has an Axis I disorder (e.g., schizophrenia), other siblings need to know very specific information about the disorder, particularly the prognosis, and about how to deal with difficulties in communication and problem solving with their siblings (Landeen et al. 1992).

Enculturation of offspring. Parents teach the younger generation the basic adaptive techniques of their culture. They must transmit ways of thinking, feeling, and acting that are culturally appropriate. These include basic communication skills but also beliefs, values, and attitudes. For minority or oppressed groups, this is particularly problematic—for example, an African American family must teach both pride of heritage and ways of understanding and dealing with white privilege and racism. Social class attitudes are transmitted through the family, as are beliefs about the proper place of men and women. Parents who are themselves outside the mainstream culture (e.g., recent immigrants) must allow their children to find a way to learn mainstream culture as well or the children will be disadvantaged. To the extent that the children learn both cultures, they will be bicultural, which has advantages and disadvantages. Families that wish their children to remain outside mainstream culture (e.g., Amish, Lubovitch) generally require a powerful and overarching community to provide boundaries.

Family Belief Systems

Over the family's life course, characteristic beliefs and patterns of behavior evolve among family members. For example, in one family both parents may believe that neatness is very important. Everyone, including the children, learns to put things away and keep them clean. The family judges others by how organized they are and takes great pride as a family in its organization. This may be a way of carrying on an extended family tradition of neatness and organization (e.g., certain cultural groups emphasize this behavior). Conversely, such behavior may be a way for the family to differentiate itself from a chaotic (and messy) extended family. In a different family, the mother may value neatness whereas the father may want a house that is emotionally warm and not focused on order. As the parents struggle, the children may take sides with one or the other, or they may shuttle between sides, playing peacemaker.

Key areas of belief revolve around what constitutes loyalty and proper behavior; however, all areas of family life include a system of beliefs. Family beliefs centered around fundamental issues determine what choices are considered normal or acceptable in times of change. A therapist who does not consider family beliefs in framing the problem or solution is likely to miss critical aspects of the situation.

Summary

Each family should be approached as a unique cultural system that is influenced by ethnicity, race, religion, social class, and immediate social context. To develop a clinically meaningful picture of family functioning, the family therapist should evaluate the three dimensions of family functioning we have presented in this chapter: family structure, family life cycle, and the family's ability to accomplish tasks. The goal of a family systems assessment is to account for the salience of these factors and then to generate a kinetic understanding of the couple's or the family's general functioning. This assessment evolves through the generation of a series of systemic hypotheses or explanations and the systematic testing of each hypothesis with the family (see Section 3).

There are many paths to healthy family adjustment and effective functioning. In Chapter 4 we discuss what might be considered alternatives to the fast-disappearing traditional two-parent family. Many, if not all, of the characteristics of healthy functioning that pertain to the families described in this chapter hold true for single-parent families, divorced and remarried families, and other family types.

Suggested Readings

Beavers R: Successful Families: Assessment and Intervention. New York, WW Norton, 1990
  Summarizing the Beavers-Timberlawn approach, this book offers another view of normal family functioning and how it relates to family treatment.

Falicov C (ed): Family Transitions: Continuity and Change Over the Life Cycle. New York, Guilford, 1988
  This edited volume enriches the family developmental framework described earlier in this chapter. The chapters are well written, and many can stand alone as excellent references for their respective topics.

Walsh F (ed): Normal Family Processes, 2nd Edition. New York, Guilford, 1993
  This edited volume concentrates on understanding normal family processes rather than only psychopathology.

References

Duvall E: Family Development. Philadelphia, PA, JB Lippincott, 1967, pp 44–46

Feldstein M, Rait D: Family assessment in an oncology setting. Cancer Nurs 15: 161–172, 1990

Guttman HA, Beavers WR, Berman E, et al: A model for the classification and diagnosis of relational disorders. Psychiatr Serv 46:926–932, 1995

Hetherington EM, Law T, O'Connor T: Divorce: challenges, changes, and new chances, in Normal Family Processes, 2nd Edition. Edited by Walsh F. New York, Guilford, 1993, pp 208–234

Landeen J, Whelton C, Dermer S, et al: Needs of well siblings of persons with schizophrenia. Hosp Community Psychiatry 43:266, 1992

Lewis JM: For better or worse: interpersonal relationship and individual outcome. Am J Psychiatry 155:582–589, 1998

Lidz T: The Family and Human Adaptation. New York, International Universities Press, 1963

Lively P: Moon Tiger. London, Harper Perennial, 1989, p 43

Rapoport R: Normal crises, family structure and mental health. Fam Process 2:68–80, 1963

Reiss D, Plomin R, Hetherington M: Genetics and psychiatry: an unheralded window on the environment. Am J Psychiatry 148:283–291, 1991

Talan J: Living happily ever after? Newsday, April 12, 1988

Thomas A, Chess S: Temperament and Development. New York, Guilford, 1985

Thomas V, Olson D: Problem families and the Circumplex Mode: observational assessment using the Clinical Rating Scale (CRS). J Marital Fam Ther 19:159–176, 1993

Tolstoy L: Anna Karenina. New York, Bantam, 1960, p 1

Walsh F: Conceptualizations of normal family processes, in Normal Family Processes, 2nd Edition. Edited by Walsh F. New York, Guilford, 1993, p 45

Reclining Chiricahua Mother, Allan Houser, 1980. Courtesy of the artist and The Gallery Wall Inc., Phoenix, Arizona. Used with permission.

CHAPTER 4

Understanding the Functional Family: Alternative Family Forms

With Richard M. Patel, M.D.

Objectives for the Reader

- To understand the structure and function of family forms that include unmarried couples (i.e., those in cohabiting or serial relationships) and families that develop during changes in marital status (i.e., through separation and divorce), including binuclear and single-parent families and remarried or stepfamilies
- To be able to delineate the salient methods of coping of these alternate family forms

Introduction

In this chapter we describe the family system, life cycle, and functional characteristics of alternative family forms (i.e., alternatives to the traditional marital form). These are the families resulting from shifts in companionship status: 1) cohabitation and serial relationships, 2) the family during separation and divorce, 3) binuclear and single-parent families, 4) remarried or step-families. As the life cycle lengthens and people can expect 50–70 or even more years of functional adulthood, the possibility that an individual will have only one partner, chosen in the individual's early 20s, decreases.

Although many married people can grow and change together, some may change at very different rates. People may find they want or need different partners later in life, especially when they married very young before the changes of adulthood began in earnest. Many people are marrying later in life, after several serious relationships. Some individuals choose marriage and never divorce; others marry and then divorce, sometimes two or three times; and still others choose never to marry at all, preferring serial relationships. Divorce can be a painful and difficult process, and as the divorce rate has climbed, life has become more complicated. These changing marital patterns produce nontraditional family forms.

Serial Relationships

Before 1960, the typical life cycle included long courtship and a long-term marriage begun in the couple's early 20s. This pattern is based on a belief that the best way to self-fulfillment is through marriage. It is still the pattern that most people strive toward. Some people develop a life pattern of sequential relationships that includes several long-term serious relationships and may include several marriages with the creation of two or three family units. It is often difficult to tell whether this model indicates emotional problems and fear of commitment, or whether it represents personal growth for the persons involved. A person who picks the same type of partner several times, or who goes directly from one partner to another without an effort to understand himself or herself or what happened to the earlier relationship, is more likely to choose this model out of dysfunction.

Cohabiting

In the United States, living together as unmarried lovers has gone from being scandalous to normative in less than a generation. In Oregon, for example, marriages preceded by cohabitation rose from 13% to 53% between 1970 and 1980 (Cunningham and Antill 1995). In other parts of the world, such consensual unions have been common for centuries. Couples cohabit for many reasons, ranging from convenience to a trial marriage to a permanently committed relationship for emotional or economic reasons that avoids a legal marriage contract. Cohabiting couples have both the advantages and the disadvantages of a looser relational contract, including a sense of freedom, aliveness, and uncertainty. Although the basic tasks of couple coalition (e.g., dealing with intimacy, power, boundaries, and sexuality) are present, by definition cohabitation implies less agreement on beliefs about permanence (e.g., what the couple's status means) and also implies more permeable boundaries with the outside world than are found among married couples. A central issue with most couples who are living together is the decision about whether to continue the relationship. The median length of cohabitation in the United States is reported at 1.3 years, ending in marriage for 59% of the couples; more than 80% of cohabiting relationships end within 4 years (Graefe and Lichter 1999). When the choice of cohabiting represents a situation in which one member wants a permanent commitment and the other doesn't, the situation is inherently unstable.

Early research on cohabitors suggested that those who married after cohabiting were more likely to divorce (Messinger 1976). The reasons for this finding were never quite clear, although in the 1960s and 1970s one common explanation was that people who were unconventional enough to cohabit were more willing to behave in other unconventional ways, for example, by seeking divorce. In more recent cohorts in which cohabitation is more frequent, the differential in dissolution rates has been declining and has even reversed slightly (Schoen 1992). Approximately 40% of cohabiting couples live with children from one or both partners. Research (e.g., Isaacs and Leon 1988) suggests that living with a biological parent and the parent's lover is an extremely difficult situation for children, who are asked to relate to a person who may leave them and has no real rights to discipline or parent them yet who cannot be ignored. Evidence suggests that both physical and sexual abuse are more likely with a biologically unrelated adult in the house. While children from former relationships are in the house, cohabitation should be limited to permanent or soon-to-be-married couples, whenever possible.

Marital Separation

Separation is a relatively common crisis of marital life. Although it is emotionally traumatic for the individuals involved, it can serve as an opportunity to reassess the marital contract and individual goals and sometimes can lead to a renewed and more functional marriage. Depending on the phase of marriage that is involved, different precipitants may have brought about the separation;

therefore, different issues may need to be addressed. Separation in the early stages of a marriage may be caused by the partners coming down from their earlier infatuation "high," with subsequent disillusionment and a wish to flee from the task of working things out. For those who married in response to an unplanned pregnancy, later recriminations or second feelings about the reasons for the marriage may bring about a stormy period. Some people marry to get away from their parents' home or in desperation about their inability to ever attract anyone else who will be seriously interested in them. When these underlying motives lose their force, the foundation of the marriage may be undermined. The many other reasons for separation include severe psychological problems in one or both partners, bad fit, or marital affairs.

For some couples, differences in adult development lead to a situation in which the partners no longer have much in common. Spouses whose children are grown and have left home may not easily become accustomed to living alone together as a marital couple. With the parental role diminished or absent, there may be little emotional or functional viability left in the marriage.

Although it is natural to think of marital separation as an unfortunate event, it can also be viewed as symptomatic of the marital-system problems that need attention. In this sense, separation and its subsequent resolution may offer the potential for growth and change for the better. Trial separations can be useful to provide a cooling-off period for couples whose difficulties seem insurmountable. It offers the partners the opportunity to examine their relationship more objectively. At the same time the individuals can test their ability to adapt to living alone. This separation, together with new life experiences of various sorts (which may not have taken place had the couple stayed together), will often enable the husband and wife to change their behavior and feelings toward each other by the time they attempt a reconciliation. Sometimes one of the spouses may use the separation to manipulate the other spouse, or the separating person may move immediately into a new relationship. If the partners are unable to communicate with each other or learn about themselves, the separation will not be much help, regardless of whether the couple reconciles.

Clinical experience suggests that about half of those couples that separate get back together; of those couples, about half divorce later on.

Divorce

As we indicated in Chapter 2, the divorce rate in most developing countries has been rising, although since the mid-1980s it has shown signs of leveling off. According to Weiss (1975, p. 3), "Divorce is an essential adaptation to the conflict between the value we place on commitment to a mate versus the value we place on self-realization." If the relationship has been long enough for true *attachment* to take place (about 2 years is usually considered long enough), divorce is one of the most painful experiences in anyone's life. The ambivalence that ex-spouses feel about each other is probably more extreme than that in any other human relationship, with the possible exception of feelings about parents.

Divorce is a process, not an event, with its own developmental path. It usually represents one in a series of transitions that began with marital dissatisfaction and may or may not end with remarriage. A number of authors (Kessler 1975; Salts 1979) have delineated stages of the divorce process. In summary, these stages include the following:

1. A predivorce phase involving growing disillusionment and dissatisfaction with the marriage and arrival at some consideration of divorce.
2. The separation itself, including moving out of the house and dealing with immediate grief. For many people, this is a period of great emotional distress, confusion, and grief—so-called crazy time.
3. A period of 1–2 years during which the couple deal with reorganizing of their life structure, parenting issues, financial and family reorganization, community status, and legal issues. Negative life stresses are most marked during the first 2 years following divorce. Children are most likely to experience diminished parenting during this period because of the parents' preoccupation with divorce issues. Children are likely to respond with noncompliant, angry, demanding, or depressed behavior.
4. For each spouse, reforming of an identity from being part of a couple to being a single person (i.e., the psychic divorce) occurs next. Because this phase occurs during the latter part of the process, issues with children also settle down unless partners continue to use the children as weapons in the divorce proceedings. The legal aspects of the divorce itself may take from 3 months in some states with an uncontested divorce to several years, depending on the laws and the amount of anger, but the psychological issues have their own time table. If the couple have children, they must find ways to remain connected as parents while separating as partners.

Although for some couples the divorce is mutual and relatively guilt free, in most couples one member wants the divorce far more than the other. In these cases, the rejected party feels enormously wounded and hurt, whereas the rejecter often reacts with guilt and is therefore unable to mourn the very real losses associated with the divorce. The sense of narcissistic injury may be profound for one or both partners. Later events may include fierce fighting over custody, money, or the story of what went wrong—this fighting may serve the purpose of punishment or revenge, or it may be a way of staying connected to the spouse. For many spouses, attachment may last long after love or respect is gone, leading to very confusing attempts to reconnect. The process of coming to grips with the self, recognizing one's own part in the marital dissolution, and beginning to date again often provokes a great deal of anxiety. Regardless of how bad the marriage was for both spouses, many divorced people find that the transition to living alone is very painful.

What about the children of divorce? There is a great deal of controversy about this issue. Although the majority of children will show great distress at some point in the process, many children of divorce do not appear to be damaged permanently. This conclusion is difficult to prove because long-term outcomes with children remaining in conflictual homes must be contrasted with children remaining in well-functioning homes. Research varies depending on the stage in the divorce process when the study was done, the age of the children, and the sex of the children. During the first 2 years children of both sexes are apt to exhibit problem behavior; boys may exhibit problems for a longer period of time than girls. Adolescent girls may have problems with precocious sexual behavior. As with any other crisis, divorce can offer a potential for growth. Children in this situation may be forced to cope with parental distress and economic uncertainty, which may require them to behave in a more adultlike or helpful way. Situations likely to lead to more severe problems include postmarital fighting between all the adults over the children, with persistent custody battles, disappearance of or irregular contact with the noncustodial parent, poverty due to a decrease in income in a single-parent family, and the unavailability of any parental supervision if the parents are acutely distressed and struggling to make ends meet.

The Functional Single-Parent Family

One of the most dramatic social statistics of the 1990s (see Chapter 2) is the increase in the number of *single-parent families*, defined as units in which only one parent is available because of death, divorce, separation, or births outside of marriage. In the case of divorce, the other biological parent is often available and involved—these are often referred to as *binuclear families* (i.e., two households each headed by one parent), and in them the childrearing is still a shared responsibility even in different households (see next section). For all except the rarest cases, divorced couples with children will spend some time as either single-parent or binuclear families before one or both spouses remarry.

In families in which one parent has sole or almost sole responsibility for the children, that parent is the mother in 90% of the cases. In 1955, almost one-third of all families were maintained by single mothers (U.S. Census Bureau 1997). These families share some similar characteristics but may present a variety of different issues depending on whether another adult is in residence, such as a grandparent or a lover, or whether the parent and children are alone in the house and answerable only to one another. A family with two adults available usually experiences less financial stress, and the parent may have more emotional support. Families with only one responsible adult may decrease the hierarchical structure common to two-parent families and give the children more responsibility and more power. This is not a problem unless the children are given responsibility beyond their capacity without enough affection or support. Some parents, particularly custodial fathers, may find themselves closer to their children than they were before because they are directly responsible for the daily care of their children for the first time. In other cases, particularly those of mothers with no financial or family support, the need to work full time while trying to carry on any sort of adult social life may decrease the parent's time with and energy for the children. Binuclear families face the task of dealing with two parents who are angry with each other but who must collaborate, despite possibly having very different childrearing styles.

Single-parent households formed after a divorce or a death go through a transition period during which family structures have to be completely rethought and reformed. Depending on the needs of the remaining parent, there may be a period of chaos before the tasks of providing food and shelter, organization, and discipline are restructured. The questions of who is in the system (e.g., grandparents, lover, ex-spouse) and how the family will be structured are very complex. In these cases, parental support from the family, community, and in many cases a therapist is critical. Evaluation of the effect of an absent spouse on the rest of the family unit must take into account the phase of family development during which the absence occurred and the total length of the absence, the feelings of the remaining family members about the absent member, and the mechanisms the family has used in coping with its reconfiguration.

All of this may seem overwhelming at first. After a time, however, the family unit may have reorganized itself and may have reached a new equilibrium, calling on resources that were not readily apparent earlier. Single-parent families in which the father is the head of the household appear to do just as well as those in which the mother is the main figure. The effectiveness of parenting depends not on the sex-stereotypic role but on the qualities of the specific parent.

Single-parent families that began with just the mother and children develop stable ways of family life from the beginning. Depending on the capacity of the mother and the system, these families will go through the stages of family life as do two-parent families.

Being the only parent, or the only custodial/residential parent, creates family issues that may include the following:

- Social isolation and loneliness of the parent
- Possible awkwardness in dating and jealousy from the children
- Demands by small children for the continuous physical presence of the sole parent
- Children fending for themselves and carrying a greater share of the domestic responsibilities because the sole parent is working
- Children feeling different from other children because they are members of a single-parent family
- Less opportunity for a parent to discuss pros and cons of decisions and to get support and feedback when decisions are made
- Crises and shifts caused by the introduction of a potential new mate or companion

However, for many women, self-esteem and self-confidence rise after divorce. Freed of marital conflict or abuse, the woman may parent more easily and confidently. Many questions remain about whether identity formation is more difficult for children of divorce, whether love relationships are more complicated for them, and whether the somewhat increased incidence of problems is the result of acrimonious divorce and financial stress.

Mother-Headed Single-Parent Families

Mother-headed single-parent families may be those in which the father is basically uninvolved after the divorce or has never been present. If the partner is involved, the family should be considered binuclear (see next section).

Some of the stresses of mother-headed families include task overload, financial stress, social isolation and loneliness, and a need for time-out. These stresses may be greater for mothers than for fathers if the mother has custody, particularly because women's income has been shown to drop 30%–70% after divorce, whereas men's income tends to remain stable or even rises. In addition, men are offered more community support, are more apt to date, and particularly after age 35 years are more apt to get remarried. Widowed women are more apt to have some financial reserves from insurance, for example, and more social acceptance. The question of identity formation, cognitive development, and social skills in children in mother-headed families has been reviewed but is still confusing. Male children are more apt than female children to get into cyclic arguments with their divorced mothers. Children with vulnerabilities such as a difficult temperament or poor cognitive competence will have more trouble in a stress situation such as that associated with divorce; temperamentally easy children with some supports already in place may experience growth and social competence.

Part of the problem for custodial mothers is that some noncustodial fathers do not make complete child support payments and over time become less and less involved with their children, leading to great frustration on the part of both mother and child. Hetherington et al. (1979) reported that only one quarter of children see their noncustodial fathers once a week or more, and over one third do not see them more than a few times a year. Several studies have suggested that inconsistent or absent fathers make a number of developmental issues more problematic. Kellam et al.'s (1977) study on the risk of social maladaptation and psychological ill health in children of disadvantaged families (many of which were formed from births outside of marriage rather than from divorce) suggests that 1) mother-alone families entail the highest risk, 2) the presence of certain second adults has an important ameliorative function (e.g., mother-grandmother families are nearly as effective as mother-father families, and mother-stepfather families are similar to mother-alone families with regard to risk), and 3) the absence of the father was less crucial than the aloneness of the mother in relation to risk. This study suggests that having another adult to share the tasks and responsibilities of childrearing is beneficial to child development. Many single-parent families without a second live-in adult create a network of friends and relatives to provide support. Without further research it is difficult to compare disadvantaged families with middle-class ones, especially on issues that involve maternal stress and involvement.

Father-Headed Single-Parent Families

Thirteen percent of fathers are awarded sole custody of their children at the time of divorce, most often when the mother is deemed incompetent or male adolescent children are involved, although in some cases the mother has left to pursue her career or another relationship. Other father-headed families occur because of the wife's death, a highly traumatic event for everyone. More divorced men are demanding the right to have at least partial custody of their children. Noncustodial mothers are more apt to maintain contact with their children than are noncustodial fathers. Many American children younger than 18 years (many of them preschool age) now live with their fathers, and the numbers are increasing. With many more men taking over instrumental roles in parenting, fathers are arguing that they are just as capable and as indispensable to a child's development as are mothers.

Men who head families have problems and concerns that are different from those of women who head families. In general, most fathers are less comfortable in assuming custody of children than are mothers. This is because in most cases, childrearing and domestic tasks are primarily the mother's responsibility. After an initial period of apprehension, however, fathers seem capable of assuming the nurturing role with effectiveness equal to that of mothers (Friedman 1980). It is worth highlighting for the novice therapist that the father and mother each may (or will) have their own style, methods, and values about the nurturing role. The therapist's task is to stay neutral and help the family (and each of its members) to function. The father needs to develop not only a set of childrearing and domestic skills but also a method of coping with the mother's feelings about their respective roles (the stereotype being that only women can raise children). To the extent that both parents can achieve collaboration (while living apart), the children's adjustment will tend to be positive.

Binuclear Families

If both parents are interested in being involved after divorce, the question of sharing time and decision making is crucial. In the 1960s there were many questions over the issues of the child's residence. The legal axiom "in the best interest of the child" proposed that one parent should have full charge of all custody and decision making. Studies showed that this led consistently to higher degrees of complete noninvolvement by the noncustodial parent—usually the father. When parents agree, and are not at war with each other, joint legal custody has become the generally accepted arrangement in many states. However, this means only equal decision-making power over issues such as school placement. Joint physical custody, in which the child spends an approximately even amount of time in each parent's home, has both advantages and disadvantages. There are many ways to set up joint physical custody. For example, when geographically feasible, the children can alternate the weeks or the days on which they visit either parent. Despite the objection that such an arrangement will confuse and upset the children, this appears to be an acceptable solution for some children.

The most important issue for the children may be to have ongoing regular contact with each of their parents; this advantage may outweigh the disadvantages of their having two homes. However, if the parents cannot find a way to parent amicably, the sense of disloyalty to each parent and the chaos of moving between two very different lifestyles are very hard on children, and single residential custody with ample visitation should be reconsidered.

The factors to be considered when deciding on custody arrangements should include the personal qualities of each parent and the age, sex, and particular needs of the offspring. Careful evaluation by judges, lawyers, and other professionals is beneficial. It is also critical that parents be flexible enough to alter the custody arrangement as circumstances or child development dictates. For example, arrangements for a 6-year-old may not be appropriate when the child becomes an adolescent.

The family therapist, by virtue of his or her interest and expertise in the family system, brings a new viewpoint to the evaluation and outcome of custody and other childrearing issues. In assessing the parents, the family therapist should not be guided by societal biases and prejudices in assigning custody, especially when both parents are involved in childrearing and the family has suitable, adaptable, and workable options. The family therapist can clarify relevant options and possibilities to increase the function of families experiencing single- or shared-custody parenting.

Remarriage and Remarried Families (Stepfamilies)

With John S. Visher, M.D., and
Emily B. Visher, Ph.D.

As suggested in Chapter 2, concurrent with the change in divorce rate (nearly 1 million people get divorced every year) is the increase in the number of people remarrying. Four out of five divorced people remarry. The *remarried family system* is created by the marriage (or living together in one domicile) of two partners, one or both of whom had been married previously and were divorced or widowed, with or without children who visit or reside with them. The couple and the children (residential or visiting) comprise the remarried family system. The *supra-family system* is composed of the remarried family plus former spouses, grandparents, aunts, uncles, and others who may have significant input into the remarried family system. The children are part of each of their biological parents' household systems. Both the remarried family system and the supra-family system have now become permanent variations of family networks.

Becoming a remarried family requires a complex set of developmental adjustments that take several years to gel (Visher and Visher 1996). The family begins after many losses and changes, with incongruent individual, marital, and family life cycle issues. Each child carries with him or her a different set of issues, values, and beliefs from the original family. Family tasks for remarried families include forming a new parental coalition, establishing new traditions, negotiating different developmental needs, and developing a system that allows for many continuing shifts in household composition and in the larger family system.

Structurally, membership in a nuclear family usually is well defined, with clear boundaries and a limited and clear extended family. For the nuclear family, the expectations, rules, roles, tasks, and purposes are clear, with generational boundaries and sexual taboos defined by society. In contrast, membership in the remarried family system is much broader and less clear. For example, are the parents of the ex-wife, who are still grandparents to the children of the father, part of the remarried family system? Membership is open to interpretation—some members may belong in two systems or may feel they do not belong in any family unit. The system has permeable (i.e., open) boundaries, and input from significant others in the supra-family—not only former spouses, grandparents, and children but also institutions—can have a marked effect on the remarried family's viability and functioning.

The sheer number of people at widely differing life stages who are involved in remarried families adds enormous complexity as well as possibilities. In the midst of this transition, the new couple must somehow find a space to define themselves as a couple and as lovers. They must also find the emotional energy to connect with the children and to continue to take primary responsibility for their own biological children rather than assuming that the stepparent will act like a biological parent (Glick 1989).

The Remarried Couple

The old assumption in the psychiatric and sociological literature was that people tended to re-create the same patterns they had in their first marriages. With further study, this assumption appears not always to be true. There is great possibility for personal growth during a first marriage or in its aftermath. Simply becoming several years older, with more experience of self and others, is sometimes enough to give an individual a new sense of his or her own needs and possibilities. If the individual in the meantime deals with his or her own unfinished business with a parent, that individual is less likely to repeat the struggle with a marital partner. Consider the following example:

> A man with a distant, critical mother married a distant, critical woman, believing that if he could make her love him, he would be happy. She continued to be distant and critical, and he became depressed. In his second marriage, after he learned to like himself better, he chose a warm, giving person to whom he didn't have to prove anything.

If a remarried person has learned patience and compromise, he or she is apt to be happier, and the marriage is apt to be friendlier and more egalitarian. However, the tendency of divorced men to choose women 5–10 years younger in their second marriages means that the power differential may be quite great.

If the remarried person is still deeply emotionally involved with his or her ex-spouse or is so bitter and distrustful from the divorce that he or she cannot feel part of a new couple, the new marriage will be in trouble from the beginning. Most of the stress of the new marriage, however, will come from the blending of families with children, especially if there are ongoing custody battles or if a child is deeply opposed to the new marriage (Pasley et al. 1996). Add to this the number of people who become divorced because of major personality difficulties, and it is no surprise that 59% of second marriages end in divorce.

Stepfamilies

We define a *stepfamily* as a household in which there are two married adults, at least one of whom has a child by a previous relationship (Visher and Visher 1996). The number of stepfamilies in the population is closely linked to the divorce rate, which in the United States has more than tripled since the early 1960s. Half of all marriages currently end in divorce, and this statistic does not include the dissolution of cohabiting relationships (Larson 1992). Approximately 75% of persons who have dissolved their marital relationships eventually remarry or form new cohabiting relationships. About 65% of these couplings involve children from prior marriage, and thus stepfamilies are formed. The presence of stepfamilies in the population is pervasive. For example, 35% of all children in the United States born in the 1980s will live with a stepparent before their eighteenth birthday, and it is estimated that more than half of the entire population will have personal experience as a part of a stepfamily during their lifetime, as a stepchild, a stepparent, a step-grandparent, or a remarried parent. Demographers predict that stepfamilies will be the most common type of family by the year 2010.

There are important differences between the structure of stepfamilies and other types of families that are generally not well understood by those in stepfamily situations. These differences often lead to a high amount of stress as stepfamilies attempt to integrate into a functioning stepfamily unit (Visher and Visher 1996). Each of these structural differences imposes specific tasks on stepfamily members that must be mastered before successful integration can occur. Consider the following examples:

- Families must deal effectively with many losses and changes.
- Incongruent individual, marital, and family life cycles must be negotiated. For example, if a 55-year-old man with two grandchildren marries a 35-year-old woman with two young children, he may be a grandfather, a new husband, and a new father all at once.
- Children and adults all come to the stepfamily with a history of experiences and convictions from previous families about what is right and wrong, which may lead to differences of opinion that must be resolved so that new traditions can be established.
- Parent-child relationships predate the new couple relationship, so that a solid couple bond and new relationships with others in the stepfamily must be developed consciously.
- The presence of a biological parent elsewhere in actuality or in memory challenges new stepfamily members to work out cooperative parenting relationships.
- Children are often members of two households, and everyone must learn to deal with shifting household composition and complicated relationships. Children are frequently caught in loyalty conflicts.
- There is little or no legal relationship between the stepparent and stepchildren, so that there is a perceived risk in forming new relationships with little legal and societal support.

The dynamics of stepfamily life are different from those of other types of families, and there tends to be a lack of satisfactory understanding of these differences, thus depriving stepfamily members of needed information, education, and support. Many stepfamily members who lack information about these issues decide prematurely to dissolve their new relationship before the rewards and satisfactions of stepfamily life can become apparent.

Forming new relationships and finding solutions to stepfamily challenges take time, and family members typically go through predictable emotional stages before achieving integration (Figure 4–1) (Papernow 1993). The length of time depends partly on the ages of the children (e.g., teenagers take longer than do younger children). In general, stepfamilies start from a position in which the adults expect everything to go smoothly—the so-called fantasy stage. The adults try to make the fantasy come true, but as a rule there are tense times, and stepparents start to feel that something must be wrong with them and the way they are feeling and doing things. When things go wrong the family splits along biological lines and pressures build.

The stepparent is often the one (as a rule) who begins to see changes that need to take place in the functioning of the family, for example, the need for more teamwork between the adults in situations involving the children. The stepparent may feel left out and as though the parent-child coalition is the only important alliance. The parent who has remarried feels caught in the middle between his or her spouse and children. Children often exploit the split between the two adults.

> The stepparent is often the one who begins to see changes that need to take place in the functioning of the family.

Often the stepparent finds support outside the household for his or her reactions and becomes more vocal about dissatisfactions. The adults may become very upset and find it impossible to understand each other's feelings. They argue and often seek therapy at this point. Getting past this stage is difficult and takes time and understanding. As things become clearer and the two adults begin to work together as a parenting team, changes take place in the household so that biological divisions begin to blur.

It is hoped that step-relationships develop and deepen positively, that the stepparent becomes an "intimate outsider" in the family unit, and that the difficulties come to seem more manageable. Satisfactions develop as relationships shift over time. A stepparent can develop multiple types of relationships with a stepchild: friend, "aunt" or "uncle," or a truly parental connection. The sense of having mastered difficult interpersonal situations results in increased self-esteem for both children and adults. Situations rooted in the structure of stepfamilies tend to arise from time to time, especially around nodal family events—for example, graduations, marriages, holidays, or deaths—and the family may experience old feelings and behaviors, but they work them out more quickly than before and return to a family equilibrium.

One of the major difficulties for stepfamily members is that their basic human needs for belonging to an accepting group, receiving individual support from someone who really cares about them, and having some control over their life may be denied by the structure of the stepfamily. Those families that work out ways of satisfying these needs tend to become integrated more quickly.

Most of those involved in stepfamily life eventually achieve satisfaction and find the experience rewarding. A positive outcome can be anticipated in a majority of remarriages. Many families get help from support groups, pastors, other stepfamily members, therapists, and counselors. The Stepfamily Association of America in Lincoln, Nebraska, is a national organization that offers educational materials, sponsors conferences and seminars, and gives guidance to those seeking help through support groups or local chapters.

Grandparent-Headed Families

When both parents have died or when a single parent has become incapacitated by drugs or illness, children are often taken care of by grandparents. This has become more common in inner-city areas where AIDS and crack cocaine have taken a major toll. The incongruent developmental needs of an aging person and an active young child, plus grief for the lost parent, make this system difficult although viable. It is helpful if an extended family is available for support. Therapy tasks include determining the role of the parent in the child's life if the parent is alive and maintaining social and financial support for the grandparents.

Gay and Lesbian Families

Gay and lesbian families are increasingly demanding the right to have their children from former marriages with them, to adopt children, or in the case of

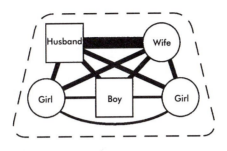

A. Nuclear family

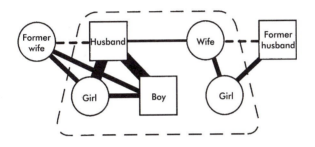

B. New stepfamily

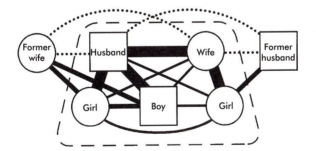

C. Integrated stepfamily

FIGURE 4–1.   Changes in family relationships.
Source.   Visher EB, Visher JS: *Old Loyalties, New Ties: Therapeutic Strategies With Stepfamilies.* New York, Brunner/Mazel, 1988, p. 13. Reprinted with permission.

lesbians to have children within the union. These families face several unique tasks, including defining the role (both legal and emotional) of the nonbiological parent and dealing with the effects of homophobia on the child and the family. There is no evidence that these families produce a higher proportion of gay or problematic children. We discuss this type of family in more detail in Chapter 23.

Family Vignettes

In the mid-1980s we found brief life vignettes written (anonymously) 25 years after graduation in the annual reports of two colleges (Ideas and Trends 1986). The following four vignettes encapsulate nicely some of the concepts we have discussed in Chapters 2–4—such as lifestyle, tasks, and systems.

For years I had a dream of a full-time career, which I tempered with responsibilities to family. I now have full time to devote to my challenging career as a tenured professor. The biggest disappointment since college was my bitter divorce from my college sweetheart. He ran off with my best friend after 14 years of marriage, and it was a very low point for me. He was threatened by my desire for a career. He wanted a housewife. I found the women's movement and went through consciousness-raising, a life-saving experience. I will be eternally sad that my children are from a broken home, but I found a second chance at a marriage. I have a successful and satisfying career, two wonderful daughters, a loving husband, and good health. Isn't life wonderful?

College professor, California

After college I went to seminary, where I met my husband. I became the minister's wife in a small town and had a son. For years I enjoyed this, but I slowly realized that I desperately missed my work in science, which I had given up part way through college. When I was 35 I fell in love with a woman in my husband's congregation. I never told her about it, but I knew then that the interest in women I had experienced as a teenager had not gone away. With great difficulty I left my husband and moved to Chicago, where I went back to graduate school. I left my son with my husband. I was very depressed for almost a year. Now I am living with a woman and finishing training in research. I am more happy than I thought I could be, but I miss my son a great deal.

Scientist, Arizona

Like many of us, I suspect, I work too hard. From the beginning of my career at a big Wall Street firm all the way up to the present at the New York City practice I started with my two present partners 15 years ago, I regret having spent too much time working and not enough enjoying my beautiful wife and two wonderful daughters. I wish that I hadn't found it so consistently necessary to do all the things that kept me away from them. I'm glad that many lawyers care about the problems of IBM and AT&T, but I confess that the presence of a close human relationship is most important to me. As a result, most of my clients are friends with whom I have shared some significant experience. I've incorporated their dreams, sat on their boards, negotiated their deals, sold their stock, created their trusts, and probated their wills. It's been grand, and it's getting better. It's also been grand watching my wife transform herself from housewife and mother without a clue about the nature of a debenture into a highly sophisticated investment banker. In fact, although neither of us are where we thought we'd be 25 years ago, we're both delighted and immensely grateful for our healthy, beautiful children and our busy but interesting lives together.

Attorney, New York

When I was 25, I decided not to work with my father. I moved to Philadelphia and opened a restaurant. It did really well, and I opened another. I got married. I got diabetes. We had no children, and I lived at the restaurants because they were so much fun. I should have paid more attention to the business side. When I was 39 my wife left me, and I got depressed. The restaurants went bankrupt. Now I'm living in a rented apartment trying to decide what to do. I'm not sure it's possible to start over at 40. My girlfriend wants me to live with her, but I'm not ready to be with anyone yet.

Former businessman, Delaware

We discuss new family forms further in Chapter 21. In contrast to our focus on function here, our focus in Chapters 19 and 21 is on dysfunction and its treatment.

Suggested Readings

Ahrons C: The Good Divorce: Keeping Your Family Together When Your Marriage Comes Apart. New York, Harper Collins, 1994

This well-written book offers a sensitive and practical guide for parents facing divorce. Based on two decades of solid research, it assesses the consequences of divorce and proposes the hopeful and useful notion of the binuclear family.

Carter B, McGoldrick M: The Expanded Family Life Cycle: Individual, Family and Social Perspectives, 3rd Edition. Boston, MA, Allyn & Bacon, 1998
This book is the newest and most complete version of the classic text on the family life cycle, with a multisystemic perspective.

Visher E, Visher J: Therapy With Stepfamilies. New York, Brunner/Mazel, 1996
Focused on stepfamilies, this book offers clear and straightforward guidelines for clinical assessment. The therapeutic framework is practical for all families in transition.

References

Cunningham J, Antill J: Current Trends in Non-Marital Cohabitation: In Search of the POSSLQ (Persons of the Opposite Sex Sharing Living Quarters). Edited by Wood J, Duck S. Thousand Oaks, CA, Sage, 1995, pp 148–173

Friedman HJ: The father's parenting experience in divorce. Am J Psychiatry 137:177–182, 1980

Glick PC: Remarried families, stepfamilies, and stepchildren; a brief demographic profile. Family Relations 38:24–28, 1989

Graefe D, Lichter D: Life course transitions of American children: parental conhabitation, marriage, and single motherhood. Demography 36:205–217, 1999

Hetherington EM, Cox M, Cox R: The development of children in mother-headed families, in The American Family: Dying or Developing. Edited by Reiss D, Hoffman HA. New York, Plenum, 1979, pp 117–156

Ideas and Trends: The class of 1961 offers some dissertation on itself. The New York Sunday Times, July 13, 1986

Issacs M, Leon G: Remarriage and its alternatives following divorce: mother and child adjustment. J Marital Fam Ther 14:163–173, 1988

Kellam SG, Ensminger ME, Turner RJ: Family structure and mental health of children. Arch Gen Psychiatry 34:1012–1022, 1977

Kessler S: The American Way of Divorce: Prescription for Change. Chicago, IL, Nelson-Hall, 1975

Larson J: Understanding stepfamilies. American Demographics 14:360, 1992

Messinger L: Remarriage between divorced people with children from previous marriages: a proposal for preparation for remarriage. J Mar Fam Couns 2:193–200, 1976

Papernow P: Becoming a Stepfamily: Patterns of Development in Remarried Families. San Francisco, CA, Jossey-Bass, 1993

Pasley K, Rhoden L, Visher EB, et al: Stepfamilies in therapy: insights from adult stepfamily members. J Marital Fam Ther 22:343–357, 1996

Salts CJ: Divorce process: integration of theory. Journal of Divorce 2:233–240, 1979

Schoen R: First unions and the stability of first marriages. Journal of Marriage and the Family 54:281–284, 1992

U.S. Census Bureau: Statistical abstract of the United States. Washington, DC, U.S. Government Printing Office, 1997

Visher EB, Visher JS: Therapy With Stepfamilies. New York, Brunner/Mazel, 1996

Weiss RS: Marital Separation. New York, Basic Books, 1975

Escape, Naoko Matsubara, 1991. Private collection.

CHAPTER 5

Problems and Dysfunction From a Family Systems Perspective

Objectives for the Reader

- ல To understand the characteristics of dysfunctional families
- ல To understand theories of the development of family dysfunction
- ல To understand theories of how one individual family member becomes the identified patient
- ல To obtain an overview of how symptoms and problems in a couple, family, or individual are viewed from a family systems perspective

Introduction: The Dysfunctional Family System

In the preceding chapters we described the organization and behavior of the functional family, using the concept of the family as a system with its own life cycle and tasks. In this chapter (and again in Chapters 19, 20, and 21) we focus on the disturbances in these areas and the ways in which families become dysfunctional. We discuss the types of disturbances manifested by dysfunctional family systems, including problematic family beliefs and myths, individual symptomatology, life cycle stressors, and the inability of the family to accomplish family tasks.

How do problems become problems? What leads to symptoms? Who begins to realize that a problem is distressing enough to require outside intervention? These are issues that intrigue family theorists (and individual theorists before them) and will preoccupy the family therapist as he or she begins the assessment of a couple or family.

In order to contrast systemic explanations with more traditional perspectives, it is interesting to briefly revisit the psychoanalytic and biological approaches to the development of symptomatology. Freud focused on data obtained from the verbalizations of patients about their internal thoughts, feelings, and experiences. He saw psychopathology as relating both to internalized conflict between wishes and desires and to the control mechanisms within the psyche. He noted astutely that the dysfunctional patterns and defenses that hinder the life of the patient (and at times the analyst) were reenacted within the therapy in similar forms, most commonly in the form of transference toward the psychoanalyst. (*Transference* is the unconscious tendency of a person to assign to others in the present and immediate environment feelings and attitudes linked originally with significant figures in the person's early life.) Freud's psychoanalytic approach emphasized the individual patient, and his clinical focus was on internal experience, which was thought to have its roots in the early history of the individual.

Current biological views of psychiatric illness also focus on the individual, but instead of centering on the mind, they examine the individual's genetic inheritance and neurophysiology in order to relate psychobiological changes to changes in mood, thinking, and behavior. The most sophisticated model relating family process to genetic expression is the one now being studied by Hetherington, Plomin, and Reiss in a multisite study (Figure 5–1; D. Reiss, personal communication, 1999).

In general, family theorists only recently incorporated psychodynamic and neurobiological aspects of illness into their thinking. The systems perspective emphasizes what is called *circular causality*, in which symptomatic behavior is maintained by circular feedback loops within the family system. It is argued that with living systems, one cannot simply assign one part of the system as having a direct causal influence on another part; in other words, there may be different routes to the same endpoint, or similar events may lead to different outcomes. In this regard, the systemic perspective offers a comfortable stance for clinicians who have adopted the biopsychosocial perspective (see Chapter 1). Not only must these factors be accounted for in the assessment of a patient system, but narrow interventions must be contrasted with those that explicitly address biological, psychological, and social dimensions.

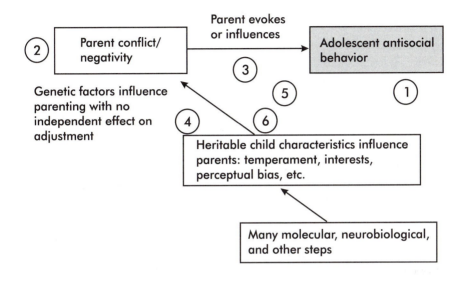

FIGURE 5–1.   Role of family process in genetic expression.

A Systems Approach to Problems and Dysfunction

Just as reductionistic views have emphasized the individual's inner life and neurobiological system, it is equally important to open the lens and look at the same phenomena from an interpersonal and systems perspective. Because current psychoanalytic theory and practice have been moving toward an interpersonal and systems perspective steadily over the past two decades, the renewed focus on context is not tied only to the field of family therapy. Indeed, it represents part of a larger swing within the field of psychiatry and psychotherapy proper.

Historical Perspectives

Freud's microscope was focused on the individual and the individual's inner life. We will not go deeply into the history of the family systems view of symptoms but simply highlight in a simplified way a few crucial steps along the way. At this point it would be helpful to review the basic concepts of systems theory (see Chapter 1).

Systems theories of etiology, as applied to Axis I disorders such as schizophrenia, are now dated. For the sake of understanding these theories, we summarize them here. One of the pioneering interactional concepts about symptomatology was Bateson et al.'s (1956) articulation of the *double-bind*. The term double-bind described a communication impasse between individuals in a relationship system, which hypothetically gave rise to responses in one individual that were labeled schizophrenic. Rather than being a disorder of reality testing, schizophrenia was viewed as the individual's best effort to cope with a reality of disturbed communication. In other words, schizophrenia made sense when understood in the context of disconfirming and disqualifying communications and behaviors.

Jackson began to look at family norms and values that were maintained by what he viewed as homeostatic mechanisms (Jackson and Yalom 1965). In his initial work, he proposed that symptoms served a homeostatic function; that is, they functioned to keep the family operating within the same narrow range of behavior. As a result, dysfunctional families used only some of the full range of behaviors available to them in order to maintain the status quo, which produced the symptomatic behavior in the first place.

At the National Institute of Mental Health, Bowen and later Wynne were also trying to understand the etiology of schizophrenia from a systems perspective. Bowen (1978), who studied whole families of schizophrenic patients, concluded that two-person relationships (e.g., marriages) were intrinsically unstable. He proposed that when confronted with stress, a two-person emotional system may draw in, or triangulate, a third person. Anxiety between the original twosome is shifted to the third person. Although it is hypothesized that triangulation occurs in all families, pathology is associated with those families in which there is a rigidity about such triangles under change or stress. This triangulation process may spread to the entire family and even peripheral family members and outsiders as the emotional contagion grows.

Wynne and his colleagues attributed psychopathology to deviant family communication processes and properties of families that blocked the young person's natural development (Wynne et al. 1982). Among the processes they noted were unreal qualities of both positive and negative emotions (i.e., *pseudo-mutuality*, which masks conflict and blocks intimacy; and *pseudo-hostility*, which obscures splits and alignments), rigid family boundaries (so-called rubber fences), and distorted patterns of communication (i.e., communication deviance). Consider the following case example:

> The A family consisted of a father in his late 40s; a mother in her early 40s; and their son, in his early 20s. The son was the identified patient. Mr. and Mrs. A,

although seemingly close, had given up sexual relations and attending social functions together. Their son had dropped out of school and was staying in the house, playing his guitar, and watching television. Mrs. A, a housewife, had given up on many household tasks. Mr. A managed his work as a salesman by routinely following the same pattern he had for many years and was barely eking out a living. The family members never seemed to disagree with one another on anything. Individual members seemed unable to allocate separate time for themselves but always did everything together. They were afraid to deal with differentness. There was a pervading sense of emptiness: Mrs. A spent much of her time in bed, Mr. A complained of not getting satisfaction from his work or his family, and their son felt hopeless.

Jackson's, Bowen's, and Wynne's theories are still key components of understanding most family dysfunction. As we discuss later in this chapter, these theories aid our understanding of general couple and family dissatisfaction and of the family contribution to much nonpsychotic symptomatology. Although these types of family dysfunction do not create psychosis, they produce levels of stress in family members that can produce other symptoms or magnify and maintain psychotic processes in vulnerable individuals.

Finally, Lidz (1963) grounded his initial investigations in psychoanalytic theory, challenging the prevalent view (at that time) that maternal rejection was the distinguishing feature in psychopathology. He looked at the role of fathers and at problems in marital roles. In particular, *marital schism* was identified as the chronic failure of accommodation or role reciprocity, whereas *marital skew* reflected marriages in which psychopathology was present in one partner, who dominated the other. Other psychoanalytically informed pioneers (e.g., Ackerman 1958) believed that family problems arose in response to the immediate environment and to the individual psyche.

Current Perspectives

The biological determinants of most of the major psychiatric disorders have been identified, using imaging, neuropathological, and neurochemical methods. The idea that rearing alone, or the current family system alone, is responsible for these disorders is now outdated, much to the relief of the families that were blamed for their members' pain. However, family stress or dysfunction certainly is involved in the onset and maintenance of symptoms. The person with psychosis puts stress on the family, and certain types of family dysfunction, such as triangulation and rigid family boundaries, put stress on the ill person. Levels of family dysfunction must be investigated as part of the evaluation and treatment of psychosis.

Family systems explanations for symptoms are as numerous as the schools of clinical theory and practice in the field, yet a small group of hypotheses seem to be endorsed commonly. In this section, we define symptoms as problems that distress others in the family and, usually, the person who has them. Symptoms possess the following characteristics:

- They may emerge as a result of problematic communication or interactional patterns in a family.
- They may signal an impasse at a particular developmental point in the family's life cycle.
- They may be part of solution behavior that is failing at its task.
- They may reflect problems in family structure and organization.
- They may be expressed when aspects of a family's life are denied or dissociated.
- They may represent a lack of validation, may be an expression of an underlying medical or psychiatric illness, or may simply relate to misfortune and bad luck.

The strongest predictor of overall life satisfaction is the quality of a person's central relationship. Not only that, but "a good and stable relationship buffers against the genetic vulnerability to both medical and psychiatric disorder" (Lewis 1998).

In the remaining sections of this chapter, we examine some of the more influential perspectives on family systems problems. Each of the following approaches may be thought of as an hypothesis that the clinician may test in approaching a new case.

Structural Problems

Sometimes symptoms in an individual may be viewed as a reflection of organizational problems existing within the marriage or family. According to Minuchin (1974, p. 51), family structure is "the invisible set of functional demands that organizes the ways in which family members interact. A family is a system that operates through transactional patterns. Repeated transactions establish patterns of how, when, and to whom to relate, and these patterns underpin the system." In Minuchin's influential structural approach, a pathological family could be one "who in the face of stress increases the rigidity of their transactional patterns and boundaries, and avoid or resist any exploration of alternatives." As the family's range of choices narrows, family members develop predictable and stereotyped responses to one another and to the extrafamilial environment. The family then becomes a closed system, and family members experience themselves as controlled and impotent (Papp 1980). From the structural perspective, the family therapist's definition of a *pathogenic family* is one whose adaptive and coping mechanisms have been exhausted. Symptoms of unhappiness in a family member are embedded in the problematic family function because symptoms can represent the family's groping for new solutions during a period of transition.

As we mentioned in Chapter 3, dimensions of family structure that warrant attention are family boundaries, hierarchies, and coalitions. Minuchin considers boundaries on a continuum ranging from enmeshment to disengagement. Enmeshment refers to a style of family involvement in which boundaries within the family are highly permeable but those between the family and the outside world are usually rigid. At the extreme, this style can become a handicap in that a heightened sense of belonging may require a major yielding of autonomy. In more disengaged families, only a high level of stress (e.g., caused by serious illness or a suicide attempt) can reverberate strongly enough to activate the family's supportive systems. If the concept of boundaries addresses proximity, the dimension of hierarchy is defined in terms of authority or relative influence that family members exercise in relation to one another.

Problems in alliances or coalitions represent another facet of structural difficulties. In a three-person system, ample opportunities exist for two of the members to be allied against or to exclude the third member. Minuchin has described three different types of triangles:

1. *Triangulation,* in which the parents make equally strong but different demands on the child, and the child responds by being unable to choose between the parents' demands, by moving back and forth between the parents (i.e., acting as a go-between), or by being rebellious.

2. *Detouring,* in which parental conflict is put aside to attend to the child, either to care for the child because he or she is needy or ill (i.e., protective behavior) or to attack the child because he or she is misbehaving (i.e., hostile and blaming behavior). Detouring requires that the child continues to be problematic so that the parents can avoid the conflict.

3. *Stable coalition* between one parent and a child, in which the parent and child are tied closely to each other, either in response to the other parent's inadequate involvement or in order to block the other parent's involvement.

Problems in family structure can be likened to structural problems in a house: Left unattended, symptoms gradually emerge and can worsen.

The Solution as the Problem

In the solution-as-the-problem approach, symptoms are explained as problems in the rules of the systems or patterns of repetitive interaction. All families are faced with everyday problems in living—for example, how to get household tasks completed, how to get children to go to school or do their homework, and how to compromise when differences occur. In addition, all families face some difficulties at some time or other in their lives. In facing a problem, each family member tends to approach the problem with characteristic ways of thinking, feeling, and acting. These initial responses may or may not be effective for the specific problem. If the family members are unable to modify their problem-solving behavior when it doesn't work, they may continue to repeat the same ineffective behavior to the point that a small or even nonexistent problem turns into a major one. Consider the following case example:

> Mrs. B believed that children should eat specific kinds and amounts of food. When her children did not do this, she punished them. The oldest child, a compliant boy with a good appetite, responded by eating in the way she required, so Mrs. B felt like a good mother. The younger child, however, was temperamentally more of a fighter and had a very uncertain appetite. She refused to eat. Mrs. B continued to apply the same problem-solving behavior, that of punishment, and the result was a pitched battle and eventually an eating disorder—exactly what Mrs. B had not wanted to accomplish.

This model posits that mishandling of the original problem occurs when 1) the solution involves denying that a problem exists, and nothing is done; 2) change is attempted for something that is unchangeable or nonexistent; or 3) action is taken at the wrong level (Watzlawick et al. 1974). In the preceding case example, one could consider several possibilities:

1. The child's original eating behavior was not, to many observers, a problem, in that she was healthy and not losing weight. The problem was Mrs. B's belief system (see section on family belief systems later in this chapter) that to be a good mother you should feed a child well and demand discipline around eating.
2. If the child needed to eat more, action could have been taken at a different level—that of discussing with the child what and how she needed to

eat—rather than at the level of discipline. If the child was not eating because of anxiety over her parents' quarreling, then the problem needed to be solved by treating the parents.

3. When Mrs. B's attempts at discipline failed, rather than change her solution (i.e., demanding obedience), she escalated her previous behavior. If, when the child developed a serious eating problem, Mrs. B refused to believe it and insisted that this was simple disobedience, the problem would continue to worsen. This outcome would illustrate our first point—symptoms occur when the solution involves denying that a problem exists.

Sometimes the problem is a conflict in problem-solving behaviors between family members. Consider the following case example:

> A child stayed home for a week with the flu. She had a fine time with her mother, who was lonely and bored and was happy to have her at home. When she recovered from the flu, she protested and said she was still sick. Her mother wanted to keep her daughter home, and her father began to shout and say that the mother was spoiling the child and that the child had to go to school. This argument raised the child's anxiety and she began to throw up. She was allowed to stay home again. Eventually she developed a school phobia. If this process resulted in her forming a coalition with her mother against her father, we could say that the problem had changed the family structure.

Sometimes the problem is very real, but the solution is ineffective. Consider the following case example:

> When Mrs. C's husband began drinking, she tried to protect him by covering for him, calling in sick for him, and so on. This allowed him to continue his drinking behavior and also created a new problem—she became depressed by the situation. When she no longer supported him and instead said that she would leave him if the behavior continued, she became less depressed. He also stopped drinking.

When the attempted solution becomes the problem, the way to change the situation is to do something else. In most cases it becomes the therapist's job to realize that the solution has become the problem and to help the family find alternative methods of behavior. This involves both understanding the beliefs that underlie behaviors and make it difficult to change (see next section) and conducting a careful examination of the communications of all family members to determine how and why the problem-solving behavior is failing.

When the attempted solution becomes the problem, the way to change the situation is to do something else.

Family Beliefs and Myths

Individuals and families have belief systems that, in part, determine their feelings and behaviors. These subterranean structures have been referred to as *family myths*. They are often found to be important contributors and maintainers of family difficulty, and family therapists must be aware of them if they are to understand family behavior that might otherwise seem inexplicable. For example, in the C family case example, the wife's belief that a good woman must stand by her man made it impossible for her to stop covering for her husband. Only when the wife became very depressed and her husband lost his job as a result of alcoholism was she able to change her belief to "In the end you cannot allow another person to destroy your life" and set some limits. Ferreira (1963) defined family myths as "a series of fairly well integrated beliefs shared by all family members, concerning one another and their mutual position in the family, which go unchallenged by everyone involved, in spite of the reality distortions which they may conspicuously imply." The implications of Ferreira's definition involve very personalized and specific myths for each family, in which individual family members are singled out for particular slots, roles, or self-fulfilling prophecies, such as "Mother is the emotional one in the family" or "Our son misbehaves continually."

Papp (1980) and Imber-Black (1991) have noted that behavioral cycles are governed by a "belief system that is composed of a combination of attitudes, basic assumptions, expectations, prejudices, convictions, and beliefs brought to the nuclear family by each parent from his/her family of origin" (Carroll 1960). Some beliefs are shared, whereas others complement one another. Beliefs, just as behavioral cycles, can be constraining of new experimentation by family members. The family's beliefs and themes (Papp 1980), constructs (Reiss 1981), and myths (Ferreira 1963) provide an added framework for the clinician who wants to go beyond interactional data to understand the ways in which family members are blocked in their accomplishment of tasks and aims. Consider the following case example:

A grandmother is deserted by her alcoholic husband and raises her daughter to distrust men. Her daughter marries a man who seems to provide the money and security she lacks, but he eventually has an affair. The family story, some variant of "no man can be trusted," will be passed down in different ways to male and female children. Subsequently the granddaughter may be caught in a loyalty bind—how can she trust her husband and be loyal to her mother?

The same situation can create different myths depending on the players. For example, a family in which several members become seriously ill but survive can label itself a family of survivors or a family of failures and sick people. This will sharply affect the level of anxiety and dysfunctional behavior when the next person gets sick. This model assumes that a family's construction of the problem is as vital as its overt behaviors. It also opens the way for the therapist to construct more positive stories with the family.

In addition to specific family myths, a variety of myths are promulgated by the culture. As a result, many of these myths will be shared by family members and perhaps by the therapist. Each therapist must work out his or her own values with respect to these issues. The therapist must be sensitive to, and deal appropriately with, those attitudes and beliefs that seem to be deleterious to a family's functioning and, conversely, must understand that some myths aid functioning. In the next several sections we discuss some examples of myths or beliefs.

If life has not worked out well for you as an individual, getting married will make everything better. No matter how unfortunate one's life experience has been in terms of career choice or relationships with parents and peers, how satisfied one is living alone, or how dissatisfied one is with one's genetic endowment or social and economic situation—getting married is usually not the answer. This myth is often shared by both partners. If the marriage does last, each spouse bears the resentment that the other feels for not making it a happy one and for not overcoming all the obstacles that existed prior to the marriage.

Marital and family life should be totally happy, and each individual therein should expect either all or most gratifications to come from the family system. This romantic myth dies hard in some quarters. Many of life's satisfactions are found outside the family setting. There is a whole range of gratifications that families need to work out to fit their own particular needs and personalities.

The togetherness myth. This myth states that merely remaining in proximity or jointly carrying out all activities will lead to satisfactory family life and individual gratification. Again, there will probably be great variation from one family to another. Most people need areas of separate interest to avoid a feeling of losing the self.

Marital partners should be completely honest with each other at all times. In its modern guise, this idea may be derived from self-help guides and talk television, in which people are encouraged to express their feelings freely (especially negative ones, it seems) and also from the concept that what is suppressed will eventually damage us. Full and open frankness in feeling, action, and thought may cause at least as much harm as good. Honesty can be enlisted in the service of hostility, or it can be a constructive, problem-solving approach. It is important to approach sensitive topics with care and gentleness. Many hurtful statements, especially regarding factors that cannot be changed, are perhaps best left unspoken.

A happy marriage is one in which there are no disagreements, and when family members fight it means they hate one another. It seems inevitable that family members will have differences with one another and that these differences will often lead to overt disagreements. Such disagreements may lead to fights or arguments, but if they are dealt with constructively, clarification and resolution can be found without anyone losing self-esteem. Many families, however, seem afraid to disagree and therefore cover up differences. In contrast, some families fight all the time about almost every issue but seemingly are unable to resolve any disagreements; instead, they seem to resort to personal attacks on one another's motives and veracity.

The marital partners should see eye-to-eye on every issue, and they should work toward being as identical in outlook as possible. The first part of this myth is just about impossible to achieve, and the second part is of questionable benefit. Open recognition of inevitable differences may be helpful and constructive. Many married couples seem either unwilling to accept or incapable of recognizing their inevitable differences with respect to past experience, basic attitudes, and personality styles. Instead, there often seems to be a marked projection of one's personality attributes, both positive and negative, onto the partner with relatively little ability to see the partner realistically.

Marital partners should be as unselfish as possible and give up thinking about their own individual needs. In most successful marriages, the partners seem able to reconcile the needs of the separate individuals with those of the needs of the family unit. Some individuals, however, live as if they do not have personal needs and satisfactions but are there only to serve the larger family system. After a time, they frequently become angry or depressed. Successful family units recognize that space must be made in one's life for individual needs as well as one's role as a marital partner and a parent.

When something goes wrong in the family, one should look around to see who is at fault.   At times of stress, many people react almost reflexively by blaming themselves or others. This often is not a useful response; instead, it may be more productive to look toward other frames of reference. When things go wrong in nongratifying family interactions, it may be because of the interactional properties of the entire system, which can be examined with a problem-solving approach in a relatively nonpersonalized, nonblaming manner. Each family member can be encouraged to assess his or her own role in the situation and in the solution to the problem. When two pieces of a jigsaw puzzle do not seem to fit well together, which of the two pieces is to blame?

When things are not going well, it will often help to spend a major part of the time digging up past and present hurts.   Arguments that involve endless recriminations about past disappointments and difficulties may give temporary relief by allowing the parties to air their resentments. This can often lead to futile escalation of the argument into a sort of "Can you top this?" discussion. Besides usually making things worse rather than better, this approach detracts from any constructive attempts at problem solving. Often one of the first jobs of the family therapist is to act as a kind of traffic cop in stopping these nonproductive family maneuvers. Nothing can be done to change what happened in the past. Focusing on the past rarely does much good by itself, unless it leads to increased understanding and modification of present patterns.

In a marital argument one partner is right and the other is wrong, and the goal of such fights should be for the partners to see who can score the most points.   Obviously this is not the case. When one marital partner wins a fight, it is usually the marriage as a whole that loses. Competitiveness in the marital relationship is not usually preferable to a cooperative working together in which neither marital partner necessarily scores points but in which the outcome is such that the individuals and the marriage itself stand to gain.

A good sexual relationship will inevitably lead to a good marriage.   Everyone has seen examples of individuals who married when they were physically infatuated with each other but who woke up after the honeymoon to discover that in respects other than physical, they were relatively poorly suited to each other. A good sexual relationship is an important component of a satisfactory marriage, but it does not necessarily preclude the presence of difficulties in other areas. The sexual relationship in a well-functioning marriage may still need specific attention. It cannot be taken for granted that a good marriage and good sex go together. Difficulties in the sexual sphere do seem to lead to difficulties in the rest of the marital relationship. Specific sex therapy for the couple may be indicated, after which other, basically secondary difficulties may diminish.

Because marital partners increasingly understand each other's verbal and nonverbal communications, there is little or no need to check things with each other. This may sometimes be the case in functional, nonproblematic families, but it is often strikingly untrue for families in trouble. Marital partners and other family members may assume that what they have said or done was understood. They may also believe that they are able to read someone else's mind or know what someone else really means. When they are encouraged in therapy to check some of these assumptions with each other, they are often shocked at their own misperceptions and misinterpretations.

In marital systems, positive feedback is not as necessary as negative feedback. Many married individuals have gotten out of the habit of letting their partner know when he or she has done something pleasing. There is often less hesitancy in commenting on something that has caused hurt or disappointment. Positive reinforcement of desired behavior usually increases its occurrence and is usually a much more effective behavior-shaping technique than is negative feedback or punishment.

"And then they lived happily ever after." A good marriage should just happen spontaneously and should not need to involve any work on the part of the participants. This is perhaps another carryover from the romantic idea of marriage as some type of blissful, dreamlike state. The sad but realistic truth is that marriage involves day-to-day and minute-by-minute interaction between the people involved, as well as constant negotiation, communication, and solving of problems. Members of dysfunctional families may spend only a few minutes a week talking with one another about anything meaningful.

Any spouse can (and should) be reformed and remodeled into the shape desired by the partner. In many marriages an inordinate amount of time and energy is spent in the effort of molding the spouse to a desired image. This is commonly done with little or no recognition that basic personality patterns, once established, are not easily modified. Attempts to do so lead mainly to frustration, anger, and disillusionment, although certain characteristics may be moderated or even rechanneled, and partners can be made to be more sensitive to each other's reactions. Such marriages may work out satisfactorily as long as both partners consent to play the requisite roles involved, but futile arguments about personal qualities and lack of cooperation may still occur. It would be better for a spouse to look inward in order to assess which personal characteristics should be modified to best profit the marriage.

A stable marriage is one in which things do not change and in which there are no problems. To be alive is to face continual change. Systems that attempt to remain fixed in some unchanging mold will sooner or later become out of phase with current needs. Systems have a tendency toward a dynamic equilibrium in which certain patterns and interactions repeat themselves, giving a sense of continuity and stability. At the same time the entire system is moving inevitably onward.

Everyone knows what a husband should be like and what a wife should be like. This statement may have been truer in the past than it is now. There is increasingly less agreement on this subject, with a constant flood of conflicting messages. The lack of a preconceived or defined notion of marital roles presents a possibility of greater confusion, but it also offers an opportunity for much greater development of each partner's and the marriage's potential.

If a marriage is not working properly, having children will rescue it. Although the arrival of children may often temporarily make the spouses feel somewhat more worthwhile and give them a new role (that of being parents), children are not the cement that will hold poor marriages together. Instead, children often become the victims of marital disharmony. Children bring increased stress to marriages even when the partners love being parents.

No matter how bad the marriage, it should be kept together for the sake of the children. It is not necessarily true that children thrive better in an unhappy marriage than they do living with a relatively satisfied divorced parent. If the marriage partners stay together, the children may bear the brunt of the resentment that the partners feel for each other, with the parents feeling they have martyred themselves for their children's sake.

If the marriage does not work, an extramarital affair or a new marriage will cure the situation. Although sometimes this is true, what may often happen is that the new partner is uncannily similar to the rejected one, and the same nongratifying patterns begin all over again; only the names of the players have been changed.

Separation and divorce represent a failure of the marriage and of the individuals involved.   This has almost always been the traditional view held by marital partners, family members, friends, and professional counselors. Individuals in a marital union, however, may be poorly matched at the outset or may grow too far apart as each changes over time. Separation, divorce, or both may represent a creative and positive step rather than a failure for the partners, although it may increase the stress on the children.

Summary.   The common denominator of these myths is the idea that there is some substitute for the slow, painful, but ultimately exciting work of knowing the partner as a separate person and oneself as a person with separate ideas and needs for aloneness and togetherness. The important things to remember are that everyone needs positive feedback, and no one can read minds well enough to substitute for clear communication. Similarly, separation and divorce may or may not be best for the children and may or may not be a failure of the individual (although it feels like one to most people). A belief in the myths described in the preceding sections is often one cause of marital breakdown.

The Larger Social System and Dysfunction

Systems theory encompasses not only the family but also the wider community. The family is basically a subsystem of the community and of the culture in which it is embedded.

Families do not live in a vacuum. Often the culture around them puts enormous pressure on the family system. The fit between the family and the culture, in certain locations or in cases of immigration, may be problematic. For example, the only Jewish family living in an anti-Semitic small town may develop boundaries that in another situation would be called enmeshed but in this case are necessary to protect the children. A couple in an arranged marriage with a very traditional role structure who come to the United States can be torn apart if only the woman is able to get a job and be exposed to the new culture, thereby turning the family hierarchy upside down.

Traditional gender roles strongly affect the direction of family life. For example, a family with an overinvolved mother and a distant father is not just a family with problems; it is the end result of a historical and cultural pattern in which husbands are encouraged to see their worth as economic and wives are seen as the children's caretakers and keepers of hearth and home. In rigid or vulnerable families, this will create a huge gulf between the partners.

Commentary—The Development of Symptoms in a Particular Person

Marital and family systems, like individuals, have characteristic patterns of coping with stress. The family's first line of defense is usually to evoke, strengthen, and emphasize characteristic adaptive patterns that the family unit has used in the past. If these patterns are inappropriate or maladaptive, the type of disturbance resulting in the family may be similar to the rigid inflexible character of an individual with a personality disorder.

If characteristic adaptive mechanisms are not available or fail to deal adequately with the situation, one or another family member may also develop overt symptoms. These symptoms in the family member may cause the individual to be labeled as being bad or sick. The appropriate social institutions (police, child welfare, community mental health centers) may become involved with that individual in an attempt to deal with the particular symptomatic expression. The individual then takes on the role of the *identified patient*. More often than not, the family context from which the individual's symptoms emanate will be overlooked entirely, deemphasized, or inadequately attended to. The so-called bad, sick, stupid, or crazy individual family member will be treated and will be found either intractable or improved. If improved, he or she may soon become symptomatic again when returned to the family context or may cause another family member to become symptomatic. The underlying family disturbance will have to be treated. Often the symptom bearer is biologically vulnerable.

A major tenet of family therapy is that the symptomatic family member may be indicative of disturbance in the entire family system (Ackerman 1958; Bateson et al. 1956; Bell 1961; Carroll 1960; Counts 1967). If the therapist overlooks or deals inadequately with the more general family disturbance, family members are likely to continue to be symptomatic. Consider the following case examples:

> Mr. and Mrs. D found that over the course of 12 years of marriage their sexual relationship had become more and more unsatisfactory. They contemplated divorce. At about the same time, their son began to do poorly in school, and they sought help for this problem. Concurrently they felt less concerned about the dysfunctional nature of their marriage. As their son's schoolwork improved, the marital problem returned to the foreground.

Dr. E brought Mrs. E for individual psychotherapy because she had "headaches and depression." Her headaches always occurred after he had problems with his patients. Dr. E was a hardworking but rigid person who believed firmly in male superiority. Things had gone well for the couple in the early years of their marriage, until Mrs. E became dissatisfied with the role of number two in the marriage and pressed for equality. At that point, Dr. E intensified his authoritarian approach, especially when he felt helpless or unsuccessful at work, and rather than fighting back, Mrs. E became depressed.

The patterns of interaction within a family cannot always be clearly related to any specific dysfunction. The reasons that a specific type of disturbance is manifested in a family system or family member are not understood clearly, but certain innate tendencies and life circumstances probably favor the development of one or another symptomatic expression in a particular instance. Similarly, the reasons why one family member rather than another becomes symptomatic have not been definitively settled, although several reasons have been suggested to account for this phenomenon:

1. *Individual susceptibility, that is, genetic predisposition.* Biological disposition to an Axis I disorder such as schizophrenia, bipolar disorder, or attention-deficit/hyperactivity disorder, or a learning disability in a child, creates an increased vulnerability to illness in comparison with those born without such lesions. Inborn temperamental differences may contribute (Thomas and Chess 1985).

2. *The situation in the family at the time of birth.* For example, a parent whose own parent died around the time of the birth of a sibling might feel helpless about parenting.

3. *Physical illness of the child.* Family problems may be projected onto a child who is chronically ill whenever he or she has an acute episode. In addition, the amount of care needed by the ill child may skew family function, leading to infantilization of the ill child and to anger and resentment in well siblings.

4. *Precipitant in the extended family.* An accident or a death that relates somehow to one child more than another (e.g., an eldest daughter who was with her grandmother the day the grandmother had a heart attack) may make one family member the focus for family problems.

5. *Sex of a child.* A child's sex may correspond to a particular difficulty of the parent. For example, if a father feels particularly inadequate with other males, his son may become symptomatic.

6. *Birth order of siblings.* The eldest child may receive the major parental

pressure to mature quickly and perform well, whereas the youngest child is often babied and kept dependent.

7. *Family myth attached to a specific individual.* Certain family members may be known as the stupid one, the smart one, the lazy one, the good-looking one, or the ugly one. First names of children and nicknames may reveal these myths. Children are sometimes named after godparents or other people significant in the parents' past, and these children may carry along a myth attached to their namesake.

The symptomatic family member may be the family scapegoat, with family difficulties displaced on him or her, or this family member may be psychologically or constitutionally the weakest, the youngest, or the most sensitive family member, unable to cope with the generalized family disturbance. The identified patient may be the family member most interested or involved in the process of changing the family. For example, some teenagers want to "save" their parents because they are not getting along with each other. One hypothesis about family functioning is that these children may begin to steal in order to get caught, so that the entire family can be referred for help.

Life Cycle Problems and Dysfunction

Although some families may struggle with problems continually over their lives, others will experience difficulties only at specific life cycle periods. A family is subject to inner pressure coming from developmental changes in its own members and subsystems, and to outer pressure coming from demands to accommodate to the significant social institutions that affect family members. Episodic family problems may be related to 1) an inability to cope adequately with the tasks of the current family phase; 2) the need to move on to a new family phase; 3) the stress of unexpected, idiosyncratic events; or 4) all of these problems.

In the case of normative, expectable family life transitions, a family's inability to master the present tasks may be cause for the expression of symptoms. For example, two people optimally need to reach a certain stage in their own personal development, and in their relationships with their families of origin, before being ready as two independent individuals to consider marriage. To the extent that this and other prior stages are not mastered, the individuals and the marital unit will be hampered in dealing with current challenges. This same hypothesis can be applied to each of the family phases, wherein a family's skill at a particular stage may not necessarily transfer to similar capacities at the next developmental stage (e.g., a couple competent with younger children may find themselves overwhelmed and inadequately prepared for the challenges of adolescence).

Although expected developmental transitions may be stressful for family members, unexpected or idiosyncratic changes can be more difficult to handle. Unusual events in the family life cycle may overwhelm the coping capacities of family systems to handle developmental changes. Common examples of such events include unemployment, catastrophic illness, accidents, violent crime, or a death in the family. Any of these events may require the family to explore news ways of organizing itself temporarily to manage the additional strains posed by the event. Marital and family systems, like individuals, have characteristic patterns of coping with stress. As we have said, the family's first line of defense is usually to evoke, strengthen, and emphasize characteristic adaptive patterns that the family unit has used in the past. However, if these do not work, the family patterns may disorganize. From this may come serious dysfunction or a creative new solution.

Whatever the particulars of a family's dysfunction, by outlining the family's individual life cycle, the therapist helps in elucidating the family's idiosyncrasies and provides a framework from which successful therapy can begin (Carter and McGoldrick 1988).

Unresolved Grief

The death of a parent or a child, especially when mourning does not occur, commonly leads to family problems. Often the family development stops at the point of the death and the family remains in limbo, unable to move on or to truly grieve. This is often expressed in family ritual—for example, if a child died near Christmas, the family may be unable to celebrate for years to come, or the family may insist that the Christmas ritual be exactly the same as before the child died, long past the point at which the ritual would have changed to accommodate the other children. Death from stillbirth or miscarriage may have the same effect. Most often the family needs help to talk about the death and to find some way to grieve and continue living.

Toxic Secrets

Families may have secrets that some members know but others don't (e.g., the mother and daughter, but not the father, may know the daughter was raped), secrets that everyone knows but no one admits (e.g., the father has alcoholism), or secrets that most family members suspect but don't want to know about (e.g., the mother is having an affair). Secrets prevent clear communication, skew coalitions, and mystify children who know something is wrong but not what. Secrets contribute an air of unreality to the family, which is bad for children's development and reality testing. Thus, as part of life cycle problems at a certain point in time, a secret may result in dysfunction.

The therapist must find a way to uncover the secret carefully, giving time to support everyone in the family. It is seldom in the family's best interest for people to keep a major family secret. We return to this topic in Chapter 14 (on the subject of resistance) and again in Chapter 31 (in the context of ethics).

Task Performance in the Dysfunctional Family

Various deficiencies in carrying out the family's functions will lead to strains and distortions, problems, and symptoms in family life. The three major family tasks, as we discussed in Chapter 3, are 1) to provide for basic needs, 2) to develop a working marital coalition, and 3) to rear and socialize the offspring. In the dysfunctional family, these tasks either are not handled or are handled differently and less adaptively than in healthy families. In Chapter 3 we detailed some of these processes and outcomes for both functional and dysfunctional families.

Task performance in the family may be compromised by an unendurable environment, by the individual physical or mental illness of one or more family members, or by serious conflict among family members, particularly the marital dyad or adult caretakers.

Providing for the Family's Basic Needs

An inability to provide for the family's basic needs is common in times of war, poverty, or economic depression. Maintaining family integrity in the face of severe poverty requires ingenuity and endurance, which are hard to maintain on a daily basis if the adults become incapacitated or depressed. However, inability to provide for basic needs may occur in the face of adequate finances if the caretaking adults (especially the mother, who is most often left in charge of daily family functioning, even when ill) are absent due to drug or alcohol addiction, psychosis, or violence or are so caught up in their own concerns as to be oblivious to those in their care.

Maintaining a Functional Marriage: Issues of Sex, Intimacy, and Commitment

Marriage is one of the few human relationships that functions profoundly on two levels: as an intense love relationship and as a functional, daily economic partnership or small business. It requires a complex set of skills and feelings and the ability to switch from one functioning mode to another. It is possible, although not pleasant, to have a marriage in which intimacy has gone but the couple functions well on a "roommate" level to parent and keep the home going. In these couples, problem-solving skills and communication may be clear, but intimate contact is absent. These marriages often break up when the children leave. It is also possible to have a marriage in which sex and passion are very much present, but fierce battles over power and control issues make it very hard to get much done. As the couple becomes more dysfunctional, anger and rage overwhelm positive feelings, communication, and task completion, leaving the couple in a constant battle, isolated and silent, or with one spouse completely dominating the other. These couples are likely to triangle in a child, parent, or lover to deal with the stress.

Rearing and Socializing of Children

It is difficult to deal with the constant needs of children when one is overwhelmed by marital strife, individual illness or addiction, or racism and poverty. The more parents are disconnected from the part of themselves that is capable of nurturing, the more the children are neglected or become used to taking care of the parents—by being responsible for household tasks, providing emotional support to the parents, or by supporting one parent against the other. The ultimate form of using the child is incest, in which the child becomes a substitute sexual object. Children as young as 4 or 5 years can be inducted into trying to cheer up a depressed parent, making their own food because the parents have forgotten, or trying to shield a younger child from abuse.

Members of very troubled families may demonstrate styles of thinking and communication that are particularly difficult for children to understand, including intrusive, projective, or bizarre thinking. In some families the children's emotions are consistently denied, contradicted, ignored, or punished, leading to depression, rage, or numbing in the children.

It needs to be said, however, that some children are very difficult to deal with and make the task of childrearing formidable. Children with a difficult temperament, attention-deficit/hyperactivity disorder, or some forms of child psychosis require of their parents extraordinary reserves of patience and attention and have little ability to maintain impulse control or soothe themselves. The parents must maintain a calm, structured environment in the face of constant testing. If the parents do not share a commitment to put in extra time, or if they cannot reach agreement on ways to deal with the child, these children can cause major rifts in marriages that otherwise would function within the normal range. Other children might not be difficult for every parent but temperamentally are a bad fit with a particular parent. For example, a very active, mischievous boy might be a bad match for a fearful and depressed mother, who might have done better with a more docile and quiet child. Or a boy child who is shy and retiring might be a great disappointment to a tough, demanding, athletic father, who may try to toughen him up by being harsh in a way that leaves permanent emotional scars.

Summary

In this chapter we described 1) the process of how a family can become dysfunctional, 2) the systems perspective, 3) and how an inability to negotiate life cycle transitions or perform family tasks causes problems or symptoms. We return to this model in Section 4 (on treatment).

A dysfunctional family seldom has the internal resources to change because of the unwritten rules by which it operates. If it were to have these resources, then it could change and the family would not be dysfunctional. A member of the family may ask for external help for himself or another family member may try to harm herself, someone, or something and thus come to the attention of an external agency. To take the identified patient at face value and to deal only with that person, without seeing the rest of the family, would represent a distorted and limited perspective of the dysfunction inherent in the family.

A functional family is like an orchestra playing a beautiful symphony: Each of its members plays a different instrument, but together they add up to an overall configuration of harmony that is effective and fulfilling. Conversely, in a dysfunctional family this harmony is lacking, and there is a pervasive negative mood of unrelatedness. A dysfunctional family is like a poker game in which each player holds certain cards, yet no one will put them on the table. As a result, the same old game keeps being played. Because no one will risk losing (or winning) by playing a new card, in effect no one wins and no one loses, and the game becomes a pointless exercise. Alternatively, one player may win the same hollow victory repeatedly, and another may always be identified as the loser. These sequences characterize a couple or family in distress.

Suggested Readings

Clarkin JF, Miklowitz DJ: Marital and family communication difficulties, in DSM-IV Sourcebook, Vol 3. Edited by Widiger T, Frances AJ, Pincus H, et al. Washington, DC, American Psychiatric Association, 1997, pp 631–672
This book provides comprehensive background material summarizing data on family communication difficulties and the development of symptoms and problems.

Jacobson N, Christensen A: Integrative Couples Therapy: Promoting Acceptance and Change. New York, WW Norton, 1996
Using a cognitive-behavioral model of family dysfunction, the authors of this clearly written and easy-to-follow book discuss evaluations, formulation, and treatment.

Minuchin S: Families and Family Therapy. Cambridge, MA, Harvard University Press, 1974
This classic book clearly describes the structural approach to family therapy, focusing on both how to assess dysfunction and how to intervene with couples and families.

References

Ackerman N: Psychodynamics of Family Life, Diagnosis and Treatment in Family Relationships. New York, Basic Books, 1958

Bateson G, Jackson D, Haley J, et al: Toward a theory of schizophrenia. Behav Sci 1:251–254, 1956

Bell JE: Family group therapy. Public Health Monograph No 64. Washington, DC, Department of Health, Education and Welfare, Public Health Service, 1961

Bowen M: Family Therapy in Clinical Practice. New York, Jason Aronson, 1978

Carroll EJ: Treatment of the family as a unit. Pa Med 63:57–62, 1960

Carter B, McGoldrick M: Conceptual overview, in The Changing Family Life Cycle: A Framework for Family Therapy, 2nd Edition. Edited by Carter B, McGoldrick M. New York, Gardner, 1988, pp 3–25

Counts R: Family crisis and the impulsive adolescent. Arch Gen Psychiatry 17:64–71, 1967

Ferreira AJ: Family myths and homeostasis. Arch Gen Psychiatry 9:457–463, 1963

Imber-Black E: A family larger system perspective, in Handbook of Family Therapy, Vol 11. Edited by Gurman A, Kniskern D. New York, Brunner/Mazel, 1991, pp 583–605

Jackson DD, Yalom I: Family homeostasis and patient change, in Current Psychiatric Therapies. Edited by Masserman J. New York, Grune & Stratton, 1965, pp 155–165

Lewis JW: For better or worse: interpersonal relatinships and individual outcome. Am J Psychiatry 155:582–589, 1998

Lidz T: The Family and Human Adaptation. New York, International Universities Press, 1963

Minuchin S: Families and Family Therapy. Cambridge, MA, Harvard University Press, 1974

Papp P: The Process of Change. New York, Guilford, 1980

Reiss D: The working family: a researcher's view of health in the household. Am J Psychiatry 139:11–22, 1981

Thomas A, Chess S: Temperament and Development. New York, Guilford, 1985

Watzlawick P, Weakland J, Fisch R: Change: Principles of Problem Formation and Problem Resolution. New York, WW Norton, 1974

Wynne LC, Gurman A, Ravich R, et al: The family and marital therapies, in Treatment Planning in Psychiatry. Edited by Lewis JF, Usdin G. Washington, DC, American Psychiatric Association, 1982, pp 225–286

SECTION 3

Family Evaluation

The family therapist's first task is to evaluate the family's areas of function and dysfunction. His or her next task is to formulate an evaluation of what is wrong and finally what can be done about it.

In Chapter 6 we examine the *process* of conducting the family evaluation. In Chapter 7 we look at the *content* of the evaluation (i.e., what areas to cover). In Chapter 8 we discuss how to formulate the case, plan the therapeutic approach, and establish a treatment contract. We include in Chapter 8 a case example illustrating the process. Finally, in Chapter 9 we describe supplementary evaluation techniques that can be useful, depending on the clinical situation.

Andean Family, Hector Poleo, 1943. Courtesy of the Museum of Modern Art of Latin America, Organization of American States, Washington, D.C. Used with permission.

CHAPTER 6

The Process of Evaluation

Objectives for the Reader

ॐ To be able to gather historical data

ॐ To be cognizant of the progression and choice points of the evaluation interview

ॐ To understand the role of individual and family diagnoses in gathering data

Introduction

The evaluation of a married couple or a family should be understood as a continuing process, begun at the first contact but not necessarily completed at any particular point. Some initial formulation (i.e., an understanding of what is wrong) can help the therapist to gather data and form hypotheses, but in a larger sense the evaluation is often an inextricable part of the therapy itself. If patients can hear and analyze their histories, their present situations will change.

As data are gathered, the therapist forms hypotheses based on a conceptual frame of reference. The therapist should assign priorities and weights to the contributory variables, while setting up an overall intervention strategy. The particular intervention tactic(s) will, it is hoped, lead to desired therapy goals. In this process, further data are obtained that are used to confirm, modify, or negate the original hypotheses, strategies, and tactics. These later formulations are then tested in the matrix of the family sessions as further data are obtained. We describe details of this strategy and its tactics in Section 4, in which we explore in more depth various family therapy techniques.

Role of Historical Material

Several points of view exist regarding the type and quantity of historical data that should be gathered. Some family therapists begin with a specific and detailed longitudinal history of the family unit and its constituent members, that is, the *genogram*, which may span three or more generations (see Chapter 7). This method permits the family and the therapist to review together the complex background of the present situation. The therapist will begin to understand unresolved past and present issues, will usually gain a sense of rapport and identification with the family and its members, and may then feel more comfortable in defining problem areas and in planning strategy. The family benefits by reviewing together the source and evolution of its current condition, which may be a clarifying, empathy-building process for the entire family. The good and the bad are brought into focus, and the immediate distress is placed in a broader perspective. If a family in crisis is too impatient to tolerate exhaustive history gathering, lengthy data gathering must be curtailed.

Other therapists do not rely heavily on the longitudinal approach. They prefer to begin with a cross-sectional view of family functioning, delineating the situation that led the family to seek treatment at the present time. This cross-sectional view attempts instead to understand the current problem and to obtain a cross-sectional view of the family's present functioning. This procedure has the advantage of starting with the problems about which the family is most concerned and is not as potentially time-consuming nor as seemingly remote from the present realities as is the longitudinal method. The therapist, however, may not emerge with as sharp a focus on important family patterns, because much of the discussion may be negatively tinged as a result of the family's preoccupation with its current difficulty.

A minority of therapists may severely curtail history gathering and may also minimize formalized discussions of the family's current situation. They may begin instead by dealing with the family's important characteristic patterns of interaction as they are manifested in the interview setting. They may tend to use primarily or exclusively the immediate here-and-now observable family transactions, interpreting these to be characteristic of the family. They may clarify and comment on these transactions, intervening in a variety of ways. Observation of the interactions among family members provides the therapist with raw data rather than historical reconstruction.

A family's biography is an altered history bent through the prism of the person telling the story. History reported by involved individuals must be considered as potentially biased secondhand information because the therapist is not witnessing the dysfunction described. The information will vary sharply among the historians, and key pieces of information may be omitted. Despite a caution about using parents' retrospective recall of early events, Robins's (1983) work comparing recall and records demonstrated that recall correlated well with the records, which suggests that retrospective reporting might be sufficiently valid to produce information useful for the family therapist. This correlation held true for all age groups surveyed. Life history material collected in a single interview, even about behaviors occurring many years previously, is strongly predictive of recent symptoms. This includes events that the reporter has no reason to believe are related to those childhood behaviors. In addition, because beliefs about an event or situation affect behavior, an individual's story, accurate or not, is a crucial part of that person's history.

A present-oriented approach has the advantage of initiating treatment immediately, without the usual delay of history gathering. There is often a heightened sense of emotional involvement, which may cause more rapid changes to occur. Sometimes families are overwhelmed by such an approach, however, feeling threatened and defensive. When specific information and patterns are allowed to emerge in this random fashion, the therapist does not always have the same degree of certainty as to whether the emerging family patterns are indeed relevant and important. As a result, such an approach is not usually recommended for beginning therapists.

To a considerable extent these differences in technique may mirror differences in therapists' training, theoretical beliefs, and temperaments. Most therapists probably use combinations of these approaches as the situation warrants, for there is no evidence that one technique is superior to the others. We recommend reviewing both past and present and gathering a three- or four-generation genogram.

We recommend reviewing *both* past and present and gathering a three- or four-generation genogram.

Whom to Include in the Family Evaluation

An early and strategic question involves which members of the family to include in the evaluation sessions. From the very first contact, usually by telephone call, the therapist often talks to one individual who represents the family and presents the problem. Sometimes the problem is presented as a family problem; other times the problem is presented as an individual's problem that is disturbing other family members. We assume here that, from the first telephone call or contact by a family member, the therapist is considering the possibility of family intervention. Thus the question arises of who to include in the evaluation sessions. Most family therapists would agree that it is important, from the first session, to include all members of the family in the evaluation sessions. This usually means all members of a nuclear family, that is, mother, father, and children who reside under the same roof. Relatives living with the family should probably also be included at some point. It is obviously impractical and often unnecessary to include, for example, an adult child who lives 2,000 miles away from his or her parents, at least for the first sessions. In addition to nuclear family members, significant others must be included if they are living with or deeply involved with the children. This is especially true in single-parent or stepparent families. Therapists seeing a custodial parent and child need to make a very serious effort to include the noncustodial parent at some point early in therapy.

Clinical experience suggests that it is easier to include all family members for evaluation sessions at the beginning than it is to wait until later to do so. This provides a clearer picture of family dynamics and allows better evaluation of family problems. If the therapist begins with all family members, including the couple and the children, then he or she can hold subsequent sessions with one subsystem alone.

Particular circumstances may occur when the therapist would not want to include the whole family in the evaluation sessions. For example, a couple who are having sexual difficulties should be seen as a couple without their children. Likewise, the couple may be seen alone for what they identify as marital difficulties without involving the children, although the children may be included later, if appropriate. Many therapists will see both spouses together in an initial evaluation session, followed by an individual session with each spouse alone. Although some authors would say that such a situation encourages one spouse to tell secrets to the therapist, others suggest that the only way for a therapist to proceed is to have all information at the beginning. Some therapists would have individual sessions with each spouse but indicate before the session that it is not confidential to the couple sessions, thus precluding the forming of coalitions and yet possibly discouraging the full disclosure of information. Some parents will insist on "checking out" the therapist before bringing the children in.

A practical consideration that often arises is the issue of evaluation sessions when one or more central family members are absent. Missing family members often have crucial roles in the problem, and their absence must be discussed and the members' presence brought about. Napier and Whitaker (1978) provide an interesting clinical illustration of a family in which the initial evaluation session is stopped because of a missing son and the family's task becomes insisting on his participation. It is probably not an uncommon practice of family therapists to refuse to proceed with the evaluation until the missing member is present; however, some therapists will do a few sessions without a missing member, focusing on how the missing member could be convinced to come in as one of the treatment issues. If, for example, a major family problem has been a couple's inability to put limits on their 16-year-old son, refusing to treat them until they bring him in would result in their giving up on treatment. A better move might be to make the focus of treatment with the couple a discussion of how they could set enough limits to get their child to come in.

Progression of the Family Evaluation Interview

Several authors have discussed the sequential progression of the family evaluation interview (Haley 1976; Minuchin 1974). Most would suggest that the first interview task is to greet each of the family members and to begin to accommodate to the family. This *accommodation* is accomplished by noting the power system of the family and using the family vocabulary that surfaces. Next, the interview can proceed to some delineation of the family problem as each family member sees it.

Reiss (1981) has provided a helpful analysis of the choice points that a clinician faces in the initial assessment of a family. He distinguishes substantive or theoretical choice points from technical choice points.

The first substantive choice point is whether to focus on the cross-sectional view (i.e., current functioning of the family) or to give more attention to the longitudinal developmental history of the family unit and its individuals. A second choice point is whether to focus on the family as the central shaping force or to focus on the extended family system or larger community/social systems that influence the family. The latter would include focus on the network of kin and friends, the school, and so on. A third choice point concerns crisis versus character orientation. The former is a focus on the current immediate concrete problem or symptom that brings the family in, whereas the latter is a focus on the more enduring patterns of self-protection, cognitive and affective style, and deficits that the family manifests. Another choice point is whether to focus on the pathology or the functional competence of the family unit. A fifth choice point concerns the basic theoretical understanding of the evaluator and his or her emphasis on finding family themes versus looking at concrete behaviors and their consequences. In the psychodynamic tradition, there is an emphasis on discovering the thematic or underlying structures that give family life and behavior their meaning and thrust. In contrast, therapists with a behavioral orientation focus on the problem behaviors and their antecedent and consequent events.

The first technical choice point concerns the pacing of the assessment. Some authors advocate a thorough assessment before beginning treatment, with a clear marker between the assessment and the treatment; others emphasize that assessment and treatment merge, especially because assessment involves intervening and assessing how the family responds. A second technical choice point involves individualized measurement of the family (emphasizing the uniqueness of the family) or standardized measurement of the family (focusing on major dimensions relevant to all families). In Chapter 8 we discuss another choice point involving assessment: the issue of dimensionalizing the data (e.g., how does the family rate on communication), focusing on the typology of the family (e.g., the enmeshed family). Another choice point is the clinician's perspective of being "inside," emphatically feeling what it is like to be with this family, versus observing as objectively as possible (as an outsider) how the family performs and carries out functions. A final choice point is whether to focus on the children or adults, and whether the method should involve talking or an activity.

These choice points are not either-or situations, and depending on the situation, the evaluation will emphasize different areas. But these choice points must be faced (in the time-limited setting of conducting evaluations).

For those fortunate enough to work in training centers or nonsolo practices, an effective way of evaluating families is with a team behind a one-way mirror. The experience of being behind a mirror and watching is fundamentally different from being in the room. Although subtle emotional cues or anxiety or connection is often missed by not being in the room, the overall pattern, including the relationship of the therapist to the family, is more clear. With a team, one can obtain many differing viewpoints. It is humbling but invaluable to see how the understanding of a family is affected by the personality, age, and gender of the viewer, and the process opens up many different realities for the therapist.

Role of Individual and Family Diagnoses

In deciding who to include in the family assessment, the question must be expanded to consider the purpose for which an individual is included in the assessment. In this book our bias is that both the family and the individuals in the family unit are important in the diagnostic equation.

In psychiatry an imperfect relationship exists between individual diagnosis and treatment planning because often the diagnosis itself does not give enough information to plan the interventions. This imperfect relationship between diagnosis and treatment planning is compounded in the area of family therapy, where one must have enough information to give an individual diagnosis (especially if there is a clearly identified patient) and also make a family diagnostic statement.

The first implication is that in assessing families one must obtain enough individual information to be able to give individual DSM-IV (American Psychiatric Association 1994) diagnoses to members exhibiting pathology that meets the diagnostic criteria. There is no central place in DSM-IV for family pathology; however, Axis I does include a section titled "Other conditions that may be a focus of clinical attention" (Table 6–1). Subsumed (or embedded) in this section is the category of relational problems (Table 6–2).

In practice, DSM-IV has had a narrow limit of usefulness for many family therapists. From the point of view of the framers of DSM-IV, its lack of any emphasis on the classification of family pathology was necessary, given both the purpose and the individual orientation of DSM-IV and the current lack of research evidence correlating various methods of classifying family pathology and outcome. Axis IV, the rating of psychosocial stressors and environmental problems, may be most helpful in indicating patients for whom family problems are prominent. Although there are many proposed typologies of family functioning, we think that family typologizing is less helpful than dimensional statements concerning the family and its functioning, as outlined in the family diagnostic outline we present in Chapters 7 and 8.

We discuss these issues again in Chapter 8 as they relate to case formulation and in Chapter 24 in the context of the relationship between the family and individual psychiatric disorders. For now, let us emphasize that although not all family therapists use DSM-IV criteria, we believe that family members must be assessed at least enough to determine the presence of serious psychopathology and the need for medication.

TABLE 6–1. DSM-IV Axis I clinical disorders

Disorders usually first diagnosed in infancy, childhood, or adolescence (excluding mental retardation, which is diagnosed on Axis II)

Delirium, dementia, and amnestic and other cognitive disorders

Mental disorders due to a general medical condition not elsewhere classified

Substance-related disorders

Schizophrenia and other psychotic disorders

Mood disorders

Anxiety disorders

Somatoform disorders

Factitious disorders

Dissociative disorders

Sexual and gender identity disorders

Eating disorders

Sleep disorders

Impulse-control disorders not elsewhere classified

Adjustment disorders

Other conditions that may be a focus of clinical attention

Source. *Diagnostic and Statistical Manual of Mental Disorders,* 4th Edition. Washington, DC, American Psychiatric Association, 1994. Copyright 1994, American Psychiatric Association. Reprinted with permission.

TABLE 6–2. DSM-IV relational problems

Code	Diagnostic category
V61.9	Relational problem related to a mental disorder or general medical condition
V61.20	Parent-child relational problem
V61.10	Partner relational problem
V61.8	Sibling relational problem
V62.81	Relational problem not otherwise specified

Source. *Diagnostic and Statistical Manual of Mental Disorders,* 4th Edition. Washington, DC, American Psychiatric Association, 1994, pp. 680–681. Copyright 1994, American Psychiatric Association. Reprinted with permission.

Suggested Readings

Haley J: Problem-Solving Therapy, 2nd Edition. San Francisco, CA, Jossey-Bass, 1991

This clearly written book presents a practical, learnable framework for thinking about problems from a systemic perspective and intervening directly to change family patterns. The format for first interviews remains a standard after many years.

Imber-Black E: A family larger system perspective, in Handbook of Family Therapy, Vol 2. Edited by Gurman A, Kniskern D. New York, Brunner/Mazel, 1991, pp 583–605

Understanding the larger systems context of the family's problems is an overlooked aspect of family assessment. This chapter presents concisely some of the rationales for a broader systemic view and offers concrete suggestions for how to obtain these data.

Kerr M, Bowen M: Family Evaluation. New York, WW Norton, 1988

This book presents the clearest description of Bowen's family systems theory approach. The authors explain in straightforward language clinical concepts such as differentiation of self, and they describe elegantly the framework for clinical intervention.

Reiss D: The Family's Construction of Reality. Cambridge, MA, Harvard University Press, 1981

This book describes the logic underlying the clinical evaluation congruent with the family's view of function and dysfunction.

References

American Psychiatric Association: Diagnostic and Statistical Manual of Mental Disorders, 4th Edition. Washington, DC, American Psychiatric Association, 1994, pp 13–24

Haley J: Problem-Solving Therapy, 2nd Edition. San Francisco, CA, Jossey-Bass, 1991

Minuchin S: Families and Family Therapy. Cambridge, MA, Harvard University Press, 1974

Napier A, Whitaker C: The Family Crucible. New York, Harper & Row, 1978

Reiss D: The Family's Construction of Reality. Cambridge, MA, Harvard University Press, 1981

Robins LN: Lecture I: How population studies changed our view of psychiatric disorder. Lecture II: New findings on childhood conduct problems. 51st Thomas William Salmon Lectures. New York Academy of Medicine, December 1, 1983

Crossroads, Juannie Eng, 1998. Private collection.

CHAPTER 7

The Content of Evaluation

Objectives for the Reader

- To be aware of the information needed (i.e., the dimensions for each category in the family evaluation outline)
- To be aware of the salient content areas of family evaluation

Introduction

In Chapter 6 we indicated that there is more than one potentially useful way to evaluate a family, depending on the situation. The procedure we offer in this chapter combines useful aspects of the longitudinal and cross-sectional approaches we discussed in Chapter 6. In Chapter 9 we explore other evaluative techniques. These approaches combine both verbal and nonverbal techniques for obtaining information. In Chapter 13 we discuss in greater detail the process of gathering information over the course of therapy.

Because one cannot evaluate everything about a family without getting lost in the details, both the trainee and the experienced family therapist need an outline that indicates not only what to evaluate but also the priorities of evaluation. Such an outline is analogous to the outline used for assessing individual patients (i.e., chief complaint, present illness, and so on), which every medical student and resident has committed to memory. The theory of family functioning and its relationship to the cause and maintenance of pathology in an individual family member should in part guide and prioritize such an evaluation.

Dimensions of Family Function

Because of its thoroughness, operational definitions, congruence with the major areas of family functioning or dysfunction mentioned in Chapters 3–5, teachableness, and relevance to treatment planning, we recommend a modified version of the McMaster model of family evaluation (Epstein and Bishop 1981). According to this model, five dimensions of family functioning must be assessed. These dimensions are congruent with the concepts of functional and dysfunctional families (enumerated in Chapters 3–5) and are congruent with the consensus areas of importance across family models. These dimensions are communication, problem solving, roles and coalitions, affective responsiveness and involvement, and behavior control. The therapist must also carefully evaluate the family members' beliefs about themselves and about the problem. Finally, the family's cultural background and its patterns of beliefs and values must be assessed.

Family Evaluation Outline

Drawing heavily from the McMaster model and integrating other aspects, we developed the evaluation outline presented in Table 7–1. This outline offers a practical alternative to either gathering an extensive history or plunging into the middle of the family interaction. Although far from exhaustive in scope, this outline provides some anchoring points for initial understanding and planning. It is not meant to be inflexible or unchangeable, and it certainly can be expanded or contracted as the situation warrants. We cover the first two outline topics in this chapter and the third topic (i.e., formulating the family problem areas) in Chapter 8. In Section 4 we discuss the last topic, relating to treatment.

Gathering Identifying Data and Establishing Current Phase of Family Life Cycle

Family members' names, ages, and relationships and the family's composition, ethnicity, socioeconomic status, and living arrangements should be obtained early. To identify the current phase of the family life cycle, the therapist will ascertain the ages and relationships of those family members living under one roof, adult children living separately, and ages of grandparents. An important criterion for understanding the family's structure is knowing each phase the family has reached in its developmental cycle. Each phase is associated with unique stresses, challenges, opportunities, and pitfalls. By be-

TABLE 7–1.   Family evaluation outline

I.   Gathering identifying data and establishing current phase of family life cycle

II.   Gathering explicit interview data:

     A. What is the current family problem?

     B. Why does the family come for treatment at the present time?

       1. Recent family events and stresses

     C. What is the background of the family problem?

     D. What is the history of past treatment attempts or other attempts at problem solving in the family? What other problems has the family had?

     E. What are the family's goals and expectations of the treatment? What are its strengths, motivations, and resistances?

III.   Formulating the family problem areas:

     A. Rating important dimensions of family functioning:

       1. Communication

       2. Problem solving

       3. Roles and coalitions

       4. Affective responsiveness and involvement

       5. Behavior control

       6. Operative family beliefs and stories

     B. Family classification and diagnosis

IV.   Planning the therapeutic approach and establishing the treatment contract

Source.   In developing this outline, we adapted material from three major sources: 1) Gill M, Newman R, Redlich F: *The Initial Interview in Psychiatric Practice.* New York, International Universities Press, 1954. 2) Group for the Advancement of Psychiatry: *The Case History in the Study of Family Process.* Report No 76. New York, Group for the Advancement of Psychiatry, 1970. 3) The McMaster Model, found in Epstein NB, Bishop DS: "Problem-Centered Systems Therapy of the Family," in *Handbook of Family Therapy.* Edited by Gurman AS, Kniskern DP. New York, Brunner/Mazel, 1981, pp 444–482.

ing alert to these, the therapist is in a position to observe and explore phase-specific tasks, roles, and relationships for the family. The therapist can also discover to what extent the family members clearly recognize and are attempting to cope with issues relevant to the family's current developmental phase. For many married couples and families, the basic difficulty underlying the need for professional help can be related to their inability to cope satisfactorily with their current developmental phase or with the transition into the next phase. The A family (see the first case example in this chapter) is a good example of the type of problem arising in a later stage of marriage—the empty-nest syndrome—in which the parents could not cope with the separation of their child from the home, in part because of their fear of being alone as husband and wife.

One or both parents may be going through an individual developmental phase that powerfully affects the family life cycle. For example, the birth of a baby to a 40-year-old mother and a 60-year-old father may be in conflict with the father's sense of aging and his thoughts of ease and retirement. Alternatively, it might bring both parents a sense of renewed youth and empowerment.

Gathering Explicit Interview Data

What is the current family problem? The interviewer asks this question of each family member, in turn, with all family members present. The interviewer attempts to maintain the focus on the current family problem, rather than on one or another individual, or on past difficulties. Each family member receives an equal opportunity to be heard, without interruption, and to feel that his or her opinions and views are worthwhile, important, and acknowledged. The interviewer will begin to note what frames of reference the family members use in discussing their difficulties. By *frames of reference* we mean whether there exists a family or an individual problem, which individuals seem to be bearing the brunt of the blame, how the identified problem members deal with their role, who has overt power in the family, where the alliances exist in the family, who seems to get interrupted by whom, who speaks for whom, who seems fearful or troubled about expressing an opinion, who sits next to whom, and so forth.

A family's nonverbal communication is a key to family patterning. It is also often more difficult to follow and interpret than verbal communication. Videotaping a family interaction is one way to closely observe nonverbal communication, which may be expressed by a child who twiddles his thumbs in the same way as his mother, a father whose facial expression and bodily movements indicate the opposite of what he is saying, or a parent who stares off into space when his adolescent daughter yells. All of these observations are as valuable as some of the verbal comments that the family may make to the interviewer.

Why does the family come for treatment at the present time? The answer to this question helps to shift the focus of difficulty closer to the current situation and also provides an opportunity for further specifying of the factors that led to family distress. Various types of last-straw situations usually present the important patterns of family interaction in a microcosm (i.e., what may have been going on for long periods). Consider the following case example:

Mr. and Mrs. A's son, age 25 years, has had symptoms of paranoid schizophrenia for many years. His parents allowed him to sleep in their bedroom at night. On the day after he moved out to his own apartment, Mr. and Mrs. A began to blame each other for their son's behavior and sought attention because their son was "out on the streets where anything could happen." Their son had maintained an uneasy balance between the parents by staying in the parental bedroom at night, thus obviating their need for intimacy or sex. It was only when he moved out that the parents' problem came into sharp focus.

The clarification of why the family is seeking treatment *now* also helps alert the therapist to any acute crisis situation that may need either the therapist's or the family's immediate intervention. The answer will be relevant, too, in assessing the goals the family has in mind for the therapy and the degree to which it is motivated to seek help.

Most often it is the wife who requests psychotherapy for herself or who brings the family under protest. This most commonly reflects the wife's greater sense of responsibility for the family's emotional functioning, her willingness to accept blame or guilt, and her willingness to seek and accept expert help, rather than being a reflection of a greater degree of intrapsychic disturbance. With the popularization of therapy and family therapy, in particular since the 1970s, men have become more attuned to family issues and more comfortable with therapy as a possible solution. The therapist must understand that there are usually very different levels of motivation in different family members, whether split on gender or other lines.

The therapist must be sure to determine the referral context and history. This includes referral source(s), conflict and agreement among family members or referral source(s), current involvement in other treatment (including medical), history of treatment (type, hospitalization, outcome, and satisfaction), and presence of other informal advisors such as extended family members or clergy.

What is the background of the family problem?

1. *Composition and characteristics of the nuclear and extended family, such as age, sex, occupation, financial status (including differences between husband's and wife's income, and joint financial status), race, class, and ethnicity.* Couples from ethnic groups with widely differing traditions or communication styles will often have communication problems. If the couple have moved up or down a social class from their parents' generation, this is important to note. The therapist can use a three-generation

genogram. (See section "The Family Genogram" later in this chapter, where genograms are discussed and are shown in Figures 7–1 and 7–2).

2. *Developmental history and patterns of each family member.* The therapist should evaluate individual family members' life histories in terms of patterns of adaptation, including an impression of how the individual manages affects, frustration, and identity outside the family. Although somewhat outside the scope of a family therapy text, our bias is that the evaluator should not underestimate the importance of individual styles of adaptation, the use of defenses and resistances, tolerance of stress and ego strengths, signs and symptoms of any mental disorder, and the capacity of each person to be supportive and empathic to his or her partner.

3. *Developmental history and patterns of the nuclear family unit.* The therapist should explore the longitudinal course of the family unit with reference to the role of the spouses' individual expectations, values, goals, and conflicts in their relationship; the effect of each partner's adaptive patterns on the other partner; how gender roles have been expressed over time in the family; the need for control by one partner or the other, including how control is obtained and maintained; the existence of mutual trust and ability to share; the importance of individual and mutual dependence issues; and the family's ability to deal effectively with its earlier life phases (in the family's life cycle).

4. *Current family interactional patterns (internal and external).* Here the therapist considers and rates dimensions of family function by observation. The therapist also questions the family about their sense of these patterns. Is the power structure flexible, rigid, or chaotic? Are the generation boundaries intact, blurred, or broken? Is there an affiliative or oppositional style? What degree of individuation is noted? Is there clarity of communication, tolerance for ambivalence and disagreement, respect for others' differentness versus attempts at control or intrusiveness, responsiveness to others, ability to deal realistically with separation and loss? Do the family beliefs seem congruent to the situation? What is the overall family affect: that of warmth, humor, caring, hope, tenderness, and the ability to tolerate open conflicts, or that of constricted, unpleasant, hostile, depressive, or resentful behavior?

This part of the evaluation—the background of the family problem—lends itself to expansion or contraction, depending on the circumstances. For example, a very specific examination of a particular part of the family's current functioning or history might be thought relevant in a particular instance. In another situation, only a brief amount of background data might be gathered initially, with the feeling that more would come out as the treatment sessions proceeded. In any event, the therapist would always want to identify the important participants in the family's current interactions, the quality of the relationships, and the developmental patterns of the family unit over a period of time.

What is the history of past treatment attempts or other attempts at problem solving in the family? It usually is illuminating to understand the circumstances that have led a married couple or a family to seek assistance in the past, from what sort of helpers this assistance was elicited, and the outcome of the assistance. Experience in previous help-seeking efforts illuminates more clearly the family processes and possible therapist traps, and it delineates useful strategies. Past help-seeking patterns are often useful predictors of what the present experience will be both in family therapy and in other therapies.

> Mr. and Mrs. B presented for treatment with the complaint that they could not get along with each other and were contemplating divorce. They gave a history of being in family therapy several years earlier. They had some 20 sessions, which "of course led to nothing." In discussion with the couple and the former therapist, the present therapist discovered that the couple had spent most of the sessions blaming each other and attempting to change each other, rather than making any change in their relationship or in themselves. In addition, Mr. B, who was quite authoritarian, had persuaded the former therapist to line up on his side and say that his wife was quite unreasonable. This treatment had been unsuccessful. The strategy in this case was to go over, in detail, the past problems in treatment, suggest that the present therapist would not be a judge, and explain that the focus was to be on the couple's relationship and on each partner's own responsibility for change in the self rather than on what the other partner would have to do.

Often one spouse has been in intensive individual psychotherapy to seek help with the marital relationship. When this therapy has been unsuccessful, both therapist and patient may blame the failure on the spouse not in treatment. This situation may exacerbate the difficulty and lead to separation or divorce.

> Mrs. C sought individual therapy because she felt her husband was inadequate. Her own life had been replete with difficulties, starting from the time her parents had died in an automobile accident when she was 2 years old. She had lived in various orphanages, had been married twice by the time she was 22 years old,

and experienced periodic bouts of alcoholism and depression. She felt that her present marriage of 5 years was acceptable until she had children. She felt that although she had some difficulty in raising the children, the real problem was with her husband. She went into individual psychotherapy three times a week and in the course of this therapy began to "see quite clearly what a loser he was." Although Mrs. C's therapist struggled valiantly to point out her own difficulties at first, he, too, began to see the difficulties in the husband. The husband himself was never called into therapy, and after 2 years of treatment the couple were still experiencing the same problems and were contemplating divorce. A consultant suggested marital therapy.

What are the family's goals and expectations of the treatment? What are its members' motivations and resistances? Some families come to treatment with short-term goals, such as finalizing a fairly well-thought-out separation between husband and wife. Others come with more long-term goals, such as making a basic change in how the family functions. Other families come because of an individual-oriented goal (e.g., mother's depressed; they are there to help her), whereas still others come because of a family goal (e.g., "the family isn't functioning right"). If the goals are individual oriented, the therapist's task is to translate for the family the relationship between the symptoms and the family process. Initial goals may be at times unclear or unrealistic. In such instances the therapist and the family must work out from the beginning an appropriate and clear set of goals (see Chapter 11).

The married couple or the family presumably will have certain types of positive hopes and motivations for seeking help but at the same time will have some hesitations, doubts, and fears. One of the therapist's tasks is to explore and reinforce the positive motivations, to clarify them, and to keep them readily available throughout the process of therapy, which at times may be stormy and stressful. In marital therapy the motivation of each partner for conjoint therapy should be evaluated. The evaluation should include the partners' stated commitment to the marriage, the evaluator's opinion of their commitment to therapy, the reality of their treatment expectations, and the opinions of other interested parties (e.g., parents, friends, and sometimes lovers), as related by the pair.

The positive expectations, goals, and motivations keep the family members in treatment, and every effort should be made to ensure that each family member will benefit from the family therapy sessions both as individuals and as concerned members of the family. It is helpful for family members and the therapist to work out these expectations explicitly.

Ideally each involved family member will understand the positive reasons for his or her own participation and understand the more general family system goals. At the same time the therapist must be aware of individual and family resistance before they undermine the successful implementation or continuation of treatment. The therapist's clinical judgment will suggest when such fears and resistances need immediate attention and when they only need to be kept in mind as potentially major obstacles.

Such resistances may be of various sorts. Although some may be specific to particular families, many are general concerns. Among these is the feeling that the situation may be made worse by treatment; that some member of the family will become guilty, depressed, angry, or fearful as a result of the treatment; that a family member may go crazy; that the family may split up; that there is no hope for change and it is already too late for help; that shameful or damaging family secrets may have to be revealed; or that perhaps it would be better to stick to familiar patterns of family interaction, no matter how unsatisfying they may be, rather than attempt to change them in new and therefore frightening directions. (Chapter 14 is devoted to a more detailed review of resistance to treatment.)

> Mrs. D felt that to continue in marital treatment after her recovery from an acute psychotic episode might mean that she would go crazy again. She believed that she and her husband would have to explore their unsatisfactory marriage and that this might lead to separation or divorce. She also felt that she would have to be strong and powerful to prevent her husband from committing suicide as his father had done. Mr. D, for his part, had a very obsessional personality structure with little interpersonal sensitivity or emotional awareness. He felt angry at psychiatrists and was insecure and threatened by the therapist as a male role model. The therapist working with this couple would need to look for and stress the couple's strengths and allow them to avoid discussing areas of maximal sensitivity before they were ready.

The Family Genogram

Even in the absence of a comprehensive assessment scheme such as our family evaluation outline, the family genogram remains an extremely useful tool for the assessment of couples and families. The genogram, developed by Bowen (1978), is a graphic depiction of the patient and several generations of his or her family, noting important dates (e.g., births, deaths, marriages, separations), occupational role, and major life events such as illness. The genogram uses symbols and conventions to note the important information, as shown in Figure 7–1. A good example of a genogram is shown in Figure 7–2. For the sake of clarity, the example is drawn without symbols. Usually the genogram

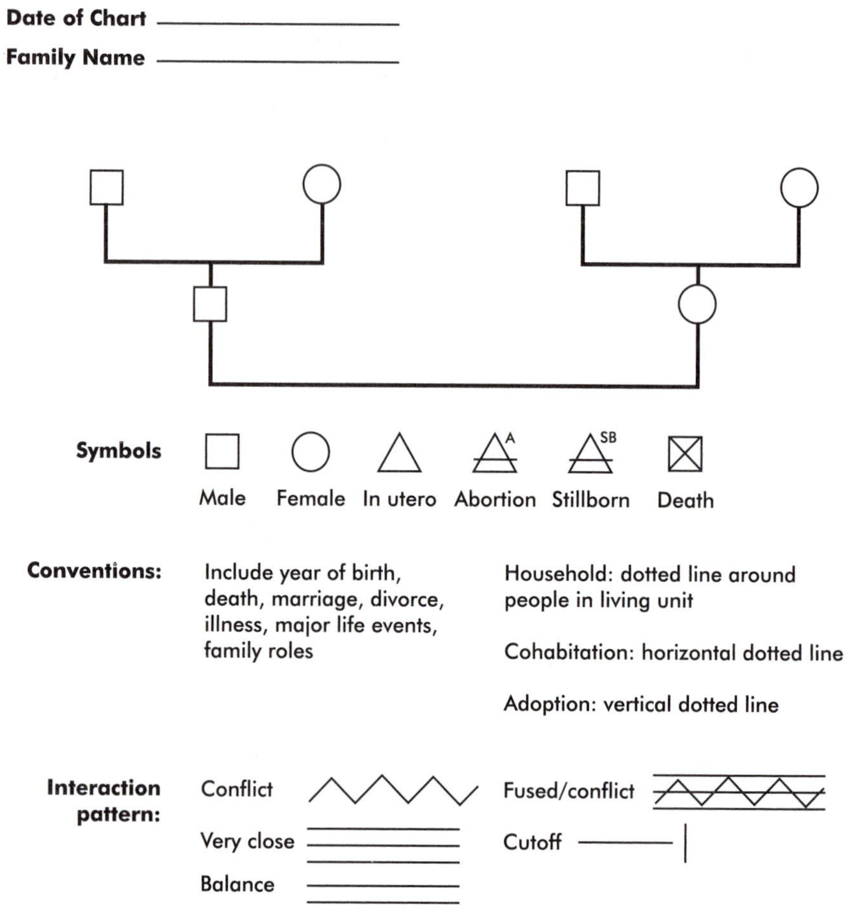

Date of Chart ——————————————

Family Name ——————————————

FIGURE 7–1.   The family genogram and symbols.

is completed during the beginning phases of treatment and serves many purposes, related to both process and content:

1. It provides the patient, family, and family therapist with a structure with which to explore current difficulties and their background.

2. It gives the therapist background information with which to put current difficulties in context.

3. Through the process of gathering the information, it may give the patient some conception, distance, and control over the emotional tugs and pulls created by the family.

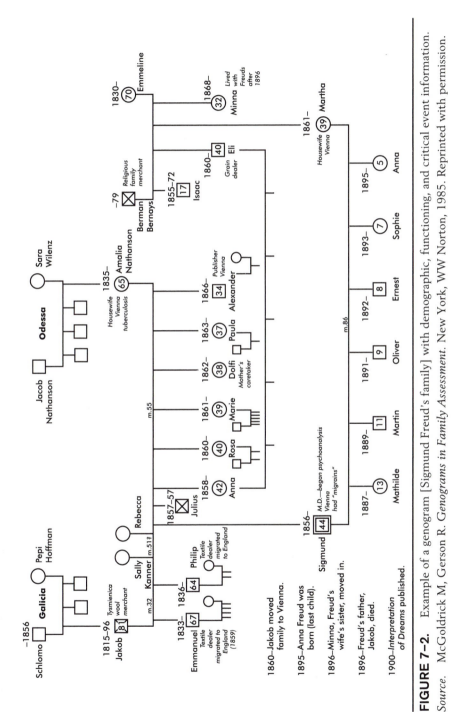

FIGURE 7–2. Example of a genogram [Sigmund Freud's family] with demographic, functioning, and critical event information.

Source. McGoldrick M, Gerson R. *Genograms in Family Assessment.* New York, WW Norton, 1985. Reprinted with permission.

4. It can be used later in the therapy to set realistic goals for dealing with the emotional strains of the family system in the future.

The genogram displays information about the family in an accessible graphic fashion so that the therapist and family can begin to understand how present family circumstances may be linked to the family's evolving context of relationships. McGoldrick and Gerson (1985) have written the most comprehensive text to date on using the genogram. They provide a format for the standard genogram symbols and outline the principles underlying the effective application and interpretation of the genogram. Figure 7–1 shows the genogram form used in the Couples and Family Therapy Clinic at Stanford University Medical Center. Therapists routinely collect this information from the couple or family, often on a whiteboard, so that family members can observe it unfolding and make additional contributions. Clinicians then transcribe the data onto the form shown in the figure and include them in the patient's clinical chart. Genograms should be a routine part of any assessment.

Final Note

A family therapist must be competent and knowledgeable about a variety of evaluation techniques while remaining maximally flexible and comfortable in adjusting his or her methods to make an evaluation work for the individual family.

Suggested Readings

Bloch S, Hafner J, Harari E, et al: The Family in Clinical Psychiatry. Oxford, England, Oxford University Press, 1994
Written for clinicians, this book has an excellent chapter on family assessment, including a discussion of genograms and circular questioning.

McGoldrick M, Gerson R: Genograms in Family Assessment. New York, WW Norton, 1985
This manual provides the best practical introduction to constructing genograms. It is easy to read, nontechnical, and straightforward. The genograms of famous people alone make the book worth reading.

Weber T, McKeever J, McDaniel S: A beginner's guide to the problem-oriented first family interview. Fam Process 24:357–364, 1985
Family therapy trainees routinely find useful this step-by-step introduction to problem-focused interviewing.

References

Bowen M: Family Therapy in Clinical Practice. New York, Jason Aronson, 1978

Epstein NB, Bishop DS: Problem-centered systems therapy of the family, in Handbook of Family Therapy. Edited by Gurman AS, Kniskern DP. New York, Brunner/Mazel, 1981, pp 444–482

McGoldrick M, Gerson R: Genograms in Family Assessment. New York, WW Norton, 1985

Family Group, Henry Moore, 1948. Courtesy of the Hakone Open-Air Museum, Hakone, Japan. Used with permission.

CHAPTER 8

Formulating an Understanding of the Family Problem Areas

Objectives for the Reader

⟡ To be able to detail the clinically significant dimensions of family functioning and dysfunction in order to formulate an evaluation of the family

⟡ To examine the process of treatment planning and establishing the treatment contract

⟡ To be able to formulate important problem areas in preparation for planning and choosing the therapeutic approach

⟡ To be able to apply the concepts of treatment planning to a clinical case

Introduction

Meeting with the family, the therapist experiences its patterns of interaction and uses the data obtained to begin formulating a concept of the family's problems. These formulations come from historical material and from direct observations made during contact with the family. The data gathered should permit the therapist to pinpoint dimensions or aspects of the family functioning, and its individual members, that may require special attention. As data are gathered, the therapist notes areas of health and dysfunction and creates a priority list for addressing problems. Prioritizing a family's problems allows the therapist to focus on the relative severity of the problems, establishing the order in which they should be addressed. The data also enable the therapist to have greater clarity about therapeutic strategies and the tactics indicated for the particular phases and goals of treatment.

Rating Important Dimensions of Family Functioning

Using the explicit interview data (see Chapter 7), and drawing heavily from observation of the family in interaction during the evaluation sessions, the therapist is in a position to formally or informally summarize and rate the important dimensions of family functioning. (We discussed these dimensions in greater detail in Chapter 7, and in Section 4 we examine them from the point of view of treatment strategies.)

Communication

> Listening is a magnetic and strange thing, a creative force. The friends who listen to us are the ones we move toward, and we want to sit in their radius. When we are listened to, it creates us, makes us unfold and expand.
>
> Karl Menninger

With regard to communication, the major focus is on the quality and quantity of information exchange among the family members. Can they state information clearly and accurately? Is that information listened to and perceived accurately by the other family members? Can some family members do this, whereas others cannot? Is the tone of the communication (i.e., the command aspect) respectful? Affirming? Demanding? Insulting?

Problem Solving

Every family faces problems. One difference between nondistressed and distressed families is that the latter do not come to effective agreement and action on problems, which then accumulate. The family has come for evaluation with at least one problem, and by asking about current and prior attempts to solve this problem, the interviewer gets a sense of where and how the family has started to deal with it. Many authors (e.g., Jacobson 1981) have delineated the steps of effective problem solving, and some have made teaching of these problem-solving steps a major ingredient in family intervention. For example, Falloon et al. (1988) have used this model with the families of schizophrenic patients, and many authors have used these steps for less ill populations, including dysfunctional couples (Gottman 1994; Jacobson and Christensen 1996; Markman et al. 1993) and couples seeking marital enrichment [Guerney 1977 (one of the pioneers)]. In the assessment the interviewer should note whether the family is capable of each of the following steps in the problem-solving sequence: 1) stating the problem clearly and in behavioral terms, 2) formulating possible solutions, 3) evaluating the solutions, 4) deciding on one solution to try, and 5) assessing the effectiveness of that solution.

Roles and Coalitions

As we detailed in Chapters 3 and 4, the family unit must manage certain tasks: 1) to provide for basic needs, 2) to develop a working marital coalition, and 3) to rear and socialize the offspring. The notion of roles refers to the recurrent patterns of behavior by various individuals in the family through which these family tasks are carried out.

Furthermore, as the individuals in the family carry out their functions, how do they coordinate and mesh with others in the family? How rigidly are roles assigned by age or gender rather than by ability? Who assumes leadership, especially regarding decision making? To what extent does the family seem fragmented and disjointed, as though made up of isolated individuals? Or do its members appear to be undifferentiated? How are boundaries maintained with respect to family of origin, extended family, neighbors, and community? To what extent is the marital coalition functional and successful? To what extent are cross-generational coalitions stronger than the marital dyad? How successfully are power and leadership issues resolved?

Affective Responsiveness and Involvement

With regard to affective responsiveness and involvement, the clinician assesses the family's ability to generate and express an appropriate range of feelings. To what extent does the family appear to be emotionally dead rather than expressive, empathic, and spontaneous? What is the family's level of enjoyment, energy, and humor? To what extent does there appear to be an emotional divorce between the marital partners? To what extent does the predominant family mood pattern seem to be one of depression, suspicion, envy, jealousy, withdrawal, anger, irritation, or frustration? To what extent is the family system skewed around the particular mood state or reaction pattern of one of its members? Are the expressed emotions consonant with the behaviors and context?

Affective involvement refers to the degree of emotional interest and investment the family members show toward one another. This could range from absence of involvement to involvement that is devoid of positive feelings to narcissistic involvement, warmth and closeness, angry intrusiveness, or symbiosis (L. C. Wynne, personal communication, 1987).

Behavior Control

Behavior control is the pattern of behavior the family uses to handle physically dangerous situations (e.g., when a child runs into the road, or when a family member drives recklessly), to express psychobiological needs and drives (e.g., eating, sleeping, sex, aggression), and to engage in interpersonal socializing behavior. Control in these areas can range from rigid to flexible to laissez-faire to chaotic.

The single most important initial assessment and intervention involves the prevention of physical harm to the family members or the therapist. Abused children, battered wives, and sometimes battered husbands or abused grandparents are all too common. Remember, too, that most families are afraid of psychotic individuals, even when there has been no violence or threat of it. The therapist must also be aware that violence directed toward therapists is not uncommon, particularly with patients who are angry, paranoid, alcoholic, or impulsive. Neither the family nor the therapist can work on other issues when they are afraid.

If a family member makes threats, the available community resources must be considered and employed when appropriate. Encouraging family members to call the police when threatened, to seek shelter when abused, and to inform the appropriate authorities of child abuse should be regarded as the beginning of family therapy and as necessary for its success. Little can be accomplished when family members are too frightened to speak openly. The family, however, may not be willing to take any of these steps until it trusts the therapist. In some circumstances the therapist is required to call child protection services whether or not the family wants it.

Operative Family Beliefs and Stories

Families and individuals function with a set of conscious and unconscious ideas pertaining to what the family is about, what the family's history tells about the roles of men and women, what values are important (e.g., money, education, endurance), and what adults and children should do and be. Some of these beliefs are clearly cultural or class bound, such as whether family loyalty or career advancement is more important, and whether obedience or initiative is valued more in children. Some beliefs are related to issues in the family's history, such as a story of occupational success or failure, or a parent who has been in a war or the Holocaust. Some beliefs are about a particular child, in terms of whether the child is considered good, bad, talented, or pretty, labels with which others, outside the family, might disagree. Some beliefs are about therapy itself and whether people should accept help, do it on their own, or deny and endure problems. These beliefs markedly influence how the family functions and copes. Not all family members share each belief. A knowledge of these beliefs is essential to finding ways to help the family to develop new behaviors.

Recent Family Events and Stresses

As we discussed in Chapter 7, in answering the question of why a family comes for treatment at a particular time, the therapist carefully reviews any recent changes in family composition (e.g., births, deaths, recent marriages), location (e.g., when a child leaves home), or stress (e.g., severe illnesses) and life cycle transition points.

Family Classification and Diagnosis

Several generations of family therapists have attempted to find a reliable and agreed-on way to classify family functioning. Such attempts usually focus on problem-centered descriptive diagnoses, as exemplified by the relational problems and problems of abuse and neglect, which we consider relational issues, listed in DSM-IV (American Psychiatric Association 1994) (Figure 8–1) and by the more complete Group for the Advancement of Psychiatry (GAP) Committee on the Family's classification of relational disorders (Guttman et al. 1996) (Table 8–1). The conditions described in these systems are serious ones (e.g., family violence with abuse of children). They are called *relational diagnoses* in that they involve interactions of one or several of the participants (remember, though, that not all families have a diagnosis). Clarkin and Miklowitz (1997) have completely reviewed the data relevant to family and relational disorders.

Several dimensions of the family are important for the family therapist: the location and type of the problem (e.g., marital conflict, parent-child conflict with violence); the severity of the identified problem and the severity of general family dysfunction; and the description of the problematic system,

RELATIONAL PROBLEMS

Relational problems include patterns of interaction between or among members of a relational unit that are associated with clinically significant impairment in functioning, or symptoms among one or more members of the relational unit, or impairment in the functioning of the relational unit itself. The following relational problems are included because they are frequently a focus of clinical attention among individuals seen by health professionals. These problems may exacerbate or complicate the management of a mental disorder or general medical condition in one or more members of the relational unit, may be a result of a mental disorder or a general medical condition, may be independent of other conditions that are present, or can occur in the absence of any other condition. When these problems are the principal focus of clinical attention, they should be listed on Axis I. Otherwise, if they are present but not the principal focus of clinical attention, they may be listed on Axis IV. The relevant category is generally applied to all members of a relational unit who are being treated for the problem.

V61.9 Relational Problem Related to a Mental Disorder or General Medical Condition

This category should be used when the focus of clinical attention is a pattern of impaired interaction that is associated with a mental disorder or a general medical condition in a family member.

V61.20 Parent-Child Relational Problem

This category should be used when the focus of clinical attention is a pattern of interaction between parent and child (e.g., impaired communication, overprotection, inadequate discipline) that is associated with clinically significant impairment in individual or family functioning or the development of clinically significant symptoms in parent or child.

V61.10 Partner Relational Problem

This category should be used when the focus of clinical attention is a pattern of interaction between spouses or partners characterized by negative communication (e.g., criticisms), distorted communication (e.g., unrealistic expectations), or

(continued)

FIGURE 8–1.   DSM-IV relational problems and problems related to abuse or neglect.
Source. Diagnostic and Statistical Manual of Mental Disorders, 4th Edition. Washington, DC, American Psychiatric Association, 1994, pp. 680–682. Copyright 1994, American Psychiatric Association. Reprinted with permission.

noncommunication (e.g., withdrawal) that is associated with clinically significant impairment in individual or family functioning or the development of symptoms in one or both partners.

V61.8 Sibling Relational Problem

This category should be used when the focus of clinical attention is a pattern of interaction among siblings that is associated with clinically significant impairment in individual or family functioning or the development of symptoms in one or more of the siblings.

V62.81 Relational Problem Not Otherwise Specified

This category should be used when the focus of clinical attention is on relational problems that are not classifiable by any of the specific problems listed above (e.g., difficulties with co-workers).

PROBLEMS RELATED TO ABUSE OR NEGLECT

This section includes categories that should be used when the focus of clinical attention is severe mistreatment of one individual by another through physical abuse, sexual abuse, or child neglect. These problems are included because they are frequently a focus of clinical attention among individuals seen by health professionals. The appropriate V code applies if the focus of attention is on the perpetrator of the abuse or neglect or on the relational unit in which it occurs. If the individual being evaluated or treated is the victim of the abuse or neglect, code 995.52, 995.53, or 995.54 for a child or 995.81 or 995.83 for an adult (depending on the type of abuse).

V61.21 Physical Abuse of Child

This category should be used when the focus of clinical attention is physical abuse of a child.

Coding note: Specify 995.54 if focus of clinical attention is on the victim.

(continued)

FIGURE 8–1. DSM-IV relational problems and problems related to abuse or neglect. *(continued)*
Source. Diagnostic and Statistical Manual of Mental Disorders, 4th Edition. Washington, DC, American Psychiatric Association, 1994, pp. 680–682. Copyright 1994, American Psychiatric Association. Reprinted with permission.

V61.21 Sexual Abuse of Child

This category should be used when the focus of clinical attention is sexual abuse of a child.

Coding note: Specify 995.53 if focus of clinical attention is on the victim.

V61.21 Neglect of Child

This category should be used when the focus of clinical attention is child neglect.

Coding note: Specify 995.52 if focus of clinical attention is on the victim.

Physical Abuse of Adult

This category should be used when the focus of clinical attention is physical abuse of an adult (e.g., spouse beating, abuse of elderly parent).

Coding note: Code
    V61.12 if focus of clinical attention is on the perpetrator and abuse is by partner
    V62.83 if focus of clinical attention is on the perpetrator and abuse is by person other than partner
    995.81 if focus of clinical attention is on the victim

Sexual Abuse of Adult

This category should be used when the focus of clinical attention is sexual abuse of an adult (e.g., sexual coercion, rape).

Coding note: Code
    V61.12 if focus of clinical attention is on the perpetrator and abuse is by partner
    V62.83 if focus of clinical attention is on the perpetrator and abuse is by person other than partner
    995.83 if focus of clinical attention is on the victim

FIGURE 8–1.   DSM-IV relational problems and problems related to abuse or neglect. *(continued)*

Source.   *Diagnostic and Statistical Manual of Mental Disorders*, 4th Edition. Washington, DC, American Psychiatric Association, 1994, pp. 680–682. Copyright 1994, American Psychiatric Association. Reprinted with permission.

TABLE 8–1.   Proposed classification of relational disorders (CORD)

I. Relational disorders within one generation
    A. Severe relational disorders in couples
        1. Conflictual disorder with and without physical aggression
        2. Sexual dysfunction
        3. Sexual abuse
        4. Divorce dysfunction
        5. Induced psychotic disorder (folie à deux)
    B. Severe relational disorders in siblings
        1. Conflictual disorder
        2. Physical and/or sexual abuse
        3. Induced psychotic disorder (folie à deux)
II. Intergenerational relational disorders
    A. Problems relating to infants, children, and adolescents
        1. With overt physical abuse or neglect
            a. With intrafamily child sexual abuse
            b. Without sexual abuse
        2. With problems in engagement
            a. Overinvolvement
                i. Intrusive overinvolvement
                ii. Emotional abuse
                iii. Family separation disorder
                    a. Preadolescent type
                    b. Adolescent type
            b. Underinvolvement
                i. Reactive attachment disorder
                ii. Failure to thrive
        3. With problems in control
            a. Undercontrol
            b. Overcontrol
            c. Inconsistent control
        4. With problems in communication
            a. Communication deviance (for example, high expressed emotion)
            b. With lack of affective or instrumental communication
    B. Problems relating to adult offspring and their parents
        1. With physical abuse or neglect
        2. With problems in engagement
            a. With burden
            b. With overinvolvement
        3. With problems in communication
            a. With cutoffs
            b. With severe verbal conflict

Source.   Guttman HA, Beavers WR, Berman E, et al: "A Model for the Classification and Diagnosis of Relational Disorders." *Psychiatric Services* 46:926–932, 1995. Reprinted with permission.

TABLE 8–2. A comprehensive evaluation schema

	Type of formulation	For the family	For the individual(s)
Diagnosis	Functional	*A*	*B*
		A systemic formulation	Behavioral or individual psychodynamic model and/or biological model
	Descriptive	*C*	*D*
		DSM-IV conditions not attributable to a mental disorder that are a focus of attention or treatment (e.g., parent-child problem, family typology)	DSM-IV classification for each family member on Axis I, II, or III, as appropriate

which includes both the history and the current patterns of communication, role, affect, and so on. As we mentioned in Chapter 7, it is critical to determine whether the problem is heavily weighted toward issues of the individual (e.g., a child with schizophrenia in a reasonably well-functioning family) or toward issues of the family (e.g., a marital relational disorder with violence, in the throes of a divorce).

The therapist's task includes making a diagnosis, meaning systemic and dynamic formulations for both the individual and the family, as well as descriptive diagnoses. Table 8–2 offers a schematic way to address the key questions the therapist must answer:

1. How can the problem best be explained (cells A, B, C, D)?
2. What is the level of family functioning, and how does the family function; that is, what are the family problems and processes (cell C)?
3. Has any family member been given a DSM-IV Axis I, II, or III diagnosis (cell D)?
4. If a serious psychiatric disease is present in any family members (cell D), how is the family involved (cell A)?
5. How can systems concepts help clarify the problem (cell A)? What roles do individual biology and individual psychodynamics (cell B) play in the problem?

Saying it another way, the therapist can

1. Use DSM-IV or the GAP diagnostic scheme for a descriptive diagnosis, if applicable.
2. Describe the functioning of the family, using the dimensions listed earlier in this chapter.
3. Make a judgment as to the salience of individual pathology.
4. Determine the severity of the family problem, using the Global Assessment of Relational Functioning (GARF) Scale (Figure 8–2). This instrument was also developed by the GAP Committee on the Family (Dausch et al. 1996; Guttman et al. 1996). It is a dimensional scale that describes features of a relationship along a health-to-dysfunction continuum. For example, communication is one of the dimensions. The GARF Scale permits the clinician to characterize the overall functioning of a family or other ongoing relational unit on a hypothetical continuum: from competent, optimal performance to disorganized, maladaptive functioning. (Contrast the GARF Scale with the severity of psychosocial stressors scale [Axis IV], which is dimensional. Axis IV is concerned only with the individual's experience; it rates only stressors and dysfunction, not the protective, health-enhancing factors that help individuals cope more effectively.) The GARF Scale includes only three areas of family functioning: problem solving, organization, and emotional climate. As a global scale, the GARF Scale cannot characterize all of the features of families and other relationships that might be important to specialists assessing and treating families, but it is still very useful.

This method, albeit imprecise, represents our recommendation for how to assess a family, formulate a working diagnosis, and draw implications for goals and treatment. To reemphasize, just as individual, psychodynamic theories maintain that symptoms are the result of internal forces, dynamics, and fantasies, so family theories maintain that symptoms are the result of, or are maintained by, the properties of an interaction or the functioning of a family system and the characteristics of the individuals involved.

The key task is to determine how much each of these theories contributes to an understanding of the development and maintenance of the problem and, even more important, what approach is most likely to foster change at the present time. A purely physical symptom such as invalidism after a heart attack can be maintained by the way family members treat the patient, and a problem such as difficulties in shared decision making can be the result of individual dynamics. If the therapist has decided that the family is involved in the problem, and he or she believes that intervening with the family may pro-

Global Assessment of Relational Functioning (GARF) Scale

Instructions: The GARF Scale can be used to indicate an overall judgment of the functioning of a family or other ongoing relationship on a hypothetical continuum ranging from competent, optimal relational functioning to a disrupted, dysfunctional relationship. It is analogous to Axis V (Global Assessment of Functioning Scale) provided for individuals in DSM-IV. The GARF Scale permits the clinician to rate the degree to which a family or other ongoing relational unit meets the affective or instrumental needs of its members in the following areas:

A. *Problem solving*—skills in negotiating goals, rules, and routines; adaptability to stress; communication skills; ability to resolve conflict

B. *Organization*—maintenance of interpersonal roles and subsystem boundaries; hierarchical functioning; coalitions and distribution of power, control, and responsibility

C. *Emotional climate*—tone and range of feelings; quality of caring, empathy, involvement, and attachment/commitment; sharing of values; mutual affective responsiveness, respect, and regard; quality of sexual functioning

In most instances, the GARF Scale should be used to rate functioning during the current period (i.e., the level of relational functioning at the time of the evaluation). In some settings, the GARF Scale may also be used to rate functioning for other time periods (i.e., the highest level of relational functioning for at least a few months during the past year).

Note: Use specific, intermediate codes when possible, for example, 45, 68, 72. If detailed information is not adequate to make specific ratings, use midpoints of the five ranges, that is, 90, 70, 50, 30, or 10.

81–100 Overall: *Relational unit is functioning satisfactorily from self-report of participants and from perspectives of observers.*

Agreed-on patterns or routines exist that help meet the usual needs of each family/couple member; there is flexibility for change in response to unusual demands or events; and occasional conflicts and stressful transitions are resolved through problem-solving communication and negotiation.

(continued)

FIGURE 8–2.   Global Assessment of Relational Functioning (GARF) Scale.
Source.   American Psychiatric Association: *Diagnostic and Statistical Manual of Mental Disorders,* 4th Edition. Washington, DC, American Psychiatric Association, 1994, pp. 758–759. Copyright 1994, American Psychiatric Association. Reprinted with permission.

There is a shared understanding and agreement about roles and appropriate tasks, decision making is established for each functional area, and there is recognition of the unique characteristics and merit of each subsystem (e.g., parents/spouses, siblings, and individuals).

There is a situationally appropriate, optimistic atmosphere in the family; a wide range of feelings is freely expressed and managed within the family; and there is a general atmosphere of warmth, caring, and sharing of values among all family members. Sexual relations of adult members are satisfactory.

61–80 Overall: *Functioning of relational unit is somewhat unsatisfactory. Over a period of time, many but not all difficulties are resolved without complaints.*

Daily routines are present, but there is some pain and difficulty in responding to the unusual. Some conflicts remain unresolved but do not disrupt family functioning.

Decision making is usually competent, but efforts at control of one another quite often are greater than necessary or are ineffective. Individuals and relationships are clearly demarcated, but sometimes a specific subsystem is depreciated or scapegoated.

A range of feeling is expressed, but instances of emotional blocking or tension are evident. Warmth and caring are present but are marred by a family member's irritability and frustrations. Sexual activity of adult members may be reduced or problematic.

41–60 Overall: *Relational unit has occasional times of satisfying and competent functioning together, but clearly dysfunctional, unsatisfying relationships tend to predominate.*

Communication is frequently inhibited by unresolved conflicts that often interfere with daily routines; there is significant difficulty in adapting to family stress and transitional change.

Decision making is only intermittently competent and effective; either excessive rigidity or significant lack of structure is evident at these times. Individual needs are quite often submerged by a partner or coalition.

Pain or ineffective anger or emotional deadness interferes with family enjoyment. Although there is some warmth and support for members, it is usually unequally distributed. Troublesome sexual difficulties between adults are often present.

FIGURE 8–2. Global Assessment of Relational Functioning (GARF) Scale. *(continued)*

Source. American Psychiatric Association: *Diagnostic and Statistical Manual of Mental Disorders*, 4th Edition. Washington, DC, American Psychiatric Association, 1994, pp. 758–759. Copyright 1994, American Psychiatric Association. Reprinted with permission.

21–40 Overall: *Relational unit is obviously and seriously dysfunctional; forms and time periods of satisfactory relating are rare.*

Family/couple routines do not meet the needs of members; they are grimly adhered to or blithely ignored. Life cycle changes, such as departures or entries into the relational unit, generate painful conflict and obviously frustrating failures of problem solving.

Decision making is tyrannical or quite ineffective. The unique characteristics of individuals are unappreciated or ignored by either rigid or confusingly fluid coalitions.

There are infrequent periods of enjoyment of life together; frequent distancing or open hostility reflects significant conflicts that remain unresolved and quite painful. Sexual dysfunction among adult members is commonplace.

1–20 Overall: *Relational unit has become too dysfunctional to retain continuity of contact and attachment.*

Family/couple routines are negligible (e.g., no mealtime, sleeping, or waking schedule); family members often do not know where others are or when they will be in or out; there is little effective communication among family members.

Family/couple members are not organized in such a way that personal or generational responsibilities are recognized. Boundaries of relational unit as a whole and subsystems cannot be identified or agreed on. Family members are physically endangered or injured or sexually attacked.

Despair and cynicism are pervasive; there is little attention to the emotional needs of others; there is almost no sense of attachment, commitment, or concern about one another's welfare.

0 Inadequate information.

FIGURE 8–2. Global Assessment of Relational Functioning (GARF) Scale. *(continued)*

Source. American Psychiatric Association: *Diagnostic and Statistical Manual of Mental Disorders*, 4th Edition. Washington, DC, American Psychiatric Association, 1994, pp. 758–759. Copyright 1994, American Psychiatric Association. Reprinted with permission.

TABLE 8–3. Setting goals after evaluation

	Type of formulation	For the family	For the individual(s)
Diagnosis	Functional	*A*	*B*
		A systemic formulation	Behavioral or individual psychodynamic model and/or biological model
	Descriptive	*C*	*D*
		DSM-IV conditions not attributable to a mental disorder that are a focus of attention or treatment (e.g., parent-child problem, family typology)	DSM-IV classification for each family member on Axis I, II, or III, as appropriate
Goals	Based on diagnosis	Specify for each problem	Specify for each problem

duce change, then he or she should discuss this with the family and agree on a contract for consultation or therapy.

> The key task is to determine how much each of these theories contributes to an understanding of the development and maintenance of the problem and, even more important, what approach is most likely to foster change at the present time.

Planning the Therapeutic Approach and Establishing the Treatment Contract

After the evaluation data have been gathered and formulated into diagnostic hypotheses, the therapist and family together can formulate goals regarding important problem areas (Table 8–3 is a continuation of Table 8–2). Note that in Table 8–3 goals are set *after* the diagnostic evaluation. The therapist is then ready to consider the appropriate therapeutic strategies (see Chapter 12).

The therapist should make a concise, explicit statement of the family problem using language the family can understand. Such a formulation will be determined by the treatment model the therapist is using. For example, a behavioral therapist might say to the family, "You two have gotten into the habit of criticizing each other so much that you have neglected to comment on the good things the other one does, or to give each other what each of you needs. We will try to help you communicate more clearly and take care of each other in ways that you both want." A therapist using a more dynamic approach might say, "Each of you had a mother who was depressed and a father who was working too hard to be available. So each of you assumes that if the other one doesn't give you what you want, they must be unavailable or unloving. It makes both of you become tense and withdrawn a lot. Perhaps we can find a way to help you separate your past from your present and learn to take care of each other better." A therapist with a problem-solving approach might say, "You seem to be trying to explain to each other what you need in ways that make each of you angry. So your attempts to solve this problem have been making things worse. Perhaps we could find a better way to do it, by focusing on a new solution or on the solutions that have worked at least some of the time."

As we mentioned earlier in this chapter, if it appears from the initial family evaluation that any family members have an individual disorder, as in cell C of Table 8–3, this must be noted and taken into account in the formulation and treatment planning. The most common way a family gets to the family therapist is through an individual. Common situations include those in which one spouse has a diagnosable depression or phobia, a family member appears to have a severe personality disorder, a member has a serious substance abuse problem, schizophrenia is present in one of the young adults living in the parents' home, or childhood or adolescent antisocial behavior is present. The initial suspicion of a diagnosable disorder in one individual may necessitate further evaluation either in the family setting or individually in order to carefully assess the nature and extent of the individual symptoms as enumerated in DSM-IV. Our assumption is that important components of both the individual and the biological models interact with each other and with the family model.

At this point, a beginning contract with regard to goals and treatment should be established (Shankar and Menon 1993). The contract should include who is to be present; the location, times, estimated length, and frequency of meetings; the fee; and contingency planning with respect to absent members and missed appointments. It is usually not possible to determine in the first sessions how long treatment will take. Some therapists contract for

10 sessions and renew; others leave things open-ended. For some families, treatment will be very brief and crisis oriented, lasting only one or two sessions, whereas for other families treatment may continue for months or occasionally years when the resources to maintain treatment are available.

Some therapists may want to refer families to the book *Solving Your Problems Together: Family Therapy for the Whole Family* (Annunziata and Jacobson-Kram 1994), which was written specifically for the lay market:

> This illustrated book for children, adolescents, and adults is designed to answer typical questions and address feelings of reluctance that arise when a family is considering family therapy: Does our family need therapy? What are the sessions going to be like? Will what we talk about be confidential? If our child has a problem, why must the whole family go? How can I find the right family therapist for us? What if a family member refuses to go?
>
> Families are introduced to the idea of family therapy as a safe place in which strengths can be used and skills can be learned to help solve problems, improve communication, and handle stress more effectively. By not advocating any one school of family therapy, the book is helpful to potential clients regardless of the theoretical orientation of the therapist they may choose.

Case Example Illustrating the Outline

The following case example illustrates the use of the family evaluation outline (see Table 7–1).

> The R family is a working-class, Irish family consisting of a father, a 55-year-old manual laborer; a mother, a 44-year-old housewife; a 17-year-old daughter, who is a senior in high school; a 20-year-old son, who is a part-time college student; and a 22-year-old son, who is working part time. All three children still live at home. Both mothers-in-law are actively involved in the family. They have been referred for family therapy after Mrs. R's hospitalization for paranoid symptoms following barbiturate withdrawal.

☙ 1. Gathering Identifying Data and Establishing Current Phase of Family Life Cycle

The therapist notes that although the identified patient is Mrs. R, the family is also approaching the empty-nest phase, in which the parents will have to face being alone together. The therapist begins to wonder and to ask to what extent the couple has emphasized the parental role rather than the marital relationship, and to what extent they have discouraged the development of the children's ability to move out of the house and complete their maturation and separation from their parents. The older son, a month prior to intake, had indicated that he was moving out of the house and in with his girlfriend.

☜ 2. Gathering Explicit Interview Data

A. What Is the Current Family Problem?

The older son said that the family problem was his mother because she had recently stopped using barbiturates on the advice of her doctor and subsequently began having ideas that people in the family were trying to harm her. Mr. R added that his wife had always been the problem. He was joined in these sentiments by the daughter and by the younger son. Mrs. R, however, said that the problem was that nobody would help her around the house and that she could not get any cooperation from the family members.

The therapist then asked the family to think in terms of what the current family (not individual) problem was. The younger son said he thought that maybe the problem was not the mother but the fact that nobody in the family was communicating or was happy.

B. Why Does the Family Come for Treatment at the Present Time?

The family reported that about the time the older son announced that he was going to move out, the parents' quarreling, which had been long-standing, intensified. Mrs. R went to a family doctor for a tranquilizer. The doctor said that she appeared confused and suggested that she stop taking the barbiturates she had also been using, and she stopped taking them all at once. She then became suspicious and had a fight with her husband in which they threw pots at each other. At this point, everybody felt that she should see her family physician, who recommended admission to an inpatient psychiatric unit. She remained there for a week until her symptoms stopped.

C. What Is the Background of the Family Problem?

1. Composition of household.

Mr. R works as a manual laborer in a shipyard. Although he spent a year in college, he has not advanced in his job and is concerned about finances and worried about retirement. Mrs. R is a housewife. She has never worked outside the home. The older son works part time in a record store. The younger son is a part-time student at a local college. The daughter is finishing high school. Mrs. R's father is dead, and her mother is a frequent visitor in the home. Mr. R's parents are alive. He is close to his mother.

*2. Developmental history and
patterns of each family member.*

Mrs. R's father was manager of a cemetery, and she described her mother as being sick all the time. Her parents' relationship revolved around her father taking care of her mother through much of the marriage because of her sickness. Mrs. R gave a history of being chronically sick, like her mother. She had been born prematurely and developed sinusitis and asthma at an early age. She had one older brother. She felt ignored by her mother and father and was often called on to care for her mother when her father was absent. She often dreamed of someone to take care of her. In adulthood, she and mother became very close.

Mr. R's father was the foreman in a factory, and Mr. R was close to his father, but he described his mother as "overprotective" and said that his father essentially catered to his mother. Both parents had hoped that their children would exceed them educationally and professionally and had tried the best they could to encourage this.

Mr. R was the oldest of four children and took care of two younger siblings who were "always sick." He resented this caretaking and tended to stay in his room or work on his car as he grew older. He never quite lived up to his parents' expectations. He attempted college but quit, did not want to move out of the house, and dated very little before he met Mrs. R.

*3. Developmental history and
patterns of the nuclear family unit.*

Mr. and Mrs. R were introduced by relatives. Most of their courtship involved family social events, and there was little intimacy during their courtship period. Mrs. R described the marriage as somewhat disappointing. She indicated that she had married for stability and someone to take care of her. He had said that he thought she would provide some of the spark that he lacked. He saw her as an independent person who would not ask too much of him. Both partners stated that they had no knowledge of contraception, and their older son was born in the first year of the marriage. They had had very little experience being alone together as husband and wife.

After they had the other two children, Mr. R began spending more and more time at work. Mrs. R found herself becoming sick more frequently with various respiratory and other ailments. They had to turn to their own mothers: his for financial support, hers for help in raising the children and taking care of herself. Mrs. R. felt uncared for by her husband, and Mr. R became increasingly resentful that his wife was sick and angry rather than the "spark plug" he had married. As the children grew up, Mr. R increasingly retreated, neither helping Mrs. R nor supporting her in her attempts to get the children to cooperate with her. Mr. R also experienced his own sense of failure in that he had never moved up in his job and believed his wife was disappointed in him for not earning more money. She became angry, then anxious, at this withdrawal and then began to take barbiturates. In addition, they had many arguments over the children: Mrs. R wanted them to work harder in school, and Mr. R would tell her to leave them alone.

4. Current interactional patterns.

The situation had worsened progressively during the 2 years prior to referral as the two boys reached adulthood and Mrs. R reached an increasingly depressed middle age. Mr. and Mrs. R found themselves drifting further apart and spending less time together, barely talking to each other. Mr. R was working much more than before, which made Mrs. R suspicious that he was chasing other women. Mrs. R continued to complain of physical symptoms, to take more medications, and to become less able to perform childrearing or housekeeping tasks. The more Mrs. R attempted to get Mr. R's attention, the more he retreated. The older son began to experiment with psychedelic drugs, the younger son had difficulty with his grades, and the daughter attended school less frequently and did poorly when in class. The two mothers-in-law fought over who was helping the family more, each placing the blame for the family problems on the other's child.

It appeared that Mr. R had abdicated his role as a parent and a spouse. The marital coalition was almost nonexistent; instead, the daughter and her father were on one side and the younger son and mother on the other. The older son, although a mediator in the family, had in many ways withdrawn from the battle by using drugs.

D. What Is the History of Past Treatment Attempts or Other Attempts at Problem Solving in the Family?

Mrs. R had been seeing the same internist for the past 15 or 20 years. The doctor had frequently suggested psychiatric treatment, but Mrs. R had refused. Instead, he prescribed barbiturates to help her sleep. She went for individual psychotherapy over a 3-month period but quit. She explained, "It didn't make my husband better." Mr. and Mrs. R also consulted their local clergyman on several occasions, and he counseled tolerance and patience. The children had not been involved in treatment.

E. What Are the Family's Goals and Expectations of the Treatment? What Are Its Strengths, Motivations, and Resistances?

The family's motivations at first were to help Mrs. R so that she could get better. During the evaluation interview, they hoped she would "stop being sick and take care of us."

The primary resistances apparent during the evaluation interview were the family members' scapegoating of Mrs. R and a reluctance to change themselves, the latter quite evident in Mr. R's saying that he could not get to treatment sessions because of his job, no matter what time the therapist suggested for the meeting. Although it was less apparent than the resistance, each person in the family did seem to recognize that there was something wrong with the overall functioning of the family and with its individual members and that this problem could be worked on.

❧ 3. Formulating the Family Problem Areas

A. Rating Important Dimensions of Family Functioning

1. Communication.

There was little or no spontaneous interaction or communication between Mr. and Mrs. R. The children seemed somewhat at odds, but they were united in a struggle to prevent their parents from taking power. Even when the therapist tried to get the parents to talk to each other, it was impossible, as Mrs. R felt that Mr. R never listened to her, and Mr. R felt that Mrs. R was always complaining and could not do anything. There was very little communication follow-up from one to the other, thus leaving them without continuity of communication or closure. The parental communication was mainly nonverbal. It consisted of Mrs. R clutching her stomach, grabbing her chest near her heart, or rolling her head back, as though she were about to have a stroke or a heart attack, at which point Mr. R would move his chair farther away from everyone in the family. Positive feedback has been virtually abandoned in this family for years. Communication was best between Mr. R and the daughter and between Mrs. R and the younger son.

2. Problem solving.

The family had difficulty agreeing on anything, even the making of a list of problems. The topic of the list led to various arguments involving many family members. Sometimes they would follow the lead of the older son.

3. Roles and coalitions.

Mrs. R, who was currently a daughter, wife, and mother, had been unable to move out of her family of origin to her present family. She seemed almost childlike in her presentation and her functioning. She seemed to be overly involved as a daughter and less involved as a wife and mother. Mr. R was likewise very involved with his family of origin. He had essentially given up his role as husband and turned over the role of father to the older son, who had been managing the family finances, bringing in extra money, and making the kinds of family decisions that Mr. R used to make.

There had been a reversal of generational roles, with the daughter taking over when Mrs. R was ill and doing the housecleaning and cooking. The daughter also fulfilled part of a spouse's role, in that she and Mr. R frequently went to the movies together, whereas Mrs. R stayed home with her headaches. The strongest coalition in the family appeared to be father-daughter instead of the more usual husband-wife.

The main alignments and communication patterns pitted the father and daughter against the younger son and mother, with the older son being a mediator. In his role as mediator, the son was the center of all communication. All fights seemed to be resolved in his "court." This seemed to be taking a toll on him. He said he was having trouble finding himself and was having great difficulty in making a job decision or career choice. It became clear that this son's leaving home would be a grave crisis for the family.

4. Affective responsiveness and involvement.

The therapist noted that the general emotional tone of the family was one of anger and frustration. Any sign of positive emotional expression between family members was lacking.

5. Behavior control.

There seemed to be no difficulty in this area, as there was no inappropriate expression of aggressive or sexual impulses.

6. Operative family beliefs and stories.

In the R family the theme of illness and caretaking was central. Both spouses had ill parents for whom they had been caretakers. Mrs. R entered the marriage wanting someone to care for her. Mr. R also had been a caretaker but hated it and was hoping his wife would take care of him. Over time Mrs. R's requests for caretaking were rejected, and she became seen as sick or a nag, while Mr. R became helpless and silent. In one way or another, the children then became involved as caretaker (daughter), assistant man of the house (older son), or good boy (the younger son—the only one to attempt college).

The family operated under the cultural myth that a happy marriage is one in which there are no disagreements. Mrs. R lived with the fantasy that everything should be calm and that any flaws or problems were to be avoided and not to be discussed. This meant that the painful realities of both partners could not be addressed directly. In addition, both partners believed it was possible to change the other by nagging enough. Mrs. R wanted her husband to be a charming prince, and Mr. R wanted his wife to be a happy and supportive spouse who would make up for his feeling of inferiority. Mrs. R also felt that both marital partners should be as unselfish as possible and that she had sacrificed her life for her children and husband. In contrast, Mr. R felt that he had worked himself to the bone to bring home the money to keep the family going, sacrificing everything for everyone else. Mr. R could not see that his wife wanted his presence and support more than the money, and Mrs. R could not see that her anger at his withdrawal made it impossible for her to support him or make him feel better about himself or his work. The children, faced with an ill, scapegoated mother and a retreating father who felt like a failure, could neither succeed themselves nor leave home.

Mrs. R was the scapegoat in the family. Whenever anything went wrong, everyone turned on her. If what she had done did not seem to be an adequate explanation of the problem, an explanation was found that took into account her past transgressions. Her position as the bad person, on the one hand, and as responsible for much of the family's functioning, on the other, is a classic gender bind (note that when she did not do the caretaking, her daughter stepped in). The fact that she had been tranquilized to help her avoid her reasonable frustrations is not unusual.

It was clear that what at first looked like an individual medical illness was predominantly a family problem.

B. Family Classification and Diagnosis

CORD classification: Couple conflictional relational disorder (without violence)
Score on GARF Scale: 50

C. Individual Diagnoses

Mrs. R met criteria on DSM-IV Axis I for barbiturate abuse (code 304.1). At the time of evaluation most of Mrs. R's symptoms of barbiturate withdrawal had ceased and she was on no medication. She appeared sad but did not meet the criteria for addiction or major depression. Her physician assured the therapist that her other medical symptoms, particularly the respiratory ones, were present but minor and that she needed no special treatment at this time. Mr. and Mrs. R met criteria for personality disorder features on Axis II (Mr. R, dependent; Mrs. R, histrionic). The older son met criteria for substance abuse.

⟶ 4. Planning the Therapeutic Approach and Establishing the Treatment Contract

The therapist's first decision was to approach the R family's problem from a family standpoint rather than by treating Mrs. R, the identified patient, as an individual, isolated from her family. The family seemed to be in a crisis, facing the imminent departure of the older son, the family mediator. The parents seemed unable to handle this separation. Mr. R seemed to be behaving in an ineffective manner, and both parents still had a dependent relationship with their own families of origin.

The basic strategy was to strengthen the marital coalition by increasing interaction between the marital dyad, by attempting to decrease the intensity of the interaction between these two people and their families of origin, and by attempting to decrease the cross-generational ties between these two people and their children. The therapist encouraged the mother not to take any tranquilizers, which she was happy to do when she felt that the family was being attended to. The older son made a treatment contract with the therapist to stop taking drugs.

The therapist treated the family as a unit, and he also met with the marital dyad alone for many of the sessions; for a time, the children also had a few sessions as a sibling group. A decision was made to exclude the parents' in-laws from treatment and to encourage the marital dyad to take over the parental role that they had abrogated not only to the older son but also to their own parents. In the sessions in which just the marital dyad participated, positive attention was given to reinforcing communication patterns between husband and wife. They were taught to pick up emotional cues and to respond to each other, rather than to withdraw or to somatize. Each was encouraged to find ways to take care of and praise the other.

Mrs. R was encouraged to reassume executive functions in the house and to consider whether she wanted a part-time job to help out with finances and to give her a focus of interest separate from the house and children. Mr. R was encouraged to share decisions with Mrs. R rather than retreating and then criticizing her. He also spent some time dealing with the question of whether his own life has been the failure he felt it to be. The older son was steered toward his girlfriend and a career choice, letting his father make the decisions the son had once made. The daughter was encouraged to improve her failing schoolwork and to stop doing the housecleaning and cooking. The younger son was supported in his plans for college and began to deal with the question of what would happen if he surpassed his father educationally. He was also encouraged to do his share of chores around the house as long as he lived at home.

Suggested Readings

Guttman HA, Beavers WR, Berman E, et al (Group for the Advancement of Psychiatry Committee on the Family): Global Assessment of Relational Functioning Scale (GARF), I: background and rationale. Fam Proc 35:155–172, 1996

This article offers a detailed approach to diagnosis and treatment planning based on the Global Assessment of Relational Functioning Scale.

Pinsof W: Integrative Problem-Centered Therapy. New York, Basic Books, 1995
This book integrates important concepts from biological psychiatry, individual therapy, and family therapy in providing an excellent, accessible framework for conducting brief therapy from a biopsychosocial perspective. The problem-centered focus is sensible and practical.

References

American Psychiatric Association: Diagnostic and Statistical Manual of Mental Disorders, 4th Edition. Washington, DC, American Psychiatric Association, 1994

Annunziata J, Jacobson-Kram P (contributor): Solving Your Problems Together: Family Therapy for the Whole Family. Washington, DC, American Psychological Association, 1994

Clarkin JF, Miklowitz DJ: Relational problems, in Psychiatry, Vol 2. Edited by Tasman A, Kay J, Lieberman JA. Philadelphia, PA, WB Saunders, 1997, pp 1355–1368

Dausch BM, Miklowitz DJ, Richards JA: Global Assessment of Relational Functioning Scale (GARF), II: reliability and validity in a sample of families of bipolar patients. Fam Proc 35:175–189, 1996

Falloon IRH, Hole V, Mulroy L, et al: Behavioral family therapy, in Affective Disorders and the Family: Assessment and Treatment. Edited by Clarkin JF, Haas GL, Glick ID. New York, Guilford, 1988, pp 117–133

Gottman J: Why Marriages Fail. New York, Simon & Schuster, 1994

Guerney B: Relationship Enhancement. San Francisco, CA, Jossey-Bass, 1977

Guttman HA, Beavers WR, Berman E, et al (Group for the Advancement of Psychiatry Committee on the Family): Global Assessment of Relational Functioning Scale (GARF), I: background and rationale. Fam Proc 35:155–172, 1996

Jacobson NS: Behavioral marital therapy, in Handbook of Family Therapy. Edited by Gurman AS, Kniskern DP. New York, Brunner/Mazel, 1981, pp 556–591

Jacobson N, Christensen A: Integrative Couple Therapy. New York, WW Norton, 1996

Markman H, Renick M, Floyd FJ, et al: Preventing marital distress through communication and conflict management training: a four year follow-up. J Consult Clin Psychol 61:70–77, 1993

Shankar R, Menon MS: Development of a framework of interventions with families in the management of schizophrenia. Psychosocial Rehabilitation Journal 16:75–91, 1993

Home, Ignacio Iturrea, 1987. Private collection.

CHAPTER 9

Tools for Evaluation, Including Rating Scales and Tests

Objectives for the Reader

❧ To know when and how to use special evaluation techniques such as medical examinations, structured tasks, and home visits

❧ To be able to select clinical self-report instruments and rating scales for couples and family assessment

Introduction

As we discussed in Chapter 8, there is a working consensus about the most important areas of family functioning that must be assessed for effective family intervention. In this chapter we examine a sample of rating scales, self-report instruments, and tests that assess some aspect of those dimensions. In addition, we describe how home visits and a medical examination (when indicated) can round out the evaluation.

In contrast to purely verbal techniques, these tools may be useful for the clinician who is interested in measuring the effects of change over the course of treatment and in providing an additional perspective in assessing a couple or family. Given the increased attention focused on patient outcomes by managed care organizations, many therapists use self-report measures to assess the nature of the individual and/or family pathology and efficacy of their ongoing work. Because what families report, how they actually feel, and what they do may often be quite different, the clinician must reconcile these different sources of data in arriving at a picture of the couple's or family's functioning. Because verbal techniques rely on both the family's ability to give information and the therapist's ability to elicit it, there may also be great variance in the information given from interview to interview. The family therapist, therefore, may use more than one technique to gain information over the course of treatment.

Medical Examinations

In order to rule out physical problems as the cause of individual or family dysfunctions, medical examinations may need to be completed for each family member when indicated. Consider the following case example:

> Mr. A, a successful musician in his late 40s, was noted to have become progressively more paranoid and quarrelsome. His family therapist felt that his paranoia was related to his wife's love of dancing (sometimes with his friends), her younger age, and the reality of their children leaving home. Even with competent family therapy over 3–4 months, the situation worsened. Mr. A began complaining of headaches and double vision. A neighbor suggested that he consult a physician, who, after a medical workup, found that Mr. A had a brain tumor. After the tumor was removed, Mr. A's paranoia decreased dramatically, as did the problems between him and his wife.

The message for family therapists is that major psychiatric illness should be evaluated using traditional history taking and mental status examination. Physical illness, however, must also be kept in mind.

Home Visits

In some instances a family therapist might choose to visit the family in its own home, with as many family members present as possible. Sometimes, the reason may be that a critical family member is disabled or housebound. At other times, home visits can be considered when the therapist senses a gross discrepancy between the interactions observed in the office sessions and the reports of what is taking place at home.

Home visits enable the therapist to see the family on its own turf and may lead to a better understanding of its interactional patterns. Some families feel that the therapist is more interested when he or she is willing to make a home visit. However, there are possible disadvantages to home visits. For example, the family may see the visit as an intrusion or may try to convert the therapy into a purely social situation. In such cases, the time consumed may be uneconomical. In general, the rationale and timing of the visits can vary depending on their purpose, but they should always be discussed with the family and agreed to in advance.

Structured Family Tasks

Assessment techniques have been developed that involve the entire family in a structured task. For example, the therapist may recommend that the family plan a picnic together or furnish a room together (using hypothetical furniture and a fixed amount of money), so that he or she can observe the family's problem-solving processes, coalitions among family members, roles, and areas of conflict. Such techniques give the family therapist useful ways of evaluating families in which verbal interventions are not the common communication method. Therapists should continually look for ways to assess and intervene in the couple's or family's process by suggesting activities (e.g., discussing a difficult issue), watching the process unfold, supporting what is functional, and gently challenging what is not. These approaches provide the therapist with useful data because they result in a behavior sample that most approximates the family's behavior outside the session.

Therapists also can assign tasks or homework in between sessions to assess the couple's or family's motivation, flexibility, and resourcefulness. For example, asking a highly verbal, cognitively oriented family to go bowling together may provide the family members with an alternative way to enjoy one another while letting the therapist learn about their willingness to engage in novel behaviors. Tasks can be playful (e.g., "Each time one of you remembers to compliment the other, you get a penny"). They can also be very serious, as when the therapist asks parents to track the antecedents and consequences of problem behaviors shown by their school-aged child during the week.

For the clinician who wants a view of the actual ecology of the family, mealtime is notable as a microcosm of the family in sociological and dynamic terms. Direct observations of family mealtime planning, preparation, and consumption can be made. Alternatively, the family therapist can ask the family to describe the seating and behavior at a typical family meal. Sometimes family members will not eat together. Children rather than parents may prepare the meals. An adolescent who is angry with his or her parents will often take meals alone—if the parents allow this. One child might be used as a mediator between the parents and be asked to sit between them, whereas other siblings are not so involved in the parental drama. In a situation in which one parent cannot function (e.g., a drinking father), that parent may take meals in the bedroom. Such observations are often helpful in determining the family patterns. Either in session or between sessions, family tasks are a rich source of clinical data.

Family Rating Scales

Although assessment is an ongoing process in marital and family therapy, these methods can be used early on to develop a treatment plan, at the midpoint in therapy to assess progress and goals, or at termination to show the gains that have been made. Many of these tools are research instruments, but they can also be beneficial to the clinician. Because the clinical situation can be so complex, the additional data drawn from these diverse sources can greatly assist the practicing family therapist.

Self-Report Instruments

A number of brief and useful self-report measures of overall marital adjustment/satisfaction and family functioning exist that can be quite useful to the practicing clinician (Table 9–1). In general, patients fill out these instruments before the first session either in the waiting room or at home; they provide additional data and feedback to the overall evaluation and treatment program. We list some of our favorite instruments in the sections that follow. Because these instruments undergo revision continually, it is best to look for the most recent version of each measure along with the scoring manual. These can usually be obtained from the authors who devised the scales.

Dyadic Adjustment Scale (DAS). This brief self-report measure is intended to assess the quality of marital or dyadic relations (Spanier 1976). It measures the specific dimensions of satisfaction, cohesion, consensus, and affectional expression.

TABLE 9–1.   Self-report instruments and dimensions of family functioning assessment

	Dimensions of family functioning				
Instrument	Communications	Problem solving	Roles/ coalitions	Affectivity	Behavior control
Dyadic Adjustment Scale (DAS)	×			×	×
Family Adaptability and Cohesion Evaluation Scales (FACES III)	×	×		×	
McMaster Family Assessment Device (FAD)	×	×	×	×	×
Family Assessment Measure III (FAM III)	×		×	×	×
Family Environment Scale (FES)	×			×	×

Family Adaptability and Cohesion Evaluation Scales III (FACES III). Olson (1986) developed a family typology around two major dimensions: family adaptability and cohesion. *Family adaptability* is the capacity of the family when confronted with situational or developmental stress to change its rules, power structure, role relationships, and styles of negotiating. *Family cohesion* is defined as the emotional bonding between members of the family and relates to issues such as independence, autonomy, and family boundaries central in the family theory literature.

McMaster Family Assessment Device (FAD). This screening instrument assists in the initial process of evaluating a family for intervention (Epstein et al. 1983). Each family member (over age 12 years) fills out a pencil-and-paper questionnaire on the family functioning in six areas: problem solving, communication, roles, affective responsiveness, affective involvement, and behavior control. The instrument is easy to administer (it takes 15–20 minutes to complete) and provides a measure of areas of family functioning/dysfunction that could be targeted for intervention. Miller (1994) has developed a clinical rating scale based on the FAD dimensions.

Family Assessment Measure III (FAM III).   This is another self-report pencil-and-paper instrument that can be used to assess the whole family (Skinner et al. 1983). Based on a model of family functioning quite similar to the McMaster model, the FAM III provides scores on task accomplishment, role performance, communication, affective expression, involvement, control values, and norms and provides a general overall rating of family functioning. The instrument takes approximately 30 minutes to complete and can be done by all family members age 10 years and older.

Family Environment Scale (FES).   This scale was developed to assess three dimensions of families: 1) relationship (e.g., family cohesion, expressiveness, conflict), 2) personal growth (e.g., independence, achievement orientation, intellectual-cultural orientation, active-recreational orientation, moral-religious emphasis), and 3) system maintenance (e.g., organization, control) of families. The FES gives a picture of the family's interests and features without the kind of clinical depth that some other self-report scales offer, yet it remains useful for capturing these aspects of a family's experience (Moos and Moos 1981).

Other self-report instruments.   Additional measures such as the *Family Inventory of Life Events (FILE)*, the *Family Crisis Oriented Personal Evaluation Scales (F-COPES)*, and the *Parent-Adolescent Communication Scale* all provide more specific data about family stresses, methods of family coping, and parent-child communication. They can be used in tandem with other more general scales to develop a more differentiated view of the family (McCubbin and Patterson 1981).

The *Marital Precounseling Inventory (MPCI)* was developed to elicit from both spouses material on an extensive range of marital issues: identification of target problems, common interests, satisfaction with communication, rules for decision making, reinforcement power, general satisfaction, and optimism regarding the future (Stuart and Stuart 1972).

The clinician can also use the observations of each spouse in order to complete the assessment of marital interaction. Although it can be argued that the spouses' observations might be inaccurate, it is eminently useful for the clinician to know in what areas the spouses' observations seem biased and distorted. Thus comparing each spouse's observations with the other's and with that of the clinician is quite helpful in planning for treatment focus. The *Spouse Observation Checklist (SOC)* and the *Areas-of-Change Questionnaire (AOCQ)* examine this area.

Developed by the Oregon Research Institute, the *Spouse Observation Checklist* covers 12 categories of behavior—including companionship, affection, consideration, sex, communication, coupling activities, child care and parenting, household responsibilities, financial decision making, employment-education, personal habits and appearance, and self and spouse during the previous 24 hours—and indicates only those behaviors that were experienced as either pleasing or displeasing (Patterson 1976). The data can be used to pinpoint displeasing behaviors, provide a baseline for pretherapeutic efforts, and focus interventions aimed at increasing positive behavior.

The AOCQ asks each spouse to list behaviors of the mate in which change would be desirable (R. S. Weiss et al. 1973). It asks for an indication of major areas for change, including a prediction of what change the partner will desire. The AOC score is highly correlated with the Locke-Wallace Marital Adjustment Test and provides information on target areas of treatment.

Therapist-Rated Marital and Family Interaction Instruments

We mentioned the *Global Assessment of Relational Functioning (GARF) Scale* in Chapter 8. The GARF Scale provides a global rating scale similar to the individually oriented Global Assessment of Functioning (GAF) Scale (for reporting overall functioning on Axis V in the DSM-IV system) but focuses on relational adjustment. In addition, a simple and reliable global scale is now available to measure the quality of the family environment (Rey et al. 1997).

The *Beavers Timberlawn Rating Scales (BTRS)* are completed by an outside observer of family functioning across a number of areas, including overt power, parental coalitions, closeness, mythology, goal-directed negotiation, clarity of expression, responsibility, invasiveness, permeability, range of feelings, mood and tone, unresolvable conflict, empathy, and global health/pathology (Thomas 1977).

In the clinical assessment of marital interaction, clinicians may present the couple with a problem-solving task that can be rated on a variety of dimensions included in the *Marital Interaction Coding System III (MICS III)* (R. L. Weiss and Tolman 1990). Although the coding system is quite complex, simply reviewing the dimensions of the MICS may help the clinician to pinpoint the couple's difficulties (Heyman et al. 1995; R. S. Weiss et al. 1973). Gottman's *Couples Interactional Scoring System (CISS)* and *Specific Affect Coding System (SPAFF)* also provide the clinician with useful categories for classifying the couple's interactions and emotional styles (Gottman 1989; Gottman and Levenson 1986).

In addition to these measures of couples' interactions, the *Structural Analysis of Social Behavior (SASB)*, based on both interpersonal and systems theories, provides a detailed view of how family members' interactions complement one another (Benjamin 1996). As noted earlier in this chapter, a clinical version of the McMaster FAD also offers therapists more global indices of family functioning (Miller et al. 1994).

Summary

The marital and family therapist can choose to complement standard family interviews with a range of assessment approaches to gain a more comprehensive perspective on individual and family functioning. Every clinical contact provides the opportunity for ongoing evaluation and intervention, and the judicious clinician will select carefully from the assessment methods described in this chapter. As family members begin to see themselves in a different, sometimes more objective, ligh, they also may benefit from the additional data generated by these tools and techniques.

Suggested Readings

Clarkin JF, Glick ID: Instruments for the assessment of family malfunction, in Measuring Mental Illness: Psychometric Assessment for Clinicians. Edited by Wetzler S. Washington, DC, American Psychiatric Press, 1989, pp 211–227
This chapter reviews constructs and related instruments useful in family assessment.

Jacob T, Tennenbaum D: Family Assessment: Rationale, Methods, and Future Directions. New York, Plenum, 1988
This volume of research-based chapters presents and assesses many of the available measures for couples and family assessment. It is a good resource for family researchers.

Sprenkle D, Moon SM: Research Methods in Family Therapy. New York, Guilford, 1996

Long-time family researchers, the authors have done a fine job of presenting and synthesizing the most current research methods in the field. It is a "must read" for any serious researcher or consumer of quantitative and qualitative rating scales.

References

Benjamin LS: A clinician-friendly version of the Interpersonal Circumplex: Structural Analysis of Social Behavior (SASB). J Pers Assess 66:248–266, 1996

Epstein N, Baldwin L, Bishop DS: The McMaster Family Assessment Device. J Marital Fam Ther 9:171–180, 1983

Gottman JM: Toward programmatic research in family psychology. Special Issue: Current issues in marital and family assessment. J Fam Psychol 3:211–214, 1989

Gottman JM, Levenson R: Assessing the role of emotion in marriage. Behav Assess 8:31–48, 1986

Heyman RE, Mark JN, Weiss RL, et al: Factor analysis of the Marital Interaction Coding System (MICS). J Fam Psychol 9:209–215, 1995

McCubbin H, Patterson J: Systematic Assessment of Family Stress, Resources and Coping: Tools for Research, Education, and Clinical Intervention. St. Paul, University of Minnesota, 1981

Miller IW, Kabacoff, RI, Epstein N, et al: The development of a clinical rating scale for the McMaster Model of Family Functioning. Fam Process 33:53–69, 1994

Moos R, Moos B: Family Environment Scale: Manual. Palo Alto, CA, Consulting Psychologists Press, 1981

Olson DH: Circumplex Model VII: validation studies and FACES III. Fam Process 25:337–351, 1986

Patterson GR: Some procedures for assessing changes in marital interaction patterns. Oregon Research Institute Bulletin 16:1–7, 1976

Rey JM, Singh M, Hung S, et al: A global scale to measure the quality of the family environment. Arch Gen Psychiatry 54:817–822, 1997

Skinner H, Steinhauer P, Santa-Barbara J: The Family Assessment Measure. Canadian Journal of Community Mental Health 2:91–105, 1983

Spanier GB: Measuring dyadic adjustment: new scales for assessing the quality of marriage and similar dyads. J Marriage Fam Couns 38:15–28, 1976

Stuart RB, Stuart F: Marital Precounseling Inventory. Champaign, IL, Research Press, 1972

Thomas EJ: Marital Communication and Decision-Making. New York, Free Press, 1977

Weiss RL, Tolman AO: The Marital Interaction Coding System—Global (MICS—G): a global companion to the MICS. Behav Assess 12:271–294, 1990

Weiss RS, Hops H, Patterson GR: A framework for conceptualizing marital conflict, technology for altering it, some data for evaluating it, in Behavior Change: Methodology, Concepts, and Practice. Edited by Hamerlynck LA, Handy LC, Mash EJ. Champaign, IL, Research Press, 1973

SECTION 4

Family Treatment

Once the therapist achieves an understanding of what is wrong, the next step is to set treatment goals (Chapter 11). For the reader, however, it is necessary first to understand the current competing models of understanding and treating family disorder—each with its unique mediating and final goals. We review and compare each in Chapter 10.

In Chapter 12 we get to the essentials of how to do family treatment, and in Chapter 13 we examine what treatment looks like over time. In Chapter 14 we review the resistances that can occur during a course of treatment and highlight the elements that may be most crucial to make it all work—the therapeutic alliance.

In Chapter 15 we cover some of the ground rules, that is, the issues that are of major interest to beginning therapists. Among these issues are determining who to include in the treatment, choosing to work with another therapist or as a member of a team, establishing where and how to see and schedule families, setting fees, keeping a record of treatment, deciding whether to include family therapy in combination with other psychotherapeutic and pharmacological treatments, and coordinating treatment with helping agencies and other health care professionals.

We close Section 4 by devoting individual chapters to brief therapy, an increasingly common type of family work (Chapter 16); to the factors (e.g., the patient's culture, ethnicity, race, gender, class, and career) that influence strongly the therapy undertaken (Chapter 17); and to the special issues associated with one particular cultural/ethnic group (Chapter 18).

Family Group, Olivia Glick, 1999. Private collection.

CHAPTER 10

Major Schools of Family Therapy

Objectives for the Reader

- To be able to outline in broad strokes the major schools of family therapy
- To differentiate the strategies, techniques, stance, goals, and database used in each school

Introduction

An observer of the general psychotherapy scene has stated, "In picking up the textbook of the future, we should see in the table of contents not a listing of School A, School B, and so on—perhaps ending with the author's attempt at integration—but an outline of the various agreed-on intervention principles, a specification of varying techniques for implementing each principle, and an indication of the relative effectiveness of each of these techniques, together with their interaction with varying presenting problems and individual differences among patients/clients and therapists" (Goldfried 1980). We agree wholeheartedly, as we have emphasized throughout this book, although this seems like an ideal to strive for rather than a full possibility at present.

In the spirit of Goldfried's idea, we present in this chapter (and in Chapter 11) the general schools[1] of family intervention by focusing not primarily

---

[1]We use the terms *schools* and *models* interchangeably in this chapter.

on their originators but on their mediating and final goals and related strategies of intervention.

Much has been written about the diverse schools of family intervention, often formed around the so-called first generation of charismatic leaders such as Minuchin, Satir, Haley, Bowen, and Ackerman. Different classifications of the schools exist, each with its own assumptions about the origin and maintenance of pathology; goals, strategies, and techniques for intervention; and indications for use. Especially for the twenty-first century, it is necessary for the student of family intervention to have some general conceptual understanding of these schools, their history, and the contemporary personalities involved (Table 10–1).

Insight-Awareness Model

The insight-awareness orientation has also been known as the historical, the psychodynamic, or the psychoanalytic school. In a real sense, this is the oldest school of family therapy because it grew naturally out of the psychoanalytic tradition. One of the earliest family therapists was Ackerman, a child analyst who used his analytic background to inform and lend substance to his approach and understanding of families. One has only to read the transcripts of his sessions to appreciate the influence that analytic thinking and techniques had on his work with families and couples (Block and Simon 1982). The marriage counseling movement of the 1930s and 1940s also drew from this tradition.

The theoretical underpinnings of this model are the familiar ones of psychoanalytic thinking, including especially topographical concepts of conscious, preconscious, and unconscious; constructs of the id, ego, and superego; and concepts that focus on the interaction of individuals, such as secondary gain, transference, and projective identification. Although early analysts (e.g., Ackerman) who opted for a more interactional model criticized this model for its lack of attention to, and language for, interactional data, others in the analytic tradition of object relations have applied these concepts to the understanding and analytic treatment of these interactional problems (Dicks 1967).

By changing the transference distortions, correcting the projective identifications, and infusing insight and new understanding into the arena of interpersonal turmoil and conflict, this school of family therapy attempts to change the functioning and interrelationships of the members of the family or marital system. The database is derived from historical material of the cur-

TABLE 10–1. Models of family treatment

Treatment approach (school)	Representative therapies	Strategies and techniques	Stance	Goals	Database
Insight-awareness (a.k.a. historical, psychodynamic, or psychoanalytic)	Ackerman Boszormenyi-Nagy & Spark Paul Nadelson Bowen	Observe Clarify Interpret	Therapist is listener Therapist keeps "therapeutic distance" Therapist maintains therapeutic stance of technical neutrality	Foster understanding and insight to effect change	History Unconscious derivatives Transference
Systemic-structural (a.k.a. systems, communications, or structural)	Palo Alto Group (Jackson, Bateson, Haley, Satir) Sluzki Bowen Minuchin Erickson Palazzoli	Alter family structure and behavior Observe and transform using directives	Therapist observes and moves in and out of process	Change structure, communication pattern, and roles, which change perception and behavior	Sequences Communication Rules History
Cognitive-behavioral	Weiss Jacobson Patterson Falloon	Teach communication skills and problem-solving skills Use contingency contracting	Therapist is collaborator in the development of interpersonal skills	Eliminate dysfunctional behaviors and learn to utilize new and more effective interpersonal behaviors	Observation of overt behaviors Functional analysis of problematic behavioral sequences

(continued)

TABLE 10–1. Models of family treatment *(continued)*

Treatment approach (school)	Representative therapies	Strategies and techniques	Stance	Goals	Database
Experiential-existential	Whitaker Bowen Boszormenyi-Nagy Satir	Design or participate with family in the emotional experience Empathize	Therapist offers himself or herself for interaction to minimize distance between family and therapist	Change ways family members experience (and presumably react to) each other Growth and differentiation	Observed verbal and nonverbal behavior Shared feelings (including the therapist's feelings)
Narrative	White Epston	Externalize the problem Map influence of problem over family and influence of family over problem	Therapist collaborates with family on a therapeutic conversation	1. Develop an alternative narrative story about the problem 2. Liberate the family from being controlled by the problem toward authoring their own study	Linguistic behavior

Note. a.k.a. = also known as.

rent and past generations, from transference and countertransference phenomena, unconscious derivatives, and resistances. A basic assumption is that intrapsychic conflict, interpersonal problem foci, and defensive and coping mechanisms are modeled and played out within the family system. Portions of the database that are of paramount interest to the practitioners of this model are dream and fantasy material, fantasies and projections about other family members, and transference distortions about other family members and the therapist. Understanding the history and mutations of these dynamics over time is considered crucial to understanding current dysfunction.

The terms *transference* and *countertransference* are used broadly here. Such phenomena can be understood in terms of transference in at least five directions: 1) man to woman, 2) woman to man, 3) woman to therapist, 4) man to therapist, 5) couple (or family) to therapist. Just as there are multiple transference reactions, there are multiple countertransference responses. It is assumed that understanding of unconscious derivatives and their resistances is usually necessary to effect change.

The major therapeutic techniques of the insight-awareness model include clarification, interpretation, and exploration of intrapsychic and interpersonal dynamics and development of insight and empathy. Using such analytic techniques with an individual in the presence of a spouse or other family member represented a unique development in its time. However, more important is the understanding of mutual distortions and projections in the couple's process.

> The goal is to foster understanding and insight in order to effect change in individuals and in the family unit.

Family of Origin Model

Allied with the insight-awareness model is the family of origin model, pioneered by Framo, Bowen, Boszormenyi-Nagy and Krasner, Williamson, and others. As in the insight-awareness model, historical data are important. This group of theorists is most interested in the realities of the three- and four-generation family—its themes, beliefs, and loyalties from past generations and the current functioning of adult patients and their parents rather than patient fantasies about them. In this model the spouses are encouraged and coached to deal with their issues directly with members of the family of origin so as not to project them onto their spouses. This model encourages understanding of the parents and individuation within the family rather than confrontation.

Each of the pioneering theorists is identified with a different model within a broad range of interest in looking at the reality of the three-generation family. Bowen (1978) developed family systems theory, in which he focused on the role of the family emotional system in the etiology of individual dysfunction. His theory concentrated on the need to differentiate oneself in the family by distinguishing between intellectual process and the feeling the person is experiencing; he focused on family triangles, the family projection press, and multigenerational transmission. Using his approach, the therapist works with the individual, coaching him or her in how to differentiate while within the family. Framo (1992) is usually grouped with object relations therapists, whereas others are more interested in seeing the whole family of origin together and concentrating on reconnection. His model starts with the couple but has each spouse separately explore the relationship with all family members. Framo also developed a model of working with couples groups. Boszormenyi-Nagy and Krasner (1986) developed contextual therapy, which emphasized loyalty, balance, and relational justice.

Boszormenyi-Nagy, Williamson, and Framo all work with multigenerational families in the therapy room. Advantages to these models are their emphasis on personal and family growth rather than pathology, their inherent commonsense appeal to many people. These innovators pioneered the active and creative use of the genogram (Boszormenyi-Nagy and Krasner 1986; Bowen 1978; Framo 1992; Williamson 1986).

Systemic-Strategic Model

As systems theory developed, a variety of therapists decided to see how far they could take a therapy in which the only emphasis was on the here-and-now system and current relationships between people. In these models it is assumed that the individual is governed and regulated by the system and that changing the repetitive patterns of communication and behavior between them in the present will eliminate symptomatology. Various models were proposed for symptom production, including the idea that the symptom was needed for the homeostasis of the system, or that the family's efforts to solve the problem had led to more problems (i.e., the solution had become the problem). The ultimate goal of the therapy is to change the pattern. Insight or understanding is not a goal of this therapy, although often it occurs as a result of treatment. In these models it is considered the job of the therapist to understand the problem and find a solution, as opposed to models that are seen as more collaborative.

Treatment techniques in this model include focusing on, exaggerating, deemphasizing, or relabeling symptoms; clarifying communication; interrupting repetitive interactional patterns; or prescribing symptoms (i.e., requesting a family member to continue to do what he or she is already doing so that the behavior is, in effect, controlled by the therapist). For example, the family may come in with the complaint that the daughter does not obey the mother and is becoming impossible to discipline. If the father and daughter look at each other and smile whenever the mother attempts to make a statement, the therapist could ask the mother and daughter to speak directly to each other and ask the father to support the mother. He or she could also *exaggerate* the problem by telling the father that every time the girl disobeys her mother, he should congratulate her or give her a dime. This would bring the problem out in the open and force the father to disown his covert support of the girl's behavior. Or the therapist could *label* the daughter's behavior as spoiled instead of psychiatrically troubled and ask why father was letting his daughter behave in this way. None of these interventions requires history or insight. We discuss these techniques in more detail in the next four chapters. Needless to say, systems theory has limitations (Merkel and Searight 1992).

Structural Model

The structural model, pioneered by Minuchin and Fishman (1981), is probably the most known and most used of the systems theories. It is less focused on the details of communication and more on the family structure. Minuchin is particularly interested in hierarchy (e.g., parental subsystems should be in charge of child subsystems) and clear boundaries, so that each member has a sense of self and privacy but also a sense of family-ness. It is important to understand, however, that boundaries, hierarchies, and coalitions are not things but repetitive behaviors (both verbal and nonverbal) that are determined by the family's operational rules and beliefs. These patterns arrange or organize the family's function. The structural model is particularly good at setting up situations in which the new structure is modeled in session (e.g., "Mrs. A, you and Mr. A sit next to each other and decide how to handle this problem with your child") or in which the family is given tasks to continue the structure at home.

The models of systems theory in which present-oriented and family-focused techniques are used exclusively have been modified extensively since the 1980s. Most practitioners see the system as composed of subsystems that must be understood, including the biological system of each individual and the internal myths, stories, and beliefs by which each individual modifies incoming communications. Most therapists today are interested in how a person's story of his or her past affects present behavior and how the individual uses this knowledge in reframing the current situation or in developing directives.

Cognitive-Behavioral Model

The behavioral model grows out of the behavioral orientation that has historically flourished in parallel and in reaction to the psychoanalytic tradition. The database for this orientation is quantifiable, measurable behavior, whether internal (thoughts) or external (actions). Explanatory concepts are those of the learning theories traditions, for example, stimulus and response, and concepts such as classical conditioning, operant conditioning, schedules of reinforcement, and so forth. With the behavioral model being applied increasingly to interactional systems such as the family, other concepts have been introduced to expand the model into the interpersonal sphere. Perhaps the most influential theory has been Thibaut and Kelley's (1959) behavior exchange model, in which it is postulated that there is a cost-benefit ratio for each individual in an exchange situation (e.g., marriage). The value of that ratio has a major influence on the course and outcome of that relationship. For example, if one spouse receives (what is perceived as) only a little benefit for a lot of effort, the risk of the marriage failing would increase. Jacobson has been the most influential creative practitioner of this approach (Jacobson and Margolin 1979).

The goal in this model is to effect change in discrete, observable, measurable behaviors that the individuals seeking assistance consider to be problematic. As opposed to the insight-awareness model, which often seems to have more ambitious goals of character change and insight, this model tends to focus more on discrete problem areas defined by clear behavior patterns. Thus treatment in this model tends to be briefer and more circumscribed. Emphasis is placed not on pathology but on behavioral deficits and excesses that are to be changed. If undesired behaviors are eliminated (e.g., husband hitting wife), it is not assumed that more social behaviors will necessarily emerge spontaneously but rather that the therapist might be required to teach new and more adaptive behaviors to the spouses or family members.

Techniques in this model include helping family members learn means of effecting the desired behavior in another member. Some of the major tactics used are behavioral contracting based on good faith or *quid pro quo* agreements (e.g., If you do this, I will do that), training in communication skills, training in effective problem solving, and combining positive reinforcement with a decrease in destructive interchanges. Since the 1990s cognitive issues have been given more attention, especially the meaning of behavior (e.g., Is he doing it because he loves me or because he is forced to?) and the cognitions behind behavioral choice (e.g., I must not say I am sorry, even though I am, because it makes me feel less of a man). Therapists using this model have also been more willing to focus on the gender problems that make negotiating more difficult—for example, can the couple really negotiate as equals an agreement on behavior when the husband earns a million dollars a year and the wife has no skills or training and believes she cannot leave the marriage? The inherent inequality makes change more difficult.

The therapist's stance is quite active because he or she sees his or her job as a means to introduce behavior change into the family members' repertoire. The increased focus on cognitions and meanings is beginning to result in an increase in writings on individual and family resistances to their therapists' suggestions. Recent writings have focused more on systemic interventions such as reversals or restraint of change.

This school of family therapy in general does not concentrate on eliciting much historical material or expression of buried feelings or on interpreting psychodynamics. Understanding and insight are much less important in producing change. Active suggestion, direction, and homework are its hallmarks.

Although most family therapists would not call themselves cognitive-behavioral therapists, these techniques are used to some extent by almost all therapists at one time or another.

Experiential Model

Experiential therapy involves a search for meaning through *mutually shared experience* on the part of the therapist and family. Whitaker and Satir were two of the best-known therapists following this model. Both had as a goal the idea of increasing the family members' capacity to experience their lives more fully by sharing with the therapist the struggle with the here and now.

Whitaker's approach, symbolic experiential therapy, worked to strengthen the unconscious symbolic processes that foster their maturation (Napier and Whitaker 1978). The approach emphasizes the therapist's participation as a whole person rather than as an interpreter or director in the process. Assumptions include the following:

1. Growth in families occurs spontaneously and with the mastery of successive developmental tasks.
2. Prior sets of assumptions must be dissolved before new ones can replace them.
3. Therapy should work to catalyze this process rather than impose a predetermined structure.
4. Symptoms are regarded as frustrated attempts at growth.
5. Symptom removal is not the primary goal of therapy but more likely the byproduct.
6. Integration of the aspects of the family's experience out of their collective awareness is the main objective.

The therapist uses both technical skills and knowledge, and nonrational responses (e.g., intuitions, fantasies, dreams, affect), that affect the family at a powerful level and evoke their latent symbolic conflicts. In Whitaker's model the assumption is that if the family disorganizes by talking about usually hidden things, it will let go of its logical defensive structures and reorganize in more constructive ways. His model, intuitive and idiosyncratic, is difficult to teach but thought to be powerful in practice.

Satir's model operates less in the fantasy dimension and more in the here and now (Satir 1964). These models remind us that structure and problem solving are not the only possible goals of family therapy but that a warm and connected listener who is listening for deeper structures and meanings has much to offer.

The goal is to change the way family members experience and presumably react to one another. A secondary goal is growth and differentiation of family members.

Narrative Model

Among the newer additions to the field of family therapy is a set of assumptions falling loosely under the rubric of constructivism, part of the postmodern movement in philosophy and psychology. It is based on the work of a series of theorists from epistemology, biology, and cybernetics who see reality as constructed by the observer rather than as a truth to be discovered. Translated into the field of therapy, this suggests that the family's reality is in its shared *narratives and meaning systems,* that the personal story or self-narrative provides the principal frame of intelligibility for our lived experience, and that the therapist's assumptions about the family are also constructed rather than truth. The job of the therapist, then, is to help the family explore and reevaluate its own assumptions, beliefs, and meaning systems. In this model, a dysfunctional family has constructed a series of meanings that are not working in allowing the family flexibility and functioning. For example, if the mother is defined as bad, any move she makes toward either comforting or disciplining will be ignored, meaning the children get neither comfort nor discipline. If the family constructs the mother's story differently (e.g., she is doing her best to function despite her difficulties), she will be able to take care of the family members because they will accept her care.

This model allows the therapist and the patient together to deconstruct confining family stories that produce stasis or sadness and to consider new ones. Rather than the therapist producing a reframe and convincing the family of its correctness, this model emphasizes the importance of collaboration and mutual respect in the therapeutic alliance. Treatment is conceptualized primarily as a conversation about problems in which new meanings and new behaviors can be considered. Unlike those schools that highlight the family's history or its structural organization, these approaches highlight the strengths and competencies of the family that are often occluded by the family's and therapist's tendency to focus on the problems that bring the family to treatment.

Different therapists have used these ideas in different ways to attack family problems. The solution-oriented approach has been championed by deShazer (1988) and O'Hanlon (O'Hanlon and Weiner-Davis 1989). Its aims are to build on the growth-enhancing part of people's lives. These therapists focus on specific solutions to problems, rather than on personal growth, and help the client find new stories by focusing on exceptions—times when the problem did not occur. This allows for the development of new and more competent stories.

White and his group in Australia (White and Epston 1990) have developed a model of externalizing problems so that the problem becomes a separate entity, external to the person who has it. This allows for a move from a problem-saturated story about the person or family to a person or group of people working together to defeat it. These therapists might ask, for example, "How is bulimia working to keep you from your friends?" Problems are viewed as oppressively intruding on people's abilities to lead more fulfilling lives. These problems are also seen as unacknowledged, insidious extensions of both historical and sociocultural influences (e.g., inequities related to gender, race, class, ethnicity, sexual orientation).

In some ways the constructivist position has returned us to our roots, by elevating meaning to a position at least equal in importance to behavior patterns and by increasing the attention given to our own meaning and value systems. Discussion continues over whether "relativism" can be taken too far, meaning that any solution acceptable to the family is acceptable to the therapist.

Conclusion

Various strategies are available for treating families. Each may emphasize different assumptions and types of interventions. Some therapists prefer to operate with one strategy in most cases, whereas others intermix these strategies, depending on the type of case and the phase of treatment. At times the type of strategy used is made explicit by the therapist, whereas in other instances it remains covert. Regardless of whether a therapist specializes in one or another approach or is eclectic, some hypotheses will be formed about the nature of the family's difficulty and the preferable approach to adopt.

Some therapists emphasize reconstruction of past events, whereas others choose to deal only with current behavior as manifested during the therapy session. Some therapists favor verbal exploration and interpretation, whereas others prefer using an action or experiential mode of treatment, either in the session itself or by requiring new behavior outside the interview. Some therapists think in terms of problems and symptoms and attempt to decode or understand possible symbolic meanings of symptomatology, whereas other therapists focus on the potentials for growth and differentiation that are not being fulfilled. Some therapists use one or a very limited number of methods in dealing with a whole range of problems, whereas others are more eclectic and attempt to tailor the treatment techniques to what they consider to be the specific requirements of the situation.

Therapists may choose one school or another based on their training or their personality. For example, a very organized and directive person would probably prefer cognitive-behavioral methods, whereas a person who preferred long-term emotional intensity over problem solving might gravitate to experiential models. Individuals and families also may prefer some ways of working over others. This text encourages the integration of a variety of techniques, depending on the particular problem and personalities of the family. It also encourages the therapist to look beyond the problem at hand (i.e., the presenting complaint) to issues of power, intimacy, and personal growth. Our approach is to emphasize models that have empirical data.

This text encourages the integration of a variety of techniques, depending on the particular problem and personalities of the family.

With the therapeutic focus on one person, the emphasis is often on the individual's perceptions, reactions, and feelings and on the equality of status between the individual and the therapist. When the operative system involves two people, attention is directed to interactions and relationships. Therapists who think in terms of a unit of three people look at coalitions, structures, and hierarchies of status and power. The number of people involved in the interviews may not be as important as how many people are involved in the therapist's way of thinking about the problem.

Suggested Readings

Gurman A, Kniskern D (eds): Handbook of Family Therapy, Vols 1 and 2. New York, Brunner/Mazel, 1981
These edited volumes provide an excellent introduction to the major models of family therapy. The books are well organized, and chapters are written by noted representatives of each of the "influential schools."

Lebow J: The integrative revolution in couple and family therapy. Fam Process 36:1–19, 1997
This article examines the present status of integrative models of therapy, including specific conceptual developments and directions, and demonstrates the direction in which the field is headed.

References

Block D, Simon R (eds): The Strength of Family Therapy: Selected Papers of Nathan W. Ackerman. New York, Brunner/Mazel, 1982

Boszormenyi-Nagy I, Krasner B: Between Give and Take: A Clinical Guide to Contextual Therapy. New York, Brunner/Mazel, 1986

Bowen M: Family Therapy in Clinical Practice. New York, Jason Aronson, 1978

deShazer S: Clues: Investigating Solutions in Brief Therapy. New York, WW Norton, 1988

Dicks HV: Marital Tensions. London, Routledge & Kegan Paul, 1967

Framo JL: Family of Origin Therapy: An Intergenerational Approach. New York, Brunner/Mazel, 1992

Goldfried M: Toward the delineation of therapeutic change principles. Am Psychol 35:997–998, 1980

Jacobson N, Margolin G: Marital Therapy. New York, Brunner/Mazel, 1979

Merkel WT, Searight HR: Why families are not like swamps, solar systems, or thermostats; some limits of systems theory as applied to family therapy. Journal of Contemporary Family Therapy 14:33–50, 1992

Minuchin S, Fishman HC: Family Therapy Techniques. Cambridge, MA, Harvard University Press, 1981

Napier AY, Whitaker CA: The Family Crucible. New York, Harper & Row, 1978

O'Hanlon WH, Weiner-Davis M: In Search of Solutions: A New Direction in Psychotherapy. New York, WW Norton, 1989

Satir V: Conjoint Family Therapy: A Guide to Theory and Technique. Palo Alto, CA, Science and Behavior Books, 1964, pp 162–167, 175–176

Thibaut JW, Kelley HH: The Social Psychology of Groups. New York, Wiley, 1959

White M, Epston D: Narrative Means to Therapeutic Ends. New York, WW Norton, 1990

Williamson D: The Intimacy Paradox: Personal Authority in the Family System. New York, Guilford, 1986

La Familia, Lorenzo Homar, 1967. Courtesy of the artist and the Division of Education of the Committee of Puerto Rico. Used with permission.

CHAPTER 11

Goals

Objectives for the Reader

- To be able to set the mediating and final goals of family treatment
- To be able to individualize treatment goals
- To relate the goals of treatment to strategies and interventions
- To relate the goals of treatment to process and content of treatment issues

Introduction

If you would hit the mark, you must aim a little above it:
Every arrow that flies feels the attraction of the earth.

—Henry Wadsworth Longfellow

In this chapter we examine the issue of goals from five perspectives:

1. Mediating and final goals as they relate to family therapy schools

2. Individualizing goals with the family

3. Goals and their relation to process and content issues

4. Mediating goals and their related strategies

5. Goals and related strategies common to all family therapy schools

Mediating and Final Goals as They Relate to Schools

A convenient way to conceptualize types of treatment goals is to distinguish the final goals (i.e., the ultimate results desired) from the mediating (or intermediate) goals that must precede the final results. Although one would conceptualize unique and specific goals for each individual family, we present more general mediating and final family therapy goals in this chapter. These goals are relatively broad areas that allow for considerable flexibility according to the specifics of each particular family or marital unit, and they are not mutually exclusive but often are intertwined. These broad areas help clarify the therapist's idea of what is to be achieved, and they suggest potential treatment strategies and timing of interventions.

The Most Common Mediating Goals

1. *Establishment of a working alliance.* Patients and families size up therapists very quickly, and those early attitudes are likely to persist. Thus the early connection between family therapist and each family member is crucial to the ultimate outcome of the work. Setting up such an alliance in individual therapy seems relatively simple in comparison with setting up an alliance with the multiple members of a family, who themselves often do not get along with one another. The therapist also must find a way to connect with each person rather than favoring certain family members.

2. *Specification of problem(s).* This would include a detailed delineation of family members' feelings and behaviors regarding the symptoms or problems that brought the family to treatment.

3. *Clarification of attempted solutions.* It is very likely that many families have attempted solutions to their problems before coming to the conclusion that they need outside intervention. Because almost by definition these are solutions that failed, the therapist should determine what did not work (as indeed some would say that many problems are simply ordinary situations to which poor solutions were applied).

4. *Clarification and specification of individual desires and needs as they are expressed, mediated, and met in the total family or marital environment and network of relationships.* It is the lack of clarity, and conflict (either overt or covert), about such needs and desires that leads to or constitutes family pathology itself.

5. *Modification of individual expectations or needs.* Almost always, families

need/want too much change, too soon. The therapist titrates the rate of family change.

6. *Recognition of mutual contribution to the problem(s).* Although therapists differ in how early they think this recognition must come or how explicit it must be, the very acceptance of the family intervention format (i.e., most or all family members coming to most sessions) implies the family has some recognition that more than one family member may contribute to the problem or at least to solutions.

7. *Redefinition of the problem(s).* Redefining a problem completely and redefining it into various parts, some of which are problematic and others not, are steps to possible solutions. By way of an example, the therapist might say, "You are not 'bad' people; you are responding to stress with anxiety or anger." In this example, the problem is redefined as a need to find alternative ways to respond to stress.

8. *Improvement in communication skills.* This includes an improvement in listening and expressive skills, a diminution of coercive and blaming behavior with an increase in reciprocity, and the development of effective problem-solving and conflict-resolution behaviors.

9. *A shift in disturbed, inflexible roles and coalitions.* This may include helping to improve the autonomy and individualization of family members, to facilitate the more flexible assumption of leadership by a particular family member as circumstances require, and to facilitate general task performance by one or more members.

10. *Increased family knowledge about serious psychiatric illness.* In families in which any member has serious Axis I pathology such as schizophrenia or recurrent affective illness, a common mediating goal is to increase family information about the illness, its course, and its responsiveness to environmental, including familial, stresses.

11. *Insight.* The mediating goal of developing and improving insight regarding historical factors related to current problems or about current interaction patterns may be relatively important in psychodynamically oriented family or marital work but be absent in other orientations. However, other orientations may reframe particular stories about the family's history as a way of changing interaction.

The Most Common Final Goals

1. *Reduction or elimination of symptoms, or symptomatic behavior, in one or more family members.* Symptoms may include major or minor symptoms of mood and affect (e.g., anxiety and depression), thought disorder, dis-

ruptive behaviors in children and adolescents, marital conflict and fighting, and sexual disorders.

2. *Resolution of the problem(s) as originally presented by the family.*

3. *Increased family or marital intimacy.*

4. *Role flexibility and adaptability within the family matrix.*

5. *Toleration of differentness and differentiation appropriate to age and developmental level.*

6. *Balance of power within the marital dyad, with appropriate sharing of input and autonomy for the children.*

7. *Increased self-esteem.*

8. *Clear, efficient, and satisfying communication.*

9. *Resolution of neurotic conflict, inappropriate projective identification, and marital transference phenomena.*

The problems of families and the goals specific to these problems, both mediating and final, should determine the therapeutic strategies. Table 11–1 follows sequentially Tables 8–2 and 8–3 in making this concept clear, and the assumptions embodied in this table are central to the rest of the text.

Unfortunately the therapist's theoretical background and convictions too often dictate the techniques used (rather than the needs of the family). If research has specified the behaviors that cause or maintain a problem or specific symptoms, the mediating goals of the treatment should be adapted to focus on these behaviors. Several examples come to mind from recent research. Because prolonged contact between an individual with schizophrenia and a family member who is hostile and critical leads to the reappearance of symptoms and often rehospitalization (see Chapter 24), a specific treatment goal with such an individual and his or her family would be the reduction of such stress. In another area, research suggests that antisocial behavior in adolescents is related to coercive behavior exhibited by parents who lack parenting skills (Patterson 1982). Treatment in such situations would therefore involve mediating goals of reducing parental coercive behavior and instigating more appropriate parental behaviors of appropriate limit and boundary setting. These two illustrations are meant only as indications of the kinds of research that will specify needed mediating and final goals in order to change symptomatic constellations. In such a way, so-called schools of family intervention will give way to specified mediating goals that require proven strategies to accomplish desired goals.

TABLE 11–1. Determining strategies after goals are set

	Type of formulation	For the family	For the individual(s)
Diagnosis	Functional	*A*	*B*
		A systemic formulation	Behavioral or individual psychodynamic model and/or biological model
	Descriptive	*C*	*D*
		DSM-IV conditions not attributable to a mental disorder that are a focus of attention or treatment (e.g., parent-child problem, family typology)	DSM-IV classification for each family member on Axis I, II, or III, as appropriate
Goals	Based on diagnosis	Specify for each problem	Specify for each problem
Strategies	Based on goals	Specify for each goal	Specify for each goal

Individualizing Goals With the Family

The therapist forms a concept of the family's difficulties based on the evaluation of the family's history and interaction (see Section 3). The treatment often begins with the issues that seem to be most crucial to the family; that is, the treatment at the outset helps the family to deal with an immediate crisis situation. Only after some stability and rapport have been achieved is it possible for the therapist to begin to help the family in other ways that also will be beneficial. The work is sometimes slow and gradual, but often a few sessions are enough to get the family's own adaptive mechanisms operating again. At most family therapy clinics, the average number of visits is 6–10. At the extremes are some families that come in for only a few sessions and others that come in for many more. One hallmark of family therapy is the belief that rapid change is possible. Sometimes a family comes in for a brief period for one problem and comes back later to work on deeper issues. Family therapists do not consider this a failure. When one family member is seriously ill, therapy may be long term, intermittent, and supportive.

In setting goals it is helpful to think not only of the family as a whole and of the various interpersonal dyads and triads but also of the individuals who make up the system. Each individual will have a history, a personality, and a set of coping mechanisms. A thorough knowledge of individual personality theory and psychopathology is essential for knowing what to expect from the individual atoms and from the family molecule. At times it will be necessary to provide specific treatment for, or to direct specific attention to, the needs of an individual family member (e.g., when a family member is floridly psychotic) with individual sessions, somatic treatment, and sometimes hospitalization (see Chapter 24).

Even under ordinary circumstances, however, a thorough understanding of the strengths and weaknesses of each family member (e.g., basic personality patterns, reactions to stress) will help to determine the goals and techniques of the family therapy. Especially when separation or divorce impends, the assessment of individual issues becomes critical.

In setting goals it is also important to assess the needs of the larger family system, that is, those who may be deeply involved in the family but not in the room. For example, if the wife's mother hates her son-in-law and wishes her daughter would divorce, this is a critical issue affecting the nuclear family. In addition, the possibilities within the larger social system must be considered. For example, is it possible for a couple to marry if it means losing a significant amount of money from welfare or alimony?

> In setting goals it is also important to assess the needs of the larger family system, that is, those who may be deeply involved in the family but not in the room.

The goals of family treatment must be in some way congruent with what the family members seem to desire and what they are realistically capable of achieving. The therapist's views of the appropriate therapeutic possibilities, however, may differ from those the family members envision initially. For example, the family may wish for a home with no conflict, whereas the therapist may see a need for more effective ways of disagreeing.

Overall goals encompass the entire family system and its individual members. Ideally, the entire family should function more satisfactorily as a result of family therapy, and each family member should derive personal benefit from the experience and results of the therapy. The family therapist, for example, should not be in the position of taking the focus off a scapegoated member (saying, for instance, "It's not Dad's withdrawal that is the problem") only to consistently refocus on one or another family member as the cause of the family's difficulties. Nor should the family as a whole feel blamed for one member's problems.

Families traditionally enter therapy because of symptomatic difficulty. In the family's eyes this is often related to one family member, who has already been labeled as the identified patient. For example, a marital partner may blame the spouse for causing his or her distress or may feel guilty because the children are not behaving properly. Similarly, a child may be singled out as the only problem in the family. Sometimes a specific family member has a problem (e.g., alcohol, cancer, retardation) around which a family system organizes.

Less commonly, family members talk about system difficulties as marital troubles or family unhappiness. One family member may have instigated the seeking of help, or, much less often, the family as a whole may have discussed the difficulties and agreed to seek professional assistance. Families may come into treatment on their own with varying levels of motivation and expectations, or they may be referred by other agencies or individuals.

Some families today are seeking professional help, not for these more traditional reasons but for clarification of family roles and as a growth-enhancing experience. Of course, this is less common because of managed care, unless the family is able to pay for treatment on its own. In such cases, a problem-solving model seems less appropriate than a growth-development model.

The therapist will relate the goals of treatment to what has been learned during the initial evaluation period and to whatever develops as the therapy progresses. All specific mediating and final goals need not be spelled out clearly at the outset of treatment. In some schools of therapy, goals are left somewhat vague, with details being clarified only later or perhaps never being discussed explicitly. The particular areas to be dealt with, and a determination of the priority in dealing with them, must be considered carefully. Some family therapists are relatively comfortable with allowing goals to develop as the therapy proceeds. Such treatment sometimes appears as a sequence of short-term problem resolutions. Other therapists attempt to delineate major goals early in the course of treatment, including those aimed at helping the family to cope better with problems that cannot be reversed.

Goals and Their Relation to Process and Content Issues

The relative importance of structure and process, as compared with its content, is an issue sometimes raised by family therapists. The more traditional view tends to favor substantive content issues, whereas the newer, holistic view looks more closely at the characteristic patterning in an interpersonal network, with less emphasis on the subject matter. In some ways this may be an artificial dichotomy. For example, the communication process may become the most important subject matter of the therapy. Any attempt to deal with a specific content issue inevitably brings process issues to the surface (and vice versa).

> Mr. and Mrs. A requested help because their 19-year-old son, Ted, who was living at home, was very angry at Mrs. A and was being verbally abusive and refusing to help the household in any way. The problems started when Ted was supposed to go to college but refused. In sessions that included Mr. and Mrs. A, Ted, and his younger brother, Ted would talk angrily and dominate the sessions, and Mrs. A would complain about him whenever he stopped talking. Mr. A and Ted's younger brother watched silently.
>
> An initial goal was to alter the communication pattern to bring the rest of the family into the session and decrease the intensity between Mrs. A and Ted. The content of what Mrs. A and Ted talked about was less relevant than the context and pattern of the communication. The therapeutic interventions were to insist that Ted make room for the other members of the family, to get Mr. A to support Mrs. A, and to connect the sibling subsystem. Only when the communication pattern was altered did it become clear that Ted had stayed at home because of fear of failure (he had always had some trouble at school, and college would be a big step) and because he was afraid his father's diabetes would worsen and he would be needed at home.

Sometimes major emphasis is placed on a particular process technique and goal such as clarifying a family's communication patterns or helping family members deal with their feelings. Family therapists may see such process goals as being primary, either on ideological grounds or because of the appropriateness to a particular family, with the family being encouraged to deal with content issues as they arise after the family has the general process tools to do so. Other family therapists, perhaps because of differing conceptual bases applicable to different types of family goals, will tend to work in the other direction—that is, from the more specific content issues toward the more general process issues.

Trainees often feel uneasy about setting goals for family therapy because they are afraid of being perceived as too authoritarian by taking away from the family its right to set its own goals. Indeed, families should be encouraged to set their own goals to the greatest extent possible; however, the therapist's ability to reframe a problem may lead to different goals (e.g., "Your kid isn't bad, but he seems to be very reactive to your marital conflict; perhaps we could look at how he responds to the stress and how you might deal with each other better"). With disorganized families, the therapist will need to be more structured and active.

Mediating Goals and Their Related Strategies

The intersection of appropriate mediating goals with the most efficient therapeutic strategies and techniques at the most propitious moment and in the right sequence is by definition the art of psychotherapy. Future research will help specify such combinations, but clinical skill and creativity will always play a role. For heuristic and instructional reasons, Table 11–2 presents a general scheme of family intervention that relates mediating goals to strategies. In later chapters we delineate more fully the specific techniques of family intervention.

Goals and Related Strategies Common to All Family Therapy Schools

Although repetitive with material presented in Chapter 10, we think it is heuristically useful to conceptualize the broad strategies of intervention that cut

TABLE 11–2.   Mediating goals of family therapy and their strategies

Mediating goals	Strategies
Increased knowledge, decreased guilt, redefinition of problems, increased use of adaptive coping mechanisms	Supporting adaptive mechanisms
Appropriate emotional experience and communication	Expanding emotional experience
Use of communication skills, problem-solving skills, parenting skills	Developing interpersonal skills
Clarification of boundaries, setting of appropriate boundaries between familial subsystems and family of origin	Reorganizing the family structure
Insight regarding current transactions and historical factors, decreased conflict	Increasing insight
Work on family of origin issues	Constructing an alternative reality or story

across the various schools of thought because, in practice, strategies are combined in different ways to treat the individual family. We summarize here the various ways to conceptualize overall strategies of family intervention.

1. *Strategies for supporting adaptive mechanisms.* There are a number of ways to assist families in using existing strategies and developing new strategies for coping. For example, the therapist could provide the family with information (i.e., psychoeducation) about illnesses in family members or about parenting skills. Supportive advice and encouragement of existing coping mechanisms are also included here, as is the strategy of bearing witness (i.e., acknowledging and understanding the family's experience or emotional pain or trauma). These strategies are of critical importance.

2. *Strategies for expanding emotional experience.* The basic skills are listening, labeling, and encouraging supportive family responses to feelings. Sharing the therapist's own response or that of others (e.g., "Many people would feel great pain in that situation") is a common way of validating and encouraging feelings. Therapists may at times use fantasy, humor and irony, direct confrontation, family sculpting, or choreography (prescribing sequences of what a family should do) to open up new areas of immediate emotional experiencing for the family.

3. *Strategies for developing interpersonal skills.* By a multitude of techniques, including modeling of intent listening to others, insisting that only one person speak at a time, questioning the exact meaning of what others are saying and wishing to communicate, and providing explicit instruction in communication skills, the therapist brings the family to a better communication level. This improvement can be an end in itself, or it can be used to solve specific problems that brought the family to treatment in the first place.

4. *Strategies for reorganizing the family structure.* Reframing of the problems as presented by the family, enacting the family problems with their attendant interactional sequences (step-by-step enactment of a family, behavior; e.g., father over "A," mother over "B," son over "C," and so on), marking boundaries, and restructuring moves (changing the structure of a family; e.g., bringing in another family member, such as grandmother, to help change a problem behavior, such as mother's cocaine abuse) can all be used to change the structured family behaviors judged to be causing or contributing to the family distress. Paradoxical techniques (which are discussed in Chapter 12), although used less frequently than in the past, can be used for families that are resistive or at an impasse.

Effective family structure is predicated on the idea that parents work together and that appropriate generational hierarchy be maintained. By insisting in the session that parents make joint decisions about the children rather than leaving the mother in charge and the father passive, insisting that parents take charge of children rather than allow them to control the session, and delineating responsibilities of grandparents and other family adults, the therapist allows families to experience new types of structure. Homework assignments that encourage clear boundaries, such as making sure the parents' bedroom door is closed at night, reinforce these messages.

5. *Strategies for increasing insight.* Traditional techniques of psychodynamic psychotherapy, such as clarification, confrontation, and interpretation either in the here and now or of genetic material, can be used in the marital and family treatment formats in order to bring underlying conflicts to the fore and reduce conflict-laden interactions. Insight here must be relational in terms of how the person's past affects the present and the response of the other. Direct questioning of the parents and analysis of current relationships by family of origin work are other useful ways of developing insight.

6. *Strategies for helping the family understand and modify its narrative.* These strategies involve helping the family tell its story and find alternative and less problem-saturated narratives that offer novel solutions. The therapist and family members look for redefinitions (e.g., enthusiastic rather than noisy, survivor rather than victim), understandings (e.g., fear of failure rather than laziness), and novel outcomes (e.g., how about the times it doesn't fail—what happens then?).

Conclusion

There are short-term goals (see Chapter 13) and long-term goals. Examples of goals can be found in the R family case example presented in Chapter 8, and we discuss short- and long-term goals for different types of families in Chapter 24.

The beginning therapist is cautioned against trying to produce instantaneous behavioral change that may prove to be evanescent. As Winston Churchill said, "It is a mistake to look too far ahead. Only one link in the chain of destiny can be handled at a time." The chronicle of unconventional psychotherapies is replete with claims of being able to change behavior in the short term. In contrast, family therapists should aim for a more permanent, long-term change in family structure and function but should do it step by step.

These differences in outlook and practice can be bewildering to the inexperienced therapist who is not aware of the underlying rationales and guidelines. Given the current state of the field, with no unifying theory of family pathology, nomenclature, or even of treatment, each new situation represents an experiment of sorts, in which the therapist is required to clarify and test hypotheses.

Suggested Readings

Steinglass P: Family therapy, in Comprehensive Textbook of Psychiatry/VI, 6th Edition, Vol 2. Edited by Kaplan HI, Sadock BJ. Baltimore, MD, Williams & Wilkins, 1995, pp 1838–1846
This volume is a clearly written guide to treatment and goal setting.

References

Patterson GR: Coercive Family Process. Eugene, OR, Castalia, 1982

"The Interrupted Marriage" by Rigaud Benoit, 1972.
Humor, social criticism in an Arabian Nights setting.
COLLECTION, THE AUTHOR

The Interrupted Marriage, Rigaud Benoit, 1972. Private collection. Used with permission.

CHAPTER 12

Family Treatment: Strategies and Techniques

Objectives for the Reader

- ☜ To understand the common elements of psychotherapy as they apply to family treatment
- ☜ To become familiar with the general strategies of family therapy and their related techniques
- ☜ To become familiar with the notion of treatment packages for specific situations and disorders

Introduction

Before describing how to treat families, we first examine family therapy in the general context of the strategies and techniques of psychotherapy. In this chapter, we recommend treatment modalities that look beyond the notion that success is merely an unconditional acceptance of life and what it brings. Subjective and objective improvement should occur in behaviors, emotions, and individuals' capacities to live. We conclude the chapter with reference to current treatment packages for various diagnostic or problem situations that families face.

General Elements of Psychotherapy and Their Relationship to Family Therapy

Most schools of psychotherapy share the following elements:

1. An effective patient-therapist relationship

2. Release of emotional tension or development of emotional expression

3. Cognitive learning

4. Insight into the genesis of one's problems

5. Operant reconditioning of the patient toward more adaptive behavior patterns using techniques such as behavioral desensitization

6. Suggestion and persuasion

7. Identification with the therapist

8. Repeated reality testing or practicing of new adaptive techniques in the context of implicit or explicit emotional therapeutic support

9. Construction of a more positive narrative about oneself and the world

10. Instillation of hope

Family therapy involves all of these elements, but it does so in the context of the whole family, with the goal of improving the entire group's overall functioning. The particular mix of therapeutic elements will vary with the family's specific needs. There are few, if any, specific techniques used in other therapy formats (i.e., individual and group) and orientations (e.g., insight-awareness, cognitive-behavioral, systemic-strategic, experiential-existential) that could not in some way be adapted for use in family intervention.

Somewhat parenthetically, the question is often asked "Can a 'psychotherapy,' such as family therapy, change the brain?" Gabbard (1998) pointed out "that the brain is characterized by considerable plasticity and that genes are not static but responsive to environmental factors which we are only beginning to understand." Kandel (1998) suggested that by producing changes in gene expression, psychotherapy may alter the strength of synaptic connections. Biological and psychosocial factors appear to have equal weight in development. There is a reciprocal effect of gene expression on environment and environment on gene expression in every family system. We can no longer afford reductionism in either a biological or a psychosocial direction.

Basic Strategies of Family Intervention

Because much overlap exists among the schools of family intervention (both in theory and techniques), and because our bias is that the field must advance beyond strict schools to basic principles of change, we present our choice of basic strategies of family intervention. We also describe in this section the techniques used in each strategy:

- Supporting adaptive mechanisms and strengths, including imparting new information, advice, suggestions, and so on—the so-called psycho-educational approach
- Expanding individual and family emotional experience
- Encouraging explicit development of interpersonal skills (e.g., communication skills, parenting skills, problem-solving skills)
- Reorganizing the family structure
- Increasing insight and fostering intrapsychic conflict resolution
- Helping the family find new and more positive ways of understanding its situation (i.e., the narrative approach)

Even these strategies, abstractly stated in terms of their aim or goal in treatment, are not mutually exclusive. To some extent, they represent different frames of reference for understanding and dealing with the same family phenomena. Nevertheless, each strategy seems to offer something unique in its conceptualization and execution. The choice of strategy depends on the goals (see Table 11–2). In general, however, all families can profit from review and support of their strengths.

In a clinical situation, the therapist will be hard-pressed to remain a purist. For example, a therapist's efforts to clarify communication may produce shifts in family coalitions or may initiate an exploration of family myths that may lead to a considerable outpouring of previously concealed emotion.

Although we list specific therapeutic strategies here, there is no one magical technique that will "cure" the family. Interventions are instead a series of repetitive maneuvers designed to change feelings, attitudes, and behaviors. If the overall goals and strategy are kept in mind, specific interventions will suggest themselves and be modified by the family's circumstances and the therapist's own style.

> **W**hat is unique in family therapy is not so much the specific techniques used but rather that these techniques are used not with an isolated individual but within a relationship and that the overall focus and strategy aims to evaluate and produce a beneficial change in the entire family system.

Techniques for Supporting Adaptive Mechanisms and Strengths

First and foremost, the therapist uses many techniques to support the active or latent positive coping mechanisms the family has at its disposal. Every family has some degree of health, and that should be acknowledged and actively encouraged. Empathic listening and concern, positive feedback about the use of adaptive defenses (such as healthy denial in the face of terminal illness), education about poorly adaptive defenses, and well-timed advice are all helpful to the family in distress.

The therapist is constantly in the role of a teacher, either directly or indirectly. Without saying a word, he or she is modeling mood, tempo, and interpersonal acceptance. The therapist also teaches values, often implicitly. For example, in structuring the treatment so that only one person in the family speaks at a time, the therapist is modeling good communication but is also indicating implicitly the value of respecting the thoughts of every person in the family.

More recently there has been a growing emphasis on providing explicit information that might be helpful to families in their coping. This approach has been most obvious in the psychoeducational strategies used with families in which a member has been given the diagnosis of a disorder such as schizophrenia or mood disorder (Anderson et al. 1986; Goldstein 1996). Information can be communicated through written material, in lectures and discussions in family groups, and in workshop format. Anderson and colleagues have described a day-long survival skills workshop, which the family attends without the patient. During this workshop, information is provided on the nature of schizophrenia (e.g., the history and epidemiology of the disorder, its biological basis, and personal experiences of patients and family members), the available treatments (e.g., medication and psychosocial treatment), and the role of the family (e.g., family reactions to the patient and the illness, methods for coping with the condition). Consider the following case example:

Ms. A, a 20-year-old single, female college student, had long-standing double depression (i.e., major depressive disorder and atypical depression) since her teens. She was in the midst of an 8-month episode of acute depression characterized by psychomotor retardation, cognitive slowing, lability, and overeating. She was being treated with a combination of individual therapy, family therapy, and antidepressants. Although she had been ill for 3 or 4 years, she had never understood her illness. Her physician spent time explaining in detail the multiple roots of her depression. She reported that before receiving the psychoeducation, when she thought about her illness it was "like a huge something I didn't understand." After psychoeducation, she said, "I could pick apart pieces of the illness, ask questions about it, and understand it, and I felt better immediately after the session." When asked why she felt better, she said her thoughts were now more cohesive and thus she could better cope with her illness.

In Ms. A's case a second nuance of psychoeducation involved the family therapist's focus on her parents' perception that she was lazy because she spent so much time on the couch watching television. The intervention directed to Ms. A and her family was partly psychoeducational (i.e., it was explained that leaden paralysis is a cardinal symptom of atypical depression and that weight gain is a side effect of antidepressants) and partly dynamic and systemic.

The psychoeducational approach need not be limited to situations in which there is a clear diagnosis of a condition that has biological components in its etiology. Communication skills and problem-solving skills are taught in many forms of marital therapy. For example, Patterson (1982) provides information to parents with antisocial children so that they can improve their family management skills (described later in this chapter). In some situations therapists give advice to families that function relatively well. This may include discussing parenting alternatives such as discipline styles or helping the family to make difficult decisions (e.g., determining whether a child should go away to school or stay at home).

The use of psychoeducation should not lead to an exclusive focus on either biology or behavior. As Hunter et al. (1988) have pointed out, "Family therapists should not abandon a concern with the inner lives of severely ill patients and their families 'after they are educated about an illness.'" Families that have been asked about their experience in therapy repeatedly cite as helpful the therapist's ability to listen respectfully, to notice their strengths, and to be active—that is, to offer suggestions and advice but in a way that is respectful and not commanding. Families need to have the sense that their therapist has ideas they can try but that the therapist will not be hurt or angry if they don't agree with the plan.

Families that have been asked about their experience in therapy repeatedly cite as helpful the therapist's ability to listen respectfully, to notice their strengths, and to be active—that is, to offer suggestions and advice but in a way that is respectful and not commanding.

Techniques for Expanding Emotional Experience

Techniques used to help individuals and family units expand their experience repertoire tend to focus on the here-and-now experience in the sessions themselves. These techniques are designed to help the individual family members to quell anxiety, slow their reaction process, and maximize the emotional and cognitive experience of the moment, experiences that may have been denied, defended against, and missed in the past. In many families, feelings are either avoided or detoured. For example, some members of the family, or the entire family, may not admit to feelings because they are afraid of hurting other family members. Alternatively, certain feelings may be avoided or denied, so that, for example, anger instead of sadness may be expressed. Rebellious or inappropriate behavior may be used as a nonverbal protest (e.g., forgetting, daydreaming, or bowel control problems may occur as a way of demonstrating helpless rage or anxiety).

In some families the affect, especially rage or anxiety, may appear all too obvious and overwhelming, but invariably there are also hidden feelings and silent family members. Some families may appear too full of affect, and some families may seem to have none. The therapist's job is to slow down or speed up the family's process and allow the variety of feelings to surface in a safe environment, allowing everyone to feel heard and to see how hidden or detoured feelings, or long-standing rage or anxiety, have affected the family's functioning. Often the most important thing for an individual family member is to know that other family members understand how he or she feels, even when they cannot fix it. For a child especially, the most difficult thing, even worse than disagreement or punishment, is to be disconfirmed—that is, to have a feeling of being completely ignored.

Often the most important thing for an individual family member is to know that other family members understand how he or she feels, even when they cannot fix it.

The therapist's main role is to look for the family's underlying feelings and, using empathy and clarification, to help family members to express them. Simple examples of such expression include "That really must have hurt," "How did you feel then?" or "I hear you were angry, but you also look sad; why is that?" The therapist may also use disclosure, by saying, for example, "That story makes me feel sad." This approach is especially helpful in younger patients who are less experienced in expressing emotions, especially strong emotions that are often feared by children to be overwhelming. The therapist then asks how other family members felt or reacted because the issue in families is not only the feeling but the reaction or anticipated reaction of other family members. For example, the therapist could use the following series of questions: "Did you tell your mom or your dad how you felt? What did they say? How did you feel, Mom? Dad? What happened next? Were there other people in the family who felt differently? Why? If you didn't tell them then, how do you think they feel when you tell them now?" The therapist acts as witness and support, making sure that everyone is heard and protected.

The therapist examines which feelings are acceptable in the family and which are not, and whether only certain family members express feelings for other family members (e.g., only the mother expresses anxiety, and she is told she is crazy). This is a particularly important technique in marital therapy, in which the spouses' feelings about each other form much of the basis of the therapy. The sense that one partner is not heard or respected by the other is a common underlying reason for divorce in a society in which the fulfillment of emotional needs is the center of marriage. The use of this technique is critical when violence, acting out, or mourning is present. When the feelings are of great grief, or there is great anger and a need to forgive, rituals are often designed to support or accentuate the process. For example, families that have been unable to mourn may be asked to prepare a new memorial service, to share stories and perhaps pictures of the deceased with the therapist, or to design a new holiday celebration that would include memories of the person who died but allow for new activities.

A number of techniques adapted from other therapies are powerful emotional catalysts. Such techniques include psychodrama and the techniques adapted from it (e.g., role-play, gestalt, family sculpting), family marathons, and guided fantasy. Although these techniques are all interesting and often extremely powerful, they are best left to those with special training. In the long run there are few techniques as powerful as a therapist who can sit with a family, hour after hour in the face of its pain, and bear the pain with the family and help it find ways to heal.

Techniques for Developing Interpersonal Skills

Many families and marital units do not use basic skills of communication, parenting, or general problem solving, either because they never learned such skills as a result of poor or absent parental modeling or because of interpersonal conflicts that interfere with the use of such skills.

The therapist is by training an expert in communication and thus can help family members express their thoughts and feelings more clearly to one another. These are not skills traditionally learned in residency, and beginning therapists do not always have these skills. The therapist should be certain that he or she is familiar with these techniques, and he or she should have attempted to use them at a personal level before teaching them to others. The therapist tries to promote open and clear communication, emotional empathy, a positive rapport between family members, and good problem-solving skills. Good problem solving requires an additional set of skills beyond the clear communication of feeling. Problem solving is different from sharing feelings in that the emphasis is on cognitively finding solutions to problems rather than simply expressing feelings about them. Although expressing feelings may involve great positive or negative affect, problem solving needs calm. Communication requires both a speaker and a listener (or a communicator and a receiver, in the case of nonverbal communication) and consists of not only the message sent but also the message intended and the message received. The therapist's goal is to help the family look at intended messages, the way the messages are sent and their content, and what the receivers think about them. Although it is impossible not to communicate in a family (even silence plus nonverbal signals present a powerful message), many troubled family members spend very little time talking meaningfully with one another. Both thoughts and feelings can be distorted, hidden, negated, or blurred. The person sending the message may or may not be aware that his or her intention and the message do not match. Unless the person sending the message asks, he or she will never know what the other person understood.

Although expressing feelings may involve great positive or negative affect, problem solving needs calm.

The therapist supplies an arena for family discussion, being cognizant of the different levels of meaning in messages and how these levels of meaning influence and sometimes contradict one another. The therapist does not allow anyone to monopolize a session or to speak for someone else. The therapist helps the family look at how messages are sent, what messages are hidden, and why it is often hard to hear them. A common technique to slow down a conversation so that it is clearer is to insist that before someone can reply to a communication, he or she has to repeat it, first verbatim and then in paraphrase. The therapist attempts to encourage interpersonal sensitivity and empathy and tries to help each person become more aware of his or her own thoughts and feelings. Consider the following examples:

Example of a problem.

Husband: I was really upset that you didn't do the dishes last night.

Wife: You think I'm a bad wife and mother! Well, you didn't do the breakfast dishes either.

Example of communications practice.

Husband: I was really upset that you didn't do the dishes last night.

Wife: You were really upset that I didn't do the dishes?

Husband: Yes, that's what I said.

Wife: That makes me angry, and I think you think I'm a sloppy person.

Husband: I don't think you are sloppy, but you promised to do them. I am upset because you broke your promise to me, and that makes me feel as if you don't care about me.

The therapist encourages family members to be specific, to state who did what to whom (e.g., "Dad hit me with a stick," rather than "He did it"). The therapist encourages more productive and supportive communication. He or she emphasizes finding both positive and negative ways of saying things and noticing nonverbal messages. He or she helps parents speak to their children in ways appropriate to each child's age. The therapist looks for family members who speak for others (e.g., a mother who always answers for her daughter) and for family members who don't speak to one another (e.g., a son who speaks only to his father, not his mother). He or she works to get family members to speak for themselves (i.e., using "I" statements) and to get family members who have issues with another family member to speak directly to that member rather than through a third person. The therapist stresses that individuals are held accountable for their actions. He or she fills in gaps in communication, points out discrepancies, and deals with nonverbal communication. The therapist points out nonproductive verbal and nonverbal family communication patterns and tries to identify the implicit, unstated patterns or attitudes that may be causing trouble. Through these efforts the covert is made overt, the implicit made explicit. Blocked channels of communication and feeling can be opened. The therapist counsels that good communication includes listening. Often three or four family members are heard talking at exactly the same time during a session, presumably to avoid hearing thoughts and feelings other than their own. In such a situation the therapist may function as a communication traffic cop or referee.

Marital and family life is filled with problems, large and small. In many cases distressed families have no more problems than do nondistressed families, but nondistressed families use effective problem-solving techniques so that problems are handled and do not multiply. Distressed families can be taught problem-solving methods. The steps of problem solving are 1) defining a problem, 2) brainstorming, 3) negotiating, and 4) making clear the behavioral contract.

In general, distressed families have trouble with problem solving not only because of skill deficits but also because of hidden agendas, many of which involve power issues. For example, if a wife wants her husband to share the work around the house more and he doesn't want to, a behavioral contract about how many nights he is to wash dishes isn't much help. He is likely to forget, do the job badly, and be angry, even if she agrees to do something for him in return. The problem must be defined as a larger issue about equality in family life, and if the husband is strongly against doing any more than he is already doing, it is difficult to solve this problem. It will have to be clear to him that he will get something of equal value that will not injure his sense of self-esteem or manliness (the cognitive issue behind the behavioral problem). A couple or family that comes up with seemingly reasonable solutions that are not put into practice needs to spend time with the therapist redefining the problem and looking for the issues behind the issues.

Distressed families have trouble with problem solving not only because of skill deficits but also because of hidden agendas.

In addition to the communication and problem-solving skills needed by a marital dyad, other skills are needed to raise children effectively. Patterson (1982) has referred to these skills as family management skills and has devised techniques for teaching these skills to families with an antisocial child. The family management skills that can be taught include rule setting, parental monitoring (detection and labeling), and parental sanctions, including the appropriate use of positive reinforcement and punishment. Each of these skills must be carefully taught, role-played, and supervised.

In the social learning theory tradition, Stuart (1980) has outlined a behaviorally oriented marital therapy approach that begins with assessment and proceeds through so-called caring days (i.e., each partner offering specific requested caring behaviors). Techniques are organized to increase 1) small, high-frequency, conflict-free behaviors; 2) communication skills; 3) contracting procedures; 4) training in problem-solving skills; 5) training in conflict containment; and 6) strategies for maintaining the changed interaction. Stuart gives as a clinical example a holistic agreement in which several behaviors by one spouse are exchanged for several by the other, with no requirements that the offerings by one exactly match those of the other:

> An agreement arrived at by Mr. and Mrs. B negotiated and put in writing by the two, for example, looks like this: Mrs. B would like Mr. B to mow the lawn, initiate lovemaking, take responsibility for balancing their checkbooks, and share washing the dishes. Mr. B would like Mrs. B to have dinner ready by 6:30 nightly, weed the rose garden, and call him at the office daily. It is contracted and expected that each will do as many of the items requested by the other as is comfortably manageable, ideally at least three or four times weekly.

This model is workable only if the therapist has evaluated carefully the power, intimacy, and justice issues underlying the problematic behaviors. Most behaviorally oriented marital therapies stress cognitive issues (e.g., How does this fit with my picture of myself? Is this acceptable behavior in my culture?) and the careful and gradual increase of positive and caring behaviors. We believe that systemic and cognitive approaches are gradually converging (see Dattilio et al. 1998 for a discussion of this development).

Techniques for Reorganizing the Family Structure

In many ways, the unique contribution of the family orientation is the recognition of structured (i.e., repetitive and predictable) behavioral sequences in family groups that cause or maintain symptomatic behaviors. Figure 12–1 provides a graphic representation of common family coalitions. In the figure, a typical four-member family is taken as the unit, with the squares representing the males and the circles the females. The larger symbols stand for spouse/parent, and the smaller symbols represent the offspring/siblings. The solid straight lines joining these symbols are intended to represent positive communication, emotional, and activity bonds between the individuals involved, in a semiquantitative fashion, according to the number of straight lines used. Dotted lines are used to represent the relative absence or negative quality of the interactions.

In example A, the functional family, the marital coalition is the strongest dyad in the family, the generational boundary is intact, and all other channels are open and about equal to one another in importance. In contrast to this example are various types of dysfunctional families (see Chapter 3).

In example B, the marital coalition is relatively weak or absent, and instead there are strong alliances across the generations and sexes—between father and daughter and between mother and son—with a relative absence of other effective channels. In example C, cross-generational alliances exist between same-sex parent and child. Examples B and C can be thought of as representing types of the schismatic family.

Examples D and E depict skewed families in which one family member is relatively isolated from the other three, who form a fairly cohesive unit. Example F represents the generation-gap family, in which the marital unit and the offspring both form a fairly cohesive duo, with little or no interaction across the generational lines. Example G represents the pseudodemocratic family, in which all channels seem to be of about equal importance, with the marital coalition and the parental role not being particularly well differentiated. Example H, the disengaged family, represents an extreme case in which each family member is pretty much cut off from every other member, and in which one would expect very little sense of positive interaction, feeling, or belonging to a family unit.

Clearly these representations are highly oversimplified and are pictured only for a two-generation, four-member family. Infinite variations could be added. Such representations enable the therapist to conceptualize more clearly the nature of the coalitions in a particular family and to begin planning a strategy to bring those coalitions into a better functional alignment, pre-

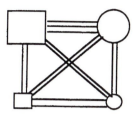

A. Functional

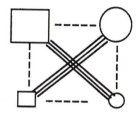

B. Schismatic

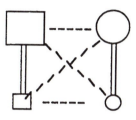

C. Schismatic

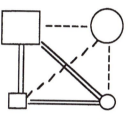

D. Skewed

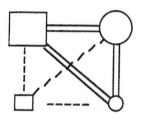

E. Skewed

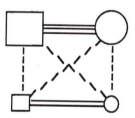

F. Generation gap

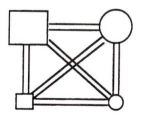

G. Pseudodemocratic

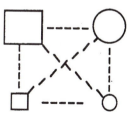

H. Disengaged

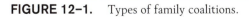

FIGURE 12–1. Types of family coalitions.

sumably more closely approximating example A. In example B, for instance, the therapist might focus on activating the marital coalition, the coalitions between parent and offspring of the same sex, and those between the offspring themselves. Also, the therapist might attempt to attenuate the force of the existing cross-generational, cross-sexed interactions.

The tactics and strategies of family therapy, viewed in this light, might include changes in the marital coalition (very commonly the case) and in the parent-child dyads. Although triads are not considered to any great extent in this model, an isolated family member might be brought into interaction with the rest of the family unit. In some of the families depicted in Figure 12–1, the problem is an overly connected triad, in which case decreasing less functional coalitions will automatically make space for the isolated family member. Looking outside of the nuclear family for a moment, it is critical to consider coalitions and cutoffs with the extended family (e.g., parents and siblings of the adults and other significant family members) and to examine relationships with other significant systems (e.g., peers of children, therapists, other helping professionals in the system, secret relationships such as affair partners). Remarried families in particular will have immensely complicated structures, and it is critical that the therapist uses a genogram to include all members of the family (see Chapter 7). When outside interactions, especially those with in-laws, seem problematic, modifications should be considered. Sometimes outside interactions may need to be encouraged, especially if no one has contacts outside the family.

Temporary triads, for example, incorporating the therapist, are often purposely formed in order to produce structural change. In example D, the father is connected primarily with his son, and both men are disrespectful to mother and daughter. If the daughter enters therapy with depression, rather than treat the daughter's depression in isolation, the therapist looks at how the father's disrespect and mother's passivity have made her feel hopeless. The therapist encourages the husband to insist on his son being respectful (i.e., fathers teach their sons respect) and works with the parents to encourage the mother to speak up for herself and the father to look at why he is treating his wife badly. (Perhaps he is really angry because she is paying attention to her own mother and not to him.) The parents are encouraged to support their daughter and to deal with their own issues. The daughter's depression lifts because she no longer has to be her mother's support.

Techniques that enable the family therapist to interrupt and change such structured family behaviors are central to reorganizing the family structure (Minuchin 1974; Minuchin and Fishman 1981). The techniques include the following:

- *Reframing.* Each individual frames reality from his or her own unique perspective. When the therapist perceives and understands the patient's or family's frame and then counters this frame with another, competing view, this is called a *reframe* (Watziawick et al. 1974). Such a therapeutic move can be sudden, dramatic, or humorous and often models a more relaxed, less conflicted, or more positive view of the world and the basic details of family life. The goal of a reframe is to allow the family to find different ways of behaving. For example, if the parents of a misbehaving child label the child as being sick or creative, they may not discipline him, but if they label him as being spoiled, then they may find more creative but firm ways of getting him to behave.
- *Enactment.* It is one thing for a family to describe what has happened, and it is another thing for the family to enact what happened in front of the therapist. *Enactment* is the technique of eliciting during the therapeutic hour the playing out of interpersonal problems of which the family complains. Enactment enables the perceptive therapist to observe the interpersonal behaviors in the problem sequence, rather than hearing the typical censored versions of what goes on, as offered by each participant.
- *Focusing.* The individual therapist is flooded with a multitude of data from the patient. With the recent developments in the brief therapy field, literature has accumulated on patient ability and therapist factors in focusing the sessions. This multiplicity of data is compounded in family therapy by the number of individuals involved. For there to be organization, highlighting, and progression in the treatment, someone must focus the group's attention. From multiple inputs, the therapist must select a focus and develop a theme for the family therapy work (Minuchin and Fishman 1981). According to Minuchin and Fishman (1981), there are three major techniques to challenge the structure of the family: 1) boundary making, 2) unbalancing, and 3) creation of a systemic reality.

  - *Boundary making.* Boundary-making techniques are ways of focusing on and changing the psychological distance between two or more family members. A common example is when the therapist moves the mother away from the daughter and insists that the daughter speak. In triadic interactions, a typical situation is one in which the unresolved conflicts between the parents are acted out by the misbehavior of a child, who then either sides with the mother or the father or becomes a judge or go-between for the two parents. The therapist can intervene in the session by distancing the child verbally or physically from the mother-father dyad. The therapist can make boundaries through verbal reconstructions (e.g., he or she could say, "Mom and Dad, you are the bosses of your children; now act like it"), the giving of tasks, special re-arrangements of seating in the sessions, or nonverbal gestures and eye contact (Minuchin and Fishman 1981).

- *Unbalancing.* The family therapist uses unbalancing techniques in order to change the hierarchical relationship of members of a family system or sub-system. There are three basic ways of unbalancing the existing family hier-archy and power distribution: 1) affiliating with certain family members, 2) ignoring family members, or 3) entering into a coalition with some fam-ily members against others. A therapist unbalances the family's existing power system by, for example, allying with a family member low in the power hierarchy. Unbalancing is a technique that is somewhat controver-sial because many therapists prefer either a more neutral stance or one that supports all family members equally. Unbalancing may have unintended consequences and needs to be done with a clear sense of its use and an awareness of whether the intervention is working.

- *Creation of a systemic reality.* By using mainly cognitive interventions, the family therapist attempts to help the family members perceive and understand the workings of their mutual interdependence and member-ship in an entity (i.e., the family) larger than themselves. Family mem-bers generally perceive themselves as acting and reacting to one another, rather than seeing the larger picture of the family dance (or family script) over time.

The family therapist commonly challenges the family's usual rhetoric (i.e., formulation) in three areas: 1) the family notion that there is only one identi-fied patient, 2) the family notion that one person is controlling the family system, or 3) the family's time-limited vision of its interactions. First, even if one person is obviously symptomatic, the therapist introduces the notion that family interactions are probably helping to maintain the problem. Sec-ond, the therapist counters the idea that one person controls the system with the conception that each person provides the context for the other. That is, symptoms in one person are maintained by the interpersonal context. Finally, the therapist helps the family achieve an understanding of its interactions over a large time frame so that it (the family) can perceive (i.e., bring into their awareness) the family rules that transcend (i.e., govern) the individual family members.

- *Paradoxical techniques.* These techniques are called paradoxical because they appear to be opposite to common sense. They are based on the fact that although people are often aware of the reasons they want to change, hidden reasons for not changing keep the symptom going. Faced with a symptom that does not respond to support, insight, logic, and so on, the therapist may suggest that the person keep the symptom to study its effects, make a list of all the reasons the symptom is useful or cannot be changed, or increase the symptom frequency in order to make sure it is working (thereby proving that it is also under the person's control). For example, a couple who have been unable to either make a commitment or split up may be told that their current arrangement of indecision is the best process, giving reasons that are believable and yet slightly off base (e.g., each needs the sense of distance and remoteness, the tension is good for their work, they are not yet ready to give up their mothers). They are given the task of planning how to remain in this ambiguous state for a long time. The therapist must give this intervention with seriousness, which means he or she must believe in its inherent truth. This injunction to hold on to the symptom usually jars the continuing process and helps the couple focus more clearly on what is going on; it may also unite the couple against the therapist and cause them to rebel, which would also break the logjam. (Because it seems manipulative, many family therapists have argued against this type of intervention.) Although it is possible to conduct a whole therapy in this manner, most therapists reserve this type of intervention for more resistant couples (Weeks and L'Abate 1982).

A common intervention is to request that the family members (or individuals) intensify the occurrence of the symptoms. When the family does this, the symptoms begin to lose their autonomy, mystery, and power. Whereas the symptoms previously seemed to have been out of control, they now appear to come under the therapist's and the family's control. The participants, in increasing the behavior, become more conscious of it, and often the disruptive behavior begins to lessen or disappear. Consider the following example:

> Mr. and Mrs. C, a married couple that have engaged in nonproductive arguing, now find that the therapist has asked them to continue fighting and even to increase it. She tells the couple to fight about the menu before dinner, so that they can enjoy the food. After the first few fights Mr. and Mrs. C decide that this ruins dinner. They refuse to fight. The therapist expresses doubt that this is a good idea, that is, remaining in the no-change position relative to her own suggested intervention. The couple now insist that they can and will stop fighting—taking the change position relative to the intervention. The resistance to

change is now coming from the therapist, leaving Mr. and Mrs. C free to experiment with change.

If the therapist gives directives or homework, he or she is obligated to follow through to make sure that the directions have been followed in the way that was intended. The therapist does so by seeing the family in his or her office on an ongoing basis and by asking more than one family member what changes have taken place. In some situations the therapist may choose to make a home visit, but this must be done with considerable care and preparation.

Techniques for Increasing Insight and Conflict Resolution

Although the experiential-existential and insight-awareness schools of psychotherapy have different goals, they both use techniques to further the emotional-cognitive horizons of the patient(s), with the assumption that such expansion will lead to behavior or character change. In family therapy with dynamic and expressive undertones, the therapist uses the context of relative therapeutic neutrality (and empathic support) to use techniques such as clarification, confrontation, and interpretation (see below), either with the individual or with the marital dyad or family unit.

In family therapy, insight is always given in a family context. In general, family therapists are clearer than other types of therapists that insight is more constructed than revealed. The goal is to link past with present reality of the family in such a way that family members can stop trying to solve the past with the present.

- *Clarification.* In using the technique of clarification, the therapist asks the family members to elucidate their understanding or emotional reaction to present and past events.
- *Confrontation.* Confrontation is the pointing out of contradictory aspects of the patient's behavior, often between verbal and nonverbal behavior.
- *Interpretation.* Interpretation is the elucidation by the therapist of links between present contradictory behavior and present or past distortions that are out of the patient's awareness. In making interpretations, often immediately preceded by clarification and confrontations, the therapist is providing a conceptual link for the patient and the family. The interpretation should connect current behavior (as distorted or guided by internal templates) and past experiences (distorted by anxiety and defense mechanisms) timed so as to maximize cognitive and emotional affect.

Interpretations can be made in the here-and-now interaction between family members or between therapist and family member(s), or interpretations can link current behavior to past experiences. Probably the former are of more use in family intervention. Ackerman (1958) was a pioneer in using dynamic techniques (along with a multitude of others) in a family therapy format in order to interrupt intrapsychic conflicts being played out in the interpersonal sphere (e.g., if you are mad at a parent, you take it out on your spouse). Dicks (1967) has more than any other author spelled out the use of dynamic techniques in interventions with married couples.

> Mr. and Mrs. D, a couple in their 30s who are married and have three children, came into therapy complaining that Mrs. D was not interested in sex. Although she was honestly very busy with three young children, that did not seem to be the central issue. It was noted that Mr. D was very depressed and critical and had serious depressive symptoms for years. He was treated with fluoxetine with excellent results. As Mr. D's irritability lessened, Mrs. D realized that she responded to his annoyance with fear and anxiety far beyond the usual response. At that point she began to discuss her abusive father and how if she made him angry, he would hit her, or go into a total rage, and how desperately she had tried to be good. She was projecting onto her husband her fears about her father. Mr. D's mother had been intrusive and anxious, and when his mother became anxious, his father would retreat, as he was doing with his wife. As each saw their projections, they began to learn to reassure the other, and Mrs. D was able to relax and have satisfactory sex.

In the preceding case the issue was not oedipal (i.e., resulting from repressed sexual feelings toward the father) but rather was the projection of an old family interaction into the present. Similarly, Dicks (1967) describes the brief marital therapy case of H, a 45-year-old man, married for 20 years to W [the names Mr. E and Mrs. E are used here]:

> Mr. E and Mrs. E had three adolescent children. The presenting complaint was Mr. E's sexual impotence of 10 years' duration and his depressive moods and irritability, especially at his wife and children, all of which threatened his marriage.
>
> In the initial diagnostic interview with Mr. E alone, he was asked about his early sexual attitudes. His associations shifted to his parental home and its atmosphere, noting that his sulking did not work as it did for his father, as he knows it is wrong. This was followed by an interpretation by the therapist: There seemed to be a similarity between general sulking and sexual withdrawal. The patient's next association was to his wife, whom he saw as having her own way as to times for intercourse. He then described the many talents of his wife

in contrast to himself. Another interpretation was offered: Mr. E feels inadequate in comparison to Mrs. E, as if she has all the potency, much as it was in Mr. E's parents' case.

In the diagnostic interview with Mrs. E, she described a strong bond to an idealized father, who died when she was 17, and a scarcely concealed hostility toward a weak mother.

In the first conjoint marital session, it appeared that the couple had a stereotyped and unvarying pattern of simultaneously attempting intercourse and anticipating failure, followed by some symptomatic behavior on the wife's part. In the second conjoint session, Mrs. E suggested that they discontinue sleeping together, as the strain left her without sleep and constantly tired. An interpretation was made: Her symptoms showed her emotional frustration, which might reflect her disappointment that Mr. E was not the strong, potent man she expected. She had tried to improve him, and Mr. E had met this attempt with anxiety and resistance. Mr. E conceded that he left his office cheerful, but when he entered the home, he felt depressed, nagged, and belittled. Mrs. E responded by saying that it was not she but the children who received the brunt of his moods. She described her husband's belittling and sarcasm toward the children. Another dyadic interpretation was given: There is a vicious circle around power and control. Mr. E feels Mrs. E is trying to control him, whereas he is feeling a great need to control the family through the children. Mrs. E becomes anxious and resentful because she would like to run things her way. This battle has invaded their relationship, and the struggle to contain the urges to dominate has produced mutual strain and pushed out affection. Mrs. E responded to this interpretation by conceding that she is driven to control and that she sees how Mr. E responds by becoming controlling with the children.

At this point the therapist suggested that this pattern may relate to earlier experiences in their families of origin. Mrs. E recalled that she felt a lack of support from her mother and a devotion to her prematurely deceased father, a need to support and control the weak mother, and a desire that in marrying Mr. E he would make up for it all. An interpretation was made that she must feel very complicated about Mr. E's sexual difficulty and his feelings as the weak one. She now saw him not as the interested, inspiring father for her children in whom she saw her own needs mirrored. This interpretation was followed by a show of great feeling on the part of Mrs. E, in which she recalled that her father was not only loving but had also been very demanding and sarcastic, the latter so intolerable to her in Mr. E's behavior toward their children. Another interpretation: Perhaps Mrs. E had not seen the similarity before between her feelings for Mr. E and for her father, with great disappointment that like her father Mr. E had weaknesses that she must control because she could not bear them.

Mr. E responded with some emotion about how as a child he had been very strong willed and strove to compel his mother to give in to him. This was followed by a final dyadic interpretation: It was the strong-willed part of Mr. E that Mrs. E liked. Because of his fear of weakness, the failure in sex, which could have happened to anyone under the circumstances, was quite disproportionately seen by Mr. E as an utter failure, with a compensatory need to be in control in the home. Mrs. E, attaching her aspirations for strength and success to Mr. E, felt disproportionately disappointed in him because it destroyed her fantasy that he was like her father. Her reaction to disappointment, both in the past and now, was to take control.

By the third session, the couple reported that their general relationship was much improved and that Mr. E had been completely potent on a number of occasions.

Techniques for a More Effective Construction of Family Reality

The critical issue for understanding the family's story is a respectful conversation in which the family members are asked to consider their beliefs and ideas about the problem (White and Epstein 1990). The therapist must have on hand a number of alternatives that can be offered to the family to see if a consideration of these ideas would offer new possibilities. To the extent possible the family should participate in the creation of a new story. Consider the following case example:

> Mrs. F is distressed by her husband's unwillingness to talk about problems, and Mr. F is distressed by his wife's constant talking. They both assume the worst—Mrs. F sees Mr. F as withholding, and Mr. F sees Mrs. F as demanding. After discovering that Mr. F is from the midwestern United States and that Mrs. F is an Italian woman from New York, the therapist points out that these are ethnic and regional differences that must be understood, rather than hated, and reminds the couple that Mr. F had originally liked Mrs. F's energy and Mrs. F had liked Mr. F's calm. The couple were then engaged in a discussion of how they could turn their differences to their advantage.

Treatment Packages

Clinical work and research suggest that so-called treatment packages, which contain a combination of techniques delivered in a specified sequence, are effective with targeted patient populations. These packages include the prescribed use of various techniques from the major strategies outlined in this chapter. Many of these packages have manuals that add to an abstract listing of strategies and techniques by indicating the overall goals (mediating and final) of the treatment for the targeted families, with a rationale for the timing and sequencing of the intervention techniques. Much psychotherapy research is focused on investigating treatment packages as they are applied to specified disorders. We discuss these packages in more detail in Chapter 24 and in other parts of the text.

Indications for Differential Use of the Basic Strategies

Family therapy trainees are often uncertain about the circumstances in which various strategies and techniques are to be used. As we discuss in Chapter 29, this is an unresolved area, not only in family therapy but in all psychotherapy. Clinical writers often do not specify the situations in which their proposed strategies and techniques are indicated. Clinical research that compares one therapy technique with another indicates that by and large no one technique is clearly superior. It remains for future research to clarify the differential application and effectiveness of the techniques. In the interim, clinical decisions about the thrust of strategies in family intervention must be made on every case and in every session.

In order to choose a strategy, the therapist must consider both motivation and family style. Families that enjoy talking and analyzing, for example, may prefer a dynamic model, whereas action-oriented families may want specific homework and a behavioral model. Many, if not most, families want some educational interventions—families want and need information. The therapist also must consider speed. For example, low-motivation families need intervention more quickly, so that brief therapy techniques are often the first ones to try. Many apparently low-motivation families increase their motivation when they see results and begin to trust the therapist. The therapist should always remember the following basic rule: try the simplest thing first. The simplest thing is usually an explanation of the problem and some suggestion for making it better. Before the therapist offers an elaborate discussion of why a couple has become more distant, it is helpful to prescribe 15 minutes of talking to each other every night and see what happens. Sometimes it's all that's needed. If not, the therapist will gather a lot of information from observing how the couple avoided or sabotaged the task. We will look at this topic in more detail in Section 7, in which we discuss guidelines for therapy.

Patient diagnostic issues are beginning to factor into recommendations for the type of family therapy techniques to be used. For example, patients with serious Axis I pathology, such as schizophrenia or bipolar disorder, and their families should receive psychoeducation about the illness and how to cope with it. It has also been argued that because the schizophrenic individual is by the nature of the disorder vulnerable to cognitive and emotional overload (and this seems more true of males than females), family therapy strategies that stir up family emotional conflict should not be used, at least during certain phases of the disorder (Heinrichs and Carpenter 1983). It remains to be seen whether family classification schemes and typologies can be useful in guiding decisions about whether to use the family therapy format and which strategies and techniques to use.

> What the family wants is an important consideration. Most critical, however, is the family members' sense that they are heard, understood, and respected and that the therapist believes the problem is solvable or at least can be made more tolerable.

Some family therapy strategies have received research support for their effectiveness, whereas others have been the focus of very little if any research. Because most therapy research has found little differential effect for the various treatment strategies and techniques, some researchers have argued that elements common to the various strategies are most important (Hoberman and Lewinsohn 1985). These elements include careful assessment, focus as negotiated by the therapist, a reasonable rationale for proceeding, the generation of hope that intervention will help, and orientation to a goal. From this point of view, the organized approach of the family therapist is more important than the specific strategies and techniques. One clinical application of this notion is that the family therapist should not be eclectic in strategies to the point of shifting constantly from one set of strategies to another. A clear focus on the central family problems with a combination of a limited set of strategies is probably more efficient, less confusing to the family, and more effective than is a less focused approach. This is congruent with the fact that negative outcomes in family therapy are associated with a lack of therapist structuring and guiding of early sessions and with the use of frontal confrontations of highly affective material early in treatment (Gurman and Kniskern 1978).

Conclusion: Beyond Techniques

It has been wisely noted that a therapist, not unlike an artist, spends years of hard practice acquiring and honing techniques. Once acquired, these techniques become relatively invisible (Friedman 1974). During the last two decades of the twentieth century, family therapy has seen a great deal of outcome research, from which many manuals have been written. "The manuals attempt to carefully describe treatments, and therapists are taught to perform as the manuals describe. And, yet, with this careful attention to scientific rigor, researchers have noted that the same technique in the hands of a 'pro' and a 'neophyte' (despite years of practice) can have quite different effects on the patients" (M. Weissman, personal communication).

Suggested Readings

In this chapter we have offered an integrative model for couples and family treatment. The following references provide an additional perspective on integrating models:

Dattilio F: Case Studies in Couple and Family Therapy. New York, Guilford, 1998
    This book presents a series of case studies using a cognitive-behavioral model. It includes a good discussion of the theory of cognitive-behavioral work and how it interfaces with other models.

Pinsof W: Integrative Problem-Centered Therapy. New York, Basic Books, 1995
    This book integrates important concepts from biological psychiatry, individual therapy, and family therapy in providing an excellent, accessible framework for conducting brief therapy from a biopsychosocial perspective. The problem-centered focus is sensible and practical.

If you are interested in exploring in further depth the particular viewpoints of other clinical theorists, we recommend the following books:

Kerr M, Bowen M: Family Evaluation. New York, WW Norton, 1988
    This book presents the clearest description available of the family systems theory approach developed by Bowen. Clinical concepts such as differentiation of self are explained in straightforward language, and the framework for clinical intervention is described eloquently.

Minuchin S, Fishman C: Family Therapy Techniques. Cambridge, MA, Harvard University Press, 1980

For readers interested in the techniques associated with structural family therapy, this older book is the most useful. It breaks down the interventions into specific skills that can be learned, especially if one understands the thinking behind them.

Whitaker C, Bumberry W: Dancing With the Family: A Symbolic-Experiential Approach. New York, Brunner/Mazel, 1988

This book presents a nice introduction to Whitaker's clinical thinking and approach to treatment. It follows a case from beginning to end and has both transcripts and commentary that illustrate his fundamental, guiding ideas.

References

Ackerman N: The Psychodynamics of Family Life. New York, Basic Books, 1958

Anderson C, Reiss D, Hogarty G: Schizophrenia and the Family. New York, Guilford, 1986

Dattilio F, Epstein N, Baucom D: An introduction to cognitive-behavioral therapy with couples and families, in Case Studies in Couple and Family Therapy. Edited by Dattilio F. New York, Guilford, 1998, pp 1–37

Dicks HV: Marital Tensions. London, Routledge & Kegan Paul, 1967

Friedman PH: Outline (alphabet) of 26 techniques of family and marital therapy: A through Z. Psychotherapy: Theory, Research and Practice 11:259–264, 1974

Gabbard GO: The impact of psychotherapy on the brain. Psychiatric Times XV:1, 26, 1998

Goldstein MJ: Psychoeducation and family treatment related to the phase of a psychotic disorder. Int Clin Psychopharmacol 11:77–83, 1996

Gurman AS, Kniskern DP: Deterioration in marital and family therapy: empirical, clinical and conceptual issues. Fam Process 17:3–20, 1978

Heinrichs D, Carpenter W: The coordination of family therapy with other treatment modalities for schizophrenia, in Family Therapy in Schizophrenia. Edited by McFarlane W. New York, Guilford, 1983, pp 267–287

Hoberman HM, Lewinsohn PM: The behavioral treatment of depression, in Handbook of Depression: Treatment, Assessment and Research. Edited by Beckman EE, Leber WR. Homewood, IL, Dorsey, 1985, pp 39–81

Hunter DE, Hoffnung RJ, Ferholt BF: Family therapy and trouble: psychoeducation as solution and as problem. Fam Process 27:327–338, 1988

Kandel ER: A new intellectual framework for psychiatry. Am J Psychiatry 155:457–469, 1998

Minuchin S: Families and Family Therapy. Cambridge, MA, Harvard University Press, 1974

Minuchin S, Fishman HC: Family Therapy Techniques. Cambridge, MA, Harvard University Press, 1981

Patterson GR: Coercive Family Process. Eugene, OR, Castalia, 1982

Stuart RB: Helping Couples Change: A Social Learning Approach to Marital Therapy. New York, Guilford, 1980

Watziawick P, Weaklund J, Fisch R: Change: Principles of Problem Formation and Problem Resolution. New York, WW Norton, 1974

Weeks G, L'Abate L: Paradoxical Psychotherapy, Theory and Technique. New York, Brunner/Mazel, 1982

White M, Epstein D: Narrative Means to Therapeutic Ends. New York, WW Norton, 1990

Family Portrait, Baron von Stillfried. From *Once Upon a Time: Visions of Old Japan*, 1984. Courtesy of the publisher, Les Editions Arthaud, Paris, France. Used with permission.

CHAPTER 13

The Course of
Family Treatment

Objectives for the Reader

- To acquire techniques for gathering history
- To become familiar with some of the processes of each phase of family treatment
- To identify various opportunities and interventions appropriate to each phase of family treatment

Introduction

In this chapter we review the phases of a typical course of treatment—somewhat arbitrarily dividing them into an early phase, a middle phase, and a termination phase. By necessity, some material in this chapter overlaps material in earlier chapters—here it is presented in relation to the course of family treatment. Readers may also wish to refer to the R family case example in Chapter 8.

Early Phase

The early phase is the most difficult of the phases, especially for trainees. Before the early phase of treatment begins, the therapist needs to consider the following issues:

- Identifying objectives of the early phase
- Choosing strategies to get started
- Distributing the available time
- Gathering history and simultaneously building a treatment alliance with the family
- Noting special issues in evaluation
- Distinguishing evaluation from treatment

We discuss each of these issues in the sections that follow.

Identifying Objectives of the Early Phase

The primary objectives of the early phase include the following:

- Detailing the primary problems and nonproductive family patterns
- Clarifying the goals for treatment
- Solidifying the therapeutic contract
- Strengthening the therapeutic relationship
- Shifting the focus from the identified patient to the entire family system
- Decreasing guilt and blame
- Increasing the ability of family members to empathize with one another
- Assessing the family's strengths
- Assessing the family's preferred style of thinking and working
- Defining who is in the family
- Getting a clear idea of the ethnic and cultural issues that are part of the family's functioning
- Determining the life cycle phase for each individual and for the family

Choosing Strategies to Get Started

Before describing in detail the techniques that enable the therapist to achieve the final goals of family intervention, it is important to note the general strategies used in beginning work with the family. These skills are basic, assumed by all orientations, and crucial for the new therapist to master. Without such skills, a therapist is likely to find families dropping out of treatment, which precludes the possibility of change.

1. *Accommodating to and joining the family.* The family is a biological-psychological unit that over time has evolved rules (overt and covert), procedures, and customary interactional patterns. The therapist must

join this group by letting the family members know that he or she understands them and wants to work with them for their better good. Every family therapist will use his or her own unique personality, combined with sensitivity and warmth, to join with the family in distress.

2. *Interviewing subgroups, extended family members, and other networks.* Family therapy is by definition a therapeutic approach that emphasizes the tremendous power and influence of the individual's social environment. This social environment includes immediate family, family of origin, extended family, neighborhood, school, and community. A crucial decision that often takes place early in treatment is which parts of the social environment to include directly in the treatment. Various groups of individuals can be included for assessment only or can be more involved in the ongoing treatment. We discuss this topic further in Chapter 15.

3. *Negotiating the goals of treatment.* The family or couple usually come to treatment with their own goals in mind. Unlike individual therapy, however, in which one individual comes with his or her own goals, the family comes with a few individuals having specific goals, often for other people (not themselves) to change, and with some individuals not wanting to be there at all.

Distributing the Available Time

If the therapist is engaged in short-term crisis intervention, 30 minutes may be all the time that is available for evaluation. The therapist must join the family group quickly and will evaluate the family only for the presenting problem, with further evaluation occurring during the intervention. In a training or practice setting, with no fixed time limit for treatment, the therapist may be able to allot more time for thorough evaluation (e.g., to complete a quick genogram). Some clinicians take the time at an initial phone contact to gather detailed biographical and historical information. This may save time initially, but it is not a substitute for a complete interview with the entire family.

Gathering History and Simultaneously Building a Treatment Alliance With the Family

Styles and techniques of gathering history are very much related to the crucial task of building a treatment alliance with the family. These techniques vary depending on the phase of treatment. Although we covered some of this material in earlier chapters, we repeat it here in the context of the course of family treatment.

We recommend that most therapists obtain a fairly extensive history, perhaps mainly in the opening sessions. Some family therapy models, such as those that are solution focused, place less emphasis on an extensive history diagnosis and more emphasis on the here and now, working more with what happens in the session and gathering longitudinal data only as needed during the course of the meetings.

The therapist may decide to hear from each family member in turn on certain important issues or may let the verbal interaction take its own course. The therapist should allow for at least a few minutes of unguided conversation among family members in order to see their patterns of interaction. However, to allow fighting among family members to go on for too long, once the therapist has seen the pattern of the fight, is demoralizing to the family. A decision may be made to call on one parent first, then the other, and then the children in order of descending age. Or it may appear more advantageous to call on the more easily intimidated, weaker, or passive parent (or spouse) first, or to allow the family to decide who speaks first. The therapist may decide to use first names for all family members to help put everyone on an equal footing, or he or she may prefer to be more formal in addressing the parents in order to strengthen relatively weak generational boundaries and parental functioning. Some therapists may encourage the family members to talk with one another, whereas others may focus family members' conversation largely through the therapist, at least during the first sessions or at times of stress or chaos.

The assumption is made that the family's behavior in the office and at home is similar. This is not always true: The family's behavior is usually modified in some ways in the office by the therapist's presence. In the beginning the therapist is somewhat the outsider, whose main function may be to allow everyone, including the weakest members of the family, to be heard. Some family members will often be on the attack, whereas others will be defensive at first. An identified patient who is an adolescent will often demand changes at home because those in this age group are often the ones most interested in change. An angry, frustrated spouse will demand that the marital partner change. Some therapists may point out that they will not be decision makers for the family but will help the family members clarify their problems and help them with their decision-making processes. Such therapists may act as communication referees or traffic cops when necessary, making sure that one person speaks at a time, that no one person is overwhelmed by attacks during the sessions, and that nonconstructive family patterns are not allowed to continue unchallenged during the therapy sessions. They create an atmosphere that encourages the verbal expression of feelings toward constructive ends.

The therapist should indicate to the family that, in an unhappy family, everyone hurts and therefore everyone wants to get something positive out of the sessions. The therapist should convey the feeling that all the family members are doing the best they can and that each family member needs to understand his or her motives and the motives of others. The therapist also should explain that well-intentioned attitudes and actions sometimes have less than completely positive outcomes.

Families vary considerably in their readiness to move from a discussion of the current crisis situation to an exploration of their patterns and histories. The therapist will follow the family's lead in this respect. For example, a couple may refuse to discuss issues related to themselves as a couple, focusing only on the children. Or a therapist may be willing to start the sessions even though the father is absent and may sense that the family members need some time to talk about the "badness" of one of the children.

The therapist must get an idea of the family's mode of operations in order to convey a sense of respect for and understanding of the family's initial point of view. At the same time, the therapist will need to guard against being so passive and accepting that nothing new will be added to the equation. The family's experience in the therapy hour should not be merely a repetition of the nongratifying interactional patterns for which it originally sought help. It may be helpful to indicate to the family members that individual problems are often related to family problems and that they all need to find out more about the family as a whole, in order to enable each member, and the family as an entity, to benefit from the treatment.

As we discussed in Chapter 6 (in the context of choice points), it may be desirable to move on to a longitudinal, chronological narrative of the family's history (perhaps through three generations) or alternatively to begin with a cross-sectional inventory of how the family currently functions. Which of these areas will be discussed first depends on the therapist's predilections, the family's distress, and the nature of the difficulty. The major longitudinal data to be gathered will refer to the parents' courtship, engagement, wedding, honeymoon, and early years of marriage prior to the arrival of children as well as changes in the family as a result of the first child and each subsequent child and so on through the family cycle.

The therapist may start with the courtship period (which is, in part, predictive of marital patterns), move on to the marriage, and then work backward, with each partner going back to his or her original family. The therapist can discuss the life history prior to the marriage for each partner, including any previous marriages. In going back to the couple's families of origin, the therapist gets a picture of the functioning of those previous families. This picture serves as a foundation for understanding the present family and its problems. Careful attention must be given not only to recollections of the past and to expressions regarding attitudes and values but also to overt behavior. Difficulties in sexual adjustment should be delineated carefully by taking a complete sexual history. It is our experience that such a history is rarely taken in the field of family therapy, as though sexual problems are regarded as only secondary to other interpersonal difficulties. The timing of the sexual history is critical, even with presenting sexual problems. Consider the following two rules of thumb: 1) The history of sexual problems should be taken after other history is known, and 2) it is best not to begin taking a sexual history in the last half hour of the session. The sexual history should not be taken with children present.

Noting Special Issues in Evaluation

Although we discussed evaluation in earlier chapters and revisit it in Section 5, on couples treatment, we emphasize a few points here as they affect the course of therapy. Each of the topics is discussed in greater detail in subsequent chapters.

Should the therapist allow the family to present the history, or should the therapist structure the history with an outline? Most therapists seem to combine these approaches. It is often helpful to let the family members talk until they have told their story in their own way. In contrast, the therapist has expertise in helping families with problems and can help them in structuring a history. What is not mentioned, or doesn't emerge because of the structuring, we believe will emerge as time goes on, but what is missed by not asking (e.g., by not taking a sexual history) may *never* be revealed.

Sexuality. Primary difficulties in sexual adjustment will often sour the rest of the marital relationship. Sometimes sexual difficulties are the major area of difficulty for the married couple and perhaps the one most difficult for them to deal with. Some couples appear to need and benefit from specific therapy directed toward improving their sexual adjustment. To the extent that this can be done satisfactorily, other areas of marital and family interaction may then improve markedly. The sexual adjustment of the married couple should be evaluated as carefully as other areas of marital and family interaction. It is not safe to assume that any sexual problems are secondary and will always resolve themselves more or less spontaneously when other areas of family difficulty have been overcome. Parents' sexuality is not (usually) discussed in the presence of the children. With teenagers, the particulars of their sexual experience are also discussed in private, but families need to discuss the guidelines for teen sexual behavior within the family. It is the family therapist's task to set the guidelines for discussion and to help the family state clearly its beliefs on sexual activity, sexual safety, and respect and love for the partner.

> It is the family therapist's task to set the guidelines for discussion and to help the family state clearly its beliefs on sexual activity, sexual safety, and respect and love for the partner.

Money.   Another area often overlooked or slighted in the evaluation phase is that of the family's dealings with money. We have found this to be an important issue in marital and family friction. As with sexuality, this issue is not always merely secondary to other marital problems. Some married couples have never been able to work out a satisfactory way of managing money as a marital pair. Any other marital problem may be reflected in fights about money, just as they may be reflected in sexual maladjustment.

Gender.   All couples operate within a larger social system that in general privileges men, but their individual ways of dealing with power differentials and gender-based communication differences vary greatly. The therapist needs to gain an understanding early on of whether men or women are devalued in a particular family and what kinds of power are available to each partner.

Ethnicity.   Whereas the therapist may see subtle ethnic differences, the participants may see major fault lines. For example, Irish Catholics and Italian Catholics have some very different traditions about home and family. Couples who have crossed ethnic, racial, or class lines in marriage may experience additional stress either because of the differences between themselves or because of disapproval within their families of origin.

Individual diagnoses.   The therapist must be alert to the possibility of major mental illness, addiction, or dysthymia in one or more family members. Sometimes both members in a couple have a mood disorder. The therapist must decide whether an individual diagnostic workup is necessary.

Phase of the family life cycle.   The amount and type of data to be assembled will be influenced strongly by the current phase of the family life cycle.

It is appropriate to concentrate on material relevant to that particular phase of family life. The relative emphasis, and some of the specific content of the history to be gathered, would be quite different if the therapist were dealing with a couple in the first year of marriage rather than a family in which the last child is preparing to leave home.

Distinguishing Evaluation From Treatment

For clarity's sake, we have separated the discussions of family evaluations and family treatment. In practice this rarely happens and is not particularly desirable. A process of continual evaluation and hypothesis testing takes place throughout the course of therapy, with the therapist constantly checking his or her perceptions. At the same time, every session should have some beneficial outcome. The more skillful and experienced the therapist is, the less rigid the approach, the more total the blend of evaluative and therapeutic aspects, and the more extensive the use of improvised variations, condensations, and extensions on some of the themes.

> Mr. and Mrs. A, a young couple in their early 20s, came for treatment because their marriage was in trouble. An evaluation was completed (using the format described in Chapter 7). At the beginning of the session the following week, the therapist asked the couple what had happened since the evaluation. Mr. A said he realized that they were not communicating, but they had made a point of increasing communication during the week. Mrs. A said that she thought the session had not done anything, but she had recognized for the first time that there was a communication problem.

During the early phase, the therapist comes to a better understanding of the life of the family, making contact and promoting empathy and communication. Major nonproductive patterns are spotlighted, and scapegoating is neutralized. The painful shift begins to move the focus away from the identified patient and to direct attention toward the entire family system.

Middle Phase

The middle phase of treatment is often considered to be the one in which the major work of change takes place. Because Section 4 is devoted to treatment, we will say less here regarding this phase. What the therapist does during the middle stage will vary, depending on the goals that have been identified. During this phase the therapist may repeatedly discuss common examples of persistent, nongratifying interpersonal patterns and attitudes, preferably drawn from recent or here-and-now interactions. He or she challenges old, nonfunctional coalitions, rules, myths, and role models and presents the possibility of alternative modes. New habits of thinking, feeling, and interacting take time to develop, and much repetition is often required. At the same time resistance to change comes to the fore and must be dealt with accordingly (see Chapter 14).

The initial focus may be on the identified patient, but the focus then moves to the family. Often the identified patient may improve before the family does. A crisis often develops when the problems that have been hidden away or have been too painful to face are brought to the conscious awareness of the family members. Consider the following case example:

> In the B family the identified patient was Mr. B, who had chronic anxiety and depression. Mrs. B was a loyal but suffering housewife. They had two young children. Mrs. B had been doing most of the childrearing. The couple socialized very little. When the family was brought together, Mr. B talked about his wife's chronic hostility toward him. She responded by saying, "Look what I put up with." As communication finally opened up over a period of weeks, the anger escalated until the couple was talking about divorce. This crisis was used to change the patterns of family participation on the part of both parents. Mr. B, after beginning to take medication, started to share some of the family tasks, such as getting the kids to school on time and helping them do their homework. Mrs. B had more time for herself. She returned to work as a biochemist. Feeling better about herself and about her husband's ability to be part of the family, she suggested to her husband that they go out to movies and concerts.

In the early phase of treatment, the situation may appear to worsen rather than improve. The therapist must monitor the situation carefully and frame the situation as potentially positive.

In the middle phase of treatment, symptomatology may accelerate, new symptoms may arise, and families may talk about quitting treatment. This upheaval usually is related to the family's barely perceived awareness that for things to get better, some family member will have to change. Rather than change, a family member may accentuate or exaggerate symptoms. Family therapy changes have to be made sequentially. For example, a family cannot let go of an offspring until the marital couple has found increased satisfaction in their own lives and in their relationship.

As for the process of doing therapy, at the start of therapy the therapist must meet the family where it is coming from and gradually draw it toward the therapeutic scenario. Figure 13–1 illustrates this process.

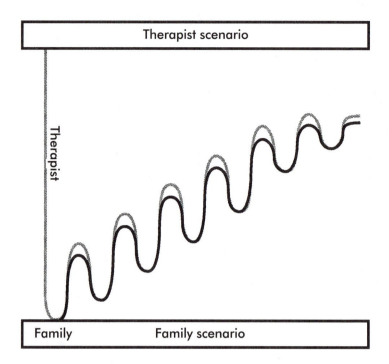

FIGURE 13–1.   Schematic of the joining of therapist and family scenarios. *Source.*   Marion Forgatch, Oregon Social Learning Center, 1997. Reprinted with permission.

In this figure, the family (bottom of the figure) has its own scenario of what it thinks the problem is. Similarly, the therapist (top of the figure) has his or her own scenario of what he or she thinks the problem is. If the family is left to its own devices, its patterns are scripted, repetitive, and unchanging. The same can hold true for the therapist. That is, without interaction with the family, the therapist's scenario does not vary. The essence of the therapy is to bring together the two scenarios, beginning at the top left of the diagram as the therapist and the family interact. Presumably, the family's behavior changes as the family interacts with the therapist's strategies. The figure also points out that therapy is never a smooth line. As it continues, frequent oscillations occur. The point is that therapy should be moving forward to achieve the goals that were established earlier in the process (see Chapter 11).

Termination Phase

In the termination phase the therapist reviews with the family the goals that have been achieved and those that have not. It is often useful to review the entire course of therapy, including the original problems and goals. A useful technique is to ask each family member to say what he or she would have to do in order to make the situation the same as it was at the outset of treatment. For example, the father would have to yell at the mother, who would have to yell at the daughter, who would have to stop going to school. In essence, the family reconstructs the sequences leading to the pathology. Videotape playback may be helpful at this time, so that the family can see what it looked like at the start of treatment, compared with its present state. It is important to acknowledge that some behavior cannot be altered and that life will continue to change, that is, unexpected and periodic problems will occur. The family should be provided with the skills for solving future conflicts and challenges.

What are the criteria for suggesting termination of therapy? If the original goals have been achieved, the therapist may consider stopping the treatment. When the treatment has been successful, new coping patterns and an enhanced empathy by family members for one another will have been established. There will be recognition that the family itself seems capable of dealing satisfactorily with new situations as they arise. There may be little to talk about during the sessions and little sense of urgency. Nonproductive quarreling and conflict will have been reduced; the family will be freer to disagree openly and will have methods of living with and working out its differences and separateness. The family will seem less inflexible in its rules and organization and appear more able to grow and develop. Individual family members will be less symptomatic, and positive channels of interaction will be available between all family members. There will be improved agreement about family roles and functions.

Even if the goals have not been achieved but have been worked out to the best capabilities of therapist and family, therapy can stop. If the therapist feels stuck but believes more change is possible, it is helpful to consult with another therapist before ending therapy.

Families often cannot or do not recognize changes that have occurred during therapy. A therapist should check carefully for any change and amplify it, giving positive reinforcement. If a family can produce a small change, then bigger changes may be possible. With some families, no change may occur until the therapy is completed.

After a successful therapy, when termination issues have been resolved, the family may experience a recurrence of presenting symptoms. For example, a son may begin hallucinating again, coincident with the father's reduction in communication with the mother (after losing his job), or the son may stop taking his medication and begin hallucinating, and the parents may begin arguing about it. These eruptions are usually short-lived and may represent a temporary response to the anxiety of terminating treatment, rather than being a sign of treatment failure or a new problem. Such anxiety is part of the separation process, which is a key issue to be worked on in termination and which in some theoretical orientations may represent the major theme of the entire therapy. One way to deal with this is as follows: The family is encouraged to experience the recurring symptoms to see if it wants to keep any of them. If the family says no, it is encouraged to examine how symptoms occur and to review what happens on the days when symptoms do not occur. The family is encouraged to see this as a review or final examination.

Final Note

We have gone to considerable lengths to describe the processes involved in an entire course of family therapy. This is because during training, therapists rarely see a case from beginning to end (primarily because of the dropout problem). The point is that treatment (like anything else) has a certain natural course (i.e., rate of change), and therapists must be aware of it.

Suggested Readings

Haley J: Problem-Solving Therapy. New York, Harper & Row, 1976
This book offers practical ideas for thinking about family therapy as it evolves over time.

Napier A, Whitaker C: The Family Crucible. New York, Harper & Row, 1978
This book, by two expert therapists, offers a thoughtful and readable description of the entire course of treatment.

Spirit of Life, Robert I. Russin, 1970. Courtesy of the artist and the Palm Springs Desert Museum, Palm Springs, California. Used with permission.

CHAPTER 14

Promoting Change in Family Treatment: Issues of Alliance and Resistance

Objectives for the Reader

- To understand how the connection between the therapist and the family facilitates change
- To understand how to build an alliance with a family and to know those factors that make it more difficult
- To be aware of and understand family resistances to treatment and change
- To understand therapist reactions to the family that interfere with progress in treatment
- To identify strategies for countering resistances

Introduction

In this chapter we discuss two issues that at first glance may not seem related: the therapeutic alliance and resistance. By *therapeutic alliance*, we mean the collaborative relationship between therapist and family aimed at promoting change. By *resistance*, we mean, broadly speaking, the processes in the patient or family that impede change. Both issues are central to the process of therapy, and without the therapeutic alliance, it is almost impossible to deal with resistance.

The Therapeutic Alliance

The family unit is often portrayed as sanctified. Certainly, popular politics touts it thus, celebrating the importance of family values as a means to alleviate a variety of societal ills. Much like in a religion, those within the intimate sect of the family use the utmost caution in questioning the rules governing its functioning. The therapist is an outsider, initially unaware of the family's complex (and often dysfunctional) rules. As has been proven throughout history, religious convictions are remarkably resistant to change, especially if suggested by someone outside the church. To alter the system one must first be accepted by the system. This is also true in marital and family therapy.

The success of any therapeutic endeavor depends on the participants establishing and maintaining an open, trusting, and collaborative relationship or alliance. In marital and family therapy, the therapeutic alliance offers the opportunity for corrective experience and is a necessary condition for therapeutic change. A growing body of empirical evidence demonstrates that the therapeutic alliance is the best predictor of psychotherapy outcome in individual therapy, and a similar line of clinical research in relation to marital and family therapy has begun to emerge. The functions of a therapeutic alliance include instilling hope in the family and creating an environment safe enough for the family to engage in new behaviors that take it past its comfort zone. The family members must believe that the therapist not only has the skills to help them through the problem but also respects and appreciates them as people. The family therapist faces the following issues in establishing an alliance:

- The therapist must form at one time an alliance with several people, who often have quite different feelings and agendas.
- The therapist must keep in mind the need to adopt a conceptual framework to account for interactions within triangles or systems of three (or more) people.
- The system will operate in powerful ways to induct the therapist into it.
- Because multiple participants are present, people with different motivations, goals, and beliefs about how to change must all be attended to. If the participant has come involuntarily, as with many adolescents and most court-ordered patients, the situation is even more complicated.

Sessions with any family tend to be more complex and more openly conflicted than are most individual sessions. The therapist must work to develop a connection with each person, with the various subsystems, and with the family as a whole. In this process, the therapist must be constantly aware of the presence of triangles among family members and among himself or herself and family members: No dyadic relationship in therapy can exist outside a series of interlocking triangles. This means that, for example, if the therapist develops a strong relationship with one spouse, the other may feel left out or angry. Any move the therapist makes may be seen from a variety of different angles.

N o dyadic relationship in therapy can exist outside a series of interlocking triangles.

The therapist joining the system experiences the pull of the system—that is, the request to operate within the system's rules and beliefs—to help the family members change the problem without changing the system. This process is subtle and very strong. If the therapist, for example, buys into the family's definition of the problem as "We have a bad child," he or she may not pay attention to the marital problems or to the problems of the child who is labeled as being good. The therapist must see the constraints on behavior (e.g., this cannot be talked about, this cannot be changed) as information to use in understanding the system, and he or she must remain separate enough not to be bound by these constraints.

Alliance formation for the therapist is complicated by multiple countertransference reactions. The therapist may be drawn to, or prefer, some family members. Family dynamics may replicate the therapist's family in some way, producing wishes to save, or punish, certain family members. In addition, the therapist can see how badly one person is treating another, in a way that does not happen in individual therapy. Watching a parent verbally abuse a child in session, the therapist may find it difficult to ally with the parent and the child, but unless the therapist can connect with all family members in some way, the family will exclude him or her.

Different family theorists use forms of connection and joining that are related to their overall model. For example, Satir and Baldwin (1983) modeled warmth, support, and respect for give-and-take and emphasized that therapist and patients are equals in learning. Bowen's (1978) model took the position that the therapist is coach, or researcher, and should stay more distant to avoid being affected by the family's emotional process. In Bowen's work, most of the session is focused on one individual. The therapist seldom sees the whole family together. Haley and Hoffman (1967) and many solution-focused models use the therapist's position as expert. These models differ in their beliefs about the use of the therapist's power and the level of appropriate closeness. At one end are therapists who see themselves as defining the problem and having the job of fixing it. At the other end are (with the family) co-constructors of a new reality for the family—who hope to change the family's perception of their family life. This second group of therapists are quite humble about their suggestions. The position that a particular therapist chooses will relate both to the therapist's model of therapy and to his or her specific personality and situation. The therapist's ability to form an alliance with a particular family is partly skill and partly a matter of style and tolerance for certain kinds of interaction. Beginning therapists will find certain families dramatically harder to ally with than others. Different therapists, by virtue of their position with certain patients, will be able to take some positions more easily than others. For example, a 50-year-old male physician working with a young couple in their 20s will be more able to take an expert position than will a 25-year-old female social worker, who might more effectively work from a position of one-down, conversational (in contrast to speaking from authority), or equals-in-learning model.

Models for Dealing With Families That Have Trouble Forming an Alliance

In the family therapy field there are at least four different models for dealing with families who present difficulties in forming a therapeutic alliance.

Medical Model

In the medical model it is assumed that the identified patient has an illness, such as schizophrenia or a major affective disorder, and that the family is not the only, nor necessarily the principal, factor in the etiology of the illness. With this assumption, the major strategy in reducing family resistance to treatment is psychoeducation for the family members, in which they are taught about the symptoms, etiology, and course of the illness. In this model it is emphasized that the family did not cause the illness, thus reducing the family guilt and resistance to meeting with the therapist. The family therapist takes on the role of a teacher who instructs the family about the illness and what the family can do to ensure optimal coping.

Coaching Model

Therapists who work in individual and family formats that use behavioral techniques tended until recently to ignore the concept of resistance in their writings. Instead, they emphasized that individuals in families must learn certain basic social, communication, and negotiating skills for harmonious interactions and that individuals lacked these skills because of deficiencies in prior learning. In this model it was assumed that the therapist was a coach and rational collaborator who elicited the cooperation of the patient and family in learning skills that were missing. More recently behavioral therapists have become interested in what prevents learning of these skills and have developed cognitive-behavioral models that consider the role of the cognitive meaning of behaviors, so that resistance is also examined as a series of cognitive distortions and beliefs that impede learning (e.g., "If I'm nice to her and give in, I won't be a real man," or "He is really a bad person, so why should I give him anything?").

In a coaching model it is assumed that the therapist helps the couple locate problem areas and address them in a rational and focused way. Resistances in learning skills, such as failure to do homework or diverting attention from practice during the session, may be met first with rational argument (e.g., "You need these skills in order to function well"), encouragement, and positive reinforcement. Therapists also work with the couple or family to uncover distortions and replace dysfunctional cognitions with more functional ones.

Conflict Model

In a continuation of the psychodynamic tradition, the conflict model assumes that particular individuals in the couple or family system may exhibit resistance to intervention and change based on their own internal conflicts and defense mechanisms. In this model the family therapist, like the individual dynamic therapist, uses techniques of confrontation and interpretation of the here-and-now interaction, especially negative interactions that might destroy the therapeutic relationship and the very survival of the therapy itself.

Strategic Systems Model

A unique contribution of the family therapy field is its theoretical position regarding the strength of a pattern of family interactions that shape and mold the behavior and psychopathology of an individual member of that group. In this orientation it is assumed that family systems in homeostasis, even when the homeostasis involves severe problems, will resist change. When faced with resistance of a whole system, the therapist may use strategic interventions to change not individual behaviors but a pattern of systems behaviors. Consider the following case example:

> The A family sought treatment after the younger son, age 25 years, refused to leave home or get a job. The son was not psychotic or handicapped, and he had worked previously. Mr. A was subtly encouraging his son to stay. The therapist suggested that the son should not leave because, after all, he was a good companion for his father, and the family had plenty of money. The therapist began to discuss building an addition onto the house so that the son would be more comfortable, implying that this would certainly be a permanent plan. He talked about how pleasant it would be that the son would keep his parents company into their old age and that even though it meant the son could not marry, it would be a small sacrifice. At this point Mrs. A, who had remained quiet, said that she would begin house hunting because one of them was leaving, either she or her son. Within a week the son was looking at graduate school catalogues, and within a month he had left home.

The concept of prescribing the symptom, or encouraging the no-change position, is a helpful alternative to the therapist being the voice for change. If the therapist pushes too hard for change, the family will become the keepers of the no-change position. Once the therapist backs off, the family's demand for change can be activated. For example, the family can be asked to list all the negatives that would occur if the supposedly desired change occurred (e.g., "If we gave up arguing, we might get too close, and I would feel vulnerable," or "If we gave up arguing, we might not have anything to say," or "If we gave up arguing, I wouldn't feel angry and I might feel depressed").

Problems in Creating Change: Resistance and Disconnection

Resistance in family therapy is usually defined as those forces within the patient or family that impede apparently wished-for change. Although resistance is usually seen as negative, it is also clear that because personal and family stability depend on certain consistencies of thought and behavior, psychological mechanisms and family rules are not designed for instant change. In general, families are likely to have an idea of what changes they want to make and are confused about why they cannot make these changes. The task of the therapist and family then becomes understanding the specific ideas and fears that stand in the way of change. Some families are not open to change at any level at a particular point in time. However, lack of change in therapy is often attributed to family mechanisms when the real problem is a disconnect between the therapist and the family, meaning that the therapist is not correctly assessing the system or has lost the family's trust. Problems in creating change during therapy can come from the family, from the therapist (e.g., as a result of inexperience, mistakes in judgment), or from disconnects in the therapist-family system.

> **R**esistance in family therapy is usually defined as those forces within the patient or family that impede apparently wished-for change.

Problems in Creating Change: From the Family

Families fear change for many reasons. Most problem behaviors were originally adaptive mechanisms that are now failing but are frightening to let go of unless something can replace them. For example, if an overly close relationship between a mother and her daughter made up for the mother's poor marital relationship with the father, the mother will need to believe she can change the relationship with her husband, or feel better herself, before she can wholeheartedly let her daughter go. Similarly, if a father believes that his son will be a sissy unless he yells at and bullies him, the father will have to change that belief before he can change his behavior.

Sometimes the family has a toxic secret that it is afraid to reveal. For example, no one may be willing to speak about the father's sexual abuse of his daughter because they are afraid he will retaliate with violence, so they are unable to mobilize themselves to change any of the resulting problems.

Certain conditions in individuals make change far more complex. For example, alcoholism or drug addiction sometimes responds to family interventions, but if these conditions do not, only limited change is possible. Similarly, with severe mental illness in a parent, family therapy must be accompanied by appropriate psychiatric medical management, or the situation will be difficult to change.

Problems in Creating Change: From the Therapist

Therapists face many challenges, including their own powerful countertransference feelings, as they begin to deal with a family. Therapists who become angry at or too connected to some members of the family will be unable to form the necessary alliance with the whole system. Therapists may blame the family for the symptoms of one member, as did many early practitioners who treated schizophrenia, making their hostility so apparent that the family members were unable to take anything useful from them.

Basic therapist mistakes will make it appear as though the family is resisting. For example, failing to diagnose attention-deficit/hyperactivity disorder in a child, the therapist may insist that the problem is an overprotective mother and spend time working to get her less involved, when the child actually needs both medication and more structure. Similarly, if a couple presents for treatment of wife abuse, and the therapist concentrates on communication and does not directly interdict the husband's violence, it is unlikely that much will change. Even if the therapist correctly understands the family system, problems ranging from the therapist's failure to be clear about goals and directions, or to explain his or her theory to the family, to the therapist's failure to give tasks small enough and clear enough for learning to occur to the therapist's inability to control the session will result in inability to move the family forward.

In summary, in the spirit of our integrated model, let us quote from William Vogel (1998, p. 972):

> The issue of countertransference is, arguably, even more important in couples therapy than in individual treatment. The patient-couple is ever alert to the danger that the therapist might favor (or disfavor), or be more identified with, one of the two partners; the wise therapist will ever be alert to the same possibility. The therapist's differential response may be a function of any combination of almost an infinity of factors and will, of necessity, determine his or her response to the couple, as well as to the outcome of the treatment.
>
> To give one obvious example, a therapist who, all unaware, tends to behave seductively with the same-sex (or opposite-sex) member of the patient-couple, or who, conversely, disfavors the same-sex (or opposite-sex) member of the couple is a therapist who will always be in serious difficulty. The fact that the therapist is simultaneously dealing with two patients immeasurably complicates all of the problems that are associated with countertransference.

Problems in Creating Change: From the Therapist-Family System

1. *Mismatch between therapist and family.* Although most therapists learn to work with a variety of patients over time, some therapist-patient systems are too difficult to manage, especially for beginning therapists. For

example, a very young female therapist, who was newly married, was assigned to work with a midlife couple in sex therapy. The wife, who was depressed, angry, and feeling unlovable because of years of sexual disinterest on the part of her husband, could not stand being treated by a woman she saw as a rival and who did not have the life experience necessary to understand midlife issues. The couple did well when transferred to an older therapist who could connect more directly with the couple's life experience and circumstances. Sometimes the therapist's style of functioning is too far from the needs of the patient system (e.g., too aggressive, too passive, too distant).

2. *Disagreement as to treatment goals.* Problems can occur if the therapist believes that one goal is central and the family wants to focus on another goal. For example, the therapist may see couple issues as critical, whereas the family wants to talk only about the child. If the therapist moves too fast or does not wait to see if the family has accepted the new goal, treatment will stall.

3. *Inclusion in the system of others besides the nuclear family and the therapist not taking this into account.* Common systems to be considered include family elders (e.g., grandparents or other relatives), who may have very definite ideas about what should be done; the school system; the legal system; and the medical system (e.g., if a family member is physically ill). Families with multiple problems are often involved with several caregivers who may have very different ideas about the problem's definition and solution—this may involve child welfare, the school, a social worker, legal services, or other therapists seeing family members. If the therapist is working in an agency, another set of systems is involved. For example, the family may be suspicious of therapists working in social welfare or probation agencies, seeing them as agents of social control rather than support. In addition, the treatment that the family or the therapist desires may be in conflict with agency rules or with the therapist's supervisor.

Problems in Creating Change: At Evaluation and Early in Treatment

The therapist's first task is to set the structure within which the family intervention can occur. Many resistances can surface during this process of negotiating the structure with the family. In contrast to individual therapy, family or marital therapy necessitates the attendance of a number of people, most of whom do not have overt symptoms. The therapist must first decide whether to insist on seeing the whole family. Napier and Whitaker (1978) describe their approach in doing family therapy (with a mother, father, and three adolescents) in which all family members were required to attend. In an initial session, when the adolescent son did not appear, the therapists refused to begin therapy even though the parents were concerned that the adolescent daughter was suicidal. The therapists assessed the situation, felt that the suicide potential was not significant, and told the parents to return with the whole family. In this case it was felt that to let the family dictate the terms of the therapy would result in a loss of what the authors called the battle for structure. However, some families would not return after such an experience.

At times it is best to begin work with whoever comes to treatment first and to support the family member(s) in getting the rest of the family to come. In general it is best to insist on seeing the whole family as close to the beginning of therapy as possible. Getting fathers into and involved in family therapy has classically been seen as the most difficult task, especially for inexperienced therapists (Forrest 1969; Shapiro and Budman 1973). Until recently fathers did not see their role in the emotional life of the family as significant and often were afraid of their own vulnerability in a setting in which words and feelings were paramount.

Strategies for getting fathers (and other important family members) to sessions include the following: reassuring the missing member of his or her importance, pointing out that changes depend on his or her presence, noting that his or her absence can sabotage therapy, providing flexibility in scheduling, and spacing appointments (Anderson and Stewart 1983; Napier and Whitaker 1978). If it seems appropriate, the therapist can refuse to continue without the family member. Stanton and Todd (1981) generated a number of principles to ensure attendance in starting family intervention with drug addicts and their families (these principles are probably appropriate for other symptom groups):

- The therapist, not the family, should decide which family members will be included in the treatment.
- Whenever possible, family members should be encouraged to attend the evaluation interview.
- The identified patient alone should not be given the task of bringing in the other members of the family.
- The therapist should obtain permission from the identified patient and personally contact the family members (fathers in particular should be contacted personally).
- The therapist should contact the family with a rationale for family inter-

vention that is nonpejorative and nonjudgmental and that in no way blames the family for the symptoms and problems of the identified patient.

Often the critical issue is in supporting the overtly symptomatic patient to ask for help from the family. Consider the following case example:

> In the B family, the identified patient was Mr. B, who had a long history of unipolar depression. After his depressive episodes had been regulated with medication, he told the therapist that his wife was unhappy with their relationship. The therapist suggested marital therapy. Mr. B said that this was his cross to bear because Mrs. B would not come in for therapy. The therapist suggested that he again try talking to her about this. Surprisingly Mrs. B appeared for the next session and said that she was unhappy with the relationship but had never been asked to come in for therapy. Mr. B said that he had asked her but admitted he might have "mumbled the invitation."

Families in which one member exhibits current self-destructive behaviors (e.g., suicidal threats, gestures, and attempts; anorexia or bulimia; drug abuse; physical violence) present special challenges in the initial structuring of the therapy. Clinicians vary in how they address these behaviors in the early structuring of the treatment. Although there is little research evidence as to the most efficacious approaches, it is our clinical opinion that from the beginning, even in the very first session, the family therapist must address his or her responsibilities and the family's responsibilities if and when these destructive behaviors occur. The therapist must often spell out in great detail what he or she will and will not do when these behaviors occur. The therapist can also help the family members plan how they will behave. If this is not done, the first resistance will come in the form of destructive behaviors that derail the possibility of change.

As we mentioned earlier in this chapter, disagreement about treatment goals is an area of potential resistance and deadlock in the early phase of treatment. We also addressed this issue in Chapter 13 in our discussion of the process of bringing together the family's and the therapist's views of the problem (see Figure 13–1). The family members themselves may disagree about the problem and the goals of treatment. For example, the family of an identified adolescent patient may see the adolescent as the only problem, whereas the adolescent sees no problem in himself or herself and sees the parents as authoritarian, narrow, and hostile. Similarly, covert disagreement about the problem and especially the goals of intervention occur in marital therapy when one spouse wants the marriage improved and the other secretly wants out and is intending to leave the spouse, using the therapist for assistance in the breakup.

Strategies to overcome family differences about the problem include searching for a new definition of the problem with which all family members agree, labeling the disagreement as part of the problem, and asking the family to give up idiosyncratic notions about its version of truth and reality. Covert goals can be approached by encouraging family members to say what has remained unsaid.

Disagreement about goals of intervention can also occur between the therapist and the family. This seems most prominent when the therapist sees the problems of the identified patient as related to the interactions of the family, whereas the family sees no contribution of its own and wants the identified patient changed or cured. The therapist can approach this problem by initially accepting the family's view of the problem, or at least not challenging this view, or by broadening the family's definition to include other aspects of interaction.

In families in which a member has been hospitalized for the first time with the emergence of psychotic symptomatology subsequently diagnosed as either schizophrenia or mood disorder, a common resistance of the family is to deny either the presence of the illness or its severity. If such denial persists, the family is in danger of avoiding follow-up care for the patient and family and furthering expectations for the identified patient that are unrealistic and thus cause stress for the vulnerable individual.

A particularly troublesome resistance for the beginning family therapist, especially if he or she is a psychiatric resident, psychology intern, or social work student, is the family's attack on the therapist's competence or personal characteristics (e.g., age, sex, race, socioeconomic level). These resistances can come in subtle barrages (e.g., "You're so good for a youngster, but you probably don't know much about older people") and not so subtle barrages (e.g., "This is probably your first case, and we are not making any progress. Have you talked to your supervisor about this?"). Contact with an experienced and level-headed supervisor is most helpful in these situations. The therapist, if able to see the remarks in the context of resistance, can explore the meaning of the questions about competence by empathizing with the family's concern. With equilibrium and, at times, humor, the therapist can admit differences and limitations (e.g., youth, relative inexperience), appeal to the family for its assistance and help, and ask for a period in which to give the therapy a chance to succeed.

If it is clear that the family cannot tolerate the situation, a transfer to a therapist it has requested (e.g., older, younger, different race or gender) is indicated. Either when the family was correct in its assessment that it needed something different or once the family has proved it has some control in a situation, the family may feel it is safe to begin work.

Problems in Creating Change: In Ongoing Treatment

It is extremely common for a therapy to move rapidly in the early weeks and then stall. This is the point at which old habits reassert themselves, the natural homeostasis of the family takes over, and small failures begin to seem insurmountable. The process of working through change is difficult. The therapist needs to review the treatment and decide whether to change direction or to simply support the idea that change is sometimes difficult and continue in the same direction.

Anderson and Stewart (1983) have listed several situations that threaten treatment:

- A family member who is consistently too talkative and dominant
- A family member who refuses to speak
- Chaotic and disruptive children
- Use of defenses such as intellectualization, rationalization, and denial
- Constant focus by one or more family members placing blame on others
- Unwillingness to do assigned tasks or homework that is necessary for change

The therapist can limit overly talkative family members or can encourage other family members to do so. Parents of chaotic children can be educated by words and by the therapist's modeling of limit setting in the sessions. Most important is the therapist's understanding of why the behavior is occurring. If the behavior serves a purpose, it will be less amenable to requests to stop it, unless the underlying meaning is addressed. However, if the therapist can create a different experience in the session, such as getting a quiet husband to talk while his wife listens, the family may be able to repeat the experience at home without needing to have specific insight into why things have changed.

When couples argue as a regular pattern, usually they are not trying to understand what each other is saying. More likely feeling defensive and out of control, the partners listen for weaknesses in logic to leap on or selectively mishear what each other says. Such couples misread each other's intent, feel defensive, and believe if they don't attack first, they will be injured. Behind this behavior is a deep sense of hurt. The truth is more likely to be found in the complex middle than in the simplified extremes. Therefore, the therapist must discuss the process of the argument and its underlying meanings.

If tasks are not being completed, then the therapist can challenge the couple or redesign the task. Refusal to do homework should always be discussed because the discussion will contain cues about what is really going on.

Several techniques are available for handling defenses, not unlike those one might use in individual or group therapy. For example, to counteract intellectualization and rationalization, the therapist can go with the theme by emphasizing the intellectual aspects of the therapy or by giving intellectual explanations. Relabeling of feelings as facts may help. A family in denial can be slowed down so as to emphasize aspects of the interactions before they are glossed over. Nonverbal and experiential techniques can also be used to get to denied material. As a last resort, the therapist can focus on and support a no-change position as a way to eventually get change.

Problems in Creating Change: At the Termination Phase of Therapy

Often after a successful therapy, the family experiences a resurgence of symptoms when termination begins. This usually indicates anxiety over ending rather than a new problem. The family can use this time to review its progress and understand its issues further. The family may be encouraged to have the symptoms to see if it would like to keep any of them. It may use the situation to understand how the symptoms occur and when they are avoided, so as to lock in new behaviors. The therapist should be alert to the idea that the family is asking for more support and should plan appropriate follow-up care.

Problems in Creating Change: Family Secrets

Individual family members often have secrets that in most cases are known but not acknowledged by other family members. They may involve overt behaviors that one marital partner feels he or she has been able to conceal from the other (e.g., marital infidelity), or they may involve thoughts, feelings, and attitudes that family members believe others are not aware of. For example, parents may not realize (or may deny) that their children pick up the general emotional tone existing between mother and father. They may act as if marital discord is hidden from their children and may want to keep that discord secret. The family can also keep secrets from the therapist, as in the following case example:

> The C family consisted of a hospitalized adolescent, the parents, and two older siblings. For 10 weeks, the family therapy seemed to be bogged down. The fam-

ily stopped treatment. Two months later the family therapist discovered a secret that the entire family already knew—the identified patient had been having sexual relations with a ward nurse. The patient had told his siblings, who told the parents, who then signed the patient out of the hospital. The secret served the purpose of denigrating the hospital staff (including the family therapist) and effectively halting the family therapy.

Helping the family bring these secrets into the open usually results in a clearing of the air and eventually leads to a sense of relief and greater mutual understanding. Interestingly, it is commonly the children who talk openly in the family sessions about what was thought by others to be a secret. The therapist should be prepared to deal with acute shock waves at the time the secret emerges. When a family member requests an individual session for the purpose of revealing a secret, the therapist may listen and try to explore the consequences of discussing the issue within the family setting. If, for example, one of the spouses has an incurable illness and the other spouse does not know about it, the reasons for the secrecy would be examined and the spouse would be encouraged to share the information with the whole family. If the secret does not seem critical to the relationship, the therapist might take a more neutral stance. Imber-Black (1993) provides a good discussion of secrets and the distinction between secrets and power. The therapist must guard against becoming a repository of secrets. He or she has the right to tell the patient the therapy will end unless the secret is told. It is not recommended that therapists themselves reveal a family secret unless a no-confidentiality agreement has been made in advance.

At times a family member may insist on total honesty, either because of emotional insensitivity or as an active way of hurting another family member. For example, a parent might report to a child every negative feeling that crosses his or her mind in the guise of honesty. Needless to say, the therapist must be alert to these kinds of resistances (i.e., "honesty") in the service of stopping the treatment. Usually the therapist will reframe the behavior and place it in context so that the family can work with the issue.

Techniques to Deal With Resistances in Stalled Therapy

Regardless of the type of resistance or when it occurs, a therapist can do several helpful things:

1. *Announce to the family that the therapist feels stuck and ask if the family does.* Sometimes the family is doing fine and only the therapist is anxious. If everyone feels stuck, then everyone can work on the problem together.

2. *Retake a history.* The most common reason for problems in therapy is that the therapist does not have all the facts and so has not formulated the problem or the solution properly. Sometimes information is not shared with therapists until late in therapy when the patients are more trusting. Sometimes if a family came in crisis, the original history was too sketchy. The best way to regroup is to start over, preferably with a more complete genogram related to the problem (see Chapter 7).

3. *Go up or down a system level.* Often the problem is that too many or too few people are involved. If the therapist is seeing a couple, he or she can go up a level by involving more people (e.g., the couple's children or parents). Likewise, the therapist can go down a level by doing some individual work.

4. *Do the opposite of what has been done so far.* With therapy, as with life, sometimes the solution becomes the problem. If pushing hard doesn't work, the therapist can prescribe the symptom. If the therapist has been gentle and nonconfrontational, he or she can try pushing harder.

5. *Request a consultation.* A consultation serves notice to everyone that there is a problem and opens up the system for new ways of thinking. Consultants can often see a problem or blind spot because they are less connected to the family system and can visualize the therapist-family system as a whole.

In the same vein, Alves (1992, p. 8) suggested that

therapists often refer to their families as being "stuck" when movement in the therapy process breaks down. Often, when this occurs, it is the therapist who has gotten off track and contributed to, if not directly reinforced, the lack of progress. Therapists have a major responsibility in getting the therapy process back on track. A return to a few basic, fundamental principles often dislodges even the most stubborn roadblocks to progress. Here are a few trusty stand-bys on which we rely.

Assume nothing: As we have said, it goes without saying that a thorough assessment of a family's presenting problems and overall functioning is key to the therapy process. However, problems in therapy presented in supervision can often be traced back to a hurried, haphazard assessment. Therapists either don't ask all the questions or jump to conclusions based on limited information. Assumptions by therapists on family treatment goals will typically create blocks to progress if the family has not agreed to such goals. A quick check of this area often reveals that what the therapists once labeled "family resistance" is in fact a lack of clarity on the therapists part.

Collaboration: Without collaboration between family members as well as between the family and the therapist there is no therapy. Collaboration is an active process, with each step in the treatment needing to be negotiated and agreed upon. It can happen that family members will change their minds in the midst of treatment. If not addressed, this can result in a breakdown in progress.

Family responsibility: Therapists will describe a sense of "working too hard" with some families. In such cases, shifting the balance of responsibility evenly between the therapist and family is necessary. Ultimately, it is the family who must do the work necessary to reach their desired goals. It is the therapist's responsibility to facilitate an environment in which that change can take place.

Focus on the present: Session after session discussing the same issues over and over again. Therapists expressing frustration in "getting nowhere with the family." These are tell-tale signs that the work is more focused on "talking about" rather than "acting on." The past is useful only to the extent that it affects today's functioning. Allowing families to continuously wallow in the unfortunate water that has gone under the bridge is not only unproductive but can be dangerous. Inadvertently, the therapist may be facilitating a sense of hopelessness in the family.

Final Note

Doing family therapy is very different from doing individual treatment. Therapists are usually apprehensive at first, but as they gain experience, they are excited by the challenge and fascination of working with family units. Many therapists find themselves uncomfortable doing family work and should not force themselves to undertake it. In some ways, the experience for the therapist is like sitting in between the couple in the play *Who's Afraid of Virginia Woolf?* or in the middle of the family in the play *Long Day's Journey Into Night*, or it can be like watching a three-ring circus. The therapist has to pay attention not only to the feelings of individuals in the family system but also to the tone in the family unit and at the same time must be aware of his or her own feelings toward the family. The task is to stay focused on the objective to be achieved with each family.

Suggested Readings

Anderson C, Stewart S: Mastering Resistance: A Practical Guide to Family Therapy. New York, Guilford, 1983
This book is useful for clinicians interested in converting resistance into opportunities for learning. Case examples and vignettes illustrate concrete strategies for engaging couples and families in treatment.

deShazer S: Keys to Solutions in Brief Therapy. New York, WW Norton, 1985
This book describes ways to sidestep resistance. The author emphasizes the importance of communicating with patients in a way that will invite their cooperation with treatment.

Nichols MP, Schwartz RC: Family Therapy, Concepts and Methods, 3rd Edition. Boston, MA, Allyn & Bacon, 1995, pp 512–513
This book provides extensive discussions of treatment models and resistance.

References

Alves JW: Back to Basics Is Good Move When "Stuck" in Family Therapy. The Brown University Family Therapy Letter, August 1992

Anderson C, Stewart S: Mastering Resistance: A Practical Guide to Family Therapy. New York, Guilford, 1983

Bowen M: Family Therapy in Clinical Practice. New York, Jason Aronson, 1978

Forrest T: Treatment of the father in the family therapy. Fam Process 8:106–109, 1969

Haley J, Hoffman L: Techniques of Family Therapy. New York, Basic Books, 1967

Imber-Black E: Secrets in Families and Family Therapy. New York, WW Norton, 1993

Napier A, Whitaker C: The Family Crucible. New York, Harper & Row, 1978

Satir VM, Baldwin M: Satir Step by Step: A Guide to Creating Change in Families. Palo Alto, CA, Science and Behavior Books, 1983

Shapiro R, Budman S: Defection, termination and continuation in family and individual therapy. Fam Process 12:55–67, 1973

Stanton MD, Todd TC: Engaging resistant families in treatment. Fam Process 20:261–293, 1981

Vogel W: Enriching therapy for couples and families. Psychiatr Serv 49:972–973, 1998

Work and Rest, Jean Charlot, 1971. Private collection.

CHAPTER 15

Family Therapy: General Considerations

Objectives for the Reader

- To be able to decide which family participants to include in treatment and to be aware of the guidelines for including children, adolescents, grandparents, and others
- To know the advantages and disadvantages of various therapist combinations
- To be aware of the variety of settings in which family therapy has been used
- To be able to manage the complexities of combining family treatment with medication or with other psychotherapies
- To know the similarities and differences between family therapy and individual or group therapy

In a family you live close to people that you otherwise may not even want to talk to. Over time, you learn their most miniscule, most private habits and characteristics. Today, professionals are preoccupied with the dysfunctional family. But to some extent all families are dysfunctional, with most having serious problems. A family is a microcosm reflecting the nature of the world; a place which runs on both virtue and evil. You can not change this, you can only learn to live in it.

Thomas Moore, *Care of the Soul*

Introduction

By now the reader should have some understanding of how families function and how their difficulties may be conceptualized. In addition, we have presented material relevant to the evaluation of troubled families and to the setting up of appropriate treatment goals. In this chapter we consider more general features of marital and family therapy, namely, the participants, the setting, the scheduling of treatment, and the use of family therapy in combination with other treatment methods and helping agencies. Finally, we compare family therapy with other therapy formats.

Family Participants

In practice it is often preferable to begin treatment by seeing the entire family together. The family can be defined broadly to include all persons living under the same roof; all those persons closely related to one another, even though they do not live together; or even more broadly, all persons significant to the family, even though not related to them—including friends, caregivers, or the family's social network.

Sometimes family therapy is carried out with the same therapist meeting with the whole family and with *each* family member individually. This approach, termed *concurrent family therapy*, is uncommon today. At other times two therapists who maintain some contact with each other, but who do not work jointly, may both see separately one or more members of a family in what is known as *collaborative family therapy*, which is also rare. *Conjoint family therapy* has been defined as family therapy in which the participants include at least two generations of a family, such as parents and children, plus the therapist, all meeting together. *Conjoint marital therapy* is limited to the two spouses plus the therapist meeting together.

The preferred model for family therapists is to see the whole family together for most of the sessions, occasionally having sessions with one of the subsystems (e.g., parents alone, siblings alone, father-son) as needed. Therapists who are interested in family-of-origin work will also have some sessions with one of the spouses and the spouse's parents. Opinion is divided over whether individual therapy with one or more family members should be done while family therapy is in progress and whether the individual therapist should also be the family therapist. Concurrent individual therapy is sometimes done by a different therapist, who it is hoped has some communication with the family therapist. Frequently a child's or spouse's therapist will suggest family therapy and then continue to treat his or her patient while family therapy is ongoing.

The preferred model for family therapists is to see the whole family together for most of the sessions, occasionally having sessions with one of the subsystems (e.g., parents alone, siblings alone, father-son) as needed.

Although it often seems desirable to meet with all family members present, in practice this may be impossible or even contraindicated. For example, children should not be present when their parents' sexual adjustment is being discussed. (We discuss the issue of taking a couple's sexual history more fully later in this chapter and in Chapter 20.) Often, too, the therapist will be unable to include certain family members because of illness, divorce, or death or because one or more family members temporarily or permanently refuse to participate. In the latter case, a decision will have to be made, either at the outset of treatment or after the evaluation, as to whether it is worthwhile and possible to continue working with the incomplete family. Hard-and-fast rules as to when such therapy is worthwhile are not easy to give, but our bias is that if the pros and cons are about equal, it is better to give treatment a try even if the family is incomplete.

Sometimes individuals will feel uncomfortable talking about certain topics in front of other family members. The family therapist will then have to decide whether individual interviewing might be indicated. Such an approach might be taken, for example, with the goal of eventually bringing the material from the individual session to the entire family group. However, there may be family secrets that cannot be productively shared with other family members and that should be kept private between an individual family member and the therapist. For example, one of the most complex current issues is whether children should be told they are products of artificial insemination or assisted pregnancy (e.g., surrogate mothers). Current thinking is that the emotional problems for the family caused by not knowing or by having a secret are worse than the emotional problems associated with dealing with the secret, but there is no real proof for this conclusion. (We discuss more fully the issue of secrets in Chapters 14 and 31.) On the issue of secrets, too, no rigid guidelines can be established. Consider the following example of an un-shared family secret[1]:

> Ms. A, the identified patient, was a 20-year-old woman with schizophrenia. After Ms. A's birth her mother experienced a postpartum psychosis, during which she jumped in front of a train, resulting in bilateral amputation below the knees. Ms. A's grandmother had also experienced a postpartum psychosis after the birth of her daughter, Ms. A's mother. Ms. A had not known about these secrets. Her father revealed the story in a family session that did not involve Ms. A. She was not informed of her mother's psychosis, based on the judgment of all concerned that she was not psychologically capable of dealing with this material at that time. However, because this information surely affected Ms. A deeply, the therapist might choose to share it with her when she is in a more compensated state.

The family concept can be extended to cover nonrelated people who have an effect on the individuals in treatment. These might be friends, neighbors, professional helpers, or custodians. Such people often do not have the same kind of emotional impact and influence that the natural family unit has, but at any one particular time these significant others may be quite important.

Many experienced family therapists believe that the probability of improvement increases as the number of nuclear family members involved in treatment increases. We tend to agree.

Extended Family and Significant Others

Family therapists include grandparents or in-laws as participants when these individuals seem to influence significantly the family's difficulties (see Chapter 12). Grandparents and other extended family members play vital roles in many families. In some families they may provide important help financially and functionally in carrying out the family's tasks. They may be a repository of emotional support and warmth, available in times of crisis and need. Their contributions and participation may at times be viewed as interference or infantilization. They may create or demand obligations in return for their involvement. The grandparents may provide money with strings attached, which may be in the form of rules and regulations concerning the rearing of their grandchildren; such aid may also imply an obligation that the family visit the grandparents on a prescribed schedule. The 1976 film *Lies My Father Told Me* provides an excellent example of a family in which a child may feel

---

[1]We are indebted to Pamela Ingber, M.D., for this example.

much closer to a grandparent than to his father or mother. In this film, a 7-year-old boy is being raised by a mother who is totally devoted to a rather insensitive, chronically inadequate spouse. The boy spends most of his time with his grandfather, who acts as a father substitute.

The question of whether a friend, fiance(e), boyfriend, or girlfriend should participate in a therapy session is raised occasionally. Sometimes the inclusion is vital, and such individuals should be included if their involvement is judged to be important to the progress of the therapy. However, there are potential drawbacks of including such outsiders. For example, they may be less motivated to change than are family members, thus hampering the usefulness of the family therapy; they are more likely to drop out of family therapy; and they may learn more intimate knowledge than is appropriate in a noncommitted relationship.

Caregivers

Caregivers (e.g., baby-sitters or housekeepers) are playing an increasingly important role in the function of families, especially in families in which both parents work. They are sometimes usefully included in treatment. Consider the following case example:

> In the B family, Mr. and Mrs. B were separated. Mrs. B had great difficulty functioning as a mother and in general, secondary to her depression. Mr. B, therefore, had custody of the children. Care of the children, ages 14, 12, and 10 years, was left to a baby-sitter, who was the 21-year-old sister of Mr. B's current girlfriend. Feeling despondent, Mrs. B attempted suicide. It was at this point that attempts at family therapy were initiated, but Mr. B refused to attend because he was angry with his wife. At the outset of family therapy, Mrs. B complained that she was unable to get the children to attend. They were on Mr. B's side. The children refused to attend when the therapist called them, saying the baby-sitter would not let them travel to the sessions. The baby-sitter was, of course, on the father's side. Furthermore, once the children began to attend therapy, the baby-sitter would, after each session, belittle the mother to the children. They would then berate their mother, who would again become suicidal. Only after the husband, the baby-sitter, and the husband's girlfriend were included in family therapy could this sequence of interactions be understood and modified.

Pets

Pets often serve important functions in the family (Feldman 1977).

1. As safe, faithful, intimate, noncompetitive, nonjudgmental love objects and friends

2. As substitute children for childless couples or for those whose children have left home; couples planning to have children may find that practicing their parental skills first on pets is desirable

3. As ways of compensating for personal deficiencies by identification with the pet's strength, courage, assertiveness, attractiveness, size, playfulness, directness, animality, dependence, or independence

4. As scapegoats or allies in intrafamily conflicts

5. As a means for children to learn responsibility and compassion

Consider the following two case examples:

Ms. C was from a family based on dyads (mother-father, older sister–younger sister). Ms. C's dog served as her "confidante" during her emotional crisis. When she left home to attend school, the dog developed a rash and lost his hair. He manifested the symptoms during the beginning of his empty-nest syndrome. There was also a family crisis about who should take care of the dog.

In the D family, Mr. D was unable to express any affection to his wife, son, or daughter, but he spent long hours caressing, talking to, and grooming his five dogs.

Veterinarians have observed the relationship between the neurotic behaviors of pets and those of their owners. One veterinarian has taken a family approach, stating, "You can't change a dog's behavior without changing the dog owner in terms of how he relates to the dog" (Campbell 1975).

The family therapist may want to include a pet, at least temporarily, as part of the therapy to observe and discuss the pet's role in the family system. A pet may be used as a more neutral way of getting into the family's dynamics because it may be easier to talk about the pet than to talk about the problems involving the human beings in the family.

Including Children and Adolescents in Family Therapy

With James Lock, M.D., Ph.D.

It would seem obvious that family therapy would be a useful modality in the treatment of the problems and disorders of children. Children are usually brought by their parents to mental health professionals for help. The child's family is often involved with and affected by the problem. Family members are concerned, usually motivated, and may have their own theories about the causes expressed in terms of some family dysfunction. It is common for parents to blame themselves for their child's problem.

Historically, child psychology and psychiatry have been shaped principally by theories of the individual, the development cycle, and the psychoanalytic model. These theories might have a similar point of view, as does family systems theory, with regard to the family's role in causing the problem, but when it comes to therapeutic intervention, the theories lead to very different approaches. Family systems thinkers believe that family treatment involving the child and various family members is the optimal way to produce change. In recent years, psychoanalytic thinking has taken a less central role in psychiatry training. Increased emphasis on family and systems issues is a more common component of child psychiatric training programs (Ravenscroft 1991). Nonetheless, studies confirm that although instruction in family therapy is required in child psychiatry training programs, most training does not include it (Detre 1989). A new concern has arisen, with the advent of managed health care, that an emphasis on medications as the only approach may undermine the gains family therapy has made within child psychiatry.

Working with families that have children compels the family therapist to first think developmentally. Some theorists have looked at families as the laboratories in which children are socialized and first learn about order, discipline, respect, cooperation, conflict resolution, and enjoyment. At the same time, every clinician has working models of the tasks that families with children of varying ages encounter and must master. For example, parents of young children must make room for their children, learn new parenting roles, and guide their children's behavior through rules and words. As children enter school and progress through adolescence, the parent-child relationship is based less on parental authority and more on parent-child collaboration.

For the family therapist, it is important to understand that the stable family and/or marital partner is a good buffer (possible healer) of childhood psychiatric disorder (Lewis 1998).

Diagnostic Family Evaluation

All children require careful medical, neurological, and developmental evaluations by professionals qualified to do them (Gardner 1993). To assume that a symptom has an interactional basis or that it is acting as a metaphor for the systems problem is premature and unprofessional. In addition to these evaluations, any evaluation of a child must include a family assessment. But family assessment means different things to different people. A family therapist would interview all family members and significant others at the same time. He or she would believe that such a procedure would give the most information about the child's and family's problems and that a child psychiatrist, who interviewed the parents and child separately and excluded siblings, was getting less information and not doing a family evaluation. Many good mental health professionals who work with children intuitively work with families. For example, individual psychotherapy for a 15-year-old adolescent who exhibits school avoidance won't produce change if the child psychiatrist missed the family evaluation and didn't pick up that the adolescent's 6-year-old sister is being abused by the parent. Conversely, child psychiatry has a lot to offer the family therapy field. For example, family therapy for that same adolescent won't help if the family therapist misses the adolescent's severe learning disability. Child psychiatrists, who in addition to being trained to evaluate and treat individual children are competent in family therapy, become fine generalists capable of working in both modalities of treatment.

Most family therapists assume that assessment of the family environment is crucial when a child presents with emotional-behavioral symptoms. By looking at the problem in its natural context, such as the home, the therapist can determine how family members' responses to the child's behavior may be contributing to the problem's persistence. For example, a child with oppositional behavior may elicit contradictory reactions from his or her parents. The father may react by punishing the child whereas the mother tries to modify what she views as her husband's extreme reaction. The astute family therapist will choose to see the problem in action, asking the family to show the problem rather than simply describe it. The therapist, guided by a developmental framework, may then identify the problematic pattern that maintains the child's difficulties, clarify the parents' conflict over discipline, help the parents to define a common strategy with which they both feel comfortable, and coach them in applying their plan with their child.

Many therapists prefer to involve everyone in the household, including infants (and perhaps even pets), during the evaluation period in order to observe how family members relate to one another. Helpful observations may be gathered, such as differences in how parents relate to each other with and without the infant present, how one parent holds an infant, and what the other parent's role is. After the initial evaluation is completed, the therapist must decide whether the continued inclusion of an infant or relatively nonverbal child aids or disrupts the work of therapy. An increased appreciation of the family variables involved in taking care of infants has developed in recent years (McDonough 1993).

Most family therapists would agree that infants and children should be included at least once for diagnostic purposes. Certainly much can be gained from having children present for many of the sessions, if for no other reason than that they are often more open and direct than adults and will say what they think.

Many family therapists can get confused and distracted by young children in a session, commonly maintaining that children don't sit still, that they just play. Because children's play and drawings can add much information to a family session, the therapist should keep some toys in the office. At different stages of family therapy, excluding younger children may be appropriate, just as seeing the sibling subsystem or the parental subsystem may be. Children and adolescents have delicately balanced internal psychological forces, which are in constant interaction with the external forces of the family. Where and how to intervene should come out of a careful evaluation of these factors.

As we have emphasized throughout this book, other individuals such as teachers, pediatricians, clergy, and neighbors may be important to the problem and should be consulted if they are part of the system (Furman 1986).

Treatment

Family therapists not only assess but also treat the problems of children and adolescents within the context of the family. Therapists must ally with the family, invite the family members to enact the problem, recognize the developmental tasks that need to be accomplished, and devise therapeutic interventions that assist family members in continuing through the course of normal development. In addition, therapists who work with children and families need to appreciate the important socializing roles that schools and friendships play in contributing to the positive social development of children and adolescents.

When young children are present, the parents are expected to exert appropriate behavioral control over them. If not, the therapist helps the parents to accomplish the task. The therapist explains the house rules, including behavioral limits and freedom of communication. The therapist must decide who should handle requests to go to the toilet or the water fountain. The therapist may wish to provide materials for play, such as toys, papers, and crayons.

Adolescents will be crucially involved in the family unit's concerns and interactions and often are the identified patients. They should be included in the sessions so that intergenerational conflicts and inadequate communications can be addressed. One of the primary tasks of the late adolescent, however, is to achieve increasing psychosocial autonomy from his or her family of origin. If such adolescents are consistently included in all family sessions, their involvement in all of the family's interactions is structurally reinforced. In addition, there may be little recognition of those specific interactions of the husband-wife pair that do not, and should not, involve their children. Thus it may be useful to have some sessions with only the husband and wife. Other sessions may be devoted to seeing an adolescent alone for the special purpose of reinforcing or increasing autonomy. Conjoint sessions may also be used successfully to explore issues of differentness and separation.

Occasionally a marital relationship has ruptured to the extent that treatment is stalemated. For example, two spouses may sit in the room and not speak to each other. A last-resort technique is to use adolescent children, on a temporary basis, as buffers, neutralizers, or reality testers, until such time as the couple is able to resume functioning as a dyad.

Careful recognition must be given to the readiness and ability of the adolescent and his or her family to separate. Although individual autonomous functioning is seen as a desirable goal, in some situations the therapist must be realistic with respect to the family's ability to tolerate an abrupt separation. He or she should also consider the possibility that the adolescent may have brain damage, chronic schizophrenia, or severe characterological difficulties. Child psychiatrists may face other issues, including the child's need for medication and the effect of this situation on families.

The Child in School

With Audrey J. Clarkin, Ph.D.

The function of schools has changed dramatically since the early 1980s, as family time lessens and school days lengthen with after-school day care and programs for the children of working parents. Far more than in the past, schools have become parent surrogates, expected to provide enrichment, socialization, sex education, and in some poor communities breakfast and even clothing. Schools are the child's first exposure to a hierarchical, competence-based environment and are one of the most powerful socializing factors outside the family.

Parents and school staff are partners in raising children but often experience themselves as antagonists. Schools are complex systems in and of themselves, with their own structure, hierarchy, and meaning systems. Parents and school staff may have many different relationships with one another. In private schools, where parents are often well educated, pay high tuition, and are greatly involved, the parents may see the school staff as serving them and become angry when teachers or the administration does not agree with them. In disadvantaged schools and neighborhoods, the parents may have little influence and experience themselves as without power and the school staff as critical and unhelpful. Conflicts and misunderstandings are particularly likely to occur when teachers and administrators are from a different ethnic group than are the students and parents. Parents also have their own personal, projected feelings about school, left over from their own experience as children.

Although family therapists tend to assume that children with problems are reacting to family issues, children can also develop problems in response to poor, dangerous, or humiliating school situations. The definition or locus of the problem is often confusing. Difficulties in parent-school collaboration will occur when 1) parents and the school staff cannot agree that a problem exists (e.g., the staff may report, "He's bullying others and fighting," and the parents respond, "He's a nice kid—it must have been the other kid's fault"), 2) parents and the school staff agree that a problem exists but cannot agree on a course of management and whether it should be more home or school based, or 3) school staff blame the parents for the problem and the family blames the school staff. A clear definition of the problem, its location, and previous management must be made before interventions can be effective (Rotheram 1998).

Therapists working with children in families should at a minimum request school reports if the child is having school problems. It is often helpful to request a phone conversation with the school counselor, who is usually the connecting link with the family, or if necessary the teacher(s). Plans that require monitoring, reporting, or specific behavior by the teacher should be worked out collaboratively with the teacher and counselor rather than being imposed on the school. It is often helpful to request a meeting of all involved persons, especially when multiple agencies (e.g., child social service, individual therapist, tutor, family therapist) are also involved. Most important, the therapist must conceptualize the school system as an important system in the child's and family's lives.

For the interested reader, the relationship between the family and the school is discussed in detail in a 1996 text (Booth and Dunn).

Conclusion

When the child is a focus of intervention, the fields of family therapy and child psychiatry or psychology have turf claims on the situation. In the past, McDermott and Char (1975) could say that there was an undeclared war between child psychiatry and family therapy. It would appear that the war is over, the dust is settling, and accommodation is being made on both sides. Family therapists are beginning to see that individual diagnosis is important, that not all of the variance of individual pathology and symptomatology is under the control of the family system, and that in some instances family therapy is not the primary mode of intervention. Similarly, child psychiatrists are beginning to recognize the influence of the family system on the maintenance and exacerbation of child pathology and to recommend family intervention when family factors are assessed as salient. New problems of integration may be developing now that managed health care places emphasis on the medical model as the only acceptable approach.

Therapist Combinations

Co-Therapy

Most family therapists work alone; however, some therapists still prefer to work with a co-therapist to help monitor the complexity of the transactions and to use as a system of checks and balances with the other therapist. Co-therapy is seldom used except in teaching sessions, and it poses a problem in such a setting because of the unequal balance of power involved when a student and a teacher do therapy together. One-way mirrors and video have supplanted this method as a learning technique. Some collaborative modules use one therapist for each spouse and involve periodic four-person sessions.

For training purposes, a student therapist can work with either a more seasoned veteran or a student of another discipline. Co-therapists can present an experiential model of a two-person interaction that is similar to a marital dyad by dealing openly with their own differences and by providing models for healthy communication. If, in contrast, the co-therapists feel that they need to present a united front or that they need to be identical in their attitudes and interactions with the family members they are treating jointly, the family will then be provided with a very unrealistic model.

Co-therapists may come to be seen as parents or as husband and wife by the family and may therefore be the recipients of the typical patterns, feelings, and attitudes that the family has toward people in these roles. The co-therapists may find themselves in danger of being split and having to take sides, in a manner very similar to that which takes place in family treatment. The co-therapy team must avoid falling into this trap. A solution is for one co-therapist to be sensitive to a family member who is in distress and who may need support, while the other therapist focuses on someone else. A co-therapist may in style or in behavior either complement (i.e., be different from) or be synergistic with (i.e., be similar to) the other therapist.

It is necessary to consider whether a therapist can work effectively with a co-therapist and if co-therapy is the best use of each therapist's time. An older study suggests that therapist satisfaction with co-therapy decreases as experience in family therapy increases (Rice et al. 1972). Furthermore, some authors have found that co-therapy causes problems that can impede family progress. For example, if a male co-therapist has had significant problems with his mother and is in the process of treating a family that has a difficult mother, he might have difficulty working effectively with a female therapist. Another obvious reason for the more common use of a single therapist is that it costs less.

In order to make co-therapy a successful experience, the co-therapists should know and like each other. They should have worked together, so that they are able to appreciate each other's therapy style and attitude. They should have time to discuss together what has been going on in their therapy sessions and to work out their mutual roles with respect to the family and each other. Ideally, co-therapists should get together before each session in order to review their objectives and ideas. Co-therapists should meet after each session to review what went on and to plan for the next session.

An innovative approach is the use of co-therapists from different disciplines, a desirable approach for beginning therapists. This technique has the advantage that each therapist may complement the other because each discipline has different training and may bring its own areas of expertise. This method requires the use of extra staff time, however, and to justify it, one would have to prove its differential effectiveness over family therapy as it is usually practiced.

Working as a Team

Several groups have experimented with the use of a treatment team (i.e., three or four therapists) to work with the family (Hoffman 1981; Montalvo 1973), although this practice is less common now than in the past. Typically, one or two therapists are in the treatment room with the family, while the rest of the treatment team is behind a one-way mirror. The team communicates with the therapist in the room by telephone or by having a conference (without the family) during or toward the end of the therapy hour. The team assists the therapist by providing directives to the therapist-trainee or by helping to formulate messages and tasks, including paradoxical tasks that the therapist will convey to the family.

In some settings, team members may join the therapist in the room or may send in contradictory messages (e.g., the team can insist that the couple shouldn't change so that the therapist can defend the change position). Although some families are put off by the one-way mirror and the idea of several people watching, most become comfortable with the setting and the idea that many people are involved in their care.

A treatment team is an extraordinary advantage to a trainee or even a seasoned therapist, particularly those working on the cutting edge of innovation. Having several people focus on a case at one time gives a sense of the broad possibilities for intervention and offers an opportunity to try things out, get immediate feedback, and correct course if needed. For the trainees behind the mirror, it offers a chance to see many cases in process and to work on formulating intervention. These sessions are usually taped so that work on the case can continue between sessions.

Problems can occur when no one is monitoring and supporting the team's dynamics. Sometimes the treating therapist freezes at the thought of several people watching behind the mirror or becomes so dependent on the team's interventions that he or she stops feeling as if he or she is running the session. Of course, this is also a very expensive way to do therapy, because although the patient is charged for only one therapist, many people may be involved.

Although expensive in terms of therapist resources, the team approach has the advantages of many heads being better than one and of using outside observers who are not enmeshed in the family interaction. It seems clear that with a number of team members, the team must generate its own smooth systems functioning, including clear leadership, cooperation, and so on.

Setting

Family therapy has been carried out in virtually all mental health settings, including child-guidance clinics, psychiatric hospitals, emergency rooms (walk-in or crisis clinics), outpatient clinics, juvenile probation offices, domestic relations courts, private offices, schools, social welfare services, and so on. In the past there have been cases in which entire families have been hospitalized for treatment or for research purposes (Bowen 1961). Other therapists have carried out treatment in the family's own home. In Italy most treatment contacts at some community mental health centers are made in the home (we discuss home visits in more detail in Chapter 9).

The issue of effectiveness in relation to location of treatment (e.g., in the hospital/clinic or in the home) has been raised. Some researchers feel that there is no carryover from the office to the home and have described the situation using the metaphor of training in the zoo (i.e., office) versus in the jungle (i.e., home). Although there may be a modicum of truth in this argument, in most countries practical problems associated with home visits (e.g., time and money) may make this approach a nonissue in the current treatment climate.

Time, Scheduling, and Fees

Most family therapists will see a family once a week for 45–90 minutes. In Italy many sessions last 2 hours or more. In outpatient settings a minority of therapists see a family more than once a week. In inpatient settings, family sessions may be scheduled more frequently. There is nothing sacred about once-a-week scheduling. Because the frequency of sessions is somewhat arbitrary (once a week is the most common), meeting less frequently may be strategically better for some families. In multiple-impact therapy, families are seen on an intensive basis and in different combinations—marital couple, mother and son, whole family, individuals, and so on—over a 2- or 3-day period by various members of a therapy team, consisting of a psychiatrist, a psychologist, a social worker, and a vocational counselor. Techniques focus on bringing about rapid change in the family during this time because its members have come for therapy from distant locations.

The overall duration of treatment depends in part on the treatment goals. On average, family therapy is a short-term method compared with individual or group psychotherapy or psychoanalysis. Other ground rules include the following:

1. Missed appointments should be rescheduled that week, if possible.
2. When one member of the family comes late, the therapist may start the clock at the arranged time and proceed with whoever is present. The therapist can present the position of the absent member. In contrast, many therapists don't start therapy until everyone arrives, in order to put pressure on everyone to come on time.
3. What can be done if one member of the family will not come to treatment? Often the resistance is not only from the member who will not come but also from the other family members who encourage the absence (either covertly or overtly). They may be unaware of their collusion, however, and often ask for help to get the reluctant member to participate. One possibility is for the therapist to contact the absent member.

4. Fees are usually set by time (i.e., the length of the session), not by number of family members present.

Keeping a Record of Treatment

Opinions differ as to the value of keeping written notes on the course of family treatment. Such a record may be useful in monitoring goals and in recording changes. The problem-oriented record modified for families provides a concise overall picture of the identified patient and the family and outlines problems, goals, and strategies (Deming and Kimble 1975). Ongoing progress notes record significant family developments, enable goal achievement to be measured, and provide a record of treatment and modalities used for achieving these goals. Referrals to other agencies are also noted. Such a system has a definite advantage over the traditional practice of keeping a separate record for each family member.

Many therapists focus on the process rather than the content of the sessions and therefore believe that there is no need to write down the details of what goes on. Others prefer not to keep any records of treatment to protect themselves against possible subpoenas (we discuss this issue in Chapter 31). We disagree. Our bias is to keep succinct and relevant records in all cases. We believe, too, that records are very helpful for legal and training purposes.

The American Psychiatric Association has set forth the following guidelines:

> In family therapy, although it may be preferable to keep records on a family basis, it is usually more practical to keep them in one of the participant's individual charts, as most facilities maintain records in this manner. Since authorization from the patient named in the chart is generally sufficient for the release of information, care must be taken about information included about other family members. Whether or not the record is kept on an individual or a family basis, it may be wise to have all of the involved family members sign a statement at the beginning of therapy acknowledging that it will contain information about all of them and specifying which signatures or combination thereof will be required to authorize access to the chart or release information from it. In the event of substantial family change, such as divorce or a child's reaching majority, particular care should be exercised not to release information inappropriately (Committee on Confidentiality 1987).

Family Therapy in Combination
With Other Psychosocial Therapies

At present the differential effectiveness of family therapy alone as compared with its use in combination with other therapies is just beginning to be studied (see Chapter 29).The use of family therapy in combination with somatic, individual, and group therapy has increased and is now common practice.

A *minority* of family therapists use conjoint family therapy alone. All contacts are kept strictly within the joint family setting, and the therapist will not communicate, even by telephone, with individual family members. No other treatment, including individual therapy, is used. This is done to avoid any type of coalition derived from material shared by the therapist and any part of the family system.

It is becoming more common for the same therapist to use individual psychotherapy sessions combined with family therapy. In this case the therapist has the advantage of knowing both the individual and the family. This combination, however, changes the nature of the therapy as follows: 1) The patient in individual therapy feels that what he or she reveals in the one-to-one situation may in some way (either overtly or covertly) be communicated to the family by the therapist; 2) family members may be reluctant to deal with sensitive issues in the conjoint sessions, preferring to reveal them in individual sessions; and 3) transference in individual sessions does not develop as fully because the patient can directly express his or her feelings about his or her family in the family therapy. The first two items must be dealt with directly; the last item is not a major problem because in these situations the therapy is usually not transference based. Inexperienced therapists may tend to identify with the individual patient, thus seeing the family from the patient's point of view. For example, the therapist may see all problems as resulting from a cold, passive, authoritarian father and a smoldering, double-binding, rejecting mother and from what the parents have done to the poor patient. This attitude may make it extremely difficult to work conjointly with the whole family.

In addition to conjoint family treatment, individual therapy has been carried out simultaneously in separate sessions with one or both parents. In this case individual therapy is often carried out by a colleague of the family therapist. It cannot be stressed too strongly that communication between therapists is necessary for effective collaborative treatment.

In the E family, the son, who had chronic schizophrenia, was the identified patient. He was age 20 years when he was brought for treatment because he had not left his room for a year. Mr. and Mrs. E were bringing him his meals in bed, and he had stopped attending school. The patient history revealed that there were two older sisters who were functioning well. Mr. and Mrs. E had met 25 years earlier. Mr. E was shy and withdrawn. Mrs. E was handling most of the burden and brought in most of the money. She worked as a cashier. Life for them had been good until the birth of the youngest child—the identified patient—at which point Mr. and Mrs. E stopped having sexual relations (the previous frequency had been about two times per week). Mrs. E said that she was uninformed about contraceptive methods and that because she did not want any more children, the only way she could think of was to stop having sex. Because Mr. E was a noncommunicative person, this issue had not been discussed for 19 years, until their son returned to the hospital.

Treatment intervention was initiated with an individual therapist who prescribed medication for the symptoms of the son's schizophrenia. Once the son's symptoms (negativism and autistic thinking) began to clear, treatment was directed toward his rehabilitation. To this end, and to place the patient in a work setting, the parents had to let him out of the nest. Family meetings were held with the mother, father, sisters, and the identified patient. Mr. and Mrs. E were also seen as a couple to help them rebuild their marital relationship. A series of progressive behavioral exercises markedly improved their sexual relations, which resumed with a satisfactory frequency. After this had occurred, Mr. and Mrs. E helped to find a halfway house for their son.

A major shift in the 1990s was the notion of using different formats over different stages of therapy and periods of time. A common sequence of treatment starts with the couple presenting with a sexual problem. Sexual therapy solves the problem. At this point, marital problems often come to the fore. Marital therapy is then used, and the marital relationship improves. Then one, or both, members of the couple may decide they want to explore different aspects of their own growth and development; therefore, individual sessions or therapy is scheduled. Numerous variations on this concept are possible, and this kind of sequencing represents an increasing trend.

Sugarman (1986) described some rules of thumb to follow in making decisions about combined therapy, which are still useful:

1) It is useful if it appears that different modalities would help significantly in different dimensions, such as the biological, social, and psychological; 2) if it appears that a given modality is either not helpful or of limited usefulness without an additional modality; 3) if there is significant motivation on the part of the individual or family to combine modalities; and 4) if the modalities are synergistic and enhance one another. On the other hand, the following reasons would be contraindications to combining modalities: 1) The epistemological

foundations of the various modalities are often based on contradictory assumptions. Since the goal of clinical work is to provide a coherent cognitive ordering of the world, combining modalities can at times be unproductively confusing for the patient system. 2) The additional time and money involved may be unnecessary. A single modality is often powerful enough to accomplish what is therapeutically necessary. 3) Different modalities can dilute the potential catharsis available for each separate therapeutic involvement. To the extent that there is meaning to the concept of psychic energy, it could be divided between the various modalities with not enough available in any one for the "critical mass" necessary to accomplish therapeutic work. This is similar to the concept of "diluting the transference" in psychoanalytic thought.

Individual treatment as a supplement to conjoint family therapy has also been carried out with mother and/or child. Holding individual sessions supplemented by conjoint sessions for all family members is an approach used commonly in child psychiatric practice.

Family therapy has been prescribed in combination with group therapy and with behavioral therapy. It has been used in conjunction with hospitalization and partial hospitalization for one member (usually the identified patient) or for all members of the family in both inpatient and day hospital settings and in conjunction with psychiatric medications and electroconvulsive therapy, which may be used to control the identified patient's acute symptoms. Throughout this book we stress the usefulness of the combination of medication and family therapy. In some situations, we have found that marital therapy was possible, and effective, only after one or both marital partners had been treated with antidepressants for their depressions (which predated the marriage).

Family therapy has been prescribed as an adjunct to individual therapy. In these situations it may be useful for diagnostic purposes to correct distorted perceptions and to shorten treatment. (See Chapter 1 and later in this chapter for indications for, and comparisons of, several types of psychosocial treatments.)

Family Therapy in Combination With Pharmacotherapy

Since the 1970s, new medications for the treatment of schizophrenia, depression, mania, borderline personality disorder (an Axis II disorder), and other Axis I disorders have improved the prognosis for patients and their families

(Glick et al. 1996). As these medications (e.g., atypical antipsychotics, selective serotonin reuptake inhibitors, anticonvulsants) become more effective, is therapy still useful, and how? An important part of the answer to this question is to combine psychotherapy and rehabilitation strategies, especially family intervention, with newer medication strategies (Glick et al. 1993).

Research suggests that although pharmacotherapy may be the cornerstone of treatment for Axis I disorders, it should be combined with individual and family intervention for almost all patients, and with family therapy at some point in the treatment. This suggestion has been made for the following four reasons:

1. Family dynamic issues or other stress may precipitate episodes, and therapy can help the family to prevent or cope with further stress.
2. Persons with these disorders often have lost (or never gained) social skills, or the illness has created behavior patterns that make the individuals aversive to their support systems, including, and especially, the family.
3. The illness has powerful effects on family life, and the entire family needs to cope with this fact together.
4. An ongoing relationship with the family therapist not only improves medication compliance but also provides continual support when the patient may not be on medication and provides a critical social support for persons dealing with what in many cases are chronic and potentially lifelong issues.

A modest body of controlled studies suggests that medication and family intervention are synergistic. Each approach covers different domains: Medication decreases certain symptom clusters (e.g., hallucinations, delusions), and family intervention improves interpersonal skills and relationships. By extension, an assumption is that both of these treatments improve compliance. Some obvious questions follow: Which diagnoses need which combination of therapies? In which sequence? In what doses? The following section addresses these issues.

Practical Guidelines

1. *Diagnosis.* The therapist must be sure to make a DSM-IV diagnosis, a family systems diagnosis, and an individual formulation of dynamics. Without a diagnostic map the appropriate drug will not be prescribed. Similarly, without a map of the family system dynamics, the clinician will be lost in the complexity of family issues.

2. *Goals.* The therapist must set target symptoms for all modalities. The issue here is to determine which symptoms are responsive to drugs and which are responsive to individual or family interventions. Without this delineation of target symptoms, it is impossible to know which treatment (or combination) is effective.

3. *Untoward effects.* The therapist must be aware of the side effects of drug therapy, family and individual psychotherapy, and their interaction. For example, increasing medications may enable the identified patient to discuss issues that were previously too emotionally charged for careful family discussion. Untoward effects must be monitored at each session. For example, neuroleptic medication may create side effects (e.g., sedation, dysphoria) that not only are unpleasant to the patient but also may decrease the patient's ability to socialize inside and outside the family.

   In some situations, a patient, with or without the family, may use the improvement that results from medication to avoid exploring relevant family issues. In such cases the family therapist should continue prescribing medications as necessary rather than discontinuing a treatment that is efficacious.

4. *Contraindications.* The therapist should be aware of situations in which combined family or individual treatment plus medication is contraindicated. Obviously this combination is not for everyone. We believe in the principle of therapeutic parsimony. If one modality is effective, a second should not be added. To be explicit, for some clinical situations we start with family therapy; for others we start with medication. In still others we start both approaches simultaneously and may withdraw one (or both) modalities over time. Given the shift in the field of psychiatry to psychopharmacology from psychotherapy, family therapy may be the right modality at the right time. At the very least, putting aside the power of a family intervention by itself, the family systems approach is an efficacious way to increase medication compliance.

5. *Sequencing.* The next issue is to sequence the modalities effectively and efficiently. As a first step (usually), a working therapeutic alliance must be established. Medication should be prescribed only after the therapeutic alliance is in place. Simultaneously, if appropriate, the family should be referred to the appropriate consumer group (e.g., National Alliance for the Mentally Ill, National Depressive and Manic-Depressive Association, Alcoholics Anonymous). Psychoeducation for the patient (if cognitively able) and the family is a crucial early step. This means the systematic administration over time of information about signs and symptoms, diagnosis, treatment, and prognosis. Individual supportive therapy

or family supportive intervention may begin at this point. Only later are dynamic individual or systemic family models used. Later, depending on response, rehabilitation is added to the equation.

Medication Alliance

By way of comparison with the alliance in a psychotherapy such as family therapy, let us describe what has been called the *pharmacotherapeutic alliance*, which can be defined as the manner in which active efforts are made by the physician to enlist, recruit, and involve the patient in a collaboration around the use of medication. Its characteristics are a flexible, prescriptive stance and the acknowledgment of uncertainty. Its objective is the establishment and maintenance of the alliance. The process includes shared inquiry, shared goals, and mutual participation in the use of the medication.

Family Intervention

Lam (1991) has described seven components of effective family approaches to schizophrenia, but each of these approaches can be adapted to most Axis I and II disorders:

1. A positive approach and genuine working relationship between the therapist and family
2. Provision of family therapy in a stable, structured format with the availability of additional contacts with therapists if necessary
3. A focus on improving stress and coping in the here and now, rather than dwelling on the past
4. Encouragement of respect for interpersonal boundaries within the family
5. Provision of information about the biological nature of the illness in order to reduce blaming of the patient and family guilt
6. Use of behavioral techniques, such as breaking down goals into manageable steps
7. Improvement of communication among family members

The essence of the family intervention, when combined with medication, is to educate the family about the disorder (e.g., signs and symptoms, causes, and biological and psychosocial treatments); provide communication skills training to improve the quality of family transactions and reduce family tension; provide problem-solving skills training for managing family or illness-related conflicts and reducing family burden; and resolve dynamic and systems issues created by the disorder.

The essence of the pharmacological intervention, when combined with the family intervention, is to normalize the illness (as with lithium in bipolar disorder) and to suppress symptoms in the individual. To summarize, somewhat paradoxically family therapy ultimately and indirectly can promote medication compliance, whereas medication can improve interpersonal function and compliance with family therapy.

Family Therapy in Combination With Other Helping Agencies

Family therapists often find themselves conducting family therapy at the same time that other helping agencies are also exerting influences on the family. This may create unwanted complications.

Commonly families have multiple problems that involve a wide variety of agencies (e.g., welfare, probation, school, housing). These agencies may be pulling the family in different directions. The need is often to open up communication among the various agencies and to allocate areas of responsibility. It then becomes necessary to coordinate the work of the various agencies in the service of the family's goals, thus avoiding much duplication and wasteful contradictory efforts.

In some families, treatment is being administered simultaneously by the therapist and physician of one or more members of the family (Anthony 1970). For example, one family member may be receiving cortisone for rheumatoid arthritis, which may make that member euphoric or even manic. He or she may be difficult for the family to live with. The family therapist will have to be in continual contact with the family physician to coordinate treatment in such cases.

Family members may play one agency against the other in the service of their needs. For example, the family members may need to have the identified patient remain dysfunctional so that they can get welfare or disability payments.

Comparison of Therapy Formats and Strategies

Now that we have presented the techniques of family therapy, let us again compare family therapy to individual therapy and to group therapy (see Chapter 1), only this time by type of strategies used. Table 15–1 is an expansion of Table 1–1. It reveals the relevant similarities and differences, but the

TABLE 15–1. Comparison of therapy formats and strategies

Therapy format		Strategies	
	Insight-awareness	Systemic-strategic	Experiential-existential
Family	Confrontation of family interaction Clarification of interaction Interpretation of conflict	Psychoeducation Assignment of task Marking of boundaries	Empathic contact Exploration of present family experience
Individual	Confrontation Clarification Interpretation	Assignment of individual task Cognitive restructuring Role-playing Desensitization	Empathic contact Exploration of present individual experience
Group	Confrontation of group interaction Interpretation of group and individual transference	Role-playing Behavioral rehearsal Assignment of tasks	Empathic contact Exploration of present group experience

main issue is to note the most obvious difference—the unit with which the therapist is working: in individual therapy, an individual; in family therapy, members of the same family (broadly defined); and in group therapy, persons who are not members of the same family.

Final Note

In this chapter we try to speak to the most frequent questions trainees have about the intricacies of actually doing therapy. Obviously, not every situation is addressed—the key clinical pearl is to remember that family treatment involves "the family" (i.e., it is a way of thinking about a problem). That principle should help in finding solutions to so-called impossible treatment dilemmas.

Suggested Readings

Imber-Black E: A family larger system perspective, in Handbook of Family Therapy, Vol 2. Edited by Gurman A, Kniskern D. New York, Brunner/Mazel, 1991, pp 583–605
This clearly written book presents a practical, learnable framework for thinking about problems from a systemic perspective and for intervening directly to change family patterns. It demonstrates how to think and work with families that are involved with helping systems such as welfare, hospitals, and group homes.

Thase ME, Glick ID: Combined treatment, in Treating Depression. Edited by Glick ID. San Francisco, CA, Jossey-Bass, 1995, pp 183–208
This chapter takes an in-depth look at combining family therapy with drug treatment and at how therapists of different disciplines can work together.

References

Anthony E: The impact of mental and physical illness on family life. Am J Psychiatry 127:138–146, 1970

Booth A, Dunn JP: Family-School Links: How Do They Affect Educational Outcomes. Mahwah, NJ, Lawrence Erlbaum, 1996

Bowen M: Family psychotherapy. Am J Orthopsychiatry 31:40–60, 1961

Campbell W: Owners cause dogs' mental problems. San Francisco Chronicle, October 29, 1975, p 45

Committee on Confidentiality: Guidelines on confidentiality. Am J Psychiatry 144:1522–1526, 1987

Deming B, Kimble JJ: Adapting the individual problem-oriented record for use with families. Hosp Community Psychiatry 26:334–335, 1975

Detre T: Some comments on the future of child and adolescent psychiatry. Journal of Academic Psychiatry 13:189–191, 1989

Feldman B: Pets soothe their owners' hang-ups. San Francisco Examiner, November 20, 1977

Furman E: The roles of parents and teachers in the life of the young child, in What Nursery School Teachers Ask Us About. Edited by Furman E. Madison, CT, International Universities Press, 1986, pp 3–19

Gardner RA: Child Psychotherapy: The Initial Screening and the Intensive Diagnostic Evaluation. Northvale, NJ, Jason Aronson, 1993

Glick ID, Clarkin JF, Goldsmith SJ: Combining medication with family psychotherapy, in American Psychiatric Press Review of Psychiatry, Vol 12. Edited by Oldham JM, Riba MB, Tasman A. Washington, DC, American Psychiatric Press, 1993, pp 585–610

Glick ID, Lecrubier Y, Montgomery S, Vinar O, Klein DF: Efficacious and safe psychotropics not available in the United States. Psychiatric Annals 26:354–361, 1996

Hoffman L: Foundation of Family Therapy: A Conceptual Framework for Systems Change. New York, Basic Books, 1981

Lam DH: Psychosocial family intervention in schizophrenia: a review of empirical studies. Psychol Med 21:423–441, 1991

Lewis JM: For better or worse: interpersonal relationships and individual outcome. Am J Psychiatry 155:582–589, 1998

McDermott JF, Char WF: The undeclared war between child and family therapy. Journal of the American Academy of Child Psychiatry 13:422–435, 1975

McDonough SC: Interaction guidance: understanding and treating early infant-caregivers relationship disturbances, in Handbook of Infant Mental Health. Edited by Zeanah C. New York, Guilford, 1993, pp 414–426

Montalvo B: Aspects of live supervision. Fam Process 12:343–359, 1973

Ravenscroft K: Family therapy, in Child and Adolescent Psychiatry: A Comprehensive Textbook. Edited by Lewis M. Baltimore, MD, Williams & Wilkins, 1991, pp 850–868

Rice D, Fey W, Kepecs J: Therapist experience and "style" as factors in co-therapy. Fam Process 11:227–238, 1972

Rotheram M: The family and the school, in Children in Family Contexts. Edited by Combrinck-Graham L. New York, Guilford, 1998, pp 347–368

Sugarman S (ed): Interface of Individual and Family Therapy: Family Therapy Collection. Rockville, MD, Aspen Publications, 1986

Encounter, Naomi Gerstein, 1974. Private collection.

CHAPTER 16

Brief Family Therapy: Treatment as It Is Influenced by Time Constraints

Objectives for the Reader

- To be aware of and understand the indications for brief family therapy
- To be able to describe the course of and techniques of brief intervention

Introduction

In the 1990s, under pressure from managed care companies, time-limited therapy became the rule rather than the exception—by necessity, it is a preferred model. Gurman (1981) has commented that to call family or marital treatment brief is redundant, as the typical family intervention before the 1990s lasted only for approximately 15–20 sessions. It has now become even briefer—estimated at 2–10 sessions. The current focus on time-limited therapies has resulted from a multitude of factors. Economic limitations of patients and clinics helped press for an intervention package that was time limited and cost-effective. The existence of long waiting lists of clinic patients expecting assignment to therapists also pressured clinicians to consider and experiment with shorter forms of intervention. Another reason for the increased use of brief therapy was the need for research on psychotherapy, coupled with the realization that to research 10 sessions of therapy was much more practical than observing and recording a therapy that spanned some years. Most important, some clinicians began to formulate the theoretical advantages of a short, preplanned intervention and linked it to the historical roots of the beginning of psychotherapy, pointing out that Freud's initial work, for example, was brief (Malan 1963).

Gurman suggested some interesting hypotheses as to why marital therapy tends to be brief. Because marital therapy is not based just on the insight-awareness model, the therapist focuses on the current problem rather than examining the antecedent of the problem. Many of the patients who enter marital therapy have shown themselves capable of having at least one (more or less) meaningful relationship judged by the fact that they are married; thus, these individuals are likely to constitute a selected good-prognosis population. In addition, the interpersonal or transferential aspects of the problem are not only talked about but also exhibited in the therapy sessions themselves because both parties are present. Finally, the loss of the therapist at the end of the treatment is not as threatening as the termination of an individual treatment, because the primary affect is always toward the partner rather than the therapist.

Indications for Brief Family Intervention

Indications for the use of planned, brief family or marital intervention would include the following:

1. When there is a current, relatively focused family or marital conflict. Examples include the need to separate from the family of origin (Haley 1980); to establish marital commitment; to resolve mixed feelings about intimacy and dependency; to establish modes of conflict resolution, decision making, and negotiation in the marital dyad; to clarify role expectations; to develop channels for expression of positive and negative feelings; to explore the decision to divorce or gain assistance in negotiating a separation or divorce that is least harmful to spouses and children involved.
2. When evidence indicates that family members are contributing to an identified patient's focused symptom or problem complex.
3. When family cooperation must be mobilized as an induction to another mode of therapy.
4. When the family situation is baffling, and brief therapy is chosen partly as an extended evaluation and partly as therapy.

Not only is the specific problem area important in indicating time-limited family intervention, but also the family members' specific capabilities for focused brief work factor into the decision to use this treatment mode. These capabilities include the family's ability to meet together without uncontrollable fighting, the presence of family agreement and the family's ability to focus on specific problems, and the motivation of significant family members to participate. For the most part, these capabilities are not as crucial in lengthier family work.

> Many current practitioners believe that the issue is not the presenting problem but defining the problem in such a way that it is amenable to solution (as we discussed earlier in the chapter on strategies) by highly systemic formulations. In the hands of experienced practitioners, brief therapy models have been applied with success to all family issues.

Course of Treatment

The initial referral contact and evaluation interview can be used to set the stage for the brief family treatment. The therapist in collaboration with a family can focus on specific issues, clarify the goals and expectations, and channel the interactions in ways suited to short-term, focused work. For example, if the family situation fits one of the indications listed earlier in this chapter, then the evaluation data gathering will focus on material and processes relevant to that category and its goals, and other types of data will be given less attention.

Before the end of the first session, the therapist will have made a contract with the family outlining the goals and duration of treatment. An agreement may also be made about the goals that will not be pursued. Anything else that is made explicit to the family about the process of treatment may vary, but the therapist should have a blueprint in mind.

As the therapy proceeds, the therapist will actively keep the family on track and discourage derailments of various sorts. Depending on the type of treatment involved, the family will be rewarded for continuing in the necessary stepwise sequence or for gaining mastery in a more adaptive way of dealing with an old pattern. The therapist will be conductor, traffic cop, referee, mentor, and model, using his or her knowledge of individual and group dynamics, as well as family processes.

The therapist will remind the family of the limited nature of the treatment. He or she will be aware that termination anxiety may occur, with distress reemerging as the end of the treatment approaches, even if positive gains have been made during the earlier phase of treatment. The therapist will resist attempts to prolong therapy beyond the agreed-on time. He or she will deal with the family's desire for dependence on the therapist and the family's fear of being unable to cope. The family members will be helped to summarize the gains they have made during treatment and to rehearse their future problem-solving efforts.

Techniques

In this section, we discuss specific techniques established as especially useful in brief, focused family evaluation and treatment. Although these techniques are by no means the only ones available, readers should gain from their descriptions an adequate understanding of the variety of therapeutic options available (Cade and O'Hanlon 1993). There is no necessary and absolute connection between any one technique and the five general strategies we outlined in Chapter 12, although some techniques obviously lend themselves more easily to one strategy than to another.

Experienced therapists are most likely to be flexible in what they do, from case to case and from minute to minute. The techniques we describe, then, should be thought of as freeing the therapeutic imagination rather than as restricting it with a straitjacket.

Setting Limited Goals and a Definite Endpoint

When brevity is not part of the agreed-on contract, the reasons for therapy often remain vague and ambiguous. Sessions are likely to continue with no fixed termination agreed on in advance and with goals and directions changing as treatment proceeds. Symptomatic and behavioral progress is not taken as a sign that treatment can end but rather as confirmation of the positive effects of the treatment and the desirability of continuing it.

It is essential in brief therapy that the therapist be clear as to the focused and limited goals of treatment. In every session the therapist must keep clearly in mind that the amount of contact with the family will be limited and will have a definite endpoint, in terms of either the number of hours or the achievement of a specific goal. The therapist's concept may be centered on the least that needs to be done to help the family to continue on its own rather than on more ambitious, if not grandiose, notions of the family's potential.

During the first few sessions, the therapist should state and discuss with the family the focused goals of the treatment in concrete and specific detail. The family can be asked to specify in concrete terms how family life would be 6 or 10 weeks from then if interactions in the problem area were better. This approach can flush out individual family members' grandiose or unrealistic goals, vagueness, or resistance to visualizing change. Stated in concrete and observable terms, the goals can then stand as barometers to be observed during the course of treatment and can be used to assess progress at termination, thus reinforcing the efforts of successful families and challenging the more resistant families.

The content of the goals will, of course, vary according to the situation. If the evaluation indicates that the family has been functioning satisfactorily until a recent crisis, efforts will be made to restore the preexisting equilibrium as quickly as possible. For example, crisis intervention techniques may be used in a family in which the 22-year-old son, who is living with his parents, has had an exacerbation of positive symptoms of chronic schizophrenia. The parents may panic, demanding hospitalization of their son and his permanent removal from the home. With ventilation, attention to what triggered the upset, support, symptomatic relief for all concerned, and a setting that allows for daily visits to the therapist, brief but intensive therapy may avoid hospitalization and quickly restore the family's ability to cope.

If the family's distress seems more related to long-lasting patterns of interaction, some attempt can be made to set goals in one or two crucial areas in a way that will open up new possibilities for the family to grow and develop on its own, without further reliance on the therapist. For example, when a wife's suicide attempt seems related to chronic unspoken doubts about the viability of the marriage, the therapist will work toward the goal of getting the husband and wife to express more openly to each other the extent of their current needs, disappointments, and frustrations and make at least one thing better. As soon as the couple are able to engage satisfactorily in these transactions, they may be ready to carry on without the therapist's presence. But there is always the danger of making things worse temporarily, in which case the therapy may need to be longer. Because problem avoidance was at the root of the suicide attempt, a no-treatment option is not indicated.

Setting a fixed number of sessions with the family at the beginning of treatment is often desirable, as it makes explicit and concrete the limited time in which the goals are to be achieved. It is essential that this commitment to terminate be adhered to, despite various attempts the family may make to undermine it. The essence of such treatment may be to help families begin to understand how they do not keep agreements and how they sabotage attempts at changing dysfunctional patterns.

Active Focus: Reinforcement of Family Strengths, Reconceptualization

The therapist will be alert to the need to stay on target during the course of the treatment and will continually help the family to stick to the one or two primary goals that have been agreed on. Other issues that emerge can be conceptualized as relating to the core issues in some important ways or as resistances to dealing with those issues. Alternatively, extraneous matters can be noted as important but not germane to the current focus, and perhaps they can be left for the family to deal with later, on its own. Whatever treatment focus has been selected will benefit from underlying and positive reinforcement from the therapist whenever possible.

> Family therapy requires the active contribution of the therapist, possibly more so than in some other formats of therapy. In brief family therapy, even more therapist participation is usually needed. Passivity and indecisiveness tend to activate the family's dysfunctional repetitive patterns.

Existing and emerging family strengths should be reinforced and supported, as should the concept that all family members are doing the best they can. Especially in brief therapy, in which there is little opportunity for the gradual development of rapport, the therapist must be active and encouraging and must indicate that an attempt is being made to understand the situation from each member's, as well as the whole family's, vantage point. For effective brief therapy each family member needs to feel that the therapist understands and accepts him or her. Informal moments before, during, and after sessions are invaluable for the therapist to add a personal touch of contact with each family member.

The therapist should reward successes in substituting more functional patterns during the course of the therapy. He or she should highlight indications that the family can change and should emphasize the important idea that the therapist is there to catalyze the changes and help the family learn how to carry on this process alone. The therapist may temporarily be extremely active and directive but always with the goal in mind that the family needs to learn how to monitor and direct itself. The therapist should discourage any long-term reliance on outside experts and should challenge and educate the family to take charge of itself in more gratifying ways.

Active Exploration of Alternatives: Behavioral and Emotional Rehearsal

Sometimes families need to be given permission and encouragement to consider alternative patterns to those they have been living with or feel they will be facing in the future. The mere raising of such an issue can be a liberating experience. For example, a middle-aged couple, facing the oncoming empty-nest syndrome in which their parental role will be curtailed sharply, may find it exhilarating to consider rethinking their marital contract and marital roles. Once the therapist has opened such a door, the couple may find quickly that they are able to proceed on their own.

Couples who have secretly thought about separating but have never dared to express such a thought may at first feel threatened by a therapist who openly wonders whether they have considered it. With a skillful therapist such a couple can face ideas and feelings they have been too afraid or guilty to express before, allowing for intensity and change.

During the therapy sessions, family members should be given the strength to express themselves more openly to one another than before. The therapist should make it safe for them to do so but should also explore with the family the consequences of such openness. Repeated rehearsals of possible consequences may be required before more open communication can be established as being safe.

When a child is considered to be the problem, rehearsals aimed at strengthening the parental coalition may be essential. The parents may be undermining each other's authority, which is often related to weaknesses in their marital relationship.

Homework and Family Tasks

For therapy to be effective, changes must be noted outside the treatment sessions. To speed up this process, and to maximize the effect of the limited number of sessions, family members can be asked to carry out homework assignments. These should be relatively simple and achievable and should bear on those crucial problems that are the focus of treatment. They may involve, for example, various types of marital or family communication exercises. The husband and wife may be asked to practice negotiating differences at home. They can be told to make explicit to each other their position on a given issue, with the expectation that they will repeat to each other their understanding of the other's position.

Interaction and behavioral exercises are often helpful. For example, two estranged family members can be asked to jointly plan and carry out a dyadic activity that they would enjoy and to report about it at the next treatment session. The therapist can make negative injunctions, such as prohibiting family members from bringing up recriminations from the past.

Sometimes the therapist can help a family member clarify or modify an important outside relationship, such as with that member's family of origin. For example, a wife who has felt squeezed between her love for her husband and her mother's disapproval of him can be asked to start talking to her mother about this situation in an attempt to resolve it.

To encourage rapid transactional changes, the therapist can negotiate explicit contracts between family members. For example, a mother may be asked to agree to let her teenage daughter stay out until midnight on weekends in return for the daughter's having all her homework completed by then. Such contracts can bring a temporary halt to bickering, offer a model for mutually satisfying negotiations, and allow the family sessions to move on to other issues.

The Problem-Oriented School of Brief Therapy

One school of brief therapy is based on the notion that change can be accomplished by identifying the problem and changing the family's solution to it (Watzlawick et al. 1974). The model ignores all historical material except as it pertains to why the clients have chosen a particular solution to the problem and what other solutions they have attempted. The rationale is that the family's attempted solution maintains and compounds the problem. The therapeutic intervention then is to intercept and redirect the family's solution. Other therapists may search with the family for exceptions—that is, times when the problem did not occur—and emphasize what went right at those times.

In the A family the presenting problem was that the adolescent son got into fights with his single-parent mother and refused to help with basic household maintenance. The mother's solution had been to reason with her son as to why she couldn't fulfill his demands. Her solution escalated the problem. Taking as an example the son's demands for her always to prepare meals despite her busy work schedule, she was instructed to tell her son that she wouldn't be able to get supper every night because she was not a good enough mother. This intervention pushed the mother to decide whether she was good enough. After she made a list of all that she was doing, she concluded that she was carrying 90% of the workload in the house. She could then deliver the line with a smile and a shrug. After eight sessions, mostly with the mother, the son began to be more helpful, and his fighting in the home stopped completely (as determined over a 1-year follow-up period).

Crisis Intervention

In one sense, an extreme form of brief intervention is the crisis intervention needed when a family is in acute distress that threatens the very life of an individual, the family unit, or family adjustment. This would be analogous to a serious medical emergency in which primary efforts would be directed at maintaining vital body functions, stopping any loss of blood, and providing for supportive conditions until the system stabilizes. At such a time, no definitive reconstructive or elective procedures can be undertaken.

For family emergencies, attention must be given to the carrying out of necessary family tasks, including the basic provision of food, clothing, and shelter. Physiological needs, such as sleep, may require professional intervention, and outside sources of help (e.g., relatives, friends, agencies) may need to be called on. Behavioral controls and at least a modicum of emotional stability should be sought while the therapist evaluates the specific situation that resulted in the acute family disequilibrium. Every effort should be made to eliminate, contain, buffer, understand, or conceptualize this situation so that the family can return quickly to its former level of adjustment.

After the acute crisis has passed, further intervention may not be needed or desired. Often, however, a new contract (or referral) can be made for ongoing treatment with new goals.

Suggested Readings

Bagarozzi D: The Couple and Family in Managed Care; Assessment, Evaluation, and Treatment. New York, Brunner/Mazel, 1996
This book provides a useful blueprint for the family therapist doing brief therapy and dealing with managed care.

Eron J, Lund T: Narrative Solutions in Brief Therapy. New York, Guilford, 1996
This book is a very readable text on the narrative school approach to brief therapy.

O'Hanlon W, Wiener-Davis M: In Search of Solutions: A New Direction in Psychotherapy. New York, WW Norton, 1989
This book presents a direct strategic approach to conducting brief therapy. It is written in a lively style and provides enjoyable case vignettes to illustrate the authors' clinical points.

References

Cade B, O'Hanlon W: A Brief Guide to Brief Therapy. New York, WW Norton, 1993

Gurman AS: Integrative marital therapy: toward the development of an interpersonal approach, in Forms of Brief Therapy. Edited by Budman S. New York, Guilford, 1981, pp 415–457

Haley J: Leaving Home: The Therapy of Disturbed Young People. New York, McGraw-Hill, 1980

Malan DH: A Study of Brief Psychotherapy. London, Tavistock, 1963

Watzlawick P, Weakland J, Fisch R: Change: Principles of Problem Formation and Problem Resolution. New York, WW Norton, 1974

Indians and Squaws, Caughnawaga Near Montreal, Cornelius Krieghoff, 1860. Courtesy of the Confederation Centre Art Gallery and Museum, Charlottetown, Prince Edward Island, Canada. Used with permission.

CHAPTER 17

Treatment As It Is Influenced by Issues of Ethnicity, Race, Gender, and Class

Objectives for the Reader

- To understand the functioning of families of differing races, ethnic origins, and socioeconomic status
- To be able to generate principles for accommodating therapeutically to such families
- To be aware of how cultural, racial, gender, and class issues can influence therapy with families
- To consider how discrimination on the basis of race, gender, and ethnicity affects family life

Introduction

According to the 1990 Census, approximately 60 million people (24%) in the United States are African American, Latino American, Asian American, Pacific Islander, or Native American. The Bureau of the Census estimates conservatively that by the year 2050 this population will more than double to 122 million people, or 40% of the total population. If current trends continue, at some point in the twenty-first century, white European Americans will constitute a minority group in the United States (Olmedo 1994). This has profound implications for family therapists who find themselves working increasingly with patients from differing races, cultures, and classes and who as a group are increasingly multicultural. This situation has brought an understanding that cultural and class issues are not peripheral but rather are at the heart of understanding family life. Family life transmits culture to its members, and cultural norms are embedded in the family.

Race has always been an extraordinarily complex issue in the United States, one of the most racially diverse and racially conscious countries in the world. Persons of color are denigrated minorities in this country; this experience, in addition to differing cultural norms, affects the experience of these individuals and their family life. Class, present but seldom spoken of in the United States, is linked with money, opportunities, and belief systems, affecting the family's ability to make choices, care for its members, and plan for the future. The family therapist must understand how issues of culture, race, and class influence family function and dysfunction.

Culture and Ethnicity

The cultural context in which the family functions determines, to a greater extent than is generally thought, the family's daily operations and functioning. The family's cultural background and experience determine its attitudes and beliefs about life and the political, social, and economic options and opportunities that its members are likely to have.

Culture is defined as the broad base of ways of living built up by people in a particular area that includes roles, beliefs, behavioral habits, rituals, meanings, collective goals, and ways of expressing and feeling. Family experiences defined as normal vary greatly from culture to culture. For example, in some English families, in which early independence is a positive value, children are sent to boarding school after age 6 or 7 years, whereas in many Italian families, in which being an integral part of the family is a value, children may live at home until they are married, even into their late 20s. These families have very different ideas about closeness, parenting, and what would be called enmeshment. A therapist who makes assumptions about either of these families might see severe psychopathology where the culture would see a normal family.

Cultural groups vary in their attitudes toward everything: sex; food; men, women, children; the elderly; birth; and death. Everyone in the United States carries some ethnic identity, although this identity may be multiethnic from several generations of intermarriage, and individuals may or may not have been taught to value their ethnic identity.

Regardless of their country of origin, when couples and families emigrate to the United States, they come with a set of assumptions, values, and behaviors that may be greatly at variance with American norms. Over two or three generations, immigrants find some way of blending their old culture with the new one, usually helped by members of their culture who are already in residence. When we speak of ethnicity in America, we must consider whether the person's identity is primarily American with a sense of ethnic background from another place, or whether the person's identity is primarily as an emigrant, or outsider. We also must remember that different family members assimilate at different speeds.

> Mr. and Mrs. A, a Korean couple who had lived in the United States for 20 years, came to therapy because of constant arguing. Mr. A wanted the family to "be Korean" and wanted Mrs. A to participate in Korean women's organizations, to serve only Korean food, and to be obedient to his wishes. Mrs. A saw America as a land of opportunity for women and wanted to be American, joining with the children in eating American food and having American friends. She had not, however, begun a career. She stated that she was furious with her husband and wanted a divorce. The therapist (an American woman) explained that Mrs. A could make that choice if she wished but that she needed to be clear about the legal aspects of divorce and that she would be financially much worse off. The therapist recommended trying to find areas of agreement or compromise before Mrs. A gave up. At this point, however, Mr. A insisted they drop out of therapy, because the therapist had not told his wife to obey him.

People who come from other countries bring with them different traditions that may be at variance with the new environment in which they find themselves. It is helpful to remember that dysfunctional families are often at variance with the norms of their own culture; it is critical that the therapist learn something about those norms.

Within its own cultural framework, the family may transmit certain cultural norms and fight others, but the parents and their children must acknowledge, and either accede to or work around, the roles and beliefs demanded of them. For example, the cultural pressure for white adolescent girls to be thin is very strong in the United States. Parents may agree with this idea and encourage their female child to diet, or disagree, valuing intellect or obedience more than looks, and encourage their child to fight against believing that value and body size are connected, but they cannot completely ignore it. The child must in some way deal with both the cultural pressure and the family's response. If the family's level of anxiety about the child's weight gets very high, she may develop an eating disorder. If the child is a gymnast, a dancer, or a member of a peer group that puts great emphasis on small size, she may still develop an eating disorder, regardless of parental influence. Thus cultural mores may be filtered through the family but may produce great pressures in and of themselves. In the African American community, where the pressure to be thin is not as strong (although in this community there are also class differences in attitudes toward weight), the frequency of eating disorders is lower and the family issues around food are different.

As we described in Chapter 3, functional families share certain characteristics. In this chapter, we emphasize that a knowledge of the particular issues associated with race, class, gender, and ethnicity, as they interact to provide a direction and context for each family, is critical for rapid and effective treatment.

> **A** knowledge of the particular issues associated with race, class, gender, and ethnicity, as they interact to provide a direction and context for each family, is critical for rapid and effective treatment.

Guidelines for Understanding Family Patterns in Different Cultures

In this section we provide an itemization and a summation of some of the ways in which families of different cultures may vary. For beginning therapists, obtaining this information from each family provides a general approach to thinking about variations in pattern.

1. *Role and family membership.* Who is considered a family member? Is only the nuclear family part of the family, or are aunts, uncles, or informally adopted members part of the decision-making system? How are family members perceived in terms of their roles? The role of father, for example, may be quite different from one culture to another in terms of power and authority.

2. *Interpersonal relationships and reciprocity.* How does the family handle interpersonal relationships and reciprocity? In some cultures there may be a strong sense of interpersonal reliance and mutual obligation within the family unit, whereas in other cultures the trend may be toward independence, with each person doing his or her own thing.

3. *Power, age, and gender relationships.* In some cultures the man is clearly head of the household in all areas; in others the woman has greater decision-making power within the area of home and children. The current direction in Westernized cultures is toward a more egalitarian relationship between the spouses, although true equality is seldom reached. Cultures also vary in terms of the generation that has the most family power. In many Asian cultures the oldest members of the family, usually the grandparents, have the most power. In some cultures it is the spouses, or the caregiving parent, and in some families, although it is not a cultural norm, child-centeredness becomes so strong that the children appear in control.

4. *Propriety.* Cultural standards of right and wrong are important components of family functioning. Families in some cultures have a rigidly defined set of acceptable behaviors, whereas families in other cultures may rely on a more pragmatic and flexible style of behavior. Overt public shaming of wrongdoers is a common form of chastisement in some cultures; an internalized guilt system is more common in others.

5. *Time and relationships.* In traditional cultures, extended family clans may institutionally reinforce the feeling of family continuity over a period of many generations, even centuries, so that generational history is very salient. However, many American families cannot trace their history further back than grandparents. In more Westernized cultures, very poor families are sometimes more present oriented and middle-class families more future oriented.

6. *Expression of feelings and symptoms.* Culture, race, and class may have a marked influence on the expression of feelings. In some middle-class families feelings are expressed openly, whereas in many upper-class families one is expected to keep a stiff upper lip. In some lower-class families expression of physical symptoms may be more acceptable than the expression of certain feelings. Some cultural groups are more apt to express sadness or upset psychosomatically, whereas others are more likely to express these feelings in words. Cultures that are more expressive verbally and that value emotional expression (e.g., Hispanic peoples) may be seen as symptomatic (i.e., hysterical or out of control) by a therapist from a more stoic culture, whereas people who value stoicism and silence may be seen as pathological in certain therapy settings.

7. *Models of mental illness.* In different cultures families will conceptualize mental problems in different ways. In some cultures psychological problems and symptoms are more stigmatizing than obviously physical ones.

Differences may exist that create strains between generations in the same family. These differences are accentuated when families migrate, for example, when African American families move from the rural South to the urban North. These families are often more comfortable in discussing their difficulties in their own style than they are in the manner of the predominant culture. Although cultural issues play an important role, they may not be the sole cause of the problem. Sometimes issues that appear to be primarily culture related are related primarily to specific family issues. Consider the following case example:

> In the A family, the wife (who was Catholic) and the husband (who was Jewish) recently began fighting about how to celebrate December holidays, to the point that all of December became a battleground. Exploration revealed that neither member of the couple had been very religious before marriage and had seldom celebrated holidays extensively. When Mrs. A's father died and her mother became depressed, she began to spend more and more time with her mother, a very religious woman, and was less available to her husband. Conflict over Mrs. A's return to her family of origin was being expressed symbolically by the couple's inability to form their usual compromise over a religious cultural ritual.

Descriptions of any culture are vague at best, and the patient remains the best source of information.

Therapy Considerations

Therapy issues include the following:

- Including the right people
- Sharing respect for cultural differences
- Raising cultural issues as factors in problems
- Normalizing problems as culturally determined
- Tailoring interventions to preferred cultural styles

For a full discussion of culture and the family, we recommend publications by McGoldrick et al. (1996) and Tamura and Lau (1992).

Race

The definition of *race* is complicated. Physical trait differences (e.g., skin color, facial features, hair) are the usual basis for differentiating race, but race is to a surprising extent a social construction. For example, by the end of the Civil War there was enough intermingling of Caucasian and African American genes (frequently from white slave owners having children with slaves) that the following socially constructed definition was created: Anyone with ⅛ (or ¹⁄₁₆, or even ¹⁄₃₂, depending on the state) African blood was considered to be black. Many such people, of course, had Caucasian skin and features; fear of so-called racial impurity was so strong that is was made a crime to "pass." The ability to pass and the concept of passing make it clear how much of a social construction race can be.

Racial identity can also be the subject of individual and family construction and may differ from the cultural construction. For example, many people who are designated African American in the community insist on a multiracial heritage. For example, the golfer Tiger Woods identifies himself as a person of color but includes in his definition of himself his Thai and Native American heritage.

In the United States we tend to lump people into racial/cultural groups for convenience, and some groups accept these identities for several reasons. For example, there are many different physical types and skin color variations in Asia, but in the United States they are commonly all designated as Asian. This is extremely frustrating to many people who are clear on their own national and ethnic identity and who feel lost and unseen by the refusal of others to recognize difference. The same is true for Central and South Americans, whose cultural differences have been collapsed into the idea of the Hispanic or Latino/Latina. However, this confusing ascribed identity may be accepted for a number of reasons. In a discussion of the use of Hispanic versus Latino to describe Central and South American peoples, Shorris (1992) stated "the use of a single word to name a group including people as disparate as Mexican and Cubans conflates the culture, and whatever conflates cultures destroys them. Nevertheless, there will have to be a name, for political power in a democratic society requires numbers, and only by agglomeration does the group become large enough to have a voice in national politics." He goes on to explain that the group cannot be defined racially, because it includes people whose ancestors came from Asia, Europe, and Africa. Religion and culture vary widely. "All that is left is the language itself" (Shorris 1992).

To designate by race not only labels a difference but also makes a statement about power and status. In the United States a person of color is a denigrated minority, facing daily experiences of racism and discrimination. Since the civil rights movement, racism is no longer expressed as directly in segregation, lynchings, and miscegenation laws but is still obvious in hiring practices, living arrangements, and daily small experiences of disrespect. This situation takes a toll on families of color, who often feel unable to protect their children and must teach them how to deal with such experiences. The development of a positive racial identity is a key to dealing with oppression. We address this issue for African Americans in more depth in Chapter 18, but similar processes are necessary for any minority group. The situation is also difficult for multiracial families, in which some members may be more privileged than others because of variations in skin color among family members.

In the United States and elsewhere, there is generally prejudice toward immigrant people, unless they are white and economically well to do. People who have been conquered or particularly devalued by the majority population, particularly dark-skinned ones, are assimilated last—witness the plight of Native Americans and African Americans in the United States. Asian and Hispanic peoples occupy a complex middle ground depending on their skills, finances, and living situations. Each early generation of immigrants faces issues of acclimating to the culture while maintaining their own traditions and are usually seen by the majority population as being not good enough. Families must decide how much they wish to assimilate and how much they wish to remain separate.

Therapy Considerations

In addition to the guidelines we already described in this chapter (and in Chapter 27), the therapist must be able to discuss directly the family's experiences with racial, cultural, and religious prejudice. The most complex situations are those that are ambiguous. For example, is a child having problems at school because of prejudice, because of personality problems, or because of home stress? How do these factors combine? If a couple is interracial, what hidden prejudice or devaluation is at work? How do the extended families deal with the racial issues? Are lighter children more privileged than darker children? What is the relationship between the race of the therapist and that of the family? If the therapist feels comfortable raising the issues, the family will usually begin to express its concerns. For many families, unless the therapist raises racial concerns, they will likely go unremarked even though everyone is aware of them.

Gender

As we have pointed out elsewhere in this book, family roles are highly strati-fied by gender, with women still performing most of the emotional caregiving in the family. Even if both parents are working full time on identical career tracks, the mother is expected to provide the emotional center to the family. Mother blaming is still rampant in the psychiatric literature and at home (Kaplan 1989). For example, in many cases in which sexual abuse has oc-curred, the children are often angrier at the mother for not protecting them than at the father for actually abusing them. This is true even if the mother is also being abused.

Gender issues are present in the differential developmental paths for boys and girls and in differential experiences of power in the family and the cul-ture. Although the mother may be seen as powerful within the family—both for her role as the children's caregiver and for her ability to make her husband feel good about himself—her power in the world outside the family may be limited. Most often, especially after children are born, she will cut back her outside work to take care of the children, thereby making less money and de-veloping less of an occupational network. Should she divorce, she faces a legal establishment that in general has not been kind to women or children. Should violence occur, the wife is more likely to be seriously injured or killed than is her husband (see Chapter 25).

Gender issues also vary with different cultural groups. Japanese women, for example, are expected to be more deferential to men than are American women and have less power in Japanese society than American women do in the United States.

Therapy Considerations

Gender-aware or feminist therapy (McGoldrick et al. 1989) is not a series of techniques but more a series of awarenesses. Therapists who take gender into account will pay attention to, and educate patients about, the effects of gen-der socialization. They will ask about how the couple were socialized to femi-nine and masculine behavior, what each partner believes good wives and husbands should do, and how their differential incomes affect their ability to argue. They will not take it for granted that a man who has a busy career should be allowed to leave all the parenting to his wife, or that a woman should automatically sacrifice her career goals for her children. They will push men to own their feelings in words and push women to own their own voice and wishes, and their competence. They will ask specifically about marital violence and emotional abusiveness. They will, to the extent possible for the client's personality and cultural group, suggest more egalitarian models of behavior. They consider the effect of their own gender on each partner and make this explicit. They consider the cultural norms that privilege men, even when the couple are trying to be egalitarian. The key issue for gender-aware and culture-aware therapy is the therapist's ability to see problems as based in cultural norms as well as personal pathology or system dysfunction. Once this is seen and addressed, it becomes part of the therapy package (Chaney and Piercy 1988).

> The key issue for gender-aware and culture-aware therapy is the therapist's ability to see problems as based in cultural norms as well as personal pathology or system dysfunction.

Class

Class is difficult to define in a culture in which inheritance of money and name is not the central mechanism for its determination. Class is most often defined in the United States by a combination of money, education, social prestige, and political power. Class issues are very complex and seldom talked about in the United States, because our pride in not having a rigid inherited class structure is strong and has been transmuted into a myth of a classless society. What we have instead is a society with a real but somewhat fluid class structure in which people define themselves (and others define them) by class, but because of differing financial and educational attainments it is possible that people will be in a different class than their siblings or children. An individual's perception of his or her own class determines to some extent how that individual feels about self and others. The concept of class is complicated by the fact that because the prevailing myth is that one can rise in class if one works hard enough and is gifted enough, the corollary is that if one is lower class, one deserves it.

Class plays a role in three types of situations that may be seen in family therapy (Ross 1995):

1. When a family member achieves significantly more or less than others and does not fit into the family of origin group because of envy, change in in-

terests, or decreasing contact. For some parents, a child who achieves significantly more than the parents did may be seen as looking down on the parents or as disloyal by moving away.

2. When a family member marries someone who is up or down in social class from the family of origin and experiences conflict over which spouse's social-class standards and customs will become the family of heritage. The person from the lower class may feel loyal to his or her previous customs (such as frugality or less formal ways of dressing) but guilty because he or she should be assimilating into a higher class. The person from the higher class may secretly (or not so secretly) look down on the lower-class spouse or his or her family members. Either family of origin may attempt to exclude the other spouse.

3. When divorce or remarriage causes class differences between children and one parent. For example, if a father achieves a great deal financially after a divorce, and the mother remains or becomes much less affluent, the child moving between the mother's and father's homes is likely to have problems.

The therapist's main task is to name the issue—that is, to help the couple admit and discuss class issues as real. Questions of class loyalty, money, and inclusion, once mentioned, can be dealt with more easily.

Wealthy Families

Wealthy families should be differentiated between upper class (so-called old money) and new money. Families in which there has been money for several generations, and the families experience themselves as upper class (in the United States often tracing their ancestry back to the 1700s), are not very visible in this country. They tend to keep to themselves, socializing and marrying within their social group. In this group, more than in most groups in this country, who you are, or who your parents were, is as or more important than what you do. Many of the men and most of the women do not work at a career, instead serving on charitable boards, going into politics, or acting as gentleman farmers. In some families, childrearing is performed more by nannies and paid help, and both mothers and fathers are busy with social functions. The problem of creating a life structure and meaning when work is not necessary to earn money is a difficult one: Although many people from old money become our best public servants, others drift aimlessly. A family therapist for such families must be sensitive to their tendencies to escape difficulties through the use of money and their ability to bribe the therapist with high fees while (unless the therapist is also upper class) perceiving and treating him or her as a servant.

Families in which wealth has been made recently, in the current or parent generation, have the characteristics of whatever ethnic group they came from plus the problems of being in a different economic group from their families of origin. People vary greatly in their ability to handle the stresses and advantages associated with a great deal of money. They may ignore their children, or greatly overgratify them, giving them too many material things and no responsibility. Alternatively, they may use the extra advantages to give their children a more hands-on and loving rearing. A common pattern in suddenly wealthy families is that of a hard-driving businessman father who works very long hours and is far more interested in, and compelled by, work than family life. All of the family life is handled by the wife, who usually does not have a career and devotes herself to the children. These fathers are absent spouses and parents who focus very little on the emotional needs of their families and are hard to engage in therapy. They may also harbor unrealistic expectations for their children, particularly their older sons, to achieve as much or more than they have. Beyond the problem of engagement (many of these couple come in only when the children are at serious risk and even then with reluctance), the issues of money, class, and meaning in life need to be discussed.

Disadvantaged, Lower-Class, or Poor Families

Those who have been called poor or disadvantaged are a highly diverse group of people varying by age, race, ethnicity, and values; by whether they live in rural areas or the city; and by how they understand and make sense of their situation. Race, gender, and class interact in critical ways. Most of our social and political focus has gone into the urban African American and immigrant communities, ignoring other communities under stress such as the rural poor.

Poverty can be temporary or permanent. Many working-class employed people (and the working poor, or as they were called in the nineteenth century the "deserving poor") exist in a precarious financial position. A serious health crisis, a fire, or a layoff may place them in a condition of serious poverty, including a loss of home and safety. Many suddenly divorced women with young children and no family supports may go very quickly from being in the middle class to being on welfare.

Poor people may also be categorized as unemployed, chronically unemployed, or underclass. The unemployed are those persons who are currently out of work but have a work history of having been employed for at least 5 of the past 7 years. The chronically unemployed are those persons who have been unemployed for at least 5 of the past 7 years and have ceased to look for employment but may still continue to value work as a measure of self-esteem and survival. The underclass has been defined as that group of individuals who have been unemployed for at least 5 of the past 7 years and who have a value system that makes their effective reincorporation into the world of work unlikely. (This definition is currently controversial.)

If parents continue to experience occupational failure, the family may eventually reorganize itself into a new homeostatic balance, with parents who assume they will not work and who are disconnected in major ways from mainstream working culture. If the family members see themselves as being unable to influence or control their lives, and without a sense of future, they may disorganize, becoming less able to protect the children in the family or provide them with the tools needed to succeed in school or life. Family members may become depressed. If the neighborhood or community is made up primarily of a group of people in similar straits, violence or criminal behavior may become part of community culture.

Poverty is confounded by culture and gender. Most immigrants to the United States begin in poverty. Their ability to escape it depends on community supports and how their abilities fit with mainstream culture. In general, several generations are required to assimilate, but extended kin systems and values of very hard work are helpful. Most immigrants retain a strong extended kin system for two or three generations, because it is so difficult to survive as an isolated nuclear family when very poor. As the children from these families move into the middle class there is a strong tendency to move out of the family neighborhood and into a more separated life style, with a series of gains and losses associated with that move.

Women who are raising children on their own are at a serious disadvantage. Women earn less than men and have fewer supports, and the United States, alone among Western, industrialized countries, has no easily available federally funded child care alternatives. Most of those in poverty in the United States are women with children.

Severe psychiatric illness may lead to poverty if the person is temporarily or permanently unable to work and does not have family support.

Treatment Options for Disadvantaged Families

Particularly given our consumer culture, it is difficult to be poor in the United States, unable to afford any of the objects or toys constantly on view, not to mention insurance, adequate health care, or college education for the children. People whose income is insufficient for their needs are likely to become depressed and anxious. Psychological awareness is likely to give way to survival needs in such families, and they are most likely to attend therapy only in emergencies, for example, when therapy is school mandated because children are having problems in school, when teenagers act out, or when adults exhibit Axis I disorders.

Among couples who value employment, another common reason for therapy is the sudden unemployment of the husband due to a layoff. Such experiences are a blow to the husband's self-esteem, and he may become depressed or start drinking, leaving the wife as wage earner and family emotional support. The wife's job loss is less likely to lead to problems because she likely has a second job of housework and child care. Because the husband does not have this identity to fall back on, he is less likely to be able to take over household tasks unambivalently when out of work. Obviously, if the patient is a single parent, the situation is very different.

Treatment with poor families cannot be limited to internal family affairs but must include a consideration of the family's environment and other caregiving systems with which the family may be involved. Because poverty often leads to lack of self-esteem and a reluctance to confront authority or a lack of knowledge about how to do so, the therapist must be prepared to help the family deal with various systems (e.g., school, medical, welfare), if necessary. Careful screening for depression, anxiety, and alcohol or drug abuse is crucial, regardless of the presenting problem. Alcohol and drugs are frequently used as self-medication for depression, to produce a temporary sense of ease and comfort. Education about child development and discipline is often helpful for parents so caught up in basic survival needs that they have ceased to think about their own or their children's emotional needs.

For people who have had a precipitous drop in income because of a layoff or divorce, critical ingredients of therapy include the instillation of hope and advocacy efforts on the part of the therapist to help the individuals seek retraining. Relabeling family conflicts as related to the tension caused by outside stress may enable the family to locate its own emotional resources. A search should be made for sources of support in the community—often family or friends would help if the difficulty were known. Many families can continue to function as long as a support system is in place. Function is most likely to break down when the family experiences itself as completely on its own, with no safety net.

Families that are part of the culture of poverty need a coordinated approach that includes attention to the political and economic aspects of the community. Treatment is best done in a team approach when multiple aspects of the family's life receive attention. Such families require a great deal from the therapist, including the ability to be realistic but hopeful. Therapeutic techniques should include direct and action-oriented methods (structural family therapy was developed with this group) and include all relevant kin. Outreach and home visits are often the best way to maintain such families in treatment, because they are not likely to comply easily with the rigidly scheduled appointments of standard outpatient work.

> Individual or family treatment without other types of social support for the family usually is ineffective. With such support, these families can benefit from family intervention and develop new strengths and resources.

Cultural Norms and Therapy

To a greater extent than is usually realized, cultural norms determine one's attitude toward therapy. For example, older Americans are more likely to believe therapy is for crazy people, Europeans are less likely to assume therapy is necessary, and some cultures value action techniques more than talking about it. Cultural and ethnic differences provide a normalizing frame within which partners can learn to tolerate differences.

> Mrs. B, a Jewish woman from the East Coast originally, and Mr. B, a Protestant man from the Midwest, sought therapy because they felt they couldn't communicate. Mr. B thought Mrs. B was "hysterical," and Mrs. B thought Mr. B was totally unfeeling. The therapist reviewed the gender issues and the cultural issues of each family of origin, pointing out how differently women and men, and East Coast Jews and Midwestern Protestants, handle conflict and communication. Each was encouraged to find a way to enjoy the other's different point of view (i.e., her ability to be emotional and his ability to be calm) and see these differences as nonpathological.

Therapist-Family Fit

Should the therapist be of the same race, culture, age, and so on as the family in treatment? Research strongly suggests that the closer the therapist is to the family in terms of race, ethnic background, social class, and value system, the greater the potential for mutual understanding, empathy, and sensitivity (Luborsky and Crits-Critstoph 1988). However, a background similar to that of a specific family does not guarantee the therapist's successful treatment of that family. The therapist will still need to check all presumptions with the family. It would be ill advised for the therapist to imagine that he or she can avoid the process of getting to know the family because of similar backgrounds. No family shares all culture-specific characteristics, and families that require treatment have often been found to function aberrantly according to the norms of their racial or cultural groups. In addition, class and education alter how cultural characteristics are developed. The therapist may have particular blind spots related to socioeconomic facts. He or she must learn awareness of these attitudes, because they may impede rather than facilitate working with families with similar characteristics. Also, some families, particularly those of oppressed minorities, have negative attitudes toward working with a therapist of a similar background. Some individuals seem to prefer therapists from a different background.

> There is never a perfect fit between family and therapist, but racial and cultural differences should not be a contraindication to their working together.

Suggested Readings

McGoldrick M: Re-Visioning Family Therapy: Race, Culture and Gender in Clinical Practice. New York, Guilford, 1998
This is McGoldrick's most recent book suggesting some revisions of family therapy theory and technique based on racial, cultural, and gender issues.

McGoldrick M, Anderson C, Walsh F (eds): Women in Families: A Framework for Family Therapy. New York, WW Norton, 1989
This edited volume is extremely valuable in its focus on gender as an organizing dimension for assessing families and conducting family therapy. The chapter critiquing influential family therapy models from a feminist perspective is especially illuminating.

McGoldrick M, Giordano J, Pearce J (eds): Ethnicity and Family Therapy, 2nd Edition. New York, Guilford, 1996

This edited book thoughtfully addresses how ethnicity influences normal family functioning. The chapters describe families of different ethnic backgrounds and particular therapeutic challenges that therapists can expect to encounter.

Pinderhughes E: Understanding Race, Ethnicity and Power: The Key to Efficacy in Clinical Practice. New York, Free Press, 1989
This book examines the pervasive influence of race, ethnicity, and power on the identities of practitioners and patients. Also included is a complex analysis of how these issues intertwine and ways of using these concepts in assessment and treatment.

References

Chaney S, Piercy F: A feminist family therapist behavior checklist. Am J Fam Ther 16:306–316, 1988

Kaplan P: Don't Blame Mother. New York, Harper & Row, 1989

Luborsky L: Who Will Benefit From Psychotherapy? Predicting Therapeutic Outcomes. New York, Basic Books, 1988, p 118

McGoldrick M, Anderson C, Walsh F (eds): Women in Families: A Framework for Family Therapy. New York, WW Norton, 1989

McGoldrick M, Giordano J, Pearce J: Ethnicity and Family Therapy, 2nd Edition. New York, Guilford, 1996

Olmedo EL: Testimony of Esteban Olmedo to the Subcommittee on Health and the Environment, United States House of Representatives Committee on Energy and Commerce. Reprinted in CSPP Visions 7:15–17, 1994

Ross J: Social class tensions within families. Am J Fam Ther 23:338–350, 1995

Shorris E: Latino, Si. Hispanic, No (editorial). New York Times, October 28, 1992, p A21

Tamura T, Lau A: Connectedness versus separateness: applicability of family therapy to Japanese families. Fam Process 31:319–340, 1992

Family, Mary Mayfair Mathews, 1995. Private collection.

CHAPTER 18

Treatment as It Is Influenced by Issues Specific to African American Families

With Marlene F. Watson, Ph.D.

Objectives for the Reader

- To understand how race affects individual and family development
- To consider the interaction of race, gender, and class in family dynamics
- To be able to describe treatment issues specific to African American families

Introduction

Since the early 1980s, the field of marriage and family therapy has struggled with the issue of psychotherapeutic effectiveness with ethnic minority families. The cultural movement came on the heels of the feminist movement, and like the feminist movement, it has gone through stages. Pioneers of the cultural movement focused on family therapists developing awareness of ethnic minority families (McGoldrick et al. 1996). The second wave of family therapy culturalists stressed that because treatment outcome was affected in part by "person of the therapist issues" (i.e., countertransference), it was critical for therapists to develop sensitivity by exploring their own racial, ethnic, and cultural identities (Watson 1993).

The inclusion of culture as a key construct in family systems and family relations suggests a search for new information about family organization and functioning. As such, the cultural movement called into question the assumption that because all families are the same the therapist need only treat the symptom. However, the movement also gave rise to the equally dangerous assumption that all members of a given ethnic minority group are the same. Even so, the cultural movement led to the important understanding that families differed on the basis of race, ethnicity, and culture.

Although the current stage of the cultural movement has emphasized the need to examine process variables of race, ethnicity, and culture (Comas-Diaz and Greene 1994), African American families are still frequently regarded as a monolithic group. Family therapists are not aware of, or do not acknowledge, the diversity of African Americans in the treatment process for three reasons: 1) the overall invisibility of African Americans in the larger society, with the exception of celebrities or those portrayed negatively in the media; 2) the assumption that African American families are matriarchal; and 3) the historical failure to credit African Americans for their achievements and successes.

In fact, Watts-Jones (1997) prepared a genogram specifically designed for African American families. It is based on the concept that such families have both biological and functional ties.

Race as It Affects Individual Development in the Family

Because race affects psychosocial development, it must be central to the therapeutic process. Cross (1980), a significant figure in the black psychology movement,[1] developed the Cross Model, which explored stages of racial identity formation for African Americans. The Cross Model contained five stages: 1) pre-encounter, 2) encounter, 3) immersion-emersion, 4) internalization, and 5) internalization-commitment.

---

[1]Black psychology is a body of knowledge that recognizes the effect of race on biopsychosocial functioning.

In the pre-encounter stage, the individual's world view is dominated by the majority culture. He or she holds a negative view of blackness. A personal event happens to challenge the person's world view, propelling him or her into the encounter stage, which involves rethinking one's belief system and searching for a black identity. The third stage consists of two levels. The first level (immersion) is characterized by the person's withdrawal into blackness. The individual's awareness of blackness is high, but the degree of internalization is low. The second level (emersion) results in the person becoming more open to exploring both strengths and weaknesses of blackness. The internalization stage signals the resolution of conflicts between the old way of thinking and the new world view. In the internalization-commitment stage, the person not only integrates a new identity but also demonstrates social interest toward the referent group (i.e., the individual's ethnic/racial group of origin). In addition, the individual shows appreciation and respect for multiculturalism.

The value of a racial identity model in the treatment of African American families is twofold: First, it aids in the assessment process because it reminds the clinician that within-group differences exist both among African Americans and within a given family. Second, it has utility as a solution-focused approach.

We exist in a society that labels and at times measures people on the basis of race, class, gender, sexual orientation, physical ability, age, and religion. Race is a predominant theme in the lives of African Americans because of institutionalized and internalized racism. The chronic stress of racism has a traumatic effect on African Americans. For some people, it may result in a feeling of worthlessness, psychological numbness, anger, and a poor sense of future. The effects of racism may be mediated by factors such as class and the presence of family or community supports.

The legacy of slavery and the aftermath of oppression necessitates for African Americans consciousness about one's race. Not all African Americans have conscious awareness of the effect of race on their self-esteem and identity and, consequently, their actions.

Employing a racial identity model as a lens in family therapy assists the clinician in better understanding intrafamily conflict. For example, skin color may be a hidden dimension in the problems experienced by an African American family. Sibling or parent-child coalitions may exist in the family because of lighter or darker skin. A family dynamic of this nature would indicate internalized and, most likely, unrecognized self-hatred, reflecting negative racial identity development (Cross 1980; Sue and Sue 1990). The family may express other manifestations of negative racial identity either by refusing to explore race or by blaming all problems on race.

Using a racial identity model as a framework in treatment may empower therapists to address comprehensively the effects of race on African American families. It also may facilitate more conscious awareness on the therapist's part about his or her own racial identity process and the dynamic tension that may be created when the family members and the therapist are at different stages of racial identity (Sue and Sue 1990). In many cases, the therapist may be fearful of addressing racial identity because of doubts about his or her own racial identity process, especially because therapists often feel pressured to be objective, fair, and caring human beings who are seen as colorless, genderless, and sexless.

The level of racial identity achievement for African Americans is probably correlated with other factors such as gender and socioeconomic status. For instance, some middle-class African Americans may have a sense of positive racial identity because of their perception of having made it despite the odds. Some African American women might have a solid sense of racial identity because black women have, often to their own detriment, been validated as super-beings (i.e., women who are expected to provide and care for their families without needing the help of men, reinforcing the idea of black families as matriarchal). In contrast, lower-class African Americans have been blamed for their failure to rise up by their bootstraps, suggesting that they are racially inferior. African American men have also been labeled as lazy and shiftless, conveying the message that their lack of economic success is the result of their race. African Americans may experience negative racial identity regardless of gender or social class, in part because of specific deleterious effects of racism on self-esteem and identity.

The following case example illustrates the value of using a racial identity model in therapy:

> Mr. and Mrs. A, both 34 years old and previously married, presented for couples therapy because of constant fighting. According to the partners, the fights began soon after they married. Mr. A described his wife as ideal when they were dating. They dated for 1 year and had been married for 2 years when treatment began. Mr. A met Mrs. A soon after his divorce. He related that he was attracted to Mrs. A because she was strong, assertive, and ambitious. She was also supportive of his career goals. Mrs. A stated that she was attracted to Mr. A because he seemed secure and clear about his future. She was disappointed by her former husband's dependency and lack of initiative, which eventually led to irreconcilable differences. Mr. A's ex-wife divorced him after a failed business left them bankrupt.
>
> Mr. A expressed feelings of hopelessness and reported coming to therapy

because Mrs. A wanted to. He seemed resolved to end the marriage. Mrs. A also was doubtful about things changing but was not ready to give up. The therapist hypothesized that Mr. and Mrs. A were each looking for the other to validate his or her self-worth.

The therapist used a model that posited the following: 1) Individuals need a positive self-identity in order to develop healthy relationships; 2) issues such as race, gender, class, and sexual orientation have a major effect on the identity formation process; and 3) negative valuations of African Americans occur in the larger society and within the group. The therapist asked Mr. and Mrs. A to share early memories and current thoughts about skin color in their family of origin, neighborhood in which they grew up, current community, and society at large. Mr. and Mrs. A acknowledged feelings of inferiority as children because of their darker skin. African Americans have had an informal caste system based on skin color. Although a higher value was generally placed on lighter skin, such a caste system has specific consequences for both dark- and light-skinned African Americans.

Mr. A described feelings of shame around not achieving the success his family believed him capable of and the fear of being seen as another black man who had failed. He secretly believed that his ex-wife was right when she said, before walking out, "I should have married a white man because black men are failures." Later, when she married a white man, Mr. A experienced tremendous conflict concerning his children's perception of him and their new stepfather.

Mrs. A felt pressured to achieve because of society's stereotype of African Americans as lazy and dumb. Despite her career success, she was fearful that it might not last. She appeared to have symptoms related to the impostor phenomenon, characterized by excessive worry that one's success is due to luck rather than to one's efforts. She was fearful of failure and was counting on Mr. A to be strong, courageous, and successful.

Mrs. A's feeling of insecurity interacted with Mr. A's feeling of inadequacy and vice versa. Race was a major factor in this couple's interacting feelings of inadequacy and insecurity. A racial identity model helped the therapist increase the couple's understanding of the role of race in their expectations of self, each other, and the relationship. It also helped each partner to take responsibility for his or her feelings, which is critical to effective couples therapy.

Race is a difficult and painful topic for many African Americans, particularly when they have internalized negative valuations about themselves; however, it is also influential in individual and family functioning and therefore is an essential construct in couples and family therapy. Incorporation of a racial identity model enables the therapist and the family to openly address this frequently neglected dimension of the treatment process.

Gender Dynamics in African American Families

Gender issues are often unexplored but central to dynamics in African American families. The stereotype of African American families as matriarchal frequently allows family therapists to ignore powerful gender dynamics. Family therapists who unintentionally use the stereotypical matriarchal African American family as an organizing principle in therapy assume that women have the power and that men either are not present or are not capable of being at the head of the family.

Caretaking in African American families, as in most ethnic groups, is provided largely by females. However, caretaking is a sensitive issue for African American men and women because of their imposed roles during slavery and the lasting effects of racism. Men were unable to protect women from rape and other human atrocities during slavery, as they themselves endured harsh realities. Women had to rely on themselves. The practice of not counting on men has been maintained through cultural messages, such as "black men ain't no good" and "God bless the child who's got her own."

African American women often find themselves in a difficult situation. On one hand, they are told that they must be super strong, self-sufficient, and responsible for the family. On the other hand, they are told that they should make their men feel strong, competent, and secure, despite the realities of racism that attack the men's sense of self. In addition, African American women are expected to deal with the effects of racism on their own psyche.

Because of the sociopolitical context of African American life, parents have a particular fear that their sons might be harmed. A stance of hypervigilance with male children developed as a protective reaction to the killing of black males in the aftermath of slavery, and many factors tend to contribute to the perpetuation of this stance: the vivid stories of black male lynchings passed down in families; police brutality as witnessed in the Rodney King beating; hate crimes such as the one in Jasper, Texas, that resulted in a black man being dragged to his death; and racial profiling that can end with four young black men on their way back to college being shot by New Jersey state troopers. As a result, males are nurtured and protected differently from females. Mothers seem to try to prepare their sons for life in a racist society by giving them unconditional love. For example, mothers may be more concerned about their sons' feelings because they do not want them to risk losing control in a hostile society. Concomitantly, mothers may have very high expectations of their daughters and less regard for their feelings because the mothers feel that black women must count on themselves.

This pattern in many African American families reinforces the stereotypes of the super black woman and the no-good black man. The assumptions and feelings that African American men and women have about these stereotypes are frequently integrated into couple dynamics. The following case example illustrates this point:

> Mr. B, a 32-year-old account executive, and Mrs. B, a 30-year-old lawyer, initiated treatment because of frequent arguments. Mrs. B complained that she had to do everything, and Mr. B complained that Mrs. B loved to argue. Mr. B stated that he tried to help out, and Mrs. B countered by saying that she had to go behind him and redo things. As a result of their conflict, Mr. and Mrs. B developed a couple style in which he was often quiet and withdrawn and she was overtly angry.
>
> The therapy focused on cultural stereotypes that formed the meanings given to each partner's behavior. Underlying Mrs. B's complaint that she had to do everything was the belief that black men couldn't be counted on and the hurt that she felt over not being special (African American women have historically been the caretakers for their own and others' families, with little recognition of their own need to be cared for). Underlying Mr. B's complaint that Mrs. B loved to argue was the belief that black women were controlling and domineering and his hurt over the stigma of being seen as a lazy, shiftless, no-good black man.
>
> The therapist focused the partners on their own feelings and beliefs and discouraged them from trying to manage the other partner's behavior. They began to look at their own internalized negative thoughts about African American men and women. They also began to share their feelings with each other, as opposed to being critical.

Although angry-silent couple dynamics are not unique to African Americans, the cultural messages and beliefs that served to form this destructive pattern for the couple in the preceding case example were crucial to understanding the meaning of the symptom. Thus it is as important to understand the role of culture as it is to understand the role of the family of origin, especially because the family is embedded in a larger sociocultural context. Recognizing the value of culture does not suggest ignoring or abandoning principles and techniques from the various models of systems therapy.

Social Status and Class

In contrast to other groups, in African American communities, social status may be assigned not only on the basis of material goods but also on the basis of color of skin. Skin color has long been a determinant of status and frequently promotes a power and value differential among individual family members. Although the larger society has tended to view all African Americans as the same, African Americans are extremely focused on within-group differences.

African Americans share membership in the various classes defined by society, but the attention given to poor African Americans and to the megastars in sports and entertainment constructs an image of two classes: the haves and the have-nots.

Class is a crucial issue in the treatment of African American families; however, social status is not determined only by economics. Because within-group differences have been so divisive for African Americans, lower-class family members may become anxious when another family member graduates from college. They fear losing connection with the member who is now obviously in a class above them. Consider the following case example:

Ms. C, an African American student in a master's program in family therapy, remembered that when she graduated from college, she received a letter from her grandmother (to whom she was very close). In the letter the grandmother stated that she should always remember that a college degree did not make her better than her mother. At the time, she was merely hurt. It was not until many years later that she understood the grandmother's fears.

Not only does the family become anxious around a member graduating from college but so does the person graduating.

At one point during her master's program, Ms. C began to have difficulty completing the last 50 clinical hours needed to graduate. Her supervisors were baffled because she was an excellent student. The director of the program met with Ms. C, and she shared the story of the grandmother's letter. She was the first in her family to have a college degree and was worried about how family members might view her. More specifically, she was concerned that family members would think that she thought she was better than them and reject her.

Cutoffs sometimes occur when class differences exist within a family. Class differences in African American families seem to be compounded by racism. For example, middle-class African Americans may experience family cutoffs as well as rejection by co-workers, particularly in a predominantly white workplace.

Intermarried Couples and Multiracial Children

Intermarried couples face a variety of issues based on societal prejudice and their own cultural differences. In the United States, there were state laws until 1967 that prohibited racial intermarriage. Intermarriage is occurring at triple the rate of the early 1970s (McGoldrick et al. 1996), but marriages between African and European Americans are still difficult in this culture. Prejudice from family members and the community may be very high, which can produce enormous strain. African Americans marrying those of other races or cultures may not attract as much notice in the wider culture, but gender dynamics and expectations of self and marriage may be very different. Whether each member sees himself or herself as marrying "down" or "up" may affect the power balance in the relationship.

Multiracial children who are partly African American used to develop a primarily African American identity. Many multiracial children are now creating more complex identities that express their complex origins. Parents of multiracial children need to define for themselves and their families the rituals, practices, and self-definitions the family will use. Therapists must assume that race is significant in multiracial marriage but must let the couple define how it is significant. Although the problem may be embedded in a racial context, there is no guarantee that it is central to the problem with which the couple is concerned.

Treatment Considerations With African American Families

Treatment with African American families must also take into account the extended family system. The extended family model that characterizes most African Americans is influenced by three major factors: 1) The group is emphasized more than the individual in African tradition, 2) nuclear families were separated in slavery, and 3) the nature of racism reinforces the need for mutual sharing and support.

The clinician must broaden his or her focus to consider the wider family system, which may include more than blood relatives. According to Boyd-Franklin (1989), many African American families include play mamas (i.e., "other mothers" or women who act as surrogate mothers for individuals by virtue of their nurturing relationship but have no blood or legal status for that role), aunts, uncles, baby-sitters, godparents, and neighbors who serve vital roles in family dynamics. The degree to which nonblood relatives affect family dynamics may be determined by social class and proximity to blood relatives more so today than in the past.

The therapist's first task is to understand the patient's definition of the family and to include each of these significant members in the assessment and treatment phases of therapy. It is especially important for the practitioner to also consider those family members who are not physically present but who have an enormous effect on family processes. The therapist may not appreciate fully the complexity of an extended family model, seeing instead the absence of the so-called normal nuclear family structure. An understanding of who does what, when, where, how, and for whom and of who makes the decisions can assist the therapist in assessing functional as opposed to dysfunctional extended families.

Roles and boundaries may be critical issues in an extended family model. Thus the therapist must assess familial roles and expectations and overall family functioning. Boyd-Franklin (1989) identified three typical forms of role confusion in extended families: 1) the nonevolved grandmother whose role is changing constantly, leaving her subject to burnout; 2) the three-generation family in which the roles have become blurred (e.g., the young mother cannot function in the parenting role because the grandmother governs the entire household); and 3) the parentified child.

Sibling caretaking is a crucial dynamic in African American families. It can have a profound effect on family functioning that can either enhance the sibling bond or lead to conflict. Moreover, sibling caretaking can affect familial relationships throughout the life cycle, and the sibling caretaker is especially vulnerable to role confusion and strain.

Because many negative stereotypical assumptions have been made about African American families, the therapist may be consciously or unconsciously guided by them. The therapist must have the capacity for self-confrontation regarding his or her own biases instead of rigidly adhering to the notion that the therapist is always objective. Because African American families are aware of and sensitive to society's negative portrayal of them, trust and credibility will be significant factors in the treatment process.

Conclusion

This chapter has emphasized race, class, and gender as crucial variables in the assessment and treatment of African American families. The rationale is that family therapists have used a monolithic model with ethnic minority families, resulting in inadequate treatment and premature termination. African American families, more than any other group, have been seen as a single mass with little attention given to within-group differences.

Like all families, African Americans are varied in form, structure, and class but are rarely appreciated for their diversity. This chapter is intended to facilitate a greater in-depth exploration and understanding of African American families by way of improving their outcomes.

Suggested Readings

Boyd-Franklin N: Black Families in Therapy: A Multisystems Approach. New York, Guilford, 1989

This classic book applies a multisystems framework to looking at the diversity and strengths of black families. Relying on the notion of empowerment, the author recommends specific clinical interventions for a variety of presenting situations.

References

Boyd-Franklin N: Black Families in Therapy: A Multisystems Approach. New York, Guilford, 1989

Comas-Diaz L, Greene B: Overview: gender and ethnicity in the healing process, in Women of Color: Integrating Ethnic and Gender Identities in Psychotherapy. Edited by Comas-Diaz L, Greene B. New York, Guilford, 1994, pp 185–193

Cross WE Jr: Models of psychological nigrescence: a literature review, in Black Psychology, 2nd Edition. Edited by Jones R. New York, Harper & Row, 1980, pp 81–98

McGoldrick M, Giordano J, Pearce J: Ethnicity and Family Therapy, 2nd Edition. New York, Guilford, 1996

Sue DW, Sue D: Counseling the Culturally Different: Theory and Practice, 2nd Edition. New York, Wiley, 1990

Watson MF: Supervising the person of the therapists: issues, challenges and dilemmas. Contemporary Family Therapy 15:21–31, 1993

Watts-Jones D: Toward an African-American genogram. Fam Process 36:375–383, 1997

SECTION 5

Couples Therapy

Although much overlap exists in the theory and practice of marital therapy and family therapy, for clarity's sake, we focus in this section on issues relevant to couples. In Chapter 19 we review the theory and therapy for dysfunction in a first marriage, and in Chapter 21 we do the same for subsequent forms of couple relationships. The reader must keep in mind the material from Chapters 2, 3, and 5, which is more focused on marriage as related to the nuclear family. For didactic reasons, we separate sexual issues from other marital issues and focus on couples and sex therapy in Chapter 20. We discuss in Chapter 22 the challenges presented by families with reproductive issues and problems. Issues for gay and lesbian couples are both similar to and different from those for heterosexual couples, and we review the former in Chapter 23.

Bride and Groom (ornament for wedding cake), Emily Chang and David Humphrey, 1983. Private collection.

CHAPTER 19

Dysfunctional Couples and Couples Therapy

Objectives for the Reader

- To understand marriage and marital therapy in historical context
- To understand characteristics of distressed couples
- To be able to outline general guidelines for assessing couples
- To be able to outline strategies and techniques of couples therapy

Introduction

Husband and wife form the essential subsystem of the nuclear family and a system in its own right. How this dyad functions and copes will determine in large measure how the family progresses over time. In Chapters 3 and 4, we considered how families function (and introduced the idea of dysfunction), with a special focus on how the marital coalition arises from the family of origin. In this chapter we start with a historical perspective on marriage and then consider specific dimensions and patterns of dysfunction in the marital dyad in order to formulate couples therapy goals and strategies.

Marriage in Its Historical Context[1]

The marital relationship in all societies is a peculiar combination of the most idiosyncratic and intimate and the most culturally patterned of relationships.

---

[1]We are indebted to E. Kovacs, M.D., for some of the material in this section.

Each society varies in its emphasis on the external aspects of the marriage (e.g., the mechanism for the transfer of property and privilege and for management of paternity) and on the intimate aspects (e.g., the friendship, love, and sexual issues binding the couple). In general, the more Westernized the culture, the more free is marital choice and the more important are issues of love and intimacy. Even so, strong cultural sanctions within one's race or class remain.

Westernized marriages are today characterized by freedom to choose a spouse, equality in terms of marriage vows (although not necessarily of roles), emancipation from relatives, and an increased emphasis on intimacy. Marriage is distinguished among all family relationships by the peculiar set of power differentials that are dictated by gender. The couple are equal partners in an emotional sense, at the level of intimacy and connection. The issue of power inequality in relationships bound by love is complex (Goldner et al. 1990). Reasons for inequality include man's greater power in the culture, his greater physical strength, and the fact that marital choice often involves women marrying men who are older and more financially successful. Marriage is also distinguished among family relationships by its voluntary nature. That is, although you can never truly be an ex-parent or an ex-child, it is possible to be an ex-spouse, to choose to sever the relationship. The voluntary nature of the relationship lends to it a particular complexity that is central to treatment.

Marital Difficulties, Problems, and Dysfunction

As we suggested in Chapters 3 and 4, some periods of marital dysfunction are inevitable in any long-term relationship. The burden of carrying intimate, social, and parenting roles means that people will inevitably clash over some aspects of life. It is common for marriages to undergo periodic stages of crisis and reorganization. Problems occur when couples lose faith in the marriage or lose a sense of respect and warmth for each other. Partners who have had poor role models, who have had a childhood of loss and violence, or who are poorly suited to each other by style or inclination may have increasing problems as time goes by.

A number of theories, not mutually exclusive, attempt to explain how marriages become conflicted to the point of impairment. These theories include the systems concept we discussed earlier in this book, the exchange model of Thibaut and Kelly (1959), and the object relations model of Dicks (1967). A number of writers (e.g., Sager 1976) have attempted to tie these theories together in various ways. Although certain models may explain marital conflict, they do not by themselves predict divorce. The decision to divorce is determined not only by the amount of conflict but also by a set of societal issues—the prevailing attitudes toward divorce and how easy it is to obtain, issues regarding money, the presence of children, and the individuals' assessment of whether life would be better single. Many couples in severe conflict remain together for complex reasons, living separate emotional lives without divorcing (whether this is a good solution is hard to determine). Certainly for children the experiences of divorce and of living in a high conflict home are both poor arrangements. There is not necessarily a negative correlation between high conflict levels and love. Many high conflict couples also have a great deal of positive intensity and passion for each other. Many low conflict couples are indifferent to each other. John Gottman (1994), who has extensively researched divorce prediction, lists criticism, contempt, defensiveness, and stonewalling, leading to intense marital negativity, as highly predictive of divorce.

> **A**lthough certain models may explain marital conflict, they do not by themselves predict divorce.

Individuals come to marriage with the legacy of their several-generation family of origin plus the beliefs and role models of their parents. This means they carry with them firm ideas about what marriage should be like, how men and women should behave, and what behaviors signify love and respect. From a developmental point of view, there remain unresolved needs and demands left from a childhood invested with deeply ambivalent feelings of love and hate.

In the process of mate selection, a partner may be attractive partly because he or she promises rediscovery of an important lost aspect of the subject's own personality or because he or she offers the chance to redo an unfinished conflict with a parent. When the couple join, they make a marital contract, in which each partner assumes he or she and the other partner will each do certain things (Sager 1976). Some of these assumptions are conscious and shared (e.g., you will care for the children and I will work); some are not shared; and some are secret, even from the self. For example, a person may marry to get away from home or may believe that as long as he acts like a good child his spouse will act like a good mother. Mate selection, of course, is also determined by less dynamic reasons such as physical attractiveness, family demands, financial considerations, timing, and luck. As Lewis (1998) has pointed out, relationships fail "when either the person who is more powerful feels unrewarded for that responsibility, or the person with lesser power feels that they've had enough of that relatively powerless situation."

Treatment involves increasing the intensity of the affective bonds and repairing the inevitable disruption of those bonds. That is "each spouse must have someone who listens to our experience (i.e., the 'narratives') and helps to sort them out. The prerequisites include a genuine and reciprocal liking for each other, mutual respect, a two-way valuing and affirmation" (Lewis 1998). Lewis suggests that couples need to learn conflict management mechanisms, including techniques to prevent isolation. Couple communication style (i.e., how people talk to each other) is a critical variable in affecting couple satisfaction and function. To help prevent disconnections, the therapist must teach intimate communication (focusing on how to explore difficult issues and increase empathy).

From a Dynamic Point of View

Many individuals who need assistance with marital conflict seem to have a rigidity in their personalities that forces them to deny or be blind to the existence of certain aspects of themselves. If they are confronted with a similar aspect of the partner's personality, they will ignore it or not accept it. Such people may project onto the partner aspects of their own personality with which they are uncomfortable. They are therefore prevented from seeing the problem clearly or seeking alternative solutions. Often third parties are used to deflect conflict between the partners.

Gender differences in needs and communication often make marital problems more complex. Men are more likely to wish for deference, to wish to deal with their problems by themselves first before talking about them, and to see sex as a way of solving problems. Women are more likely to wish for verbal intimacy and task equality, to prefer handling problems by discussion and feeling talk first rather than moving immediately to solutions, and to prefer sex after intimate connection has been reestablished. Women tend to experience the emotional burden of the relationship as falling on themselves. Men tend to see themselves as more responsible for the family's finances even when the wife is working. Therefore, in a fairly high number of cases the woman will find herself emotionally pursuing and sexually unhappy; the man will find himself criticized for his need to be less emotional even though he has been trained to control most of his feelings. Obviously, many individuals do not fit the gender stereotypes.

As couples struggle over different ways of behaving or different and ambivalent needs, each sees the other as unhelpful or bad and begins to become angry. This situation intensifies into a cycle of distress.

From a Behavioral Point of View

Distressed couples engage in fewer rewarding exchanges and more punishing exchanges than do nondistressed couples. Distressed couples are more likely to reciprocate each other's use of negative reinforcement and eventually go on the offensive by increasing the level of punishment regardless of the stimuli. Distressed couples are likely to attempt to control each other's behavior through negative communication and the withholding of positive communication. They strive for behavior change in the other by aversive control tactics, that is, by strategically presenting punishment and withholding rewards.

From a Systems Point of View

From a systems point of view, the solution becomes the problem—that is, more aversive control (e.g., silence or attack) produces more aversive behavior in the spouse rather than the longed-for connection. In addition, triangles form to deflect conflict, so that children, friends, parents, or lovers are drawn into the marital conflict.

From a Psychiatric Illness Point of View

Having a spouse with a serious Axis I disorder, such as anxiety disorder, mood disorder, or substance abuse, puts strain on the marital relationship. The marital interaction before, during, and after the onset of the symptoms in the spouse is influenced by numerous factors and varies greatly across dyads. It is false to assume that in all cases the interaction between the spouses brought on, caused, or even helped trigger the mental disorder and symptoms. Whatever the symptoms in one spouse, the relationship of symptoms to the marital interaction is on a continuum and can take any one of the following forms:

- The marital interaction neither causes the symptoms nor stresses the psychologically vulnerable spouse.
- The marital interaction does not stress the vulnerable individual, but after onset of symptoms, the marital interaction declines and becomes dysfunctional, thus causing more distress.

- The marital interaction acts as a stressor that contributes to the onset of symptoms in a vulnerable spouse.
- The symptoms can be explained totally as under the control and function of the interactional patterns between the spouses.

The therapist meeting a new couple therefore can entertain a range of ideas that may help illuminate and explain the couple's distressing circumstances. In the next section, we offer guidelines for assessing and treating couples. Although these guidelines do not cover all couples' problems and situations, they represent a general set of ideas that therapists may apply to the specifics of many marital issues.

Couples' Development

Dym (1993) has described how couples' relationships evolve over time. Members of couples are influenced by past and present relationships and tend to form ties that have a distinct character that emerges through regular cycles of conflict and resolution. Dym draws attention to broad, normative changes in couples, characterizing these developmental shifts as periods of expansion, contraction, and resolution. For example, in the early, expansive years of a committed, romantic relationship, the lives of two are, in a sense, woven into one, moving from "I" to "we."

Dym describes a predictable stage of contraction and a feeling of betrayal in the next years of the relationship, in which members of the couple reconnect with a need for an I. This desire can be marked by experiences of doubts, fears, and insecurities, and many couples retreat from their established routines. Partners may find themselves feeling out of sync with their own personal ambitions, describe themselves as feeling trapped or lonely, and believe they are progressing at different tempos from each other. Stormy times may ensue with bitter conflict and blame. During the resolution stage, couples may resort to compromise, negotiation, or even a more radical restructuring of their relationship in an effort to make room for both the individual and the relationship. This cyclical movement from expansion to contraction to resolution repeats several times over the course of the relationship. Dym notes that many couples have what he calls a home base where they tend to reside, in terms of the sense of "we," "I, " or "working on it. " A home base is the point in the cycle of expansion and contraction at which the couples find themselves most often. For many couples, patterns of commitment, intimacy, and passion interact over time.

Couples Therapy

Marital or couples therapy can be defined as a format of intervention involving both members of a dyad in which the focus of intervention is the problematic interactional patterns of the couple. Its similarities to family therapy are so numerous that the differences have often been overlooked.

The focus of couples therapy is on the dyad and its intimate emotional and sexual aspects, whereas family therapy is usually focused on issues involving behavior of a child or adolescent and the interactions between parents and children. In family therapy one can discern triangles involving various family members, whereas in couples therapy triangles in the family must be inferred, and triangulation in the here-and-now interaction must involve the therapist (because only two family members are present). In couples therapy, although the children may be invited during the initial assessment or later for specific issues, usually only the spouses attend the sessions.

Couples therapy is distinguished by the peer relationship of the participants, the ever-present questions of commitment, and a need to carefully attend to gender issues. In general, even if behaviorally focused, couples therapy must attend particularly to the feeling level, with the goals being positive feeling between the partners and more reasonable behavior.

The Issue of Commitment—The Problem of Affairs

The clinician must begin by assessing each partner's commitment to the marriage or, if the partners are not married, to the relationship. This also affects the partners' motivations for therapy. Varieties of motivational asynchrony include the following: one partner may feel coerced into treatment by the other; each partner's desires to improve the relationship may differ significantly; one partner may come to enlist the therapist's help in changing the other; one partner may be ready to leave the relationship, whereas the other shows a commitment to preserving it; or both may be ambivalent. Needless to say, the clinician needs to evaluate each partner's motivations and goals and try to normalize their differing expectations for treatment.

Assessing a couple's motivation becomes more complex when one spouse expresses commitment to the relationship at the beginning of therapy but is secretly having an affair and plans to leave the relationship after the final attempt at therapy requested by the spouse is completed. Although it used to be thought that one partner could not help knowing about the other's affair, further experience has taught us that with a fairly emotionally distant marriage in which some trust is still present, many things can be kept secret by a

determined person. Often marital therapy is precipitated by the partner discovering the affair. In this case it is no longer secret, but the marriage is altered profoundly.

Many therapists will not proceed with marital treatment unless a spouse
actively engaged in an affair (also called an extramarital situation) terminates
the affair immediately. Some therapists will proceed with treatment while
the affair continues if the affair is known to the other partner, at least while
the couple decide what to do next. Very few therapists will see the affair
partner unless the couple have separated and decided to divorce, because
seeing the affair partner in a sense legitimizes the new relationship. It is
thought to be impossible to do effective marital therapy when one spouse
and the therapist are keeping an affair secret from the other spouse. It is
probably also impossible for a spouse having an affair to have the energy necessary to work on the marriage. The therapist may be able to persuade the
wandering spouse to give up the affair and return to the marriage at least long
enough for a reasonable try.

Evaluation of Partners

With the obvious modification of focusing mainly on the marital dyad, the
outline for family evaluation we proposed in Chapter 6 can be used for the
evaluation of a married couple seeking assistance with their troubled relationship. This involves obtaining data on the current point in the family and marital life cycle, why the couple comes for assistance at this point in time, and
each partner's views of the marital problem. In formulating the marital difficulty, the evaluator will want to consider the couple's communication, problem solving, roles, affective expression and involvement, and behavioral
expression, especially in sexual and aggressive areas. The clinician will also
want to evaluate gender roles, cultural and racial issues, and power inequities
resulting from gender, class, age, or financial status. It is critical to ask about
alcohol, health and reproductive issues, and violence. Even if the partners do
not mention their children as a problem, it is wise to spend some time developing a sense of how the children are doing, whether there are favorites or
problems with any of them, and whether the children are being pulled into
marital conflicts. The clinician should ascertain whether a diagnosable condition, especially on Axis I, is present in either partner.

Several areas, included in the above-mentioned general categories, deserve
special evaluation attention. Such areas include each spouse's commitment
to the marital union and the couple's sexual life. Assessment is complicated
when one spouse is keeping commitment doubts or extramarital sex secret.

Conjoint and individual assessment interviews with each partner may be needed. Infidelity or serious commitment questions change the character of the marital therapy from one of how the couple manage to whether or not the couple stay together.

The complicated issue of how the therapist can get information about the degree of commitment and ongoing marital affairs, as well as other private information, can be handled in various ways. We recommend that as part of the marital evaluation the therapist hold one individual session with each partner after the first or second conjoint session. These sessions are usually considered confidential. However, the therapist may reserve the right not to continue treatment unless the spouse tells the partner relevant information, such as about an ongoing affair or HIV-positive status. The therapist may give the partner a few weeks or an extra session to plan for this disclosure but is not obligated to do therapy in situations in which such a secret makes therapeutic work impossible. Although some therapists prefer not to know certain secrets, it is our belief that to proceed with therapy in the face of an overwhelming secret as if it did not exist is futile. If the information (e.g., incest, violence, alcohol abuse) is known to the couple but is secret from the therapist at the wish of the erring partner, it is also best that the therapist hear it early, in private session, and find a way to bring it into the couples work.

It is often difficult to determine whether couples therapy is the treatment of choice and whether other therapy should be given concurrently or sequentially. For example, one partner may need concurrent medication or may be having enough other problems with work, his or her parents, or his or her own personality difficulties that no energy is left for couples work. In general, couples who come in for therapy together should be given evaluation, support, and perhaps education—plus a clear picture of how the couples issues connect with the individual issues. If appropriate, partners may be sent for concurrent individual therapy or may be asked to have individual therapy first and return for couples work later.

The couples therapist may do individual work concurrently or work on individual issues in the couples setting. Some clinicians recommend that the same therapist not do individual work with only one partner and then do the couples work, because the therapist tends to become more bonded to the person with whom he or she does the individual work. Others believe that the advantage of one therapist knowing the systems' issues—that is, doing both the individual and the marital therapy—outweighs this disadvantage. A controlled random-assignment study can settle this issue to some extent, but there is no substitute for therapist skill in a particular case. As of now, we recommend it as an option.

Couples in which active violence has been present are not candidates for couples work unless the therapist believes that the couple can hold to a clear contract that no violence will occur during the therapy. For example, a wife who is afraid of being hit will not be honest in the therapy. Violent men usually need their own therapy. Group treatment has proven effective in many cases (see Chapter 25 for a discussion on violence). In some cases, both partners are violent.

Goals

The mediating goals of couples therapy that uses an integrative model include the following: specification of the interactional problems, recognition of mutual contribution to the problems, clarification of marital boundaries, clarification and specification of each spouse's needs and desires in the relationship, increased communication skills, decreased coercion and blame, increased differentiation, and resolution of marital transference distortions. Final goals of the marital intervention may involve resolution of presenting problems, reduction of symptoms, increased intimacy, increased role flexibility and adaptability, toleration of differences, improved psychosexual functioning, balance of power, clear communication, resolution of conflictual interaction, and improved relationships with children and families of origin (Gurman 1981).

Couples therapy is often conceived of as a relatively brief therapy (though it need not be), usually meeting on a once-weekly basis, with a focus on the marital interaction. Sometimes bringing in the parents or children of one or both spouse's may be beneficial for addressing issues affecting the marriage (Framo 1981). The major indication for marital intervention is the presence of marital conflict to which both parties contribute, but other indications include symptomatic behavior such as depression or agoraphobia in one spouse. We discuss specific guidelines in Section 7. If the couples therapy seems to consistently escalate conflict, then the goals should be reevaluated.

Strategies and Techniques of Intervention

Like family therapy in general, couples therapy uses strategies for imparting new information and opening up new and expanded individual and marital experiences, psychodynamic strategies for individual and interactional insight, communication and problem-solving strategies, and strategies for restructuring the repetitive interactions between the spouses. As the divisive spirit of earlier schools of psychotherapy recedes and a sense of pluralism and clinical pragmatism grows, clinicians will attempt to integrate the various strategies into a coherent treatment approach that can be adapted to individual couples.

We advocate an integrative marital therapy model that uses psychodynamic, cognitive-behavioral, and structural-strategic strategies of intervention.

A Model for Intervention Based on Patterns of Interaction

Although couples may exhibit conflict over specific content issues, such as handling finances, spending time together, and reconciling individual and family needs, the therapist is usually confronted with repetitive patterns of interaction that will likely become the focus for treatment. For example, in one couple, the wife may try to explain something important to her husband about her need to feel emotionally connected to him; he reacts negatively to her tone of voice (saying he feels criticized) and retreats; she responds by suggesting that he is simply pushing her away and feels unloved; and so on. This pattern of pursuit-withdrawal might well occupy the attention of the therapist, who notices that it occurs irrespective of the particular topic of conversation.

Other patterns involve either complementarity or symmetry in relationships. In complementary relationships, the overfunctioning of one member may invite the underfunctioning of the other (e.g., responsible-irresponsible, nurse-patient). Because the pattern is reciprocal, the pattern description can be reversed; that is, the underfunctioning of one member may invite the overfunctioning of the other. In symmetrical relationships, the therapist encounters a power struggle in which each member is engaged in asserting his or her own position in order to gain the one-up position or to avoid feeling one-down.

As we said previously (see Section 3), data suggest that the diagnosis and symptom picture of the spouse and characteristics of the other spouse stand in complex relationship to the issues in the marital interaction and should therefore influence the planning of intervention. For example, if one spouse has a unipolar depression with no clear precipitating stressful life events, the marital interaction could be a chronic stressor and contributor to the condition. Marital therapy in this situation could well be a preferred mode of intervention. In contrast, if the spouse has a bipolar illness and experiences a manic episode, and the marital interaction was good prior to the episode, psychoeducational intervention with the couple may be in order with little or no attention to the ongoing marital interaction.

Sometimes couples have chronic histories of unresolved and unrelenting conflict. Other couples are in a state of transition, perhaps moving from the initial expansion stage of their marriage to the inevitable crisis related to the reevaluation of the contraction stage. In either case, clarifying the couples' process, that is, their reoccurring patterns of behavior, represents the starting place for couples therapy. We discuss how to interrupt these patterns in a later section.

Individual Models

Once the therapist understands the couple's specific problem and has defined it as a pattern that each partner helps to maintain, the goal is to find out what keeps the couple from making needed changes. It can generally be assumed that patterns are developed from the partners' individual models of marriage, learned in their families and in prior relationships and by their own traditions of relating to each other as a couple. In considering historical models, the therapist might suppose that each member of a couple brings his or her own images or model of how intimate relationships should proceed. The therapist can collect and organize historical data through the use of a genogram, the three-generational family tree that depicts the family's patterns regarding either specific problems or general family functioning (see Chapter 7). The genogram technique suggests possible connections between present family events and the prior experiences that family members have shared (e.g., regarding the management of serious illnesses, losses, and other critical transitions), thereby placing the presenting problem in a historical context (McGoldrick and Gerson 1985; Shorter 1977). The construction of a genogram early in treatment can provide a wealth of data that offers clues about the couple's pressures, expectations, and hopes regarding the marriage. This pictorial way of gathering a history allows each partner to learn about beliefs or themes that characterize his or her family background.

Based on the couple's own idiosyncratic experiences as individuals, the therapist can then try to help them understand how their own preferred patterns (which may relate to earlier family models) have limited their ability to adapt and change. The predictability with which they will respond to unmet needs and disappointments can be pointed out supportively so that the partners begin to understand the specific ways they each reenact the same process over and over again. If this is all the couple knows, they may become despondent at recognizing the limitations of their emotional-behavioral repertoire. However, with support and active interventions, the couple's therapist can begin to help the couple conduct experiments with each other aimed at expanding their ways of relating.

Strategies and Techniques

Like family therapy in general, couples therapy uses an array of techniques meant to create new experiences and new understanding for the couple. Although each school of couples and family therapy advocates its own emphasis on particular aspects of the change process (e.g., changing the couple's beliefs or cognitions, changing behavioral sequences, increasing differentiation, expanding emotional awareness), some relatively enduring characteristics can be identified among most marital therapies.

The focus should be primarily on the interpersonal distortions between husband and wife and not on the couple-therapist transference. However, negative transference distortions toward the therapist must be addressed quickly and overtly. There are three strategies in this focused, active treatment of marital discord:

1. As Gurman (1981) has emphasized, the therapist interrupts collusive processes between the spouses. The interaction may involve either spouse failing to perceive positive or negative aspects of the other (e.g., cruelty, generosity) that are clear to an outsider or it may involve either spouse behaving in a way aimed at protecting the other from experiences that are inconsistent with the spouse's self-perception (e.g., the husband working part time views himself as the breadwinner, but the wife works full time and manages the checkbook to shield her husband from the reality of their income and finances).

2. The therapist links individual experience, including past experience and inner thoughts, to the marital relationship.

3. The therapist creates and gives tasks that are constructed 1) to encourage the spouses to differentiate between the other's intent and the effect of his or her behavior, 2) to bring into awareness the concrete behavior of the partner that contradicts past perceptions of that partner, and 3) to encourage each spouse to acknowledge his or her own behavior changes that are incompatible with the maladaptive ways he or she has seen himself or herself and has been seen by the marital partner. These tasks also help to make the couple's narrative more positive. The last task is the most important. In the initial stage of marital treatment we ask that each partner focus on what he or she wants to change in himself or herself, not how he or she wants the other spouse to be different.

Gurman's (1981) integrative marital therapy model assumes that effective marital treatment does not artificially dichotomize individual and relationship change; rather it focuses on both. The model assumes that not all of one spouse's behaviors are under the interactional control of the other spouse, and even behavior with obvious relationship to the marital interaction is not completely under relational control. Furthermore, Gurman (1981) asserts that adoption of a systems perspective does not preclude attention to unconscious aspects of experience. Self-perceptions are the mechanisms that power the behavior-maintaining aspects of interpersonal reinforcement.

In Gurman's integrative model, the goals of assessment are to evaluate three related domains: "the functional relationships between the antecedents and consequences of discrete interactional sequences; the recurrent patterns of interaction including their implicit rules; and each spouse's individual schemata for intimate relationships. In the initial stage, alliances must be developed early between the therapist and each marital partner, with the therapist offering empathy, warmth, and understanding. The therapist must also ally with the couple as a whole and learn their shared language and their different problem-solving styles and attitudes." (Gurman 1981, p. 434)

Behavioral techniques, including giving between-session homework, in-session tasks, and communication skills and problem-solving training, can help marital partners reintegrate denied aspects of themselves and of each other. However, the focus is not on behavioral change alone, because overt behavior is seen as reflecting the interlocking feelings and perceptions of each spouse. Ideally, the process of treatment should allow each partner to consider what he or she wants to change in himself or herself as opposed to how he or she wants the other spouse to be different; to safely explore new beliefs, feelings, and behaviors; and to experiment with new patterns of interaction that are unfamiliar and even anxiety provoking.

> **"T**opics at issue between couples typically remain the same over many years. Psychoeducation is most helpful when it enables couples to label as entirely normal their continuing efforts to grapple with the same set of issues over a lifetime."
> (Lebow 1999, p. 172)

Beginning therapists sometimes feel more at ease when they have a set of questions that can help them to organize the session and the overall structure of the treatment. Table 19–1 offers one model that has been successful for advanced trainees (D. Rait, unpublished manuscript). The table includes sample questions with the specific rationale for each set of questions. After the interview, the therapist is then free to track themes (always keeping an interactional focus), invent tasks and experiments designed to provide new experiences for the couple, and evaluate the changes that occur or do not occur as a result of the couple's efforts to change their patterns of interaction.

Summary

In a nationwide survey of family therapists, marital problems were identified as the most common presenting problem seen in their practices (Rait 1988). Couples therapy also represents the most common pathway for many trainees to initially explore the field of marital and family therapy. At the same time, there is little question that developing the skills needed to work successfully with couples who present with a wide range of difficulties requires an understanding how normal couples' relationships change over time, how problems emerge and are maintained, and how focused marital treatment can alleviate distress and dysfunction. The rewards are great when therapists can assist couples in recognizing and shifting the patterns that inhibit their abilities to live rich, intimate lives together. In Chapter 20, we review issues of sex therapy and marital therapy separately and in combination.

Suggested Readings

Chasin R: One Couple, Four Realities: Multiple Perspectives on Couples Therapy. New York, Guilford, 1992
  This interesting book looks at four therapists' perspectives on treating one couple. Emerging from a conference on couples therapy, it shows the diversity of opinion in the field.

Dym B: Couples: Exploring and Understanding the Cycles of Intimate Relationships. Boston, MA, Harper Collins, 1993
  This book provides a developmental model of couples development and the problems that couples face. It provides a humane, sensible approach to assessment. The book is also full of rich clinical insights and ideas.

Gottman JM, Levenson RW: What predicts change in marital interaction over time? A study of alternative models. Fam Process 38:143–158, 1999

TABLE 19–1.   Guidelines for interviewing couples—the process

Questions	Rationale
Can you tell me about yourself? As individuals? As a couple?	Joining, forming an alliance with each member and the couple, creating a safe place
What brings you here? How do you understand the problem? What feelings does it elicit for each of you?	Developing an interactional problem focus
How does the problematic pattern actually work? Can you show me how it works?	Observing by staging an enactment
How did this pattern originate? How did you create it?	Placing the problem in context of their relationship, families of origin, and individual development
How have you maintained this pattern? What have you done to keep it going?	Placing the pattern or problem under their joint control
Tell me about what you believe should be happening.	Revealing myths, stories, ideas, and expectations about love, sexuality, marriage, and closeness
In what other ways is the pattern currently reinforced? What do your family and friends believe is the problem?	Reflecting how jobs, extended family members, and friends contribute to the pattern's resilience
Is this pattern always occurring or are there exceptions? Demonstrating how pervasive the pattern is (i.e., whether it is chronic or related to a life transition)	
What have you done to try to change the pattern?	Trying to avoid redundancy by inquiring about solution behavior
Have your efforts to change the pattern made things better or worse?	Looking at the problem as attempted solutions
What has been the influence of this problem in your lives?	Looking for the influence of the problem over their lives
How motivated are you to change the pattern now?	Assessing individual's and couple's motivation
What would happen if you succeeded in changing the pattern?	Anticipating possible consequences of change, both positive and negative
What patterns of relating have you created that you want to keep?	Identifying and honoring assets and resources
Are you ready to make a change? How about trying something different?	Preparing the couple for exploring new patterns of interaction

Gottman JM, Levenson RW: How stable is marital interaction over time? Fam Process 38:159–166, 1999

These two thoughtful articles summarize recent work on marital interaction over time with a special focus on marital stability.

Guerin P, Fay L, Burden S, et al: The Evaluation and Treatment of Marital Conflict. New York, Basic Books, 1987

This volume describes the Bowenian approach to marital problems, relying on case examples to illustrate assessment and treatment strategies. The writing is clear, and most clinicians will find the model useful.

Gurman A: Integrative marital therapy: toward the development of an interpersonal approach, in Forms of Brief Therapy. Edited by Budman S. New York, Guilford, 1981, pp 415–457

Although somewhat dated, this fine chapter integrates ideas from behavioral, psychodynamic, and systemic approaches to marital therapy. Throughout the chapter, the author's reasoning is clear and the writing is accessible.

Jacobson N, Gurman A: Clinical Handbook of Couples Therapy. New York, Guilford, 1995

This well-written and concise book provides strategies and techniques from most of the major schools of therapy.

Karpel M: Evaluating Couples. New York, WW Norton, 1994

This book is an excellent and complete guide to couples evaluation.

References

Dicks HV: Marital Tensions. London, Routledge & Kegan Paul, 1967

Dym B: Couples. New York, Guilford, 1993

Framo JL: The integration of marital therapy with sessions with family of origin, in Handbook of Family Therapy. Edited by Gurman AS, Kniskern DP. New York, Brunner/Mazel, 1981, pp 133–158

Goldner V, Penn P, Sheinberg M, et al: Love and violence: gender paradoxes in volatile attachments. Fam Process 29:343–364, 1990

Gottman J: Why Marriages Succeed or Fail. New York, Simon & Schuster, 1994, pp 68–102

Gurman A: Integrative marital therapy: toward the development of an interpersonal approach, in Forms of Brief Therapy. Edited by Budman S. New York, Guilford, 1981, pp 415–457

Lebow J: Building a science of couple relationships: comments on two articles by Gottman & Levenson. Fam Process 38:167–173, 1999

Lewis JM: For better or worse: interpersonal relationships and individual outcome. Am J Psychiatry 155:582–589, 1998

McGoldrick M, Gerson R: Genograms in Family Assessment. New York, WW Norton, 1985

Rait D: Family therapy practice survey. The Family Therapy Networker 1:52–56, 1988

Sager C: Marriage Contracts and Couple Therapy: Hidden Forces in Intimate Relationships. New York, Brunner/Mazel, 1976

Shorter E: The Making of the Modern Family. New York, Basic Books, 1977

Thibaut JW, Kelly HH: The Social Psychology of Groups. New York, Wiley, 1959

Daddy's Friend, Tom Birkner, 1998. Courtesy of the artist. Used with permission.

CHAPTER 20

Sex, Marriage, and Marital and Sex Therapy

Objectives for the Reader

- To be able to illustrate the connections between sexual problems and other family problems
- To understand the relationship between couples therapy and sex therapy
- To understand techniques of sex therapy and how they can be included in couples therapy

Introduction

Schnarch (1997) contends that for many married people the magnetic force that drew them together eventually weakens to the point that sexuality and eroticism play a minor role in their lives. Sometimes specific problems in sexual functioning affect the couple's relationship. In this chapter, we look at issues of couple sexuality and the evolving ways that marital and sex therapy can be combined.

Although DSM-IV (American Psychiatric Association 1994) and most of the early sex therapists make a dichotomous distinction between sexual function and dysfunction, sexuality is probably best thought of as a set of experiences on a continuum of satisfaction. It is possible, for example, to have a sexual life in which sexual arousal and orgasm occur, but the experience feels passionless and boring. The same functioning couple could have more passionate and exciting sex after therapy. It is possible to have an erotic sexual experience even if dysfunction is present (e.g., the male partner cannot achieve erection because of a physical illness) but the couple uses other methods of sexual expression. It is possible to have a pretty good sexual experience even if there are serious arguments between the couple about the frequency or type of sexual practice.

It has been estimated that 50% of American marriages have some sexual problems. These problems can be divided into *difficulties* (such as inability to agree on frequency), which are clearly dyadic issues, and *dysfunctions*, which are specific problems with desire, arousal, and orgasm, as listed in DSM-IV. Dysfunctions may be organic or psychological or a combination of both and may be lifelong or acquired, generalized or situational. They may be deeply embedded in relational power or intimacy struggles or may be the only problem in an otherwise well-functioning relationship. Although most family therapists believe that there is no uninvolved partner when one member of a couple presents with sexual dysfunction, that is different from saying that the relationship itself is the cause of the dysfunction. The family therapist's job is to ascertain as best as possible the etiology of the problem and to choose the most effective therapy, whether medical, individual, or relational. It is also within the therapist's purview to inquire about whether the couple would like to improve a technically functional but not very satisfying sexual relationship, in the same way that the therapist can offer to increase intimacy in a couple that wish personal growth.

> The family therapist's job is to ascertain as best as possible the etiology of the problem and to choose the most effective therapy, whether medical, individual, or relational, or some combination.

Diagnosis—Systems Issues

Sexual dysfunction or dissatisfaction is seldom caused by a psychiatric disorder (although depression and anxiety may often decrease sexual desire). It is commonly caused by ignorance of sexual anatomy and physiology; negative attitudes and self-defeating behavior; anger, power, or intimacy issues with the partners; or medical conditions. Male erection problems are proving increasingly to have contributing physiological causes and to be amenable to medical treatment. It is important to remember that people vary enormously in the importance they place on the sexual, or erotic, in their lives. For example, according to Laumann and Michael (1994), about one-third of the people surveyed for their book had sex at least twice a week, about one-third a few times a month, and the rest had sex with a partner a few times a year or not at all. In general, when sex is not part of a marriage over a long period of time, the relationship has less vitality and life. However, even well-functioning marriages may have periods in which sexuality is much less a part of the couple's lives (such as after the birth of a child or during a family crisis). Different people have vastly different tolerances for such periods.

Gender Issues in Sexuality

Socially constructed gender issues play an important role in marital sexuality. In the past, men were encouraged to be the aggressive ones in the relationship and were supposed to be the more experienced partner. Women were taught to be attractive but not sexual before marriage and to be less sexually demanding in marriage. Women were trained to see sex as something they gave, men as something they took or received. (Given that the consequences for women were far more serious, particularly before easily available birth control, it is not surprising that this pattern developed.) For men outside of marriage, having sex meant proving yourself a man, for women it meant being seen as promiscuous. Men are still more inclined to separate sex from love and to see sex as recreation, whereas women more often see it as something acceptable only if the rest of the relationship is functioning well.

There has been a marked shift in recent years in the general attitude toward female sexuality. Since the 1960s, women have increasingly expected to receive pleasure from sexual activities and to achieve orgasm. They also expect to participate in a more assertive way, because their sexual interests and activities have been legitimized. Initially, some men became disturbed and sometimes dysfunctional because of the changing and increasingly assertive sexual role of women. This has been less of a problem for younger men who are used to more equal relationships. Men often feel that they must be responsible for the sexual experience and that they have failed if their partner has not reached orgasm. Couples growing in their sexual relationship learn that they must each contribute to the experience. Some women may still find it difficult to learn to ask for what they want and to feel that they are partners in the sexual relationship.

Some Parameters of Sexual Function

Healthy sexual functioning can be thought of as resulting from relatively nonconflicted and self-confident attitudes about sex and the belief that the partner is pleased by one's performance. In such a situation, a reinforcing positive cycle can be activated. When either partner has doubts about his or her sexual abilities or ability to please the other, the partner's sexual performance may suffer. This self-absorption and anxiety will characteristically produce a decrease in sexual performance and enjoyment and can lead to impotency and orgasmic difficulties. Couple or individual difficulties might then follow. A vicious circle may be activated, with worries being increased, leading to increasingly poor sexual performance.

Because each person is vulnerable to the other during sex, it is difficult to have sex when one is angry or not in a mood to be close (although some people can block out other feelings and keep the sexual area of their lives more separate). In addition, people who feel abused, mistreated, or ignored in a relationship are less likely to want to please their partner. For partners who feel that they have no voice in the relationship, lack of desire is sometimes the only way they feel able to manifest displeasure.

Couples who continue in marital or individual treatment for long periods of time can resolve some of their marital problems but can still experience specific sexual difficulties in their marriage. These difficulties may be reversed dramatically after relatively brief periods of sex therapy, even though such problems may have proven intractable following long periods of more customary psychotherapy. Sexual functioning that is suffering because the partners do not want to be close is not likely to respond to sex therapy unless other issues are also addressed.

Usually when a married couple has a generally satisfactory relationship, any minor sexual problems may be only temporary. Resolution of sexual problems in a relationship, however, will not inevitably produce positive effects in other facets of a relationship.

Marital and sexual problems interact in various ways:

1. *The sexual dysfunction produces or contributes to secondary marital discord.* Specific strategies focused on the sexual dysfunctions would usually be considered the treatment of choice in these situations, especially if the same sexual dysfunction occurred in the person's other relationships.

2. *The sexual dysfunction is secondary to marital discord.* In such situations, general strategies of marital treatment might be considered the treatment

of choice. If the marital relationship is not disrupted too severely, a trial of sex therapy might be attempted because relatively rapid relief of symptoms could produce beneficial effects on the couple's interest in pursuing other marital issues.

3. *Marital discord co-occurs with sexual problems.* This situation would probably not be amenable to sex therapy because of the partners' hostility to each other. Marital therapy would usually be attempted first, with later attention given to sexual dysfunction.

4. *Sexual dysfunction occurs without marital discord.* This situation might occur when one partner's medical illness has affected his or her sexual functioning, forcing the couple to learn new ways to manage the change. Another example might be when one partner has had a history of sexual abuse or a sexual assault that creates anxiety related to the sexual experience. Although individual therapy can be helpful in these situations, couples therapy can be especially useful in creating a safe place to address painful feelings and anxious expectations and to provide education and guidance for couples undergoing these transitions.

> When sexuality functions well in a marriage, it's a positive, integral component. However, when sexuality is dysfunctional or nonexistent, it plays an inordinately powerful role, robbing the marriage of intimacy and vitality (McCarthy 1999).

Assessment of Sexual Disorder

The therapist needs to evaluate carefully all of the couple's interactions and to conduct a physical assessment if dysfunction is present. If the basic marriage appears to be a sound one but the couple experience specific sexual difficulties (which may also lead to various secondary marital consequences), the primary focus might be sex therapy per se. In many cases, however, specific sex therapy cannot be carried out until the relationship between the two partners has improved in other respects. The sexual problems may clearly be an outgrowth of the marital difficulties. When marital problems are taken care of, the sexual problems may be resolved readily. It may be difficult to disentangle marital from sexual problems or to decide which came first. The priorities for therapy may not always be clear.

DSM-IV recognizes the following disorders as sexual dysfunctions:

- Sexual desire disorders: hypoactive sexual desire disorder, sexual aversion disorder.
- Sexual arousal disorders: female sexual arousal disorder, male erectile disorder.
- Orgasmic disorders: female orgasmic disorder, male orgasmic disorder, premature ejaculation.
- Sexual pain disorders: dyspareunia (not due to a general medical condition) and vaginismus (not due to a general medical condition). These disorders are coded separately if they are due to a general medical condition or are substance induced.

Many people have more than one dysfunction (e.g., hypoactive sexual desire disorder plus orgasmic disorder), and often both members of a couple will have a dysfunction (e.g., premature ejaculation in the man and hypoactive desire in the woman). It is important to understand the sequencing of the onset of the dysfunctions in order to understand how they influence each other. As we have said earlier, many sexual problems are not dysfunctions but are relationally based dissatisfactions.

Specific techniques have been devised for eliciting a sexual history and for evaluating sexual functioning. The marital therapist should become familiar with these techniques and obtain experience in their use. Just as many individual therapists shy away from inquiring about their patients' sexual histories, some marital therapists still are not well informed about their patients' sexual experiences. Anxieties arising from their own discomfort about such material, or from their lack of a conceptual frame of reference, handicap their ability to acquire and use sexual data. Table 20–1 lists the minimum requirements for a systemic assessment of sexual difficulties.

Leiblum and Rosen (1989) provide a thorough discussion of assessment techniques for each specific sexual problem. For readers interested in family-of-origin work, a sexual genogram is useful (Berman and Hof 1987). The sexual genogram questions are as follows:

- What are the overt/covert messages in this family regarding sexuality/intimacy? Regarding masculinity/femininity?
- Who said/did what? Who was conspicuously silent/absent in the area of sexuality/intimacy?
- Who was the most open sexually? Intimately? In what ways?

TABLE 20–1. Assessment of sexual problems

I. Definition of the problem

    A. How does the couple describe the problem? What are their theories about its etiology? How do they generally relate to their sexuality, as reflected in their language, attitudes toward sexuality, comfort level, and permission system?

    B. How is the problem a problem for them? What is the function of the problem in their relationship system? Is the relationship problem the central problem? Why now?

II. Relationship history

    A. Current partner.

    B. Previous relationship history.

    C. Psychosexual history, including information about early childhood experiences, nature of sexual encounters prior to the relationship, sexual orientation, feelings about masculinity and femininity.

    D. Description of current sexual functioning, focusing on conditions for satisfactory sex, positive behaviors, specific technique, and so on. Who initiates sex, who leads, or do both? How does the couple's sexual pattern of intimacy and control reflect or compensate for other aspects of their relationship?

III. Developmental life cycle issues (births, deaths, transitions).

IV. Medical history, focusing on current physical status, medications, and present medical care, especially endocrine, vascular, metabolic.

V. Goals (patients' and therapist's viewpoints): The task is to examine whether goals are realistic and what previous attempted solutions have yielded.

- How was sexuality/intimacy encouraged? Discouraged? Controlled? Within a generation? Between generations?
- What questions have you had regarding sexuality/intimacy in your family tree that you have been reluctant to ask? Who might have the answers? How could you discover the answers?
- What were the secrets in your family regarding sexuality/intimacy (e.g., incest, unwanted pregnancies, extramarital affairs)?
- What do the other "players on the stage" (i.e., extended family members or [sometimes] close family friends) have to say regarding the aforementioned questions? How did these issues, events, and experiences affect him/her? Within a generation? Between generations? With whom have you talked about this? With whom would you like to talk about this? How could you do it?
- How does your partner perceive your family tree/genogram regarding the aforementioned questions? How do you perceive his/hers?

- How would you change this genogram (including who and what) to reflect what you wish had occurred regarding messages and experiences of sexuality/intimacy?
- Were there inappropriate sexual behaviors by family members, such as sexual fondling of children by relatives or detailed sexual discussions in the presence of small children?
- Are any family members homosexual? How were they treated at home? Could one express nonsexual love for same-sex people?

In addition, a medical workup should be ordered for couples in whom the problems may have an organic component. This is particularly true for men, for whom small physiological changes in potency may produce anxiety that exacerbates the problem.

Children should not be present when the therapist takes the husband and wife's intimate sexual history. The process of taking a sexual history should be handled with care and regard for each person's level of comfort.

What type of language should be used when discussing sexual topics? Obviously, the therapist should not use terms that would be offensive or uncomfortable for either the therapist or the couple. At the same time, care must be taken to avoid using bland generalities that fail to elicit specific sexual information. Frankness is encouraged, and when a patient's response is vague, the therapist needs to follow up with more specific questions.

The therapist should use simple language or use the simplest technical sexual term with which the patient is comfortable. Some patients will misunderstand technical terms. For others, the therapist's use of the vernacular may be inappropriate. The problem faced in the choice of language is itself an indication of our general cultural discomfort with sexuality. The therapist's own use of a particular sexual vocabulary can be a model to help the marital partners feel comfortable in communicating with each other more openly.

Taking a sexual history of lesbian and gay couples may be particularly difficult for a heterosexual therapist, either because of discomfort with homosexuality or because of a lack of knowledge of homosexual norms and mores. In addition, the couple may have a wider or different set of sexual practices than the therapist is used to (of course, this also may be true with heterosexual couples). The therapist can educate himself or herself about homosexual sexuality (the number of books available in mainstream bookstores about gay and lesbian life has increased dramatically in the past few years), or he or she may ask the couple about their own and other common practices. If the therapist is very anxious in this situation, he or she must decide whether he or she can be an effective therapist for the couple or should refer the couple elsewhere (see also Chapter 14). Gay and lesbian couples may present with any of the dysfunctions or dissatisfactions that heterosexual couples experience. "Sex Therapy With Lesbians, Gay Men and Bisexuals" (Nichols 1989) is an excellent overview of this topic.

Treatment

Treatment of psychosexual disorders, in the form developed by Masters and Johnson (1966), consisted of a thorough assessment of the partners and the relationship, education about sexual functioning, and a series of behavioral (i.e., sensate focus) exercises. The model was based on three fundamental postulates: 1) a parallel sequence of physiological and subjective arousal in both genders; 2) the primacy of psychogenic factors, particularly learning deficits and performance anxiety; and 3) the amenability of most sexual disorders to a brief, problem-focused treatment approach. The sensate focus exercises were designed predominantly for behavioral desensitization but also taught the individual partners about their own sexual desires and served to elicit relationship problems. In these exercises, the couple pleasures each other, alternating in the role of giver and receiver, first in nongenital areas, then genitally, then with intercourse. Intercourse is prohibited during the early stages to remove performance anxiety. There are also specific exercises for each of the sexual dysfunctions. Different authors have developed different exercises and ways of approaching them. For a complete description of these exercises, we recommend Kaplan (1995), LoPiccolo and Stock (1996), and Zilbergeld (1992). This method works best when ignorance, shame, or a specific dysfunction such as premature ejaculation is present. They are difficult to complete if the couple feel angry or unloving toward each other.

Many of the patients whom Masters and Johnson treated in the 1970s had issues related to sexual ignorance and inexperience. Two decades later, the increase in premarital sex and the proliferation of easily available articles and books on sexuality had decreased the number of these couples and allowed some couples with sexual dysfunction to work on their issues at home. Recent studies of couples seeking sex therapy have shown that a higher proportion have concomitant complicated marital problems than those treated by Masters and Johnson.

Some writers, particularly Schnarch (1997), have focused on cognitive and emotional issues in sexuality, especially on the meanings attached to a particular act and the level of intimacy involved. While the field has learned a great deal about the more behavioral and organic issues related to arousal and orgasm, it is important to rethink other aspects of sex—such as eroticism, passion, mystery, and dominance or submission—that make the act itself meaningful. This is particularly true in areas of sexual boredom or situational lack of desire. These therapists do not use rigidly staged exercises but focus on the couple's relatedness during sex; however, they may suggest specific homework to help a couple focus on a particular aspect of their sexuality. The presence of organic factors must be considered. Couples wishing personal growth in the area of sexuality need to be pushed past their comfort zone to areas of greater intensity and feeling, rather than simply being helped to expand the variety of techniques used.

Although not mentioned in DSM-IV, sexual compulsions or addictions may occasionally be a couple's presenting complaint. In such cases, one partner's unceasing compulsion to think about, talk about, and have sex may be very wearing on the other partner, especially because a key component of this problem is that such persons become extremely anxious if sex is denied. Sexually compulsive persons may present with multiple affairs or with constant demands on the other partner. Most people who have affairs do not have a sexual compulsion, however. Treatment for sexual compulsions or addictions remains controversial. Some therapists use a 12-step addiction model, with group therapy; some treat it as a compulsion with individual therapy and medication [particularly selective serotonin reuptake inhibitors (SSRIs) such as fluoxetine]. Couples therapy is still a critical component part of treatment, to educate the couple, to deal with couple dynamics that are part of the problem, and if multiple affairs have taken place, to discuss the viability of the marriage.

In recent years, emphasis has shifted to the role of biomedical and organic factors in the etiology of sexual dysfunction, along with the growing use of medical and surgical treatment interventions. Focus has been given to the role of vascular disorders and neuroendocrine problems and to the tendency for many medications to affect sexual functioning. Patients must receive a thorough physical workup. Abramowicz (1992) provides a good review on the interaction of medication and sexuality.

A variety of medical approaches to the treatment of erectile disorders in men have been developed. These approaches include surgical prostheses or penile implants (seldom used in the past few years), intracorporal injection of vasoactive drugs such as papaverine, constriction rings and vacuum pump devices, and urethral suppositories. In 1998 oral medication (sildenafil [Viagra]) was introduced for the treatment of impotence. As of this writing, sildenafil appears to be revolutionizing our conceptions of sexuality and treatment. Because our understanding and treatment of impotence is developing so rapidly, it is important to stay current on new research in the field. Surgical treatments are available for the correction of arterial insufficiency or venous leakage problems. These methods may be more or less acceptable to the man and his partner. The partner's response to the husband's improved sexual function is a key element of their success. Premature ejaculation has sometimes been treated successfully with SSRIs and clomipramine; however, because these drugs may also decrease sexual desire, caution and careful monitoring are indicated (Abramowicz 1992). Yohimbine is sometimes helpful in preventing loss of sexual desire in patients treated with SSRIs (Rosen and Ashton 1993).

In women, most medical interventions have been for dyspareunia. Female dyspareunia due to the decreased lubrication associated with aging can be treated with topical estrogen cream or lubricant jelly. Even when an organic cause for dyspareunia is found and treated, the conditioned anxiety and lack of arousal associated with sex usually requires an additional course of couples therapy with a sexual focus. Hormone treatment for lack of desire has not proven effective (Rosen and Leiblum 1995).

Mrs. A had problems with anger during adolescence, generally because she felt neglected by her busy parents. She had a period of intense sexual activity during adolescence, which was related to her looking for affection through sexuality; she reported that she had no sexual problems during this time. Through twice-a-week individual psychotherapy in her 20s she worked through these problems, married Mr. A, and had a child. Mr. A was a kind but rather distant man who soon after the marriage made a series of career moves that made him extremely busy. For the first 2 years, there were no sexual problems, but then marital problems developed, and Mrs. A's desire decreased. Mr. A then became more sexually demanding. Frequency and enjoyment of sex for both partners were decreased markedly. Mrs. A refused to have sex, saying that she was too upset. When they occasionally had sex, however, both were orgasmic.

Mr. and Mrs. A had been raised in traditional backgrounds and had been taught that sex should not be discussed. Although both partners had previous sexual experiences, they were unable to talk about their sexual problems. Mrs. A also began fantasizing about other men. Although fantasies of other partners are not unusual, Mrs. A's fantasies occurred only when she was particularly angry at her husband.

Whereas at one time individual psychotherapy for Mrs. A might have been the treatment of choice, the therapist decided to use both marital therapy and sex therapy. Marital therapy helped to open communication between the couple. It was discovered that Mrs. A was feeling very abandoned by her extremely hardworking husband and feeling that she was being ignored as she had been in her childhood. In addition, she was angry at her husband for not helping with childrearing responsibilities. Her fantasies about other men, which seemed to be a way of wishing for the original affection she craved, were upsetting her and making her wonder if she loved her husband. She experienced as further withdrawal Mr. A's inability to insist on her connecting with him emotionally before he demanded sex.

The couple were encouraged to deal more directly with their differences and with the disappointments underlying their anger. Issues related to each partner's family of origin were brought up. Roles were restructured as Mr. A took over more of the childrearing responsibilities. As the marital relationship improved, their sexual problems decreased. The couple were also given a series of sensate focus exercises in which they were asked to focus on giving and receiving pleasure. They were encouraged to talk with each other about their sexual wishes and to pay attention to the connection between themselves while being sexual. They also discussed deepening their nonsexual physical connection.

Other Issues Related to Sexuality and Marriage

Homosexuality or Bisexuality

Overview. Family therapists should be adequately educated in the area of human sexual orientation and sexual identity (see Chapters 22 and 23). The terms themselves are confusing. *Sexual orientation* is another way of indicating an individual's tendency to be attracted to one or both sexes. Sexual identity is one's sense of oneself as male or female. Sexual orientation, like most psychological phenomenon, is not an absolute. One may be sexually attracted to the opposite sex, the same sex, or both. Sexual orientation falls along a continuum, with completely homosexual and completely heterosexual preferences falling at the extreme ends, and many gradations in between.

Observations of human sexual behavior, emotional attachments, erotic fantasies, arousal, and erotic preference have suggested that sexual orientation and sexual identity are not static; both may fluctuate over a person's lifetime. Sometimes changes in sexuality are considered to be phases, but sometimes they become the predominant disposition of sexual relation. Some persons change from heterosexual to homosexual or the reverse in their 30s, 40s, or 50s. Some remain bisexual during their adult lives. Regardless, deviation from heterosexuality in Western society is accompanied frequently by rejection, not only by one's immediate family but also by one's peers and, in some cases, society in general. News stories about accusations of discrimination based on sexual orientation and about violence targeted at gays appear regularly in the media. For therapists, the issue should be centered on understanding and listening to the patient's experiences even if the experiences are quite different from their own, helping the patient deal with both external and internal homophobia and choosing a lifestyle congruent with the self (see Chapter 23).

> **S**exual orientation and sexual identity are not static; both may fluctuate over a person's lifetime.

Marital issues in homosexual or bisexual individuals. Many persons who are bisexual or whose homosexuality is admitted to consciousness later in life spend some years of their lives in heterosexual marriages. Many such people are able to function well heterosexually, changing their sexual focus when they realize that something appears to be missing or that their level of desire and love is greater for their own sex. Some have low levels of sexual desire in the marriage and pursue affairs. Because there may be a great deal of love and affection between the marital partners, the discovery that one member is homosexual is very painful, and the desire to remain in the marriage may be strong on one or both sides. Although sex therapy can improve sexual functioning, no treatment has proven effective in decreasing homosexual desires and wishes. The couple must decide how to handle the situation, that is, whether to divorce, whether to remain in the relationship and allow for alternative sexual behaviors, or whether the homosexual person can remain monogamous in the marriage and give up expressing the other parts of himself or herself. Therapy can help the couple clarify alternatives and make decisions. Unfortunately, even with the most loving spouses the most common outcome is divorce, but this is not the only possible choice.

Sexual Functioning After Rape or Sexual Abuse

Rape and sexual abuse are acts of violence that may seriously affect the victim's ability to respond sexually in marriage. Both are likely to produce symptoms of posttraumatic stress disorder, with anxiety and flashbacks occurring when sex is begun, even with a loved partner. Decreased sexual desire or sexual aversion are common, although some women with a history of early sexual abuse become indiscriminately sexual, considering themselves to be used merchandise and worth something only because of their sexuality. Some women maintain good sexual function but may be wary of intimacy. Men sexually abused as children report similar problems. Some become abusers in adulthood.

Women with histories of early sexual abuse may experience periods of relatively normal sexual functioning but begin to exhibit symptoms during therapy for other effects of the abuse (such as depression). This is because memories of the abuse are brought to the forefront of consciousness during therapy. In such cases, the husband must be carefully informed of what is happening so that he can be patient in dealing with his wife's varying moods and concerns. These symptoms usually change by the end of treatment. If a previously well-functioning adult has been raped, the sexual symptoms may be either relatively brief or long-standing, depending on the circumstances of the rape, the amount of physical damage, the vulnerability of the victim, and the partner's response. Because the partners of rape victims also have a complex set of feelings, including a wish to protect, a sense of shame, and murderous rage toward the rapist, they may or may not be able to respond empathically as the woman deals with the trauma and her own feelings.

Couples therapy must be directed primarily toward helping the partners respond to each other emphatically and deal with the meaning of the trauma. Behavioral desensitization exercises may decrease sexual pressures enough to make sex more comfortable.

Marital rape was at one time considered impossible because a married man had a right to force his wife to have sex. We now know that this is a traumatic event and an illegal one in most states. Marital rape should be treated as a form of abuse.

Sexual Problems After Medical Illness

Adults treated for cancer, diabetes, heart disease, prostatitis, HIV, or chemical dependency may face special sexual challenges because of the underlying disorder, its treatment, or the effect of the illness on the couple's relationship. Two types of problems can occur. In one type, the illness can have a specific effect on sexual functioning. For example, surgery for prostate cancer may produce erectile dysfunction. This can now generally be treated medically with sildenafil; sometimes permanent dysfunction is unavoidable. Close communication with the patient's urologist is necessary. The therapist should also help partners expand their repertoire of sexual behaviors that do not involve intercourse. In the second type, sex is still possible, but the couple is anxious that having sex will injure the patient. The classic example is sex after a heart attack (Cobb and Schaffer 1975). There is no evidence that sex with a known partner in familiar surroundings is problematic for the heart. The couple should be advised to resume sex as soon as any reasonable exercise is permissible. The very few heart attacks related to sex are most likely to involve affair partners and heavy intake of food or alcohol.

Likewise, erectile dysfunction may be the predictable side effect of certain antihypertensive medications. Narcotics, such as heroin, barbiturates, and alcohol, have a similar effect. Obviously, addictive drugs should be stopped or efforts made to change necessary medications. Many of the newer antidepressants, especially the SSRIs, can decrease sexual desire and slow orgasm. In general, the treatment of choice is to lower the dose or change the antidepressant, although adjunctive pharmacological therapy is sometimes helpful in reducing these side effects. Serious illness of any kind, and treatment for certain illness such as cancer, may leave the person with no sexual interest. In such cases, the couple may have to live with the situation, and the therapist's task is to help the couple decide the best way to handle the situation within the marital relationship. Similarly, surgery, chemotherapy, or radiation for cervical, ovarian, or prostate cancer can reduce sexual desire and performance. HIV and AIDS should alter a couple's approach to sex, and the therapist must recommend safe sexual practices.

Sexual Problems in the Elderly

With the rapid growth in the number of older people in the population, interest has increased in their psychiatric and sexual problems. The family therapist can help couples realize the following:

1. Advancing years are not a contraindication to sexuality and sensuality.

2. Older men may achieve erection and orgasm more slowly and may not necessarily ejaculate each time they have intercourse. Older women may have a shorter excitement phase, and their orgasms may be less intense, with slower vaginal contractions. Both partners, however, can still have a regular, ongoing sexual life.

3. The couple should make efforts not to decrease their general level of affection and nonsexual physical connection.

Even after an elderly patient has experienced a severe disability, such as a stroke, his or her sexual life can still be maintained. The couple can be aided in adjusting to changes of sexual functioning by a thorough discussion of what positions and techniques are still possible.

Conclusion

Sexual issues are intimately and unpredictably intertwined with a couple's functioning. Couples with sexual dysfunction in one or both partners should be evaluated carefully, and the therapist should decide whether to add specific sensate focus exercises to the ongoing marital therapy. If the therapist chooses to do so, he or she must be sure to obtain adequate training or supervision.

Suggested Readings

Kaplan HS: The Illustrated Manual of Sex Therapy, 2nd Edition. New York, Brunner/Mazel, 1987 and Kaplan HS: The Sexual Desire Disorders: Dysfunctional Regulation of Sexual Motivation. New York, Brunner/Mazel, 1995
These helpful books describe the integrated sex therapy approach based on the author's triphasic model of sexual disorders. Line drawings illustrate the approach that begins with sensate focus exercises and proceeds through major sexual difficulties. The newer book brilliantly integrates couples therapy with individual therapy and psychopharmacology.

Polansky D: Talking About Sex. Washington, DC, American Psychiatric Press, 1995
This easy-to-read book provides information on a variety of topics related to sex, including treatment.

Schnarch D: Passionate Marriage. New York, WW Norton, 1997
The author's approach to sex therapy draws on family systems, object relations, and behavioral ideas in looking at the establishment of intimacy and differentiation in the sexual relationship. The book is clinically clear and is also helpful for patients.

References

Abramowicz ME: Drugs that cause sexual dysfunction: an update. The Medical Letter 34:95–111, 1992

American Psychiatric Association: Diagnostic and Statistical Manual of Mental Disorders, 4th Edition. Washington, DC, American Psychiatric Association, 1994, pp 493–538

Berman E, Hof H: The sexual genogram—assessing family of origin factors in the treatment of sexual dysfunction, in Integrating Sex and Marital Therapy: A Clinical Guide. Edited by Weeks G, Hof L. New York, Brunner/Mazel, 1987, pp 37–57

Cobb LA, Schaffer WE: Letter to the editor. N Engl J Med 293:1100, 1975

Kaplan HS: The Sexual Desire Disorders: Dysfunctional Regulation of Sexual Motivation. New York, Brunner/Mazel, 1995

Laumann E, Michael E: Social Organization of Sexuality. Chicago, IL, University of Chicago Press, 1994

Leiblum S, Rosen R: Principles and Practice of Sex Therapy, 2nd Edition, New York, Guilford, 1989

LoPiccolo J, Stock W: Treatment of sexual dysfunction. J Consult Clin Psychol 54:158–167, 1996

Masters W, Johnson V: Human Sexual Response. Boston, MA, Little, Brown, 1966

McCarthy BW: Marital style and its effects on sexual desire and functioning. Journal of Family Psychotherapy 10:1–12, 1999

Nichols M: Sex therapy with lesbians, gay men and bisexuals, in Principles and Practice of Sex Therapy, 2nd Edition. Edited by Leiblum SW, Rosen RC. New York, Guilford, 1989, pp 269–297

Rosen R, Ashton AK: Prosexual drugs: empirical status of the "new aphrodisiacs." Arch Sex Behav 22:521–543, 1993

Rosen R, Leiblum S: Treatment of sexual disorders in the 1990s: an integrated approach. J Consult Clin Psychol 63:877–890, 1995

Schnarch D: Passionate Marriage. New York, WW Norton, 1997

Zilbergeld B: The New Male Sexuality. New York, Bantam, 1992

Reconciliation of the Family, Jean-Baptiste Greuze, 1795. Courtesy of the Phoenix Art Museum. Used with permission.

CHAPTER 21
Separation and Divorce

With Richard M. Patel, M.D.

Objectives for the Reader

- To learn the principles of diagnosis and treatment of separated, divorced, single-parent, binuclear, and other family forms
- To learn treatment goals and techniques with these family forms

Introduction

In Chapter 4, we discussed the functioning of nontraditional families and some of the difficulties that separated, divorced, single-parent, and reconstituted families commonly experience and cope with. Some families, because of the multiplicity of stressors, poor coping, or psychopathology, are not able to deal with the situation and therefore seek help. In this chapter we discuss the assessment and treatment of these families.

Separation

The process of separation can be an experiment on the part of a couple who are experiencing stress, or the first step in a process leading directly to divorce. We describe in the next section in this chapter separations in which the couple are definitely ending the relationship. Trial separations in which the couple (neither of whom is having an affair) still express interest in rebuilding the marriage can be a chance for the therapist and the couple to do serious work. In general, separations are to be avoided when possible, as the best therapy can usually be done when the partners are in constant contact. Separations may be unavoidable or preferable when high conflict, violence, or alcoholism are present or when a person who married young feels as if he or she has no separate identity and needs to be alone for a period of time. During a trial separation the couple should be encouraged to have ongoing couples therapy and to have planned and scheduled times to be together during which they have some pleasant experiences and some serious talks. They should be encouraged not to date others during the separation. Some therapists suggest that each partner should also be in individual therapy during this time because part of the problem involves individual issues that are hard to address in conjoint work. Others believe that individual therapy is necessary only in certain situations. For example, when emotions are extremely intense, separate individual therapy for one or both partners, or group therapy, may be indicated to cool down a contentious relationship while marital therapy is proceeding. It is also worth mentioning that separation and divorce increase the risk of depression, more significantly in men than in women (Weissman et al. 1996). This may also require individual therapy or medication.

Separation may involve couples without children or couples with children of any age. Arrangements for children must be made. This may or may not necessitate a legal separation agreement. The therapist also needs to evaluate the relationships among the parent(s), other caregivers, and the children.

When a couple separates, the family therapist can help uncover the problems that prevented the partners from living together successfully on a sustained basis. The primary task for the marital therapist is to remain *neutral* on the decision as to whether to separate or to stay together. Having said that, the experience of the family clinician suggests that rebuilding a once-functioning relationship may be less difficult than finding and building a new one (although initially and/or in anger, it may seem easier to walk away). In some situations both couples and their therapists give up too quickly, whereas in others all parties hold on too long.

We recommend avoiding the extremes and, when appropriate, making reasonable attempts to hold together a relationship that the therapist evaluates as having once been, and having the potential to be, satisfying and functional for *both* partners. Not everything can be changed, but some things can be improved, and the therapist needs to be realistic in helping the husband and wife to accept parts of themselves that cannot be changed. It is critical, however, that the therapist not be the only one in the system trying to hold together the relationship. The decision to separate or to stay together must be made by the couple, not the therapist.

The primary task for the marital therapist is to remain *neutral* on the decision as to whether to separate or to stay together.

Couples who separate because one partner is having an active affair present a more difficult situation. The couple and the therapist must decide whether therapy is possible and whether ongoing contact between spouses is preferable. With highly ambivalent spouses, the one having the affair may move repeatedly between the relationships in a way that is distressing for everyone. (We know of one couple in which the husband returned to his home and then moved out more than 11 times over the course of 1 year. Another couple's separation continued for 8 years with multiple affairs and reconciliations before the wife finally gave up and refused to take back her husband.) Such separations leave everyone, including the children, in limbo and should be time limited if possible. Guidelines for the departing spouse regarding time spent with the children and financial arrangements should be spelled out carefully. Legal separation should be considered to prevent financial problems and to protect against later charges of abandonment, although not all couples find this necessary.

Separation Leading to Divorce

If the couple have decided that divorce is inevitable, a different approach applies. The imminent dissolution of the family as it was produces violent feelings of abandonment, grief, and loss in family members, regardless of their age (it has been said that every divorce is the death of a small civilization). Although it has always been assumed that divorce is easier after children have left home for college or work, even adults in their 30s are often deeply upset by their parents' divorce. The parents and siblings of each spouse may also experience a variety of feelings, including anger and loss. Obviously, the partners who are initiating the divorce may have other feelings as well, such as relief, but loss is always present.

We discussed in Chapter 4 a number of issues related to divorce. The most immediate of these issues have to do with finding separate living arrangements, dealing with children, and redistributing money. In general, men will have the least experience dealing with issues related to the children, and women the least experience with and the most fear related to issues of money. If the husband has left parenting primarily to his wife, he must learn quickly how to relate to his children when he is alone, and he must be actively encouraged to see them frequently and regularly and to be in contact with his wife about sharing parenting. If the wife has assumed that her husband will protect her financially, she may, even in current times, be woefully ignorant about finances and without much earning power. In her panic, she may initiate an unnecessary legal battle over money. Alternatively, she may be so sure that her husband will protect her (or may feel so guilty if she thinks the divorce is her fault) that she will not protect herself and the children financially by fighting hard enough. Another critical issue at this time is how long should the couple live in the same house. If there are children at home, they should be given a few weeks to adjust to the situation; that is, one of the parents should not move out immediately after the divorce is announced. Remaining together for months after divorce has been chosen is often destructive to both parties, although couples who are in poor financial situations, or in whom neither is willing to leave the family home, have done this. The therapist needs to be very active during the early phases of separation to make sure the children are cared for and not used by the parents as pawns. The therapist should help the couple in making coherent, not emotionally driven, decisions in areas such as the redistribution of money. It is usually best to postpone any major decisions, such as selling the house or giving up one's job, until the dust settles. Even if legal divorce has not been initiated, both partners need to seek legal advice about local divorce laws. We strongly advise mediation rather than adversarial legal procedures whenever possible.

After a couple have decided to divorce they often drop out of therapy. They should be encouraged to remain in treatment at least long enough to plan their initial moves; that is, telling the children and their families of origin, making preliminary financial arrangements, and discussing how to handle the physical separation. Some couples may want to review the course of the marriage to further understand what went wrong, but for most couples their emotions are too intense at this time. One or both partners may request individual therapy; sometimes a support group for separating and divorcing partners is also helpful. If the couple have been seen conjointly, it may be helpful to refer them to different therapists rather than have the former couples therapist do the individual work. In other cases the couples therapist may continue with one member (or rarely both). If only one person is seen by the original couples therapist, the other may feel that it is unfair, but some spouses are relieved when their former mate continues in therapy. It is almost impossible for the couples therapist to see, individually, both members of a divorcing couple, because the therapist then becomes privy to information about legal and custody battles from both sides. In addition, the spouses may see the former couples therapist as a link to the other or as favoring the other and may not be able to engage fully in their own work.

Communicating the Issue of Divorce to Children

Telling the children about impending separation is usually a traumatic event for the parents. It is useful to remember that, as with many other issues, this is a process and not a single event. Initially, most children hear very little other than divorce is impending. Children do not really know what separation will mean for them until they have gone through the experience, and they usually do not know what questions to ask at first. The parents must discuss the divorce with the children repeatedly in the ensuing weeks, as plans are made. The parents must convey the following information to the children, either all at once or over time:

> We are getting a divorce. That means we won't be living together. We will always be your parents, and we both love you. That does not change. You will not have to choose between us. (This may or may not come true, and the therapist must help the couple keep the children out of the middle.) You did not cause this divorce and could not have prevented it. As time goes on we will need to keep talking about what is happening with all of us, both the feelings and the changes in our lives. We will talk about what is happening with us, and you need to talk about what you need. You can also talk to your friends and whoever else it would help to talk to.

The children need to be told, as simply as possible in broad strokes, the reasons for the divorce. Teenage children in particular want a reasonable amount of information. If one of the parents is having an active affair, it is not unusual for one or more of the children to already be aware of it. Children tend to overhear conversations and know what is going on with their parents to a larger extent than parents are aware. It is very difficult to keep secret the major reasons for the divorce. Because children today usually have friends whose parents are divorced, there is less stigma and more knowledge than a generation or two ago. However, no child wants the details of his or her parents' sexual or intimate lives. No child wants to sit in judgment as to which parent is at fault. Children need to be reminded that at the time of their birth, their parents loved each other and that they were wanted children. This can help alleviate the children's fear that they were in some way responsible for the divorce.

Children are appropriately also concerned about the details of their daily lives—for example, who will care for me, who will pick me up at school, where do I keep my pets, will I have to leave my house. For most children, their house and their neighborhood are crucial parts of their sense of self. They need to be reassured that regardless of the living arrangements, they will be considered and cared for.

It is generally best for both parents to be present when the initial announcement is made, so that everyone hears the same information. Private talks later are also necessary and appropriate, because each parent must now learn how to parent alone. Parents need to check with each other before conveying potentially explosive information about financial changes or about an affair partner. Talks should be informational and not about the badness of the other parent.

Immediate Issues

The level of conflict during the initial year of living apart varies greatly depending on whether the divorce is sudden or long in the planning, whether one spouse opposes it, and what the level of conflict was like before the separation. Regardless of how long separation was anticipated, the many ensuing changes in feelings and life structure make the situation difficult. If the couple have a fair amount of good will left, or if one partner is so guilty that he or she agrees to almost anything, many decisions can be made quickly. Most often, each decision is complex and will be struggled over.

The early months of the separation are likely to cause irrational feelings and behavior toward the ex-spouse, regardless of how rationally the person is behaving with children or work. For many people the first months in particular are a crazy time, when everything feels upside down. The therapist's job is to keep both partners grounded, allowing them to retell the story over and over, to find some answer to the questions "How did this happen?" and "Am I still a good person?"

For the couple, mediation is often helpful in solving problems. The more the couple can make decisions themselves with a mediator's help, rather than using the judicial system, the better. However, if this does not work, it may be helpful to the couple if the therapist supports the process of finding and working with lawyers. For many people, divorce represents their first experience with the legal system. They may be overwhelmed and unable to be an advocate for their own interests with the lawyer.

Family conflict may escalate during the year after divorce, although it may decrease in high-conflict families. If the parents are having a difficult time they may temporarily find their parental skills decrease, and they may become inconsistent, less affectionate, and less focused on discipline and continuity. Parental quarreling and mutual denigration can result in the children becoming anxious, feeling that they must take sides or, in the case of school-age and early adolescent children, completely cutting off the absent parent. The risk of delinquency is believed to be greater if the parents separate or divorce than if a parent dies. The parameters of marital discord that seem most toxic for children are prolonged marital disputes, parental pathology that impinges on the children's functioning, and the child's lack of a good relationship with either parent. Rapid changes in lifestyle and finances are stressful for everyone and add to the frustration. However, things improve in many families, particularly when the parent who is leaving has been violent, alcoholic, or emotionally abusive. When fathers have left the active parenting to mothers, they may improve their parenting when they have the children by themselves. And many families do very well after an initial period of disruption.

Therapy for Families Facing Divorce

Common treatment alternatives for families facing divorce could include 1) no formal treatment, 2) marital therapy with discussion about the children, 3) family treatment with both ex-spouses and the children, or 4) therapy with the children and only one parent on issues that parent has with the children. Family therapy must have a careful agenda focused primarily on practical matters—for example, what are the living arrangements, or how do the parents handle emergencies, discipline, and child transfers between parents. Central issues include what the children need; whether they are caught between the parents; and whether they have been asked to report on parental activities, ask one parent for money for the other, and so on. Therapy must be focused clearly on problems with the children and not on rehashing the marriage. Although the same therapist can see each parent alone with the children, he or she must also have knowledge and respect for the other partner. A therapist who begins working with the custodial parent and children after the divorce, and does not speak to or meet the noncustodial parent or consider that person's concerns, is likely to worsen the struggles between the spouses. *The Difficult Divorce* (Isaacs et al. 1986) is a good reference book for therapists working with couples who have no ability to compromise or deal with each other. For the children alone, intervention is also possible but not mandatory. It may include a children's support group or individual therapy. It is also important to inform others who have contact with the children (especially at their schools) that the parents have divorced.

A difficult issue is that of introducing children to their parents' new love relationships. Children may not want to meet a parent's new lover, particularly if the lover was an affair partner for whom the parent left the marriage. Even if the children are ready, the ex-spouse may be furious about having the children meet the affair partner, whom he or she may see as immoral or evil. However, if the children are to have a relationship with both parents, they must eventually find some way to deal with the new lover, at least with regard if not affection. The therapist must help the family deal with the realities of the situation, although if a great deal of animosity is present, it is generally wise to wait at least a few months after the separation before introducing the new person. New relationships should not be introduced to the children unless the relationships are potentially serious ones. If possible, live-in status should be reserved for partners with whom marriage is planned; otherwise, their ambiguous status in the house may lead to real problems with the children. Sleepover status is a highly emotional topic, and no clear guidelines are obvious in most situations. A good rule of thumb is that new partners should not sleep over unless the relationship has reached a relatively committed status.

Divorce and Postdivorce Treatment

The presence of divorce should not lead one to think of only pathological sequelae, because an intact, conflict-ridden family can be more detrimental to children than is a stable home in which the parents are divorced. As such, divorce can be a positive solution to a destructive family situation. This seems to be especially true in the presence of a rejecting, demeaning, or psychiatrically ill parent. Most adults report positive feelings about their parents' divorce when surveyed years later and eventually conclude that their parents made the right decision. Adult children have different attitudes toward their mothers and fathers, however, and a majority of the children had at least some "very negative" feelings about their mothers. A lesser number harbored such feelings about their fathers. A crucial issue for divorce therapy is the fact that a majority of adult children report that their mothers maligned their fathers, whereas only 12% said their fathers spoke critically about their ex-spouses. This must be seen in the context that most mothers were custodial parents who were doing most of the parenting without spousal support.

As to the long-term effects of the divorce process, research is complex and somewhat contradictory. The problem is that no study has been done comparing those parents who divorce with those who are discordant and contemplating divorce but stay together or with those who are discordant but never contemplated divorce. In one of the earliest and best-known studies, Wallerstein (1988) suggested that some children of divorced families have strong feelings about it even 10 years later. She conducted a systematic follow-up study of a small sample of children of divorce (with no control subjects) and found that 1) three in five felt rejected by at least one of the parents; 2) in at least half the families both parents remained angry; and 3) as expected, children conceptualize and feel differently about the divorce, depending on their age. She suggests that divorcing parents apologize for the pain they are causing their children, express their own sadness so as to allow children to express their feelings about the ending of the relationship, and give children concrete details about future plans as soon as possible. Her age-specific comments include:

1. For the adolescent: Try not to lean on the child for support—don't get lost in one's own needs to the detriment of helping the adolescent deal with his or her own needs.
2. For children age 9–12 years: The angriest child tends to take sides and act as if he or she understands the issue even though he or she may understand very little. This child needs to be told that the parent's fight is a battle in which he or she should not get involved.
3. For younger children: The important thing to remember is to reassure the child that he or she will still have both a mother and a father. Abandonment can be a central issue for younger children. For preschoolers, continued, ongoing contact from both parents on a regular and frequent basis is best.

It must be kept in mind that these comments are generalizations. For example, although fear of abandonment is preeminent in younger children, older children and adolescents often experience similar feelings. Additionally, family stressors often cause children to regress emotionally and behaviorally to earlier stages of development. Thus a prediction of the predominant issues caused by divorce is best made on a case-by-case basis.

Many authors have issued strong challenges to the idea that divorce is inevitably harmful, pointing to the fact that at least 50% of divorced partners have amicable relationships and to the positive functioning of nontraditional families for both parents and children. Ahrons (1994) reviews this literature and describes the process of creating a functional divorce. An organization begun in 1997, the Council on Contemporary Families, has begun working to collect this research and disseminate it and to consider ways of exploring the needs of contemporary nontraditional families.

Single-Parent and Binuclear Families

"Single-parent" families may include a variety of people in the parenting system. A parent with legal custody of the children may be living with his or her parents, a lover, or a friend. Even if the noncustodial parent visits infrequently, he (usually it is a he) may still be very important in the children's lives. Alternatively, the single parent and children may form a tightly self-contained unit. In binuclear families, both biological parents are responsible for child care. Although the general rules of family therapy apply to all families, single-parent and binuclear families experience additional issues.

Hierarchy is a complex issue in single-parent families. A grandparent may take over a majority of the childrearing duties, especially if the single parent and children are living in the grandparent's house. A lover may be feel that he or she should take over disciplinary duties without any clear mandate to do so. Because the custodial parent may be overwhelmed by a combination of work and household duties, one or more of the children may act as companion to the parent or surrogate parent to younger children. In other cases, the family may operate with a high level of democracy, with all children sharing more of the power and responsibility than in a two-adult household. It is important that the therapist consider the possibilities for health inherent in nontraditional models rather than assume that the only possible functioning family is a mother who is totally head of the household. However, if conflicts occur, it should be clear that the custodial parent has final say in the matter. Children must not be overburdened with parenting responsibilities, but they are capable of taking on a reasonable share of the chores when it is obvious that help is needed. For many children, a single-parent family is one in which their contribution is needed and welcomed.

> If conflicts occur, it should be clear that the custodial parent has final say in the matter.

In therapy, it is important to speak to all family members rather than only to a parent or one child. If the family is living with grandparents, it is important to include the grandparents in at least some of the meetings. The therapist must be willing to work with the family to determine the best system available, rather than assuming the parent must carry the entire burden himself or herself.

If the custodial parent has no supports, she (or he) is prone to depression and demoralization. The therapist's job is to help the parent form a functioning support system rather than to try to be the support system.

In binuclear families the central issue involves the multiple systems in which the children must operate. Not only must the parents collaborate on clear rules for the children, but if one or both parents remarry, the new spouses also will be involved (see next section).

In single-parent families, the launching of the children, particularly the oldest, is often problematic because they have been such crucial supports for the parent and the younger children. Sometimes the oldest child becomes briefly symptomatic immediately before he or she is ready to leave for college, as a way of testing whether it is safe to go.

Stepfamilies

With John S. Visher, M.D., and
Emily B. Visher, Ph.D.

For the majority of divorcing spouses, at least one will remarry, forming a stepfamily. The question is how to treat these families. A recent study of responses to stepfamily therapy provides valuable insights into what 280 remarried couples found to be most helpful in their stepfamily therapy (Pasley et al. 1996). Besides responses that commented on the importance of therapist warmth and good basic skills, couples reported four specific types of interventions that were particularly helpful: 1) validating their feelings and normalizing stepfamily dynamics and issues, 2) supplying psychoeducation, 3) reducing their feelings of helplessness, and 4) helping them strengthen their couple relationship. Respondents were also asked to list any therapeutic elements that were not helpful to them. Nearly 50% of the negative comments concerned the therapist's "lack of knowledge about stepfamily issues and dynamics."

Goals

We suggest the following goals for therapists working with remarried couples with children:

1. To consolidate the remarried couple as a unit and their authority in the system, helping the two adults to understand and develop a modus operandi to further their romantic love requirements and their necessity to parent.
2. To consolidate the parental authority in the system among biological and stepparents, with the formation of a collaborative coparenting team.
3. As a corollary to the preceding goal, to help children deal with and minimize the continuation and exacerbation of loyalty conflicts between their two biological parents and between each biological parent and the corresponding stepparent.
4. To facilitate mourning of the nuclear family, former partner, old neighborhoods, friends, and way of life. A period of mourning prepares the way to accept and to grow with the new reality of the stepfamily.
5. To be sure there is a secure place for the children's development and to maximize the potential within both family systems. It is hoped that the two systems can be synergistic at the same time that the children learn there is more than one way to deal with many life situations.
6. To accept and integrate the children's need for individuation from both families and for more peer involvement. At the other extreme, some children may prematurely develop great peer involvement if they cannot find appropriate love and nurturance in the household systems of either biological parent. One approach may be to strengthen the bond and acceptance of the children in one if not both family systems.
7. To help family members accept and tolerate their differences from some idealized nuclear family model. These differences include the following:

    a. Lack of complete control of money and income.
    b. Shared responsibility for children; some lack of control (e.g., when child is in the other parent's home).
    c. The reality that children may neither like nor love a stepparent and vice versa.
    d. Different feeling to the families. The stepfamily will not feel the same to a participant as did his or her former nuclear family. There are different levels of bonding and different characters playing different if seemingly similar roles; these latter roles need clarification for all involved.
    e. Different rules and expectations likely to exist in the two homes. Flexibil-

ity is necessary for the children to navigate situations that do not meet their own wishes.

f. Difficulty in living in a stepfamily structure. Sometimes the stepfamily is more complex, more persons are involved, models and guidelines are less clear, and every stepfamily is in a sense a pioneer family; however, the stepfamily system can be regarded and promoted as an enriching one, enabling the children to avail themselves of more diverse parental and interactive models.

Evaluation and Treatment

Stepfamilies need to be evaluated and treated in a context of awareness of appropriate stepfamily norms (see Chapter 4). Using a nuclear family model can lead stepfamily members to pursue unrealistic goals with unfortunate consequences. In this section we discuss some issues related to stepfamilies and the implications of these issues for therapy (Table 21–1).

The complexities and intricacies of stepfamily relationships appear to require a systemic perspective even when the therapist is working with a single individual from a stepfamily (i.e., outside the system) (Sager et al. 1983). The therapist must think in terms of the family, no matter who or how many family members he or she is treating. This approach is also important when the stepfamily has multiple problems. In addition to other types of interventions (e.g., for drug abuse, chronic illness), dealing with stepfamily dynamics and issues can reduce tensions, thus giving family members more energy to deal with other difficulties.

The question of whom to see in therapy is important. It can be detrimental to see the new couple and the children together in the same session before the couple have arrived at the stage of family integration in which they have some ability to be supportive of each other and to work together on family issues. Seeing the couple alone is an important way to demonstrate the importance of the couple and to help the two individuals to strengthen their relationship. Some therapists have meetings with all those involved with the children (i.e., ex-spouses, lovers, stepparents). Unfortunately, with preexisting parent-child alliances, the parent who has remarried often feels it is betraying to these relationships to form a strong new couple bond. However, children need the family stability and modeling that can come from association with a unified, well-functioning couple.

Even when the couple are working well together, step relationships do not necessarily develop spontaneously. The family may need inclusive family therapy to work out these relationships. Communication and having special one-to-one times between parents and children, and between stepparents

TABLE 21–1. Differences between stepfamilies and nuclear families; therapeutic implications

How stepfamilies differ from nuclear families	Therapeutic implications
Stepfamilies and nuclear families have different structural characteristics.	The therapist must evaluate the family using stepfamily norms; a nuclear family model is not valid.
There is little or no family loyalty in stepfamilies.	Initially, seeing the family members together may be unproductive.
Before integration, stepfamilies react to transitional stresses.	The first focus needs to be on the transitional adjustment process, not on intrapsychic processes.
Society compares stepfamilies negatively with nuclear families.	There is a basic need for acceptance and validation as a worthwhile family unit.
Stepfamilies experience a long integration period with predictable stages.	The stage of family development is very important in the assessment of whom to see in therapy.
There is not a breakdown of family homeostasis in stepfamilies; equilibrium has never been established.	With normalization and education, stability can emerge from chaos and ignorance of the norms.
Stepfamilies have complicated supra-family systems.	The complications of the family need to be kept in mind during therapy. Drawing a genogram helps.
Stepfamilies have experienced many losses for most individuals.	Grief work may be necessary.
Stepfamilies involve preexisting parent-child coalitions.	Developing a secure couple relationship is essential. Many times, permission is needed to do this.
A solid couple relationship does not signify good stepparent-stepchild relationships.	Step-relationships require special attention, separate from the couple relationship.
The balance of power differs in stepfamilies and nuclear families.	Stepparents have very little authority in the family initially; therefore, discipline issues need to be handled by the biological parent. Children have more power, which needs to be channeled positively.
There is less family control in stepfamilies, because there is an influential parent elsewhere or in memory.	Appropriate control can be fostered to lessen the anxiety engendered by helplessness.

(continued)

TABLE 21–1. Differences between stepfamilies and nuclear families; therapeutic implications *(continued)*

How stepfamilies differ from nuclear families	Therapeutic implications
Children have more than two parenting figures in stepfamilies.	There is a need to think in terms of a parenting coalition, not a parenting couple.
Ambiguous family boundaries exist in stepfamilies, with little agreement as to family history.	These losses and stresses may require attention.
Initially stepfamilies have no family history.	Members need to share their histories and develop family rituals and ways of doing things.
The emotional climate is intense and unexpected in stepfamilies.	Empathy with other family members can be encouraged by understanding the human needs that are not being met: to be loved and appreciated, to belong, and to have control over one's life.

Source. Visher EB, Visher JS: *Therapy With Stepfamilies.* New York, Brunner/Mazel, 1996, pp 41–42. Reprinted with permission.

and stepchildren, can be important in building and maintaining relationships. For children in stepfamilies this approach can reduce the loss of more exclusive parental attention and can foster communication and bonding between stepparents and stepchildren.

The balance of power does not reside initially with the couple in stepfamilies. The stepparent joins the biological parent and his or her children but has no authority as far as the children are concerned. Many remarried biological parents make the error of expecting the stepparent to take on a disciplinary role with the children. Research indicates that the stepparent needs take on the co-manager role slowly; meanwhile, the biological parent needs to become, or remain, the active parenting adult with his or her children and also needs to require civil behavior in the household. These steps can create a climate in which step relationships can develop and stepparents can begin to take on a co-management role with the biological parent. With young children this may take 1 to 2 years (Stern 1978); with older children it usually takes longer (Papernow 1993).

Many stepfamily adults need psychoeducation about discipline and roles for stepparents. Adults are relying on their previous experiences in their families of origin and former marriage(s). Therapists can help these adults share these expectations, join them by understanding their positions, and help them to pursue more realistic stepfamily goals. If the couple is reluctant to change unproductive patterns, they may be willing to try a different approach for 3 or 4 weeks as an experiment. Frequently, positive experiences change the family dynamics so that continuing change is supported. Finally, when the stepparent is alone with the children the biological parent's authority needs to be delegated to the stepparent, as one delegates authority to a baby-sitter or other caregiver, by bringing the family together and letting the children know the stepparent is in charge when only that adult is present.

A great deal of the complexity in stepfamilies comes from the fact that there are more than two parenting adults in the children's lives. With a biological parent in another household, there may be three or four parenting adults if both parents are remarried, and children may be living part of the time in each of these two households. When parents feel insecure, they tend to fear loss of their children's love to the other parent and perhaps to that parent's new partner. Another concern is the loss of control and sense of helplessness that arises because of the mere existence of the other household, and the therapeutic task can become one of helping the couple build an adequate boundary around its household and learn to respect the boundary around the other household. Gates in the boundaries are needed for the children so that they can come and go comfortably. Adults often need help controlling the things they can control in their own household and letting go of concern about situations in the other household. Gaining control and accepting the limits of their influence is helpful in reducing the feelings of helplessness that remarried adults may feel.

Forming a parenting coalition of parents and stepparents can be difficult, but with help it is possible (Visher EB and Visher JS 1988, 1990). Ordinarily this requires the new couple to develop a solid, secure bond before they are emotionally able to form a working relationship with the children's other household. The lesser the hostility is between the households, the fewer the loyalty conflicts for the children and the greater the satisfaction for the adults. In some situations it can be helpful to bring the adults together to work on issues involving the children. Bringing them together in therapy becomes a possibility when each parent has formed a strong bond with his or her new partner. The therapist needs to make direct, personal contact with each household, state clearly the purpose of the joint meeting, and then make certain the agenda of the session does not include potentially explosive areas unconnected with the present welfare of the children. Older children may need to be included when their situation is being discussed.

The emotional climate in stepfamilies is often intense, particularly during the early stages of stepfamily integration. A helpful way to conceptualize the reasons for this intensity is to understand and recognize the inability of new stepfamilies to meet three very basic human emotional needs: 1) to belong to a group, 2) to be cared about and loved by a few special people, and 3) to have some control over one's life.

Because of all the changes and unfamiliarity in the household, stepfamily members can feel out of control, not accepted by the new people in their lives, and as though they do not belong in this unfamiliar group. Parents who have remarried frequently fear the loss of their children, whom they love and by whom they are loved. Stepparents in particular feel unloved, alienated from the group, and with little control. Children are upset by their lack of control over all the losses and events occurring in their lives.

For therapists, then, the basic task is to help family members gain an understanding of these basic emotional needs so that they can have empathy for everyone in the family and be understood in return. The family members need to find ways in which to communicate, to fill in history with one another, and to further accelerate the sense of control and belonging by developing rituals and predictable day-to-day ways of doing things. Being cared about requires the building of relationships. This takes time and positive shared memories, both on a one-to-one basis and as a family unit.

Many stepfamilies that come for therapy need the therapist to validate their feelings and the worth and viability of their families, to normalize the situations that arise in such families, to find ways to deal effectively with the challenges, and to find support for the new couple relationship. With this assistance stepfamilies can work toward satisfactory integration, deal more effectively with disruptive situations, and bring satisfaction and happiness to the adults and to the children.

Cohabiting Couples

Cohabitation, once seen as pathology, sin, or nonconformity, is now a common developmental phase for young people who are developing intimacy or for older people after divorce. About 50% of marrying couples have lived together for some time before marriage. Cohabiting couples who come for therapy are most likely to present with the need to determine the future of the relationship. Couples who have been living together for some time and are unable to make the decision to marry tend to divide into two categories: those in which one partner is committed and the other is uncommitted and those in which both partners have felt the relationship to be unsatisfactory but are afraid to be on their own.

Therapy consists of clarifying each partner's position and helping the couple think through what would have to occur in order to make the relationship go forward (or end). Each partner can be asked to take the other's position—that is, the less committed partner could explain why marriage would be a good idea, and the more committed one why it would be better to break up. Often, when pressed, the uncommitted partner can finally admit that he or she has no intention of changing, or the more committed one can admit that if he or she does not get married, and soon, he or she will leave. Faced with the real possibility of ending the relationship, one or both partners may change their positions. If both partners are unhappy, the therapist should initiate a careful exploration of the relationship, in the same way the therapist would with a married couple.

Occasionally a couple will come in with wedding plans already made and with one partner very frightened about impending marriage. Both partners should have the chance for some individual therapy time. In some cases, investigation proves that an episode of violence, or a flirtation or affair with another person, has occurred. It is within the therapist's prerogative to recommend that the wedding be postponed if he or she thinks the couple are in serious trouble. Despite the distress caused to the in-laws and the difficulties associated with canceling contracted-for wedding plans, we believe it is worse to go through with a wedding that one partner believes should not take place. Obviously, the couple often will not follow this advice, but it should be considered a possibility. Often the couple will be able to do serious therapeutic work once the furor around the wedding has quieted.

Other couples enter therapy seeking help with communication, sexuality, or children and are clear that the question of commitment is not at issue. The therapist should proceed as if this were true, although commitment issues may surface later, and a high index of suspicion is wise.

Serial Relationships

Even if a person has previously been in multiple relationships, he or she will enter treatment for a specific relationship at a specific time either alone or with the partner. The critical questions are whether the person has been making the same set of mistakes each time or has been making new ones, and whether he or she has grown developmentally. A common pattern is as follows: A man marries first a woman whom his parents approve of and who seems "safe," then someone totally different, of a different religion or race. Finally, around age 40 years, he figures out who he is and what he wants and marries someone who is like him culturally but is interesting to him emotionally. Similarly, a woman might marry cold, abusive men until she decides that she is worth something and then marries someone who respects her. A less hopeful pattern is a person who marries two or three people in succession, each with the same serious problem, such as alcoholism, violence, or mental illness. The therapist's job is to help the person work on his or her own unfinished business enough to make healthy choices in the future.

Suggested Readings

Isaacs M, Montalvo B, Abelsohn D: The Difficult Divorce: Therapy for Children and Families. New York, Basic Books, 1986
This excellent research-based book provides an extremely useful clinical model for solving problems in families facing separation and divorce. It contributes a clear, straightforward systemic perspective, and the rich case illustrations are superb.

Visher EB, Visher JS: Therapy With Step Families. New York, Brunner/Mazel, 1996
Focused on stepfamilies, this book offers clear, straightforward guidelines for clinical assessment. The therapeutic framework is practical for all families in transition.

References

Ahrons C: The Good Divorce. New York, Harper Collins, 1994

Isaacs M, Montalvo B, Abelsohn D: The Difficult Divorce: Therapy for Children and Families. New York, Basic Books, 1986

Papernow P: Becoming a Stepfamily: Patterns of Development in Remarried Families. San Francisco, CA, Jossey-Bass, 1993

Pasley K, Rhoden L, Visher EB, et al: Stepfamilies in therapy: insights from adult stepfamily members. J Marital Fam Ther 22:343–357, 1996

Sager CJ, Brown HS, Crohn H, et al: Treating the Remarried Family. New York, Brunner/Mazel, 1983

Stern PA: Stepfather families: integration around child discipline. Issues in Mental Health Nursing 1:50–56, 1978

Visher EB, Visher JS: Old Loyalties, New Ties: Therapeutic Strategies with Stepfamilies. New York, Brunner/Mazel, 1988

Visher EB, Visher JS: Parenting coalitions after remarriage: dynamics and therapeutic guidelines. Family Relations 38:65–70, 1990

Wallerstein J: Second Chances. New York, Ticknor & Fields, 1988

Weissman MM, Bland RC, Canino GJ, et al: Cross-national epidemiology of major depression and bipolar disorder. J Am Med Assoc, 1996

Birth of a Notion, Susan Kay Williams, 1974. Private collection.

CHAPTER 22

The Couple and Reproductive Issues

Objectives for the Reader

- To be aware of the complex family systems issues involved in childbearing decisions, pregnancy, and birth
- To consider the effect of reproductive trauma (i.e., pregnancy loss, unwanted pregnancy, and infertility) on the family
- To understand how assisted reproductive technology and adoption affect the family system
- To learn how to support a couple's decision making and be helpful in times of reproductive stress

Introduction

Because so much of family life is centered around having and raising children, issues of reproduction—including the decision to conceive, pregnancy and childbirth, and the reproductive trauma of pregnancy loss, unwanted pregnancy, and infertility—produce a series of critical points in the family's life. Recent and almost incredible technological changes in so-called assisted reproduction have added complex legal and psychological dimensions to age-old human concerns. Adoption, another way of creating family, has its own set of concerns.

In this chapter we review the family implications of what have been labeled in the past as women's problems. Everyone in the family, not only the husband but also existing children and the partners' families of origin, have a deep interest in the birth and rearing of children. For each reproductive issue we review the salient family responses and suggest ways in which the family therapist can help the family make decisions and deal with problems. All reproductive events include individual, couples, and larger family issues, making this area another example of the need for attention to all levels of the system.

The Wish for a Child

Until the advent of effective contraception in the twentieth century, the issue of whether one wanted a child was not open for discussion—one's choices were either to have children or to be celibate. After the scientific development of contraceptives, it was still illegal to distribute them in this country for many years. When it became possible (after an acrimonious political and legal battle) to distribute contraceptives, they were still used primarily to space children and decrease family size. Only since the 1960s has it been common for people to remain childless by choice. Most people still want children, although they are having them later and are having fewer of them. Reasons for having children range from pleasure in the company of children and a wish for family life, to more self-focused reasons (i.e., a desire for immortality or for children who will act as caretakers in later years), to a wish to please the family of origin. Parental pressure is still a powerful motivator, and for many people, pregnancy is still an accident.

For many couples, the question of children is a contentious one. Couples may disagree about when to start a family or how many children to have. Both partners may be ambivalent about having any children. The most difficult situations are ones in which one partner wants children and the other strongly does not. This may occur if the partners did not discuss their differences before marriage or if, despite the discussion, one partner believed he or she could change the other's mind. Sometimes one spouse changes his or her mind after marriage (e.g., a woman who says she can live without children at age 25 may have a very difference mental set by age 35). Reasons for not wanting children can range from believing that one would be a bad parent because of a dysfunctional childhood or one's own psychiatric symptoms, to preferring a career and lifestyle focus, to being uncertain the marriage will last, to having grown children from a previous marriage and being reluctant to begin parenting again.

The therapist's job is to help the couple find ways of resolving the conflict so that to the extent possible neither partner feels that he or she has lost completely. The therapist should discuss carefully family-of-origin issues of both partners, looking at each partner's fears and wishes and how likely they are to be realized. For example, a woman with a strong family history of schizophrenia and a psychotic mother has biological and psychological reasons to be afraid for her children and herself. Similarly, a man whose mother had a several-year postpartum depression after his birth may be afraid that his wife will also have one. The couple's current relationship must be evaluated. If the couple are arguing constantly, or if violence, alcoholism, or unemployment are present in the family, each partner may be appropriately afraid of the stress a child would bring. Finally, the therapist must examine the couple's fantasies of the future family. This enables the couple to consider more carefully their fears of what might happen and their various competencies. Although the therapist cannot make the decision for the couple, he or she can certainly add information about the joys and stresses of having children. The therapist must point out to couples when they appear to be operating on myth rather than fact. For example, the fact that one had an easy time with a first child does not mean an easy ride with a second or third. The therapist should discourage the couple from making an agreement that only one parent will be the active parent (e.g., the husband may agree to get the wife pregnant but not to do any child care). This situation is very destructive to the child, who feels abandoned by one parent, and to the parent who is doing all the child care, who invariably feels resentful.

In some cases the couple cannot resolve the disagreement about having any children and the spouse who wants a child initiates a divorce and later remarries. In other cases the couple argue until the decision becomes moot because of the wife's menopause. With the advent of better obstetrical care and the improvement in health in general, some women may be able to have children into their late 40s. However, fertility drops sharply in the 40s, and couples who delay a first child that long may face serious problems.

Pregnancy and Childbirth

The process of pregnancy is fraught with anxiety and joy. Before the twentieth century, death in childbirth was a relatively common occurrence, and despite current technology childbirth is still not a risk-free process for mother or child. Although it is a particular risk for poor mothers who lack prenatal care, anyone having a child can experience serious complications. There are also psychological risks. The dependency of the infant changes the mother's and father's internal sense of identity and competence. The process of pregnancy is different depending on the mother's circumstances. For example, a 14-year-old girl living with her mother will have an experience different from that of a 25-year-old woman living with her husband, and they will each have an experience different from that of a 41-year-old new mother whose 55-year-old husband has children by a previous marriage.

The woman's experience includes coping with the mood shifts of rapid hormone changes. Many women feel tired or depressed during the first trimester, happy during the second, and tired and irritable during the third. The woman must deal with the shifting contours of her body, which she may experience as beautiful or terrible depending on her need to be thin. The couple must deal with the wife's need for more emotional support and with her physical limitations at a time when she may be less able to take care of her husband's emotional needs. For some husbands, envy and anxiety are provoked by their wives' ability to reproduce. These men may respond by engaging in pursuits designed to prove their masculinity (from motorcycles to affairs), by developing sympathetic physical symptoms (a significant number of men experience headaches, backaches, and so on while their wives are pregnant), or by becoming deeply involved in the process of pregnancy, nest building, and so on (Liebenberg 1973). If violence has occurred within the couple, it sometimes increases during pregnancy.

First pregnancies involve issues of taking on the identity of parents, and increasing memories of one's own childhood bring up fears of being a parent or repeating the mistakes of one's own parents. The need to redo one's relationship with one's own parents to become more adult makes this a good time for family-of-origin work. Second and third pregnancies are less likely to be as emotionally stressful as the first, but they may be more difficult physically. Sexuality may be altered by the man's fear of hurting his wife, his seeing her as a mother rather than a sexual being, his discomfort with her body, or the need for different positions as the pregnancy progresses. The wife's sexuality is more hormone driven. Most women experience a decrease in desire during the first trimester, but many experience an increase during the second, and another decrease during the third.

Childbirth itself is a critical event in the couple's life. Because this is a shared event for most couples today, prenatal childbirth education classes are important. If the husband and wife cannot act as a team during this time, it may leave permanent scars. Single women must decide who they want for labor coach and who their primary support persons will be during pregnancy and afterward. With the current practice in some hospitals of allowing in the labor room other family members, including older children, the mother or couple must decide who is to be included.

Expectant couples who come to therapy are sometimes in crisis about continuing the marriage, and the usual couples issues and techniques apply. Couples with or without commitment issues also need education about how pregnancy stresses them and practical advice about dealing with jobs, parents, and planning for the labor and the first weeks at home.

Women with histories of severe mental illness often do well during pregnancy; however, symptoms may increase during the postpartum period, necessitating careful monitoring by the family and physician. Women with a history of depressive disorder must be evaluated for postpartum depression and psychosis. Severe postpartum depression and postpartum psychosis are psychiatric emergencies. Medication is almost always necessary. Infanticide and suicide can result from untreated illness (American Psychiatric Association 1994; Kaplan et al 1994). Evaluation of women with postpartum disorders includes evaluation of the family system. The therapist must ask about communication and parenting roles and values. Also, the mental status of the partner must be evaluated given the enormous stress of the situation. Couples therapy can be very effective in such situations.

The first weeks home with a new baby are a time for the couple to begin the process of renegotiating their relationship. Pregnancy and the birth of the first child alter the relationship between the partners and between the prospective parents and their parents, as each now moves up a generation, with the latter becoming grandparents. Having children also increases the number of tasks the couple must perform and limits their private time together. Because the father often feels a need to go back to work, and the mother is often breast-feeding, the couple will fall into a traditional pattern quickly (i.e., she does most of the child care, he returns to work and takes care of the baby when needed), unless the couple work specifically at having both partners involved with the baby.

Conflicts also occur about how soon the mother should return to work. Researchers vary in their beliefs about the results of early return to work on bonding between mother and child. The trend toward immediate return (4–6 weeks) is very hard for the mother, whatever its effect on the baby. Many women and some men opt to downsize career expectations or take more time off. Issues of child care must be dealt with before the mother returns to work. Child care may involve the father, other relatives, hired help, infant day care, or one or both parents staying home at least part time. These issues may become complex and acrimonious, or just difficult, and the family may need to try out several methods before finding one that meets its needs. The United States is the only Western country that does not provide organized government-supported child care. Because the gap is filled only slightly by workplace-supported child care, parents are essentially on their own. Grand-parents may be very helpful during the child's first year, or they may stress the situation further by demanding more care and affection, giving intrusive advice, or fighting over the child's name. Issues of boundaries and fairness will come up in the larger family at this time.

Premature babies need an enormous amount of care and are particularly stressful for parents. They may be in the hospital for weeks or months after delivery. When home they are often harder to soothe and feed, may need monitoring, and may at first have a high-pitched and unpleasant cry. Parents need a great deal of support to deal with the fear and the practical issues sur-rounding a very premature birth.

Miscarriage, Fetal Death, and Stillbirth

A pregnancy that ends in the death of the child is a devastating experience for the family. The reality and intensity of parental emotional attachment to the unborn child is well known. Attachment increases sharply in both parents the first time they feel the baby move. The internalized representation of the fe-tus is a mixture of fantasy and reality, with projected aspects, both desirable and undesirable, of self and spouse. In addition, the ability to carry a success-ful pregnancy feels like a test of womanhood to the pregnant woman. The more the child was wanted, the more ambivalence or disagreement there was within the couple about the pregnancy, and the longer the experience of the pregnancy, the greater the possibility of family disruption.

Early miscarriages may produce an asymmetry between husband and wife in the grief process, because during the early months of pregnancy the child may be far more real to the mother who is experiencing bodily changes than to the father who does not have this experience, and because the woman ex-periences a failure of her body. Because men often prefer to grieve in private, or if the husband is less involved, the husband may not be able to support his wife adequately, which may increase the partners' isolation from each other. The therapist should support the couple in talking about the loss, help them accept the fact that they may have asymmetric experience of that loss, and educate them that a grief process is likely to take months rather than weeks and should not be hurried. The therapist must help the couple think through the meaning and explanation for the loss.

The stillbirth of a full-term baby is an even more devastating experience. Bereavement in this instance differs from conventional bereavement because of the unusual psychological attributes of the lost object, the unique psychobiological climate in which it occurs, and the multitude of sociocultural attitudes that surround pregnancy and stillbirth (Condon 1986). The family's first needs are to have a clear explanation of the death and a chance to see and name the child. The family needs to plan a funeral or some type of service and acknowledge the child as a real person. Attempts to prevent grief by keeping the parents from seeing the dead child or by pretending it didn't really exist only serve to block mourning (Patel 1993).

Abortion

A woman who becomes pregnant when she does not wish it has a different psychological response to the pregnancy and its loss. Women who are desperate not to have a child will risk anything to avoid the pregnancy, as we know from the era in which abortions were illegal and carried great physical risks. If the woman is ambivalent, the decision to abort becomes that much harder and the sequelae more complex. Few women make the decision to abort lightly. Numerous studies have indicated that the majority of women do not have severe psychological reactions to an abortion, although many experience guilt or sadness and persistent fantasies of the child (Dagg 1991). Few have serious psychiatric difficulties. Certainly the response is not as powerful or long lasting as it is in a woman who carried a baby to term and gave it up for adoption. If the abortion is for medical reasons with a wanted child (e.g., amniocentesis reveals that the fetus has serious birth defects), the experience is often agonizing and the grief process prolonged.

If the mother and father are married or in a relationship, conflicts between the partners about whether to abort can profoundly affect the relationship. For the therapist, the issues must be to help the woman make a decision in an atmosphere of a great deal of pressure; to include the father, if possible; and, if the mother is an adolescent, to include her parents when appropriate. Therapists whose own value system is opposed to abortion must let their patients know this at the outset of treatment.

Infertility

Infertility is usually defined as the inability to conceive a pregnancy after a year or more of regular intercourse without contraceptives, or the inability to carry a pregnancy to live birth. Infertility can be primary (i.e., no successful pregnancies) or secondary (i.e., after one or more successful pregnancies). Biological causes of infertility are equally divided between men and women; in

20% of cases it is a combined problem. Now that we understand the biology of reproduction more completely, we realize that psychogenic causes of infertility, once thought to be common, are actually quite rare.

Approximately 50% of infertile couples will conceive with proper medical treatment. Infertility workups, however, can be financially and psychologically exhausting, involving the couple in increasing preoccupation with their sex and reproductive life and in increasingly painful procedures. Fertility drugs can drastically alter the infertile partner's moods for months at a time. The psychological reactions to infertility are complex. Loss of and grief for one's dreams for the future, anger at others who conceive easily, and a loss of a sense of power and control are extremely common (especially among those who are used to getting what they want by just working harder). The couple may develop a sense of isolation, especially from friends who are having children. For the partner identified as having the fertility problem, shame, loss of self-esteem, and guilt are common; for the fertile partner, anger and a loss of respect for the other partner are seldom admitted but not infrequent. Because attempts to diagnose and solve the problem may take months or even years, ongoing involvement with the medical community, endless decisions (e.g., Should we change doctors? Should we try one more round of fertility drugs? Should we give up and adopt?) mean that the couple must be constantly aware of the problem and communicate about it. Meanwhile, other life decisions may have to be put on hold (e.g., Why buy a house, if we will not have children?). One partner may demand to press forward for more studies, procedures, and so on long after the other partner has given up. Sex may stop being a source of pleasure and become only a tool for contraception.

The therapist's job is to allow a place for strong feelings, to keep the lines of communication open, to facilitate decision making, and to keep the couple connected to their normal life. The couple can be encouraged to focus on loving sexual expression during the wife's nonfertile periods to keep sexuality from being limited only to times when conception is possible. In addition, the therapist can support the couple in dealing with the complexities of the medical world. Meyers et al. (1995a, 1995b) have explained the major diagnostic and treatment issues about infertility related to the family therapist.

> The therapist's job is to allow a place for strong feelings, to keep the lines of communication open, to facilitate decision making, and to keep the couple connected to their normal life.

Assisted Reproductive Technology and Collaborative Reproduction

Many forms of assisted reproductive technology are available, depending on the source of the couple's infertility. These forms include donor insemination; egg, sperm, or embryo transfer, in which the couple's (or a donor's) egg, sperm, or embryo are placed in the wife's uterus; or surrogacy, in which the embryo is implanted in a surrogate for the purpose of gestation. The child could in theory end up with five parents: genetic mother, genetic father, gestational (surrogate) mother, and parent of rearing. In practice, for all methods except insemination with the husband's sperm or in vitro fertilization of the couple's own genetic material, at least one other person is involved in the genetic mix. The medical interventions of assisted reproduction, until recently swathed in secrecy and complexity, are difficult to deal with psychologically. When the process is kept secret from family and friends, the couple's sense of isolation is increased. In addition, the history of how the family came about will shape how family members create meaning and define who they are to one another.

The therapist may enter the picture at any point in the process, from the original infertility workup to helping the parents deal with how to tell the children the circumstances of their birth several years later. In terms of telling the children, single parents and gay or lesbian parents have no choice about early disclosure of how their children were conceived. Opinion seems to be moving toward explanation rather than secrecy for children in heterosexual families. This is because secrets such as these alter family dynamics, strain trust in the relationship, and create mystifying concerns and expectations. For health reasons a child should be entitled to his or her genetic information (Reitz and Watson 1992). Explanations are usually given as soon as the child is cognitively old enough to understand (i.e., in the early primary school years). As in adoptive families, the parents must help the child make a distinction between genetic parent and parent of rearing. See Bernstein (1995) for one of the best and only discussions of this topic. We are awaiting the results of further research into the psychological effects of assisted reproduction as the first children born of the new technology come of age.

Adoption

Adoption forms an extended system that includes the birth parents, the child, and the adoptive parents. For much of the twentieth century, attempts were made by adoption services and families to pretend that adoptive families were exactly like birth families. By making the whole adoption process closed and secret, they hoped family members would be able to forget or avoid the differences in how the family came to be. But this approach ignores the inherent losses and hope experienced in adoptive family systems: The adoptive parents (most commonly) wanted biological children and could not have them, and the birth parents felt they could not care for their children and gave them up in hopes of a better life for their child. Both the adoptive parents and their adopted children are quite aware of the differences, and most often the children strongly want to know something about their birth parents, who are biologically and psychologically part of their heritage. (Not all adopted children, of course, are interested in connecting with their birth parents.) Similarly, for most birth parents, especially mothers, the desire for knowledge about their lost children never leaves. An adoptive family's psychological boundaries are different from those of a birth family (Reitz and Watson 1992).

Certain issues acquire special salience in adoption. Self-esteem and identity formation are often complex in adopted children. Interracial children and children whose looks or temperament are dramatically different from other family members may experience a sense of disconnection or not fitting in. Families with a combination of biological and adoptive children have to deal with similarities and differences between the siblings. Families who adopt older children who have been at risk may experience special stresses in family formation. Although the majority of adoptive families do well, it is important to acknowledge their particular complexities. Informal adoptions within a kin or friendship circle, or open adoptions in which the birth parents are known to all and involved in family life, have a different set of dynamics in which all family members work out a relationship. In recent years, there has been a major effort on the part of adopted children in closed adoptions to open adoption records and look for their birth parents, especially mothers. This may be upsetting to some adoptive parents who feel that they may be supplanted in the child's affections or who see this as a disloyal act. The results of these reunions vary widely, depending on the expectations and preparations of all concerned. Disappointment may develop if the birth parents are not interested in the children or if an exploitative relationship of some kind develops. When these efforts are successful, however, the family boundaries expand widely to include the birth parents, their spouses, half siblings, and so on. Adopted children should be encouraged to think in detail about their expectations for reunion, explore the fantasies surrounding a reunion, and be prepared for all possible responses.

Conclusion

Issues of pregnancy, contraception, and parenting form the basis of the family's history and meaning. Therapists must be aware of the multiple complex issues involved and be willing to assist the couple in making decisions about whether and how to have children, in dealing with the medical establishment, and in sharing with children the circumstances of their birth.

Suggested Readings

David H, Zdenek O, Mategcek Z, et al (eds): Born Unwanted: Developmental Effects of Denied Abortion. New York, Springer, 1988
  This book covers a number of the most influential European studies of denied abortion and reviews much of the rest of the literature.
Reitz M, Watson K: Adoption and the Family System. New York, Guilford, 1992
  This book is a good review of adoption from multiple points of view, covering a wide range of age and adoption situations.
Shapiro C: Infertility and Pregnancy Loss. San Francisco, CA, Jossey-Bass, 1988
  This book is a good guide for therapists.

References

American Psychiatric Association: Diagnostic and Statistical Manual of Mental Disorders, 4th Edition. Washington, DC, American Psychiatric Press, 1994, p 386
Bernstein A: Family Therapy News, February, 1995, pp 9–11
Condon J: Management of established pathological grief reaction after stillbirth. Am J Psychiatry 143:987–992, 1986
Dagg P: The psychological sequelae of therapeutic abortion—denied and completed. Am J Psychiatry 148:578–585, 1991
Kaplan H, Sadock B, Grebb J: Synopsis of Psychiatry, 7th Edition. Baltimore, MD, Williams & Wilkins, 1994, pp 494–496
Liebenberg B: Expectant fathers, in Psychological Aspects of a First Pregnancy. Edited by Shereshefsky P, Yarrow L. New York, Raven, 1973, pp 103–114
Meyers M, Diamond R, Kezur D, et al: An infertility primer for family therapists, I: medical, social and psychological dimensions. Fam Process 34:219–129, 1995a
Meyers M, Weinshel M, Scharf C, et al: An infertility primer for family therapists, II: working with couples who struggle with infertility. Fam Process 34:231–240, 1995b
Patel RM: Small, perfect circles. JAMA 270:21, 1993
Reitz M, Watson K: Adoption and the Family System. New York, Guilford, 1992, pp 3–13

Family Group, Phillip Levine, 1966. Courtesy of the artist and the private collection of Julius and Florence Myers. Used with permission.

Chapter 23

Lesbian and Gay Couples

With Laura Markowitz, B.A., and
John T. Patten, M.D.[†]

Objectives for the Reader

- To be able to describe characteristics of lesbian and gay relationships
- To become familiar with treatment issues for same-sex couples
- To understand the issues related to AIDS and gay relationships

Introduction

Since the 1970s, the amount of reliable information available concerning homosexuals has increased (Bell and Weinberg 1978), and as more and more lesbians and gays come out of the closet, their growing visibility has caused family therapists to become aware of and sensitive to the range and diversity of the homosexual population.

Understanding what is normal for lesbians and gays is vital for marital and family therapists for two reasons: first, same-sex couples are not just like opposite-sex couples, and a clinician must factor specific differences into treatment; second, by providing a point of comparison, an understanding of

[†]Deceased.

the functioning of same-sex couples sheds light on the way gender roles, sexuality, and relationship styles affect heterosexual couples (Table 23–1).

Coming Out and Coupling: Stressors and Challenges

Several studies have looked at same-sex relationship patterns (Blumstein and Schwartz 1983; Duffy and Rusbult 1985/1986; Mendola 1980; Peplau 1982; Symposium 1982), although the realities of same-sex couples have been submerged because most homosexuals in our society continue to lead covert and vulnerable existences. Since 1973, when homosexuality was removed from DSM and therefore depathologized by the mental health professions, lesbians and gays have been more forthcoming to researchers interested in studying aspects of their lives.

The process of commitment in a same-sex relationship requires intrapsychic and interpersonal shifts similar to those occurring in opposite-sex couples. Individuals must reconcile self-awareness with concern for the partner and with the couple as an entity. Superficial playfulness has to make room for emotional intimacy, and physical passion has to be joined by caring and tenderness. There is a concomitant need to reallocate previous involvement with family and friends (Morrison 1980). However, for same-sex couples, there are also the special characteristics of being members of an often disliked group and acquiring a positive gay or lesbian identity. Given the profound and pervasive antihomosexual bias in our society, these transitions are fraught with considerable psychological and social hazards. We outline some of the old myths about gay relationships, discussing them in light of recent

TABLE 23–1. Comparison of opposite-sex and same-sex couples

	Opposite-sex couples	Same-sex couples
Societal models and support	Present	Limited
Involvement of extended family	Present	Limited
Offspring	Present	Limited
Rapport (producing closeness and affection) (stereotype)	Low	High
Contrast (producing complementarity and sexual interest)	High	Low
Traditional masculine/feminine roles	Present	Absent

changes. We compare lesbian and heterosexual couples and briefly discuss the implications of the new issues for clinical practice.

Although it would seem that committing oneself to a same-sex relationship would presuppose coming to terms with a gay or lesbian identity, some individuals strive to acquire this identity in the context of a same-sex relationship. In treatment, clinicians can explore the stage of coming out that each partner may be in to determine the degree to which an individual has integrated a lesbian or gay identity; however, this is not always a cut-and-dried phenomenon. Individuals who have experienced same-sex attraction since early childhood might nevertheless consider themselves bisexual. Similarly, individuals who are heterosexually married might still identity themselves as gay or lesbian, despite being in monogamous, opposite-sex relationships and perhaps never having had a same-sex sexual experience. Because the nature of sexual attraction and identity is subjective and therefore defined by the individual, a clinician can be of use to the patient by asking questions that will help the patient clarify to his or her own satisfaction the question of identity and affiliation, including a discussion of heterosexism and the role internalized homophobia plays in decisions about partnering and identity.

In the process of coming out to oneself, at whatever age, it is customary to be reluctant to admit to oneself the true nature of one's same-sex orientation because of the antihomosexual bias of most cultures. Having perhaps fought actively to suppress, hide, and convert one's sexual orientation to heterosexual, a gay or lesbian person comes to terms with being homosexual and, either during or after this phase of coming out, may become involved in a sexual and emotional relationship with someone of the same sex. Joining a gay or lesbian relationship is a step toward exploring the forbidden side of oneself and involves both a personal and a social change of identity. Often lesbians and gays begin to access the lesbian and gay community, if one is available near where they live. Identifying with other lesbians and gays, and being identified as a member of the community, can be important to individuals who need positive role models and support, and to couples, who also need support and a sense of normalization that they cannot find in heterosexual society.

As same-sex couples become recognized as entities in the gay or lesbian subculture to which they have access, it may become more difficult and less desirable to hide their homosexual identity from colleagues and neighbors, particularly as the relationship develops and partners decide to live together. But because of the absence of protection from discrimination based on sexual orientation, it is often economically hazardous, as well as physically threatening, for homosexuals to come out in their workplaces, neighborhoods, churches, synagogues, schools, and even families of origin. The result is an uncomfortable compartmentalization, in which a homosexual may be forced to keep his or her same-sex relationship completely separate from the other aspects of his or her life.

All same-sex couples are challenged to thrive in an atmosphere of denigration. In order to shape a more helpful and realistic view of these couples, clinicians must be cognizant of the misguided stereotypes that oppress same-sex couples. In the next section, we outline these myths and offer a brief discussion of the implications for clinical practice.

Myths About Same-Sex Couples

Myth: Lesbian and gay relationships don't last and are doomed to failure. This false notion arises from many sources; for example, all gay males are thought to be sexually promiscuous and incapable of monogamy. Gay male sexuality is generally portrayed as hedonistic and superficial, and gay males have been characterized as incapable of anything but anonymous sexual encounters. For many heterosexuals, the term *gay life* conjures an image of a singles bar, the culture of which is taken to be the prototype for all gay male relationships. Although there certainly are gay bars and gay men having anonymous sex (as there are straight pick-up bars and heterosexuals having anonymous sex), there is also another side of gay life that includes long-term monogamous couples; long-term nonmonogamous couples; couples with children; and couples caring for elderly parents—in short, the same assortment of relationships found among heterosexual couples. Because gay couples often lead private lives, they are often hidden even from single gay men, who might worry that no such gay couples exist. If a gay man has come to believe, on the basis of internalized cultural homophobia, that he is destined to be emotionally unstable and unhappy, such an attitude will have a negative consequence for his ability to establish a successful relationship.

There is nothing inherent in male or female homosexuality that precludes the establishment of meaningful and continuing partnerships (Silverstein 1981). Such relationships exist in large numbers. For example, recent studies indicate that almost all gay males had been involved in at least one continuing physical/emotional relationship. Of gay men in their 20s, 40% were currently involved in such a relationship that had lasted an average of 2–3 years.

Although gay men are stereotyped as being hypersexual, lesbian relationships are burdened with the sexist notion that a real sexual encounter cannot occur without a penis. Lesbians are presumed to have long-term, monogamous, nearly stifling relationships that lack any sexuality and therefore have failed. Early psychoanalysts dismissed lesbianism as an immature sexual expression, as if lesbians were somehow stunted in their sexual growth, and this myth persists. When measured against other couple configurations, lesbian couples have been found to have less sex within the relationship than heterosexual or gay couples. Although the researchers defined sex for lesbians as involving genital contact, there remains a question of heterosexual bias in the assumptions underlying the definition of sex. Because lesbianism is the only opportunity we have to view sexuality outside patriarchal (male-defined) norms, it may be that lesbians express a more true and accurate female sexuality, whereby sex is not merely defined by genital contact and orgasm but by sensuality and sexuality. But because their sexuality is routinely pathologized and dismissed, and because it may not resemble heterosexual or gay male sexuality, lesbians may experience a lack of self-esteem and doubts about the sexual health of their long-term relationships.

Myth: Same-sex couples lead isolated lives, cut off from families and community. Gay and lesbian couples have strikingly less social and institutional support for the maintenance and continued fidelity of their relationships. Religious, legal, and economic considerations (including tax, inheritance, and estate laws) do not serve to stabilize same-sex couples as they do opposite-sex couples. Often tenuous or broken ties with extended family may leave same-sex couples isolated from multigenerational support and modeling; at the same time, the inaccessibility—particularly for gay men—of a same-sex couples culture (as opposed to a singles culture) leaves newer couples feeling as if they are inventing same-sex couplehood for the first time. Because of the inappropriate fit of a heterosexual model of couplehood, which is so often structured around gender and sex roles, same-sex couples must negotiate their relationship based on individual needs and desires.

The absence or disapproval of family of origin often leads same-sex couples to look to extended friendship networks for support, and these families of choice become essential support systems, something that clinicians must keep in mind. For example, when creating a genogram (a "map" of the family relationships) with same-sex couples, it may be useful to also chart the extended friendship network as a possible resource for the couple. Although some families react strongly and negatively when a member reveals his or her homosexual orientation, many become staunch supporters of their homosexual relatives. It should not be assumed that lesbians and gays don't have any family contact or support. Parents and relatives of homosexuals go through stages of adjustment when a member comes out as gay or lesbian, and the relationship may change and improve over time.

Lesbians and gays have a healthy subculture, providing community support and advocacy. In most major cities there are sports clubs, religious groups, self-help groups, publications, social clubs, political organizations, and health clinics for lesbians and gays. Like any minority groups, lesbians and gays find emotional relief and enjoyment in being with other lesbians and gays and not having to hide or try to fit in to a heterosexist world. For same-sex couples, these outlets allow the couple more breathing room and the chance to develop healthy connections and find support for their relationship.

Although social stigma and discrimination—and antigay violence and harassment—continue to be significant stressors for lesbians and gays, the past decade also has included some significant and positive changes. For example, lesbians and gays are also increasingly depicted in a positive way in movies and on television. As health care companies offer domestic partner benefits and society becomes more accustomed to same-sex couples, there is increasing comfort, visibility, and participation of some lesbians and gays in mainstream society. The findings are inconclusive whether closeted same-sex couples do better than those who are out. There is reason to believe that those who are open about their sexual orientation feel better about themselves and more confident and positive about their entitlement to be fully respected members of the mainstream. Often this leads to increased validation of their couple status from supportive heterosexual family, friends, co-workers, and acquaintances. There are still dangers—both physical and economic—in coming out, and those who feel unsafe about doing so should not be pathologized.

The presence or anticipation of offspring often acts as a glue for opposite-sex couples, holding the relationship together and linking them to the larger community through schools, religious institutions, and neighborhoods. Couples with children make a transition from focusing on the self and the present to focusing on others and the future. The absence of offspring in heterosexual and same-sex couples may diminish opportunities for this intrapsychic and social shift. However, many lesbians and gays do have offspring—either from previous heterosexual relationships or from alternative insemination, adoption, surrogacy, or known sperm donor arrangements. In these cases—and the number of lesbian and gay parents is growing—clinicians must examine the effects of heterosexism and homophobia on the functioning of the entire family system, assessing the developmental stages of the children and the level of safety the family experiences in the community, extended family, and neighborhood.

Myth: Lesbians and gays are childless or only have children from previous heterosexual marriages. Although this may have been true 20 years ago, it is no longer the case that lesbian and gay families are necessarily childless. In the past 5 years, there has been a surge of interest and community and social support within the gay and lesbian culture for having children. Alternative insemination by anonymous or known donors, surrogacy, and adoption are all avenues of parenthood for lesbian and gay individuals and couples. Once they become parents, lesbians and gays must deal with having to come out of the closet to teachers, pediatricians, neighbors, and parents of other children. They must negotiate coming out to their children and find language to explain to the children how they were conceived. The same-sex coparent's role, which makes perfect sense to the children, will have to be explained over and over to the outside world, and no appropriate descriptor yet exists. In addition, discriminatory laws make it impossible for most nonbiological or nonadoptive coparents to become legal guardians of the children they are raising. This may create feelings of alienation and insecurity among coparents, who have no legal rights in the event of a breakup and may be denied access to their children. In addition, the lack of legal status makes it difficult for them to assert their parental role in the schools or with other institutions in their children's lives. For example, if a child is in the hospital emergency room, a nonbiological mother would not be allowed to see her son or daughter.

It is useful to put the families in touch with national support groups such as the Gay and Lesbian Parents Coalition International, Children of Lesbians and Gays Everywhere, and other local groups organized through lesbian and gay community centers. The need for contact with other families like their own is expressed repeatedly by same-sex parents and their children. Clinicians can help concerned parents normalize their experience of childrearing as there may be a tendency to wonder if all the developmental challenges of their children are somehow caused by the parents' homosexuality rather than behaviors that are normal and appropriate for children of that age.

Myth: Same-sex couples are shaped by the fact that both partners are homosexual, rather than by their gender and learned sex-roles. In many respects an individual's relationship attitudes and behaviors are more highly correlated with his or her background and gender role as a male or female than with a particular sexual orientation. Why is this important? Because same-sex relationships must be viewed not as unusual entities that have no resemblance to opposite-sex relationships but as configurations whereby gender and sex roles have a significant influence on the functioning of the couple. For example, although it may be true that gay men find it easier to engage in sexual acts without emotional commitment (i.e., they can separate love from sex), is this because they are gay or because they are men? In contrast, for lesbians, romantic involvement more often precedes sexual contact, but isn't this true for American women in general? Coming from a stable family and having a history of good psychosocial functioning may be more crucial indicators of successful partnership than one's rating on the Kinsey scale (a scale used for measuring sexual orientation and understanding heterosexuality, homosexuality, and bisexuality as existing on a spectrum).

It has been said that compatibility in a couple requires both rapport and resistance. *Rapport* is a similarity of response and outlook, which is important to develop closeness and affection. *Resistance,* consisting of tension, distance, and dissimilarity, is the matrix for complementarity and sexual interest. According to this view, opposite-sex couples would be low on rapport (similarity) and high on resistance (contrast). Because there is greater social sex-role differentiation between the partners, problems for opposite-sex couples often stem from lack of empathy and excessive differentness, which lead to major conflicts.

For same-sex couples, in contrast, one would expect high levels of rapport and low levels of resistance. Such a configuration results in an easy initiation of gay relationships but also an early detection of possible mismatch—the excessive similarity may result in relational fatigue (i.e., a feeling of being bored in a relationship). Alternatively it might result in a satisfying level of fusion such as lesbian couples often describe. Fusion has been characterized as an unhealthy, restrictive level of closeness whereby each partner is unable to separate her own needs, wants, and desires from the other's, and differentiation is stalled or thwarted. But lesbian-feminist theorists criticize this negative view of fusion, believing that although some excesses require intervention, there is also a level of fusion that generates closeness, intimacy, and a sense of safety that lesbians find highly satisfying and enjoyable (Slater 1995). Clinicians needn't dismiss lesbian fusion as an undesirable relationship characteristic; indeed, it may be a resource for couples who find themselves under siege in a culture that is hostile to lesbians. It has also been pointed out that the traditional definition of fusion may be more male defined than female defined and therefore not as applicable to partnerships of two women as it might be in gay male or heterosexual relationships.

In couples composed of two men, each partner has undergone a socialization process leading to his adopting a predominantly traditional masculine social sex-role, even though his sexual orientation may be atypical. Of course, what is considered traditional for males varies from culture to culture, but all males go through some level of socialization into their roles as males. In cultures in which males are socialized to be competitive, independent, unemotional, unaffectionate, and goal oriented (rather than process oriented), females are assigned the role of keeping the heterosexual relationship together. Women are trained to be the nest builders, whereas men are the explorers. Women are taught to monitor their own and others' emotions and be caregiving and empathic. In same-sex relationships, in which partners have the same sex-role socialization, relationships may tend more dramatically in one direction or another (see Table 23–2). In lesbian relationships, couples tend to stay together longer on average than in gay relationships. Lesbians, predictably, show more fusion; sex is equated with love, and monogamy is often valued. Bell and Weinberg's (1978) closed-coupled style is modal for lesbians, whereas the open-coupled style is modal for gay males. Some observers have attempted to account for these dissimilarities by pointing out that in the lesbian couple, both women have been socialized into female roles (Krestan and Bepko 1980; McCandlish 1981/1982; Tanner 1978).

Myth: All same-sex couples divide into stereotypical butch-femme roles.
It is a commonly held belief that in same-sex relationships one partner becomes the masculine or butch partner, and the other takes on the role of feminine or femme partner, thereby approximating heterosexual couples. In contrast, a great deal of diversity exists among same-sex couples. Some couples do divide their roles into butch and femme—in terms of sexual activity and their home life. The literature on this phenomenon is quick to point out that, for example, a butch woman is not necessarily longing to be a male but is comfortable with the male sex-role characteristics including independence, competition, and emotional distance. A gay man who takes on a femme role is not necessarily longing to be a female but enjoys the role of homemaker and emotional nurturer and enjoys having permission to express vulnerability.

The majority of same-sex couples don't adopt butch-femme roles in their relationships. Gender-role allocation is based on a variety of factors:

TABLE 23–2.   Comparison of gay and lesbian couples

	Gay couples	Lesbian couples
Individuation	High	Low
Fusion, clinging	Low	High
Sex and intimacy	Sex precedes intimacy	Intimacy precedes sex
Sex and love	Often unrelated	Usually related
Fidelity	Open relationship or unattached	Monogamy

for example, a gay man may be active in certain areas and passive in others. Each partner chooses the chores he or she likes, and the couple compromises on the others. Chores such as fixing the car or cooking are assigned according to preference and ability. Most same-sex couples reject the models of traditional, heterosexual marriage and social sex-roles. Indeed, this is often cited as one of the benefits of being in a same-sex relationship: There is freedom to define oneself apart from assigned sex roles. There is a marked tendency toward egalitarianism, with sharing of power, responsibilities, and tasks. Sex-typed role-playing is more typical of heterosexuals than homosexuals.

Myth: Sexual monogamy helps bind couples together, whereas non-monogamy destroys the relationship. For lesbians, this may be true, but for gay men, sexually open (nonexclusive) relationships often increase the stability of long-term relationships. Although the AIDS epidemic has made sexual encounters more risky, male couples still negotiate open relationships, including establishing rules for safe-sex encounters and limits on behaviors and discussing extra-relationship affairs. These couples may renegotiate their decision to be monogamous and nonmonogamous at different times in the relationship, showing more flexibility and fluidity than opposite-sex or lesbian relationships. In the 1970s, before the AIDS epidemic, 156 gay male couples who had been together for 18 months to 30 years were studied (Mendola 1980). In the early phases of their partnerships, they were more likely to be monogamous than in later stages. Not one of the couples who had been together for more than 5 years remained monogamous (this may be different now, with the fear of contracting HIV inhibiting many gay men from having sexual encounters outside the relationship). Successful couples found that sexual exclusivity was less satisfying than was including outside sexual relationships, which enhanced the partners' sexual attraction to each other. Far from destroying the relationships, sexual nonexclusivity served to keep couples happily together. Fidelity became redefined as emotional commitment rather than sexual exclusivity. Because some gay men are able to split off sex from love, this did not present a contradiction in terms.

Couples develop rules and etiquette to maintain the boundary of the couple even with outside sexual activity. For example, there may be an agreement that these sexual encounters take place on a partner's own time, when the other partner is not around and in such a way as to not bring the matter to the other's attention. Contacts may be limited only to sex, and the specifics of these encounters are not shared between partners. Other couples may decide to open their relationship to a third person and invite someone into the relationship for a three-way sexual encounter. Again, the ability to negotiate and discuss the arrangement and expectations and fears beforehand is key to the longevity of these couples.

Myth: A successful same-sex relationship is one in which couples experience no conflict. The idea persists that enduring relationships stem from an early period of enthrallment and that this state of infatuation remains, unchanged, throughout the couple's life. Of course, this romantic notion is contrary to the experience of same-sex and opposite-sex couples alike. It unrealistically denies the concept of differentiated stages in a relationship related to the life cycle of the individual and the couple, with phase-specific stresses that require adjustment, change, and growth on the part of each partner.

Like heterosexual couples, same-sex couples stay together because the partners discover and develop mutual compatibility and because they share the same values, sense of humor, and sexual attraction for each other. As early passion wanes, partners work on living in increasing harmony by communicating and negotiating more effectively. The issues of autonomy and attachment, for example, may be continually in flux over the course of a couple's life together.

Issues in Therapy With Same-Sex Couples

Same-sex couples inevitably face the same kinds of challenges that any other type of couple faces (McWhirter and Mattison 1981/1982). These challenges may revolve around communication, role allocation, power, sex, money, and so on. Partners in same-sex couples report most of the same reasons for breaking up as heterosexual couples. The most frequent reasons are "nonresponsiveness and emotional distance" (Kurdek 1991).

Certain themes are unique to same-sex relationships. These themes concern attitudes toward being homosexual, and the partners' relationship to the straight world. For example, to the extent that the partners themselves feel negative about being lesbian or gay, these attitudes and associations will have a detrimental effect on the relationship. To the degree that they feel isolated as a result of societal homophobia and heterosexism, the partners may be forced to become largely dependent on each other, causing considerable strain on their partnership.

Partners in a couple may be at different stages in their self-acceptance as homosexuals and may be at different points in their coming out process, which may create instability in the relationship. If one partner, for example, wants the other to come to the office holiday party, but the other is afraid of being known as a lesbian, a certain amount of friction will result.

Same-sex couples who unthinkingly accept traditional heterosexual models for their own relationships may be faced with unnecessarily restrictive options. For this reason, many same-sex couples and homosexual individuals do not feel comfortable working with heterosexual clinicians. As with all differences between therapist and patient, the more the clinician initiates useful dialogue about the differences, the more open and honest the communication can become. If a clinician is uncomfortable with the notion of same-sex attraction, he or she may become uncomfortable during the course of treatment when issues of sexual practices or problems arise and may even steer the sessions away from such anxiety-producing topics. Alternatively, a clinician may feel unsure about how to handle transference and countertransference issues that may arise. For straight therapists who don't know much about these issues, a body of important literature exists, including magazines such as *In the Family*, which explores lesbian, bisexual, and gay families using the insights and wisdom of the mental health professions; theoretical books such as *The Lesbian Family Life Cycle* by Suzanne Slater; and newsletters such as the *Gay and Lesbian Quarterly*, which sums up relevant research about lesbians and gays.

Significant Factors in Treating Same-Sex Couples

All same-sex couples, no matter how openly they live as homosexuals, are subjected to the burden of what has been called *heterosexism*. Heterosexism is the privileging of heterosexuality, which results in the denigration of same-sex affection, orientation, and relationships. Because there is relatively little or no positive mirroring for lesbians and gays in the mainstream—including popular movies, books, films, and news—these individuals are burdened with predominantly negative internalizations. This negativity has been actively promoted by most cultures for centuries, often through religion. For example, consider the following biblical passage: "And if a man lie with mankind, as with womankind, both of them have committed abomination: they shall surely be put to death; their blood shall be upon them" (Leviticus 20:13). Similarly, and possibly more alarming, as recently as three decades ago a psychiatrist writing in the *Journal of the American Medical Association* called homosexuality "a dread dysfunction, malignant in character, which has risen to epidemic proportions" (Socarides 1970). As a result, when a same-sex couple forms, each partner will often have some degree of internalized prejudice and antihomosexual beliefs that is at odds with his or her own life and affiliative identity. Individual, couples, and family therapists must take into account the effects of internalized *homophobia* (fear of homosexuality) in assessment and treatment.

A related factor that must be addressed in treatment with homosexuals is social prejudice. Because homosexuality is vilified in this country and homosexuals continue to be denied basic civil rights such as the right to protection against discrimination, the right to marry, and in some states (e.g., Utah) the right to assemble in schools, considerable psychological stress results. The everyday effects of social heterosexism and homophobia must be discussed and explored in treatment with couples and individuals, including ways in which the lack of positive social recognition and affirmation affects the couple's relationship. Slater (1995) has found that high levels of fusion among lesbian couples (described in the "Myths" section later in this chapter) are caused in part by the couple viewing the outside world as dangerous and hostile, causing the women partners to bond together more tightly and make their relationship a sanctuary.

When working with any special treatment population, there are no easy answers or cookie-cutter techniques. It may be useful for straight clinicians who work with lesbian, gay, or bisexual clients to seek some guidance, supervision, or peer advice from a homosexual colleague. Rather than feeling intimidated, or striving to hide one's ignorance from the patient, it can be a rewarding and healing experience for clinician and patient when differences can be negotiated openly, honestly, and with respect.

All of the basic family therapy techniques described in this book may be useful in treating same-sex couples, depending on the clinical situation. The task for the therapist is to apply the techniques as the situation demands, that is, keeping in mind the issues described in this chapter.

AIDS and the Gay Community

Perhaps the two greatest influences on the gay community in the last two decades have been the gay liberation movement on the one hand, which has allowed gay and lesbian people a far greater degree of freedom, and AIDS on the other, which has profoundly altered all aspects of the community's life. As of 1995, the total death toll from AIDS in this country was 350,000. More than half of the dead were gay men, and the total number of HIV- and AIDS-affected people is much greater. In the United States, AIDS is now the leading cause of death in people under age 35 years.

For many gays and lesbians, the death toll in their immediate group of friends and lovers is huge. Some people have seen several lovers and as many as 100 other friends and acquaintances die a slow and painful death at a young age. It is probably not possible to be gay in the United States and not have firsthand knowledge of this disease. Dealing with this level of grief as a constant is an exhausting and ultimately numbing experience.

The older gay community has actively pressed for research in AIDS and has altered its sexual behaviors, practicing safe sex, decreasing the number of casual partners, and increasing the number of relatively monogamous couplings. Some groups of younger gay men, seeing the amount of death around them, have become certain they will die young and have deliberately refused to take precautions to protect themselves. The incidence of AIDS in the lesbian community is much lower, but the same issues are very much a part of their lives.

In same-sex couples in which one partner becomes HIV positive, the question of who will take care of the ill partner and how that partner and his parents relate becomes of central importance. If the other partner becomes HIV positive and has clearly contracted the virus from the already-ill partner, issues of guilt make the situation even more complicated. Because the ill partner eventually cannot work, the questions of who will pay for treatment and for living expenses also must be determined. AIDS is an expensive illness.

Treatment Issues

Because of recent treatment advances, HIV infection is now frequently a chronic illness. A couple may have anywhere from 6 months to 10 years between the time HIV is diagnosed and the infected partner dies—a long time to deal with issues of illness, grief, and whether and how to maintain a sexual relationship. Additionally, new combination therapies have been successful in reversing and stabilizing the downward course of the disease. Thus individuals who were once planning or prepared for death now face the dilemma of regaining health and preparing for an uncertain future.

For the parents of the AIDS patient, grief is paramount. If the patient had not previously come out to his parents, the parents must deal with the initial shock and perhaps shame they feel about having a gay child and with the possibility of their child's death. For most families, this is a time for reconciliation, but for some there is a complete cutoff from the ill person. They may see their child's partner as a resource or they may attempt to completely cut him off from contact. The family needs help over a long time in using its resources to do the best it can.

Each city has a variety of AIDS support groups and services, and therapists must familiarize themselves with local resources. The family therapist's task is to help the AIDS patient and his families—of choice and of origin—to live with the illness and to find meaning in the individual's life and death.

> The family therapist's task is to help the AIDS patient and his families—of choice and of origin—find the capacity to live with the illness and find meaning in the individual's life and death.

Suggested Readings

Laird J, Green RJ (eds): Lesbians and Gays in Couples and Families: A Handbook for Therapists. San Francisco, CA, Jossey-Bass, 1996
This book offers a distillation of the more recent applications of family systems work to same-sex couples and their families. The volume abounds with theoretical and clinical ideas—including critical aspects of couple and family development and family processes—that will benefit every therapist.

References

Bell AP, Weinberg MS: Homosexualities: A Study of Diversity Among Men and Women. New York, Simon & Schuster, 1978

Blumstein P, Schwartz P: American Couples. New York, William Morrow, 1983

Duffy SM, Rusbult CE: Satisfaction and commitment in homosexual and heterosexual relationships. J Homosex 12:1–24, 1985/1986

Krestan JA, Bepko CS: The problem of fusion in the lesbian relationship. Fam Process 19:277–289, 1980

Kurdek LA: The dissolution of gay and lesbian couples. Journal of Social and Personal Relationships 8:265–278, 1991

McCandlish BM: Therapeutic issues with lesbian couples. J Homosex 7:371–378, 1981/1982

McWhirter D, Mattison A: Psychotherapy for gay male couples. J Homosex 7:379–392, 1981/1982

Mendola M: The Mendola Report: A Look at Gay Couples. New York, Crown, 1980

Morrison C: Made in heaven: coupling (and uncoupling) the gay way. Blueboy, November 1980

Peplau LA: Research on homosexual couples: an overview. J Homosex 8:3–8, 1982

Silverstein C: Man to Man: Gay Couples in America. New York, William Morrow, 1981

Slater S: The Lesbian Family Life Cycle. New York, Free Press, 1995

Socarides CW: Homosexuality and medicine. JAMA 212:1199–1202, 1970

Symposium on homosexual couples. J Homosex 8:1–83, 1982

Tanner DM: The Lesbian Couple. Lexington, MA, DC Heath, 1978

Family Treatment When One Member Has a Psychiatric Disorder or Other Special Problem

We discuss in this section the differences in evaluation and treatment made necessary by the presence of a psychiatric disorder or other special problem in a family member. In Chapter 24 we discuss how the family is affected when one member has a psychiatric disorder, and in Chapter 25 we examine how treatment techniques must be modified for special but common situations such as the problematic family in which aggressive, abusive, or suicidal behaviors are frequent.

In Chapter 26 we discuss how family behavior can be organized around acute or chronic mental illness and why the therapist must be aware of the typical patterns and responses of families in these situations. We also discuss treatment in settings such as the psychiatric hospital or the community mental health center, in which these problems are (or should be) managed from a family perspective.

Gypsy Family, Jack Reed Royce, 1973. Private collection.

CHAPTER 24

Family Treatment in the Context of Individual Psychiatric Disorders

Objectives for the Reader

☞ To be aware of family interaction patterns associated with individual psychiatric disorders

☞ To know the indications for, and techniques of, family intervention in combination with other treatment methods in specific psychiatric disorders

Introduction

In this chapter we demonstrate how family, individual, dynamic, and physiological issues intersect in Axis I disorders, and how family therapy is conducted when a family member has a specific disorder. We concentrate on those diagnoses in which we believe family issues are most often part of the total picture. We also propose treatment guidelines and strategies for each disorder.

If the identified patient has a specific major psychiatric diagnosis, treatment will usually include individual therapy and, most often, medication. For example, antipsychotic medications are used to treat the positive symptoms of schizophrenia. In most instances, treatment is also indicated for the family problems and interactions accompanying these conditions. Some of the family problems may be related to the etiology of the individual illness, some may be secondary to it, others may adversely affect the course of the illness, and still others may not be connected at all. For example, if schizophrenia has developed in a spouse early in the marriage, the therapist's attention must be directed not only to treatment of the mental illness but also to the nature of the marital interaction, including its possible role in exacerbating or ameliorating the illness. If a major psychiatric disorder occurs in one family member, attention must be paid to the family's ability to cope with the illness. For example, a child may respond to his or her mother's severe depressive illness by becoming a caretaker to younger siblings, at risk of his or her own development, or the child may begin acting out. The symptoms of depression may also cause marital stress. Conversely the depression may have been symptomatic of severe marital or family stress.

Family interventions for many psychiatric disorders are one component of a multimodal prescription, and those interventions may be crucial to success.

The Family Model and Individual Diagnosis

In medicine, psychiatry, and related fields, the traditional focus of healing and treatment has been on disease and disorder. Diagnosis as a rubric implies a model that includes signs and symptoms, etiological theories, treatment, and prognosis. For some family therapists, any kind of labeling of the individual is inappropriate, because it locates the problems in the individual while ignoring the role of family members and other environmental conditions and stimuli. For others the concept of diagnosis according to DSM-IV (American Psychiatric Association 1994) is acceptable but inadequate, in that it ignores family systems issues. The giving of a diagnostic label does not necessarily imply a treatment. For example, depression as a broad concept has been treated successfully with medication, cognitive therapy, or couples therapy depending on the circumstances, degree of severity, and treating professional.

Weinstein (1983) has explored the issue of patient and family reactions to receiving a diagnosis in the hospital. As expected, patients are strongly negative toward generalized labels of mental illness. Contrary to popular belief, however, current and former patients think more favorably than expected about mental illness (including their diagnosis) and their hospital and posthospital experiences. Also, patient attitudes do not become more unfavorable during or immediately after hospitalization. Nor are they less favorable than nonpatient attitudes. The issue for the therapist is to relate to patients as real people who have problems or illnesses rather than to dehumanize them.

With increasing evidence of the multiple causes (including genetic, neurochemical, individual, and environmental ones) of many psychiatric syndromes, attention must be paid to both individual diagnosis and family interactions (see Chapter 8 for a fuller discussion of this issue). In this chapter we discuss the syndromes described in DSM-IV (American Psychiatric Association 1994) and ICD-10 (World Health Organization 1992) that most commonly interact with family issues. The system is multiaxial as follows:

- Axis I: clinical disorders and other conditions that may be a focus of clinical attention (V codes)
- Axis II: mental retardation and personality disorders
- Axis III: general medical conditions
- Axis IV: psychosocial and environmental problems
- Axis V: global assessment of functioning

The system is devised to categorize the pathology of the patient, with only relatively minor attention given to environmental factors in the patient's condition, including family factors.

Individuals who do not have a diagnosable condition based on their symptom pattern or personality traits but who complain of discomfort due to family issues are classified under the rubric of other conditions that may be a focus of clinical attention (i.e., the V codes referred to on Axis I). These are the situations in which a family most often comes to a family therapist for help, that is, when one or more members do not have a diagnosable condition, and the issue is a systems problem. Even when an individual has a diagnosed condition, family evaluation may be helpful. Assessment tools are helpful in both types of situation. V codes cover the variety of relationship issues with which marital and family therapy is most concerned. Because they are not individual issues and are on a separate axis, they often have been seen as less important by psychiatrists and are not reimbursable diagnoses for many insurance and managed care companies.

Several attempts to give this set of diagnostic criteria (i.e., relationship issues) more status as a separate axis in DSM-IV have been unsuccessful. By themselves, these proposed criteria were judged not to be sufficient as a "diagnostic group" for family therapy. A number of diagnostic schema have been proposed (Guttman et al. 1995) but have not been generally adopted. It is hoped that an axis for relational context will be developed that will be as important as Axis I.

Schizophrenia

With Lisa Dixon, M.D., M.P.H.

Rationale

From the early days of the family therapy movement, clinicians have had a fascination with schizophrenia and the families of patients with the disorder. In the 1990s the family approach has changed dramatically in this area, relating to these most seriously ill patients and their family interactions.

Early family theorists were interested in the family's role in the etiology of schizophrenia. These writers emphasized concepts such as the schizophrenogenic mother (Fromm-Reichman 1948), faulty boundary setting, and family interactions such as double bind (Bateson et al. 1956, 1963), pseudo-mutuality (Wynne et al. 1960), and schism and skew (Fleck 1960). Current conceptualizations have been influenced by subsequent research concerning the multiple factors in the etiology of schizophrenia. Schizophrenia is now understood to be a brain disorder with strong familial links. Specific brain area functions show abnormalities. The familial aggregation of persons with schizophrenia appears to be largely from genetic causes (Wahlberg et al. 1997). Changes in brain function may precede adolescence. A vulnerability-stress model of schizophrenic episodes was proposed in the 1980s (Nuechterlein and Dawson 1984), emphasizing individual deficits (e.g., information-processing deficits, autonomic reactivity anomalies, social competence and coping limitations) in combination with stressors (e.g., life events, family environmental stress, substance abuse as it affects the brain). This model still seems relevant to the development of psychotic episodes (see Figure 24–1).

A number of historical and scientific trends have contributed to the development of the psychosocial interventions recommended today for families of persons with schizophrenia. One trend is the development of the construct of expressed emotion. In 1962 a team of British investigators reported that patients who returned to live with their families after psychiatric hospitaliza-

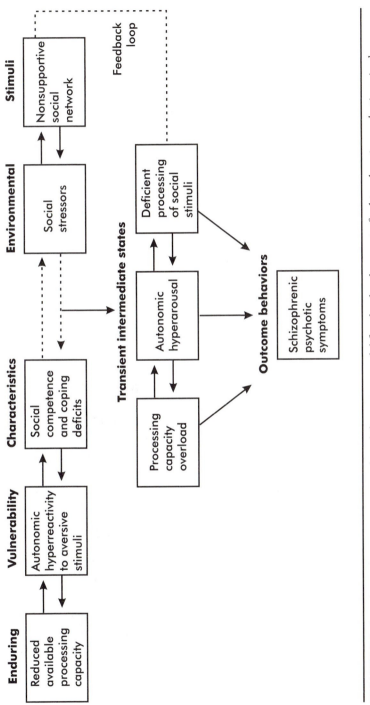

FIGURE 24–1. A tentative, interactive vulnerability-stress model for the development of schizophrenic psychotic episodes.

Source. Nuechterlein K, Dawson M: "A Heuristic Vulnerability/Stress Model of Schizophrenic Episodes." *Schizophrenia Bulletin* 10:300–312, 1984. Reprinted with permission.

tion were more prone to rehospitalization than were those patients who went to boarding homes and hostels after discharge (Brown et al. 1962). To explore these interesting leads, this group developed a semistructured interview to quantify the family environment to which the patient would return. This instrument, the Camberwell Family Interview, provides measures of what these researchers have termed expressed emotion, which is primarily an index of the family's criticism of, and overinvolvement with, the identified patient. Although researchers commonly refer to high expressed emotion families, it is important to understand that the rating of expressed emotion is based on observations made of a single cross-sectional interview of one family member and the patient. In subsequent years, it has been found both with British and American samples that the percentage of patients in families with high expressed emotion who relapse, or are rehospitalized, is significantly higher than the percentage in the low expressed emotion families.

The concept of expressed emotion has been dissected further. In the long term (i.e., after the acute episode), emotional overinvolvement is associated with a better social outcome in patients because it is part of the increased care that these disabled patients need (and desire) (King and Dixon 1996). The concept of expressed emotion may be detecting excess stress in the environment of the person with schizophrenia; however, much more needs to be learned about how the patient may contribute to this family response, how expressed emotion changes over time, and how it varies across cultures. Somewhat parenthetically expressed emotion has been found important in understanding and preventing relapse not only in schizophrenia but also in both mood disorders and eating disorders (see later in this chapter) (Butzloff and Hooley 1998).

This work has led to very specific family therapeutic approaches concerning schizophrenia. Influenced by such work, researchers have put together treatment packages with the specific goals of reducing familial hostility and overinvolvement in the acute phase. These studies will not only provide data on a potential intervention strategy but also might provide experimental evidence that expressed emotion indeed has some causal relationship to the course of the illness. This work has been carried on in the United States and in England (Leff et al. 1989). This therapeutic approach has been used with chronic schizophrenia on an outpatient basis (Falloon et al. 1982), with more acutely ill schizophrenia in inpatient settings (Glick et al. 1993), and in brief therapy immediately after hospitalization (Goldstein et al. 1978). We describe these studies in Chapter 29, in our discussion of family treatment outcome.

Treatment Considerations

Modern family interventions have been based partly on the concept of expressed emotion and partly on the increasing evidence that schizophrenia is a disease of the brain. Children with a genetic predisposition to schizophrenia appear to be more sensitive to environmental influences (i.e., parents) than are children who do not have a genetic predisposition (Wahlberg et al. 1997).

The shift in caretaking burden to families after the deinstitutionalization movement of the 1950s and 1960s led to the rise in the family advocacy movement. Families demanded services for their family members and themselves that did not blame them for the illness. Because families may perceive the concept of expressed emotion as a form of blaming, an alternative term that appreciates the complexity of this phenomenon is "expressed exasperation." Family therapists acknowledged that traditional family therapy techniques were not working and had caused many family members to complain and revolt (i.e., they did not want to be treated by family therapists, preferring biologically oriented professionals).

A number of guidelines exist for the treatment of schizophrenia using a family approach. The family approach has shifted dramatically from the early conceptualization of the family as part of the problem to the family as part of the treatment team.

First and foremost, the family intervention must be combined with medication. Figure 24–2 provides a quality treatment equation (i.e., the elements of what must be done for most Axis I disorders). Second, different formats of family intervention must be used at different phases of the illness (Table 24–1). Third, the approach must be mostly psychoeducational rather than systemic but can shift in later phases of the illness.

As we discuss in Chapter 26, during acute episodes when the patient is psychotic and may need hospitalization, contact is not only helpful to the family but is also beneficial for later collaboration with treatment personnel (Glick and Clarkin 1997). The family is involved from the first contact. The main focus is psychoeducational to teach the family about the symptoms, di-

FIGURE 24–2.   A quality treatment equation.

TABLE 24–1. Alternative formats for psychoeducational family treatment

Individual family unit (Falloon et al. 1982; Goldstein et al. 1978)
Individual family plus relatives' groups (Leff et al. 1982)
Relatives-only groups (Leff et al. 1989)
Multiple family groups (McFarlane et al. 1995)
Parallel patient and relatives' groups (Kissling 1994)

Source. Goldstein MJ: "Psychoeducation and Family Treatment Related to the Phase of a Psychotic Disorder." *International Clinical Psychopharmacology* 11:77–83, 1996. Reprinted with permission.

agnosis, treatment, and prognosis with and without treatment and about the family's role in management. The family therapist should take a positive, interested, supportive, undemanding, and uninterpretive stance toward the family during this phase. The acute psychosis may last for several weeks or months, during which time hospitalization or crisis intervention may proceed with use of neuroleptic medication. Conjoint family meetings with the patient during this period may be contraindicated as being too stimulating for an acutely psychotic patient but sometimes yield helpful information about family patterns during the psychotic phase. Family meetings with the patient for psychoeducational purposes should be started and the family referred to the National Alliance for the Mentally Ill (NAMI). NAMI and its local affiliates frequently offer family support groups that can be very helpful. NAMI also sponsors a family education and support program called Journey of Hope, which is designed specifically to help families cope with having a family member who has severe mental illness. These programs are generally free of charge and are available in many communities.

During the subsequent stabilization phase, when symptoms are subsiding, the family's feelings (e.g., guilt, anger, worry) are more likely to emerge. In this phase (lasting 3–9 months) the patient's florid symptoms give way and expose negative symptoms such as lack of initiative and apathy. At this point the family needs further information and support in dealing with the chronic condition. The psychoeducational approach should be started early and continued during this phase. The approach consists of individual meetings with the family, educational workshops with other families, family support groups, and so on.

Individual sessions focus heavily on concerns of a particular family, whereas family groups and workshops focus on more generic issues linked to the diagnosis. As the illness becomes stabilized and the clinical team moves into the maintenance phase, multifamily psychoeducational groups become more important. This is probably because other families that are coping with the same kinds of problems are extremely helpful to the individual family that has a member with schizophrenia. McFarlane et al. (1995) conducted a controlled study of individual versus multifamily groups and found that the multifamily group format is more efficacious than the individual format for some types of families (e.g., Caucasian). B. McFarlane (personal communication, 1998) has developed an excellent list of "family guidelines" for families of patients with chronic schizophrenia:

> Here is a list of things everyone can do to help make things run more smoothly:
>
> 1. GO SLOW. Recovery takes time. Rest is important. Things will get better in their own time.
> 2. KEEP IT COOL. Enthusiasm is normal. Tone it down. Disagreement is normal. tone it down too.
> 3. GIVE EACH OTHER SPACE. Time out is important for everyone. It's okay to reach out. It's okay to say "no."
> 4. SET LIMITS. Everyone needs to know what the rules are. A few good rules keep things clear.
> 5. IGNORE WHAT YOU CAN'T CHANGE. Let some things slide. Don't ignore violence.
> 6. KEEP IT SIMPLE. say what you have to say clearly, calmly, and positively.
> 7. FOLLOW DOCTOR'S ORDERS. Take medications as they are prescribed. Take only medications that are prescribed.
> 8. CARRY ON BUSINESS AS USUAL. Reestablish family routines as quickly as possible. Stay in touch with family and friends.
> 9. NO STREET DRUGS OR ALCOHOL. They make symptoms worse.
> 10. PICK UP ON EARLY SIGNS. Note changes. Consult with your family clinician.
> 11. SOLVE PROBLEMS STEP BY STEP. Make changes gradually. Work on one thing at a time.
> 12. LOWER EXPECTATIONS, TEMPORARILY. Use a personal yardstick. Compare this month to last month rather than last year or next year.

Not everything can be accomplished with psychoeducation. Tables 24–2 and 24–3 cover issues relevant to patients experiencing their first psychotic break and what can and cannot be taught in psychoeducation. Some sessions must be directed to family dynamics. Adding family intervention cannot replace adequate medication. Schooler et al. (1997) found convincing evidence that the standard dose of medication is the best dose strategy, in comparison with a low dose or a targeted medication strategy, and that adding family intervention is insufficient to lower a particular dose.

TABLE 24–2.　Special issues in carrying out psychoeducational family programs with patients experiencing their first psychotic break

Diagnostic ambiguity
　Presence of striking affective features
　Need to acknowledge diagnostic uncertainty
　Education cannot be as specific as with chronic patients
Impact on family different compared with chronic cases
　No previous experience with psychosis
　Acuteness of episode more mystifying
　Limited readiness of patients and relatives to seek support outside family

Source.　Goldstein MJ: "Psychoeducation and Family Treatment Related to the Phase of a Psychotic Disorder." *International Clinical Psychopharmacology* 11:77–83, 1996. Reprinted with permission.

TABLE 24–3.　Factors affected and not affected by a brief family education program

Factors affected	Factors not affected
Feeling of support from treatment team	Information retention
Family's sense of responsibility for the illness	Perception of symptoms
	Interactions with patient
Understanding of the illness	Burden from illness
Awareness that the patient's behavior is not intentional	Hope for the future
	Hours per week spent with patient
Rejection of the patient	

Source.　Goldstein MJ: "Psychoeducation and Family Treatment Related to the Phase of a Psychotic Disorder." *International Clinical Psychopharmacology* 11:77–83, 1996. Reprinted with permission.

Glick et al. (1993) randomly assigned 84 schizophrenic patients either to an inpatient family intervention plus medication in the context of standard hospital treatment or to medication and standard hospital treatment without family intervention. They found positive effects for female patients with schizophrenia and their families at discharge and at 18-month follow-up for those that received the family intervention. Male patients were unaffected or did worse, probably either because the brain disease was worse than in females or because females have been socialized to be more compliant with treatment (both with family therapy and with medication) and therefore do better than males. Perhaps women are more responsive to family environment improvement. This is also true in couples therapy for depression (i.e., women did better, men did worse).

Schizophrenic patients living with or supported by families of origin. Because the majority of schizophrenic symptoms, including first psychotic break, occur in the late teens and early 20s, the majority of young patients with schizophrenia will be unmarried and living with or connected to their families of origin. For these families the onset of symptoms is cause for enormous fear, helplessness, and guilt over whether they have damaged their child. Early individual therapists and early family therapists blamed the family for the child's schizophrenia. Individual therapists often kept families ignorant of the treatment process, and family therapists burdened the family with the full responsibility for the child's recovery. Many of these families were doubly traumatized. Current assumptions are that although families are not responsible for the illness, they can aid in (or derail) the recovery process and need to be given as much information as possible, while being supported in the huge burden of caring for their child and mourning the loss of the child's healthy self and possible future. The current state of health care has increased the burden on families, who can no longer rely on the health care system to respond adequately to psychotic symptoms and who can seldom get a child hospitalized unless violence to self or others has occurred. Because schizophrenia has a large genetic component, it is important to consider the mental health of other family members and their ability to support or contain the manifestations of illness. Chronic illness in a child exacerbates marital conflict, and because marital conflict exacerbates stress at home, the parental unit also must be evaluated.

> Families need to be given as much information as possible, while being supported in the huge burden of caring for their child and mourning the loss of the child's healthy self and possible future.

One of the most complicated issues with these families is a decision about when the child is well enough to leave home to work or live on his or her own. Parents who are understandably concerned about their offspring managing alone in an apartment may be labeled incorrectly as enmeshed; in contrast, parents can infantilize children who could manage in the world with help. For these families the process of leaving home can be complicated and protracted, with many attempts before some form of independent living is managed.

Landeen et al. (1992) found that siblings of patients with schizophrenia have a special need for information and benefit from workshops with other well siblings. This is because of the emotions they commonly experience—guilt, fear, shame, and anger. Without some help, their most common defense is flight from the family and emotional constriction.

Schizophrenic patients who are married, with or without children.   Although the rate of marriage among patients with schizophrenia is lower than that of the general population, many do marry and have children. Many of these are patients with periods of relatively good functioning between psychotic breaks. Some patients develop symptoms after marriage. The spouse of such a patient lives with the constant anxiety that another episode will occur, plus the oddness or difficulties with intimacy characteristic of the majority of these patients. Isolation and stigma also take a toll. Because some patients attempt self-medication with alcohol or other drugs, intoxication or addiction is a concern. Violence during psychotic episodes may occur. The rate of separation or divorce is quite high among schizophrenic individuals.

Children faced with psychotic parents who cannot care for them, or parents whose thinking is far from consensual reality, face a series of problems growing up. A parent who changes suddenly from a loving caretaker to a helpless or dangerous being is an enormous source of fear for a child. If the healthy spouse cannot tolerate the situation and becomes emotionally absent or leaves the family, very young children may become caretakers for their ill parent. If the family cannot explain to the child what is happening, or insists that everything is normal, the child's own grasp of reality is compromised. Needs of offspring of patients with schizophrenia and other serious mental illnesses have also received increasing attention at family organizations such as NAMI. We recommend referral to such organizations in almost all cases.

The therapist must evaluate the family and the family's support system, make sure children are provided for and adequately informed, and ensure that the family is supported in its functioning. The therapist must approach the family with a supportive, nonblaming attitude. Families will blame themselves and need help to become constructive participants in the management of the schizophrenic patient.

Bipolar Disorder

Rationale

Bipolar disorder is a severe, recurrent, usually chronic mental disorder that affects approximately 1% of the United States population. Patients with this disorder experience an average of 12.3 episodes during what are typically the most productive years of adulthood. Pharmacological treatments are effective; however, medication treatment alone may not be sufficient, at least for a subgroup of bipolar patients. Factors relevant to the effectiveness of medication treatment include noncompliance, the relationship of stress to relapse, and limits of medication effects on symptoms and functioning in the family.

> Medication treatment alone may not be sufficient, at least for a subgroup of bipolar patients.

Rates of medication noncompliance among bipolar patients are as high as 53%. Medication adherence is associated with many patient variables (e.g., increasing age, being married, chronicity of illness). Health system issues such as convenience of clinical setting, continuity of care, and extent of supervision by others have also been implicated. Noncompliance is associated with living alone, having unstable and nonsupportive families, a more complex treatment regimen, and higher numbers and costs of medications. Psychosocial factors contribute substantially to medication noncompliance, and psychosocial interventions may be effective in dealing with the problem (Clarkin et al. 1988).

Even when taken in adequate doses, medication may have a limited effect on impaired social function, and even with medication, psychosocial stress may provoke relapse and recurrence. Research demonstrates the need to specify more precisely the critical psychosocial variables that mediate medication compliance and, therefore, medication effectiveness.

Because psychosocial stress is an important determinant of relapse and recurrence in major affective disorders, it needs to be addressed both theoretically and pragmatically in the development and evaluation of treatment models. Although the characterization of high levels of expressed emotion as a response or adaptation to the stress of caretaking is still under debate, the usefulness of expressed emotion as a predictor of relapse and rehospitalization in schizophrenia and unipolar depression is now well established. More recent work with bipolar or manic patients shows that expressed emotion, along with affective style, predicts clinical outcome at 9 months postdischarge (Miklowitz et al. 1996).

The first manic and depressive episodes are likely to occur in young adulthood, when patients are beginning to establish their own lives. Patients with bipolar disorder are more likely than schizophrenic patients to maintain good personality function between episodes; bipolar patients also marry more often and divorce less often than those with schizophrenia. If episodes are mild, the disorder may not be diagnosed. If episodes are severe, they are likely to wreak havoc on the family, especially in the manic phase when the patient's judgment is impaired and he or she may spend the family's money, lose jobs and friends, or become angry and paranoid. Severe depression brings the possibility of suicide. The family must be involved, particularly in monitoring early symptoms and promoting medication compliance.

Because of genetic inheritance and because children of bipolar parents may experience chaos and parental loss periodically in the family, they are highly vulnerable to psychiatric disorders in adulthood. They may show early signs of bipolar illness that may not be understood and treated unless the family is evaluated. In one family three out of six children of a bipolar patient developed mood disorder symptoms by their early 20s, and at least one had been depressed periodically since age 8 or 9 years.

Bipolar patients who are not in the acute phase, or cyclothymic patients without frank psychosis, often have personality issues and subsyndromal symptoms. Individual and couples therapy is often helpful when the patient is in remission or maintained on medication. Consider the following case example:

Mrs. A, a 50-year-old married mother of eight children, experienced her first psychiatric disturbance 8 years earlier. At that time a depressive episode characterized by profound lethargy, weeping and sadness, inability to complete minimal household tasks, and eventual withdrawal to bed led her to outpatient treatment with tricyclic antidepressants for a period of 2 years, with little change. The depression had occurred soon after the marriage of Mrs. A's oldest child and only daughter. A full-blown episode of mania led to an extended hospitalization, which lasted 1 year. During that time Mrs. A was treated unsuccessfully with various antidepressants, including monoamine oxidase inhibitors, carbamazepine, and lithium carbonate. Since being discharged from the hospital, Mrs. A has continued to cycle unrelentingly, with periods of hypomania lasting 2 weeks and alternating with similar-length periods of severe depression. She is currently taking low doses of lithium and carbamazepine, which have altered the severity of the episodes slightly but not changed their frequency.

The history obtained from Mr. A presented a premorbid picture of an energetic and intellectual woman who was resourceful and well liked in the community where the family lived. Mrs. A's father, who committed suicide when she was age 16 years, and her paternal grandfather had histories of pronounced mood swings and are assumed to have had bipolar illness. The paternal grandfather lived in the family home until his death, and Mrs. A vividly recalled the profound effect this model of depression and hypomania had on her childhood.

By the time family therapy began, Mr. and Mrs. A's older children had assumed responsibility for cooking the meals, managing the shopping and the laundry, and generally attending to the needs of the younger children so that they were properly dressed and sent to school. During the first four family sessions, all of the children were present. They discussed the resentment they felt when their mother's mood switched from depression to hypomania, especially the resentment of her attempts in the first few days of mood elevation to reestablish her standards and control. They felt that she was oblivious to what was happening in the family and explained that her unavailability during a depression, when they had to be responsible, was experienced as an abandonment. Mr. A was noted to be quite passive. It became clear that despite resenting their mother's seeking to reclaim control during the first hypomanic days, the children nonetheless preferred her to be hypomanic, when fantasies could be acted out, no limits were set, and the children were swept along by Mrs. A's infectious high spirits.

During hypomanic periods, Mr. A perceived his wife as untrustworthy, a spendthrift, and neglectful of him and the children. He also seemed to prefer the hypomanic phase, which is unusual because many bipolar spouses prefer the period when the patient is depressed and less active. Mr. A resented his wife's threats of divorce, which occurred invariably during her hypomanias and were linked to her lack of access to money and credit cards, which Mr. A controlled. He experienced comfort and gratification from the high energy level and the excitement of Mrs. A's hypomanic phase. He was pleased by the increase in sexual activity and was excited by Mrs. A's plans and ideas, which though sometimes bizarre were perceived as sound and reasonable enough to be tolerable.

While Mrs. A was in the hospital, the family was seen weekly. After that, Mr. A and the children came in only when there was a marital- or family-focused problem or when they felt a need for support during a particularly trying episode. Mrs. A continued as an outpatient in individual therapy for many years. Over time the sessions focused on the despair she felt about her relentless illness, her losses, and her sense of being a useless person. In individual sessions, she articulated conflictual and ambivalent feelings, areas that became available because of the family work. During good periods, she would talk about the possibilities that she could reintegrate and become a functioning person again. With two exceptions, she remained out of the hospital. One hospitalization entailed a brief stay when she was admitted for reevaluation of her medication. The other occasion, also brief, occurred when the therapist who had treated Mrs. A and her family throughout this period announced her departure from the area. Shortly afterward, Mrs. A had an episode in which she smashed and destroyed objects in her house, and the therapist was summoned in the middle of the night. Mrs. A insisted that the destructiveness had nothing to do with the coming loss of the therapist—that it merely represented anger felt toward Mr. A, who happened to be away on a business trip. Needless to say, this painful incident was also invaluable in the psychotherapy in working through the termination.

Mrs. A continues to have cycles and remains severely impaired by her illness; however, the marriage is intact and the children are coping relatively successfully in high school and college and have dealt well with the possible heritable aspects of the illness. Mrs. A continues to take her medication, which at best alleviates her symptoms only slightly, and has begun therapeutic work with a new and interested therapist.

Treatment Considerations

Psychosocial treatments for aspects of other serious mental disorders, such as schizophrenia, suggest that the combination of psychosocial interventions with medication treatments may also be useful in bipolar disorder. Recent reviews (Miklowitz et al. 1996) indicate that the seriousness of bipolar disorder has not been addressed by investigations of treatment efficacy. The growing research on the medication treatment of this crippling disorder is in sharp contrast to the relative absence of research on crucial behaviors associated with seeking treatment and the outcome of treatment, such as medication compliance, symptom monitoring, and stress management. Clinicians have not yet systematically incorporated psychoeducation of patients and their families into the treatment of bipolar disorder, as has been done for schizophrenia. Only recently have there been controlled studies of the combined medication and psychosocial treatment of patients with bipolar disorder and their spouses. The fact that psychoeducation has been linked with greater medication compliance among bipolar patients underscores the importance of investigating this approach.

A combination of inpatient psychosocial and pharmacological treatments can result in improved work and social functioning in bipolar patients (Clarkin et al. 1988, 1990; Miklowitz 1996). Clarkin et al. (1990) randomly assigned bipolar patients and their families to either standard acute inpatient treatment or standard treatment plus inpatient family intervention. The family treatment was brief (approximately six sessions) and included a psychoeducational component. Goals included accepting the reality of the illness, identifying precipitating stresses and likely future stresses inside and outside the family, elucidating family interactions that produce stress on the patient, planning strategies for managing or minimizing future stresses, and bringing about the family's acceptance of the need for continued treatment after hospital discharge.

Patients receiving inpatient family intervention showed less symptomatology at discharge. There was no rehospitalization of patients in either treatment group at 6 months after discharge. However, at 18 months significantly fewer patients from the inpatient family intervention group had been rehospitalized (2/12) compared with the standard treatment group (4/8) ($P < 0.05$). Work or primary role functioning was significantly better for inpatient family intervention patients at both 6 and 18 months. Social role functioning was significantly better for the inpatient family intervention patients at 6 months.

Reviews of these psychoeducational treatment programs (Goldstein 1996) have identified two common features: 1) They all aim to ameliorate the course of the illness and reduce relapse rate rather than to cure the condition, and 2) they try to attain these goals via clearly defined types of family intervention that are largely educational in nature (Anderson et al. 1986). Psychoeducational interventions are those aimed at obtaining the family's help in working with the patient, educating the family as to the nature of the illness and what can be expected, and helping the family to modify stressful interaction patterns.

Psychoeducational marital interventions. For the family therapist we suggest an approach called psychoeducational marital intervention. It is based on the belief that the following four variables mediate outcome: 1) medication compliance, 2) engagement in the psychoeducational marital intervention treatment, 3) change in spousal negative attitudes, 4) and increase in problem-solving skills. Clarkin et al. (1998) conducted a controlled study of psychoeducational marital intervention and found that this treatment may be most useful with patients who have more severe illness and have a personality disorder. Less severely ill bipolar patients without personality disorder may respond adequately to medication without the need for family intervention.

Other specific psychosocial interventions. Behavioral family management is a treatment for patients who have recently been hospitalized for an episode of mania. It is based on a home-centered psychosocial treatment for schizophrenia (Falloon et al. 1988). The treatment includes psychoeducation, communication skills training, and problem-solving skills training. Although definitive trials of behavioral family management have not been completed, preliminary evidence suggests that the treatment approach, in concert with adequate pharmacotherapy, leads to a substantial decrease in relapse rate.

Miklowitz (1996) reported a pilot study of the effect of family therapy and psychoeducation (in addition to pharmacological and milieu treatment) on patients with bipolar disorder. Patients who were assigned randomly to the family therapy group (compared with a control group) had lower rates of family separations, greater improvements in level of family functioning, higher rates of full recovery, and lower rates of rehospitalization for 2 years following family treatment.

In summary, drug and family psychoeducational intervention seems mandatory. Whether systemic family therapy in the prevention phase is useful remains to be tested.

Dysthymia and Major Depressive Disorder

Rationale

DSM-IV major depression has a substantial heritable component, and there is little evidence of an effect of shared family environment on development of an episode (McGuffin et al. 1996). Where an association exists between family conflict and depressive disorders, it can be understood in a number of possible ways (Akiskal et al. 1978, 1983):

- Family stressors may elicit or precipitate depressive symptoms in a biologically vulnerable individual.
- Family stress or the lack of a sufficiently supportive intimate relationship may potentiate the effects of other environmental stressors.
- Depressive symptoms may trigger maladaptive behaviors and negative responses from family members, thus eliciting conflict.
- Subclinical depression or characterological traits, behavior patterns, and so on may potentiate family discord, which tends to trigger a depressive episode.

A major depressive disorder may develop, slowly or quickly, in a person with previously good mood and social functioning. These patients may progress to complete inability to function at home or work. Although these depressions sometimes remit spontaneously after several months, most last 6–12 months untreated. Appropriate treatment, usually including medication, will restore function quickly in most patients. Research has indicated that depression is in many cases a relapsing problem. If multiple episodes occur, the patient may develop personality changes and social maladjustment. In patients with dysthymia, a slow course of depressed mood, lack of concentration, sleep disturbance, and so on occurs over a period of months. These patients may have an intact or mildly impaired ability to function. They receive diagnoses and treatment less often than those with more severely impaired function. Shyness, low self-esteem, and anxiety or a depressive personality style may precede either a major depressive disorder or dysthymia.

Depression in adolescents and young adults.   Undiagnosed depression is a major cause of adolescent suicide and alcohol and drug use. Because adolescents are trying to separate from their parents they may be reluctant to share their distress, see a therapist, or accept treatment. Depression in adolescents may occur without obvious cause, especially in children with a family history of depression, or it may occur secondary to family factors such as parental divorce, alcoholism, or conflict; parental mental illness; or child abuse or neglect. Because the peer system is so important and the teen's identity shaky, difficulties in love relationships are particularly likely to precipitate depressive episodes, especially if the adolescent has a history of parental loss or neglect. Serious depression in young adults can also seriously compromise the launching process. If a child believes he or she is needed at home to protect a parent, depression provides an excuse to be home instead of out in the world. Even if the parents are ready for the child to leave, the child may be overwhelmed by the choices inherent in setting up a home and life of one's own and may require more parental support. In those who complete the launching successfully, difficulties in love relationships (especially for women) and work relationships (especially for men) may precipitate depression in vulnerable people.

Depression in partnered or married people.   Depression in marriage is a common outgrowth of the complex nature of the relationship. The fact that two out of three depressed people are women has led to considerable questioning about the role of hormones; the role of female role conditioning for passivity, caretaking, and low self-worth; and the role of chronic stress and discrimination as precipitants for depression. Because women are particularly attuned to relational contexts and draw much of their self-worth from intimate relationships, marital and family dysfunction or overload are particularly likely to generate depressive symptoms in a vulnerable woman. Verbal and physical abuse especially are likely to lead to depression. Severe environmental stress—such as job loss leading to alcohol intake in one or both partners, a very ill child or parent who requires care, or multiple interpersonal losses—can lead to depression. Men who become depressed within marriage sometimes present with masked depression, in which they become irritable and withdrawn but deny sadness or feelings of poor self-worth. At other times they may present a classic depressive triad (i.e., I am bad, the world is bad, and it won't get better).

How depression in one partner affects the marital interaction has been clarified (Haas et al. 1985). The depressed person gives and receives aversive stimulation (i.e., irritable or negative responses) at higher rates than do other family members. Depressed partners and mates engage in negative exchanges more frequently than do nondistressed normal couples. In social situations depressed people tend to avoid others, which is associated with the tendency for others to avoid them. This further narrows their interaction field and leads to problems at work and with friends, putting additional stress on the marriage. Systemic patterns commonly seen in depressed couples include the following:

- *Both partners are depressed.* Often one partner is more angry and the other more sad. Neither has time or energy to care for the other. This pattern often occurs when there has been severe family trauma such as the death of a child.
- *One partner is depressed, and the other is the caretaker.* The depressed person is labeled incompetent, helpless, and in need of cheering up and support. He or she is allowed to avoid unwanted activities because of the depression. The caretaker may be angry or take on the role of saint or superperson. Because both of these roles involve many positive attributes, they may be hard to give up.
- *One partner (most often the man) is demanding, coercive, and abusive, and the other (most often the woman) is depressed.* This pattern is common in abusive relationships. The depression is often a response to the abuse and control; it may also mask the anger that, if expressed, would lead to more abuse.

Depression in parents. Considerable evidence indicates that a mother depressed enough not to respond empathically to her infant puts the infant at some risk. Because the infant is dependent on the parent's ability to return nonverbal cues, a parent who cannot do so may cause the infant to give up on the possibility of response. Depressed persons have less energy for their children and are more apt to be less encouraging and more irritable and unavailable. In addition, they model a depressive world view and low self-esteem. Female children of depressed mothers are particularly likely to become caretakers in the home. The marital discord found in families with a depressed mother may have a larger negative effect on the child than does the parent's mood disorder itself.

Depression in middle-aged and older adults. Because depressive episodes become more frequent as people age, many middle-aged and older people with previously adequate functioning develop depression secondary to life stresses or losses. Middle-aged depression may be a factor in midlife divorce, as one partner blames his or her sadness on the spouse and determines to leave. Major depression or dysthymia may also be the result of divorces, especially for middle-aged women whose primary job was homemaking and who did not want the divorce. Retirement is another cause of depression, particularly in men. When older adults become depressed, they are often a burden on their adult children, who may respond with a mixture of guilt and anger or who may refuse to help at all. This can often affect all generations of the family system, including the grandchildren.

Treatment Considerations

The temporal and functional relationships between depression and aspects of family interaction have important implications for the design and implementation of family treatment of depressive disorders. Family conflict is often reported as the primary precipitant in episodes of clinical depression. In such cases, family therapy would be indicated for treatment of the interpersonal problems, often directed at reducing the frequency of aversive communications between partners, inducing more frequent mutual reinforcement, and modifying distorted cognitive and perceptual responses to the partner's behavior (Prince and Jacobson 1995). Antidepressant medication can be combined with these therapies for symptom relief without risk of compromising their effectiveness. If family conflict appears not to be a contributing factor in the depressive episode, the identified patient should be treated with appropriate medication and then reevaluated for psychotherapy. The addition of short-term supportive family therapy may be useful in helping to engage the patient in the recommended medication regimen.

With more severe depression in which the identified patient's function is severely impaired, a two-phase program of family intervention is needed. During the initial phase, psychopharmacological treatments are begun and short-term supportive family therapy is introduced to ameliorate the family's negative reactions to the symptoms (thus reducing secondary stress reactions) and to educate the patient and family as to the nature of the disorder, the recommended treatment, and strategies for coping with residual symptoms and possible relapse. The family can be helpful either directly to the patient or indirectly in maintaining its own homeostasis by early recognition of symptoms (especially hypomania); by monitoring the patient's mood; by being aware of early signs of medication toxicity such as nausea, vomiting, diarrhea, ataxia, and dysarthria; and by encouraging medication compliance. An objective family therapy helps the family develop new patterns necessary as a result of changes in the patient's role and function that stem from the illness and the medication.

Only after the florid symptoms have diminished and the patient and family have reached a plateau or relatively stable stage of adjustment can a second phase of therapy be initiated. Efforts to modify maladaptive communication patterns and problem-solving strategies, to deal with resistances, and to effect structural changes are best reserved for this phase of intervention. Consider the following case example:

> Mr. B was a 46-year-old lawyer, and his wife, Dr. B, was a 45-year-old physician. They had three children, ages 6, 9, and 12 years. The couple were referred for marital treatment (as a last resort) because of dissatisfaction with the marriage. The spouses saw divorce as the only solution. Over the previous year the couple's fighting (and mutual blaming), which dated to the beginning of their marriage some 20 years earlier, had intensified. Areas of conflict included money and childrearing. Mr. B's need for control of the relationship was evident in financial and parenting issues. To accomplish this, he would criticize his wife's attempts in both areas. For example, Dr. B would discipline the children, and Mr. B would say she should not have been so tough on them. When she did not discipline them, he would proclaim that she was negligent.
>
> The couple's history revealed that both had been brought up in Europe in what they described as chaotic households, with parents who fought more than their peers' parents. Each partner had a parent who experienced depressive episodes. The history of treatment attempts revealed that both husband and wife had had separate, classical psychoanalyses, which they described as "helpful but not enough to end the marital fighting." Both partners met criteria for a diagnosis of major depressive disorder, recurrent type.
>
> When couples treatment started, Mr. B and Dr. B were extremely depressed, manifesting symptoms of loss of interest and pleasure, low self-esteem, and lack of energy. Treatment sessions centered around mutual blaming for each partner's symptoms. Three sessions led to no improvement. At that point, antidepressant medication was instituted. After 6 weeks, both partners experienced considerable improvement in mood and activity level.
>
> This change afforded the therapist two tactical advantages. First, with their mood and cognition improvements, the couple could conceivably begin to examine and alter behavioral interactions that might build a viable relationship.

Second, the therapist was now viewed as an expert who could prescribe tasks (e.g., taking the right medication) that were effective and thus was in a position to prescribe interpersonal tasks to change the previously described negative feedback systems such as Dr. B's control, Mr. B's criticism, and their resulting morass of further depression and lowered self-esteem. At this point, the therapist took advantage of this position by guiding the couple to interpersonal changes that led to further marital improvement.

The preceding case example illustrates how psychopharmacotherapy may enhance the efficacy of marital therapy. We also believe that marital therapy is likely to enhance psychopharmacotherapy in many depressive patients.

Controlled studies have shown that psychosocial treatment with families can have significant effects on patient outcome (Prince and Jacobson 1995). Well-controlled clinical research on unipolar depression has demonstrated that outpatient psychotherapy used in conjunction with pharmacological treatments can improve patient functioning in the areas of social, family, and work adjustment. Jacobson and colleagues (1991) treated depressed females and their spouses with a cognitive-behavioral therapy, behavioral marital therapy, and a combination of the two. The results depended on the presence or absence of marital conflict. Without marital conflict, behavioral marital therapy was less effective than cognitive therapy in reducing depression. In contrast, when marital conflict was present, the two treatments were equally effective in reducing depression, but behavioral marital treatment was also effective in improving marital satisfaction. The combined treatment was the only treatment condition to reduce aversive behavior in the husband and wife and to increase facilitative behavior in the wife. On follow-up study (Jacobson et al. 1993), relapse rates did not distinguish between the treatments. The nature of the husband-wife interaction related to relapse. Reductions in dysphoria in the husband and wife and increases in facilitative behavior in the wife during therapy predicted recovery. High rates of facilitative behavior in the husband at follow-up was associated with recovery.

Keitner et al. (1995) showed a clear association between better family functioning and recovery from major depression over the long term. Different aspects of family life respond differently to the depressive illness; no one family dimension was uniquely related to outcome.

In their study of adolescent depression, Brent et al. (1997) compared cognitive therapy, individual supportive therapy, and systemic behavioral family therapy. All three treatments reduced suicidality and functional impairment, but cognitive therapy was more efficacious on a number of other parameters including credibility to the parents and more rapid relief of depression.

Borderline Personality Disorder

Rationale

Borderline personality disorder is a complex disorder, the etiology of which is still being debated. Research has indicated the possibility of a biological vulnerability in many people. There is an increased risk of substance-related disorders, mood disorders, and borderline personality disorder among first-degree biological relatives of individuals who have borderline personality disorder. In addition, both antidepressant and neuroleptic treatments have been associated with considerable improvement in some patients. There are strong indications that parental and family pathology plays a role in etiology. Parental issues include a high incidence of alcoholism, affective disorder, and Cluster B personality disorders, which often result in families with a high level of emotional neglect and impulsive and chaotic family environments. Among patients given the diagnosis of borderline personality disorder, there is a high frequency of significant separation from parents in early childhood because of marital separation or death. It has been hypothesized that physical and especially sexual abuse is extremely common in the history of these patients.

Women represent approximately 75% of borderline personality disorder patients. It is not clear whether this is because of the higher incidence of abuse among female children, whether the characteristic family patterns that produce borderline personality disorder in girls are more likely to produce antisocial personality in boys, or whether other reasons related to the etiology of the disorder are at play.

Borderline adolescents and young adults at home. Individuals undergoing a difficult adolescence may exhibit characteristics of borderline personality disorder, including unstable and intense interpersonal relationships, identity disturbance, impulsivity and affective instability, feelings of emptiness, and inappropriate anger. In most teenagers these characteristics alternate with periods of better function and a sense of developing self. Borderline personality disorder is generally not diagnosed until young adulthood, when it is clear that the symptoms do not represent a stage or a crisis but are a stable state. Young people with borderline personality disorder are usually deeply involved in highly aversive and intense relationships with their families, involving early, ineffective, and protracted launching with inability to truly individuate. Relationships with peers and lovers are often intense and unstable, leading to rage or suicide attempts.

Borderline partnered and married people.   Borderline patients are likely to withdraw from others or engage in highly intense and dramatic relationships. Marriages are likely to be highly conflicted and unstable. In some couples both spouses have borderline personality disorder; in most others one spouse has significant psychopathology. Borderline patients as parents run the gamut from reasonably functional to intrusive, hostile, and neglectful.

Of note, the association between expressed emotion and patient outcome may be different for patients with borderline personality disorder: one study did not find that relative's criticism and hostility predicted outcome. In fact, emotional overinvolvement predicted *better* clinical outcomes (Hooley and Hoffman 1999).

Treatment Considerations

Psychotherapists have struggled for years to treat borderline patients, whose shifting symptom picture and difficulties with relating make a treatment alliance difficult. Individual therapy and medication are usually part of the treatment package. Family therapy is complex and depends on the family's situation. For example, if a young adult with borderline personality disorder is living at home in a chaotic household, the entire family needs to be treated as the patient. In a family that is apparently running smoothly except for the identified patient, a decision must be made about whether to focus on basic psychoeducation (i.e., what can be expected, what types of support are sensible) or whether the patient is the truth teller or symptom bearer (e.g., in the case of a family that looks functional but in which the father has abused his daughters). In some families, whatever the issues or neglect of the early years, the rest of the family members have experienced good development and are now being overwhelmed by the demands of the borderline patient and by their own guilt. These families must be supported in setting limits on the amount of help they will give. Because borderline patients are at risk for suicide the issues of risk must be discussed with the family at length.

Couples may have stormy relationships or may include one borderline spouse (usually the woman) and an apparently stoic or saintly caretaker. Therapy with these couples is slow and involves creating an atmosphere of support and consistency. These individuals try the therapist's tolerance and patience. The therapist must interview the children and consider their support system. Because many borderline women are single parents, particular attention must be paid to adequate support for the children. Glick et al. (1995) reviewed in detail the subject of the family and borderline personality disorder.

Anxiety Disorders

DSM-IV groups together the following anxiety-related disorders: panic disorder with and without agoraphobia, agoraphobia without panic disorder, specific phobias, social phobia, obsessive-compulsive disorder, posttraumatic stress disorder, generalized anxiety disorder, anxiety due to medical conditions, and substance-induced anxiety (American Psychiatric Association 1994). These disorders seem to be related to underlying high levels of activation of the nervous system, which are probably related to alterations in γ-aminobutyric acid receptor function. Anxiety disorders can be treated with medication, cognitive-behavioral therapy including desensitization, or both.

Many of these disorders have a far higher incidence in women, and family stress or the loss or disruption of close personal relationships often precipitates attacks. Most of these patients marry, and the considerable morbidity associated with anxiety disorders strains both marital relations and parenting practices. The symptoms are often deeply embedded in the family's way of operating, and the anxious person is sometimes a symptom bearer for the family. This is particularly true with panic disorder, generalized anxiety disorder, and agoraphobia. Consider the following case example:

> Mrs. C, the mother of two young children, had low self-esteem and a family history of anxiety. Mr. C was a rather controlling husband who held a demanding academic job. After a number of years as a homemaker, Mrs. C decided to return to school to finish her degree. Mr. C was very unsupportive and declared that Mrs. C could go back to school only if she made all the child-care arrangements and continued to care for the house. After her first exam at school, on which she did adequately but not spectacularly, she became acutely anxious and subsequently depressed. For a number of weeks she was so consistently anxious that she could not function at home at all, forcing her husband to take over the household and child care. Her anxiety could be construed in several ways: It expressed her rage at his unsupportiveness, it was a way of going "on strike" that he could not combat with logic, and it represented her hopelessness over her inability to either find the intimacy and support she wanted from her husband or do brilliantly at school to support her self-esteem. She was treated with a combination of antidepressants, antianxiety medication, brief couples therapy (her husband would not tolerate more), and supportive individual therapy over a period of 3 months. At the end of treatment she was back at school, and her husband was functioning more supportively, grateful that he no longer had the full burden of the house.

Although the therapist in the preceding case example initially thought that the patient should be stabilized on medication before couples therapy was started, it was not until couples therapy had been initiated and the patient's husband had begun to take his wife's concerns seriously that the symptoms subsided. This has been true of the majority of patients seen in our practice. We recommend early evaluation of the entire family system with the rapid initiation of couples work if it appears indicated.

Panic Disorder

Of all the anxiety disorders, panic disorder with or without agoraphobia may be one of the most conducive to combined treatment. Agoraphobic individuals fear the recurrence of another panic attack, usually fearing to be alone or to go certain places. A variety of theories have been proposed to explain this disorder, including that family influences play an important role in its etiology. A mutually reinforcing system may exist in which the agoraphobic person is kept in a dependent state by a significant other, usually a spouse, to cover up the latter's anger and dependence. The symptom bearer finds a symbolic, dysfunctional way of communicating with and controlling the spouse (e.g., a wife who refuses to leave the house thus forces her husband to stay home and take care of her).

Does the removal of the agoraphobia in one spouse affect the adjustment of the other spouse? The answer is not simple. In a study of behavioral treatment in women with agoraphobia, there was no evidence of symptoms arising in the nonagoraphobic spouse (Cobb et al. 1984). In contrast, in a study of the marital interaction of 36 married agoraphobic women treated over a period of 3 years, 7 of the husbands displayed abnormal jealousy that adversely influenced the wife's response to treatment (Hafner 1979). Improvement in the wives was associated with increased jealousy in the husbands. In a study of the husbands of 26 agoraphobic women, before and after intensive in vivo exposure treatment of the wives for agoraphobia, Hafner (1984) found that most husbands had experienced transitory negative reactions including anxiety and depression. These negative reactions often coincided with large, rapid improvements in the most severely disturbed patients. Hafner suggested that negative effects were most likely in those men who were hostile, critical, and unsupportive of their wives and who had adapted to their wives' disability as part of a sex role–stereotyped view of marriage.

Antianxiety and antidepressant agents are effective for panic disorder, agoraphobia, and social phobia. Marital therapy (or behavioral therapy) in combination with medication can be extremely effective. Individual behavior modification is not as effective as family behavior modification because it is easy to overlook the reinforcing nature of the interpersonal interaction

(Hafner 1984). This complicated treatment picture suggests that in some situations the patient with panic disorder can be successfully treated individually with behavioral interventions with no need for marital intervention. In other situations, however, especially when the spouse without panic disorder is hostile and has some investment in his or her partner's symptom picture, involving the spouse in the treatment may be necessary.

The addition of the spouse as a co-therapist in the behavioral treatment of the agoraphobic spouse may enhance the treatment effect for nonsystems reasons. For example, Munby and Johnston (1980) followed 66 agoraphobic patients 5–9 years after their involvement in a behavioral treatment. Patients who had a home-based program using the husband as a co-therapist fared somewhat better than those involved in programs that did not involve the husband. The authors suggest that this is because the patient and spouse learned to deal with the agoraphobic problem themselves with less need for further professional intervention.

Obsessive-Compulsive Disorder

Obsessive-compulsive disorder has strong genetic roots. The disorder places major burdens on the families of patients who have it, including physical, financial, and emotional burdens and marital and family problems. Treatment consists of medication plus family intervention to deal with disruption of family life. If the family believes, and genuinely feels, that the patient is not motivated to change, excessive arguing and being drawn into the ritualizing behavior will result. The family's attempts to accommodate the patient's symptoms cause global family dysfunction and stress but are best viewed as the family trying to reduce the patient's anxiety. Psychoeducation is crucial so that the family's behavior can be reframed as its attempt to get along and to change the accommodating behavior, allowing the whole family to function better (Calvocoressi et al. 1995). In addition to family therapy, workshops and support groups are helpful.

Posttraumatic Stress Disorder

Except in the case of "incest," posttraumatic stress disorder is by definition a diagnosis that is seldom caused by the family system. The symptoms are very distressing to the family and to the patient, and other members of the family can have violent reactions to a trauma befalling a loved one, including anxiety, depression, and posttraumatic stress disorder (as a result of witnessing the trauma or the result). The therapist must evaluate the family and provide support and education about the disorder.

Delirium, Dementia, Amnesia, and Other Cognitive Disorders

Rationale

The most common of the cognitive disorders are those associated with presenile or senile brain disease or with chronic atherosclerotic brain disease. A variety of other syndromes (e.g., Alzheimer's disease or cerebral vascular accidents) incapacitate patients and create problems for the family. Because these disorders are of slow onset, they are sometimes confused with depression or marital problems in the early stages. Chronic dementias are among the most painful issues that any family has to face. Because of the patient's cognitive deficits, family is crucial in providing the history necessary for the differential diagnosis.

Watching a loved one decline mentally, becoming incapacitated and confused while in good physical health, is an almost unbearable grief. The constant caretaking required drains a family of its resources—money, time, energy. Because many years may elapse between early symptoms and death, the family must manage a situation that worsens constantly over many years. For the person losing function gradually, the pain and anxiety are often severe. It is not surprising that some of these situations end in suicide or euthanasia.

Assuming that the illness occurs in a person with grown children and a spouse, the first questions are apportioning caretaking duties. These usually fall to the spouse first and then to the women in the family—daughters, daughters-in-law, sisters. Members of the extended family vary in their responses. Often the ones farthest away, and least helpful, are the most critical of family care. Decisions that must be made are many, from when to take away the car keys, to when the person needs constant care, to who is in charge of the nurses or caretakers, to whether the parent should be placed in a hospital or nursing home. Questions about whether a senile parent will be taken into the home of an adult child, particularly one with children still at home, are complex and there are no comfortable answers. Guilt and anger are often paramount. Often the child who had the worst relationship with the parent and the most unfinished business is left as caretaker, stirring up further anger over having to care for a parent who did not care for him or her.

Treatment Considerations

The family therapist's job is to assist the family members in working and making decisions together, to support them in getting adequate medical care, to encourage them to use the many uncoordinated helping agencies that are available, and to help them use well the time left with the loved one. Often many years of partial function are left, during which time the family can find ways to help the person compensate for his or her memory loss and remain part of the family. The therapist must also allow time for grief. Consider the following case example:

> Mrs. D, a 60-year-old executive secretary, presented for a diagnostic evaluation because of memory loss. She gave a 3-year history of progressive inability to do her work because she was forgetting things and was irritable on the job (a marked change from her previous premorbid personality as a quiet, careful person). Her 65-year-old husband, Mr. D, quit his job in order to take care of her, and for several months things went reasonably smoothly. However, her functioning continued to decline and she developed hallucinations, confusion, and paranoia.
>
> Medications did not help the situation. Multiple consultations suggested that Mrs. D had senile dementia due to vascular causes and recommended nursing home placement. Mr. D vehemently opposed this, saying that the illness was temporary and that he could not be away from his wife. His two daughters, one living in the same city and one several states away, were violently at odds. The younger daughter, who lived close by and saw her parents often, was very frightened by the situation and pushed for placement. The older daughter, who lived far away, and who had been father's favorite, insisted that Mrs. D be kept at home to make Mr. D happy. Mr. D was also beginning to show signs of forgetfulness, and it was unclear whether this was due to depression over the wife's illness, sleep deprivation (his wife no longer slept much at night), or beginning organic brain disorder of his own.
>
> The family therapist held a meeting that included the father, both daughters, and their husbands. The more distant daughter was asked to stay in her parents' house for several days to evaluate the situation, at the end of which she was far more aware of the problems her father faced. At the end of the several-session consultation it was agreed that the two daughters and Mr. D would pay for 24-hour care in the parental home to keep Mrs. D at home as long as possible, with nursing home placement to be discussed again in 3 months or earlier if certain specified crises occurred. Mr. D was evaluated for depression and placed on a low dose of an antidepressant. With the antidepressant and the presence of another adult in the house, Mr. D was able to sleep. He was encouraged to return to work part time in order to have some respite from the situation.

Eating Disorders

Rationale

Eating disorders, including anorexia nervosa and bulimia nervosa, have a typical onset in adolescence or early adult life, predominantly in females, and with seemingly increasing frequency in American culture. According to DSM-IV they "appear to be far more prevalent in industrialized societies, in which there is an abundance of food and in which, especially for females, being considered attractive is linked to being thin" (American Psychiatric Association 1994, p. 542). Preoccupation with food has reached epidemic proportions in the United States. Almost 70% of women have been on diets, often beginning as early as age 10 years, and about 80% of American women consider themselves overweight. There is some suggestion that as women have moved into the labor force, and men have become less valued for their economic ability, men have also become more preoccupied with their appearance, and the incidence of food-related disorders in men has increased (Woodside et al. 1993).

Within the societal preoccupation with food, there is a strong suggestion that eating disorders, especially anorexia, occur in individuals with particular psychological vulnerability. Some of this vulnerability may be genetic. First-degree female relatives of anorexic patients have increased rates of anorexia, and families of patients with bulimia have increased rates of substance abuse, affective disorders, and obesity.

Many women are preoccupied with food to an extent that appears obsessive, and many women who do not binge nevertheless overeat compulsively. These food issues are linked to the fact that although food is basically a comfort mechanism for many people, control of desire to eat is linked with the concept of goodness in this society (Yager et al. 1989). Thus many people have considered an addictions model for compulsive overeaters and for bulimic individuals. The fact that one cannot abstain from food as one can from alcohol or drugs makes this a more difficult model from which to work in clinical practice.

Anorexia nervosa. Anorexia nervosa is a life-threatening illness that is complex and difficult to treat. Most often it begins slowly, often in families in which there is great concern about appearance, weight, or eating issues in other family members. As the individual consumes progressively smaller amounts of food, a preoccupation with food and ritualization of the eating process occur. Food and weight become the anorexic patient's total preoccupation. These patients are aware of hunger and pride themselves on being able to master it. Many anorexic patients cook a great deal and feed other people. Many use laxatives to induce more weight loss and exercise constantly to keep their weight even lower. In a few cases the patient may drink large quantities of water in order to stop eating (e.g., one young woman raised her liquid intake to several gallons a day). The family may be pleased initially by the weight loss, and the patient may achieve quite a low weight before the family notices that something is wrong. When the patient is unable to stop losing weight, the family may become angry, frightened, or helpless. Family members may allow themselves to be drawn into complex eating rituals in order to induce the patient to eat. Few young anorexic patients present for treatment on their own, until the family insists that something be done.

Bulimia nervosa. Bulimia nervosa is not life threatening, but it can result in serious health problems, including esophagitis, serious dental problems, and malnutrition. It can also result in a loss of focus on the rest of life because of preoccupation with food. Bulimia is common in certain social contexts. For example, in some college dormitories students model this behavior for one another. It has been reported that in some dormitories, one-quarter of the female students have been bulimic at some time. Bulimia and compulsive overeating are more common when the individual is experiencing stress, high anxiety, and a need for the comfort that food provides. The purging that frequently follows a binge often relieves anxiety and anger. Because much of the individual therapy is directed at understanding and dealing with the emotions that the binge is in some way covering, family therapy is thought to be critical in uncovering key conflicts that fuel the problem.

Treatment Considerations

Treatment of anorexia on an outpatient basis usually consists of individual therapy, family therapy, and often medication (Work Group on Eating Disorders 1993). Family issues involve marital conflict in the parent generation, parental obsession with perfection or weight, and control issues. A family secret such as abuse or alcoholism is often present. When treating older, married anorexic patients, the therapist must consider how the disease affects the patients' marriage and children. (Although severe anorexia stops menstruation, many married anorexic patients eat enough to maintain fertility, and they generally eat enough during pregnancy to protect their babies.)

Therapy is tailored to the family's specific issues. Education about the illness is necessary. Even if the predominant type of therapy is family or individual, the therapist must weigh and medically monitor the patient and periodically check electrolyte balance, which can change rapidly in very ill patients and is a serious medical issue. Starvation produces difficulties in thinking that make therapy or living even harder. The question of when to hospitalize the patient is always an issue in very-low-weight anorexic patients. Hospitalization usually is a continuation of previous treatment. Sometimes a hospitalization provides the crisis needed for the patient and family to break through established patterns. Many models of therapy, including insight-awareness, cognitive-behavioral, and supportive, have been applied in the treatment of these disorders. Eating disorders are best approached with a treatment team, whether inpatient or outpatient, consisting of a nutritionist, internist, therapist, and an experienced supervisor or team leader.

The Work Group on Eating Disorders (1993) has summarized treatment studies. In one study patients with anorexia nervosa with onset at or before age 18 years and with a duration of less than 3 years showed greater improvement 1 year after discharge from the hospital with family therapy than with individual psychotherapy; in contrast, older anorexia nervosa patients did better with individual therapy than with family therapy (Russell et al. 1987). Patients in this study were not assigned to both family and individual treatment, a combination frequently used in practice. For bulimia, family therapy was reported as being helpful in a large case series (Schwartz et al. 1985). Although no systematic studies of the approach exist, some patients have found Overeaters Anonymous and similar groups to be helpful in recovery, in part because of the networking, sense of connectedness to a group, and 24-hour-per-day support against food cravings that they offer (Malenbaum et al. 1989; Pope et al. 1983). Controversy exists regarding the role of 12-step programs that do not address nutritional considerations and psychological or behavioral deficits when used as the sole intervention in the treatment of eating disorders (Vandereycken 1990).

The year 2000 American Psychiatric Association practice guidelines now recommend that for bulimia, "family therapy should be considered whenever possible, for adolescents still living with parents or older patients with ongoing conflicted interactions with parents" (p. 25) and for patients with marital problems. Likewise, for anorexia nervosa, family and couples therapy are useful (Work Group on Eating Disorders 2000).

Disorders Usually First Diagnosed in Infancy, Childhood, or Adolescence

Mental Retardation

Mental retardation has a variety of possible causes, but in most instances secondary family problems occur. In addition to the real problem of social development and functioning of the identified patient because of his or her possibly damaged biological equipment, associated family reactions require attention. The family may feel antipathy, guilt, social isolation, or anxiety about caring for the child's usual health needs (Adams 1972). Family members may make the mentally retarded child a scapegoat to cover up unresolved conflicts between mother and father or between parents and children. Help must be focused on the identified patient's specific needs and on the family's attitudes and behavior. In addition to medication (if indicated), psychosocial treatments that provide support for the family's sense of loss and helplessness, education about the appropriate use of community resources, psychoeducation about mental retardation, and behavioral strategies for managing destructive behaviors are most likely to bring relief and success to these families.

Pervasive Developmental Disorders: Autistic Disorder

Pervasive developmental disorders comprise a heterogeneous group of disorders that includes autistic disorder, Asperger's syndrome, and others. Thinking about autistic disorder has shifted considerably since the past two decades. Family members are now recognized as being profoundly affected by this disorder. The issues of loss for parents of a child with autistic disorder are monumental, and family therapy can provide a place for couples to talk openly about their sadness, helplessness, and anxiety. At the same time, family meetings are important in consolidating a plan for advocating for the child's needs (e.g., obtaining adequate educational and therapeutic resources), learning specific strategies for teaching the child and promoting language development, and building in time for parents to focus on their needs and practical needs of others in the family. Because autistic disorder can take a large toll on families, family support is viewed widely as crucial in terms of acute and long-term adaptation.

Attention-Deficit/Hyperactivity Disorder

Attention-deficit/hyperactivity disorder (ADHD) (formerly called attention-deficit disorder in DSM-III) is among the most common problems encountered in working with children and adolescents. These disorders occur primarily in two family situations, one that is child focused and one that is adult focused (American Academy of Child and Adolescent Psychiatry 1991). The more common situation is where the child is the identified patient and becomes a severe burden on the family because of symptoms including irritability, restlessness, lack of attention, impulsivity, and aggression. ADHD is often associated with discrete learning disabilities. The standard treatment is a combination of medication (usually a psychostimulant such as methylphenidate) and therapy for both the child and family. Although medication and tutoring can modify many of the symptoms, behavioral interventions in the classroom and in the home (e.g., structuring) should also be used to reduce stimulus overload and to help the child to develop greater self-monitoring and self-control. Family intervention is necessary to provide psychoeducation about ADHD (parents commonly blame each other or the child for what is primarily a pathophysiological disorder), and instruction in behavioral techniques may be quite useful (American Academy of Child and Adolescent Psychiatry 1991). Consultation with the family is often crucial in alleviating a family crisis or long-term turmoil.

The less common situation results when the disorder continues through adulthood and involves a married couple. ADHD in adults has found new acceptance as a diagnosis, and more adults are taking stimulants for this disorder than ever before. As with children, multimodal treatments combining medication and therapy are the recommended approaches. With successful combined treatment, most patients notice that they are more productive at work and can spend more quality time with the family. Psychoeducation for spouses and other family members can be helpful in identifying realistic expectations for behavior, organization, and attention. Consider the following case example:

Mr. E, a 27-year-old man, met the DSM-IV criteria for ADHD, residual type, marked by impulsivity, irritability, inattentiveness, and motor restlessness. When treated with imipramine, 250 mg/day, he experienced a marked decrease in target symptoms, and within 10 days of his starting the imipramine regimen, Mr. E and his wife noted a dramatic decrease in domestic violence, hostility, anxiety, and irritability. His attention span lengthened, and he was able to complete household projects that had been left unfinished for years. In his words, "I can never remember feeling so calm." He had previously taken low-dose neuroleptics and benzodiazepines without benefit. Mr. E, his wife, and the treatment team considered the treatment with imipramine to be successful.

Although Mr. and Mrs. E were thrilled initially with Mr. E's improvement, they soon began to experience increased marital tension. Before Mr. E began to take imipramine, the couple's primary focus had been on his symptoms. With the initiation of medication and the subsequent amelioration of those symptoms, this focus was no longer relevant. The couple had previously communicated through arguments, affective storms, and at times outright physical aggression. While taking the imipramine, however, Mr. E found that his mood was less labile and hostile, and Mrs. E began to complain bitterly that she "couldn't get a fight out of him anymore." She sought marital separation. Outside the home, Mr. E expressed confusion over his newly acquired ability to "stop myself from hitting people—I have a few seconds now to think before I act."

Although the target symptoms had diminished, Mr. E and his wife did not adjust readily to the change. In the absence of symptoms as a major focus in the marriage the couple were disarmed; their accustomed pattern of interaction was also disrupted (Satel and Southwick 1987).

The preceding case highlights the potential for a different set of difficulties to arise after the acute symptoms are resolved by medication. The partners have to relate to each other in different ways. Family therapy is an excellent adjunct to the treatment that not only helps the patient but also helps the couple to change. The same principle holds true for other Axis I disorders, when rapid changes in treatment occur.

Conduct Disorders

Conduct problems are the most common behavioral disorders presenting in mental health settings. Conduct disorder and oppositional defiant disorder are more common in boys than in girls and are extremely difficult for families and schools to manage successfully. Antisocial behavior in adults may be an expected outcome of uncontrolled conduct disorder in adolescence.

Behavioral and structural interventions have been most successful in altering patterns of antisocial and oppositional behavior in children and adolescents. These treatments focus on the establishment of clear rules and consequences, a family structure in which the parents are in an executive position, the appropriate use of community resources, parent training in behavioral techniques, and attention to marital adjustment. Although resistance to treatment is especially prominent in these disorders (Chamberlain and Rosicky 1995), results are generally supportive of family therapy.

Anxiety Disorders

Anxiety disorders in childhood include separation anxiety disorder, avoidant personality disorder, and overanxious disorder. A survey of child psychiatrists in the United States indicated that family and individual therapy, often in combination, are the most frequently used interventions for childhood anxiety (American Academy of Child and Adolescent Psychiatry 1991). Behavioral techniques in both family and individual treatment are especially useful. School phobias are ideal situations for family therapy. Commonly, when mother and child find it difficult to separate, there may be an underlying marital problem. With all types of phobias, treatment of the individual by behavior modification or medication should be considered, possibly using the parent as a co-therapist who assists with the behavioral techniques.

Mood Disorders

Although we discussed mood disorders earlier in this chapter, we must add a caveat here. Recent research has demonstrated that depressive and bipolar disorders may start in childhood or more commonly in adolescence. Mood disorders that first appear in adolescence usually continue into adulthood—a fact that should be shared with the family. Otherwise, the patient and family will deny existence of the illness and focus mostly on the secondary family problems. In fact, Rueter et al. (1999) recently reported that parent-adolescent child disagreements predict onset of both depressive and anxiety disorders (i.e., a direct relation among stress, symptoms, and onset of disorder).

Consider the following analogy: In certain infections it is not the direct destruction of the cell by the virus but the response of the host that is responsible for producing the disease. Similarly, in psychiatry, certain behaviors are not pathogenic by themselves, but the response of the family system creates what we now call pathology. Recognition and prescription of medication combined with psychoeducation and family intervention (when indicated) provides the best basis for healthier individual and family coping.

Substance-Related Disorders

With Robert A. Matano, Ph.D.,
Amy Bronstone, Ph.D., and Diana M. Doumas, Ph.D.

Rationale

According to a 1994 Gallup Poll, 27% of Americans report that alcohol has caused family problems (McAneny 1994). This statistic is not surprising when one considers that approximately 19 million of the adult population in the United States are problem drinkers and approximately 8 million are alcohol dependent (Clark and Midanik 1982; Winick 1992). Similarly, a 1988 National Institute on Drug Abuse survey reported that 14.5 million Americans had used marijuana, cocaine, or other illicit drugs within the past 30 days (National Institute on Drug Abuse 1990). Further, current estimates suggest that 5%–6% of Americans experience drug dependence at sometime in their lives (Winick 1992).

To understand fully the effect of substance abuse, the therapist must understand alcoholism and drug addiction as diseases that affect the entire family. The ways in which alcoholism and addiction affect family members are varied and pervasive, ranging from the disruption of daily meals to the negative effect on child development. Alcoholism and addiction can produce severe health problems in the individuals with these disorders and in other family members. Families with an alcoholic or addicted member overuse health services (Holder and Hallan 1986). Addiction not only has psychological causes but also results from specific changes in serotonin and dopamine function and from receptor dysfunction.

> Conversely, the family environment affects vulnerability to abuse. Tsuang et al. (1998, p. 967) found evidence for a shared or common vulnerability factor that underlies the abuse of marijuana, sedatives, stimulants, heroin or opiates, and psychedelics. This shared vulnerability is influenced by genetic, family environmental, and nonfamily environmental factors, but not every drug is influenced to the same extent by the shared vulnerability factor.
>
> Marijuana, more than other drugs, was influenced by family environmental factors. Each category of drug, except psychedelics, had genetic influences unique to itself (ie, not shared with other drug categories). Heroin had larger genetic influences unique to itself than did any other drug.

The sections that follow focus on the family therapy of alcoholism and drug addiction. In our experience, family therapy approaches to alcoholism and drug addiction are much more similar than different; thus the same methods and procedures described for treating alcoholism can generally be applied to the treatment of drug addiction.

Treatment approaches before family therapy. A substantial body of research has described the effects of substance abuse in the family (Cronkite et al. 1990; Kaufman 1985). There was a time, however, when alcoholism was not thought of as a family illness. Thus past treatment approaches focused mainly on the alcoholic individual, usually in isolation from his or her family. For example, an alcoholic patient who was fortunate enough to identify his or her problem would be referred to a quiet place in the country to detoxify and dry out. After a number of weeks in a serene setting, the patient would return to the family setting, only to be confronted with the damage and legacy of his or her drinking. Such a treatment approach would not address the resentment, shame, and guilt felt by all family members. This situation, among other factors, contributed to a rapid relapse. Current research suggests that involving significant others or family members in the treatment process is very important in ensuring a favorable prognosis (Edwards and Steinglass 1995; McNabb et al. 1989; Moos et al. 1990).

Physical dependence on drugs such as barbiturates, cocaine, and heroin was previously thought to be extremely resistant to family therapy interventions. Current research suggests that family therapy is an effective treatment for drug dependency. Some facilities treat nonaddicted drug users by using family therapy as a primary form of treatment. This approach is based on the rationale that the drug use is in part a symptom of disturbed functioning and communication within the family.

Early theories regarding the importance of family involvement in alcohol and drug treatment suggested that the personality of the spouse played a vital role in causing and maintaining the addictive behavior (Kaufman 1985). Domineering wives were said to cause alcoholism in their husbands because of their need to infantilize them. Although this idea may seem outlandish today, the acceptance that family members might play a role in the problem was a significant development at the time.

The development of family therapy approaches. Early theories regarding family functioning led to more sophisticated models in which the family was viewed as a system with its own power. In the late 1970s and early 1980s, the application of family systems theory to conceptualizations of addiction suggested new clinical approaches. The work of Salvador Minuchin and Jay Haley became the foundation for Stanton and Todd's (1982) family therapy model with drug addicted individuals. Other authors began to describe features of the alcoholic family in detail (Steinglass 1980; Steinglass et al. 1987). These elaborate models focused on so-called wet versus dry family functioning, specific roles played by different family members (e.g., hero, scapegoat, enabler, mascot), and specific rules characterizing dysfunctional families.

The development of family systems theory, which posits that a family consists of a dynamic interplay and equilibrium of forces that affect all family members, dramatically altered approaches to alcohol and drug treatment. Based on this model, alcoholism was hypothesized to play a dynamic function in the family, involving all family members. For example, alcoholism or drug addiction could protect family members from confronting difficult issues such as fear of intimacy, mistrust, fear of independence, and so on. The negative consequences of drug use could prevent real communication or intimacy among family members who might fear this type of contact, thus keeping the family in an unhealthy, albeit balanced state of equilibrium.

Related to family systems approaches was the development of the intervention pioneered by the Johnson Institute (Johnson 1986). This intervention focused on the idea that the family system could be harnessed to motivate the alcoholic individual to accept treatment by coaching the family members to set limits with the alcoholic member about the drinking.

Another widely used treatment approach, cognitive-behavioral therapy, is based on social learning principles such as reinforcement, consequences, and modeling. Cognitive-behavioral models suggest that family dysfunction can be treated by teaching specific skills to help families learn to communicate more effectively and improve conflict resolution and problem-solving skills. Family members are taught to reinforce the alcoholic or addicted individual for periods of sobriety and provide negative consequences for substance-using behavior. Cognitive-behavioral approaches also emphasize psychoeducation about addiction and codependency, exploration of family behaviors that maintain or decrease alcohol or drug use, and relapse prevention strategies (e.g., behavioral contracting).

Most clinicians recognize the power of the family system in the etiology and maintenance of addiction. Most family therapy approaches recognize the life-threatening and progressive nature of the disease of alcoholism. In addition, most approaches are informed by the idea that addiction can generate family dysfunction. It becomes vital to arrest the progression of addiction as a first step in treating the family. We strongly believe that it is ill advised to focus on the interpersonal aspects of family therapy in the context of active alcohol or drug use; however, harnessing the family system to help motivate the alcoholic or addicted individual to stop drinking or using drugs can be a powerful means of initiating change.

Assessment and Treatment Guidelines in a Phase-Oriented Approach

Drinking or drug use phase. Because of the life-threatening quality of alcohol and drug dependence, it is necessary to assess the nature and severity of the alcohol and drug use before constructing a treatment plan. Brief screening instruments such as the CAGE (Mayfield et al. 1974) and S-MAST (Selzer et al. 1975) can be useful tools to augment the initial assessment.

Another efficient, comprehensive assessment tool is the Addiction Severity Index (McLellan et al. 1983). It is useful for both clinical and research settings and provides a thorough review of alcohol and other drug use and a limited but useful review of related problems. Compared with other assessment tools, the Addiction Severity Index is relatively long and might be best used after a brief assessment has indicated a problem.

The therapist must assess the patient's risk for suicide, violence, and other life-threatening factors such as comorbid medical illnesses and impulsivity. Assessment of the ways in which family members have been affected by the substance use should also occur in this initial evaluation. Should the therapist determine that the substance use poses an acute danger to the patient or others, the first step of the family therapy will be to involve the family in confronting the patient so that he or she will seek treatment. Either a formal intervention or unilateral family therapy (defined as therapy with the nondrinking family member) may be used to initiate this step; both strategies have been identified as efficacious in facilitating the entrance of the patient into treatment (Edwards and Steinglass 1995).

In the intervention model (Johnson 1986), family members, friends, and employers receive training to confront the patient. Those involved in the intervention are coached to describe the problematic behaviors that have been observed, the consequences of those behaviors, and their concern for the patient. The patient is then asked to enter treatment and is presented with the consequences that will occur if he or she refuses treatment (e.g., he or she will have to leave the home or will lose his or her job). Because such formal interventions can involve threats that are not always carried out, they are best used as a last resort because of the long-term negative consequences to the family.

Most often the same outcome can be achieved through the use of brief unilateral family therapy with the aim of getting family members to become clear about their intolerance of active substance abuse in their family. The therapist gathers information about previous responses to drinking or drug use, strategies used to stop the substance use, and the effect of the substance use on the family. He or she provides psychoeducation to the family members, who are then coached to decrease codependent and enabling behaviors (i.e., behaviors that continue rather than decrease the substance use), to reinforce sobriety and provide negative consequences for substance use, and to confront the patient. The therapist also helps the family members deal with their own emotional distress, set limits, and detach from the patient. The therapist should not be surprised by and should even anticipate high degrees of resistance to setting limits on the part of any or all family members. For example, family members may, during a family therapy session, agree to withdraw financial support from the patient, but individual family members may later give the patient money for fear that he or she will end up on the street.

If the therapist assesses the acute danger of the drinking or drug use to be minimal, then he or she can proceed in a more deliberate and careful manner in arranging the family therapy and engaging each of the family members, including the patient, in the goals of the therapy. A more gradual approach affords the therapist the opportunity to work in a less coercive, confrontational style, while building rapport with the patient and clarifying the function of substance abuse in the family system.

One of the first steps in assessing the family is to obtain a detailed account of how the family has responded to the substance abuse, in particular the strategies the family has used to deal with both the using and the nonusing periods and whether other family members are addicted. The therapist should evaluate the so-called positive functions that alcohol or drugs serve in the family and the negative consequences. For example, drinking alcohol or using drugs together may be one of the only means a couple have of connecting with each other.

The assessment should also include questions about family members' previous experiences with addiction. Many spouses of alcoholic patients have grown up in a family with an alcoholic parent. When this is the case, the spouse may reexperience feelings similar to those experienced with his or her parents, such as rejection, isolation, helplessness, betrayal, self-blame, and anger. The family must be helped to recognize the role that substance abuse in the family of origin plays in the current family system.

One of the most immediate challenges to a family therapist working with substance abuse is to address the problem of active substance abuse. A central goal is to maintain an alliance with both the family, which despite ambivalence at times, desires to have the drinking or drug use cease, and the patient, who wishes to continue to use the addictive substance. It is our experience that, without being fully aware, many family members are ambivalent about the patient's continued drug use. For example, a wife may express horror in response to her husband's verbal abuse and overtly criticize his drinking. At the same time, her negative view of her husband may protect her from having to deal with her fear of intimacy. Abused spouses (usually wives) may be unable to stand up for themselves, both spouses may drink, or the abused spouse may believe that her role is to stand by her man and protect him and that making demands on him is unwomanly. Clearly, getting the family to set limits or to take a stand about the drinking or drug use is not a straightforward task. If the substance abuse is not an acute danger, the first goal of the therapy is to build rapport and to explore the entire family's investment in continued use. Pressuring the family to take a stand prematurely will lead to the increased likelihood of treatment failure.

Typically family members have a long history of aborted threats and confrontations with the patient, and these encounters undermine the confidence of the family members to deal with the problem. The family's hopelessness about or investment in continued drinking or drug use produces resistance to taking yet another stand. The clinician needs to take an active stance in reducing hopelessness. This can be achieved by educating the family about the effect of drinking or drug use on the family. Family members are often relieved to understand that their responses are part of a well-defined progression of the family illness of substance abuse. The clinician should give literature to the family describing the phases of this progression. Al-Anon is one resource for obtaining this written material.

The main goal to be accomplished in the drinking or drug use phase is to help the family resolve not to live with the active substance abuse. As soon as this resolve has been achieved, family therapy should focus on facilitating the entrance of the patient into treatment. This phase is usually completed by the entrance of the patient into treatment and the family members into Al-Anon or a family component of a structured treatment program.

Early recovery phase. The main goal of treatment in the early recovery phase is to promote abstinence. This phase of treatment usually involves the entrance of the patient into a structured treatment program. The structure can vary in intensity, ranging from an acute care inpatient setting to a structured outpatient program. The most effective programs have a structured family intervention consisting of an educational and a therapeutic component. These family components educate the family about substance abuse as a family illness and help the family members integrate this understanding into their ways of interacting.

Common themes that emerge in this phase are fears of relapse, anger about being forced into treatment, mistrust, and enabling behaviors in which the family engages. In many cases, these structured approaches, along with referrals to Al-Anon, are sufficient to help the family reestablish normal functioning. However, we sometimes recommend that families undergo long-term family therapy to address relationship dynamics that interfere with the recovery process. In the course of family therapy, it may become clear that different family members have their own clinical difficulties requiring individual attention. For example, as an alcohol-dependent wife becomes more assertive, confident, and independent, her husband's insecurity may become more apparent and serve to sabotage the treatment process unless dealt with. If it becomes clear that the relationship itself is so dysfunctional as to detract from the recovery process, we recommend initiating intensive family therapy even in the early phase of recovery. Conversely, we do not recommend making the relationship the focus of treatment in the early phase of recovery because the priority in this phase is to build supports for each of the family members separately.

When family therapy is indicated in early recovery, two commonly used treatment models are family systems approaches and behavioral marital therapy. Family systems approaches focus on the interaction among family members. Addiction is sometimes (secondarily) serving a function in the family. Therefore, when alcohol or drugs are removed from the family, homeostasis is disrupted. Treatment strategies focus on the identification of roles family members have in the family system. The goal is to establish a new homeostasis in the family without alcohol or drugs. In contrast, behavioral marital therapy models focus on the exploration of behaviors that reinforce abstinence versus substance use and teach communication, problem-solving, and conflict resolution skills. Behavioral contracts are also used to outline clear consequences for substance use or to establish new behaviors that will promote sobriety.

Research suggests that both approaches may yield higher rates of abstinence than individual treatment alone (Edwards and Steinglass 1995). Some evidence supports the use of a treatment-matching strategy in which individual or conjoint therapy is recommended after a careful assessment of family dynamics. When the patient perceives a low level of spousal support for sobriety, individual treatment alone may be better than family treatment in promoting abstinence (Longabaugh et al. 1995). If marital satisfaction is very low, individual treatment alone may be more effective than couples therapy.

Ongoing recovery.   As the patient completes a structured chemical dependency program, anxiety about relapse is heightened in the family. The trauma of addiction often results in family members not being able to trust their own feelings and perceptions. In the early stages of family therapy, family members should begin to identify and examine their individual issues, in particular their relationship to the patient's active addiction. As with the patient, family members by now should have achieved some stability in their own support system. One of the best guards against relapse in the family is the patient's awareness of the family members' willingness to live without the patient, should substance use resume. Rebuilding trust is also a central theme at this stage. The therapist should explore and reinforce ways to rebuild trust in small, steady steps. If, for example, a couple have been separated, the therapist can recommend small steps toward reunification instead of sudden decisions to completely reunite. Another way to build trust at this stage is to continue to focus on developing a mutual understanding of family functioning and to have all of the family members agree on the role that active addiction has played in their lives. For example, a daughter may find great relief in hearing her father admit to being alcoholic, using this admission to explain why he disappointed her in the past.

A basic idea established in early recovery is that individual support systems are vital for all the family members. Family members may access their support independently of any other family member. As the patient becomes more independent, family members may experience feelings of resentment, jealousy, and insecurity. The principle here is that it is nearly impossible to have a healthy relationship if both parties do not have strong, separate support systems. It can be shocking to the therapist when the patient, having achieved a level of stability, experiences the overt or covert sabotage of family members. In this situation, we recommend that the therapy focus on the family's investment in continued substance use. Reasons for family members' investment in continued substance use may include motivating factors such as avoidance of intimacy, a need to maintain control, and denial of their own addiction, among others. If the patient is using a support group (e.g., Alcoholics Anonymous) to avoid intimacy, this needs to be addressed.

One of the most difficult adjustments in recovery is for family members to satisfactorily relate to one another without alcohol or drugs. As we have discussed earlier, alcohol or drugs often serve many positive functions in families. The family members usually have not developed other ways of dealing with their feelings and conflicts. Presented with the host of fears and anxieties around intimacy, anger, shame, and guilt, the family is left without its primary coping mechanism—alcohol or drugs. The family must learn new tools in order to function. Again, the temptation to relapse rather than develop positive means of interacting are strong. The therapist should take an active stance in identifying negative coping styles and teaching positive ones. This process often involves teaching family members communication skills so that they can relate to one another more effectively. In addition, especially if the patient has been abusive or cruel or has lost much of the family's money, questions of apology and forgiveness must be addressed directly. It takes much time and work to reestablish trust.

Research supports the use of family therapy in the ongoing recovery phase of treatment to promote attendance in aftercare programs and to maintain abstinence (Edwards and Steinglass 1995). Teaching couples to change the way they behave with each other promotes abstinence and improves marital satisfaction. Including the family in aftercare maximizes the maintenance of gains made in treatment in early recovery and decreases the risk of relapse.

Assessing need for ongoing family therapy.   At this phase, the therapist should evaluate the relative stability of each of the family members' support systems and the relative functionality of the family relationship and determine whether the relationship poses a threat to recovery. Recovery often requires building a stronger relationship than the one that existed previously. Continued family therapy is often indicated if either partner has problems with intimacy, feels infantilized and resentful, has a history of physical abuse, or is afraid of hurting others. We recommend aggressive treatment in this area because stable family relationships are one of the best prognostic indicators for successful recovery.

Not all alcoholism or drug addiction follow a chronic course. An intermittent increase in drinking or drug use is often a response to a problem within the family. In these cases substance use can be treated appropriately with family therapy. Similarly, people who do not have an alcohol or drug dependency problem may drink excessively or abuse drugs in response to a family conflict. In these situations, family therapy may be indicated to identify areas of conflict that trigger substance abuse and to identify alternative coping strategies to deal with family conflicts. Consider the following case example:

> In the F family, the identified patient was Ms. F, a single, 36-year-old filing clerk. She was hospitalized on the medical service because of acute gastritis secondary to a prolonged bout of alcohol intoxication. She had a 20-year history of alcohol abuse. Medical staff noted that the alcohol abuse was now complicated by alcohol withdrawal symptoms and poor treatment compliance. Ms. F began drinking at age 14 years to, like her father, calm her nerves and deal with her lowered mood. She had several episodes of major depressive disorder since age 20 years. Recent episodes seemed related either to quarrels with her mother or to the anniversary of her father's death. She was taking no medication for her mood disorder. Ms. F's mother had lost her job 20 years earlier and had been homebound since then. She and her daughter were in a continual struggle for control, with Ms. F exhorting her mother to become more socially involved and the mother encouraging Ms. F to stop drinking and get a job. A maternal aunt was supporting both the identified patient and the mother.
>
> The therapist's understanding of the case was that the alcohol abuse was preventing Ms. F and her mother from functioning more independently. Treatment goals focused on breaking up the symbiotic family system to allow the mother to socialize with her peers and to allow Ms. F to become more independent and work more consistently. The treatment prescribed was antidepressant medication combined with family therapy, Alcoholics Anonymous, and Al-Anon.

Care must be taken that the nonaffected spouse does not prompt the alcoholic patient's drinking (Deniker et al. 1964; Rae 1972). The spouse can be the supplier and the victim simultaneously. Consider the following case example:

> In the G family, the identified patient was Mrs. G, who had been given a diagnosis of alcohol abuse and dependence. Mr. and Mrs. G came to treatment complaining that they never went out together. After months of therapy, Mr. G, who had cyclothymic disorder and had elevated mood at the time, took Mrs. G to a wine-tasting festival. She promptly relapsed after months of sobriety. The pattern involves a continual reenactment of provocation, misbehavior, remorse, and atonement (Dinaburg et al. 1977).

Children of Alcoholic Parents

Children who are living with an alcoholic parent face an environment that is unpredictable and often verbally or physically abusive. They are often told that what they are observing is something else (e.g., "Nothing's wrong with dad, he's just tired."). If there are several children, they will often be given or accept narrow and specific roles. One, usually the oldest, will be the overly responsible caretaker in the family (e.g., protecting siblings and the mother if the father is violent, or doing child care and cooking if the mother is drunk and unavailable). One will often become "sad or bad," one the angry truth-teller, and one or more will hide out or become the family clown and cheerer-upper. Many children of alcoholic parents enter adult life with their thinking organized around unpredictability, distrust, survival, vigilance, hyperresponsibility, and isolation of affect. Most of the time at least one of the siblings also develops alcohol or substance abuse, and at least one becomes terrified of alcohol. Many children, especially the overly responsible caretaker, are at risk for later mood disorder. Often at least one of the children will marry an alcoholic individual. Children should be evaluated for depression and questioned about abuse. Many children benefit from Al-Anon. Adult children should at some time point in the therapy be referred to Adult Children of Alcoholics groups or literature.

Other Substance Use

There is a difference between chronic use of drugs that cause physical dependence, such as barbiturates, cocaine, and heroin, and casual use of nonaddicting agents. The former category had been thought to be extremely resistant to family therapy intervention used alone, but a classic combined therapy study changed this view. By randomly assigning male heroin addicts (under age 36 years) to one of four treatment categories—1) paid family therapy, 2) unpaid family therapy, 3) paid family movie (a placebo condition), or 4) individual counseling plus methadone—Stanton and Todd (1982) showed the superiority of family intervention.

As interesting was the nature of family intervention used. For this study, the typical family structure was a very close and dependent mother-son dyad with a distant, excluded father. In approximately 80% of the cases, a parent had a drinking problem. The therapist kept the sessions focused on drug use until stable improvement had been achieved. An overall strategy was to alter the repetitive interactional patterns that were seen as maintaining the drug taking. In practical terms, the most basic restructuring move was getting the parents to work together in relating to the addicted patient, lest the triadic conflictual pattern persist and treatment fail. In the typical situation of mother-son overinvolvement, a common technique was to get the father to take charge of the son. Family crises were common, and the general treatment strategy was to contain them within the family and thus avoid the necessity of hospitalization, increasing medications, or removing the addicted individual from the home precipitously.

Parental crises sometimes emerged during the treatment, especially marital problems or heavy drinking by one parent. The general strategy was to keep the parents working together and not to separate or divorce until the identified patient's addiction was under control. Thus the focus was on the parents as a parental system rather than a marital system during the first phases of treatment. Once the identified patient was stabilized and drug free for some time, the intervention could focus on the marital pair.

Such drug users are sometimes removed from their sociocultural milieu, and family therapy is often not possible until the patient is detoxified. Because many cases of cocaine and heroin dependence are chronic, they will require family intervention. Some facilities are treating the nonaddicted drug user (even those, for example, with occasional mixed use of alcohol, marijuana, amphetamines, and psychedelics) by using family therapy as a primary form of treatment. This approach is based on the rationale that the drug use is a symptom of disturbed functioning and communication within the family.

Conclusion

Psychiatric illness affects one out of five Americans. Like other medical illnesses, it is an intense private and individual experience and in most situations is also clearly a family illness.

Suggested Readings

Brown S, Lewis V: The Alcoholic Family in Recovery: A Developmental Mode. New York, Guilford, 1999
This recently published book provides a comprehensive discussion of the effect of alcoholism and recovery from the perspective of the family system. It also provides an excellent in-depth discussion of the stages of recovery and the clinical implications for therapists.

Clarkin J, Hass G, Glick I: Affective Disorders and the Family: Assessment and Treatment. New York, Guilford, 1988

Combrinck-Graham L (ed): Children in Family Contexts: Perspectives on Treatment. New York, Guilford, 1989
This book does a good job of sensitizing clinicians to the developmental and family contexts of children. The systems approach is delineated clearly and acknowledges the limitations of the professional settings developed to help children and adolescents.

Keitner G (ed): Depression and Families: Impact and Treatment. Washington, DC, American Psychiatric Press, 1990

McFarlane W, Beels C: Family Therapy in Schizophrenia. New York, Guilford, 1983
This book is a classic compilation of excellent articles by both authors and a distinguished group of contributors. Psychoeducational approaches highlighting the need for reduction of expressed emotion and support for family coping are outlined beautifully.

Meuser KT, Glynn SM: Behavioral Family Therapy for Psychiatric Disorders. Boston, MA, Allyn & Bacon, 1995
This book presents a clear, focused approach to Axis I disorders.

Milkowitz D, Goldstein MJ: Bipolar Disorder: A Family Focused Treatment Approach. New York, Guilford, 1997
The preceding three books review the effect of depression and mania on family functioning and offer systems, cognitive-behavioral, and psychoeducational interventions. These are excellent resources.

Perlmutter R: A Family Approach to Psychiatric Disorders. Washington, DC, American Psychiatric Association Press, 1996
This volume looks at psychiatric diagnosis and family therapy, two areas that the author contends have much to teach each other. The book systematically presents a chapter on family therapy for each of the major DSM-IV Axis I disorders.

Steinglass P, Bennett L, Wolin S, et al: The Alcoholic Family. New York, Basic Books, 1987
This book goes into depth on alchoholic family systems and provides thoughtful guidelines for both assessment and treatment. It is considered a classic.

Todd T: Family Therapy Approaches With Adolescent Substance Abusers. New York, Prentice Hall, 1990
Adolescent substance abuse is difficult to treat because of the developmental and motivational issues faced in many cases. This book explains how the clinician can engage the adolescent and family and gives prescribed steps for treating the substance abuse.

References

Adams M: Social aspects of the medical care for the mentally retarded. N Engl J Med 286:635–638, 1972

Akiskal HS, Bitar AH, Puzantian VR, et al: The nosological status of neurotic depressions: a prospective three- to four-year follow-up examination in light of the primary-secondary and the unipolar-bipolar dichotomies. Arch Gen Psychiatry 35:756–766, 1978

Akiskal HS, Hirschfeld MA, Yerevanian BI: The relationship of personality to affective disorders: a critical review. Arch Gen Psychiatry 40:801–810, 1983

American Academy of Child and Adolescent Psychiatry: AACAP practice parameters for the assessment and treatment of attention-deficit hyperactivity disorder. J Am Acad Child Adolesc Psychiatry 30:1–3, 1991

American Psychiatric Association: Diagnostic and Statistical Manual of Mental Disorder, 4th Edition. Washington, DC, American Psychiatric Association, 1994

Anderson C, Reiss D, Hogarty G: Schizophrenia and the Family. New York, Guilford, 1986

Bateson G, Jackson DD, Haley J, et al: Towards a theory of schizophrenia. Behav Sci 1:251–264, 1956

Bateson G, Jackson DD, Haley J, et al: A note on the double bind—1962. Fam Process 2:154–161, 1963

Brent DA, Holder D, Kolko D, et al: A clinical psychotherapy trial for adolescent depression comparing cognitive, family, and supportive therapy. Arch Gen Psychiatry 54:877–885, 1997

Brown GW, Monck EM, Carstairs GM, et al: The influence of family life on the course of schizophrenic illness. British Journal of Prevention and Social Medicine 16:55, 1962

Butzloff RL, Hooley JM: Expressed emotion and psychiatric relapse. Arch Gen Psychiatry 55:547–551, 1998

Calvocoressi L, Lewis B, Harris M, et al: Family accommodation in obsessive-compulsive disorder. Am J Psychiatry 152:41–443, 1995

Chamberlain P, Rosicky JG: The effectiveness of family therapy in the treatment of adolescents with conduct disorders and delinquency. (Special Issue: The Effectiveness of Marital and Family Therapy) J Marital Fam Ther 21:441–459, 1995

Clark W, Midanik L: Alcohol use and alcohol problems among U.S. adults, in National Institute on Alcohol Abuse and Alcoholism: Alcohol Consumption and Related Problems. Washington, DC, U.S. Government Printing Office, 1982, pp 2–52

Clarkin JF, Haas GL, Glick ID (eds): Affective Disorders and the Family: Assessment and Treatment. New York, Guilford, 1988

Clarkin JF, Glick ID,Haas GL, et al: A randomized clinical trial of inpatient family intervention; V. results for affective disorders. J Affect Disord 18:17–28, 1990

Clarkin JF, Carpenter D, Hull J, et al: The effect of psychoeducational marital intervention for bipolar patients and spouses. Psychiatr Serv 49:531–533, 1998

Cobb JP, Mathews AM, Childs-Clarke A, et al: The spouse as cotherapist in the treatment of agoraphobia. Br J Psychiatry 144:282–287, 1984

Cronkite RC, Finney JW, Nekich J, et al: Remission among alcoholic patients and family adaptation to alcoholism: a stress and coping perspective, in Alcohol and the Family: Research and Clinical Perspectives. Edited by Collins RL, Leonard KE, Searles JS. New York, Guilford, 1990, pp 309–337

Deniker P, DeSaugy D, Ropert M: The alcoholic and his wife. Compr Psychiatry 5:374–384, 1964

Dinaburg D, Glick ID, Feigenbaum E: Marital therapy of woman alcoholics. J Stud Alcohol 38:1247–1258, 1977

Edwards ME, Steinglass P: Family therapy treatment outcomes for alcoholism. J Marital Fam Ther 21:475–509, 1995

Falloon IRH, Boyd JL, McGill CW, et al: Family management in the prevention of exacerbations of schizophrenia: a controlled study. N Engl J Med 306:1437–1440, 1982

Falloon IRH, Hole V, Mulroy L, et al: Behavioral family therapy, in Affective Disorders and the Family: Assessment and Treatment. Edited by Clarkin JF, Haas GL, Glick ID. New York, Guilford, 1988, pp 117–133

Fleck S: Family dynamics and origin of schizophrenia. Psychosom Med 22:333–344, 1960

Fromm-Reichman F: Notes on the development of schizophrenia by psychoanalytic psychotherapy. Psychiatry 11:267–277, 1948

Glick ID, Clarkin JF: Family support and intervention, in Acute Care Psychiatry: Diagnosis and Treatment. Edited by Sederer LI, Rothschild AJ. Baltimore, MD, Williams & Wilkins, 1997, pp 337–354

Glick ID, Clarkin JF, Haas GL, et al: Clinical significance of inpatient family intervention; VII. conclusions from the clinical trial. Hosp Community Psychiatry 44:869–873, 1993

Glick ID, Dulit RA, Wachter E, et al: The family, family therapy and borderline personality disorder. Journal of Psychotherapy Practice and Research 4:237–246, 1995

Goldstein MJ: Psychoeducation and family treatment related to the phase of a psychotic disorder. Int Clin Psychopharmacol 11:77–83, 1996

Goldstein MJ, Rodnick EH, Evans JR, et al: Drug and family therapy in the aftercare treatment of acute schizophrenia. Arch Gen Psychiatry 35:1169–1177, 1978

Guttman HA, Beavers WR, Berman E, et al: A model for the classification and diagnosis of relational disorders. Psychiatr Serv 46:926–932, 1995

Haas G, Clarkin JF, Glick ID: Marital and family treatment of depression, in Handbook of Depression: Treatment, Assessment and Research. Edited by Beckham E, Leber W. Homewood, IL, Dorsey, 1985, pp 151–183

Hafner RJ: Agoraphobic women married to abnormally jealous men. Br J Med Psychology 52:99–104, 1979

Hafner RJ: Predicting the effects on husbands of behavior therapy for wives' agoraphobia. Behav Res Ther 22:217–226, 1984

Holder H, Hallan JB: Impact of alcoholism treatment on total health care costs: a six-year study. Advances in Alcohol and Substance Abuse 6:1–15, 1986

Hooley JH, Hoffman PD: Expressed emotion & clinical outcome in borderline personality disorder. Am J Psychiatry 196:1557–1562, 1999

Jacobson NS, Dobson K, Fruzzetti AE, et al: Marital therapy as a treatment for depression. J Consult Clin Psychol 52:497–506, 1991

Jacobson NS, Fruzzetti A, Dobson K, et al: Couple therapy as a treatment for depression; II. the effects of relationship, quality and therapy on depressive relapse. J Consult Clin Psychol 61:516–519, 1993

Johnson VE: Intervention. Minneapolis, MN, Johnson Institute, 1986

Kaufman E: Family systems and family therapy of substance abuse: an overview of two decades of research and clinical experience. International Journal of Addiction 20:897–916, 1985

Keitner GI, Ryan CE, Miller IW, et al: Role of the family in recovery and major depression. Am J Psychiatry 152:1002–1008, 1995

King S, Dixon MJ: The influence of expressed emotion, family dynamics, and symptom type on the social adjustment of schizophrenic young adults. Arch Gen Psychiatry 53:1098–1104, 1996

Landeen J, Whelton C, Dermer S, et al: Needs of well siblings of persons with schizophrenia. Hosp Community Psychiatry 43:266, 1992

Leff JP, Berkowitz R, Shavit N, et al: A trial of family therapy versus a relatives' group for schizophrenia. Br J Psychiatry 154:58–66, 1989

Longabaugh R, Wirtz PW, Beattie MC, et al: Matching treatment focus to patient social investment and support: 18-month follow-up results. J Consult Clin Psychol 63:296–307, 1995

Malenbaum R, Herzog D, Eisenthal S, et al: Overeaters anonymous. Int J Eating Disord 7:139–144, 1989

Mayfield DG, McLeod G, Hall P: The CAGE questionnaire: validation of a new alcoholism screening instrument. Am J Psychiatry 131:1121–1123, 1974

McAneny L: Alcohol in America: number of drinkers holding steady, but drinking less. The Gallup Poll Monthly 345:14, 1994

McFarlane, Link B, Dushay R, et al: Psychoeducational multiple family groups: four-year relapse outcome in schizophrenia. Fam Process 34:127–144, 1995

McGuffin P, Katz R, Watkins S, et al: A hospital-based twin register of the heritability of DSM-IV unipolar depression. Arch Gen Psychiatry 53:129–136, 1996

McLellan AT, Luborsky L, Woody GA, et al: An improved diagnostic evaluation instrument for substance abuse patients; the Addiction Severity Index. Journal of Mental Disorders 168:26–33, 1983

McNabb J, Der-Karabetian A, Rhoads J: Family involvement and outcome in the treatment of alcoholism. Psychol Rep 65:1327–1330, 1989

Miklowitz DJ, Frank E, George EL: New psychosocial treatments for the outpatient management of bipolar disorder. Psychopharmacol Bull 32:613–621, 1996

Moos RH, Finney JW, Cronkite RC: Alcoholism Treatment: Context, Process, and Outcome. New York, Oxford University Press, 1990

Munby M, Johnston DW: Agoraphobia: the long-term follow-up of behavioral treatment. Br J Psychiatry 137:418–427, 1980

National Institute on Drug Abuse: National household survey on drug abuse—main findings, 1988. Bethesda, MD, National Institute on Drug Abuse, 1990

Nuechterlein KH, Dawson ME: Information processing and attentional functioning in the development course of schizophrenic disorders. Schizophr Bull 10:160–203, 1984

Pope HG Jr, Hudson JI, Jonas JM, et al: Bulimia treated with imipramine; a placebo-controlled, double-blind study. Am J Psychiatry 140:554–558, 1983

Prince SE, Jacobson NS: A review and evaluation of marital and family therapies for affective disorders. J Marital Fam Ther 21:401, 1995

Rae J: The influence of the wives on the treatment outcome of alcoholics: a follow-up study at two years. Br J Psychiatry 120:601–613, 1972

Rueter MA, Scaramella L, Wallaace LE, et al: First onset of depressive or anxiety disorders predicted by the longitudinal course of internalizing symptoms and parent–adolescent disagreements. Arch Gen Psychiatry 56:726–732, 1999

Russell GF, Szmukler GI, Dare C, et al: An evaluation of family therapy in anorexia nervosa and bulimia nervosa. Arch Gen Psychiatry 44:1047–1056, 1987

Satel S, Southwick S: Consequences for the family of abrupt reduction of chronic symptoms (letter). Am J Psychiatry 144:1362, 1987

Schooler NR, Keith SJ, Severe JB, et al: Relapse and rehospitalization during maintenance treatment of schizophrenia: the effects of dose reduction and family treatment. Arch Gen Psychiatry 54:453–463, 1997

Schwartz RC, Barrett MJ, Saba G: Family therapy for bulimia, in Handbook of Psychotherapy for Anorexia Nervosa and Bulimia. Edited by Garner DM, Garfinkel PE. New York, Guilford, 1985, pp 280–307

Selzer ML, Vinokur A, Van Rooijen L: A self-administered short Michigan Alcoholism Screening Test (SMAST). J Stud Alcohol 36:117–126, 1975

Stanton MD, Todd TC: The Family Therapy of Drug Abuse and Addiction. New York, Guilford, 1982

Steinglass P: A life history model of the alcoholic family. Fam Process 19:211–226, 1980

Steinglass P, Bennett L, Wolin SJ, et al: The Alcoholic Family. New York, Basic Books, 1987

Tsuang MT, Lyons MJ, Meyer JM, et al: Co-occurrence of abuse of different drugs in men. Arch Gen Psychiatry 55:967–972, 1998

Vandereycken W: The addiction model in eating disorders: some critical remarks and a selected bibliography. Int J Eating Disord 9:95–102, 1990

Wahlberg KE, Wynne LC, Oja H, et al: Gene-environment interaction in vulnerability to schizophrenia: findings from the Finnish adoptive family study of schizophrenia. Am J Psychiatry 154:355–362, 1997

Weinstein RM: Labeling theory and the attitudes of mental patients: a review. J Health Soc Behav 24:70–84, 1983

Winick C: Epidemiology of alcohol and drug abuse, in Substance Abuse: A Comprehensive Textbook, 2nd Edition. Edited by Lowinson JH, Ruiz P, Millman RB, et al. Baltimore, MD, Williams & Wilkins, 1992, pp 15–31

Woodside DB, Shekter-Wolfson LF, Brandes JS, et al: Eating Disorders and Marriage: The Couple in Focus. New York, Brunner/Mazel, 1993

Work Group on Eating Disorders: American Psychiatric Association practice guidelines for eating disorders. Am J Psychiatry 150:212–225, 1993

Work Group on Eating Disorders: Practice guidelines for the treatment of patients with eating disorders (revision). Am J Psychiatry 157 (suppl):1–39, 2000

World Health Organization: International Statistical Classification of Diseases and Related Health Problems, 10th Revision. Geneva, World Health Organization, 1992

Wynne LC, Ryckoff I, Day J, et al: Pseudo-mutuality in the family relations of schizophrenics, in A Modern Introduction to the Family. Edited by Bell NW, Vogel FF. Glencoe, IL, Free Press, 1960, pp 573–594

Yager J, Landsverk J, Edelstein CK: Help seeking and satisfaction with care in 641 women with eating disorders; I: patterns of utilization, attributed change and perceived efficacy of treatment. J Nerv Ment Dis 177:632–637, 1989

Quarrel Between Mr. and Mrs. Latimer, and Brutal Violence Between Them Were the Natural Consequences of the Too Frequent Use of the Bottle, from "The Bottle," George Cruikshank, 1847. Reprinted in "Temperance Tales: Antiliquor Fiction and American Attitudes Toward Alcoholics in the Late 19th and Early 20th Centuries." *Quarterly Journal of Studies on Alcohol* 38:1327–1370, 1977. Reprint courtesy of, and used with permission of, the *Quarterly Journal of Studies on Alcohol.*

CHAPTER 25

Family Treatment in the Context of Other Special Problems— Violence to Self and Others

Objectives for the Reader

To be able to use the family model in the context of family issues such as violence, incest, and suicidal behavior

Your parents were fighting machines and self-pitying machines. Your mother was programmed to bawl out your father for being a defective money-making machine, and your father was programmed to bawl her out for being a defective housekeeping machine. They were programmed to bawl each other out for being defective loving machines. Then your father was programmed to stomp out of the house and slam the door. This automatically turned your mother into a weeping machine. And your father would go down to a tavern where he would get drunk with some other drinking machines. Then all the drinking machines would go to a whorehouse and rent fucking machines. And then your father would drag himself home to become an apologizing machine. And your mother would become a very slow forgiving machine.

Kurt Vonnegut, Jr., *Breakfast of Champions*

Introduction

In Chapter 24, we described the family model in situations in which the family has a member with a diagnosable psychiatric disorder. In other situations a family member may engage in violent behaviors to self or others that disrupt family functioning such as suicide attempts, verbal or physical abuse, or sexual abuse (i.e., incest). We have grouped these problems for discussion because they so clearly involve the whole family and because such behaviors cut across traditional diagnostic lines. In addition, they require very specific and aggressive treatment by the family therapist and other health care providers.

From both an individual and a family perspective, these behaviors serve multiple functions. A suicide attempt, for example, might be an effort to coerce or control another, an expression of despair, an attempt to get love and support, an expression of anger, or all of the above. The attempt may mobilize a family to change or may be part of the family's usual homeostasis (e.g., every time the father threatens to leave, the adolescent daughter attempts suicide). Violence, although highly coercive, may arise from a calculated attempt at control or may be an expression of internal feelings of helplessness, and it may be part of a familiar violence cycle or a single event of sudden rage. For example, sometimes the only way one spouse knows how to handle browbeating is to explode or to threaten suicide or homicide.

The Family Model and Violence

With Amy Bronstone, Ph.D.,
Robert A. Matano, Ph.D., and Diana M. Doumas, Ph.D.

Description of the Problem

Definition of family violence. Since the early 1990s, there has been an increasing awareness of the prevalence and consequences of family violence in the United States. Family violence is a widespread problem that affects people from all racial, ethnic, religious, geographic, educational, economic, and social backgrounds. Family violence is more than just a family problem; it is associated with social, financial, and legal sequelae that extend to society. Economic costs related to family violence include the increased need for police, courts, correctional facilities, and mental health resources (Seppa 1996).

Family violence is an umbrella term that may refer to physical, verbal, or sexual abuse against an intimate partner, child, or elder. *Physical violence* is an act that in some way directly threatens a family member's safety (e.g., hitting, throwing an object, threatening with a weapon). *Verbal* or *emotional abuse* consists of behaviors that symbolically threaten family members (e.g., threatening to abandon a family member, verbally derogating a family member, destroying property, abusing pets to hurt a family member). *Sexual abuse* refers to acts that are sexually aggressive, coercive, or exploitative (e.g., rape, incest). In violent relationships, violent episodes often involve a combination of assaultive acts, verbal abuse, sexual aggression, and threats (Walker 1984).

Once assaultive behavior occurs in a relationship, it usually develops into a stable pattern over time (O'Leary et al. 1989). Assaultive behavior may (and often does) become worse with time and can end in murder. In particular, attempts by a battered woman to separate from an abusive husband may end in killing. The phenomenon of violence is gender linked. More violence, more severe violence, and more murder are committed by men against women. In considering the violent family, it is important to understand whether the pattern is mutual physical violence, verbal aggression on the part of the woman combined with physical aggression on the part of the man, or a completely controlling husband with a severely victimized and silenced wife. Although violence perpetrated by a woman against a nonviolent man does occur, it is a much less common pattern.

Prevalence of family violence. Accurate estimates of the prevalence of family violence cannot be obtained because of sampling biases and the significant underreporting of the problem (Browne 1993). Based on limited data, family violence appears to be a widespread problem in the United States.

About 16% of married couples report having experienced at least one episode of physical violence during the preceding year, and 28% report at least one episode at some point in the duration of their relationship (Straus and Gelles 1990). This leads to estimates that 8.7 million couples experience domestic violence annually. Some researchers have reported evidence that nonmarried cohabiting couples and dating couples have even higher rates of violence than married couples (Miller et al. 1989). Other research demonstrates that nonmarried dating couples have similar rates of violence during courtship, ranging from 20% to 52% (Arias et al. 1987). The area of partner-related problems with physical abuse has been reviewed in depth by O'Leary and Jacobson in the *DSM-IV Sourcebook* (1997) and by Eisenstat and Bancroft (1999) in a detailed journal article.

Although more than 650,000 children are confirmed to have been abused or neglected each year, the actual number of children abused or neglected annually in the United States is likely at least one million (National Center for Child Abuse and Neglect 1986). In a random survey of households, 3.5% of parents admitted that they had acted in a violent manner (i.e., committing an act that could likely have caused injury) toward one of their children during the past year (Gelles 1978). Interviews with national probability family samples indicate that 63% of parents report having been violent (defined as including spanking), and 11% report having committed a severe violent act (i.e., more serious than spanking, slapping, or pushing) toward one of their children during the past year (Straus and Gelles 1986).

Causes of family violence.   Family violence has multiple causes. The strongest predictor of spousal abuse is having witnessed spousal violence in one's family of origin (Hotaling and Sugarman 1986). Similarly, having a history of being maltreated as a child is a major vulnerability factor for committing child abuse (Egeland 1993). Other factors believed to be important in the genesis of family violence include sociocultural values and norms, sex role socialization, and social isolation. The culture of masculinity in the United States encourages the devaluation of women and, in some subcultures, the idea that violence is a good way to keep women in line. In addition, many men believe they are valued less for their verbal skills than for their ability to fight, drink, and be tough—this pattern encourages men to use anger as an all-purpose emotion with which to replace fear, hurt, or helplessness. The role that individual psychopathology may play in the etiology of family violence is unclear. Studies linking psychiatric diagnoses (e.g., antisocial personality disorder, depression) with spousal abuse have generally been flawed methodologically; however, the amassed evidence suggests that higher rates of psychopathology are found among batterers than among nonbatterers (Hamberger and Hastings 1988).

Relationship between family violence and alcohol or drug abuse.   With few exceptions (Barnett and Fagan 1993) the bulk of the evidence indicates that domestic violence and alcohol or substance abuse are associated strongly (Flanzer 1993; Kyriacau et al. 1999). National survey data indicate that 70% of the husbands who reported severely assaulting their wives reported being drunk one or more times during the survey year, as compared with 50% of the husbands who had moderately assaulted their wives and 31% who did not assault their wives (Kantor and Straus 1987). Perpetrators of domestic violence are also more likely to have alcohol problems (Pan et al. 1994), binge drink, and have an earlier onset of alcohol use than nonviolent men (Murphy and

O'Farrell 1994). Research indicates that alcohol use interacts with personality variables, such as hostility and aggressive personality styles, to create violence (Heyman et al. 1995).

Available data often do not make it possible to determine whether alcohol consumption is causally related to violent behavior or merely associated with violence. In order to determine causality, the temporal relationship between violent behavior and alcohol use must be clarified. National survey data indicate that although there is a positive correlation between excessive drinking and spousal abuse, alcohol was not used immediately prior to the violent incident in 76% of domestic violence cases (Kantor and Straus 1987). This observation indicates that the relationship between alcoholism and conjugal violence may not be a direct one in which alcohol consumption always precedes domestic violence. Thus we cannot yet state with certainty that alcohol is a causal agent that leads to domestic violence.

The picture is equally unclear regarding the relationship between victim intoxication and domestic violence. There is evidence that a high proportion of female victims have been drinking prior to the abusive event or have patterns of heavy drinking. National survey data indicate that 46% of severely assaulted women reported being drunk one or more times during the survey year as compared with 36% of the minor violence victims and 16% of the nonvictimized women (Kantor and Straus 1987). In addition, alcoholic women are subjected to higher levels of violence than nonalcoholic women even after controlling for alcoholism in the spouse (Miller et al. 1989). Women who are battered report drinking more than women not exposed to spousal domestic violence (Barnett and Fagan 1993). Other researchers have not found an association between victim alcoholism and domestic violence (Van Hasselt et al. 1985).

As with the relationship between alcohol use and domestic violence in the perpetrator, the temporal relationship between victims' use of alcohol and their experience of violence remains unclear. Several relationships are possible. First, women who experience violence may use alcohol to medicate themselves after being victimized. Second, alcohol may disinhibit female drinkers who then may unintentionally provoke the abuser. Third, women's alcohol use and experience of violence may be coincidental and may be explained by a third variable such as the abuser's use of alcohol. Walker (1984) reported that women who reported heavy drinking patterns tended to be involved with men who also abused alcohol.

Finally, evidence suggests a link between alcoholism and child abuse, although more methodologically rigorous research is necessary to determine the strength of this association. Although multiple studies have demonstrated that approximately 50% of abusive parents abuse alcohol, estimates of the proportion of confirmed child abuse cases associated with some sort of parental substance abuse problem have ranged widely. A recent study using the National Institute of Mental Health Epidemiologic Catchment Area data revealed that respondents who reported either physically abusing or neglecting their children were much more likely than matched control subjects to report substance abuse (Kelleher et al. 1994).

How Violent Acts Occur: The Cycle of Violence

Walker developed in 1980 the cycle theory of violence in spousal abuse. She identified three stages in the pattern of behavior: 1) a tension-building period, 2) an acute battering incident, and 3) a tension-reducing period characterized by kindness and contrite loving behavior. This cycle can develop in many ways. In some families the abused spouse (usually the woman) tries to stop the abuse by being good and trying more and more desperately to do the other's wishes. In other families the wife stands up to her husband and violent quarrels occur. In some of these couples, violence occurs in a context in which the wife refuses to leave the room at a point when her husband is clearly becoming more and more upset. Occasionally, most often in couples in which less severe violence occurs, the wife considers herself to have won if she can get her husband to lose control and prove that he is not in control of himself. Although it is usually thought that the husband is out of control at the time of the violence, Goldener's work has suggested that in some men a cognitive process takes place at the violent moment in which the man essentially gives himself permission to lose control and that this point can be understood and worked with in therapy (Goldener et al. 1994). In the third stage both partners are upset and the husband is loving or at least not apparently dangerous. If this is a period of warmth and intensity, the couple may bond even more closely, making it easy to deny the possibility of further violence and harder for the woman to leave the system. Many battered women do not wish to leave their husbands even when they have the financial means to do so. Although much of this hesitation results from early conditioning to family violence, fear, and learned helplessness, some is due to genuine attachment and a deep connection to the intensity of the marriage.

Violent acts do not have to be frequent to be frightening. A man who has injured his wife once may only have to threaten her to control her behavior, and she may be unaware of how much of her behavior is based on the need to avoid further violence. Violence against things (e.g., breaking objects in the home, throwing things) may also be frightening, and the entire family's behavior may become completely oriented toward averting the angry spouse's rage. Wives' violent behavior is less often seen as frightening by husbands.

Child abuse is most likely to occur in a context of alcohol and high stress. The fewer resources the caretaking adult has, and the more emotional intensity the child has, the greater the chance of trouble. For many parents, abuse occurs in the context of a child who cannot stop crying or who is talking back. The line between acceptable discipline and child abuse varies to some extent with culture. For example, in the United States "spare the rod and spoil the child" was a common childrearing belief during much of the nation's history. The question remains of whether spanking is abuse or normal punishment. Beyond that gray area, however, it is usually clear what constitutes unacceptable behavior. Later in this chapter we discuss child abuse from the point of view of the pediatrician.

Assessment of Individual and Family Systems Issues

The first step in the treatment of family violence consists of a comprehensive assessment of individual and family functioning. The clinician must be flexible and shift his or her focus between individual and family systems issues. Although the treatment of family violence usually should be approached from a systems perspective, the clinician should be aware that individual factors also may be playing an important role. Psychiatric diagnoses such as organic mental conditions, affective disorders, psychosis, and personality disorders may be at the root of the violence and should be treated appropriately (e.g., medication, individual therapy). It may not be possible to conduct family therapy unless individual psychopathology is stabilized first. Another important issue is the motivation of the violent family member to change his or her behavior. Perpetrators of violence must be motivated enough to accurately report the extent of their behavior and to acknowledge their behavior as problematic. These criteria may not be present at the beginning of treatment but may represent a preliminary treatment goal. It is unlikely that significant therapeutic progress can be made without the existence of these basic criteria. Identifying potential motivating factors for the participation of a violent family member in treatment (e.g., avoiding jail, preserving the relationship) is an important task to complete during the initial assessment.

If after a careful assessment the therapist believes that the perpetrator is not motivated to stop violent behavior or if the violent behavior cannot be brought under control, family treatment is not an appropriate treatment strategy. Instead, referrals should be made for individual treatment for both the perpetrator (e.g., an anger management group) and the victim (e.g., individual treatment aimed at empowering the victim, battered women's group). Under these circumstances the therapist should advocate actively for the abused partner to leave the relationship.

While taking the initial history of a violent family, the clinician should use not only interview skills but also observational skills. In observing the family, the clinician should note whether any family members exhibit apparent injuries. If the family's explanation of an injury is suspect, the clinician's suspicions regarding potential family violence should be heightened. Other behavioral signs that may suggest family violence include clingy and fearful behaviors such as hypervigilance and a strong hesitancy to speak.

Any thorough assessment of a family or couple should include questions designed to assess the presence of family violence. The clinician must be sensitive when inquiring about this issue because a good deal of stigma and secretiveness are associated with the problem. By using empathic statements about how difficult it can be to cope with feelings of frustration, hopelessness, and anger, the clinician can help to create a nonjudgmental atmosphere. The clinician should be aware that the victim of violence may be unable to acknowledge the violence in the presence of the perpetrator. If the clinician suspects this is the case, he or she should conduct individual interviews to assess for violence. If an individual family member reveals in the individual interview that family violence occurs, the clinician should work with that family member to determine whether he or she feels safe discussing the problem in a conjoint meeting.

When assessing violence between intimate partners, it is helpful to ask questions such as the following: What does a typical fight look like? How are disagreements resolved? Do things ever get out of hand (out of control) when you fight? Do either of you have a short fuse or lose your temper easily? How do each of you express anger? These questions should be followed by more specific questions about the occurrence of violent behaviors (e.g., Did you ever hit your partner?). Questions should also assess the severity of injury sustained by the victim (e.g., What is the worst you have ever been injured by your partner? Have you ever sought medical attention for an injury inflicted by your partner?). The couple should be questioned about the presence of guns in the home.

When inquiring about child abuse, it may be helpful to begin asking the parents how they discipline their children, whether they have ever felt out of control with their children, and whether they have ever been so frustrated that they felt they might hurt their children. Again, specific questions about violent behaviors should be asked (e.g., Have you ever touched or caressed your child in what others would call a "sexual" manner? Have you ever hit your child with an object other than your hand? Have you ever left marks or bruises on your child?). The therapist can sometimes identify abuse by asking about or observing child behavioral indicators such as aggressive behavior, agitation, temper tantrums, withdrawal, hyperactivity, blunt affect, a wariness of adult contact, fearfulness, self-blaming statements, sleep disturbance, or regression from age-appropriate behaviors (e.g., becoming enuretic or encopretic) (Veltkamp and Miller 1994). Obviously, these symptoms are most often related to issues other than abuse, but a reasonable amount of suspicion is warranted.

Physical and psychological consequences of violence. Although both men and women can be verbally and physically abusive, women are much more likely to suffer injuries as victims of physical violence. One half of all injuries suffered by women seen in emergency rooms are the result of a partner's physical abuse (Stark et al. 1981). In an analysis of homicides occurring from 1976 through 1987, Browne and Williams (1993) found that 61% of women were killed by their male partners and 39% of men were killed by their female partners. Women partners were more likely to murder in self-defense. Physical effects of child abuse may include damage to the brain, vital organs, or other body parts that may result in mental retardation, blindness, deafness, or arrested development. If the clinician discovers that a family member has been physically abused, the victim should be referred for a physical examination. Undetected brain trauma or other injuries may have significant implications for the treatment of the family.

Victims of family violence may demonstrate emotional and behavioral symptoms of trauma. These symptoms may include a startle response, hypervigilance, psychic numbing, memory loss, denial of the traumatic event, depression, and anger. The clinician should be careful to observe all family members for these symptoms. Husbands with low self-esteem may be at risk for perpetrating both wife and child abuse, and abused wives and children are at risk for low-self esteem. Abused wives also frequently present with problems of anxiety, depression, and somatic complaints. Abused children frequently present with both internalizing and externalizing behavior problems, including aggression, anxiety, impulse-control problems, self-destructive behavior, and antisocial behavior.

How to assess the degree of danger. If the clinician has evidence that some form of violence has occurred in the home, it is important to assess the perpetrator's danger to self and others. This assessment should include questions regarding risk for suicide and homicide. Steps must be taken to ensure immediate safety in the home. In order to assess the degree of danger, the clinician should inquire about the severity, nature, and frequency of the violence. The clinician should also note the degree to which the perpetrator is capable of controlling his or her hostile or aggressive tendencies and the extent to which he or she acknowledges the behavior as problematic. Finally, the clinician should determine what weapons are available. Research indicates that a gun in the home adds substantially to the risk of family violence. An individual living in a home with a gun (roughly 50% of the homes in the United States) is eight times more likely to kill or be killed by a family member or intimate acquaintance than is an individual in a home without guns (Seppa 1996).

During this information-gathering process, the clinician should note the behaviors of family members. If a family's argument begins to escalate during the interview and the family is unresponsive to the clinician's interventions, the clinician may need to conduct separate interviews. The clinician should take a proactive role when dealing with a violent family and not allow arguments to escalate. Through careful observation and questioning, the clinician determines the relative risk for physical harm. If the risk is low, creating a no-violence contract with the family members may be helpful. If the risk is high, the clinician should consider working with the family members to help them establish separate living arrangements until the risk becomes lower.

Treatment

Mandatory Reporting Laws

The clinician should be aware of the mandatory and optional reporting laws for spousal, child, and elder abuse in the state in which he or she practices. In addition, the clinician should inform patients of the limitations of confidentiality prior to beginning therapy. It is often helpful to do this in an office information form that describes the policies and procedures of the clinician's practice. This ensures that patients will not have grounds to be surprised if the clinician informs them that a mandated report will be made. If the clinician believes that a mandated report is required, he or she must never be persuaded by the family not to make the report.

Making a mandated report of abuse raises significant clinical issues that must be addressed. A family may react to the clinician in a hostile manner and refuse to take responsibility for the problem. In cases in which the therapeutic relationship is damaged significantly by breaking confidentiality, the clinician may need to refer the family to another clinician for continued treatment. It is sometimes possible to use the mandated reporting process as a means to strengthen therapeutic leverage. For example, the clinician might enlist family members' cooperation by informing them that it would be most beneficial for them to remain in family therapy and that the clinician could act as their advocate with the adult or child protective agency if they complied with the treatment recommendations. This may be facilitated by the clinician allowing the family to be present in the room when he or she makes the report by phone or by having a family member make the report himself or herself while the clinician provides support. Making a report of family violence can be an empowering act that helps family members begin to take control of their lives. It may also be helpful for victims of violence to watch others taking a stance against violent behavior by reporting it to authorities.

Safety as a First Step

The primary goal of the family assessment and subsequent therapy is to stop the violence. Even if the clinician determines that the family does not need to be separated physically, he or she should initiate a discussion of separation as an option if the violence increases. Getting family members to discuss what they imagine a worst-case scenario might look like may help to empower the family to work toward change. The development of an escape plan for the victim to use if conflict escalates is recommended to reduce stress and ensure physical safety. This plan should be accomplished individually with the victim of the violence and may include calling 911; having car keys, money, and important documents accessible; alerting friends or neighbors to the violence; setting up places to stay; and getting out of the house if the perpetrator is under the influence of alcohol or drugs. The therapist should also provide the victim with a phone number for a battered women's hotline and a list of battered women's shelters. Legal options (e.g., restraining orders) should also be discussed.

The clinician must insist that violent behaviors and threats of physical violence not occur during and after the family therapy. The therapist must take a clear stance against violent behavior, even if that means potentially alienating the perpetrator of the violence. If lethal weapons are readily available, the clinician should contract with the family to immediately remove these from the home to an inaccessible location. Asking the family members to describe the ways in which the no-violence contract might fail will help them both to take responsibility for the problem and to identify ways in which they are prone to sabotage themselves. The no-violence contract should be signed by both spouses and the therapist. It should state that one consequence of violence is that the couple will separate in order for the therapist to continue conducting therapy. Regularly checking in with the family to assess the usefulness and clarity of the contract is important. For example, the clinician might begin each session by asking whether the family was able to abide by the contract.

The clinician must understand the sequence of events leading up to the violence and identify the critical points of escalation. If alcohol or substances are involved as precipitants to violence, the clinician must be clear with the family that the substance user must agree to abstain from alcohol or substances in order for family therapy to be successful. This may require a referral to a self-help group (e.g., Alcoholics Anonymous, Rational Recovery) or to an alcohol or drug treatment facility.

The clinician's basic stance in working with violent families should be one of supportive confrontation. Violent families need help in setting limits and gaining control over their lives. Violent family members may be struggling with low self-esteem and profound feelings of powerlessness. If this is the case, an important goal of family therapy would be to increase feelings of self-esteem and mastery while rejecting the violent behavior. The clinician should reinforce the distinction between rejecting the violent behavior and rejecting the person who exhibits the behavior. He or she may need to transmit this perspective through repeated and clear verbal and nonverbal communications.

Another crucial initial goal of family therapy is the reduction of family isolation. Violent families are often closed systems that promote secrecy, mistrust of outsiders, and strong family loyalty. These factors perpetuate the violence by isolating family members from help and support. The clinician should attempt to create a more open family system by referring family members to appropriate community resources, which may include support or therapy groups (e.g., assertiveness training, co-dependency groups, groups for perpetrators of violence). Family members may demonstrate resistance to following through on referrals, in which case the clinician should help the family to examine the underlying sources of its resistance and work toward change.

Therapy Approaches

Skills training. Cognitive-behavioral models of family violence view violent behavior as a learned behavior and a skills deficit. Violence is learned through direct and indirect modeling of behavior. Once learned, violence continues to be used because it is functional for the perpetrator. These models also assume that perpetrators of violence have difficulty controlling their anger and have deficits in interpersonal and communication skills. Therefore, treatment focuses on helping the perpetrator to manage anger effectively and on teaching nonviolent alternative behaviors.

Ways to reduce violent behavior include mandating the use of time-outs (described below), coaching the family to anticipate stress, identifying conflicts, and teaching negotiating or "fair fighting" skills. Improving communication skills will be an essential goal to help family members express anger, fear, hopelessness, and other feelings without verbal or physical abuse. The family must learn new techniques for the expression of anger and the resolution of conflict. In conducting this work, the clinician should be active and directive, pacing the therapy so that it challenges but does not overwhelm the family.

The time-out procedure begins with teaching the family to identify physiological, behavioral, and cognitive cues that signal impending violence. Cue recognition can be facilitated by having family members self-monitor their feelings, thoughts, and behaviors during times when they feel angry. In this way, high-risk situations can be identified and time-out procedures are taught to help the perpetrator or victim leave an escalating conflict before violence occurs. The family is coached to return to the discussion after all family members have calmed down. A common problem that occurs is that when the perpetrator states the need for a time-out, the victim may try to prevent the perpetrator from leaving so that the conflict may be resolved. The therapist may deal with this problem by reminding the victim that the function of the time-out is not to leave an argument unresolved but to protect the victim from violence.

Once the time-out procedure is provided, families are taught new communication and conflict resolution skills. These skills include the use of "I" statements and assertive statements, expression of feelings, active listening, validation, and problem solving. Families are taught to use these skills in conjunction with the time-out procedure to avoid escalation of conflict into violence.

Exploring family dynamics. Once the violence is under control and a sufficient sense of safety is established, more intensive work focusing on dysfunctional family dynamics can take place. Family systems, intergenerational, and structural family therapies are clinically useful in guiding this work. Enhancing deficient communication skills is often one of the first steps in the treatment of family violence. Examining the intergenerational aspects of violence and other salient family dynamics can help the family view its patterns of interacting in a broader context. This process may ease questions of blame and vilification as family members take responsibility for their behavior while recognizing that their patterns of behaving may have been formed in a context in which they had little control. It can be particularly helpful to use genogram work to elucidate these intergenerational patterns by creating a detailed family history and providing a visual representation of the family system (see Chapter 7). Structural family therapy can be helpful in identifying important family subgroups, coalitions, triangles, power dynamics, and boundaries.

As we said earlier in this chapter, many families in which violence occurs are closed systems. Increasing support resources for these families is an important goal of the therapy. Family members should be referred to appropriate support resources, such as assertiveness training groups, groups for batterers or victims of battering, 12-step groups, and so on. In some closed family systems, family members also may be enmeshed and may experience ambivalent feelings about their dependency on other family members. These family members may use violent behavior as a means of creating distance between family members or as a way of releasing pent-up anger about the unhealthy dependency in the family. The goal in these cases would be to develop support resources outside of the family and healthy differentiation among family members. Violent families need help in creating appropriate boundaries and in reestablishing these boundaries quickly after they have broken down.

Another relevant issue for violent families is the extent of any power imbalance in the family. Family violence usually can be conceptualized as a means for one family member to exert control over other members. In such family systems, any direct or indirect threats to the controlling family member's power are met with intimidation and violence. The controlling family member must begin to see that his or her intimidating behavior accomplishes the opposite of the goal. For example, if the controlling family member fears that his wife will leave him, he must be made to understand that by intimidating her, he will not gain her love or trust but rather her fear and mistrust. The controlling family member must come to understand the difference between overt and covert power and demonstrate a willingness to give up overt power in order to gain more indirect forms of power. Overt power refers to influence gained by intimidation and fear. Covert power refers to influential power gained by behaving in a respectful and caring manner. This message is not likely to be grasped easily by the controlling family member. It may take considerable time before family members are comfortable enough to openly share their feelings about the controlling behavior and thus confront the abuser with the negative effect of his or her behavior on the relationship.

When working with families in which child abuse is involved, clinicians will likely incorporate parenting training as an essential component of family therapy. Educating parents about developmentally appropriate behavior for children can help to eliminate unrealistic expectations. Parents should be taught to be aware of feelings of anger and frustration and to identify cues that indicate behavioral escalation to violence. Parents should be taught to take their own time-outs and to use rational self-talk to calm themselves down. Stress reduction and relaxation exercises may be used to decrease physiological arousal. Parents should also be taught alternative methods of discipline. These methods include using time-outs with their children, using new communication skills, setting limits with their children, and applying consequences consistently. Clinician modeling of appropriate behavior and behavioral rehearsal are helpful to enhance skills and confidence. Referrals to parent-training courses in the community can reduce isolation and reinforce new knowledge and skills.

Clinical Issues for Therapists

Although the therapeutic alliance is always an issue when working with families, maintaining alliances may be particularly problematic when working with violent families (Rosenbaum and O'Leary 1986). Alliance problems are set up initially as the therapist focuses on stopping the violent behavior of the perpetrator and ensuring the safety of the victim. The therapist must be able to ally with the perpetrator. One way to accomplish this is to accept the perpetrator without accepting the violent behavior. Because abusers often expect to be rejected or judged by the therapist, the therapist needs to convey that the behavior is unacceptable without condemning the abuser as a person. Finally, while recognizing that the perpetrator is responsible for the violent behavior, the therapist must view the family dysfunction and discord as a systems issue. That is, the therapist should acknowledge and validate the provocation described by the perpetrator while emphasizing that provocation never equals justification for violent behavior.

Because perpetrators of violence often feel out of control, it is important for them to believe that the therapist can deal with them and the violence (Rosenbaum and O'Leary 1986). The therapist needs to set limits about violence. When the perpetrator tests these limits, the therapist should not show fear but should lay out the consequences for such behavior. This may be difficult for some therapists, particularly for those who are afraid for their own safety. Therapists must be concerned with their own safety when working with violent families. For example, therapists should not work with violent people when they are the only ones in the building, at the end of the work day when everyone else has gone home. If guns have been involved in the violence, it must be clear that guns may not be brought into the building where therapy takes place. (This seems obvious, but therapists are often afraid to bring it up.) For example, the therapist could say, "I can't work if there is a gun around because guns make me nervous." The therapist must have a plan if violence erupts in the office. Most important, the therapist must learn to monitor the session so that escalation points are not reached.

Working with violent families presents multiple challenges for clinicians. Therapeutic progress may be slow and gradual. Clinicians must track their countertransference reactions so that they do not impart feelings of hopelessness or negativity to their patients. Just as violent families should be encouraged to seek support resources, so should clinicians readily seek support for themselves in the form of consultation or the enlistment of a co-therapist as they feel the need.

Intrafamilial Child Sexual Abuse

With James Lock, M.D., Ph.D.

Incest is a nonconsensual sexual act between family members in which one person's abuse of power violates and victimizes others whose access to power is not comparable (Erickson 1993). In addition to the serious damage done to the abused child, the family as a whole is damaged by the boundary violations, the secret-keeping, and the knowledge of destructive and violent behavior by one of its members.

Intrafamily child sexual abuse encompasses any form of sexual activity between a child and a family or extended family member, including adults in surrogate parent roles such as a live-in boyfriend. This activity is by definition exploitative and nonconsensual, as it is imposed on children who lack the emotional, physical, and cognitive ability to protect themselves. A child may appear to acquiesce to a particular sexual act for the purpose of gaining love or attention, avoiding violence, or protecting another. In some cases incest may occur between an adult child and a parent or adult sibling. This situation is rare and tends to occur after a history of childhood incest. Individual, family, and larger system dynamics interact to create a climate in which incest is possible, and it is impossible to examine incest within the family without examining all three systems.

Intrafamily child sexual abuse encompasses any form of sexual activity between a child and a family or extended family member, including adults in surrogate parent roles such as a live-in boyfriend.

Sexual contact between siblings is the most common form of incest, although father-daughter incest is more commonly reported to the authorities than are other forms. Male siblings are overwhelmingly the perpetrators. Sibling incest in some cases is experienced as less traumatic, especially when the siblings are close in age. Studies indicate that most sibling contact occurs before age 12 years and is associated with parental absence or overly stimulating sexual behaviors. Father-daughter incest is by far the next most common type. Men constitute about 95% of the perpetrators in abuse of girls and 80% in abuse of boys.

Father-son incest and mother-child incest are, to our knowledge, far less common, although underreporting has probably seriously skewed these statistics. Mothers implicated in incestuous relationships are more likely to have obvious and severe psychiatric disorders than are fathers.

Individual Issues

Key individual issues are a history of abuse in the lives of the parents and alcoholism, psychosis, violence, or pedophilia in the perpetrator. Sibling perpetrators may be violent, angry, confused, and sexually immature, using their siblings to shore up their sense of power and meet their sexual needs. Once the abuse begins the abused child will often exhibit symptoms of depression, withdrawal, or sexual precocity. Older girls may begin acting out sexually, believing that they have been damaged or that they are so worthless that sex is the only thing good about them. Many girls begin to split off parts of themselves, appearing completely functional during the day and experiencing the problems at night. These girls are later subject to severe dissociative disorder and multiple personality disorder.

Family Issues

Families in which abuse occurs are frequently disorganized, rigid, and socially isolated. The parents themselves, more often than not, have histories of neglect and abuse. This means they are unlikely to know how to get their own dependency needs met and are unlikely to be able to give much to dependent children. As the marriage progresses and the marital relationship becomes more difficult, fathers (and occasionally mothers) may turn to their dependent children for sex and affection. Two major patterns of interacting have been described with father-daughter incest. In one pattern, a rigid family is led by a domineering father who uses force and coercion to maintain his role. In the other pattern, the mother is dominant and the father develops incestuous relations to secure feelings of power and self-worth in the family. Both patterns involve closed and avoidant family systems and feelings of powerlessness in the man, although the feelings are managed in opposing ways. If the parent is a pedophile, is disinhibited by substance abuse, is a victim of abuse himself, or is under severe stress, he is vulnerable to progress to more and more explicit sexual contact with the most vulnerable people in the family, the children. Because children do not want to admit that a person who loves them could betray them, and because the cost of reporting the abuse is so high (e.g., loss of the parent, loss of family income, loss of trust, public shame), the victim is less likely to tell anyone of the abuse, and family members are likely to deny and minimize the problem. Many victims are told that they, other family members, or their pets will be killed if they tell. For the mother, the cost of not believing the abuse is to betray her child, but the cost of believing it means she may lose her spouse, break up the family, and perhaps descend into poverty. The ensuing denial creates secrecy, isolation, and shame within family members. Sibling abuse is easier to report in some ways, but this involves enormous shame and the fear of retaliation from the perpetrator. Abuse by the mother is perhaps the hardest to report; virtually all children abused by their mothers do not report the abuse at the time.

Larger System Issues

Incest takes place more commonly in any society that gives males power over females and condones many types of exploitation. The assumption that a man has a right to the women in his family allowed such a society (until recently) to deny the possibility of incest or marital rape. For many men any affection has sexual overtones, so that a woman or a child being affectionate must be "asking for it." Because men are often encouraged not to act feminine, or dependent, and are encouraged to be dominant, strong, and invulnerable, the only way for some men to meet their dependency needs is through sex. Such men are not taught to be empathic or sensitive to the needs of those around them but rather to control and be taken care of by women. When the man is a live-in boyfriend or stepfather, the lack of genetic connection may be taken as a license to abuse. Because most women are considered the gatekeepers for the family's emotional life, when incest does occur, society is more likely to blame the woman for not protecting the children than the man for the abuse, even though the woman may have no power in the relationship and no ability to make her husband do what she wants.

Assessment

Abuse must be considered when alcohol and drug use are present, when the family is secretive and depressed, when a small child begins speaking knowledgeably about sexual material with which he or she should not be familiar, when a major personality change occurs in a child who was previously functioning well, or when the child reports abuse. Although false allegations of incest are uncommon, when it occurs, it usually is in the context of a custody or other divorce proceeding, or in a chaotic home with an adolescent girl who is angry at her father or stepfather. The clinician should be alert for this possibility but should also err on the side of protecting potential victims.

Evaluation of the family in which incest occurs involves several stages. The key first stage involves identifying the degree of incest and the need for protection of family members from ongoing abuse. This may involve child protective services intervention and other legal decisions depending on the local reporting laws. The next stage takes place after the safety of family members has been established; the therapist's job is to evaluate the family as a system and each individual member. He or she must consider whether alcohol or drug abuse, violence, psychosis, or pedophilia are present. Finally, it is particularly critical to allow abused children to talk about their feelings (good and bad), about the abuser, and about themselves. If one child has been abused, the siblings likely know about it and have likely been abused as well.

Treatment

Treatment must be organized around stopping the individual and systemic dynamics that maintain the incest and understanding the crucial distinctions between incest and other dysfunctional dynamics. In addition, treatment must be dedicated to stopping not only the physical aspects of the abuse but also the other exploitative and intimidating behaviors in the perpetrator and the family. The therapist must be prepared to deal with a perpetrator mourning the loss of his or her abusive power and the family mourning a major, unexpected, and unwanted loss of its self-image and of family members. The family may be facing the mandated loss of either the abuser, who has been separated from the family, or the abused child to foster care. Legal, social work, and other uninvited health professionals have suddenly invaded their lives. Treatment will likely be mandated rather than chosen freely; therefore, these families often respond with shock, anger, and denial. The family therapist must find a way to work with many members of the helping community who may disagree about how to help or who should be punished. The legal system will often encourage the perpetrator to deny the offense and avoid entering treatment until litigation is completed, which may take months. The therapist must attend to these dynamics while dealing with the family.

In abusive families the initial impulse is to deny the facts, deny responsibility (e.g., It was my wife's fault for not stopping me), or deny the effect (e.g., It was only once and didn't matter). This may be very frustrating to the therapist who does not understand the needs that prompt this denial. The therapist must be clear and explicit about the negative consequences of the abuse while supporting the family's wish for connection and whatever strengths are available. The perpetrator is often sent to a group for perpetrators that can challenge him or her directly. The family is encouraged not to blame the nonprotective parent (usually the mother) more than the perpetrator and to understand the nonprotective parent's own powerlessness and fear. Efforts must be made to support that parent's growth and his or her ability to parent. The abused child needs adequate individual support to deal with dissociative phenomena or other symptoms (e.g., posttraumatic stress disorder) that have already occurred and to find a way to deal with the loss and shame. The complexity of treatment demands patience and willingness to work in complex systems.

Countertransference feelings of anger, disgust, and wishes to rescue the victim and family from the perpetrator are common responses in the family therapist. The therapist must be self-aware and resolve these feelings if he or she is to be effective with these families. It is often helpful to work in a team or to have an outside therapist review these cases.

Outcomes

Incestuous trauma of whatever type is not limited to the victim. Studies of sexual trauma indicate that members of the entire family are at risk for ongoing difficulties, including somatic complaints, posttraumatic stress disorder, mistrust, poor self-esteem, depression, suicidal behavior, increased aggression, impaired peer relationships, poor school performance, substance abuse, and disturbance of sexual behaviors. Families that receive appropriate early and continued assistance as they recover from the trauma of incest are likely to have the best outcomes and thereby mitigate the development of some of these problems. Kaplan and Pelcovitz (1997) have reviewed extensively the area of incest as it relates to the family.

The Family Model and Child Abuse

With Harvey S. Kaplan, M.D.

Child abuse is a major clinical problem throughout childhood. Child maltreatment occurs in families from all social classes and ethnic groups, although there is a bias toward the identification and reporting of child abuse in lower socioeconomic status families. Ultimately society must share some of the responsibility for recognizing and providing for the basic needs of its children and for reducing the level of violence played out in many aspects of daily life (Chavez et al. 1989). Each year 3 to 4 million reports of suspected child abuse are made in the United States. An estimated 5,000 deaths per year result from all forms of child abuse; the highest mortality involves head trauma in infants younger than 2 years (Chavez et al. 1989). Child neglect is the most frequently reported form of abuse but can also be linked to the family's capacity to provide basic needs such as shelter, food, and health care. In the view of some clinicians, maternal substance abuse and domestic violence directed at the pregnant mother may constitute the earliest forms of child abuse (Chavez et al. 1989).

Diagnosing accidental versus abusive forms of injury during early childhood requires evaluating the age and developmental ability of the child and the seriousness and likely mechanism for the injury. In addition, a careful history is needed to detect inconsistencies. Infants are especially likely to sustain intracranial bleeding from severe intentional shaking because of muscle weakness and their relatively large head size, which creates sufficient force momentum to tear vessels and cerebral matter (Alexander 1990).

> A 5-month-old boy was brought to the hospital emergency room by his parents. The chief complaint was lethargy, breathing difficulty, and vomiting for 3 hours. The infant appeared critically ill. Retinal hemorrhages were observed, and computed tomography scan showed cerebral edema and subdural hematomas of different ages. The parents claimed the infant bumped his head on a rattle and fell against the crib rail. Physical abuse was suspected because major head injury is inconsistent with minor trauma, and signs of repeat bleeding were present.

Blunt trauma to the chest and abdomen from a kick or punch can result in serious or fatal heart, liver, intestinal, or pancreatic injury. Skeletal trauma is also age related: 80% of fractures associated with abuse occur in infants younger than 18 months, and joint fractures are strong clues to nonaccidental injury (Lenenthal 1993). Toddlers and school-age children often present with suspicious bruises, burns, or human bite marks. Because common pediatric infections (e.g., ringworm, impetigo) or birthmarks have been mistaken for cigarette burns or other surface signs of abuse, a careful evaluation of each child is important to avoid false reports of abuse (Reece 1994). Bruises on the face, ears, neck, trunk, or buttocks are less likely to be accidental, and pattern bruises resembling a hand, belt, extension cord, or other object should be noted carefully and documented photographically, if possible (Reece 1990).

Of concern is the recent promotion of corporal punishment in the home, schools, and juvenile justice system as a response to the perceived need to discipline young people by harsh physical injury. This is the wrong message to send to parents who may already be prone to resort to physical abuse because of their own rigid moral and religious beliefs, abuse of drugs or alcohol, or mental illness.

Less common forms of child abuse include Munchausen syndrome by proxy, in which the parent (usually the mother) fabricates a history and secretly induces a host of factitious symptoms in the child (e.g., fever, bleeding, vomiting, diarrhea, electrolyte imbalance) to gain entrance to the hospital, ostensibly for care of the child but also to participate in the medical care system as a dedicated and devoted parent attending to a child with an illness that medical science seems unable to diagnose and cure. A team approach to uncovering this syndrome is mandatory if the child is to be protected from harm (Light and Sheridan 1990).

Failure to thrive in an infant is now viewed less as a pure sign of maternal neglect and more as a growth deficiency that requires specific measures to promote normal caloric intake and good growth (Bithoney and Dubowitz 1992). Individual characteristics of the infant such as temperament, physical health, and ability to respond to feeding cues strongly influence the mother's own response and bonding to the baby in an ongoing dynamic interaction. The consequences of child abuse are both immediate and long term. For the child who remains in an abusive environment, recurrent physical injury and the accompanying emotional abuse occur. A physically dangerous and threatening family environment focuses the child's energies on survival strategies and may leave little margin for normal emotional and psychological development. Recent studies of such children emphasize the potential for neurological impairment of the brain structure and function owing to abuse. This impairment is described as a posttrauma experience with persistence of the freeze, flight, or fight stress response that may show up later as negative personality and behavioral traits such as poor self-esteem, fear of failure, indiscriminate and shallow relationships with peers and adults, and use of aggression and violence to solve problems (Perry 1993). School-age children may show behavioral and learning problems that reflect past or present abuse.

In the 1990s reported cases of child sexual abuse increased sharply; surveys indicated that one in five adults may have been sexually molested as children. Most reported cases involve young girls; boys account for less than 20% of cases. Reported cases probably underestimate the true extent of sexual abuse. Perpetrators are mostly male and known to the child as family, friend, or caretaker. Adolescents are often victimized by peers. The sexual contact may go on over time and become progressive but is usually concealed from others. Stranger assault is less common but usually more violent and acute than is assault by a perpetrator known to the child. The child may disclose some or all of the abuse to a family member, friend, or teacher. Health care providers may encounter masked presentations such as psychosomatic symptoms, unusual or vague physical complaints, encopresis or enuresis, behavior disorders, school truancy, and adolescent pregnancy. Although not common the diagnosis of a sexually transmitted disease in a prepubertal child is a strong indicator of abuse and requires investigation.

Current procedures involve reporting suspected child sexual abuse to protective services or law enforcement authorities who conduct an initial intake investigation and may then bring the child to a specialized child protection center for a forensic interview and medical examination by trained examiners. Physical evidence of abuse of the prepubertal child may be revealed with the aid of photo or video colposcopy (external magnification and good light source), a useful tool in child sexual abuse cases that has been of great help in expanding the knowledge of normal versus abnormal findings (McCann 1990). Therapy for the victim and the family is crucial in most cases of child sexual abuse. Children need to hear the message that despite what happened to them they are still normal with intact bodies and that friends cannot tell they were abused simply by looking at them. Parents also need reassurance that although physical signs of trauma may be (but more often are not) found on examination, their children are not damaged goods. Some children require out-of-home placement for protection from repeated abuse if the caretaking parent is unsupportive of the child. Knutson and Schartz (1997) have reviewed in detail the physical abuse and neglect of children.

The Suicidal Patient and the Family

With Gretchen L. Haas, Ph.D.

The suicidal patient poses a major unresolved public health problem. In the 1990s, this problem was made even more complicated by economic and social pressures to radically reduce health care costs in the United States. An increasing focus on the use of outpatient treatment modalities as an alternative to psychiatric hospitalization has placed the clinician working with the suicidal patient in a precarious position of trying to accurately evaluate the need for emergency inpatient psychiatric treatment while counting the hours until discharge.

Whether the suicidal act is viewed as a maladaptive response to an acute family crisis (e.g., from the perspective of a family model, in which one identifies a family problem and interprets the suicidal behavior as an attempt to resolve the family crisis) or a maladaptive coping response to other stressors, engagement of the family in the treatment of the suicidal patient is an important adjunct to treatment. This is true when monitoring suicide risk and when intervening to manage risk for suicidal behavior. Suicide is the end result of a variety of Axis I and II disorders, including schizophrenia, mood disorder, and anxiety disorder; it also occurs when no major psychiatric disorder is present. Liability to suicidal behavior might be transmitted familially as a trait independent of Axis I and II disorders. The transmitted spectrum of suicidal behavior include attempts and completions but not ideation (Brent et al. 1996).

In this section we present a step-by-step management plan for the assessment and treatment of those patients who, with their families, present at a time of threatened or actual suicidal behavior. Such families most often present to the family therapist in crisis, and we begin at that point.

Acute Management

Recognizing that the truly accurate prediction of suicide risk is virtually impossible, the clinician must nevertheless make an immediate judgment of risk, as a first step in the management of an acute clinical condition. We dichotomize patients into the seemingly simplistic categories of "probably will try" and "probably will not try." In our experience, the best (although not exclusive) predictor of suicide attempts is a history of a life-threatening suicidal act (e.g., one that required hospitalization in an intensive care unit). Other indicators include a history of a medically damaging suicidal act that required medical intervention, the suicide of a close family member, or the recent acquisition of the means to commit suicide (e.g., purchasing a gun).

We believe that patients in the "probably will try" category should be managed with one-to-one, round-the-clock, family observation or hospitalization, pending collection of further information from other family members. Patients in the "probably will not try" category are thought to be less likely to require such observation. In all cases, a more extensive psychiatric evaluation and mental status examination is indicated.

The baseline evaluation of acute suicide risk (G. L. Haas and D. L. Mente, "Family factors in the assessment and management of suicide risk in schizophrenia," unpublished manuscript, 1995) should focus on current and past suicidal ideation, planning behaviors, and indicators of suicide intent (e.g., availability of a method and means, attempts to avoid detection, attempts to communicate intent). Knowledge of circumstances, events, and clinical conditions associated with current and previous attempt behavior can help in terms of identifying specific risk indicators for extended monitoring of suicide risk and determining appropriate conditions and treatment parameters for managing acute suicide risk.

Evaluating the Family

Once the decision has been made about whether to use maximal suicidal precautions by hospitalizing the patient, the next step is to obtain a family history, assessing the history of family functioning, key events of past and current stages of the family developmental cycle, and current patterns of family adaptation to problems (see Chapter 7). At this point, some families ask, "Why should we be involved?" At our hospital, we explain that our routine practice is to require that families be involved in inpatient treatment (if indicated) in order to achieve treatment efficacy. By establishing family involvement as one of the preconditions of inpatient treatment, the aim is to induce the patient and the family to pursue treatment and to minimize the risk of premature dropout from treatment and suicidal behavior. If the family does not participate, we explain that we will consider discharging the identified patient to his or her family. If the patient is not hospitalized, he or she should receive supportive care and monitoring.

The next step is to evaluate the role of suicidal behavior and the identified patient in relation to the family. Although the suicidal act is often unrelated to a family crisis or problem, in many situations suicide attempts are premeditated acts that are attempts to resolve mounting family conflict. The focus is on evaluation of the historical and developmental aspects of the family context in which the presenting problem has evolved (see Chapter 8).

A final step in the evaluation involves determining whether the identified patient has a current psychiatric disorder or a history of one. Dealing with family dynamics alone will seldom completely alter the course of these illnesses. Considering the known epidemiology of suicide and suicidal behavior, we are particularly concerned with determining the presence of a history of mood disorder, schizophrenia, and alcohol or other substance use disorders. For example, therapists have had the experience of seemingly restructuring and restabilizing a family after a suicide attempt only to discover (several years later) that the identified patient had a recurrent depressive disorder with associated suicidal ideation largely unrelated to family problems. It later emerged that the presence of severe depression was a consistent and probably causal factor in the recurrence of suicidal behavior.

Involving the Family

The next step is to involve the family in the treatment. The family often attempts to dump the patient on the hospital's (or family therapist's) doorstep as a solution to a family crisis. At this point, the therapist has increased leverage. As we mentioned earlier, we choose this point to inform the family that the patient cannot be treated without its involvement. The family is told that if it doesn't agree to participate in treatment, treatment cannot take place (i.e., start). This statement is used as a tactic to involve the family rather than (as the family may view it) as a consequence of ignoring the patient. We believe that effectiveness of treatment for the identified patient and the family is impaired seriously by lack of family involvement. Furthermore, if we collude with the family to allow uninvolvement, we tend to find that acutely suicidal patients are readmitted to the hospital over and over again (as indicated in follow-up studies).

After the family agrees to participate in the treatment, the next step is joining the family. This is a tactic by which we convey to the family that we're on its side—a tactic that facilitates the development of a treatment alliance with the therapist (see Chapter 14). If the patient is not hospitalized, the family should be given the therapist's telephone number, and intensive therapy should be started.

If the suicide attempt has been a response to a threat of divorce, it is critical to involve other family members such as siblings or parents when possible in order to form an alternative support system. If the partner has decided definitely to leave the relationship, he or she will not be much help in supporting the suicidal family member. Although suicide attempts are not an effective way of keeping a partner in a relationship if he or she does not want to be there, sometimes a suicide attempt will trigger a renewed attempt to improve a marriage. In such cases a trial of marital therapy is often useful.

Suicide attempts may trigger a great deal of anxiety in a beginning therapist or in one who does not see such cases frequently. The therapist must be clear that, just as with family members, his or her care and concern alone cannot prevent a determined person from committing suicide. Because most people who attempt suicide are ambivalent, the therapist often has a good deal of leverage but not omnipotence. Because of legal concerns and therapist worries, it is particularly helpful to treat these cases with the supervision of an experienced psychiatrist.

The therapist must understand that, just as with family members, providing care and concern alone cannot prevent a determined person from suicide.

Treating the Family

It has been our experience that the suicidal ideation gradually decreases as the family problem is addressed. At the stage of acute symptom remission, the task is to treat the family problem rather than to focus exclusively on the suicidal identified patient. For example, in many cases the suicidal act may serve as a way to wake up the family. In such cases the act represents an attempt to find a new option or solution to the family problem. Throughout this stage of treatment, the therapist emphasizes that although the focus of treatment began with the suicidal act, the act is essentially a symptom of a larger problem. Thus the message is conveyed that dealing with the other family problems is the most effective way to change the problem in the long run.

What often becomes evident at this stage is a continuing struggle between the family's need to keep the identified patient in the present role versus the family's feelings of wanting to help the patient (and to thereby move him or her out of that role). In our experience—especially with the families of hospitalized patients—family forces may be extremely powerful in maintaining the patient in the depressed, acting out, or suicidal role as an adaptation to the family conflict. Family members often feel guilty and in part want to help, but they are at a loss to find a new solution to the problem. This is the crucial stage of the therapy—a pivotal point at which the family is most amenable to working on reframing and redefining the family problem.

Discharging the Hospitalized Patient

After the family has reached a new equilibrium in which the family problem has been reframed and redefined, the patient can be discharged to the family for continued family therapy in the community using the more traditional family therapy techniques.

> Ms. A, a 16-year-old high school student, was admitted to the psychiatric inpatient service for her first suicide attempt, in which she ingested a handful of sleeping pills and told her parents she was going to sleep forever. The parents recognized the threat and rushed her to the local emergency room, from which she was transferred to the psychiatric inpatient service. In the first evaluation session she told the primary therapist that she had been sexually molested by her father since age 8 years. The abuse had started with nongenital fondling and had advanced to regular episodes of caressing and genital stimulation. Her mother, she thought, was totally unaware of this behavior. The suicide attempt stemmed from Ms. A's low self-esteem and feelings of being trapped, despite good school performance and an age-appropriate relationship that was beginning to develop with a teenage boyfriend.
>
> In individual therapy sessions with Mrs. A, a 45-year-old homemaker, and Mr. A, a 47-year-old stockbroker, the therapist confronted both parents with the situation. The mother was shocked, totally unaware of the situation, and became alternatively enraged and depressed over the ensuing weeks. The father was likewise shocked that his daughter had revealed their behavior and seemed surprised that the suicidal gesture was related. He confessed to the accuracy of Ms. A's account and pleaded for help with his daughter and his relationship with his wife.
>
> After several weeks of hospitalization and individual and family therapy sessions, Ms. A was discharged much improved. Family therapy sessions, which also included the patient's 17-year-old brother, were used to acknowledge the past and to plan for firmer family boundaries in the future. After being discharged, Ms. A continued in individual therapy, and her parents began a productive but painful period of marital therapy in which they reviewed the past and renewed their own intimate relationship.

Conclusion

Although violence, incest, and suicidal behavior are not DSM disorders, the frequency of these behaviors, the damage to individual and family life they cause, and the difficulty in detecting and treating them is considerable. As such, the clinician must understand the material in this chapter in order to provide thoughtful diagnostic and treatment intervention.

Suggested Readings

Gil E: Systematic Treatment of Families Who Abuse. San Francisco, CA, Jossey-Bass, 1995
This excellent book looks at domestic violence in a systems context. The author provides rich clinical vignettes and clear guidelines for treating these volatile situations.

Kaplan S (ed): Family Violence: A Clinical and Legal Guide. Washington, DC, American Psychiatric Press, 1996
Kaplan and her authors have written a detailed, easily understood guide for professionals and the public about all aspects of family violence across the life cycle.

O'Farrell T: Treating Alcohol Problems: Marital and Family Problems. New York, Guilford, 1993
This book offers a cognitive-behavioral approach to treating alcohol abuse in a couples and family context. This systematic approach is backed up by many studies demonstrating its efficacy.

References

Alexander R: Serial abuse in children who are shaken. Am J Dis Child 144:58–60, 1990

Arias I, Samios M, O'Leary KD: Prevalence and correlates of physical aggression during courtship. Journal of Interpersonal Violence 2:82–90, 1987

Barnett OW, Fagan RW: Alcohol use in male spouse abusers and their female partners. Journal of Family Violence 8:1–25, 1993

Bithoney WG, Dubowitz H: Failure to thrive/growth deficiency. Pediatr Rev 13:453–459, 1992

Brent DA, Bridge J, Johnson BA, et al: Suicidal behavior runs in families. Arch Gen Psychiatry 53:1145–1152, 1996

Browne A: Violence against women by male partners. Am Psychol 48:1077–1087, 1993

Browne A, Williams KR: Gender, intimacy, and lethal violence: trends from 1976–1987. Gender and Society 7:78–98, 1993

Chavez GF, Mulinare J, Cordero JF: Maternal cocaine use during early pregnancy as a risk factor for congenital urogenital anomalies. J Am Med Assoc 262:795–798, 1989

Egeland B: A history of abuse is a major risk factor for abusing the next generation, in Current Controversies on Family Violence. Edited by Gelles RJ, Loseke DR. Newbury Park, CA, Sage, 1993, pp 197–208

Eisenstat SA, Bancroft L: Domestic violence. N Engl J Med 341:886–892, 1999

Erickson MT: Rethinking Oedipus: an evolutionary perspective of incest avoidance. Am J Psychiatry 150:411–416, 1993

Flanzer JP: Alcohol and other drugs are key causal agents of violence, in Current Controversies on Family Violence. Edited by Gelles RJ, Loseke DR. Newbury Park, CA, Sage, 1993, pp 171–181

Gelles RJ: Violence in the American family, in Violence and the Family. Edited by Martin JP. New York, Wiley, 1978, pp 169–182

Goldener V, Penn P, Sheinberg M, et al: Love and violence: gender paradoxes in volatile attachments. Fam Process 29:343–364, 1994

Hamberger LK, Hastings J: Characteristics of male spouse abusers consistent with personality disorders. Hosp Community Psychiatry 39:763–770, 1988

Heyman RE, O'Leary KD, Jouriles EN: Alcohol and aggressive personality styles: potentiators of serious physical aggression against wives? Journal of Family Psychology 9:44–57, 1995

Hotaling G, Sugarman D: An analysis of risk markers in husband to wife violence: the current states of knowledge. Violence and Victims 1:101–123, 1986

Kantor GK, Straus MA: The drunken bum theory of wife-beating. Social Problems 34:213–229, 1987

Kaplan S, Pelcovitz D: Incest, in DSM-IV Sourcebook, Vol 3. Edited by Widiger TA, Frances AJ, Pincus HA, et al. Washington, DC, American Psychiatric Press, 1997, pp 805–860

Kelleher K, Chaffin M, Hollenberg J, et al: Alcohol and drug disorders among physically abusive and neglectful parents in a community based sample. Am J Public Health 84:1586–1590, 1994

Knutson JF, Schartz HA: Physical abuse and neglect of children, in DSM-IV Sourcebook, Vol 3. Edited by Widiger TA, Frances AJ, Pincus HA, et al. Washington, DC, American Psychiatric Association, 1997, pp 713–804

Kyriacau DN, Anglin D, Taliaferro E: Risk factors for injury to women from domestic violence. N Engl J Med 341:1892–1898, 1999

Lenenthal J: Fractures in young children; distinguishing child abuse from unintentional injuries. Am J Dis Child 147:87–92, 1993

Light MJ, Sheridan MS: Munchausen syndrome by proxy and apnea (MBPA); a survey of apnea programs. Clin Pediatr (Phila) 29:162–168, 1990

McCann J: Use of the colposcope in childhood sexual abuse examinations. Pediatr Clin North Am 37:863–880, 1990

Miller BA, Downs WR, Gondoli M: Spousal violence among alcoholic women as compared to a random household sample of women. J Stud Alcohol 50:533–540, 1989

Murphy CM, O'Farrell TJ: Factors associated with marital aggression in male alcoholics. Journal of Family Psychology 8:321–335, 1994

National Center for Child Abuse and Neglect: Study Findings: National Study of the Incidence and Severity of Child Abuse and Neglect. Washington, DC, U.S. Government Printing Office, 1986

O'Leary KD, Jacobson NS: Partner relational problems with physical abuse, in DSM-IV Sourcebook, Vol 3. Edited by Widiger TA, Frances AJ, Pincus HA, et al. Washington, DC, American Psychiatric Press, 1997, pp 673–692

O'Leary KD, Barling J, Arias I, et al: Prevalence and stability of spousal aggression. J Consult Clin Psychol 57:263–268, 1989

Pan H, Neidig PH, O'Leary KD: Male-female and aggressor-victim differences in the factor structure of the modified Conflict Tactics Scale. Journal of Interpersonal Violence 9:366–382, 1994

Perry BD: Neurodevelopment and the neurophysiology of trauma II. The APSAC Advisor 6:1–14, 1993

Reece RM: Unusual manifestations of child abuse. Pediatr Clin North Am 37:905–921, 1990

Reece RM: Child Abuse: Medical Diagnosis and Management. Philadelphia, PA, Lea & Febiger, 1994

Rosenbaum A, O'Leary KD: The treatment of marital violence, in Clinical Handbook of Marital Therapy. Edited by Jacobson NS, Gurman AS. New York, Guilford, 1986, pp 385–405

Seppa N: APA releases study on family violence. American Psychological Association Monitor, 1996

Stark E, Flitcraft A, Zuckerman D, et al: Wife Abuse in the Medical Setting: An Introduction for Health Personnel (Monograph No 7). Washington, DC, Office of Domestic Violence, 1981

Straus MA, Gelles RJ: Societal change and change in family violence from 1975 to 1985 as revealed by two national surveys. Journal of Marriage and the Family 48:465–479, 1986

Straus MA, Gelles RJ: Physical Violence in American Families: Risk Factors and Adaptations to Violence in 8,145 Families. New Brunswick, NJ, Transaction, 1990

Van Hasselt VB, Morrison RL, Bellack AS: Alcohol use in wife abusers and their spouses. Addict Behav 10:127–135, 1985

Veltkamp LJ, Miller TW: Clinical Handbook of Child Abuse and Neglect. Madison, CT, International Universities Press, 1994

Walker L: The Battered Woman Syndrome. New York, Springer, 1984

Abandoned by the Family, Chris Pape, 1992. Private collection.

CHAPTER 26

The Family and Treatment of Acute and Chronic Psychiatric Illness

Objectives for the Reader

ॐ To understand the role of the family in the acute and chronic treatment of one of its members

ॐ To be able to treat such a family with the goal of preventing rehospitalization and of reaching the highest functional level and quality of life for the identified patient and family

ॐ To become aware of family approaches and alternatives to hospitalization

Introduction

Now that we have examined the role of the family in individual psychiatric disorders and problems, it is necessary to address the issue of how the family model is used in acute and chronic care settings. Inpatient units are no longer the solitary sites for acute care. Crisis units now receive and evaluate the acutely ill or those in crisis. Some patients are hospitalized and some are held briefly, stabilized, and discharged to intensive (though not inpatient) levels of care. These include 24-hour residential programs, partial hospital services, and intensive outpatient treatment and home care. For patients who begin in a hospital, their stays are typically brief and they are later "stepped down" to less intensive, less costly services. For chronically ill patients, multiple treatment sites are available, from chronic inpatient units to halfway houses to community health centers, and so on.

In this context, we must point out that the nature and quality of work with the family has varied enormously throughout the history of the treatment of psychiatric illness. The regard and help given families has generally reflected prevailing theories of individual patient psychopathology and a tendency for clinicians to temporarily "adopt" patients from their families. Shorter lengths of hospital stays and a now-developed literature on family theory and practice have combined to inform us of the limits of hospital practice and the importance of including, allying, and relying on families for the effective short- and long-term care of the psychiatric patient (Glick and Hargreaves 1979; Glick et al. 1984).

In this chapter we focus on a new model for the evaluation and treatment of families. The model is empirically rather than theoretically based (where data exist). We provide general guidelines for family work and elaborate approaches for specific disorders. Table 26–1 contrasts the individually oriented model with the family-oriented model we recommend for the acute care of psychiatric patients.

Background

In many cultures (other than Western) families typically have a vital role in the psychiatric care of their members (Bell and Bell 1970). Because of the scarcity of trained professionals in these cultures, families must provide for the needs of the identified patient. Family members often stay with the patient in or near the hospital. The assumption is that the patient is an integral part of his or her family, and it is unthinkable that the patient would return anywhere but to the family (Bhatti et al. 1980).

In an article published in 1977, Anderson outlined some of the difficulties of working in acute settings, many of which still remain to some degree.

> Regrettably, however, the family therapy literature is not particularly helpful to those working on inpatient units; such concepts as "defining the family as the patient" tend to alienate the medical staff of an institution and the already overwhelmingly guilt-ridden families. The polarized approaches of family therapists, who generally operate on a "system" model, which overemphasizes interactional variables, and of psychiatrists, who generally operate on a "medi-

TABLE 26–1. Family therapy in individually and family-oriented treatment

Issue	Individually oriented treatment	Family-oriented treatment
Locus of pathology	In the neurobiological system or psychodynamics of the individual	Dysfunctional individual's behavior is related to dysfunction in family interactions and to individual neurobiological and psychodynamic factors—a biopsychosocial model
Locus of change and healing	In the biosystem or the intrapsychic system of the individual	In the individual within the family as a significant piece of the individual's ecology
Diagnosis	DSM-IV Axis I, Axis II, and Axis III	DSM-IV Axis IV and Axis V; characterization in relation to the symptoms or complaints
Role of the staff	To care for and provide therapy for the patient	To facilitate changes in education through family interaction or planned interactions with patient
Role of family therapy	A modality to work on those aspects of the patient's problem that seem to be related to family functioning	The orienting therapy of the overall treatment program
Discharge planning	Related to the condition of the individual and his or her ability to function	Related to the condition of the family and its ability to provide safety and continued growth for members

Source. Group for the Advancement of Psychiatry: *The Family, the Patient, and the Psychiatric Hospital: Toward a New Model.* (GAP Report 24) New York, Brunner/Mazel, 1985. Reprinted with permission.

cal" model, which overemphasizes individual variables, disregard the complex and complementary interplay of biological, psychodynamic, and interactional factors. (p. 697)

Anderson's (1977) comments highlight the problem of integrating theories of etiology and pathogenesis, a problem shared by patients, families, and hospital staff. To be sure, advances have been made since 1977. For example, research on expressed emotion in the family environments of schizophrenic patients has demonstrated the interplay between biology and environment, thereby focusing treatment (Schooler et al. 1997). In addition, research designs that include pharmacotherapy in various doses combined with family intervention (Glick et al. 1993a; M. J. Goldstein et al. 1978) recognize and provide data on the importance of attacking biological and social factors simultaneously.

During the 1990s families came to be seen as "colleagues" on the treatment team. Accordingly, our prescription for acute help for families has undergone major changes. Because patients now hospitalized are typically more ill and more disabled (than in prior decades), both mentally and physically, the families of these patients tend to be more burdened, compromised, and financially depleted. They need more support than ever.

The Function of the Acute Team for the Family

Brief acute psychiatric intervention (through hospitalization and other acute residential services), which is the norm in the United States, provides a safe and controlled environment in which to treat acute symptoms of depression, mania, suicidal ideation, alcoholism, severe personality disorder, schizophrenia, and psychotic thought and behavior. In addition, acute care with residential support serves major functions for the patient's family. The identified patient is removed temporarily from an overwhelmed family environment. In an acute family crisis, removal from home can decrease behavioral eruptions and offer substantial relief to a desperate family. During this separation, a critical goal is to evaluate the family's patterns of interaction and change maladaptive ones.

Acute residential care also can provide a setting in which the problems of the patient and his or her family surface, allowing for resolution of these problems. Psychiatric intervention can disrupt a rigidly pathological pattern of family interaction, throw the family temporarily into turmoil, and create an opportunity for change that can be more rapid and substantial than without separation. Moreover, 24-hour care permits observation, evaluation, and discussion of family interaction patterns, which can motivate the family to seek marital or family treatment after discharge. Acute care also may set the stage for overt (as opposed to previously covert) consideration of separation in deadlocked marital or parent-child interactions.

In our opinion, the clinician should consider four family-relevant functions when a patient with a serious mental illness presents for treatment (Kahn and White 1989):

1. Treat the patient.
2. Evaluate the family. Identify families with special difficulties who need immediate or intense support.
3. Develop an alliance with the family, which can later be shifted to community-based care.
4. Begin psychoeducation with the family.

In performing these functions, especially the second, the clinician should identify the family's patterns of coping with the patient's mental illness and intrafamilial differences in coping that evoke conflict (e.g., when one parent sees the patient as bad and the other sees the patient as sick). The family response always must be understood in its cultural context. Finally, a good clinician needs to recognize that how families cope can change over time.

Family Responses to Mental Illness of a Family Member

Families of the Acutely Ill

Families experience a patterned sequence of responses to the occurrence of mental illness in a family member (i.e., the identified patient). These stages are as follows:

1. Beginning uneasiness: the family does not know what to expect.
2. Need for reassurance: the family hopes that everything will be all right.
3. Denial and minimizing: the family denies that anything is wrong and minimizes the patient's difficulties.
4. Anger and blame: the family begins to see the extent of the problem, and each member lays blame on the others or on the hospital staff.
5. Guilt, shame, and grief: each member perceives his or her role and feels guilt and shame.
6. Confusion in the changed family: the family adopts new roles with resultant confusion.
7. Acceptance of reality: the family adapts to a new homeostasis.

In treating families in which the identified patient has a psychiatric illness, the therapist needs to be aware of these stages in order to make effective treatment plans. For example, to ensure that the identified patient with a manic-depressive illness takes his or her lithium medication as regularly as an individual with diabetes mellitus takes insulin, the therapist needs to know how the family feels about the illness and its treatment. Later in this chapter we translate these functions into goals.

> Some families with a member who has a serious mental illness cope successfully. Clinicians should not presume that because a patient has a serious mental illness something must be wrong with the family. The National Alliance for the Mentally Ill does not accept the assertion of many family therapists that the whole family is the patient. Alliance family members prefer to serve as "members of the treatment team" (D. Richardson, personal communication).

The Family Burden in Psychotic Illness

Researchers on family factors in the major psychiatric disorders have identified several types of stressors confronted by families attempting to cope with mental illness—for example:

- The objective and subjective burdens imposed on family life by salient aspects of the illness and by the need to provide caretaking
- Family members' tendencies to respond to the patient with criticism or emotional overinvolvement (i.e., high expressed emotion), which is hypothesized to increase the stress climate for the patient (Vaughn and Leff 1976)
- Additional stress associated with psychiatric disorders in the patient's spouse, as a consequence of assortative mating

Except for a handful of studies cited later in this chapter, management of these stressors has been fruitful with schizophrenic families but has not been included in investigations of mood disorders in general and bipolar disorder in particular.

Objective burden refers to the effects of mental illness on the family's finances, use of time, living conditions, and relationships with others. *Subjective burden* refers to the emotional stresses that the illness imposes on the family. Research on both types of family burden has demonstrated that families of patients with both schizophrenic and mood disorders experience considerable emotional distress and social and financial problems in relation to their relatives' illness. Caretakers of patients with chronic schizophrenia face psychological problems much greater than those of the general population in the care of these patients. These burdens significantly affect the lives of families of the mentally ill and may be particularly prominent among the families of patients with bipolar (as compared with unipolar) disorder. Higher levels of burden are experienced in lower class families and in families of patients who are male, have negative symptoms, and who have been ill for a relatively long period before hospitalization. Symptom severity and illness chronicity have been associated with increased levels of family burden. Falloon et al. (1985) assessed levels of family burden before and after a psychoeducational intervention; this study found significant decreases in burden in the psychoeducational but not the control condition.

Rationale for Acute Treatment of Families

Although it is our belief that most family interactions are not a major or sole cause of serious individual symptoms, it seems clear that acute intervention with family members can produce both helpful and maladaptive changes for a family system. Consider the following situations:

1. The family is in crisis and uses acute care to adaptively resolve the crisis. For example, some dysfunctional couples have described the process of coping with a psychotic episode in one partner as a strongly positive experience for both partners.

2. The family extrudes an identified patient from the family by hospitalization in an attempt to solve a crisis. Consider the following case example:

> The A family consisted of a mother, Ms. A, her boyfriend, and her two teenage daughters. The older daughter had anorexia nervosa, but the younger daughter was functioning well. Ms. A had long-standing paranoid schizophrenia and was extremely dependent on her own mother. She had been divorced about 10 years previously but had recently become involved with a boyfriend.
>
> After Ms. A became very involved in this relationship and was considering

marriage, she began to argue frequently with her older daughter. When this daughter began eating less and became paranoid, Ms. A contacted a pediatrician, stating that her daughter was seriously ill and needed hospitalization. Ms. A confided to the family therapist that she was unable to take care of her daughter because caring for her daughter would prevent her from spending time with her boyfriend and thereby would threaten the relationship. Instead of a family intervention, the pediatrician (unknowingly) hospitalized the daughter.

The preceding case example illustrates how one family member can change the life of another in the service of individual needs. In order to prevent the loss of her boyfriend, the mother restructured the family by having her daughter (i.e., the identified patient) hospitalized.

3. The family uses the care system to obtain treatment for a member other than the identified patient. The identified patient is not necessarily the only sick one (nor even the sickest one) in the family (Bursten 1965). For example, the mother may be hospitalized for depression, which ignores the father's alcoholism. A family approach allows the therapist to observe and evaluate all family members and advocate for appropriate treatment (including medication) for whoever may require it. Therapists who concentrate on one individual may overlook or not have access to psychological disturbances in a close relative.

4. The family uses the care system as a means to regain a lost member. For example, an alcoholic father who is never home may finally be convinced to enter treatment. In this case, the family's motivation is to regain a functioning father and spouse.

5. For an identified patient with a chronic or deteriorating condition (e.g., childhood or adult schizophrenia), the family can turn to an acute care system as a necessary respite from family burdens.

These situations illustrate that the treatment program is inadequate unless it includes the family. Acute care psychiatry will not fulfill its responsibility to provide effective and efficient care unless treatment includes a focus on the family.

Process of Family Treatment in Acute Care

The process of family intervention involves allying with the family, evaluating the family, defining the problem, setting goals, starting treatment (in some cases), and referring the family for continued care after discharge. Intensive psychoeducation about a specific illness and a specific treatment for that illness is an essential service. Particular attention should be paid to single-parent families and remarried families that have to cope with serious long-term mental illness. The National Alliance for the Mentally Ill has found that a high proportion of its members are single parents who often express the opinion that mental illness in a child caused the marital breakup.

Allying with the family.   Contact with the family should start as early as possible. If the patient is hospitalized, contact should start preferably before hospitalization, when the family is trying to arrange admission or certainly by the time of admission. A principal focus with the family should be discharge planning. The family must be helped to understand that hospital treatment of the identified patient involves (or requires) education, support, and involvement of all family members. This may be made a condition of all acute care. A family representative should be appointed as the accountable communicating link with the primary clinician outside of formal treatment sessions.

A more relevant question is whether to treat family members using psychoeducation or a consultative approach and in which order. Grunebaum and Friedman (1989) suggest that the first encounter should be psychoeducational rather than consultative. Therapists need the family "in order to learn about the history of the patient's illness and the family's story. Families need us to help explain to them about what they are facing, often for the first time." Consultation is more appropriate later in treatment.

Evaluating the family.   Evaluation of the family should involve the identified patient unless he or she is too psychotic or cognitively impaired to be present. The evaluation follows the customary outline for acute work and begins with the construction of a family genogram (see Chapter 7). In addition, the therapist examines immediate events, especially notable family events and changes that led to the contact. The evaluation should help the therapist to determine whether family intervention is needed and, if so, with what focus.

A necessary goal of the family evaluation is to move the family from a frightened, defensive stance (in which family members presume they will be blamed) to a position of early trust and collaboration with the treatment team. The therapist also seeks to enable the family to find the best possible coping mechanisms for the patient's symptoms. Coping mechanisms must be understood by the therapist and the family as the best of difficult alternatives. Adaptation to illness is a process of building adaptive responses.

Setting goals. Keeping in mind that acute treatment is brief, the therapist must immediately focus on the general goals of family intervention and on the goals specific to the individual family. Negotiating these goals with the family should be accomplished by the end of one or two evaluation sessions. Negotiation must be done with confidence, delicacy, firmness, and empathy. Family members are upset about the patient's condition; they may see no need for their participation in therapy or may be hostile to the treatment team for not quickly curing the ill family member. In the worst-case scenario, the family consciously or unconsciously seeks to push out the patient. These varied responses often occur because of the burden of dealing with illness.

Education about the illness from all therapeutic staff members (e.g., doctors, nurses, social workers) helps to reduce family guilt. Information about the type and length of treatment, and about what can realistically change, will reduce anxiety and allow for focus. Realistic expectations can diminish subsequent disappointment and devaluation of the treatment and staff. Education about needed family assistance will help in discharge planning and treatment compliance. Family sessions can vary in length from 30 minutes to 1 hour and may be scheduled on a daily, biweekly, or weekly basis, depending on need, goals, or anticipated discharge date.

Psychoeducation rarely proceeds as smoothly as its description might imply. Families frequently resist participating in treatment, deny the patient's illness, or magnify its severity and intractability. The family sometimes is more accurate than the therapist, especially one who is too optimistic or who appears to give up. The therapist must take family concerns seriously and not assume that he or she is right, especially on first contact. These are the complexities and challenges of family intervention. The family intervention must then switch from an educational focus to an interpretive one in order to overcome or circumvent family resistance to treatment.

We discuss the other parts of this process—that is, starting treatment and referring the family for continued care—elsewhere in this chapter. For example, the issue of treatment is addressed in several sections, starting with "Particular Decisions in Acute Care and Family Intervention," and continued care is addressed to an extent in the section on community-based support groups at the end of the chapter.

Common Goals of Acute Family Intervention

Six goals dictate the focus and course of acute family intervention. Although our inpatient family intervention research (Glick et al. 1985) has focused on two major diagnostic groups (i.e., schizophrenia and mood disorders), these goals generalize to major mental illnesses.

Whatever diagnosis the patient receives, the family faces multiple tasks: 1) understanding the patient's illness; 2) appreciating the family's own influence on the illness; 3) allying with treatment staff; 4) acknowledging the course of the illness; 5) adjusting the family's expectations of the ill member; and 6) deciding on a discharge treatment plan, including the optimal living arrangement for the ill family member. Because these are enormous tasks, especially for the first episode of illness, they require considerable focused attention from the therapeutic staff.

The sections that follow describe the six goals and corresponding treatment strategies of acute family intervention that are designed to meet the family's needs. When family needs are met, the family becomes a major asset in the patient's recovery. When family needs are not met, the family will respond with aversion, hostility, and chaos and add to a patient's risk of destabilization.

Goal 1: accepting the reality of the illness and understanding the current episode. The goal of accepting the reality of the illness and understanding the current episode is the cornerstone of all other goals. Unless the family achieves some acceptance and understanding of the illness and the seriousness of the episode, it cannot aid in future treatment. If this is a first episode, the subsequent course of the illness may not be clear to anyone. The therapist must be up front about this.

The therapist can choose from a number of techniques to accomplish this goal. All techniques require a working alliance, which is accomplished by appreciating and expressing the family's burden. The therapist should ask each family member about his or her perception and understanding of the illness. Although the therapist may not agree with a family member's view, he or she can empathize with the family's attempts to cope. In order to reduce inordinate feelings of responsibility for the illness, the therapist can provide the family with facts about the illness and (especially in the case of schizophrenia and major mood disorders) articulate the biological and genetic causes. When the family members realize that the therapist is not blaming them, the family can begin to trust the therapist. The therapist then may explore the emergence of the current episode in order to identify family stresses and environmental problems. Finally, the family can be educated about the course of the disorder, including early warning signs, progression, relapse, and recurrence.

Goal 2: identifying current episode stressors. Once the family has tentatively accepted the reality of the illness, the next step is to identify precipitating current episode stressors while they are still fresh in the minds of family members. The abstract notion that stress can influence a psychiatric illness becomes a reality when the link between theory and reality is forged.

The strategies and techniques for achieving this goal are mainly educational, cognitive, and problem-solving oriented. The therapist encourages the family to think about recent stresses, within and outside the family, that may have contributed to the patient's regression. In addition, the family can rank the stresses and assign priorities for brief interventions.

Goal 3: identifying potential future stressors, within and outside the family. Goals 1 and 2 are principally concerned with the immediate and remote past and with a didactic approach to illness. If these goals are accomplished even partly, there is a natural tendency to consider the future. In some cases a future orientation (e.g., discharge) comes too early. This generally signals defensive denial that must be met with a refocus on Goals 1 and 2.

Family attitudes toward the patient and treatment have an effect on outcome. For example, positive family attitudes about hospital treatment have correlated with patient improvement, whereas resistance to treatment has correlated with discharge against medical advice (Akhtar et al. 1981; E. Goldstein 1979). In addition, Greenman and associates (1989, p. 228) found that certain parental concerns on admission to a hospital affect patient behavior. Interestingly, these concerns were gender-linked: Mothers were concerned with limit setting (i.e., preventing impulsive and self-destructive behavior), whereas fathers "had difficulty supporting treatment because they were afraid that taking such a position would anger the patient, leading to a loss of their relationship with the patient." This observation is not surprising because mothers were often home all day with the patient and they already had a deeper relationship with the patient.

Goal 4: elucidating stressful family interactions. Informing a family that it can stress a patient is both intellectual and vague. However, when a family is shown how its behavior is destabilizing the patient (e.g., causing the patient to become paranoid or disorganized or to smash an object), real learning can occur.

An impressive body of evidence has suggested that families high in expressed emotion run an increased risk of patient relapse. High expressed emotion was originally thought to be specific to schizophrenia, but recent research demonstrates this difficulty in families with chronic mood and other disorders (Miklowitz et al. 1988). We believe that increased family expressed emotion is associated with almost all chronic psychiatric illnesses.

Family techniques that lower expressed emotion result in better patient outcome.

Although Goals 1 through 3 are mediated by cognitive and educational strategies, techniques that demonstrate how family interactions stress the patient more closely approximate traditional (or systems-oriented) family therapy. The following statement illustrates a systems-clarifying technique: "Every time you criticize him, as you did just now, he puts his head down and murmurs something under his breath that sounds like nonsense." By using this technique, the therapist educates the family about how an interaction does not cause the disorder (thereby reducing guilt) but is likely to trigger current symptoms (thereby focusing controllable and adaptive behavior). The family's frustration and anger toward the patient's behavior, which lead them to criticize the patient, can then be redirected.

Goal 5: planning strategies for managing or minimizing future stressors. By the middle or toward the end of an acute episode of illness, family members may believe that their troubles are over. The next goal of family intervention, therefore, is to help families recognize that planning is needed to ensure that history does not repeat itself.

The therapist can initiate discussion of the possible return of symptoms and how the family can cope. Family members also need to be encouraged to discuss their expectations of the patient's future level of functioning. For some families, expectations must be realistically lowered; for others, hope needs to be stimulated. Families also need help anticipating potential stressors related to the patient's reentering the community, including employment, education, and social functioning. If the family members are also experiencing illness or addiction, they should be encouraged to begin treatment.

Goal 6: accepting the need for continued treatment. This goal, central to preventing relapse, brings the family full circle with Goal 1 (reducing denial of the illness). Families that have experienced repeated episodes of illness have little problem anticipating the possibility of relapse. Because these families are often discouraged and burdened, they need support and encouragement. For families going through a first hospitalization there is the danger that they will deny future illness and the need for aftercare.

The therapist can use the family technique of visualizing in the future replays of what led to the current illness. How would the patient tell the family (or vice versa) that something is the matter? What are the early signs of illness? Who would the family contact? Additional education about the course of the condition further emphasizes the need for aftercare.

Not every family will need work on all goals. Some families will be so traumatized or limited that the therapist can approach only a few of these goals.

The ultimate goal of family intervention is to extend the gains of acute care into the family. If the family can understand precipitating stressors, modulate high expressed emotion, and ensure continued treatment, the transition from intensive treatment to community care will be facilitated greatly. This is especially important in an environment in which hospitals find it advisable to reduce hospitalization in order to limit regression and, especially, to reduce health care costs through brief stays.

Particular Decisions in Acute Care and Family Intervention

Timing

The two key moments of timing are when to make contact and when to start therapy. Contact with the family should start during the decision-making process leading to acute care (e.g., in the emergency room). Family therapists typically disagree about when the patient should be present. Some therapists believe that family intervention with the patient should begin only when the active symptoms have begun to diminish. In our experience, this position rationalizes putting off family intervention and treatment. Many patients, even in a psychotic state, become more coherent during well-planned and focused family sessions.

Staffing

Who should do the family intervention? In our opinion, the primary clinician or therapist is in the best position to work with the family because he or she has an overall grasp of the case. In the hospital setting, we believe that the individual and family treatments should be done by the same therapist; however, time constraints, or the need for supervision, may make this impossible. Primary clinicians may be of any discipline (e.g., psychology, social work, nursing), but experience with families and family therapy is critical. The key issue is training; that is, whoever does the family therapy must have training in the theory and practice of family therapy and must have experience with the disorders that are prevalent in acute care psychiatry.

The partial hospital or inpatient milieu is especially advantageous for identifying patterns of family interaction. Accurate, on-the-spot observation of a family may reveal how a patient's symptoms may be aggravated. For example, a male adolescent's repeatedly re-creating problem family interactions with female staff on the psychiatric unit can present an opportunity to demonstrate to him that this is similar to the way he reacts to his mother.

Family Techniques

A variety of family therapy techniques are needed in the acute setting: individual family intervention, multiple family groups and conjoint couples groups, and family psychoeducational workshops (also known as family survival skills workshops or family support groups).

Clinical family therapy by itself is rarely used today for hospitalized or acute care patients when hospital stays are less than 2 weeks long. For psychotic patients, family intervention complements medication and rehabilitative therapies. For nonpsychotic patients, family intervention is part of a treatment plan consisting of pharmacotherapy and individual therapy. Consider the following case example:

Tom B, a 17-year-old adolescent, was admitted to the hospital after having been extremely agitated and disoriented at home, where he refused to eat or sleep. The working diagnosis was of a schizophrenic disorder. In the hospital he continued to be very paranoid, eating only with a parent and avoiding other patients. The staff met with the boy and his mother and explained their observations and concerns and discussed how a neuroleptic medication could help. They also discussed side effects and how to evaluate the effectiveness of the medication (e.g., by observing Tom's ability to think more clearly and understand what was going on around him). Tom was told that he could help the staff decide the best dose.

Tom hesitated and his mother, Mrs. B, had questions. But it was she who convinced Tom that he should begin taking medication. Two days later he reported that he felt better and wanted to stop the medication. The staff spoke again with Tom and his mother and indicated that more time was needed to keep him well. Again Mrs. B persuaded her son to continue. Some days later he said he felt better but wondered if an increased dose would help him sleep better. In another meeting with Tom and his mother a new dosage was arranged.

The medication discussions provided Tom and his mother with a cooperative, respectful relationship with each other and the staff. Decisions were not made for him; instead he was included in the decisions. As the hospitalization progressed, Tom more readily questioned his family and the staff, and the answers he received helped to clarify and quiet his psychotic confusion. The neuroleptic medication and the therapy described had worked synergistically.

The acute treatment team must choose a family treatment model: psychoeducational, insight-awareness, or a systemic-strategic approach. All three are useful but at different times in the course of a disorder or with different disorders. Because of the brief duration of acute care and the cognitive impairment of an acutely ill patient, we recommend a psychoeducational approach, reserving insight-awareness and structural approaches for continued care.

A good description of the need for psychoeducation is found in the following communication from a parent of a patient with schizoaffective disorder:

> When my daughter and son-in-law entered the clinic with their newborn son, diagnosed with spina bifida and hydrocephalus, the chief nurse said, "You will be with this child every hour of the day. We will teach you what to look for, and then you will be able to tell us what is wrong with the baby." When my other daughter accompanied her son to the allergist about the boy's asthma, the doctor gave specific instructions about the dosage of medicine, and the desired response. The doctor told her when to go up and come down with the medication dosage and what to do in an emergency. As a pathologist who has worked closely with my son who has schizoaffective disorder, I believe it is important that a parent or family member be involved equally in the treatment of mental disorders. The principle is that a patient and his family should be given medical education and training to enable them to carry out the treatment program.

The care of a mental disorder, like many persistent or unstable illnesses, requires daily attention to symptomatology, stresses, and treatment. Professional care simply is not possible at this level of intensity. The patient and family need to be educated and supported to carry out the treatment plan.

A Working Model of Acute Family Intervention

The Group for the Advancement of Psychiatry Committee on the Family has summarized the family model as follows:

> Hospitalization should be viewed in most cases as an event in the history of the family, an event that can be devastating or valuable depending upon the skills and orientation of the therapeutic team. Hospitalization viewed in this way be-

comes central in understanding the role of the patient in the family system and in supporting the family as well as the patient. The hospital becomes an important therapeutic adjunct not only for severely dysfunctional individuals and their families, but also for families stuck in modes of relating that appear to interfere with the development and movement of individual members. For these families, hospitalization aims to disrupt the family set; this disruption can be used to help the family system to change in more functional ways. (Group for the Advancement of Psychiatry 1985, p. 24)

Family-oriented programs can be implemented within existing hospital resources, and acute care environments may be designed to include family members in patient care. (This trend also is noted in other specialties, such as in obstetric and pediatric units.) Effective programs involve the staff, from admission clerks on, in building an alliance with the family. On our acute teams, we always advise families that the changes they make in relating will always increase anxiety because the status quo has been changed. Stewart (1982) describes this as "the engagement of the family with the institution in a relationship that achieves mutual understanding and support and establishes clarity, acceptance, and commitment to mutually agreed upon goals for the treatment of the hospitalized patient." This active reaching out, which can be done at all levels of acute care (not just at the hospital level), is different from a commitment to change-oriented family treatment. The family model we propose avoids staff overidentification with the patient, which can pit staff against the family. It also reduces the stigma of psychiatric treatment and thereby increases aftercare compliance.

Different types of staff-family interactions are possible and helpful. For example, alliance building or staff-family interaction around medications, visits, and formal family therapy sessions geared toward change all may have a therapeutic function (Stewart 1982). See Table 26–2 for a summary of one model of acute family intervention.

Guidelines for Recommending Family Intervention in an Acute Care Setting

The guidelines for recommending family intervention in acute care are similar to those for outpatient settings. If the family is present and available, family intervention should not be withheld.

A careful distinction has to be made between evaluation and psychoeducation, and family treatment. As a rule of thumb, every family should be evaluated and educated about illness and family treatment. When indicated, family treatment should be started in the acute care setting, although

TABLE 26–2.   Acute family intervention

Definition: Acute family intervention (AFI) is work with patients and their families together in one or more family sessions. It aims at favorably affecting the patient's course of illness and course of treatment through increased understanding of the illness and decreased stress on the patient.

Description:

I.   Assumptions

    A. AFI does not assume that the etiology of the major psychotic disorders lies in family functioning or communication.

    B. It does assume that present-day functioning of a family (with which the patient is living or is in frequent contact) can be a major source of stress or support.

II.   Aims

    A. AFI aims to help families understand, live with, and deal with patients and their illness; to develop the most appropriate possible ways of addressing the problems the illness presents and its effects on the patient; and to understand and support the necessary acute and long-range treatments.

    B. AFI aims to help patients understand family actions and reactions and to help patients develop the most appropriate intrafamily behavior in order to decrease their vulnerability to family stress and decrease the likelihood that their behavior will provoke family maladaptive behaviors.

III.   Strategy and Techniques

    A. Evaluation

        1. Evaluation is accomplished in one or more initial family sessions, with the patient present when conditions permit. Information gained from other sources also is used.

        2. The patient's illness and its potential course are evaluated.

        3. The present effect and the possible future effect on the family are determined.

        4. The family's effect on the patient is evaluated, with particular reference to the stress caused by expressed emotion and criticism.

        5. Family structure and interaction and the present point in the family life cycle are evaluated in order to determine whether particular aspects of the patient's role in the family are exacerbating or maintaining the illness or otherwise impairing the patient.

    B. Techniques

        1. The family and patient usually are seen together.

        2. Early in treatment an attempt is made to form an alliance with the family members that gives them a sense of support and understanding.

(continued)

TABLE 26–2.   Acute family intervention *(continued)*

   3. Psychoeducation: (a) The family is provided with information about the illness, its likely course, and its treatment; questions are answered. (b) The idea that stress from and in the family can exacerbate the illness is discussed. (c) The ways in which conflicts and stress arise within each family are discussed, and a problem-solving approach is taken in planning ways to decrease stress in the future. (d) The ways in which the illness and the patient's impaired functioning have burdened the family are discussed and plans made to decrease such burden.

   4. In some cases the initial evaluation or subsequent sessions suggest that particular resistances due to aspects of family structure or family dynamics interfere with accomplishing (2) and (3) above. If it is judged necessary and possible, one or a series of family sessions may attempt to explore resistances and effect changes in family dynamics. Such attempts may use some traditional family therapy techniques. Families may be encouraged to seek family therapy after the patient's discharge.

Source.   Group for the Advancement of Psychiatry: *The Family, the Patient, and the Psychiatric Hospital: Toward a New Model.* New York, Brunner/Mazel, 1985, pp. 27–28. Reprinted with permission.

most goals will be accomplished in a continued care setting.

Examples of acute situations that call for family intervention include the following:

- A suicidal and depressed adolescent living in the parental home is hospitalized following a car accident. There is some suspicion that the father is alcoholic and that the parents are not aware of the adolescent's depression nor of his daily functioning.
- A 22-year-old college student presents with an acute psychotic episode in the fall of his first year away from home. Family sessions are needed to educate the family about the unexpected illness, to help the parents and the patient evaluate their mutual expectations for his performance, and to encourage follow-up psychiatric care.
- A 39-year-old divorced woman living with her 11- and 13-year-old children is hospitalized following a paranoid psychotic break in which she stabbed herself in the abdomen in the presence of the children. Family sessions with the children are needed to help the mother, now in a denial phase, to explain her illness and to talk about the future. An urgent need also exists for the children to discuss their feelings about witnessing their mother stab herself. The treatment team needs to find more community resources for the mother and her children. The question must also be

raised as to whether the mother can care for her children or is a danger to them.

- A 23-year-old woman who lives with her parents is hospitalized following an exacerbation of schizophrenia occasioned by her younger sister leaving for college. The patient also had stopped taking her medication. The parents have high expressed emotion (they are critical of the older daughter, and one parent is with her constantly). Family treatment is started to increase the likelihood of compliance with aftercare (i.e., aftercare includes medication, family therapy, and a partial hospital program).

Indications for family intervention come from the patient, the family, and the observable interactions between the family and the patient's illness. Patient-related criteria include current living conditions (e.g., living with spouse or family of origin) and life cycle issues (e.g., patient is a young adult trying to separate or an older adult living with or dependent on the family). Family criteria include conflict that contributes to the patient's difficulties or psychiatric illness in another family member. Criteria related to the interaction of the family with the patient's illness are family denial or inadequate support of the illness, family resistance to treatment, and danger of harm to the family.

Contraindications include the individual patient who is striving (with a good chance for success) for independence from the parents and parents in severe conflict, in which case marital treatment may be indicated.

Empirical Studies

Glick and associates (1993b) have reported the only controlled study of family intervention in an inpatient setting. Inpatient family intervention (emphasizing family psychoeducation) was compared with hospitalization without family intervention for patients with schizophrenic and mood disorders. The sample included 169 patients and their families for whom family intervention was indicated. The families were randomized into the two treatment conditions. Assessments were made at admission, discharge, and 6 and 18 months postadmission, using patient and family measures from the vantage points of patient, family, and independent assessors.

Overall, family intervention in the hospital setting was found to be effective but not for everyone (Clarkin et al. 1990; Glick et al. 1990, 1993b; Spencer et al. 1988). For some patients and families, inpatient family intervention appeared not to add anything to standard hospital treatment. The positive effect of inpatient family intervention was principally in female patients with mood disorder and their families, to a lesser extent in schizophrenic patients who had good prehospital functioning, and in patients given other diagnoses.

In a follow-up study, the statistical interactions indicated that any therapeutic effect was generally restricted to female patients with schizophrenia or major affective disorder. The effect of family treatment on male patients given these diagnoses was minimal or slightly negative. The effect of inpatient family intervention on schizophrenia did not appear until 18 months postadmission, and the most striking effect was observed in the prehospital poorly functioning group. Similarly (in contrast to the discharge results), the follow-up results for patients with mood disorder revealed positive findings favoring the inpatient family intervention but only in the bipolar subgroup. Composite means showed that family treatment was somewhat better for the families of patients (primarily females) with the major psychoses, whereas families of patients given other diagnoses did better without family intervention.

Clinical research on hospital treatments has typically focused on outcomes for patients; the outcomes for families are not known. One hypothesis-generating, three-country study of family outcome after an episode of major affective disorder found that families were less financially well off (because of hospitalization costs), frequently functioned worse than before the episode, and, without psychoeducation, were unprepared for the next episode (Glick et al. 1991a).

Our clinical experience suggests that the specific interventions of psychoeducational groups can help the often demoralized family of the chronically ill patient to reestablish itself as a viable unit and lessen family members' burden of shame, guilt, despair, and isolation (Greenberg et al. 1988). As to effectiveness in outpatient settings, five studies in three countries have found that family intervention coupled with medication significantly lowers the risk of relapse for outpatients with schizophrenia. As such, one might extrapolate from these studies that family intervention may be mandatory as part of the multimodal prescription for most Axis I disorders.

Families of the Chronically Ill

With John A. Talbott, M.D.

Thirty percent of the patients discharged from mental hospitals are rehospitalized during the first year after discharge. Sixty percent of all admissions to state hospitals are readmissions. For many patients, rehospitalization occurs more than once and indeed becomes a way of life. An implication of these facts is that for many patients the family has become more involved in their long-term outcome.

We now know much more than we did several years ago regarding families of the mentally ill. For instance, of 1 million patients admitted to state, county, and general hospitals, 3,000 are married and one-half of the remainder live at home—meaning that 70% of the seriously ill have families that can or will be involved after discharge (E. Goldstein 1979). In addition, more of the mentally ill elderly are cared for at home than in institutions, and institutionalization is sought only when the elderly person's burden on the family becomes overwhelming.

The work of several British investigators on expressed emotion of family members as it affects the course of schizophrenic illness shows the critical nature of this variable. Expressed emotion remained the single best predictor of relapse in schizophrenic patients, although medication and infrequent contact with the family also protected these patients from relapse. The worst prognosis occurred in patients who were taking medication and who had high expressed emotion families with whom they had frequent contact; the best outcomes occurred in patients who were taking medication and had low expressed emotion families (Akhtar et al. 1981).

We now know much more than we used to about the expressed needs of families of the mentally ill (Greenman et al. 1989). These families want information about mental illness, symptoms, and etiology; help in handling their sick relative's behavior; knowledge of resources; respite care and services; economic relief; crisis care; rehabilitation services; and reduction of anxiety.

Families are most distressed by their ill relative's bizarre and abnormal or intrusive and disturbing behavior and by poor task functioning. They indicate the mentally ill person at home causes serious disruption to their family life (e.g., to siblings, marriages, social and personal life); the burden of caring for someone who cannot care for himself or herself; and the emotional burdens of stress, anxiety, resentment, grief, and depression. Families that cope more effectively with their mentally ill relatives are characterized by greater acceptance, less pushiness, avoidance of rigid statements, patience, better ability to listen, lack of fear, and a positive attitude (Hatfield 1981). Although symptoms are not affected by familial expectations, performance is, at least in terms of activities of everyday living (Greenley 1979).

Families seem critical to the patient's ability to survive in the community; early rehospitalization is related directly to low family symptom tolerance

(Greenley 1978). With repeated admissions, families become less willing to help (Morris 1977/1978), and subsequent hospitalizations of their relatives become related less to the family's symptom tolerance than to its dislike of the patient (Greenley 1978).

Families and mental health professionals now seem to agree that the emphasis of intervention with families of the chronically ill should be on educational approaches rather than on traditional family therapy. Since the mid-1980s the burgeoning of programs and descriptions of techniques of such psychoeducation is nothing short of amazing. Some programs are directed primarily at one effect—such as communication (Glick et al. 1990), survival skills (Stewart 1982), or attitudinal change (Spencer et al. 1988). Some are directed at families alone (Clarkin et al. 1990), others at just the patient (Glick et al. 1991b). Some take place at home and others in a clinic setting (Solomon and Draine 1995). Despite these differences, the programs share the following characteristics (Solomon and Draine 1995; Stein 1989; Wynne et al. 1987):

- Education about the disease and its treatment
- Improvement in communications
- Structured problem solving
- Development of outside resources
- Methods to increase structure and decrease disorganization
- Sharing of the experience of living with mentally ill relative
- Concern for the healthy members' lives
- Reinforcement of family boundaries
- Anticipation and handling of stressful situations
- Attempts to avoid relapse
- Emphasis on biological etiology and avoidance of blaming the family

In light of the research showing that high expressed emotion in relatives is related to increased relapse, several groups have formulated programs aimed at directly decreasing the criticism, overinvolvement, and hospitalization felt to be so critical to outcome (Glick et al. 1991b; Schooler et al. 1997). Preliminary results on the effectiveness of these psychoeducational approaches are encouraging. The results include a relapse rate nine times greater in the control subjects receiving individual treatment (Greenberg et al. 1988), no relapses versus 48% among control subjects at 6 months, 7% relapses versus 57% in control subjects at 9 months, and 2-year mean results of 3.63 days in the hospital after the program versus 83.26 days in the 2 years before to treatment (Stein 1989).

A remarkable change has taken place among the families of the seriously and chronically mentally ill. These families have organized together, shared their common experiences, sought educational information, and destigmatized their views of themselves. As a result, beginning with the American Schizophrenic Association, which stressed orthomolecular therapy, parent groups have formed throughout the country. In 1979, the National Alliance for the Mentally Ill was formed, which currently has 200 chapters. The groups are remarkably similar, seeking to end the tendency in psychiatry to blame the family, to advocate for themselves, to support one another, to increase research efforts, and to advocate for a more efficient and effective service delivery system (Falloon et al. 1985; Hatfield 1981; Terkelsen 1982). Families also are concerned that they, who know what has worked and what has not worked, are frequently not consulted by professionals during treatment planning (Hibler 1978). Families point out that their views are often different from those of their ill relatives. For example, they tend to think that hospitalization and conservatorship are too difficult, discharge is too abrupt, the system is too permissive, and patients are allowed to refuse their medication too easily. It has often been pointed out that one reason that the mentally ill have been placed in community care less successfully than the mentally retarded is because of the stigma felt by their relatives; that is, they often feel a need to hide their love because of the stigma of loving a mentally ill adult (Boggs 1981).

Families have demonstrated that their willingness to keep mentally ill relatives at home is much greater if certain systems changes are made, such as providing fiscal support, respite services, a sound social services program that reduces the family burden, and a true community care system (Segal 1979). Although most programs have described their interaction with families in general terms, further work needs to be devoted to identifying the specific coping strategies that work with the chronically ill and the attitudes and behaviors that are most useful (Kanter and Lin 1980).

Community-Based Support Groups

It is now increasingly accepted that mental health professionals should encourage family members to use the support provided by community-based support groups and to form such groups if none are available (Solomon and Draine 1995). Since the early 1990s a number of excellent books have been written for families with mentally ill members. We recommend contacting the National Alliance for the Mentally Ill for its latest list of readings for families.

Hospitals and clinics also have developed manuals for patients and families that describe management and treatment of mental illness. These manuals can serve as important homework reading for families presenting for acute care. There also should be mandatory reading prescribed by family therapists.

Controversies in Treatment

1. *Is the family in treatment, a part of treatment, or a member of the treatment team?* Our position is that good treatment involves all three. First, most families have problems coping with the identified patient's illness. Many families have problems separate from the identified patient. Second, the family's presence in the treatment process, as compared with individual or drug treatment, makes the family a de facto part of the treatment. (As a result, the therapist should obtain the family's consent for treatment.) Finally, Wynne et al. (1987) argue that the long-term nature and seriousness of recurrent or chronic mental illness and the family's experience with dealing with a particular member requires that the family's expertise be harnessed.

   At first, most families feel most comfortable as partners with the treatment team. Later the family may feel ready to become part of treatment or enter into treatment itself. Often this occurs after the patient has stabilized. Over time, clinicians will need to blend all three positions to foster the best outcome for patients and families.

2. *Should the initial goals of family therapy be oriented around family change or family consultation?* This long-standing controversy emanates from the traditional model in which the family is blamed for the patient's illness. The best way to engage family members is to contact them "where they are" (i.e., at their level of understanding of the illness), provide psychoeducation, and respond to requests for information and support. The initial consultation serves as a means to ally with the family. Change cannot occur without this first step.

3. *A few family therapists still believe that schizophrenia and other major functional psychoses are purely family systems (i.e., psychological and social but not biological problems). Are they?* This belief is based in part on the inference that improvement (or recovery) is possible without medication. We agree with Stein (1989, p. 134) that mental illnesses, "like virtually every disease, are influenced by biological, psychological, and social factors." Treating schizophrenia or any other major mental disorder re-

quires biological, psychological, and social approaches and anything else that will help.

4. *Many families believe that major mental illnesses are solely brain illnesses.* This belief creates confusion in the minds of some families when they are offered a psychosocial treatment such as family therapy. Why would a biochemical problem be treated with a psychosocial treatment? The answer is that any family, living with a member who has sustained cognitive and other brain function defects, will have major problems in the management of the disorder and with the feelings associated with chronic illness.

5. *How much does family intervention add to medication in the treatment of acutely ill patients?* Most studies indicate that each modality is additive (Glick et al. 1991a). Medication is effective for positive (and probably negative) symptoms, and family intervention helps with the complicating interpersonal problems of illness (Glick et al. 1995).

   An interesting question is whether family intervention can result in lowered doses of medication and thereby reduction in the risk of tardive dyskinesia (e.g., a side effect of some antipsychotic medications). The Treatment Strategies in Schizophrenia Collaborative Study (Schooler et al. 1997) has addressed this question. The study involved the use of a standard-dose neuroleptic, a low-dose neuroleptic, or an early intervention strategy (i.e., use of medication once the patient starts to relapse) coupled with one of two kinds of family strategies (a weekly, applied, behaviorally oriented family treatment or a monthly supportive group). The greater was the family involvement in either applied or supportive treatment, the fewer the patient's symptoms and the lesser the need for medication; however, the addition of family intervention did not interact with the drug conditions. Neither family condition lowered the amount of medication needed, and the targeted strategy was not efficacious for patients with chronic schizophrenia. Conversely, long-term drug maintenance often helps the patient participate more meaningfully in family therapy.

6. *Family treatment in the acute setting lacks evidence of effectiveness; therefore, the enormous resources in time, staff, and money should not be allocated to this modality.* Although this accusation was mostly true until recently, clinical experience and our study (Glick et al. 1993b, referred to earlier in the chapter) suggest that the controversy about the effectiveness of family treatment should be reformulated. The central questions are, Who requires intervention? and What is an effective intervention? Our work indicates that intervention works best for female patients with mood disorder (especially bipolar disorder) and female patients with

chronic schizophrenia. The families of all patients with schizophrenia and bipolar disorder seem to derive some benefit from family intervention (as opposed to family therapy). Consequently, our position is that until further studies are done, family intervention should be considered for all patients and prescribed on the basis of available knowledge and a case-by-case evaluation of the patient and the family. Other studies show consistent patterns of effectiveness (Postrado and Lehman 1995; Walling and Dott 1994).

Suggested Readings

Anderson C, Reiss D, Hogarty G: Schizophrenia and the Family. New York, Guilford, 1986
  This classic book provides one of the best introductions to family psychoeducational approaches for schizophrenia. The premises for family psychoeducation are articulated clearly, and both volumes include rich clinical ideas. Descriptions of educational workshops and multiple family therapy models are included.

Brotter B, Clarkin JF, Carpenter D: Bipolar disorder, in Handbook of Empirical Social Work Practice. Edited by Thyer B, Wodarski J. New York, Wiley, 1998, pp 287–308

Keitner G (ed): Depression and Families: Impact and Treatment. Washington, DC, American Psychiatric Press, 1990
  The two preceding references detail the latest information on the family approach to mood disorders.

References

Akhtar S, Helfrich J, Mestayer RF: AMA discharge from a psychiatric inpatient unit. Int J Soc Psychiatry 27:143–150, 1981

Anderson C: Family intervention with severely disturbed inpatients. Arch Gen Psychi 34:697–702

Bell J, Bell E: Family participation in hospital care for children. Children 7:154–157, 1970

Bhatti RS, Janikramaiah N, Channabassavanna SM: Family psychiatric ward treatment in India. Fam Process 19:193–200, 1980

Boggs EM: Contrasts in deinstitutionalization. Hosp Community Psychiatry 32:591, 1981

Bursten B: Family dynamics, the sick role, and medical hospital admissions. Fam Process 4:206–216, 1965

Clarkin JF, Glick ID, Haas GL, et al: A randomized clinical trial of inpatient family intervention, V: results for affective disorders. J Affect Disord 18:17–28, 1990

Falloon IRH, Boyd J, McGill C, et al: Family management in the prevention of morbidity of schizophrenia: clinical outcome of a two-year longitudinal study. Arch Gen Psychiatry 42:887–896, 1985

Glick ID, Hargreaves WA: Psychiatric Hospital Treatment for the 1980s: A Controlled Study of Short Versus Long Hospitalization. Lexington, MA, Lexington, 1979

Glick ID, Klar HM, Braff D: Guidelines for hospitalization of chronic psychiatric patients. Hosp Community Psychiatry 35:934–936, 1984

Glick ID, Clarkin JF, Spencer JH, et al: Inpatient family intervention; a controlled evaluation of practice: preliminary results of the six-months follow-up. Arch Gen Psychiatry 42:882–886, 1985

Glick ID, Spencer JH, Clarkin JF, et al: A randomized clinical trial of inpatient family intervention, IV: follow-up results for subjects with schizophrenia. Schizophr Res 3:187–200, 1990

Glick ID, Burti L, Minakawa K, et al: Effectiveness of psychiatric care; II. outcome for the family after hospital treatment for major affective disorder. Ann Clin Psychiatry 3:187–198, 1991a

Glick ID, Clarkin J, Haas G, et al: A randomized clinical trial of inpatient family intervention, VI: mediating variables and outcome. Fam Process 30:85–99, 1991b

Glick ID, Clarkin JF, Goldsmith SJ: Combining medication with family psychotherapy, in Combined Treatments, the American Psychiatric Press Review of Psychiatry. Edited by Beitman B. Washington, DC, American Psychiatric Press, 1993a, pp 585–610

Glick ID, Clarkin JF, Haas GL, et al: Clinical significance of inpatient family intervention, VII: conclusions from the clinical trial. Hosp Community Psychiatry 44:869–873, 1993b

Glick ID, Dulit RA, Wachter E, et al: The family, family therapy and borderline personality disorder. J Psychother Pract Res 4:237–246, 1995

Goldstein E: The influence of parental attitudes on psychiatric treatment outcome. Social Casework 60:350–359, 1979

Goldstein MJ, Rodnick EH, Evans JR, et al: Drug and family therapy in the aftercare of acute schizophrenics. Arch Gen Psychiatry 35:1169–1177, 1978

Greenberg L, Fine SB, Cohen C, et al: An interdisciplinary psychoeducation program for schizophrenic patients and their families in an acute care setting. Hosp Community Psychiatry 39:277–282, 1988

Greenley JR: Family symptom tolerances and rehospitalization experiences of psychiatric patients, in Research in Chronic Mental Health. Edited by Simmons R. Greenwich, CT, JAI Press, 1978, pp 357–386

Greenley JR: Family expectation, post-hospital adjustment and the societal reaction perspective on mental illness. J Health Soc Behav 20:217–222, 1979

Greenman DA, Gunderson JG, Canning D: Parents' attitudes and patients' behavior; a prospective study. Am J Psychiatry 146:226–230, 1989

Group for the Advancement of Psychiatry: The Family, the Patient, and the Psychiatric Hospital: Toward a New Model. (GAP Report 24) New York, Brunner/Mazel, 1985

Grunebaum H, Friedman H: Letter. Hosp Community Psychiatry 4:20, 1989

Hatfield AB: Coping effectiveness in families of the mentally ill: an exploratory study. Journal of Psychiatric Treatment and Evaluation 3:11–19, 1981

Hibler M: The problem as seen by the patient's family. Hosp Community Psychiatry 29:32–33, 1978

Kahn EM, White EM: Adapting milieu approaches to acute inpatient care for schizophrenic patients. Hosp Community Psychiatry 40:609–614, 1989

Kanter J, Lin A: Facilitating a therapeutic milieu in the families of schizophrenia. Psychiatry 43:106–119, 1980

Miklowitz DJ, Goldstein JM, Neuchterlein KH, et al: Family of bipolar affective disorder. Arch Gen Psychiatry 45:225–231, 1988

Morris R: Integration of therapeutic and community services: cure plus care for the mentally disabled. International Journal of Mental Health 6:9–26, 1977/1978

Postrado L, Lehman AF: Quality of life and clinical predictors of rehospitalization of persons with severe mental illness. Psychiatr Serv 46:1161–1165, 1995

Schooler N, Keith SJ, Severe JB, et al: Relapse and rehospitalization during maintenance treatment of schizophrenia: the effects of dose reduction and family treatment. Arch Gen Psychiatry 54:453–463, 1997

Segal SP: Community care and deinstitutionalization. Social Work 37:521–527, 1979

Solomon P, Draine J: Adaptive coping among family members of persons with serious mental illness. Psychiatr Serv 46:1156–1160, 1995

Spencer JH, Glick ID, Haas GL: A randomized clinical trial of inpatient family intervention, III: overall effects at follow-up for the entire sample. Am J Psychiatry 145:1115–1121, 1988

Stein L: The effect of long-outcome studies on the therapy of schizophrenia critique. J Marital Fam Ther 15:133–138, 1989

Stewart R: Building an alliance between the families of patients and the hospital: model and process. National Association of Private Psychiatric Hospitals Journal 12:63–68, 1982

Terkelsen KG: No proof that families cause mental illness. FAMI Newsletter, March 1982

Vaughn CE, Leff JP: The influence of family and social factors in the course of psychiatric illness. Br J Psychiatry 129:125–137, 1976

Walling DP, Dott SG: Quality of life: a pilot study—comparison of crisis stabilization and hospitalization (abstract). Psychopharmacol Bull 30:725, 1994

Wynne L, McDaniel SH, Weber TT: Professional politics and the concepts of family therapy, family consultation and systems consultation. Fam Process 26:153–166, 1987

SECTION 7

Results of and Guidelines for Recommending Family Therapy

The question we are asked most frequently is, "What are the guidelines—i.e., indications and contraindications—for family therapy?" Now that we have discussed what family therapy is, how to do it, and with whom, we can discuss these issues. In Chapter 27 we describe our version of a decision tree for differential diagnosis and therapeutics. We describe when to do evaluation and the different therapies, including the choices of type, length, and modality. In Chapter 28 we examine complicated situations and guidelines for addressing them. These guidelines are modified by factors such as the family's ethnicity, gender issues involving both family and therapist, and the family's economic status (usually meaning the money and time the family can spend on treatment) (see also Chapters 17 and 18).

Finally, we present in Chapter 29 a summary of the results of family therapy outcome studies. These studies and accumulated clinical experience in the field provide the underpinnings for the family therapy guidelines.

Untitled, Francesco Alvardo-Juarez, 1981. Private collection; photograph courtesy of the artist.

CHAPTER 27

Indications for and the Sequence of Family Therapy Evaluation and Treatment

Objectives for the Reader

ℰ To learn decision-making processes in choosing family therapy

ℰ To be able to use the general indications, contraindications, and enabling factors in order to practice family therapy

Introduction

A recommendation for family therapy, and a particular form of family therapy, is the result of a sequence of clinical decisions. In this chapter we present a decision tree to guide the clinician's thinking. Decisions about the choice and timing of treatment are complex. Some well-controlled outcome studies have examined the effectiveness of family therapy for certain problems, but in many circumstances a number of approaches are available and clinicians must use their best judgment (see Pinsof and Wynne 1995).

Family therapy is strongly indicated in the following situations:

- Marital or family problems, discord, or disorders
- Schizophrenia

- Mood disorders
- Substance abuse (alcohol or drug abuse), to enhance treatment compliance and implement treatment (American Psychiatric Association 1995)
- Medical conditions (i.e., psychosocial difficulties arising in conjunction with physical illness)
- Medical or psychiatric illness in children

A variety of situations make choice of treatment more complex today than it used to be, including pressure from managed care for efficient and low-cost treatment, the lessened availability of hospitalization for other than very short-term crisis management, newly available medications, and the variety of new psychotherapeutic approaches.

Sequence of Evaluation and Treatment Planning

Evaluation and treatment planning involve four major steps or decisions:

1. Is a family evaluation indicated? If the family requests treatment, an evaluation is always indicated. If an individual requests treatment, a decision must be made as to whether family evaluation is necessary.
2. Based on the evaluation, is family treatment indicated? If so, should other forms of treatment also be given (e.g., individual psychotherapy, pharmacotherapy), and should they be concurrent or sequenced?
3. Presuming that family therapy is indicated, on the basis of evaluation and differential therapeutics (i.e., deciding on which treatment with which situation rather than giving the *same* treatment regardless of the situation), what shall be its duration and intensity?
4. What model of family intervention is indicated?

We examine each of these decisions in more depth in the sections that follow.

Step 1: Is Family Evaluation Indicated?

Family evaluation as described in Section 3 of this book is conducted to determine how the family functions, how the system influences and is influenced by the behavior and symptoms of its individual members, and whether family work is possible and appropriate.

Family evaluation is indicated in the following situations:

- When the family or couple request treatment or define the problem as a family issue
- When the problem obviously involves two or more people in the family (e.g., when child abuse, marital conflict, or severe parent-child conflict is present)
- When the presenting patient is a child or adolescent
- When the presenting problem is sexual difficulty or dissatisfaction
- When recent stress or disruption in the family is caused by family crisis or a milestone (e.g., when the couple are approaching the empty-nest stage of their relationship)

Some therapists believe that marital evaluation is indicated for all married patients seeking individual therapy, in that the patient may not accurately report psychiatric symptoms in the spouse or problematic marital interactions that are affecting the partners' lives or mental health. As long as the evaluation is conducted in a respectful manner as a search for information and family strength rather than pathology, most couples appreciate the chance to review issues. Other therapists believe that this is intrusive and counterproductive to the individual therapy process. In most cases we recommend the former position.

Whenever psychiatric hospitalization or acute treatment for emergencies is being considered, a family evaluation is usually indicated for one or more of the following reasons:

- For history gathering
- To clarify how the family interaction is influenced by and has influenced the course of illness
- To negotiate the treatment plan with the whole family (i.e., Is hospitalization necessary, or can the family manage with outpatient help? If hospitalization is necessary, what part will the family play?)

The following are less powerful but nonetheless common and important indications for family evaluation:

- When more than one family member is simultaneously in psychiatric treatment
- When improvement in the individual patient is correlated with symptom

formation in another family member or deterioration in their relationship

- When individual or group treatment has been tried and is failing or has failed and 1) the patient is much more involved with family problems, 2) the patient has difficulty dealing with family issues unless they are demonstrated directly in the room, 3) the transference to the therapist is too intense or actualized (i.e., the transference and countertransference becomes acted out, or played out, in the session and can be brought back to realistic proportions by including family members), or 4) family cooperation seems necessary to allow the individual to change

- When the therapist decides during the individual evaluation that, although the patient presents with symptoms that are not immediately related to family issues, the primary or secondary gain of the symptoms is an important expression of family systems pathology (e.g., a wife's agoraphobia worsens when her husband works overtime)

Family evaluation is contraindicated in the following situations:

- When any family member strongly prefers or insists on the privacy of an individual evaluation (e.g., because of a family secret)

- When it appears that the individuation of a family member would be compromised by family evaluation (e.g., the therapist might want to wait until time has passed before including the family of a young adult who has recently left home for the first time)

- When a childless marriage is breaking up with little or no desire for reconciliation

- When the presenting problem is clearly the result of repetitive intrapsychic conflicts that recur in many of the individual's relationships and seems more amenable to individual intervention

- When the patient won't trust a therapist who has also seen his or her family

- When extreme schizoid or paranoid pathology is present—unless hospitalization is indicated in the context of the patient being (still) involved and (usually) dependent on his or her family (in such a case we advise therapists to continue working on getting the family to come in, especially if the patient's condition worsens or the patient is decompensating)

Many treatment facilities are structured in such a way as to unwittingly preclude the serious consideration of conducting a family evaluation when a prospective patient seeks assistance. Although family clinics, by their name and reputation, attract those who see themselves as having family problems, most clinics are organized to deal with individuals (not family or marital units) who seek help. In such contexts, the secretaries, for example, ask on the first phone call for the name of the patient and a description of the individual's problems. They routinely give an appointment time to the individual, not the family. There may be no format for a family chart. Likewise, private practitioners often have reputations as being primarily marital and family therapists or individual therapists. If care is not given to the initial steps in the help-seeking sequence, the decision to complete a family evaluation can be made by accident rather than in a deliberate manner.

Step 2: Is Family Treatment Indicated?

The process of choosing a type of therapy is complex. Research is just beginning to develop guidelines for such decisions. The therapist most often must base his or her judgment on clinical intuition, general clinical opinion, and the wishes and judgments of the people involved.

Family Therapy Versus Individual Therapy

One of the most common questions for clinicians who are fluent in both therapies is the decision about type and timing of therapy. The basic theoretical premise of family therapy is that many problems are purely relational and that individual symptoms in one person can be viewed as interpersonal in terms of etiology or problem maintenance and that these symptoms can be changed by altering the system. The basic principle of individual therapy is that problems or symptoms develop because of the biochemistry or dynamics of the individual and that change occurs in the individual (either behaviorally or because of cognitive understanding of the problems) in the presence of an intense and exclusive relationship with the therapist. Table 27–1 summarizes the relative selection criteria for both types of therapy.

For many patients both forms of therapy may be useful or necessary. Self-knowledge does not always help the person understand the complex family system and how one's behavior affects and is affected by family members, and family therapy does not allow for intense exploration of psychodynamic issues. Individual therapy also does not allow the clinician to see how the problems of other family members may be affecting the system. Consider the following case example:

TABLE 27–1. Relative selection criteria for treatment format: family versus individual

	Family	Individual
Relative indications	Family problems are presented as such, without either spouse or any family member designated as the identified patient; symptoms are predominantly within the marital relationship.	The patient's symptoms or character is based on firmly structured intrapsychic conflict that causes repetitive life patterns more or less transcending the particulars of the current interpersonal situation (e.g., family, job relationships).
	Family presents with current structured difficulties in intrafamilial relationships with each person contributing collusively or openly to the reciprocal interaction problems.	The patient is an adolescent or young adult who is striving for autonomy.
	Family has fixed and severe deficits in perception and communication: (1) projective identification so that each member blames another for all problems; (2) family using paranoid or schizoid functioning (i.e., boundaries are vague and fluctuating, parts of self are projected readily onto other family members, trading of ego functions occurs); (3) a relentless fixity of distance is maintained by pseudo-mutual and pseudo-hostile mechanisms; (4) collective cognitive chaos and erratic distancing; (5) amorphous, vague, undirected forms of communication are pervasive.	Psychiatric problem is of such a private or embarrassing nature that it needs the privacy of individual treatment, at least for the beginning phase.
	Adolescent acting-out behavior (e.g., promiscuity, drug abuse, delinquency, perversion, vandalism, violent behavior).	

	Another form of treatment is stalemated or has failed (e.g., the patient has been unable to utilize intrapsychic mode of individual therapy or uses most of sessions to discuss family problems).	
	Improvement of one family member has led to symptoms or signs of deterioration in another.	
	Reduction of secondary gain in one or more family members is a major goal.	
	More than one person needs treatment, and resources are available for only one treatment.	
Enabling factors	Motivation is strongest to be seen as a couple or family, or an individual patient will accept no other format.	The patient is comfortable in dyadic situations and is able to handle the potential intimacy of the individual treatment setting.
	No family member has psychopathology of such proportions that family therapy would be prevented (e.g., extreme agitation, mania, paranoia, severe distrust, dangerous hostility, or acute schizophrenia).	Financial and temporal resources are available for individual treatment.
	Crucial members of a defined functional social system are available for family treatment.	
Relative contraindications	The presenting problem of the individual does not have a significant etiology in or effect on the family system.	The only issue of real importance is a family problem.
	Marital problems, if present, are chronic and ego-syntonic.	The patient regresses in individual therapy relationships.
	Family therapy is used to deny individual responsibility for major personality or character illness.	

(continued)

TABLE 27–1. Relative selection criteria for treatment format: family versus individual *(continued)*

	Family	Individual
Relative contraindications *(continued)*	Massive but minimally relevant or unworkable parental pathology is present that indicates symptomatic child or adolescent should be treated alone. Individuation of a family member requires that the member has his or her own and separate treatment. Family treatment has stalemated or failed and has resolved what crises it can, and one or more individual members require additional individual treatment. There is a need for another modality of treatment prior to family therapy (e.g., detoxification, medication, individual sessions to establish trust). Motivation exists to be seen alone (e.g., an adolescent states emphatically that he or she has personal problems for which he or she wants individual help).	

Mrs. A requested individual treatment for depression. On family evaluation the therapist learned that Mrs. A's husband had an untreated bipolar disorder (i.e., he had manic symptoms). Much of Mrs. A's depression resulted from Mr. A's behavior when he was in a manic or hypomanic state, and a key factor in treating Mrs. A's depression was treating Mr. A's symptoms and having him acknowledge the truth of his wife's concerns about him.

For many people, however, symptoms occur regardless of the different systems around them over time.

Because people tend to pick partners at similar stages of differentiation, it is not unusual for people with psychological difficulties to have spouses with similar or complementary but equally severe problems. In addition to evaluating the partner, the therapist must also address directly other problems such as the couple's problems and how they relate to symptoms such as depression or substance abuse. Children in such families often have genetically based similar illnesses (such as depression), or they experience symptoms as a result of dealing with parental problems. These illnesses and symptoms are often best treated with family therapy, but this does not rule out scheduling special meetings just for the children. For many people, both types of therapy are helpful, allowing for increased pleasure with the partner and providing a context for personal and private growth.

For more severely ill patients, family therapy may be one component of a comprehensive treatment plan that includes several other modalities such as medication, individual treatment, and family group treatment. The treatment of schizophrenia is a prominent example. Because schizophrenia in a family member produces long-term effects on the family, many therapists focus the therapeutic management of this disorder around the family as a unit. It is clear from two decades of research that although medication is essential in the treatment of such illnesses, it alone will not completely alter preexisting family relationships or ways of coping with stress.

The timing of therapy is another important consideration. If the identified patient is highly symptomatic and has a problem that is usually amenable to medications, it is often helpful to begin medication and family therapy first, in order to reduce the symptoms, educate the family, and eliminate family sources of stress.

In general, the therapist tries to deal with the most acute problems first. If possible in terms of timing and finances, individual and family therapy can be conducted at the same time. Some senior clinicians recommended that different therapists do the individual and family therapies; however, it is imperative that the therapists remain in contact to avoid splitting or conflicting treatment. Some therapists, including us on occasion, have treated both the family and an individual (or individuals) in the family. There are few controlled data to settle this question.

> Our guidelines depend more on the characteristics of the family and how the members function than on the particular diagnosis or problem area.

Managed Care

Depending on the type of program, there may be a strong bias toward one type of therapy over another. For example, on inpatient units, medication is preferred over psychotherapy (because it usually has a more rapid effect). In general, managed care companies have been encouraging more medication and less of any kind of exploratory therapy. When only a few sessions are possible, brief family therapy often can stabilize the system and support the development of other family resources most quickly. However, the therapist must put his or her own sense of the patient's and family's needs first over biases about treatment—especially when definitive data are lacking. Unfortunately, many patients do not become "cured" in 10 sessions, and our goal must be to prevent, as much as possible, undertreatment or a "revolving door" (i.e., frequent readmission of the patient).

Individual, Couples, or Sex Therapy for Sexual Problems

This distinction was more clear in the late 1980s, when sex therapy was focused primarily on a specific and highly detailed behavioral protocol. Sex therapy more recently has moved in the direction of further understanding of the physiological causes of sexual dysfunction on one the hand and the cognitive-behavioral issues involved on the other. In general, sexual problems do not disappear with couples therapy unless specific attention is paid to the nature and quality of the sexual problems. We provide a more complete discussion of treatment in Chapter 20, on sex and marital therapy (see also Table 27–2). It is most effective to deal with severe conflict in a couple before beginning to deal with sexual issues directly. Sex therapy includes education, a focus on the intimacy and power aspects of sex, and usually homework assignments that in some way deal with sexual anxiety and expansion of sexual options. Individual therapy is indicated if the problems are clearly related to the partner's history (e.g., sexual abuse, hatred of women) or if the problems have

TABLE 27–2.   Criteria for sex and marital therapy

Sex therapy	Marital therapy
The marital problem is clearly focused on sexual dysfunction.	Sexuality is not an issue, or it is one of many issues in marital dysfunction.
Enabling factors:	*Enabling factors:*
The couple are willing and able to carry out the sexual functioning tasks that the therapist would assign.	Anger and resistance are too intense to carry out extra-session tasks around sexual functioning.
The partners are strongly attached to each other; both partners are interested in reversing the sexual dysfunction.	The couple are not committed to each other; covert or overt behaviors are occurring to dissolve the marriage.

occurred in multiple relationships and are not amenable to being worked on in the couple. Individual therapy is the most inefficient way of dealing with most couples-centered sexual problems. It is also important to consider the possible role of organic problems in any dysfunction.

> It is most effective to deal with severe conflict in a couple before beginning to deal with sexual issues directly.

Family Crisis Therapy Versus Hospitalization

In many parts of the United States the financial resources to hospitalize a psychiatric patient for longer than 2 weeks have all but disappeared. In most settings, hospitalization is now only a setting for triage for people who are dangerous to self or others. Keeping a very ill patient at home requires considerable support and, when possible, a crisis team. As such, family crisis intervention in outpatient settings, such as emergency rooms or clinics, may still be a crucial intervention (see Chapter 26). Table 27–3 summarizes the criteria and enabling factors for family crisis therapy and hospitalization.

Step 3: What Shall Be the Duration and Intensity of Family Therapy?

To address this question, we have outlined criteria for family crisis intervention and for short- and long-term family therapy.

Family Crisis Therapy

Family crisis therapy is an intense (as often as daily) family intervention performed during a time of crisis and for a brief duration (usually less than 1 month) to help prevent the imminent disintegration of family relationships or decompensation of one or more family members and, it is hoped, to reestablish the family equilibrium at a level equal to, or higher than, before the crisis.

This modality is indicated when an immediate crisis in the family is causing severe and urgent family or individual symptoms or grief that could result in hospitalization or risk to life, limb, sanity, or the family's ability to continue as a unit. The crisis may be triggered by a stress that is

- Developmental—for example, birth of a child, departure of a child for college, marriage of a family member, responsibility of caring for extended family, aging and retirement, return of the wife to work, acting-out behavior on the part of a teenager
- Accidental—for example, injury, sickness, death, job loss
- Interpersonal—for example, an affair, a bitter argument

Brief Family Therapy

Brief family therapy can be any type of therapy that has a specific endpoint, usually in less than 10 sessions, or it can refer to a specific type of problem-oriented strategic therapy with a duration of 6–10 sessions. Most research investigations of family and marital therapy involve treatment that is short term. Gurman and Kniskern (1978) suggested that most of the positive results of open-ended therapy were achieved in less than 5 months. In general, brief family therapy is present focused, problem focused, and very directive.

Long-Term Family Therapy

Therapists vary in terms of whether they focus exclusively on the problem brought by the family or on a more general review of family functioning. For example, if a child is brought to treatment, should the therapy end when the couple are parenting more effectively, or should it press to address the couple's long-term issues and sexual dysfunction even though the child problem has been solved? Brief therapy in particular is problem focused rather than growth focused and when possible leaves the definition of the problem to the family. We believe that when time and families allow, it is best to offer the couple and family the possibility of working on whatever seems necessary.

TABLE 27–3.   Criteria for family crisis therapy and hospitalization

Family crisis therapy	Hospitalization
The risk of destructiveness to self or others is within assumable limits.	The patient is dangerous to self or others or is gravely disabled.
The level of family disruption is relatively low.	Presence of the psychotic patient has harmful effects on the family or society.
A need exists to preserve job and family relationships.	Thorough evaluation requires 24-hour observation and medical facilities.
	The patient gets worse when with the family.
Enabling factors: The family is intact, available, and motivated.	Enabling factors: The family is highly resistant, not available, or intact enough to carry on treatment and manage the patient.

For example, a couple may present with a complaint of the wife's depression. A family evaluation that includes the children may reveal that even though the couple did not complain about it, one of the children is also depressed or has attention-deficit/hyperactivity disorder (which sometimes produces a sense of ineffectiveness and depression in the parents). The therapist should feel free to shift the focus to allow for treatment of the child.

> **W**e believe that when time and families allow, it is best to offer the couple and family the possibility of working on whatever seems necessary.

Long-term family therapy is a treatment without time limit, when short-term intervention is inadequate or goals for the family are more ambitious. Indications for long-term family therapy may be classified as those arising directly from evaluation or as those arising through referral from brief or crisis therapy.

- Directly from evaluation:
  - When a family with multiple problems is inherently unstable and will require long-term external support and integration
  - When the family is highly motivated for treatment but problems are complex and not reducible to a manageable, short-term focus

- When the family is not highly motivated for treatment and will require an induction period to establish an adequate therapeutic alliance
- When problems are likely to be chronic and not amenable to brief intervention (e.g., intense marital difficulties with mutual projection, fusion, or long-standing disagreement)
- When short-term therapy was not sufficient in the past

- Through referral from brief or crisis therapy:

  - When brief therapy was not complete enough nor sufficiently successful; if the family is motivated to continue work, there is some hope for success
  - When the family is especially receptive and responsive to family work and has enough problems to warrant continued treatment and has sufficient resources

Long-term family therapy is contraindicated when it appears that extended therapy encourages the family to avoid focusing on problems or to delay therapeutic change, or when the cost-benefit ratio is too high.

Step 4: What Model of Family Intervention Is Indicated?

Recent research has demonstrated that no one school of therapy is definitively superior to another (Shadish et al. 1995). The trend in recent years has been toward a more integrative approach, drawing from a variety of models and allowing for a more fluid type of work (Lebow 1997; Pinsof 1995). Integrative models such as the one we present in this book are likely to combine some form of here-and-now work (i.e., cognitive or behavioral) with some type of historical understanding of the patterns that led to the current problem. Child-focused problems must include some structural work; most couples problems need some attention to family of origin; and most work with seriously psychiatrically ill patients requires some psychoeducation.

Summary

As we have emphasized, family therapy is usually prescribed as part of a multimodal package. We discuss the data for these indications in Chapter 29.

Suggested Readings

Few articles deal specifically with the issue of indications and contraindications, but interested readers may want to consult the practice guidelines for a variety of Axis I disorders, published by the American Psychiatric Association (available from American Psychiatric Press, 1400 K St, NW, Washington, DC 20005), or The Expert Consensus Guidelines Series, published in the *Journal of Clinical Psychiatry* between 1996 and 1997. These guidelines cover schizophrenia, bipolar disorder, and others that are added periodically.

Glick ID: Family therapies: efficacy, indications and treatment outcomes, in Psychotherapy Indications and Outcomes. Edited by Janowsky DF. Washington, DC, American Psychiatric Press, 1999, pp 303–321
This chapter offers an overview of data and indications for family therapy.

References

American Psychiatric Association: Practice guidelines for the treatment of patients with substance use disorders: alcohol, cocaine, opioids. Am J Psychiatr 152(suppl):11, 1995

Gurman AS, Kniskern DP: Contemporary marital therapies: a critique and comparative analysis of psychoanalytic, behavioral and systems therapy approaches, in Marriage and Marital Therapy. Edited by Paolino TJ, McCrady BS. New York, Brunner/Mazel, 1978, pp 445–566

Lebow J: The integrative revolution in couple and family therapy. Fam Process 36:1–19, 1997

Pinsof WM: Integrative Problem-Centered Therapy: A Synthesis of Biological, Individual, and Family Therapies. New York, Basic Books, 1995

Pinsof WM, Wynne LC: The efficacy of marital and family therapy: an empirical overview, conclusions and recommendations. J Marital Fam Ther 21:585–613, 1995

Shadish W, et al: The efficacy and effectiveness of marital and family therapy: a perspective from meta-analysis. J Marital Fam Ther 21:345–361, 1995

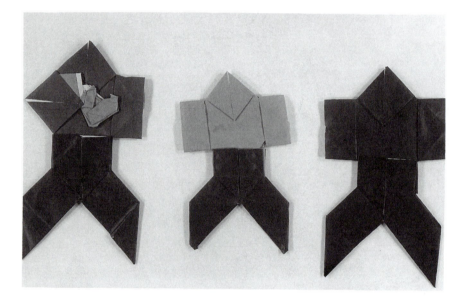

Family, Rachel Glick, 1979. Private collection.

CHAPTER 28

Controversies, Relative Contraindications, and the Use and Misuse of Marital and Family Therapy

Objectives for the Reader

☙ To be able to describe general situations in which there is disagreement in the field over the indications for marital and family therapy

☙ To recognize specific problems that make the choice of modality more complex

Introduction

Although we feel strongly that marital (or more broadly, couples) or family therapy is indicated for most marital or family problems, and that it should be included at some point in the treatment of many psychiatric conditions (including severe disorders), many questions remain unresolved in the field of family therapy. For persons with significant personal and family issues, what is the relationship among individual therapy, family therapy, group therapy, and medication? If other treatment modalities are indicated, how does the therapist decide whether to use them concurrently or consecutively? We discussed these issues in Chapter 15; here we discuss them in the context of indications and contraindications. In Chapter 27, we reviewed the situations in which family treatment is indicated; in this chapter we consider specific clinical dilemmas.

Marital Therapy

Marital Conflict and Dissatisfaction

A growing body of research has produced consistent results in the area of marital treatment. For many years it has been a prevalent clinical opinion that marital therapy is the treatment of choice for marital difficulties (e.g., Avallone et al. 1973; Greene et al. 1975). Hurvitz (1967) wrote of the dangers of doing individual therapy with only one spouse in such a situation. Gurman and Kniskern (1978a) reviewed research results that indicated conjoint marital therapy was superior to conjoint plus individual therapy, concurrent therapy, and individual therapy. We now know that another criterion for differential therapeutics is the comparative deterioration effects (i.e., worsening of symptoms or function or behavior, in contrast to lessening of positive effects over time or of not improving) of various modalities of treatment. This approaches the question of treatment choice from the negative side, that is, which treatment does the most harm? Gurman and Kniskern (1978b) found that the rate of deterioration for conjoint, group, and concurrent-collaborative marital therapies is half that of individual therapy of marital problems.

Although marital conflict and dissatisfaction seem to lend themselves especially well to conjoint marital treatment, such problems historically have been dealt with individually, especially when one partner requests individual therapy and the therapist is uncomfortable or unfamiliar with conjoint models. However, it is also true that one or both partners may have deep-seated issues more effectively worked on in private. Consider the following case example:

> Mr. and Mrs. A sought treatment because of a sense of distance and sadness in their relationship. History revealed that Mr. A had depression precipitated by his father's death 2 years earlier. Mr. A's relationship with his father had been poor and was unresolved at the time of the father's death. Possible treatment plans include the following:

- Couples work, including an in-depth discussion of both partners' early history and of Mr. A's grief and loss; medication might be included in this plan, if indicated

- Concurrent individual and couples work
- Individual work with Mr. A first, perhaps including medication, dealing with issues around his father, followed by couples therapy, if still indicated
- Family of origin therapy with Mr. A and his mother and his brother in order to do grief work and help resolve remaining family issues

Guidelines in this case include making the decision with the couple's participation and doing the most urgent thing first. Mr. and Mrs. A felt that unless the marriage was attended to, they were headed rapidly for divorce. The therapist chose to begin with couples therapy that focused on ways in which Mr. A could share his feelings with Mrs. A and; how he could be there for her despite his sadness; and on Mrs. A's grief and anger at having a depressed husband, given her own history of growing up with a depressed father. The couple then began to discuss both families of origin. Mrs. A, who knew Mr. A's family conflict well, was able to offer a number of suggestions about the origin of the problem and how grieving might begin. The therapist later saw Mr. A alone for several sessions and had two family of origin sessions with him, his mother, and his brother.

Had Mr. A presented as an individual patient requesting treatment for depression, he would in all probability have been seen individually with attention given to his depression and early life. This approach likely would not have addressed his issues with his wife, whom he was already ignoring because of his own pain. Lack of attention to couples issues in this case could have slowed Mr. A's recovery because Mrs. A's anger and withdrawal were contributing to his depression and would not have been dealt with. If the individual therapy moved slowly, and Mrs. A were not involved, she might well have reached the point of asking for a separation before too long. Even if Mr. A had presented for individual therapy, a couples evaluation was certainly indicated.

More complex situations occur when the couple is in serious conflict over goals. Such a situation is most difficult when one partner wants to preserve the marriage, and the other is very ambivalent but probably wants to divorce. In this case is it best to see the ambivalent person alone to sort out his or her feelings, or is it best to work on the marital relationship directly and deal with ambivalence within the couples work? No research is available to help the therapist sort out this kind of dilemma, and it is left to him or her to determine the best direction, on the basis of information at hand. Many therapists believe that dealing with the ambivalent partner alone supports the ambivalence and a tendency to move out of the marriage, so that a direct trial of couples therapy is often recommended, asking the ambivalent partner to behave as if the marriage is definitely going to continue so that the couple try as hard as possible to make it work. If the ambivalence seems to be part of a lifelong pattern of ambivalent behavior, if the ambivalent partner is in the midst of a midlife crisis, or if the ambivalent partner is having an affair that he or she will not give up, the indications for individual work become stronger.

Sexual Issues

Sexual issues are almost always dealt with conjointly if possible, and research suggests the therapy must be directed at both couples dynamics and the sexual symptoms (see Chapter 20). Therapy does not have to include sensate focus exercises unless indicated for specific problems. Again, however, some people need time alone to consider their previous sexual experiences, fantasies, and feelings.

Families in the Process of Divorce

Families in the process of divorce require a complicated mix of individual and family work. Although the grief work involved in a separation is best done alone, attention to the details of establishing child care, new routines, and a way to communicate requires joint work. In some middle-class families that have experienced years of conflict, the family members have acquired a sizable number of therapists by the time the divorce proceedings are impending—we have seen families involved with four or five therapists, one for each parent and one for each of the children. The goal is to reduce the number of therapists to a manageable level or at least to promote clear communication among all of them. All persons involved in the care of the children must have a chance to get together and plan so that they do not lose the sense of the entire family's needs and positions.

    In couples who are considering but are not yet at the point of divorce, the issue of couples versus individual therapy is complex. Individual therapy, which promotes personal growth in one partner without including or even informing the other, is more likely to lead to a split. Equally important, if individual therapy is indicated, the other partner (and the partner's therapist, if there is one), should be kept informed.

The Child as the Identified Patient

When the identified patient is a child, it has long been the practice of child guidance clinics to involve at least one of the parents (most often the mother), usually in collateral treatment in which both the patient and the parent are in individual treatment but with different therapists. This at least represents token recognition of the importance of the family in the problem and its resolution.

A more thorough approach seems indicated in these cases, however, with evaluation of the possible role of the child as the symptom bearer of more general family problems (e.g., unresolved marital issues). Usually the marital partners are seen as a couple for a major part of the treatment. The child may benefit from some individual attention addressed to his or her particular symptoms and psychosocial difficulties. A common sequence of events is for the entire family to start out in treatment together, and then for various individual dyads and triads to be separated out for special attention after an interval of time. Of these, the marital dyad is unquestionably the most important. Some family therapists suggest that whenever a symptomatic prepubescent child is involved, family treatment is indicated unless specific contraindications are present.

Since the early 1990s, there have been marked changes in the field of child psychiatry. Most institutions have shifted from an individual psychoanalytic focus to a family systems approach. An increasing number of childhood disorders are now being treated with family therapy. For example, school phobias are often treated with family therapy plus antidepressants.

The causes of child psychopathology are complex. Biological and genetic differences in temperament, intelligence, and ability (including attention-deficit/hyperactivity disorder and inherited tendencies to develop psychiatric disorder) interact with family dynamics and the child's cognitive and emotional development to produce child psychopathology. Controversies in this area persist as to the relative contribution of each factor in specific problems.

Within the area of parent-child interactions, conflict between child psychiatrists and family therapists has been over whether the child is best treated alone, using the relationship between therapist and child as the major change agent, or whether most attention should focus on supporting the family system to deal with the child better. In terms of family dynamics, there is also controversy over whether one must pay the most attention to the child's developmental task completion and the family's history, or whether direct attention to the here-and-now family patterns is the best focus.

The trend has been toward including the parents in treatment at some point. Part of the problem in the transition in model has been that many family therapists have not had enough training to identify psychopathology or developmental delay in children, and many child psychiatrists are not trained sufficiently in family dynamics to recognize problems and to produce change.

Another issue in choosing a treatment modality is whether the parents, even with therapy, can support the child emotionally or whether another adult is needed. In some situations, the parents are troubled enough, or their relationship conflicts are bitter enough, that family therapy cannot significantly alter the child's living situation, so that the child needs the outside support of caring adults. Although adult connections already established in the child's life (e.g., other family members, teachers) are always preferable, a troubled child may need the privacy and support offered by an individual therapist. Particularly as children get older they may need a place to consider their issues in private in addition to the public space of the family.

The therapist's recommendation should be based on an awareness that in some children psychiatric illness continues into adult life (Hechtman 1996). Many such patients remain at an impaired level of function (as in childhood), and some get worse as they age as adults. For others there is a marked discontinuity between child and adult psychopathology; that is, childhood illness does not go into adult life. With or without treatment many childhood psychiatric disorders are self-limiting. Children who are very impaired may show dramatic improvement as adults, and only 13% of children who were treated as children were rated more disturbed than controls in adult life (Cass and Thomas 1979; Vaillant 1980). Of course, the reverse is also true—many people who show normal development as children develop psychiatric illness in later life. Many patients remain ill or get worse as adults.

The Adolescent as the Identified Patient

When the identified patient is an adolescent, a focus on the family is still indicated, especially while the adolescent is living at home, before he or she has established psychosocial autonomy. A good deal of attention must often be focused on the marital partnership. The adolescent often benefits from individual attention and from the encouragement of peer-group relationships.

In treating a family that has an adolescent with an "authority problem," inclusion of the entire family group can dilute the adolescent's feelings about the therapist as an authority figure, making it easier for the therapist to make intervention(s). (We discuss these issues in different contexts in Chapters 24 and 30.)

With the family therapy field, a difference of opinion exists regarding the treatment of adolescents involved in symbiotic, mutually destructive parent-child relationships. Some therapists view this type of relationship as an indication for family treatment in order to facilitate the weaning of the teenager (Haley 1980). Other therapists believe it is difficult to promote further separation and individuation in family treatment, which brings all members together and may involve them even more in one another's lives. These latter therapists recommend that such adolescents receive individual or group treatment to demonstrate concretely their individuation and promote their growth outside the family, and that perhaps the parents be seen together to solidify their attachment to each other and their ability to tolerate the loss of their child. There seems to be some growing consensus that family therapy is most indicated when the symptomatic adolescent is exhibiting acting-out behavior. Some adolescents are seen in treatment who are not able to benefit from insight-oriented individual modes of treatment. A more focused, action-oriented family model is often more helpful.

Other Intimate Interpersonal Systems

Other systems that have been the focus of couples and family therapy include unmarried couples, and adult children and their parents.

Unmarried Couples

Unmarried couples presenting for therapy related to commitment and communication problems are treated as are any couples (see Chapter 19). More complex situations emerge when one member of the couple is still married to someone else, or when the relationship is extremely inappropriate or in its very early stages. Consider the following case example:

> A couple requested therapy after a dating relationship of 6 weeks. The young man of the couple had been in therapy for most of his life since early adolescence and used therapy in part to cope and in part as a solution for most life problems. The therapist stated that she felt a relationship of so short a duration should stand or fall on its own merits, and if the couple were still together in a few months and wanted help she would see them then. The couple broke up shortly afterward.

Family of Origin Issues

The idea of seeing adult children with their parents is little known outside the family therapy field. Adults are presumed to be able to report correctly about their childhood, and parents who have unfinished business with their children are expected to work on their own issues. Whatever the dynamics of childhood, the real relationship of adult children and their parents is very meaning-ful and is best worked on by the people involved. This is particularly true because the parent and the child may have changed greatly in the 20 or 30 years since the child grew up. This approach is in direct conflict with the psy-choanalytic model, which proposes that the agent of change is the transfer-ence relationship with the therapist and that little or no communication should be had with other family members. Years of clinical experience sug-gest strongly that family sessions, if respectful and supportive, can powerfully turn around many highly dysfunctional family dynamics and allow parents and children to make some kind of peace with one another. In addition, the process of learning about one's past from one's parents, and seeing them as the flawed but real people they are and were, rather than as the monsters of one's childhood, often speeds the process of one's own therapy.

Situations in Which Family Therapy Is Difficult and Perhaps Contraindicated

When Psychopathology in One Family Member Makes Family Therapy Ineffective

Dishonesty or manipulation of the therapy for secondary gain would consti-tute a serious handicap to effective treatment. For example, a partner might use therapy as a way to keep a spouse involved while continuing to have an af-fair and conceal it. Some persons, such as those with antisocial personality disorders, are good at convincing others of the honesty of their position while engaging in very destructive behavior (e.g., using the family's money to gam-ble, engaging in crime). Children who are lying or stealing are most likely re-sponding to family issues, which must be addressed in therapy.

If one family member is extremely paranoid, manic, or agitated, medica-tion might be initiated for behavior that is too disruptive to control, before family therapy begins. As we pointed out in Chapter 24, even quite psychotic people can be active members of the family and can profit from family work.

Controversy remains over the role of family therapy for individuals who are abusing substances (Stanton 1995). In some cases, particularly when the user is an adolescent or young adult who is not physically dependent on the drug, family therapy may be a primary treatment modality. For more deeply addicted people, family therapy must be part of a larger treatment plan in-cluding detoxification, group treatment, and specific alcohol and drug treat-ment. In doing family therapy with this population it is critical not to blame the drug use on other family members or to allow the user to blame them. For example, statements such as "I wouldn't drink if you didn't nag" are not acceptable explanations for drinking. Family therapy in which a family member is abusing substances must involve the goal of the family member stopping the substance abuse. It is ineffective to continue couples therapy with an actively alcoholic partner without dealing with the alcohol abuse and its destructive effects on the marriage. Many therapists originally believed that if they could improve communication, or the couple's sex life, the alcoholism would stop. Because the addicted person would usually prefer to keep the addiction, this model simply perpetuated the problem.

When the Family or Therapist Thinks the Risks of Therapy Outweigh the Advantages

Family members may be concerned that treatment will leave them in a worse state than when they began. This possibility should be explored at the outset, and therapy should be sensitive to this concern whenever possible.

This concern commonly arises when families apply to a child guidance clinic. Many children develop problems in relation to parental conflicts. For example, a child may develop a school phobia, may become abusive to other children, or may be encopretic whenever the parents have severe fights. The parents may want the child "fixed" but are determined not to address their conflicts because they are afraid that divorce will result. This is particularly true if the parents believe that one of them would become suicidal or psychotic if they admitted to their problems. In these cases the therapy should be addressed only to parenting issues, and couples issues should be tabled at least until the child is better. In most cases it is possible to find some way of uniting the parents around the child even when they are still in conflict. Consider the following case example:

> A 10-year-old girl whose problems included severe tantrums at home described her evenings. She would be doing her homework in the kitchen, and her parents would have screaming fights in the next room, threatening each other with divorce. Needless to say, she did not get much homework done. She would often try to stop the fights, and sometimes the parents would appeal to her to settle their arguments. The parents admitted they fought but downplayed the significance or level of verbal violence. The therapist framed the child as sensitive and told her to go to her room upstairs and close the door if her parents began to disagree. Her parents were asked to reward her when she did this, so that she would not feel she was deserting them. Because they wanted her to do her homework more than they wanted a referee, they complied. Although the

child's home life remained difficult, this approach removed her from the middle of things and allowed her some safe time, and she calmed down considerably. The parents' concerns could then be addressed, to the extent they were willing to do so. They chose to end therapy shortly thereafter.

A family that truly believes that therapy will result in divorce will not enter treatment. For couples and families in pain the real issue is how hard and when to push issues they are afraid to discuss. For example, encouraging a woman who has been subservient to stand up for herself may provoke serious reprisals from a husband who needs a very acquiescent wife. As we describe in Chapter 31, on ethics, this is both an ethical decision and a therapeutic one. It is best to discuss with the couple the pros and cons of relationship change. Often the couple will elect to stop therapy at the time and return to treatment later when the situation has deteriorated to the point that change is inevitable.

When the Family as a Whole Denies Having Family Problems

In some families, their whole way of life is oriented around denial of difficulties. Such families make therapy extremely problematic and may best be treated by brief therapy using systemic and strategic models that emphasize restraint of change and positive reframing of symptoms, what Karpel (1994, p. 181) calls defiance-based therapy.

When Cultural or Religious Prejudices Are Present

Unyielding, inflexible cultural or religious prejudices against any sort of outside intervention in the family system would make family therapy difficult. In these cases other alternatives can be offered, including working with a clergyperson, community worker, or educator, with the family therapist acting as consultant.

Skills and Attributes of the Therapist as They Affect Family Work

Many therapists are uncomfortable with family groups, or with particular types of families, and should not force themselves to treat them. Therapists must be aware of family issues and refer patients for family therapy when needed.

Mr. B, age 35 years, was in individual treatment for 6 years for his depression. His therapist believed he was passive and encouraged him to learn to speak up for what he wanted. Mr. B and his wife went to couples therapy with an unrelated therapist at the point at which his wife was ready to leave the marriage. Mrs. B said her husband had always been self-centered, but in the years since therapy started he had been impossibly critical and demanding. In the couples session, far from being passive, he was angry, condescending, and completely unempathic to his wife. The individual therapist's disinterest in Mr. B's wife's perception of the problem had led to an increasingly dysfunctional marriage and near divorce.

A decision to treat an individual should not mean ignoring couples issues. If a therapist has strong emotional ties to a family (e.g., a spouse's or friend's relative) or significant countertransference to a particular family, he or she should refer the family.

The age, sex, and race of the therapist can have significant effects on treatment, and these issues need to be considered. For example, a 50-year-old educated and status-conscious couple is not likely to respond to a 25-year-old therapist who has an M.S.W. rather than a Ph.D. Many families of color, having experienced serious oppression, are reluctant to allow a middle-class white therapist to treat them without a long period of trust building.

Conclusion

Family therapy is an approach and a world view in addition to being a specific technique. Research has defined situations in which family therapy is the treatment of choice (see Chapter 27). In other situations the therapist must use his or her clinical judgment to consider all aspects of the problems and make the best prescription he or she can.

References

Avallone S, Aron R, Starr P, et al: How therapists assign families to treatment modalities: the development of the treatment method choice set. Am J Orthopsychiatry 43:767–773, 1973

Cass LK, Thomas CB: Childhood Pathology and Later Adjustment: The Question of Prediction. New York, Wiley-Interscience, 1979

Greene BL, Lee RR, Lustig N: Treatment of marital disharmony where one spouse has a primary affective disorder (manic-depressive illness), I: general overview—100 couples. J Marriage Fam Couns 1:39–50, 1975

Gurman AS, Kniskern DP: Research on marital and family therapy, in Handbook of Psychotherapy and Behavior Change: An Empirical Analysis, 2nd Edition. Edited by Garfield SL, Bergin AE. New York, Wiley, 1978a, pp 817–901

Gurman AS, Kniskern DP: Deterioration in marital and family therapy: empirical, clinical and conceptual issues. Fam Process 17:3–20, 1978b

Haley J: Leaving Home: The Therapy of Disturbed Young People. New York, McGraw-Hill, 1980

Hechtman L (ed): Do They Grow Out of It? Long-Term Outcomes of Childhood Disorders. Washington, DC, American Psychiatric Press, 1996

Hurvitz N: Marital problems following psychotherapy with one spouse. J Consult Psychol 31:38–47, 1967

Karpel M: Evaluating Couples. New York, WW Norton, 1994

Stanton MD: Family therapy for drug abuse. Paper presented at the National Conference on Marital and Family Therapy Outcome and Process Research: State of the Science, Philadelphia, PA, 1995

Vaillant GE: Book review. Am J Psychiatry 137:387, 1980

The Storm, Inocencio Jimenez Chino, 1980. Private collection.

CHAPTER 29

Results: The Outcome of Family Therapy

Objectives for the Reader

- To become familiar with the scientific criteria for family psychotherapy research
- To be able to critically review modern studies on the outcomes of family therapy
- To be able to compare the outcomes of family therapy with other therapies and no-treatment conditions
- To be able to formulate clinical generalizations from both process and outcome family therapy data

Introduction

Does marital and family therapy work? In this chapter we provide an overview of the results of family therapy outcome studies. We also present several studies in some detail to give the reader a fuller sense of the designs, problems, and results found in family therapy research and of the criteria used to judge the quality of a research project. Finally, we draw clinical generalizations from this existing research database.

Overview of Psychotherapy Outcome Research

In 1996 the new director of the National Institute of Mental Health initiated his term by emphasizing the importance of scientifically substantiating psychiatric disorders:

> We must redouble our efforts to educate those who have not gotten the message that mental disorders are "medically valid" illnesses that affect the brain, and that the efficacy of research-based treatments for these disorders, including psychotherapies, compares favorably to the efficacy of treatments found in any other medical specialty (Hyman 1996).

The quality and quantity of research on psychotherapy, and marital and family therapy in particular, have developed dramatically since 1980. "By about 1980, a consensus of sorts was that psychotherapy, as a generic treatment process, was demonstrably more effective than no treatment" (VandenBos 1986). In general, no particular psychotherapeutic method was proved to be better than any other, and in certain Axis I disorders medication alone appeared to be better than psychotherapy in some treatment conditions. Studies have shown that family therapy is equal to or better than individual therapy over a wide variety of treatment areas. However, we are still in the early phases of understanding how families (distressed and nondistressed troubled) actually function and exactly how therapy works.

> **S**tudies have shown that family therapy is equal to or better than individual therapy over a wide variety of treatment areas.

In understanding family therapy research, and in thinking about what research can tell us and what it cannot, there are several helpful areas to consider:

1. *Specificity.* The concept that therapy works is a comforting one, but ultimately the therapist and the therapy consumer (i.e., the patient) need to know what kind of therapy works for what patient under what conditions. This area is difficult to research, and only now are outcome studies addressing it. This research is conducted primarily with between-group studies (e.g., a treatment group and a waiting-list group), but it is difficult

to do well, because it requires specificity in treatment with a homogeneous group of people. Although no specific school of therapy has proven more effective in general than others in reasonably large-scale testing, we know from clinical practice that some therapies, or therapists, work better with specific patients. Many patients have gone to multiple therapists before finding one with whom they clicked. It is not clear whether the finding of no differences between modalities is because nonspecific factors in therapy (e.g., personality match) are key, or because we have not been specific enough in matching type of problem with type of therapy. Because most therapies function at several different levels it may be that almost all therapies provide a new way of looking at the problem and a set of possible new solutions. We must also consider cost-effectiveness, that is, what is the briefest and least expensive way to get the same results? Cost-effectiveness will be a key issue in the future as cost containment efforts dominate practice.

2. *The difference between efficacy and effectiveness.* The classic distinction between efficacy and effectiveness in the public health literature is that "*efficacy* denotes the degree to which diagnostic and therapeutic procedures used in practice can be supported by scientific evidence of their usefulness under optimum conditions. Whether or not these procedures are applied adequately in practice, and whether they produce the intended results when so applied are matters of *effectiveness*" (Starfield 1995, p. 72).

This has been the ongoing struggle in trying to bring research into everyday clinical practice. In therapy done as part of a research project, subjects are recruited by the researcher and are most often homogeneous in their personal characteristics compared with the heterogeneous kinds of patients treated in clinic therapy. In clinical research, treatment is usually provided for one focal problem, and people who have multiple issues (e.g., marital conflict with coexisting medical illness or alcoholism) are screened out. Usually the therapist does one specific type of therapy, often from a manual that restricts the therapist's ability to mix methods. In the clinic or the private office, things are much messier. Patients or clients enter with multiple problems, widely differing in age and culture, and they are often less committed to the process. Treatment tends to be much more variable in length in general clinical practice. Clinicians vary greatly in their experience and are not supervised. They are specifically less likely to use behavioral marital therapy, the most studied marital and family therapy method.

Clinicians in practice often are frustrated by research findings, which seem less applicable to their specific day-to-day needs. They often use the methods with which they personally feel compatible (i.e., those they believe intuitively will work). Clinicians over time seem to become more eclectic as they struggle with complex and multilevel problems. Researchers often feel that clinicians are sloppy thinkers and uninterested in really finding out what works. It is likely that as outcome studies become more comprehensive and widely known, we will begin to see rapprochement.

3. *The difference between qualitative and quantitative, or exploratory and confirmatory, research.* *Qualitative research* is used to generate hypotheses—it is exploratory, open ended, and directed more at discovery than confirmation. It involves studying a few cases intensively with in-depth interviewing, audiotapes and videotapes, and observations of therapy through a one-way mirror. It emphasizes context, multiple perspectives, and client perspectives. The researcher is often a participant observer. This research is to designed to answer questions about the process of how therapy works. Because of its small sample size, this research cannot be considered confirmatory. *Quantitative research* is concerned with proving things—which requires data collection and analysis, objectivity, large samples, controlled conditions, and statistical analysis. Quantitative research is the method most of us think of as research. Because conditions must be controlled, this approach differs from office-based clinical work.

Both types of research must be part of the therapeutic endeavor, and the reader of a particular research article must be clear on what each type of research can and cannot do. *Meta-analysis* is a special type of qualitative research in which the results of studies (usually with small numbers of patients) are pooled and then conclusions are drawn. Of course, the better the quality of each of the studies, the more confident one is of the conclusions drawn.

4. *The difference between process and outcome research.* *Process research* describes the interactions among individuals (i.e., the process), whereas *outcome research* describes the end result (i.e., the outcome) for the family system and the individuals in the system. In family therapy research, the issues are particularly complex because there are so many variables. We are trying to understand how an entire system changes and to describe that change in order to improve the efficacy of our treatments.

Part of the problem in outcome studies of family therapy is determining how one decides the criteria for a good outcome. For example, in some marital cases divorce is a good outcome, but few studies have considered that or even defined a good divorce. Another question is whether the outcome is determined only by changes in the presenting problem (which is usually labeled as an individual problem) or by changes in family interaction patterns. Also, if multiple changes are possible, and changes occur but not in the presenting problem, is that a good outcome? For example, if a couple come in because of marital strife, and after therapy they are still unhappy but their parenting skills have improved so that their children are doing better, how do you describe this? If we assume that we are using family therapy because the problem is in some way embedded in the family, then changes in the couple and family interaction are necessary for a good outcome.

5. *The difference between moderators and mediators of outcome.* Shadish et al. (1995) have provided a detailed analysis of these concepts:

Moderating variables (i.e., under what conditions do they work better or worse, e.g., age, gender, etc.) or *mediating variables* (i.e., through what mechanisms do they work, e.g., a direct effect on the patient or via an indirect effect on the family then interacting with medication). Regarding moderators, our finding again pointed to methodological problems in interpreting marital and family therapy (MFT) outcome research. For example, behavioral treatments done in university settings yielded very large effects, but otherwise both behavioral and nonbehavioral studies all yielded small to medium effects that were not different from each other no matter where they were done. Second, the outcomes of behavioral treatments tended to depend more heavily than nonbehavioral orientations on the reactivity, specificity, and manipulability of measurement. Those outcomes were quite high with reactive or specific measure (i.e., those tailored to the treatment), but quite low with nonreactive measures, general measures, or measures low on manipulability. Nonbehavioral treatments tended to yield medium effects no matter what kind of measures were used. Behavior therapies concentrate their resources on target behaviors to the detriment of other outcomes, but nonbehavioral therapies spread their limited resources more evenly over all kinds of outcomes. Finally, our exploration of moderators found that behavioral treatments in studies with few subjects tended to have very large effect sizes compared to those with many subjects or to nonbehavioral treatment of any sample size. Taken with the preceding two sets of moderator findings, all this points to a class of behavioral studies—university-based studies with reactive measures and few subjects—that yield unusually high effects compared even to behavioral studies without their characteristics. This highlights a point implicit in our previous discussion of artifacts: how a treatment is studied may be as important to determining the effect size as what the treatment is. We may need to equate the "hows" before we can compare the "whats."

Mediational models postulate mechanisms through which treatment effects are generated: the treatment affects the mediator, which in turn affects the outcome. Shadish and Sweeney (1991) explored the mediational processes that occurred between behavioral-nonbehavioral orientation and ultimate outcome using structural equation modeling. Of the three mediational paths we studied, only one was statistically significant—behavioral orientations were published more often, and publications show larger effects than unpublished work.

Overview of Family Therapy Outcome Research

The field of family therapy outcome research has grown enormously since the mid-1970s. In 1972 a reviewer found 14 studies of family therapy outcomes (Wells et al. 1972). A few years later, Gurman and Kniskern (1978) found 200 quantitative studies, although many were uncontrolled. Less than 20 years after that, Shadish et al. (1995) summarized many more, including 163 randomized studies, 62 marital and 101 family therapy. Pinsof and Wynne (1995) in a commentary have summarized the data (Table 29–1). These studies point to the following general conclusions:

1. Family treatment is more effective than no treatment. This conclusion is manifest in studies that contrast family and marital treatment to no-treatment control groups. Roughly 67% of marital cases and 70% of family cases improve. The outcome may be slightly better if the identified patient is a child or an adolescent than if he or she is an adult. These findings were statistically significant. No one therapy method was demonstrated clearly to be better than another.

2. The deterioration rate (i.e., the percentage of patients who become worse or experience negative effects of therapy) is estimated at about 10%—lower than for individual therapy (Table 29–2). Pinsof and Wynne (1995) believe the rate is lower than 5%–10% and describe family therapy as not harmful.

3. In several areas evidence indicates that family treatment is the preferred intervention strategy. In others areas family therapy and individual therapy were tied—often in situations in which the identified patient had a serious Axis 1 problem (Shadish et al. 1995). These treatments of choice are of great importance for practitioners and students:

   A. *Couple distress or problems.* The data since 1970 suggest that couples therapy is superior to individual therapy for marital conflict situations. The strongest effects are for increasing marital satisfaction and reducing con-

TABLE 29–1. Adult, adolescent, and childhood disorders and problems for which marital therapy (MT) and family therapy (FT) have significant effects[a]

Patient age	FT > no-treatment control subjects	FT > standard or individual treatment	MT > no-treatment control subjects	MT > standard or individual treatment
Adult	Schizophrenia[b] Alcoholism[b] Drug abuse Dementia Cardiovascular risk factors	Schizophrenia[b] Alcoholism[b] Drug abuse Dementia Cardiovascular risk factors	Depressed women in distressed marriages Marital distress or conflict Obesity Hypertension	Outpatient unipolar depressed women in distressed marriages Marital distress or conflict
Adolescent	Conduct disorders[b] Drug abuse[b] Obesity Younger adolescents with anorexia of more than 3 years	Conduct disorders[b] Drug abuse[b]		
Child	Conduct disorders[b] Aggression and noncompliance in ADHD Autism[b] Chronic physical illnesses Obesity	Autism[b] Aggression and noncompliance in ADHD		

Note. ADHD = attention-deficit/hyperactivity disorder.
[a]For each disorder and problem, there are at least two published controlled studies with significant results supporting the efficacy of marital and family therapy.
[b]Indicates multicomponent packages with at least one marital and family therapy component.
Source. Pinsof WM, Wynne LC: "The Efficacy of Marital and Family Therapy: An Empirical Overview, Conclusions and Recommendations." *Journal of Marital and Family Therapy* 21:585–613, 1995. Copyright 1995, American Association for Marriage and Family Therapy. Reprinted with permission.

TABLE 29–2. Summary of reported deterioration rates in studies of nonbehavioral marital and family therapy

Therapy type or setting	Number of studies reporting improvement rates	Number of studies with "worse" category	Number of studies reporting deterioration	Studies with "worse" category reporting deterioration	Deterioration rate across studies with "worse" category
Conjoint	8	3 (37%)	1	22%	2.7% (2/72)
Individual	7	5 (71%)	4	80%	11.6% (27/233)
Group	15	7 (47%)	4	57%	16.6% (17/102)
Concurrent/ collaborative	6	4 (67%)	1	25%	3.3% (11/332)
Total	36	19 (53%)	10	53%	7.7% (57/739)
Inpatient	10	2 (20%)	0	0%	0% (0/17)
Outpatient	26	13 (50%)	4	29%	2.1% (10/477)
Day hospital	3	2 (67%)	1	50%	7.3% (7/96)
Total	39	17 (44%)	5	29%	2.8% (17/580)
Grand total	75	36 (48%)	15	42%	5.4% (17/580)

Source. Gurman AS, Kniskern D: "Research on Marital and Family Therapy: Progress, Perspective and Prospect," in *Handbook of Psychotherapy and Behavior Change*, 2nd Edition. Edited by Garfield S, Bergin A. New York, Wiley, 1978, pp 817–901. Copyright 1986. Reprinted by permission of John Wiley & Sons, Inc.

flict. These are not synonymous—some couples who have high marital conflict still report high marital satisfaction, and some couples have low conflict because the marriages are dead. Unsurprisingly, couples who are less distressed show more improvement. Some of these effects wash out (i.e., are lost) over time, as is common in chronic conditions.

B. *Sexual difficulties.* Since the 1970s, experience with treating sexual difficulties with some combination of sex and couples therapy has shown it to be consistently superior to individual therapy in the treatment of sexual dysfunction. Although Masters and Johnson's (1970) original success rates have not been repeated in later studies, 60%–95% of sexual dysfunctions can be treated, depending on the type of dysfunction. Recent advances in sex therapy have seen a movement from mostly behavioral to more integrative treatment models, with more attention given to cognitive and systemic factors and an increasing focus on organic causes and medical treatment for male dysfunction, especially erectile dysfunction (Rosen and Leiblum 1995).

C. *Mood disorder in women who have couple or marital problems.* Prince and Jacobson's (1995) review suggests that medication plus marital therapy is better than individual therapy alone. Individual therapy does little to moderate the so-called toxic marital problems that increase depression. Drugs alone are also ineffective for these types of problem. Because most therapy for depression has been done with women, we have little information on therapy for depressed married men. Some men are deeply troubled by the experience of talking about problems and prefer to work on them in private, and many depressed men have wives who are very angry, which might increase their depression if discussed in therapy. Some evidence indicates that women with other Axis I conditions respond better than men to couples therapy.

D. *Out-of-control children and adolescents.* The problems and disorders in this rubric that have been studied most are general child and adolescent conduct disorders, child aggression, global family problems, and communication/problem solving. Structural family therapy, behavioral family therapy, and an ecological approach involving the larger family system (e.g., including counselors and teachers) seem to have the most promise (or at least the most favorable studies) for treating conduct disorders and other child problems.

E. *Schizophrenia.* A well-developed body of literature demonstrates that psychoeducational therapy for the family is an important adjunct to pharmacological and supportive individual therapy in the treatment of schizophrenia (Figure 29–1). Family therapy reduces the relapse rate to the same extent (50%) as antipsychotic medication. It is less clear how and in what ways more systemic family work contributes to positive outcome in schizophrenia (see also Chapter 24).

F. *Inducing difficult-to-engage patients and family units, such as substance abusers, schizophrenic patients, and delinquent adolescents, to enter therapy.* Family therapy serves as the vehicle to induce the patient and family into treatment.

G. *Physical health problems.* Although the effectiveness of family approaches has not been demonstrated across a wide range of physical illnesses, family interventions appear to be helpful in treating chronic childhood illnesses, such as asthma and diabetes, and in enhancing the family management of other chronic illness. The new field of family systems medicine should greatly enhance the available research over the next few years (McDaniel et al. 1992; see also Chapter 30).

H. *Substance abuse.* Several different types of family intervention can engage and retain drug users and their families in treatment, may help to reduce drug use, and can improve social functioning. Most of the relevant research has concerned family interventions in adolescent, rather than adult, drug use. Broadly similar conclusions apply to alcoholism. Family therapy is often effective in motivating drinkers to enter treatment and then appears to be at least as effective as individual-based therapy in dealing with the alcohol problem (the perceived spousal support for abstinence is identified as an important variable). Recent developments in this field include the advance of family-based relapse prevention strategies.

Most researchers have agreed that for the Axis I disorders, the duration of the treatment effect dissipates rapidly after the family therapy is terminated. This should be no surprise to anyone who treats chronic medical illness. Like hypertension, diabetes, and so on, these illnesses need follow-up treatment to maintain the progress resulting from the effective intervention in the acute phase. Combining or integrating family therapy with drug therapy for most Axis I disorders seems to be an effective strategy.

Combining or integrating family therapy with drug therapy for most Axis I disorders seems to be an effective strategy.

4. Although the various schools of family intervention often claim or imply superiority, controlled research on the strategies (while holding the format of treatment constant) does not support such a view. The field of psychotherapy relies increasingly on manualized therapies, with precise specification of techniques. When these therapies are applied, often in

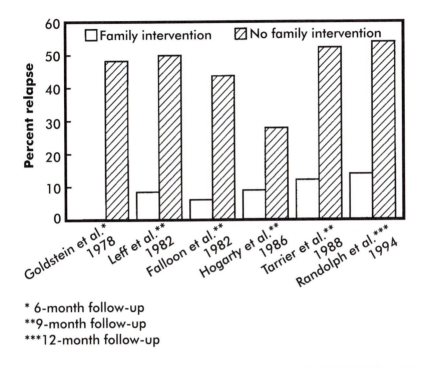

* 6-month follow-up
**9-month follow-up
***12-month follow-up

FIGURE 29–1.   Relapse rates from the six first-generation studies.
Source.   Goldstein MJ, Miklowitz DJ: "The Effectiveness of Psychoeducational Family Therapy in the Treatment of Schizophrenic Disorders." *Journal of Marital and Family Therapy* 21:368, 1995. Copyright 1995, American Association for Marriage and Family Therapy. Reprinted with permission.

usefully eclectic mixtures, results are more encouraging. They all seem to work (except for what has been labeled as humanistic therapy). Because only one study has been published on psychodynamic family therapy, it was difficult to draw a conclusion about it (Shadish et al. 1995).

Role of the Therapist in Treatment Outcome

It is our belief that not only knowledge and special technical competence but also warmth and empathy on the part of the therapist will help the family members to stay in treatment. (This, of course, leaves unanswered the issue of treatment efficacy.)

There seems to be some clinical validity to the notion that the more experienced the therapist, the better the outcome, although there is little research evidence to back up this notion. It is difficult to explain this finding. Explanations have included the personality of the therapist outweighing his or her experience and the research not being fine-tuned enough.

Prediction of Process and Outcome

Although predictions of treatment process and outcome are still extremely difficult to make, this has not deterred some senior clinicians from making them. The normative responses of the family to conjoint family therapy have been described: "Most families who accept conjoint family therapy when it is offered, and even families who might be considered unsuitable for therapy for various reasons, will enter into and participate in treatment" (Rakoff et al. 1975, p. 1015). Most family members will not initiate a move to drop out of therapy. It is difficult to predict in advance which families will be easy to treat and which will be difficult and what resistance will occur during treatment. An experienced therapist has a good chance of anticipating the common resistance of individual family members that only others in the family have troubles. It was also found that "conjoint family therapy is rarely harmful to members of the treated family" (Rakoff et al. 1975, p. 1016).

Predictions of the effectiveness of family therapy that were made to the family were uniformly underestimated by the therapist. The same underestimation occurs in the field of medicine when the internist tells the family that he or she may be able to help the patient or only to a limited degree. This is called the black-crepe effect (black crepe is used in funerals so as not to raise the family's expectations impossibly high). It is best for the therapist not to exaggerate his or her ability to help. For example, he or she could say, "I think I can help to some extent"—it will soon be obvious to all members of the system (i.e., the family and the therapist) whether the family will change (Siegler 1975).

Limitations of Family Therapy

Not all problems are the result of defects in the family. In many families the overall family structure and function are relatively healthy; nevertheless, one member has a problem. Consider the following case example:

Mrs. A, age 46 years, came with her husband and four children seeking therapy. She said that her parents died in a plane crash when she was 1 year old. Throughout her life she was raised by a series of adoptive parents and relatives. Each time one of her adoptive parents left the family, for example, when an adoptive father was drafted into the army, she would become very depressed, tearful, and angry, blaming other family members for their various deficiencies.

Family therapy was sought at this time because the family was having trouble living with Mrs. A in her depressed state—a problem that had been present for 30 years. The family therapist's task was to see what could be changed. It turned out that the precipitant was the oldest daughter going away to college. The family therapist helped the mother and the rest of the family cope with the derivatives of the mother's classical separation experience (i.e., loss of the parents at an early age as it now affected the family structure). The family therapist could not change the fact that the mother would have a strong and dysfunctional reaction to loss, but she could help the children understand it was not their fault and keep Mrs. A's husband from becoming angry and absent.

The family therapist commonly assumes that when a family comes for help with a specific problem, the cause is generally found in system problems of a more serious nature. It follows that the treatment strategy is to treat the system. The assumption is that treating the system will cause the symptom to change. Treating the system and even changing the system to function better does not necessarily mean that all symptoms in the family will improve. In practice some symptoms will be left untreated. The degree of improvement varies from family to family. Framo (1992) has written from long experience in the field:

Now that I have a more sober appreciation of clients' fears, of the complexities and difficulties involved, of the potential pitfalls, of the hard realities of intergenerational work—I have toned down my enthusiasm. For instance, I now caution that the sessions are not likely to change people's lives drastically, and I moderate some clients' unrealistic expectations about what the sessions can accomplish. For example, clients need to be prepared for not being able to fulfill fantasies of what they can get from parents or siblings.

What are the variables that limit change in families? To the extent that families or couples have not been able to cope with and master previous stages of development, they may have limitations in coping with a current phase. Other limiting factors include the degree of rigidity of chronic character traits; the couple's style (e.g., are they "screamers" or "compromisers"); and biological, physical, and social variables.

Negative Effects of Family Therapy

Any treatment that induces beneficial results must also be capable of producing harmful effects (Hadley and Strupp 1976). Although not a great deal has been written about this subject in family therapy literature, most experienced clinicians would agree that family therapy can sometimes induce negative effects. Table 29–3 expands on the following five categories of negative effects:

1. *Exacerbation of presenting symptoms during or after treatment.* In most cases there is a phase of family therapy in which problems may worsen.
2. *Appearance of new symptoms in another family member.* All members do not benefit equally. For example, if the mother challenges the father, he may become depressed. New symptoms may occur in a family member other than the identified patient.
3. *Patient abuse or misuse of therapy.* Most commonly one family member tries to use the family therapy for one-upmanship. For example, the father might say, "the doctor said that I seemed to have the best judgment in the family," and then proceed to blast his spouse and children.
4. *The family's overreaching itself.* Some therapists believe that anything is possible and encourage families to attempt tasks and try for goals that clearly are beyond their reach. Such attempts are destructive and should be avoided.
5. *Disillusionment with the therapy, the therapist, or both.* The family may try family therapy as a last resort. When the therapy does not produce beneficial change (at least in the family's terms), the family may be worse than at the start, because the members have lost their last hope.

As we mentioned earlier in this chapter, the precise incidence of negative effects resulting from family therapy is not known, but it probably occurs in 5%–10% of all cases (see Table 29–2).

What happens if the outcome of marital treatment is separation or divorce? One might automatically assume that such an outcome is deleterious and that marital and family therapy should be designed to hold the families together. On reflection, experience seems to indicate otherwise. Marital therapy allows the partners to examine whether it is to their advantage to stay together, and it gives them permission to separate if that is what they need to do.

Dr. and Mrs. B were in their 30s. He was a dentist, she was a housewife who had previously been a teacher. Mrs. B described her father as a philanderer, and

TABLE 29–3. What constitutes a negative effect?

Exacerbation of presenting symptoms	Appearance of new symptoms	Patient's abuse or misuse of therapy	Patient "overreaching" self	Disillusionment with therapy or therapist
1. "Worsening," increase in severity, pathology, etc.	1. *Generally* may be observed when (a) psychic disturbance is manifested in a less socially acceptable form than previously; (b) symptom substitution occurs when a symptom that had fulfilled an imperative need is blocked.	1. Substitution of intellectualized insights for other obsessional thoughts.	1. Two forms: (a) undertaking life tasks (marriage, graduate school, etc.) that require resources beyond those of patient; (b) undertaking life tasks prematurely.	May appear variously as (a) wasting of patient's resources (time, skill, money) that might have been better expended elsewhere; (b) hardening of attitudes toward other sources of help;
2. *Generally* may take form of or be accompanied by (a) exacerbation of suffering; (b) decompensation; (c) harsher superego or more rigid personality structure.	2. *Specific* examples: (a) erosion of solid interpersonal relationships; (b) decreased ability to experience pleasure; (c) severe or fatal psychosomatic reactions; (d) withdrawal;	2. Utilization of therapy to rationalize feelings of superiority or expressions of hostility toward other people.	2. May be related to (a) intense wishes to please therapist; (b) inculcation of unachievable middle-class "ideals;" (c) increased "irrational" ideas.	(c) loss of confidence in therapist, possibly extending to any human relationship; (d) general loss of hope, all the more severe for initial raising of hopes that may have occurred at onset of therapy.
3. *Specific* examples of symptom exacerbation: (a) depressive breakdown; (b) severe regression; (c) destructive acting-out; (d) increased anxiety; (e) increased hostility; (f) increased self-doubting; (g) increased behavioral shirking; (h) increased inhibition; (i) paranoia; (j) fixing of obsessional symptoms; (k) exaggeration of somatic difficulties; (l) extension of phobias;		3. Therapy becomes an end in itself; a substitute for action. 4. Fear of "intellectualization" prevents patients from examining their ethical and philosophical commitments. 5. Participation in more radical therapies encourages belief in irrational in order to avoid painful confrontation with realities of life. 6. Sustained dependency on therapy or therapist.	3. May result in any or all of the following: (a) excessive strain on patient's psychological resources; (b) failure at task; (c) guilt; (d) self-contempt.	

(continued)

TABLE 29–3. What constitutes a negative effect? *(continued)*

Exacerbation of presenting symptoms	Appearance of new symptoms	Patient's abuse or misuse of therapy	Patient "overreaching" self	Disillusionment with therapy or therapist
(m) increased guilt; (n) increased confusion; (o) lowered self-confidence; (p) lowered self-esteem; (q) diminished capacity for delay and impulse control.	(e) rage; (f) dissociation; (g) drug/alcohol abuse; (h) criminal behavior; (i) suicide; (j) psychotic breaks.			

Source. Hadley SW, Strupp HH: "Contemporary Views of Negative Effects in Psychotherapy." *Archives of General Psychiatry* 33:1291–1302, 1976. Copyright 1976, American Medical Association. Reprinted with permission.

she married her husband because he appeared to be reliable and stable. Dr. B described his mother as dull and masochistic, and he married his wife because she seemed exciting and interesting.

The couple came to therapy after 5 years of marriage, when Mrs. B discovered that Dr. B was having extramarital affairs. (He had left several notes from girlfriends lying around the house.) Exploration of the situation revealed that soon after marriage Mrs. B had become slowly and imperceptibly disillusioned with her husband when she found that he was very insecure about himself, was very unreliable, and characteristically lied and cheated. Dr. B perceived after a few years that his wife was not as exciting as he had thought and would not fulfill the role he had envisioned for her—that is, being enslaved to her professional husband.

The therapy allowed the couple to examine some of the original premises on which they had gotten together, and they found them faulty. The process of therapy, and not the therapist's values, gave them the necessary permission to separate.

Inability to Engage and Premature Termination of Family Therapy

The drop-out rate in the early phases of family therapy is relatively high. In one study about 30% of all the families referred for family therapy failed to appear for the first session (so-called defectors) and another 30% terminated in the first three sessions, leaving about 40% who continued (Shapiro and Budman 1973). The main reason families gave for termination was a lack of activity on the part of the therapist, whereas defectors in general had a change of heart and denied that a problem existed. The motivation of the husband appeared to play a crucial role—the more motivated he was, the more likely the family was to continue treatment (see Chapter 13).

The idea that a family that has dropped out of therapy is denying a problem may or may not be true. Because the process of entering therapy is frightening for many people and because the therapist must meet the needs of several people, it is not surprising that the process of engagement is rocky.

Patient and Family Satisfaction

There are major differences among identified patient satisfaction, family and significant other satisfaction, and outcome of treatment as judged by the therapist. Sometimes all three correlate; however, in many cases they do not. Often what the patient feels is an improvement is actually a regression by the family. Similarly, what the therapist considers an improvement is not considered so by some family members. The following case examine demonstrates these points:

> The C family, consisting of a mother, a father, and three children ranging in age from 15 to 25 years, had come for treatment after the death of one of the teenage siblings due to leukemia. Some of the problems included Mr. C's drinking and difficulties in communication between Mr. and Mrs. C and between Mr. C and the children. A long course of family therapy resulted in marked improvement in these areas. Mrs. C and the children considered it a very successful outcome. Mr. C consistently maintained that nothing had been accomplished: He could not remember changes made in the family as a result of the therapy and, therefore, felt that nothing had been done in therapy.

In this context, a survey by *Consumer Reports* (1995) found a high rate of satisfaction for patients who had been treated with psychotherapy. There was a somewhat lower satisfaction rate for marital and family therapy, most likely because it is more difficult to engage multiple family members and the therapy, by definition, demands behavioral change.

Clinical Implications of Data From Family Therapy Outcome Studies

In Chapters 27 and 28, we discuss indications for marital and family therapy. We return to that issue again by using the thoughtful (and widely cited) 1995 Pinsof and Wynne overview to provide another perspective *focused on the research data* for the family therapist. We present the following important implications for family therapists:

> The following conclusions are based on an overview of the field of MFT research primarily as presented in the articles in this Special Issue. These conclusions are provisional—the field of MFT research is not ready for definitive conclusions at this stage of its development. Even though a considerable body of empirical evidence has been accumulated, most of the findings have not been replicated systematically. Additionally, even though the field has made great progress, many methodological problems still plague the research and hinder the accumulation of a coherent and clear body of knowledge about the efficacy and effectiveness of MFT. A strong conclusion requires confirmation from at least two controlled studies. [Table 29–1] summarizes these conclusions.

1. MFT works. A clear and consistent body of evidence has been accumulated and reviewed that indicates that MFT (MT/FT) is significantly and clinically more efficacious than no psychotherapy for the following patients, disorders, and problems: adults schizophrenia (FT); outpatient depressed women in distressed marriages (MT); marital distress and conflict (MT): adult alcoholism and drug abuse (FT/MT); adult hypertension (MT); elderly dementia (FT); anorexia in young adolescent girls (FT); adolescent drug abuse (FT); child conduct disorders (FT); aggression and noncompliance in ADHD children (FT); childhood autism (FT); chronic physical illnesses in children (asthma, diabetes, etc.) (FT); child obesity (FT); and cardiovascular risk factors in children (FT).

2. MFT is not harmful. MFT does not appear to have negative or destructive effects. In all of the research reviewed, there has not been one replicated and controlled study in which patients and families receiving family or marital therapy had poorer outcomes than patients receiving no therapy.

3. MFT is more efficacious than standard and/or individual treatments for the following patients, disorders, and problems: adult schizophrenia; depressed outpatient women in distressed marriages; marital distress; adult alcoholism and drug abuse; adolescent conduct disorders; adolescent drug abuse; anorexia in young adolescent females; childhood autism; and various chronic physical illnesses in adults and children. Additionally, involving the family in engaging alcoholic adults in treatment is more efficacious than just working with the individual adults. Similarly, family involvement in aftercare for alcoholic adults is more efficacious than standard individual or group aftercare.

4. There are no scientific data at this time to support the superiority of any particular form of marital or family therapy over any other. The meta-analyses of MFT, when controlled from methodological confounds, failed to reveal any consistent effects of one type of MFT over another. Similarly, the specific reviews in this Special Issue did not reveal any consistent effects of one MFT approach over any other. The one trend and very preliminary hypothesis that emerged fairly consistently is that treatments that combined conventional family or marital therapy sessions with other interventions were more efficacious than standard family therapy approaches alone for severe disorders. It is premature to draw firm conclusions from this trend since it has not been formally tested in replicated controlled trials.

5. Data from a small number of studies indicate that MFT is more cost effective than standard inpatient and/or residential treatment/placement for schizophrenia and severe adolescent conduct disorders and delinquency. There are some preliminary data that suggest it is more cost effective than alternative treatments for adult alcoholism and adult and adolescent drug abuse. From the perspective of the health care providers and managed care, marital and family therapies may be more cost effective than individual

treatments in that more clients or patients are treated by a therapist in a single session. Additionally, the broader systemic focus of many marital and family therapies means that the therapist is focused not only on the mental and physical health of the individual client but also on the health of the other family members. This broader scope of concern theoretically expands the impact of MFT.

6. Marital and family therapy is not sufficient in itself to treat effectively a variety of severe disorders and problems. More than half of the treatments that have demonstrated efficacy involve components that go beyond the standard and conventional "family therapy session" format of MFT. All of the asterisked problems and disorders [[a]] and [b] in this volume] in [Table 29–1] involve treatments that do more than just family therapy. For instance, in addition to the family therapy component, psychoeducational therapies for schizophrenia involve medication and educational components. Similarly, the most effective treatments for childhood autism, severe adolescent conduct disorders, adult and adolescent drug abuse, and adult alcoholism involve additional treatment (group and/or individual and/or medication) and education components.

The research on these problems and treatments suggests that family involvement is a critical and necessary component in the treatment of these problems but is not sufficient in itself. An emerging hypothesis from these data is that multicomponent, integrative, and problem-focused treatments may be necessary to treat severe behavioral disorders effectively in adults, adolescents, and children. In fact, the more severe, pervasive, and disruptive the disorder, the greater the need to include multiple components in effective treatments.

Criteria for Scientific Investigation of Psychotherapies

It is useful here to consider the scientific criteria that are applied to any psychotherapy outcome study. The state of the art has certainly advanced since 1990, and the informed clinician should know how to judge journal reports of such investigations. Listed here are the criteria that would apply to any such investigation, whatever the format of treatment or the strategies and therapeutic interventions:

1. Study subjects are assigned to treatment conditions by random assignment or matching.
2. The status of the patient and family on foci of the intervention is measured before and after treatment.

3. Treatment and control groups are matched on major independent variables such as therapists' experience and competence level, enthusiasm and belief in the treatment they are administering, and equal amounts of time in therapy.
4. Patients are assessed not only at the end of treatment but also at follow-up period (e.g., 6 and/or 12 months) in order to assess the durability of the treatment effects.
5. The therapeutic techniques and strategies are described in sufficient detail (i.e., often in some form of treatment manual) in order to teach therapists the techniques, and ratings are done to see if the treatment as described is being delivered.
6. Assessment instruments are selected carefully in order to assess individual and family change; to assess those areas targeted by the two treatments as foci for change, as either mediating or final results; to judge change from the multiple perspectives of patient, family, therapist, and independent observer; and to assess positive and negative outcomes.
7. Statistical analysis is used that would assess group differences with mean scores, percentage of patients and families clinically improved in both groups, and so on.
8. Data are included on any other possible concurrent treatments.

As of this writing, the methodological issues that are important to the understanding of outcome research include *internal validity* (e.g., cases were randomly assigned, but the studies had high attrition); *statistical conclusion validity* (e.g., the studies had very low power); *construct validity* (e.g., there was very little exploration of the process of therapy—perhaps appropriate given the uncertainty about outcome); and *external validity* (e.g., the sample was mostly obtained from university settings—that is, experimenter solicited rather than using cases from clinical practice—with high exclusion rates, therefore limiting the generalizability) (Shadish et al. 1995).

Conclusion

Although outcome research still has not exactly elucidated indications and contraindications for family treatment, the clinician has a much better idea of when to do what now than he or she did in the past. A reason for continuing the push for treatment assessment is that the public is demanding proof of efficacy of all psychotherapies. Efficacy is being measured against treatments that have been shown to work, most prominently psychopharmacology. We believe the implication for the family therapist is that the day is approaching when third-party payers will attempt to reimburse for only those treatments demonstrating efficacy.

Suggested Readings

Pinsof W, Wynne L (eds): Special Issue: The effectiveness of marital and family therapy. J Marital Fam Ther 21:339–614, 1995
This edited volume contains a wealth of review articles that examine the state of the art in couples and family therapy outcome research. Specific disorders are covered in depth, and the summary pieces provide an excellent overview of each disorder. See especially the "Overview and Conclusions," pp 585–616.

Sprenkle D: Research Methods in Family Therapy. New York, Guilford, 1996
A long-time family researcher, Sprenkle has done a fine job of presenting and synthesizing the most current research methods in the field. This book is a must-read for any serious researcher or consumer of quantitative and qualitative research.

References

Consumer Reports: November 1995, p 734

Framo JL: Family of Origin Therapy: An Intergenerational Approach. New York, Brunner/Mazel, 1992, p 44

Gurman AS, Kniskern D: Research on marital and family therapy: progress, perspective and prospect, in Handbook of Psychotherapy and Behavior Change, 2nd Edition. Edited by Garfield S, Bergin A. New York, Wiley, 1978, pp 817–901

Hadley SW, Strupp HH: Contemporary views of negative effects in psychotherapy. Arch Gen Psychiatry 33:1291–1302, 1976

Hyman SE: Introduction from the new NIMH director, Psychotherapy and Rehabilitation Research Bulletin 5:1, 1996

Masters W, Johnson V: Human Sexual Inadequacy. Boston, MA, Little, Brown, 1970

McDaniel S, Kepworth J, Doherty W. Medical Family Therapy: A Biopsychosocial Approach to Families With Medical Problems. New York, Basic Books, 1992

Pinsof WM, Wynne LC: The efficacy of marital and family therapy: an empirical overview, conclusions and recommendations. J Marital Fam Ther 21:585–613, 1995

Prince SE, Jacobson NS: A review and evaluation of marital and family therapies for affective disorders. J Marital Fam Ther 21:377–402, 1995

Rakoff VM, Sigal JJ, Epstein NB: Predictions of therapeutic process and progress in conjoint family therapy. Arch Gen Psychiatry 32:1013–1017, 1975

Rosen R, Leiblum S: Treatment of sexual disorders in the 1990s: an integrated approach. J Consult Clin Psychol 63:877–890, 1995

Shadish WR, Sweeney R: Mediators and moderators in meta-analysis: there's a reason we don't let dodo birds tell us which psychotherapies should have prizes. J Consult Clin Psychol 59:883–893, 1991

Shadish WR, Ragsdale K, Glaser RR, et al: The efficacy and effectiveness of marital and family therapy: a perspective from meta-analysis. J Marital Fam Ther 21:345–360, 1995

Shapiro R, Budman S: Defection, termination and continuation in family and individual therapy. Fam Process 12:55–67, 1973

Siegler M: Pascal's wager and the hanging of the crepe. N Engl J Med 293:853–857, 1975

Starfield B: Efficacy and effectiveness of primary medical care for children, in Report of the Harvard Health Project Task Force: Children's Medical Care Needs and Treatment, Vol 2. Cambridge, MA, Ballinger, 1995, pp 71–76

Wells RA, Dilkes T, Trivelli N: The results of family therapy: a critical review of the literature. Fam Process 7:189–207, 1972

VandenBos GR: Psychotherapy research: a special issue. Am Psychol 41:111–112, 1986

Family Systems Medicine and Ethical, Professional, and Training Issues

Several important issues do not fit neatly into the previous sections of this book. The first is the expanding field of family systems medicine, which we discuss in Chapter 30, including how to diagnose and treat family problems in medical settings from the perspectives of both the family therapist and the family physician. In Chapter 31 we consider the ethical issues inherent in practicing family therapy, both within the therapist-patient relationship and outside with larger systems issues, including the managed care system. In that chapter we also discuss professional issues, that is, standards, boundaries, humanistic qualities needed, and the question of whose responsibility it is for change. We close Chapter 31 and the book, appropriately, with our thoughts about the training necessary for using the ideas and techniques we have presented throughout the book.

Death in the Sick Chamber, Edvard Munch, 1893. Courtesy of Nasjonalgalleriet, Oslo, Norway. Used with permission.

CHAPTER 30

Treating the Medically Ill Patient: A Family Systems Medicine Perspective

Objectives for the Reader

- To understand the importance of the family as a principal context of chronic illness
- To be able to define the dimensions of family systems functioning that are affected by chronic illness
- To understand a systemic approach to consultation and intervention with patients and families facing chronic illness
- For a professional in a related medical field: to be able to adapt the family model to the reader's particular needs
- For a family therapist: to understand the needs of professionals in medical fields and be able to work collaboratively with them in using the family model

Introduction

Family therapy's newest frontier is rethinking the family's place in the health care system. Family members have historically been central figures in the identification of dysfunction and illness, the delivery of health care, and the promotion of physical well-being. Since 1980, considerable research has explored the relationships between families and health, providing compelling evidence that family therapists have an important role to play in the management of physical health problems (Campbell and Patterson 1995; Rait and Lederberg 1989; see also Chapter 29). Studies examining family therapy, family psychoeducation, and family support for disorders including asthma, diabetes, pain, cancer, obesity, anorexia nervosa, cardiac problems, and Alzheimer's disease have found improvement in individual and family functioning after these interventions. Although managing acute and chronic conditions is an area ripe for family treatments, increased attention also is being paid to collaboration among patient, family, and health care providers in primary care settings.

It is well known that social support is associated with positive health outcomes, that the family is the primary source of many health beliefs and behaviors, and that treatment regimens are usually carried out and evaluated in the home by patients and family members (McDaniel et al. 1990). At the same time, studies have repeatedly established that medical illness can adversely affect both individual and family functioning (Leventhal et al. 1985). Within the field of family medicine, the family systems approach is viewed as an important extension of a broadly based biopsychosocial model (Engel 1980). Family-centered health care is also increasingly common in outpatient medical settings among both general and specialty populations (McDaniel et al. 1992). Even so, the role of the family as a primary locus for the management of physical illness has only recently begun to receive proper attention in psychiatric circles. Traditional approaches to consultation-liaison psychiatry (Hackett and Cassem 1987; Strain and Grossman 1975) have not sufficiently addressed the importance of the family, despite changing trends in health care that include briefer hospital stays, greater reliance on outpatient care, and the strengthening of community health care services. As psychiatric services continue to be integrated into primary care and hospital-based medical care delivery systems, a reexamination of the family context of both health and illness is critically important.

Premises for a Family Systems Approach

Because consultation-liaison psychiatry has concentrated primarily on the relationships among the patient, his or her illness, and its treatment, few guidelines are available for the physician contending with the patient in the family context. For example, Massie and Holland (1988) suggested that a patient's ability to manage the stresses associated with serious illness depends on the patient's prior level of emotional adjustment, his or her understanding of the illness, the threat posed to the patient's capacity to meet age-appropriate goals, the presence of social and emotional support, and variables determined by the disease. Although this standard consultation-liaison approach represents a correct starting point for a thorough assessment, it fails to account for the individual patient's interactive relationships with family members and other health care providers. In our view, a comprehensive assessment of the sick person must account for traditional features of psychiatric consultation-liaison assessment and expand them to include the broader relationships among the patient, family, and treatment setting.

One reason that clinical work based on family systems principles is still uncommon in medical settings is that the differences that distinguish this perspective have not been elaborated clearly. In order to connect the conceptual framework with practical recommendations about how health care professionals can approach the medically ill patient and his or her family, we first review four essential premises that a family systems perspective proposes:

1. The family systems perspective views medical illness as a problem that affects other family members. The family, in turn, dynamically influences the patient's experience of illness. The ensuing patterns of behavior among the patient, family, and treatment setting are interdependent.
2. The family of a medically ill patient is a family in transition. Over its course, the illness presents the family with challenges at every level of functioning, resulting in episodes of confusion and distress.
3. Families facing serious illness must strive to maintain stability and at the same time reorganize their habitual patterns of functioning. The family's solutions to the problems produced by illness can either promote the healthy adaptation of its members or encourage greater distress.
4. From a systems perspective, healthy functioning is defined in terms of both the adequacy with which essential family functions are met and the goodness of fit between patient, family, and medical setting. Effective coping includes a sense of action on the part of the individual, the family's ability to understand the illness and deny it at the same time so that the individual's needs can be met, and the family's ability to identify sources of support and use them. The fit between patient, family, and social context takes precedence over a more narrow definition of individual coping or adjustment.

In this way, the assessment of the individual's emotional resources, cognitive capacities, coping behaviors, developmental stage, illness and course, and treatment represent the fundamental building blocks for a broader, systemic formulation. The consultant must begin with a microscopic focus on the individual, his or her illness, and treatment and then add a wide-angle lens to better perceive the powerful social factors that influence and are affected by the patient's experience.

Dimensions of Family Adaptation

Each family should be approached as a unique cultural system influenced by the family's ethnicity, race, religion, social class, and immediate social context. To develop a clinically meaningful picture of a family's response to medical illness, the consultant should evaluate four additional dimensions of family systems functioning: 1) the family's developmental level, 2) the family's structure, 3) the family's system of beliefs, and 4) the family's relationship with the treatment setting. Difficulties in functioning emerge when problems in any of these interrelated domains keep the family from fulfilling the important task of attending to the sick person without impeding the growth of other family members. The goal of a family systems assessment is to account for the salience of these potential factors and generate a kinetic understanding of the patient in his or her social context. This assessment evolves through the generation of a series of systemic hypotheses or explanations and the systematic testing of each hypothesis with the family.

The Family's Developmental Level

Like the individual, the family is not static. It is evolving continually and follows its own life cycle trajectory that includes the early stage (e.g., marriage, birth of the first child, family with young children), the middle stage (e.g., entry of children into adolescence, launching children), and the family in later life (e.g., becoming grandparents, death and dying). At each stage, a realignment of relationships is required to support the entry, departure, and development of family members. The utility of this developmental framework is that it recommends specific hypotheses about the normal psychological issues facing the family at each stage (McGoldrick et al. 1993). In assessing the family of a medically ill patient, the consultant should assess two related developmental issues: the family's developmental stage and the synchrony of the illness with the family's developmental level.

Like any developmental approach, the family life cycle perspective proposes that specific developmental achievements are necessary for growth.

Each developmental stage highlights specific social and emotional tasks that must be negotiated before the family can proceed to the next stage. Stressors during any of these stages may interfere with the accomplishment of normal developmental tasks. In assessing the family's life cycle stage, the consultant can anticipate the tasks and challenges that family members of different generations normally face and can use this framework to evaluate the developmental effect of illness on the family's functioning. For example, with the diagnosis and treatment of serious illness in a family member (e.g., parent, sibling), parents may neglect a teenager's normal developmental needs for control and independence by expecting the adolescent to stay home on weekends to help out. Although these are reasonable expectations over the short run, this supportive arrangement may become dysfunctional when it begins to interfere with the adolescent's appropriate socialization. Similarly, when a grandparent becomes ill, the mother may naturally shift her energies to taking care of her ill parent. This shift reverberates through her family, as both adults and children must accommodate to support the mother's new caretaking responsibility. However, the mother's long-term avoidance of spousal or parental obligations may block normal developmental steps at home, thereby requiring an adjustment of roles and relationships.

The second developmental feature requiring attention is the extent to which the illness is synchronous with the life courses of the individual and the family. Researchers have observed that the more the illness is out of step with the family's life course, the greater the frustration, stress, and anger generated (Herz 1980; Leventhal et al. 1985). For example, life-threatening illness has a different effect and meaning in a 70-year-old grandfather than in a 40-year-old mother or her 15-year-old son. The grandfather's illness does not constitute an unexpected departure from the natural order of life, although it has a considerable effect on the family. During the grandfather's treatment, the mother might focus her energy toward her parents. In turn, her husband may be called on to manage the household. The teenagers in this family will also react to the changes, as they register the mother's grave concern and experience her as less available.

In a different scenario, if the mother were given the diagnosis of lupus, the ensuing changes might be even more dramatic. Afflicted in the prime of her life, the illness is far more unexpected. Because this woman is simultaneously a daughter to her own parents, a wife, and a mother, her condition threatens the routines of three generations. The reduction in her capabilities leaves the family with gaps that are difficult to fill without considerable flexibility. The husband may do double duty to manage the medical, economic, and practical affairs of everyday living; the children are expected to take on new jobs to help out; and even the grandmother may stay for awhile. The changes in family organization are substantial.

The limiting case of developmental asynchrony would be the diagnosis of cancer in the teenaged son in this family. As a disease mainly of older people, the diagnosis of a malignancy in a young person is a shattering event. The son's illness is out of sync with the expected order of life (Herz 1980). Caretaking routines that may have been discarded as the children reached adolescence must now be revived. Such demands might include one parent temporarily leaving a job or both parents negotiating more flexible schedules. The grandparents may also offer to help, bringing additional participants into what may have been a settled, balanced family. Finally, attention to the sick adolescent may leave the healthy children confused and neglected, or simply without a formal role to fill in this family crisis.

In each of these cases, the synchrony or asynchrony of the disease in the family's expected life course should be considered in calculating the amount of stress facing the family. The consultant must also evaluate to what extent the illness has interfered with conditions necessary for sustaining the family's normal developmental progress. Movements forward and backward, and pauses, in developmental progress should be anticipated and supported. When a family rigidly fails to resume its former course, and the developmental needs of family members are sacrificed, family intervention may be required through this transition.

Family Structure

Over the family's life course, characteristic patterns of behavior evolve between family members. A familiar example is when the mother reminds her children to take care of their chores, the children continue to show obvious irresponsibility, the father steps in and disciplines them forcefully, the mother allies with the children to protect them, and so on. An example more characteristic of troubled families involves the inability of parents to manage conflict without drawing in a third party (e.g., child, mother-in-law, physician, nurse) to deflect the tension. These habitual patterns reflect and are guided by the family's underlying structure (Minuchin 1974).

The structural approach to family functioning is concerned primarily with understanding health and pathology in the here-and-now reality of the family system. In healthy families, the basic roles and functions necessary for family adaptation are carried out successfully by its subsystems (e.g., marital, spousal, sibling). These subsystems are separated by boundaries and can be categorized according to the division of labor or psychosocial tasks within the family. For example, spouses generally offer each other social and emotional companionship and sexual intimacy, whereas parents provide nurturance, support, and guidance to their children. In the sibling subsystem, children learn to negotiate for scarce resources and develop social skills. The family's subsystems are arranged not only functionally but also hierarchically; parents typically occupy positions of authority in relation to their offspring.

In completing family tasks, ideal interactions among subsystems and their members are characterized by their range and flexibility. However, Minuchin and Minuchin (1987) observed that "when families are under stress and must explore a change in functioning, even viable families may move toward patterns that are not optimal, overshooting in the direction of their dominant style" (p. 11). According to Minuchin (1974), a pathological label should be reserved for families that, in the face of stress, "increase the rigidity of their transactional patterns and boundaries, and avoid or resist any exploration of alternatives" (p. 60). In their work with families of patients with anorexia nervosa, diabetes, or asthma, Minuchin et al. (1978) identified a common pattern of illness-maintaining features, including a lack of boundaries between family subsystems (i.e., enmeshment); overprotective parenting; the involvement of the patient in parental conflict; poor conflict-resolution skills; and rigid, repetitive family interactions.

With the diagnosis and treatment of serious illness, the family's structure is stressed, and problematic exchanges among family members can develop. The illness literally invades the family's patterns of behavior, some of which family members may be unwilling to relinquish, and compels family members to connect in new ways (Penn 1983). A common situation in the context of pediatric illnesses involves the organization of relationships formed between parents and their sick children. For example, the special bond between a mother and her fearful, anxious daughter who has leukemia can be adaptive and serve many positive psychosocial functions for the child. However, if the relationship then inhibits the child's own developmental progress and blocks the involvement of the father (or medical staff), this tie may contribute to problems in the family and treatment system (Walker 1983). In structural terms, what was formerly a healthy, protective arrangement becomes a dysfunctional coalition that may both violate the parental boundary and perpetuate overprotective behavior that may be preventing the child's behavioral symptoms from remitting.

The overall style of family involvement in relation to outsiders is also dictated by the permeability of family boundaries. A family with rigid boundaries may be isolated from social input, whereas a family with boundaries that are too diffuse may be unable to protect itself from external stresses. In general, families facing a serious threat tend to respond in directions that are habitual. For example, at the time of diagnosis, a wary family with rigid boundaries may need to relax its boundaries in order to allow the entry of medical staff. Conversely, the trusting family without clear boundaries may be vulnerable to being overwhelmed by friends, extended family, and staff. A divorced family with parents who are at odds can lose the ability to make decisions and thus overwhelm the medical staff.

In evaluating the family's structure, health care professionals must assess the family's capacity to flexibly meet the needs of its members and to accommodate to the treatment setting. The resulting formulation should include a description of the range of appropriate and varied family interactions, the adequacy of subsystem functioning, and the quality of boundaries within the family and between the family and outside. Serious illness can threaten the autonomy of family members, lead to overinvolved or distant relationships, and promote family rigidity. In contrast, the family's effective management of illness can also engender competence and well-being.

Family System of Beliefs

Although even the most minor illnesses have a limited effect on family functioning (e.g., when a sick child needs to stay home from school, changes in parental work routines are required), the changes in family structure that result from serious illness are more dramatic. For example, these changes can be maintained and even intensified by members' beliefs about and attributions regarding prior crisis, illness, and loss (Walker 1983). In entering the hospital, patients and their families bring with them lifetimes of experience that provide the blueprints for their present responses to illness (Reiss 1981). Past behavior can guide present appraisals and definitions of the stress, the means by which resources are called on and managed, and the extent to which success can be expected. Experiences with separation and loss, serious illness, and death deserve careful exploration because in times of emergency, these prototypes may serve as templates for family beliefs and behaviors.

Penn (1983) pointed out that family histories may provide important clues about the etiology of particular assumptions held by family members about illness and its prognosis. In addition, patterns around illness over several generations of a family may underscore particular values, expectations, myths, and meanings associated implicitly with illness and caretaking. Consider the following case example:

> Mr. A's despair about the possibility of a cure for his son's cardiac problem may be associated in part with his own recollection of his mother's sudden death

from a heart attack. Mrs. A's experience differs in part because she has trusted the reassurance from the physicians and has read about the advances in cardiac surgery for children. Given their different backgrounds with regard to heart problems, Mr. and Mrs. A have developed incompatible beliefs and coping styles regarding their child's illness. Although these complementary experiences could be viewed as a source of support if the couple could recognize and openly discuss their different experiences and reactions, the parents might also become more isolated from each other without explicit communication.

The family systems–oriented consultant can collect and organize historical data on the family by using a genogram, a three-generational family tree depicting the family's patterns regarding either specific problems or general family functioning (Feldstein and Rait 1992; see Chapter 7). The genogram technique lets history speak by suggesting possible connections between present family events and the experiences that family members have shared (e.g., regarding the management of serious illnesses, losses, and other critical transitions). Let us return to the A family case example:

> Further inquiry showed that in Mr. A's family, heart disease was common and that the children handled their parents' illness by fleeing from any active caretaking. The fundamental premises in his family were that the sick always die and that heart disease is incurable. Mrs. A's experience with heart disease in her family was quite different. Her own father had a bypass operation and had subsequently done well with the support of family and friends. The undisclosed premise in Mrs. A's family was that family members take care of the sick and succeed. In general, Mrs. A's family tended to be more optimistic and involved in managing medical crises.
>
> With this information providing the context for the here-and-now concerns of the A family, it is not difficult to hypothesize how the diagnosis of heart disease in Mr. and Mrs. A's child may have presented an opportunity for differences rather than support to emerge as the dominant family response. Both parents met the crisis with a history that predisposed them to react in a particular fashion that was at the same time maintained by the family's present structure. In other words, Mr. A's resignation may drive his wife into taking a more optimistic position than she would like. Alternatively, Mrs. A's positive attitude may only convince her husband that their son's inevitable death will be even more destructive if her approach is not tempered with a dose of reality. The ensuing, divided arrangement restricts each parent from experiencing a full range of reactions and ultimately may limit their opportunities to support each other as well as their child.

Although families hold beliefs about illness and crisis, their ideas about the potential effectiveness of treatment is frequently influenced by their own memory of experiences with professionals within the health care system. For example, the decision about what constitutes appropriate or humane treatment may be shaped by the dominant culture, the views of a particular ethnic group, or the family's own idiosyncratic notions that implicitly guide its attitudes (Harkaway and Madsen 1989). The consultant must evaluate the range of family members' experiences that might contribute to reflexive behaviors and invariant beliefs about illness and caretaking. If historically derived premises emerge as salient components of family maladaptation, interventions can gradually challenge these propositions and expand the range of beliefs and behaviors available to family members.

Family's Relationship With the Treatment Setting

Just as the family provides the immediate context for the patient, the treatment setting forms the immediate context for the family. The setting is composed of health care providers, extended family, and friends in the physical environment where health care is delivered. Goolishian et al. (1987) described the ensuing organization as a problem-defined system. In other words, were it not for the diagnosis of the patient's illness, this particular system would have little reason for being so constituted. The patient and family are therefore closely linked with many helpers who will influence their responses to treatment. Through their interactions with these helpers, family members indirectly affect the nature of the care offered to them. The achievement of a good fit between the patient, family, and treatment setting stands as a primary goal for the family systems consultant.

Imber-Black (1991) described how contemporary Western culture supports the entry of multiple caretakers by promoting specialization and the identification of a specific kind of helper for every aspect of a problem. For example, the patient in a modern medical center may be involved with a variety of medical specialists in addition to family, friends, and other providers of supportive care (e.g., dietitians, physical therapists, aides, nurses, fellows, consultants, attending physicians, clergy). Just as family members have particular ideas about illness and caretaking that grow out of their experience, these providers also have specific ideas about how to do their jobs, their capacity to help, and how they should be viewed. Families also differ in terms of how they interact with medical staff. Some families welcome outside helpers because they deflect attention from internal discord. Other families are suspicious of experts and block their efforts to reach the patient.

Relationships between families and multiple helpers can mirror the types of problems occurring within the family (Imber-Black 1991). With the family's introduction into the medical setting, treaters may be drawn into taking sides on issues that have been well established in the family. For example, a disagreement between adult children about a parent's treatment may expand to include disagreements between different staff members about the management of the case. The attending physician may support one child's optimistic attitude, whereas the nurses, realizing that the patient's prognosis is more guarded, may form a supportive alliance with another child. The evolution of competing coalitions that involve staff and family members can produce unwarranted stress for the patient and create obstacles to the provision of health care.

Like any social organization, the hospital can bring out the best in patients and their families. However, the technology that has emerged for patient care can also easily obscure and erode the strengths and resources of family members. With the sheer number of caretakers involved in a single case, the chances are great that contradictory advice and information will be communicated at some point during treatment. Such conflicts can functionally disable the patient and family by inducing confusion and helplessness. The relationships between patient, family, and staff are inevitable and important. Just as overly involved, intrusive parents may prompt a child to do little to care for himself or herself, overly controlling medical personnel can create an unmotivated patient or family. By the same token, patients can also elicit distressing behaviors on the part of staff members. Indeed, nagging patients can produce "deaf," unresponsive physicians.

The family systems perspective emphasizes the assessment of complementary, mutually influencing relationships at the levels of the patient, the family, patient-family interactions, and the larger treating system. The appearance of repetitive, ineffective staff-family or staff-patient interactions may signal the need for thorough assessment of the family–treatment setting interface. The consultant must seek to understand whether the treating system's exchanges with the patient and family result in dysfunction, adaptive coping, or ambiguous interactions that obscure the system's strengths and possibilities for health. As these interaction patterns are illuminated, accurate interventions can be devised to address the problems in the larger system.

Consultation and Intervention

Consultation based on family systems principles is a recent addition to modern medical settings (McDaniel et al. 1992; Minuchin and Minuchin 1987).

Common to these approaches is the assumption that problems represent a poor fit within the system formed by the patient, family, and treatment setting. Standard criteria for referrals include a family history of substance abuse, suicidal thinking or behavior, major psychopathology, or recent or difficult losses; severe reactive symptoms of anxiety, depression, phobias, nausea and vomiting, or refusal to eat; abrupt changes in behavior or mental status on the part of the patient or any family members; family reactions that include noncompliance with medical procedures, lack of support for the patient, and family conflict; and persistent staff-family, staff-patient, or internal staff discord. As in general clinical practice, medical family therapy interventions should always proceed from comprehensive evaluation and case.

Along with a recognition of the individual patient's assets, life issues, illness, and treatment, the consultant should clearly understand the stage of illness; the family's response; and the family's developmental level, structure, experiences with illness and caretaking, and relationship to the larger treatment setting. Wellisch and Cohen (1986) suggest three general goals implicit in a consultation request: 1) to solve the presenting problem, 2) to restore order, and 3) to facilitate family decision-making regarding treatment. Although anticipatory guidance and education may be sufficient for many families, some families exhibit dysfunction that requires more substantive intervention.

In many respects, the family systems approach begins with established principles of consultation-liaison psychiatry and broadens them to include the patient, family, and treatment setting. Rather than describing problems as residing in the patient (i.e., the consultation model) or the milieu (i.e., the liaison model) and intervening through individual treatments or education, the family systems consultant focuses on systemic transactions that maintain maladaptation. These connections, rarely recognized by the patient, can be elucidated thorough careful inquiry. This synthetic perspective provides a useful vantage point for conceptualizing the complex systems issues that can arise in medical settings and for generating ideas for the enhancement of patient care.

Consultation practice from a family systems perspective differs from standard psychiatric consultation-liaison in the careful attention paid to the presenting problem and the sick person in the context of a complex social system. In approaching a case, the consultant is guided by three steps: 1) assessing the nature of the referral; 2) assessing the problem in context; and 3) developing interventions that enhance the family's ability to meet the patient's needs, the staff's ability to meet the patient's and family's needs, and the patient's and family's ability to meet the staff's needs. We describe these generic points in the sections that follow.

Step 1: Assessing the Nature of the Referral

Family therapists are instructed to carefully evaluate the nature of the referral process, because the referral itself typically yields important data about the relationship between treaters and patient. For example, referrals are frequently made when constructive relationships between the patient and medical staff break down. To divert the stress already generated, a consultant may be summoned to absorb the tension on both sides. Right from the start, the consultant can begin to hypothesize about systemic patterns, as the presenting problem often condenses the difficulties of the physician and medical staff and of the patient and family. As Sargent (1985) has observed:

> The physician, who is involved in the dysfunction of the treatment system, may have resorted to blaming or cajoling the patient or family members; family and physician may be locked in a mutually antagonistic relationship where trust and collaboration are no longer possible. The family therapist should appreciate the physician's concern for the patient and be aware that referral for therapy usually occurs after genuine, and often extensive, efforts to make a treatment program effective have been made (p. 456).

Learning about the context of the referral represents the starting point for any further evaluation.

Step 2: Assessing the Problem in Context

In assessing the problem in context, the consultant must first understand the medical aspects of the case and appreciate the enormous practical and existential challenges that the family faces. We have already described important contextual dimensions of family systems assessment, consisting of its developmental stage, structure, history, and relationship to the treatment setting. These areas warrant careful evaluation, recognizing that families most in need of support will be those that exhibit the least flexible responses to their circumstances. Because the problem is generally stated in terms of a particular medical-psychiatric problem rather than problematic sequences of behavior within the family and treatment setting, the consultant must view the problem as it has been described while also mapping it onto the broader interpersonal context. The primary question to be answered is whether the family members cope in such a way that they are supporting the patient's health, meeting their own needs, and collaborating with medical personnel.

To be effective, the consultant must consider how to define his or her role in relation to the family system so that relevant information can be elicited and subsequent interventions delivered. In entering a case, the consultant should assume that the usual solutions have been attempted and have either been rejected or led to further mishap. The consultant must position himself or herself in a way that does not repeat previous failed efforts to solve the problem. Simply having an advanced degree will not enable the therapist to succeed with an approach that failed previously. Therefore, a history of the presenting problem should always include a description of prior recommendations and attempted solutions. Regard for strategic positioning offers the consultant protection from being painted with the same family brush as others who have failed.

Step 3: Developing Systemic Interventions

The central goal of the family systems consultant is to develop a system of support for the sick person and the family in the context of their specific setting (e.g., hospital, home, hospice). McDaniel et al. (1992) recommended that consultants facilitate collaboration among primary treaters, the patient, and the family. However, consultants working with the families of medically ill patients are frequently handicapped by two understandable yet limiting tendencies. First, they show a preference for offering only support, reasoning that families already so stressed should be spared the additional strain of therapeutic intervention. Second, consultants typically assume that once they have formulated the case, they personally must execute the intervention.

Family systems consultants can also support family members by motivating them to play a greater role in the ill family member's care. White and Epston (1988) have described an approach to chronic pain based on externalizing the problem and enlisting the family's talent and resourcefulness in fending off its grip over the family's experience. Because family members are often in the hospital and at home with the patient, interventions targeting changes in behavior patterns with the individuals most involved with the patient will likely produce the most immediate and lasting changes. In some cases an effective therapeutic system can be constructed only through a combination of support and challenge; however, as Minuchin and Minuchin (1987) pointed out, "the family is always healthier than the individual patient. It will always survive, and it will always respond to care and concern" (p. 15).

Family systems interventions can target interrupted developmental progress, problems in family structure, constraining belief systems or patterns of behavior, or escalating relationships with the treatment staff. As long as the family first feels ratified and supported by the consultant, standard techniques of family therapy can be used with considerable freedom, including building relationships, reframing, enactment and restructuring, coaching, systems consultation, and restraint-from-change strategies. When the capabilities and strengths in the sick person, the family, and the staff are highlighted, areas of competence that the illness obscured previously can emerge (McDaniel et al. 1992).

Minuchin and Minuchin (1987) insist that if therapy is indicated, it is generally advisable to frame the problem as a transitional issue related to the trauma of the illness. Having been destabilized, the family may be in an opportune position for exploration, mobilization, and transformation. Although an appreciation for only the tragic circumstances can engender despair and hopelessness on the part of the consultant, regard for the resiliency of those involved can stimulate the creation of imaginative and effective interventions implemented by family members, staff, or both in cooperation. The caring motivation of the family's response should be identified and preserved; the ineffective strategies that members construct to solve their difficulties may require more strenuous challenge.

Any intervention must account for the system as a whole, because the aim is to promote the adaptive functioning of the system and of its individual components. Family members and members of the medical staff typically appreciate participating in inventive treatment strategies that expand the system's flexible responses to the difficult challenges they encounter. Consider the following case example:

> Mrs. B ceaselessly tried and failed to cheer up her husband, a nervous, sad-looking man who has heart disease. Rather than reinforce the wife's devoted yet unsuccessful efforts, the consultant recommended that she listen but not respond to Mr. B's concerns for a set time period each day. This strategy connected the couple in a new way, with Mrs. B hearing Mr. B's worries but not trying to modify them. This new structure provided support for his anxiety and for her own. In turn, the couple was instructed to draw up a list of questions to be presented to the nurses at the end of the shift, thereby communicating their worries directly to the staff. The nurses would offer information and feedback to the distressed couple. Within a week, Mr. B was seen to be smiling, his wife was more relaxed, and the staff was no longer concerned about their adjustment.

Similar types of pragmatic interventions can be devised for younger patients. For example, the battling parents of an adolescent who has always been panicky about blood draws can be asked to agree on a supportive strategy before the needle is presented to the child. Staff can be enlisted to reinforce the parents' combined approach rather than offering competing advice that might induce a sense of incompetence in the couple. Rewards can be provided for the child's decreasing anxiety, and staff can emphasize the success achieved when the parents work together rather than against each other in this tense situation.

In summary, interventions that connect patient, family, and staff can effectively reduce problems through the mobilization of natural capabilities and the creation of new, facilitating patterns of interaction. Family systems interventions can also engender a more realistic view of the patient's limitations, directing the family and health care providers toward more adequate and supportive arrangements (McDaniel et al. 1992; Minuchin and Minuchin 1987). Finally, because of the episodic nature of chronic illnesses, consultants should leave open the door for patients and families to return in particularly stressful periods.

Consultation and Intervention: Summary

We have highlighted the importance of the family as a principal context of health, illness, and medical care. The medical patient's family is viewed as a family in transition because the diagnosis and treatment of disease can produce many changes that profoundly alter the lives of each family member. Families facing medical illness, especially serious illness, attempt to preserve stability while adapting to their profoundly changed circumstances. Most families can reorganize to meet the emotional and practical challenges imposed by the illness, but some families experience special difficulties in making the necessary transitions. These problems are viewed as rigidly maintained by the particular transactions occurring between the patient, family, and treatment setting.

The simultaneous consideration of patient, family, and treatment setting deserves wider application in primary care, acute care, and specialty settings, because patients and family members tend to report greater satisfaction when their biomedical and psychosocial needs are considered simultaneously (McDaniel et al. 1992). Consulting from a family systems approach is not without its difficulties, however. The conceptualization required for formulating a case at many different systemic levels—from biological to social—and devising efficient interventions initially requires reflection and flexibility, resources often in short supply in high-pressured medical settings.

The disciplined family systems consultant can extend the standard practice of consultation-liaison psychiatry in the areas of assessment and treatment. In evaluating any individual medical patient, regardless of age, diagnosis, and treatment regimen, the following dimensions warrant assessment: the family's developmental stage, the family's structure, the family's system of beliefs, and the family's relationship to the treatment setting. A systemic perspective does not limit the health care professional by limiting his or her focus. Instead, the clinician views a dynamic field that presents an endless number of assessment and entry points. He or she can evaluate the functioning of particular subsystems and then step back to see how troublesome patterns of behavior are maintained within the larger context. Although there is still much work to be done in refining the theory and practice of family systems consultation in medical settings, there is great value in developing a comprehensive, biopsychosocial viewpoint that not only enlarges the scope of assessment but also expands possibilities for patients with medical illness through systemic intervention.

The Family System and the Primary Care Physician

With Sanford R. Weimer, M.D., M.P.H.

In order to complete the picture of the system involving the patient, family, and family therapist, we must discuss the prospective roles of the primary care physician (see Table 30–1) and other specialists. Such physicians operate primarily using a medical systems model rather than a family systems model.

With the increasing predominance of the primary care physician as gatekeeper in the medical system, the primary care physician must be aware of the opportunities for medical cost offset and can benefit from maximum communication with the family systems–oriented consultant. At the same time, the family therapist must be conversant with these concepts and be able to articulate them for primary care physicians and utilization managers. Among the situations seen most commonly are the following:

- Every physician in practice will periodically meet patients and families that are chronically dysfunctional. Their lives are turbulent and unhappy, and taking care of them is problematic. In some of these families, the physiological issues are insignificant, the somatic complaints serving as a ticket of entry into the health care system (Wagner and Hendrich 1993). The system becomes the arena in which conflict and manipulation are played out. Increased use of sedative-hypnotics and tranquilizing medication often complicates the picture. The clinician's job is to recognize the

Table 30–1.   Levels of physician involvement with families

Level 1: minimal emphasis on family	Level 2: ongoing medical information and advice	Level 3: feelings and support	Level 4: systematic assessment and planned intervention	Level 5: family therapy
This baseline level of involvement consists of dealing with families only as necessary for practical and medical or legal reasons, but not viewing communicating with families as integral to the physician's role or as involving skills for the physician to develop. This level presumably characterizes most medical school training in which biomedical issues are the sole conscious focus of patient care.	Knowledge base: primarily medical, plus awareness of the triangular dimension of the physician-patient relationship. Personal development: openness to engaging patients and family in a collaborative way. Skills: 1. Regularly and clearly communicating medical findings and treatment options to family members.	Knowledge base: normal family development and reactions to stress. Personal development: awareness of one's own feelings in relationship to the patient and family. Skills: 1. Asking questions that elicit family members' expressions of concerns and feelings related to the patient's condition and its effect on the family.	Knowledge base: family systems. Personal development: awareness of one's own participation in systems, including the therapeutic triangle, the medical system, one's own family system, and larger community systems. Skills: 1. Engaging family members, including reluctant ones, in a planned family conference or a series of conferences.	Knowledge base: family systems and patterns whereby dysfunctional families interact with professionals and other health care systems. Personal development: ability to handle intense emotions in families and self and to maintain neutrality in the face of strong pressure from family members or other professionals. Skills: The following is not an exhaustive list of family therapy skills but rather a list of several key skills that distinguish Level 5 involvement from primary care involvement with families:

2. Asking family members questions that elicit relevant diagnostic and treatment information.	2. Empathically listening to family members' concerns and feelings, and normalizing them where appropriate	2. Structuring a conference with even a poorly communicating family in such a way that all members have a chance to express themselves.	1. Interviewing families or family members who are quite difficult to engage.
3. Attentively listening to family members' questions and concerns.	3. Forming a preliminary assessment of the family's level of functioning as it relates to the patient's problem.	3. Systematically assessing the family's level of functioning.	2. Efficiently generating and testing hypotheses about the family's difficulties and interaction patterns.
4. Advising families about how to handle the medical and rehabilitation needs of the patient.	4. Encouraging family members in their efforts to cope as a family with their situation.	4. Supporting individual members while avoiding coalitions.	3. Escalating conflict in the family in order to break a family impasse.
5. For large or demanding families, knowing how to channel communication through one or two key members.	5. Tailoring medical advice to the unique needs, concerns, and feelings of the family.	5. Reframing the family's definition of their problem in a way that makes problem solving more achievable.	4. Temporarily siding with one family member against another.
6. Identifying gross family dysfunction that interferes with medical treatment, and referring the family to a therapist.	6. Identifying family dysfunction and fitting a referral recommendation to the unique situation of the family.	6. Helping the family members view their difficulty as one that requires new forms of collaborative efforts.	5. Constructively dealing with a family's strong resistance to change.

(continued)

Table 30–1.   Levels of physician involvement with families *(continued)*

Level 1: minimal emphasis on family	Level 2: ongoing medical information and advice	Level 3: feelings and support	Level 4: systematic assessment and planned intervention	Level 5: family therapy
			7. Helping family members generate alternative, mutually acceptable ways to cope with their difficulty.	6. Negotiating collaborative relationships with other professionals and other systems who are working with the family, even when these groups are at odds with one another.
			8. Helping the family balance their coping efforts by calibrating their various roles in a way that allows support without sacrificing anyone's autonomy.	
			9. Identifying family dysfunction that lies beyond primary care treatment and orchestrating a referral by educating the family and the therapist about what to expect from one another.	

Source.   From Doherty WJ, Baird MA: *Family-Centered Medical Care: A Clinical Casebook.* New York, Guilford, 1987

origins of the complaint and intervene to improve family functioning, thereby reducing distress and reversing symptoms, perhaps even reducing the cost of the care (Berenbaum and James 1994).

- When a family member has an illness in which physiological disorders are prominent, the illness may be exacerbated in two important ways. In illnesses in which malfunctioning organ systems have rich autonomic innervation or sensitivity to the neuroendocrine system, family stress and conflict can aggravate the disease process, leading to increased morbidity and higher utilization of medical care (Grolnick 1972). Chronic illness frequently requires a strict adherence to doctor's orders, nutritional adjustments, and elimination of certain stresses. In a dysfunctional family, illness and the adaptations necessary to control it may become part of the family's psychosocial dysfunction, with consequent noncompliance, poor physiological control, and even outright sabotage. The outcomes may be disastrous (Frey 1984). The onset of somatic illness is correlated with life changes directly related to family functioning—for example, the death of a spouse, divorce or separation, a jail term, or even marriage itself (Holmes and Holmes 1970).

- Serious illness in a family member can evoke unexpected reactions in the patient and other family members. Cancer is an important example because of its powerful effect on families, putting all of the issues of chronic, relapsing illness in high relief. Other examples include stroke, heart disease, and metabolic diseases such as Huntington's disease . The patient, of course, has to deal with issues of disability, pain, disfigurement, sometimes stigma, and often death. An extensive review of family process and cancer (Northouse 1984) examined the associated issues and problems, from diagnosis, to adaptation, to dying and bereavement. Based on the literature and clinical experience, patients and families do better when caretakers are attuned to family issues and intervene when necessary.

- When serious chronic illness occurs in an already dysfunctional family, the consequences can be catastrophic to the identified patient's life. Several mechanisms occur commonly in dysfunctional families. The family system may reinforce the patient's ambivalence about following the medical regimen. This effect is often unseen until the other family members are brought into the interview. Consider the following case example:

Mr. C was a middle-aged epileptic patient who had a history of frequent breakthrough seizures with occasionally complicating injuries. During an interview in the neurology clinic, Mrs. C supported Mr. C's reluctance to accept his sick role and the need for regular anticonvulsants. Mrs. C used her husband's illness to foster an unrelenting depressive state and dependency in which she maintained control.

Primary care physicians must find a way to support family health and encourage medication compliance within their own time and skill constraints. As shown in Table 30–1, physicians may intervene in many ways.

Suggested Readings

McDaniel S, Campbell T, Seaburn D: Family Oriented Primary Care: A Manual for Medical Providers. New York, Springer-Verlag, 1990
This primer offers practical advice for primary care professionals interested in approaching their work from a family systems perspective. Each chapter is well organized and includes an outline of the main points. This book is a must for the practicing primary care physician, nurse, or mental health professional.

McDaniel S, Hepworth J, Doherty W: Medical Family Therapy: A Biopsychosocial Approach to Families With Medical Problems. New York, Basic Books, 1992
This book is the most thorough introduction available on medical family therapy. It provides a historical overview, a model for assessing and intervening with families, and chapters covering special topics. The authors have done a top-notch job of distilling the basic concepts and practices in this growing area of clinical work.

References

Berenbaum H, James T: Correlates and retrospectively reported antecedents of alexithymia. Psychosom Med 56:353–359, 1994

Campbell T, Patterson J: The effectiveness of family interventions in the treatment of physical illness. J Marital Fam Ther 21:545–584, 1995

Engel G: The clinical application of the biopsychosocial model. Am J Psychiatry 137:535–544, 1980

Feldstein M, Rait D: Family assessment in an oncology setting. Cancer Nursing 15:161–172, 1992

Frey J: A family systems approach to illness and maintaining behaviors in chronically ill adolescents. Fam Process 23:251–260, 1984

Goolishian H, Anderson H, Windermand H: Problem determined systems: towards transformation in family therapy. Journal of Strategic Systemic Therapies 5:1–13, 1987

Grolnick L: A family perspective of psychosomatic factors in illness: a review of the literature. Fam Process 11:457–486, 1972

Hackett T, Cassem N: Massachusetts General Hospital Handbook of General Hospital Psychiatry, 2nd Edition. Littleton, MA, PSG Publishing, 1987

Harkaway J, Madsen W: A systemic approach to medical noncompliance: the case of chronic obesity. Family Systems Medicine 7:42–65, 1989

Herz F: The impact of death and serious illness on the family life cycle, in The Family Life Cycle: A Framework for Family Therapy. Edited by Carter E, McGoldrick M. New York, Gardner, 1980, pp 223–241

Holmes TS, Holmes TH: Short-term intrusion into the life-style routine. J Psychosom Res 14:121–132, 1970

Imber-Black E: A family larger system perspective, in Handbook of Family Therapy, Vol 2. Edited by Gurman AS, Kniskern D. New York, Brunner/Mazel, 1991, pp 583–605

Leventhal H, Leventhal E, Van Nguyen T: Reactions of families to illness: theoretical models and perspectives, in Health, Illness and Families: A Life-Span Perspective. Edited by Turk D, Kerns T. New York, Wiley, 1985

Massie M, Holland J: Consultation and liaison issues in cancer care. Psychiatric Medicine 5:343–359, 1988

McDaniel S, Campbell T, Seaburn D: Family Oriented Primary Care: A Manual for Medical Providers. New York, Springer-Verlag, 1990

McDaniel S, Hepworth J, Doherty W: Medical Family Therapy: A Biopsychosocial Approach to Families With Medical Problems. New York, Basic Books, 1992

McGoldrick M, Heiman M, Carter B: The changing family life cycle: a perspective on normalcy, in Normal Family Processes. Edited by Walsh F. New York, Guilford, 1993, pp 405–449

Minuchin S: Families and Family Therapy. Cambridge, MA, Harvard University Press, 1974

Minuchin S, Minuchin P: Family as a context for patient care, in Primary Care in the Home Setting. Edited by Bernstein L, Grieco A, Dete M. New York, JB Lippincott, 1987, pp 83–94

Minuchin S, Rosman B, Baker L: Psychosomatic Families: Anorexia Nervosa in Context. Cambridge, MA, Harvard University Press, 1978

Northouse L: The impact of cancer on the family: An overview. Int J Psychiatr Med 14:215–242, 1984

Penn P: Coalitions and binding interactions in families with chronic illness. Family Systems Medicine 1:16–25, 1983

Rait D, Lederberg M: The family of the cancer patient, in Handbook of Psychooncology: Psychological Care of the Patient with Cancer. Edited by Holland J, Rowland J. New York, Oxford University Press, 1989, pp 585–597

Reiss D: The Family's Construction of Reality. Cambridge, MA, Harvard University Press, 1981

Sargent J: Physician-family therapist collaboration: children with medical problems. Family Systems Medicine 3:454–465, 1985

Strain J, Grossman S: Psychological Care of the Medically Ill: A Primer in Liaison Psychiatry. New York, Appleton-Century-Crofts, 1975

Wagner PH, Hendrich JE: Physician views on frequent medical use: patient beliefs and demographic and diagnostic correlates. J Fam Pract 36:417–422, 1993

Walker G: The pact: the caretaker-parent/ill-child coalition in families with chronic illness. Family Systems Medicine 1:6–29, 1983

Wellisch D, Cohen M: The family therapist as a systems consultant to medical oncology, in Systems Consultation: A New Perspective for Family Therapy. Edited by Wynne L, McDaniel S, Weber T. New York, Guilford, 1986

White M, Epston D: Literate Means to Therapeutic Ends. Dulwich, Australia, Dulwich Centre Press, 1988

Feeling Together, Toku Shinoda, 1980. Private collection.

CHAPTER 31

Ethical and Professional Issues in Family Therapy

Objectives for the Reader

- To be aware of ethical issues in practicing family therapy
- To be able to use informed consent procedures with a family
- To be aware of the family implications of financial issues
- To be aware of the professional issues inherent in family therapy practice
- To be able to specify family therapy training objectives and an optimal family therapy training program
- To be able to describe political and contextual issues in psychiatry residency training programs

Introduction

In this chapter, we pull together much of the preceding by applying the material to some of the issues that face family therapists in their practices at the turn of the century. They include ethical, financial, professional, and training issues. In this connection, of note, in 1997, the Association of Family Therapy in the United Kingdom did a survey of its members to determine what they (say they) are doing: they treat a broad range of issues and illnesses; they use relatively short-term therapy (five to eight sessions) regardless of whether families, couples, or individuals are involved; and they usually get supervision and/or consultation (Bor et al. 1998).

Ethical Issues Inherent in Family Therapy

The fundamental ethical dilemmas inherent in psychotherapy—confidentiality, limits of control, duty to warn/reporting of abuse, and therapist-patient boundaries—become more complex when the treatment involves more than one person. The family therapist has an ethical responsibility to everyone in the family. In some cases individual needs and family system needs may be in conflict. For example, a husband may wish to conceal a brief episode of unprotected sex with another woman, whereas his wife is better off, for health and psychological reasons, if she knows about it. A wife's wish to be divorced from a psychiatrically ill and demanding husband may conflict with his need for her care. Such clinical situations provide a set of ethical dilemmas for the therapist.

> The family therapist has an ethical responsibility to everyone in the family. In some cases individual needs and family system needs may be in conflict.

The therapist must be clear that his or her job in most cases (such as impending divorce) is to help the partners sort out their values, obligations, and options rather than to make a decision for them. In some cases (e.g., with the reporting of child abuse) the ethical decision must be the therapist's. Sometimes the therapist faces difficult gray areas that must be decided on a case-by-case basis. The therapist also has certain unalterable ethical obligations such as not engaging in dual relationships with patients (described later in this chapter) or not exploiting patients for his or her own benefit.

This section reviews common ethical dilemmas from the point of view of the family therapist. Although the operative concept is first do no harm, the questions of how one defines harm, and who will be harmed by a certain action, are complex and difficult to answer.

Conflicting Interests of Family Members

It is not unusual for the interests of each family member to conflict at some point. Boszormenyi-Nagy and Spark (1973) years ago emphasized the contractual obligations and accountability between persons in the multiple generations of a family. The family therapist in this view is uniquely attuned to the well-being of each family member (who will be affected by the treatment process) via their deep-rooted relatedness over time and through many generations. *Relational ethics* is concerned with the balance of equitable fairness between people. To gauge the balance of fairness in the here and now, and across time and generations, each family member must consider his or her own interests and the interests of each family member. The basic issue is one of equitability. That is, everyone is entitled to have his or her welfare and interests considered in a way that is fair to the related interests of other family members.

As we discussed earlier in this book, it may not always be clear who the patient is in family therapy. The symptomatic family member is often thought by the family to be the patient, but the family therapist may designate the whole family system as the patient or as involved persons in the treatment. The family therapist must be aware of the ethical issues implied in involving the family in the treatment process and in considering its contribution to the problem and the solution when it did not originally see itself as such or explicitly contract for treatment.

> The family therapist must be aware of the ethical issues implied in involving the family in the treatment process.

Because family therapy often involves meetings with all or most of the family members present, the family therapist may be in the position of asking nonsymptomatic individuals to attend sessions against their wishes. This may involve urging both resistant adults and minors to attend. This situation may become particularly troublesome if a previously nonsymptomatic individual comes to family therapy and becomes distressed.

There may be times when it is difficult to decide whether a therapeutic action or suggestion may be helpful for one individual but not helpful or even temporarily harmful to another individual. In their concern for the healthy functioning of the system as a whole, therapists may inadvertently ignore what is best for one individual. An ethical issue is how the decision is made. Should it be the therapist's concern alone, or should it be shared with the family? How much information should the family be given on the pros and cons of modalities? Our bias is to negotiate and give the family all the relevant information so that it can make the most informed decision possible [for review, see Hare-Mustin (1980) and Hare-Mustin et al. (1979)].

Secrets and Confidentiality

We discussed family secrets in Chapter 14. Let us now return to this issue in the context of ethical concerns.

Unless a therapist sees all members of a family together at all times, he or she will eventually face a situation in which family secrets are disclosed in individual sessions. Because secrets are a common source of family dysfunction, discovering and dealing with them is a frequent occurrence. As Imber-Black (1993, p.15) says, "secrets, decisions about secrecy and openness, and the management of information are woven into the fabric of our society. The paradoxes of what is to be kept secret and what is to be shared and with whom are all around us and are embedded in each encounter between family and therapist."

The family therapist needs to make a distinction between secrecy and privacy. *Privacy* is usually considered to mean information held by one person that he or she would prefer not to share but that does not directly affect his or her relationship with others. It usually implies a zone of comfort free from intrusion. *Secrecy* usually relates to feelings or information that would directly affect a relationship. Secrets are most often connected to fear, anxiety, and shame and are often shared—that is, some people in the system know them, whereas others do not. There is also a gray area in which different people have different ideas about whether the information is important. For example, is an affair that ended 10 years ago, that occurred during the marriage, private or secret?

Secrets define hierarchy and relationship, leaving the unaware mystified and out of alliance. Some secrets are helpful in that they promote differentiation and separation in less powerful members of a group. For example, a 6-year-old boy who says to his sister, "Don't tell mom we ate the cookies" is learning that parents can't read their minds and that they have some autonomy. However, some secrets are dangerous in that proper action will not be taken by the unaware. For example, the adolescent who says to his sister, "Don't tell mom we were drinking and driving without a license" leaves the parents unable to keep the children safe. Some secrets are about the past, such as an affair many years ago, and some are about the present, such as an ongoing affair or an impending bankruptcy. The majority of toxic secrets are in some way related to money, betrayal, or sex (e.g., abortions, illegitimate births).

In general, a secret should be disclosed if it seriously affects connections between people, if it poses a danger to a family member (e.g., sexual abuse), or if it shapes family coalitions and alliances. Keeping secrets is such a serious barrier that it is better to disclose them, even if painful; otherwise, the sense of mystification and isolation in the unaware is very strong. This seems to be true in many areas regarding children, such as adoption, out-of-wedlock birth, and artificial insemination, that were formerly kept secret. The issue of whether to tell depends strongly on the situation. For example, if adult children choose not to disclose their homosexuality to their parents, the matter should be considered private, because an adult's sexuality is considered his or her own decision. Even so, because such an issue maintains a large barrier between the child and his or her parents, the child should be encouraged to tell in most cases. In contrast, if a husband is bisexual or homosexual and does not tell his wife but engages in unprotected (or even protected) intercourse with men, the wife is in serious danger and needs to know. Because the husband's sexuality is definitely the wife's concern, not telling her this secret is a serious threat to the relationship.

> **A** secret should be disclosed if it seriously affects connections between people, poses a danger to a family member, or shapes family coalitions and alliances.

The therapist must carefully consider the timing and type of disclosure. Premature disclosure, before the therapist has an alliance with the family, can cause the family to leave therapy with no place to deal with potentially explosive topics. This is particularly true when the family has a history of violence or abuse. It is generally believed that if a family member refuses to disclose a secret so serious that therapy will be derailed, the therapist may terminate therapy but should not disclose the secret. In cases of potential violence to another, especially child abuse or threatened murder, the therapist is required to report the situation to the authorities and the potential victim, so that the secret will have to be disclosed. The confusion many therapists feel when faced with reporting and knowing that this may end their relationship with the family is difficult to manage; these cases must be discussed with a supervisor or mentor. Issues related to disclosure also arise when one partner has not disclosed his or her HIV-positive status to the other partner. The therapist is not legally obliged to do so; however, ethically it is extraordinarily hard not to. The patient should be urged strongly to disclose HIV status.

Therapists working with families that are involved with multiple caretaking systems (e.g., school, welfare, social services) are faced constantly with decisions about what to share with other caretakers and with the public record. Family members who have individual therapists may or may not want the family therapist to talk with the other therapists involved. It is strongly recommended that a connection be established between all therapists involved with a family to prevent splitting and mixed agendas from complicating treatment.

Confidentiality issues arise with family members outside the "family" as defined in the treatment group. For example, what information can be given a concerned grandmother about a child who might be abused? What is owed the noncustodial parent if the custodial parent and children have been the family of treatment? The therapist must help the family consider what is in its best interest. Interested parties are better brought into the therapy room as potential allies than ignored. However, the need to maintain boundaries between the nuclear family and other family members must also be considered carefully. In general, any disclosures should be discussed at length with the family.

Issues Involving Gender, Gender Roles, and Sexuality

Ethical issues connected with unequal treatment of men and women are an underexplored area in family therapy. The most critical areas involve the tendencies to blame mothers for their children's problems and to let fathers off the hook, both conceptually and in treatment strategies. Although paying more attention to the mother than the father is not unethical in the same way that is breaking therapeutic confidentiality or sleeping with a patient, it is important to consider the ethical implications of accepting traditional role assignments when they result in severely unequal treatment of men and women. For example, if a husband and wife have a relationship in which all decisions are made by the husband and the wife behaves in a completely submissive manner, to what extent does the therapist work toward a more egalitarian relationship? Similarly, if the wife is doing all of the child care and the father is doing none of it, how much should the therapist encourage the husband to take on half the child care as opposed to dealing only with the symptomatic child?

Treatment of a patient engaged in an affair involves the therapist's value system (e.g., Is it normal for a man to have a one-night stand, or is this a major therapy issue?). Ethical issues in sexuality revolve around areas in which the therapist may have very different values from the patient. Consider the following case example:

> A therapist was seeing Mr. and Mrs. A, who requested therapy for the husband's impotence. It developed that the couple were involved heavily in swapping partners and that the husband was potent with his wife but not with their joint sex partners. The therapist in this case refused to treat the problem, on the grounds that the husband's body was giving him a message he needed to listen to. The therapist made it clear that if the couple still wished therapy she would refer them to a therapist who was more comfortable with these types of relationships.

A therapist is not obligated to treat a couple whose values he or she disagrees with, whether this involves abortion, swinging, or any other issues, but the therapist is obligated to make his or her own value system clear to the couple rather than hiding it and trying to convince them they are wrong. Differences in values between therapist and patient are particularly common in family therapy because so many of the issues have to do with how one lives one's life rather than clear, diagnosable psychopathology.

Ethics in a Managed Care World

As this book goes to press, the practice of psychiatry is being changed dramatically by managed care policies that encourage brief treatment, discourage long-term psychotherapy, and make it difficult to hospitalize patients for anything other than brief stabilization. These changes have put enormous pressure on therapists to discharge patients early, to use medication as the primary form of treatment, and to treat only the presenting problem while ignoring other, perhaps equally vital, issues. They also put great pressure on families of the mentally ill, who are asked to deal with very ill family members. Confidentiality is difficult to keep when permission must be given by a managed care expert for increased sessions, hospitalization, and so on. Each therapist must consider his or her own willingness to accept the rules of a given managed care company and to fight for the patient's and family's right to adequate treatment.

Accordingly, we advise family therapists to take a proactive stance based on principles we elucidated earlier in this book. First, the therapist formulates a careful diagnosis of issues relevant to the patient and the family. Second, the therapist lays out a treatment plan based on models of intervention presented in this book. Third, the therapist presents the case to the new "member of the treatment team"—a managed care supervisor. Finally, the therapist fights for (i.e., advocates) the plan.

Informed Consent

Similar to other psychotherapy formats, family therapy does not require informed consent from the family before initiating treatment. Our bias is to inform the family of possible difficulties of treatment. If the therapist believes problems may occur, for example, in treating an Axis I disorder, it seems quite appropriate and even necessary for the therapist to clearly state and negotiate the treatment goals with the family so that the family can make an informed judgment about its desire to embark on the therapy. The negotiation should be done both at the outset and throughout the therapy.

If during the evaluation the therapist identifies family secrets to be central to the family problem, he or she may want to inform the family that those issues may need to be a focus. More important, we agree with Gutheil et al. (1984) that the sharing of uncertainty through the informed consent procedure can be a focal point in building a therapeutic alliance: "Increasingly, patients and families who experience tragic disappointment in their expectations . . . attempt to assuage their grief, helplessness, and despair by blaming . . . the physicians." This sharing can be done by understanding the family's wish for certainty and by empathizing with their unrealistic desires.

Financial Issues

Who pays the bill is relatively simple in individual treatment with adult patients, but in marital and family work the issue is more complicated. The ethical issues of who pays the bill become especially tense in marital treatment of spouses in conflict. For example, if both spouses have insurance coverage from their respective employers, whose insurance should be used? This issue becomes most delicate when the spouses have conflicting views of the matter for any number of reasons (e.g., "I don't want my secretary seeing the insurance forms" or "Using my insurance makes me the patient"). As with many concrete conflicts, the family therapist should approach the matter with a sense of fairness. The symbolic meanings of who pays should be explored thoroughly. When both partners have separate income and separate financial arrangements, they should each pay half the bill. Divorced couples may negotiate bitterly over who pays bills for family sessions. If a family session is held between adults and their parents, the question of who pays must be discussed with great care. Most often the person requesting the session pays for it.

Other financial questions involve sudden changes of fortune. For example, if a woman married to a well-to-do man divorces and her income drops severely and suddenly, is the therapist willing to continue treatment even if the husband refuses to pay? For many therapists and many clients, money is the most taboo subject, even more so than sex. It is the therapist's job to clarify his or her own understanding and feelings about money so that he or she can support discussions with patients.

Professional Issues

The Problem of Boundaries and Dual Relationships

The issue of boundaries and dual relationships is a critical one in all forms of psychotherapy. Because marital and family therapy involves more than one patient in the consulting room, there is less likelihood of inappropriate sexual contact between therapist and patient. However, there have been cases in which a therapist working with a couple began an affair with one of the spouses, either during couples therapy or after the couple separated. Therapists may also have other forms of dual relationships. For example, a therapist may agree to treat the child of a colleague. This makes a very confusing boundary for the child (e.g., the child may wonder what the therapist will tell his or her parent), and if family sessions are needed the therapist will have a very difficult time remaining neutral. Therapists who are treating students directly under them in training programs are also engaging in behavior considered to be unethical, because the patient is at a serious disadvantage as a student who must be graded or evaluated.

Other confusing issues may arise because the issues that families face are the same as the issues therapists face in their personal lives, making it very likely that countertransference issues may become ethical ones at some point. For example, it is extremely difficult for a therapist to treat a couple going through a separation at the same time that he or she is going through the early stages of divorce, and the likelihood of the therapist remaining neutral to both parties is not great. Although it is impossible for a therapist to stop treating patients while going through a divorce, he or she could certainly choose not to accept a new client whose situation is very similar to his or her own or who reminds the therapist of his or her departing spouse.

Issues of confidentiality and boundaries are mentioned in the American Association of Marital and Family Therapy Code of Ethics; we include the relevant sections in Table 31–1.

Competencies

In order to protect the public from untrained, incompetent, or unethical family therapists and family intervention, a clear delineation must exist in the competencies needed to do family therapy. In addition, ways of teaching and assessing the presence (or absence) of these competencies must be developed. Some of the qualities we think are important for the family therapist, and those required to do other therapies, include the following:

- Tolerance of family fighting
- Comfort with family secrets
- Ability to adapt to different technical models or mix different modalities together in a treatment package
- Interest in issues of gender, diversity, class, and culture
- Ability to be active and directive

We have a strong bias that in the training of family therapists, attention should be paid to the humanistic qualities of integrity, respect, and compassion for patients and their families. Our point is that attainment of these qualities is critical to the outcome of therapy. Therapists must come to realize that they are not omnipotent.

For successful long-term outcome, both the family and the therapist must play a part. For example, the therapist may recognize the family's need to be cared for, or the family's inability to make decisions, but it is not his or her responsibility to take over in these respects. Instead the therapist must help the family recognize its difficulties and start seeking solutions. Although therapists may decide to accept responsibility for providing a setting, establishing and maintaining a therapeutic alliance, and offering observations and suggestions, those therapists who take considerably greater responsibility for change are diluting what energy and motivation the family might have; these therapists are also likely candidates for burnout (Lask 1986). The everyday practice of family therapy is untidy and disorderly. At times therapists fail, make mistakes, and regret them (Spellman and Harper 1996).

TABLE 31–1.   Excerpt from AAMFT Code of Ethics

1. Responsibility to Clients: Marriage and family therapists advance the welfare of families and individuals. They respect the rights of those persons seeking their assistance, and make reasonable efforts to ensure that their services are used appropriately.

    1.1   Marriage and family therapists do not discriminate against or refuse professional service to anyone on the basis of race, gender, religion, national origin, or sexual orientation.

    1.2   Marriage and family therapists are aware of their influential position with respect to clients, and they avoid exploiting the trust and dependency of such persons. Therapists, therefore, make every effort to avoid dual relationships with clients that could impair professional judgment or increase the risk of exploitation. When a dual relationship cannot be avoided, therapists take appropriate professional precautions to ensure judgment is not impaired and no exploitation occurs. Examples of such dual relationships include, but are not limited to business or close personal relationships with clients. Sexual intimacy with clients is prohibited. Sexual intimacy with former clients for two years following the termination of therapy is prohibited

    1.3   Marriage and family therapists do not use their professional relationship with clients to further their own interests.

    1.4   Marriage and family therapists respect the right of clients to make decisions and help them to understand the consequences of these decisions. Therapists clearly advise a client that a decision on marital status is the responsibility of the client.

    1.5   Marriage and family therapists continue therapeutic relationship.

    1.6   Marriage and family therapists assist persons in obtaining other therapeutic services if the therapist is unable or unwilling, for appropriate reasons, to provide professional help.

    1.7   Marriage and family therapists do not abandon or neglect clients in treatment without making reasonable arrangements for the continuation of such treatment.

    1.8   Marriage and family therapists obtain written informed consent from clients before videotaping, audiorecording, or permitting third party observation.

(continued)

TABLE 31–1. Excerpt from AAMFT Code of Ethics *(continued)*

---

2. Confidentiality: Marriage and family therapists have unique confidentiality concerns because the client in a therapeutic relationship may be more than one person. Therapists respect and guard confidences of each individual client.

　2.1　Marriage and family therapists may not disclose client confidences except: (a) as mandated by law; (b) to prevent a clear and immediate danger to a person or persons; (c) where the therapist is a defendant in a civil, criminal, or disciplinary action arising from the therapy (in which case client confidences may be disclosed only in the course of that action); or (d) if there is a waiver previously obtained in writing, and then such information may be revealed only in accordance with the terms of the waiver. In circumstances where more than one person in a family receives therapy, each such family member who is legally competent to execute a waiver must agree to the waiver required by subparagraph (d). Without such a waiver from each family member legally competent to execute a waiver, a therapist cannot disclose information received from any family member.

　2.2　Marriage and family therapists use client and/or clinical materials in teaching, writing, and public presentations only if a written waiver has been obtained in accordance with Subprinciple 2.1(d), or when appropriate steps have been taken to protect client identity and confidentiality.

　2.3　Marriage and family therapists store or dispose of client records in ways that maintain confidentiality.

Source. Reprinted from the AAMFT Code of Ethics. Copyright 1998, American Association of Marital and Family Therapy. Reprinted with permission.

Training Issues

With Vernon Sharp, M.D.[†]

We would be remiss to conclude without discussing issues of training for both psychiatric residents and trainees in family therapy institutes. Although a tad parenthetical to the objectives of a textbook, we believe some key elements need to be mentioned in order for readers to master fully the theory and practice of family therapy described throughout the book.

As we discussed in earlier chapters, marriage and family therapy is effective across a broad range of psychopathology, including many of the severe

---

[†]Deceased.

Axis I disorders (see also Sprenkel and Bailey 1995). Family treatment is relatively brief compared to other forms of intervention and is more cost effective. These factors profoundly affect family therapy training in all of its forms. Although most psychiatry residents report a high rate of interest in the field, most programs offer inadequate quality of, or time for, such training. Wynne et al. (1988) pointed out that outside of the major academic centers, training for the most part grossly neglects work with families of persons with serious mental illness. This was still true a decade later.

The first issue is what level of mastery is desired. Some trainees desire to specialize in family therapy. Others need to know family therapy as one of multiple treatment interventions. For both kinds of trainee, the final product of the training is the demonstrated skill of the trainee in the art of family therapy. The process will be most successful, we believe, if it focuses constantly on the skills that the therapist in training needs and must gradually demonstrate.

Training in Psychiatric Residencies

For those in a psychiatric residency, we suggest (to training directors) the following series as optimal:

- In the summer, a crash course for postgraduate (PG) I's and PG II's: an introductory lecture describing the basics of the model, that is, how to evaluate couples and families and how to intervene and change the family system.
- In the PG II year: a basic course with a more detailed curriculum focusing on the basics of how to do family therapy. The clinical material comes from mostly inpatient sources. Evaluation and identification of problems is stressed (see Chapters 6–8).
- In the PG III year: a more advanced course focusing on the important schools and models and their techniques and strategies of therapy. Case material comes mostly from marital disorder couples in outpatient settings.
- In the PG IV year: family therapy electives and research opportunities may be offered for interested residents; a continuous case seminar is required in some programs.
- Supervisor seminars: all supervisors should participate in an ongoing seminar covering new work and case presentation in order to stay current.

All courses should be mandatory except for some of the PG IV offerings. In addition, all residents must carry through to completion one outpatient case, either marital or family, under supervision.

Of particular interest is that graduates of family treatment training programs were using family treatment theory and skills to a greater extent than they had anticipated during their training. But these skills were being used primarily to treat individual patients (Slovik et al. 1997). As Steinglass (1995) pointed out, there has been a remarkable paucity of articles on family treatment training in the journals. Fadden (1998) has provided a research update on psychoeducational family intervention and implications for training of family therapists.

Family Therapy Fellowships

For those trainees in fellowships (i.e., in the family therapy institutes), the emphasis is properly more focused on the family model. Goals include the following:

- Improving clinical skills in interviewing, assessing, and treating families, couples, and family networks
- Developing familiarity with current theory of family process and treatment
- Learning to provide consultation and liaison services to faculty, staff, professionals, and students from other disciplines and community agencies
- Gaining experience in teaching family concepts, and the application of family therapy, to medical students, other professionals, and community groups
- Affording opportunities for research in the general area of family therapy and family process
- Learning the linguistics of the specialty (i.e., learning in depth the basic philosophical constructs, language, and research in the field)

Intensive supervision is provided on an ongoing basis in assessment and therapy with families and couples and includes a weekly clinical caseload of 9–12 families, consultation and liaison services with other hospital and community programs, and development of videotapes for training.

Training and Licensure

Professional licensure has been a recent development in the field of marital and family therapy. The American Association of Marriage and Family Therapy has developed a consensus about a fundamental knowledge base. As a unique profession, the practice of marital and family therapy involves the application of psychotherapeutic and family system theories and techniques to the delivery of services to individuals, couples, and families in order to diagnose and treat a nervous and mental disorder. Based on this definition, a national examination in marital and family therapy now exists. This examination covers the following domains: 1) joining, assessment, and diagnosis; 2) designing treatment; 3) conducting the course of treatment; 4) establishing and maintaining appropriate networks; 5) assessing the outcome of treatment; and 6) maintaining professional standards. As of 1998, passing of the examination was required by all 41 states that required specific licensure for the practice of marital and family therapy.

Final Issues

A final issue is one we discussed earlier in Chapter 1, that is, the marginalization of the field. The key implication for the trainee is, as Kramer (1995, p. 13) has warned, that family therapy as a modality will not be reimbursed (like other forms of psychotherapy) "because it conforms poorly to contemporary models of research." Of course, the field has been working on issues of reimbursement, and trainees and supervisors need to cover this issue in the course of training so that patients can be treated properly.

Historically, as family therapy developed, differences appeared between the basic assumptions and practices of the field and the tenets of the feminist movement. Early papers challenged the family therapy establishment from a feminist perspective (Hare-Mustin 1978). Inevitably, these issues came under scrutiny in the training and supervision of students. The resulting dialogue has enriched the field and has reshaped the focus of many educational programs. Descriptions of the variety of gender differences have emerged from marital-interaction research, and a rich literature of related training practices has developed (Helmeke 1994; Libow 1985; Nelson 1991; Roberts 1991). We have discussed these issues throughout the book, especially in Chapter 17.

At the end of a family therapy training program, the trainee's education is just beginning. In a rapidly changing field such as family therapy, an individual must begin a program of lifelong self-education based on a continual awareness of the literature and course work, and on the need to evaluate his or her own work, to entertain new ideas, and to discard old ones. As obvious as this may seem, it is the inculcation of these principles that identifies the inspired and skillful clinician, teacher, or researcher.

Suggested Readings

Huber C: Ethical, Legal, and Professional Issues in the Practice of Marriage and Family Therapy, 2nd Edition. New York, Merrill, 1987

Vesper J: Ethics, Legalities, and Professional Practice Issues in Marriage and Family Therapy. Boston, MA, Allyn & Bacon, 1991

These preceding books are comparable overviews of the ethical, legal, and professional issues encountered in a clinical practice with couples and families. Both books offer case illustrations, explanations of difficult dilemmas, and careful solutions to the real-life problems one faces in practice.

Glick ID, Clarkin JF: Family, in Core Readings in Psychiatry: An Annotated Guide to the Literature. Edited by Sacks MH, Sledge WH, Waren C. Washington, DC, American Psychiatric Press, 1995, pp 63–70

Clarkin JF, Glick ID: Family and marital therapy, in Core Readings in Psychiatry: An Annotated Guide to the Literature. Edited by Sacks MH, Sledge WH, Waren C. Washington, DC, American Psychiatric Press, 1995, pp 553–560

The preceding two chapters list and annotate clinical articles on understanding and treating the family. They were written for psychiatry residents but will be of use to trainees in other programs.

References

Bor R, Mallandain, Vetere A: What we say we do: results of the 1997 UK Association of Family Therapy Members Survey. J Fam Ther 20:333–351, 1998

Boszormenyi-Nagy I, Spark G: Invisible Loyalties: Reciprocity in Intergenerational Family Therapy. New York, Harper & Row, 1973

Fadden G: Research update: psychoeducational family intervention. J Fam Ther 20:293–310, 1998

Gutheil TG, Bursztajn H, Brodsky A: Malpractice prevention through the sharing of uncertainty, informed consent and the therapeutic alliance. N Engl J Med 311:49–51, 1984

Hare-Mustin RT: A feminist approach to family therapy. Fam Process 17:181–194, 1978

Hare-Mustin R: Family therapy may be dangerous to your health. Professional Psychology 11:935–938, 1980

Hare-Mustin R, Marecek J, Caplan K, et al: Rights of clients, responsibilities of therapists. Am Psychol 34:3–16, 1979

Helmeke KL: Fostering a safe atmosphere: a first step in discussing gender in family therapy training programs. Contemporary Family Therapy 16:503–519, 1994

Imber-Black E: Secrets in Families and Family Therapy. New York, WW Norton, 1993

Kramer P: Shape of the field. Psychiatric Times, August 3, 1995

Lask B: Whose responsibility? J Fam Ther 8:205–206, 1986

Libow JA: Training family therapists as feminists, in Women and Family Therapy. Edited by Ault-Riche M. Rockville, MD, Aspen Systems Press, 1985

Nelson TS: Gender in family therapy supervision. Contemporary Family Therapy 13:357–369, 1991

Roberts JM: Sugar and spice, toads and mice: gender issues in family therapy training. J Marital Fam Ther 17:121–132, 1991

Slovik L, Griffith JL, Forsythe L, et al: Redefining the role of family therapy in psychiatric residency education. Academic Psychiatry 21:35–41, 1997

Spellman D, Harper DJ: Failure, mistakes, regret and other subjugated stories in family therapy. J Fam Ther 18:205–214, 1996

Sprenkel DH, Bailey CE: Family therapy effectiveness: current research and theory. J Marital Fam Ther 21:339–340, 1995

Steinglass P: Wither family therapy training. Fam Process 34:vii–viii, 1995

Wynne LC, Bernheim K, Wynne AR: Key issues for training in family therapy with the long-term, seriously mentally ill and their families. Paper presented at the National Forum For Educating Mental Health Professionals to Work With the Long-Term Seriously Mentally Ill and Their Families. Washington, DC, September 16, 1988

Shiva and Parvati (?), artist unknown. Khmer, Baphuon style, late 11th century A.D. Courtesy of the Avery Brundage Collection, Asian Art Museum of San Francisco. Used with permission.

Subject Index

Page numbers in **boldface** *type refer to tables or figures.*

Abortion, and couples therapy, 445
Accommodation
  early phase of treatment and,
    268–269
  family evaluation and, 143
Acute care, for psychiatric illness. *See
  also* Psychiatric disorders
  definition of, 563–564
  difficulties of, 564, 566
  family responses to mental illness
    and, 567–569
  family treatment and, 569–577
  function of for family of patient,
    566–567
  individual and family-oriented
    treatments compared, **565**
  working model of family
    intervention for, 578–582
Adaptation
  dysfunctional family and, 125
  goals of treatment and, 234
  as key concept, 16–17
  medical illness and, 660–667
  techniques for supporting, 242–243
Addiction Severity Index, 512–513
Adolescence and adolescents
  antisocial behavior and coercive
    behavior by parents, 228
  borderline personality disorder and,
    495, 496
  depression and, 491, 495

divorce and, 425
effectiveness of family therapy for,
    637
family life cycle and, 73
historical trends in family structure
    and, 30
as identified patient, 620–621
inclusion of in family sessions,
    306–312
medical illness and family
    adaptation, 662
mood disorders and, 509
Adoption, and couples therapy,
    447–448
Adult children. *See also* Children
  cognitive disorders in elderly and,
    501
  family life cycle and, 73–74
  family-of-origin issues and,
    621–622
  medical care and, 667
  postdivorce treatment and, 424–425
  relational disorders and, **175**
  secrets and, 687
Adult Children of Alcoholics, 519
Affective bonds, and marriage, 380
Affective responsiveness, and family
    evaluation, 169–170, 188
African Americans. *See also* Race and
    racism
  class and social status, 367–368

Author Index